Arctic and Northern Waters

including Faroe, Iceland and Greenland

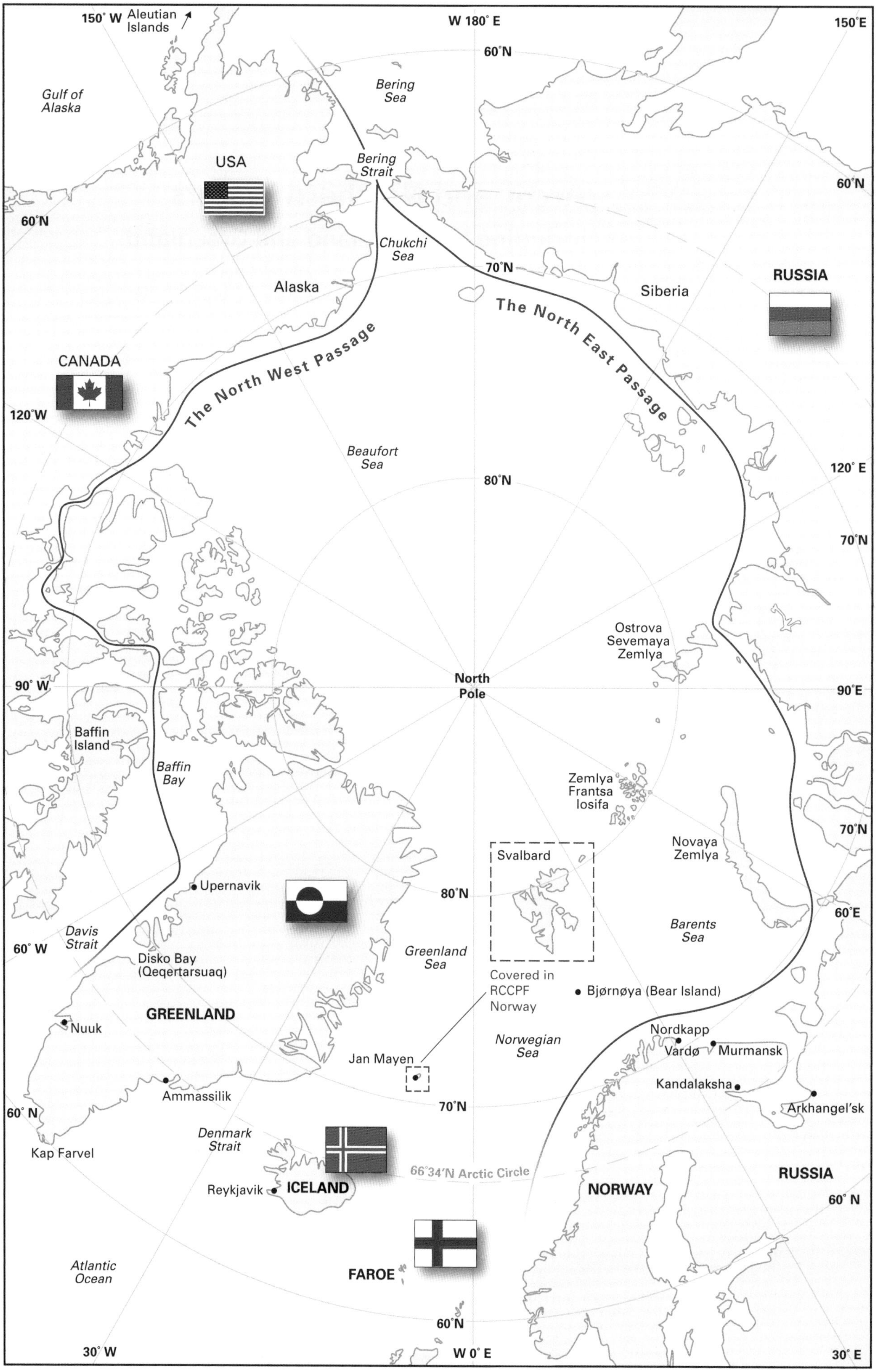

Note: This book does not give detailed information about Svalbard or Jan Mayen. These are covered in depth in RCCPF *Norway*.

Arctic and Northern Waters

including Faroe, Iceland and Greenland

RCC PILOTAGE FOUNDATION

Edited by Andrew Wilkes

Imray Laurie Norie & Wilson Ltd

Published by
Imray Laurie Norie & Wilson Ltd
Wych House The Broadway St Ives
Cambridgeshire PE27 5BT England
✆ +44 (0)1480 462114
Fax +44 (0) 1480 496109
Email ilnw@imray.com
www.imray.com
2016

First edition 2014
Revised first edition 2016

ISBN 978 184623 828 4

British Library Cataloguing in Publication Data.

A catalogue record for this book is available from the British Library.

British Library Cataloguing in Publication Data.
A catalogue record for this title is available from the British Library.

Printed in Croatia by Zrinski

ICE HAZARD

Despite the recent pattern of relatively warm summers, areas of the Arctic with a high density of ice remain a significant, life-threatening hazard to sailors. Anyone intending to sail via the northern passages is advised to gain prior ice experience in more open waters in the approaches to the Arctic.

Any yacht intended for ice voyaging should be appropriately equipped and built or modified to cope with severe impact, including impact on the rudders and propellers.

Many Arctic harbours and anchorages are subject to being closed off by ice, becoming inaccessible. If a yacht becomes trapped within a harbour or anchorage it is possible that it may remain trapped for an extended period of time.

Plan for the worst and assume a need to be entirely self-sufficient and self-reliant for the duration of your voyage.

Updates and supplements

Any mid-season updates or annual supplements are published as free downloads available from www.imray.com. Printed copies are also available on request from the publishers.

Find out more

For a wealth of further information, including passage planning guides and cruising logs for this area visit the RCC Pilotage Foundation website at www.rccpf.org.uk

Feedback

The RCC Pilotage Foundation is a voluntary, charitable organisation. We welcome all feedback for updates and new information. If you notice any errors or omissions, please let us know at www.rccpf.org.uk

CAUTION

Whilst the RCC Pilotage Foundation, the author and the publishers have used reasonable endeavours to ensure the accuracy of the content of this book, it contains selected information and thus is not definitive. It does not contain all known information on the subject in hand and should not be relied on alone for navigational use: it should only be used in conjunction with official hydrographical data. This is particularly relevant to the plans, which should not be used for navigation. The RCC Pilotage Foundation, the authors and the publishers believe that the information which they have included is a useful aid to prudent navigation, but the safety of a vessel depends ultimately on the judgment of the skipper, who should assess all information, published or unpublished. The information provided in this pilot book may be out of date and may be changed or updated without notice. The RCC Pilotage Foundation cannot accept any liability for any error, omission or failure to update such information. To the extent permitted by law, the RCC Pilotage Foundation, the author and the publishers do not accept liability for any loss and/or damage howsoever caused that may arise from reliance on information contained in these pages.

Positions and Waypoints

All positions and waypoints are to datum WGS 84. They are included to help in locating places, features and transits. Do not rely on them alone for safe navigation.

Bearings and Lights

Any bearings are given as °T and from seaward. The characteristics of lights may be changed during the lifetime of this book. They should be checked against the latest edition of the UK Admiralty *List of Lights*.

Contents

THE RCC PILOTAGE FOUNDATION

The RCC Pilotage Foundation was formed as an independent charity in 1976 supported by a gift and permanent endowment made to the Royal Cruising Club by Dr Fred Ellis. The Foundation's charitable objective is "to advance the education of the public in the science and practice of navigation".

The Foundation is privileged to have been given the copyrights to books written by a number of distinguished authors and yachtsmen. These are kept as up to date as possible. New publications are also produced by the Foundation to cover a range of cruising areas. This is only made possible through the dedicated work of our authors and editors, all of whom are experienced sailors, who depend on a valuable supply of information from generous-minded yachtsmen and women from around the world.

Most of the management of the Foundation is done on a voluntary basis. In line with its charitable status, the Foundation distributes no profits. Any surpluses are used to finance new publications and to subsidise publications which cover some of the more remote areas of the world.

The Foundation works in close collaboration with three publishers – Imray Laurie Norie & Wilson, Bloomsbury (Adlard Coles Nautical) and On Board Publications. The Foundation also itself publishes guides and pilots, including web downloads, for areas where limited demand does not justify large print runs. Several books have been translated into French, Spanish, Italian and German and some books are now available in e-versions.

For further details about the RCC Pilotage Foundation and its publications visit www.rccpf.org.uk

PUBLICATIONS OF THE RCC PILOTAGE FOUNDATION

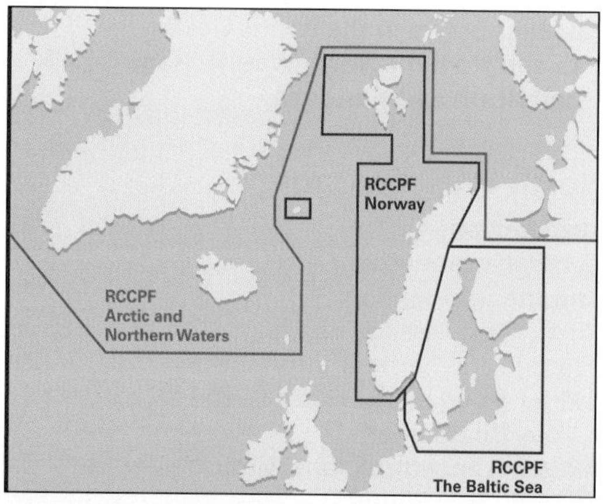

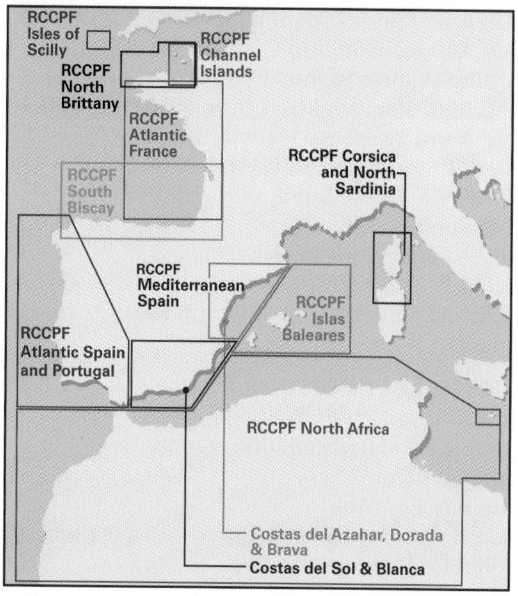

Imray
Arctic and Northern Waters
Norway
The Baltic Sea
Channel Islands
North Brittany and the Channel Islands
Isles of Scilly
Atlantic France
South Biscay
Atlantic Islands
Atlantic Spain & Portugal
Mediterranean Spain
 Costas del Sol and Blanca
 Costas del Azahar, Dorada & Brava
 Islas Baleares
Corsica and North Sardinia
North Africa
Chile
Black Sea

Adlard Coles Nautical
Atlantic Crossing Guide
Pacific Crossing Guide

On Board Publications
South Atlantic Circuit
Havens and Anchorages for the South American Coast

The RCC Pilotage Foundation
Supplement to Falkland Island Shores
Cruising Guide to West Africa
Argentina

RCCPF Website www.rccpf.org.uk
Supplements
Support files for books
Passage Planning Guides
ePilots - from the Arctic to the Antarctic Peninsula

Foreword

The number of sailing yachts heading into Arctic waters has seen a steady increase in the last few years. The trend of decline in the extent of summer sea ice limits has dramatically improved the chances of completing a successful voyage through the North West Passage. Transits of the North East Passage remain very few, but this is due to the prohibitive paperwork and regulations as well as the barriers posed by ice.

High latitude sailors are benefitting from changes in other factors: GPS has improved the accuracy of navigation in an area notorious for its magnetic anomalies. Satellite telephones and improved data access have revolutionised the communication links and allowed better access to ice charts and weather information. Specialist clothing has also improved, allowing a greater degree of comfort in extremes of cold.

Realising the new possibilities in the far North, this book began when my predecessor, Martin Walker, asked me to make good use of some Arctic material sent in to the Pilotage Foundation by Phil Hogg and Alex Whitworth. My research led me to a wider group of willing Arctic contributors and culminated in the web publication of Arctic and Northern Waters on the Pilotage Foundation website. It was a tremendous privilege for me to work with this group of Arctic experts.

In my current role it has been a great pleasure to hand the publication over to Andrew Wilkes, whose input and enthusiasm was pivotal in the creation of the web pilot. Based on Andrew's own Arctic experience and contacts, the information in this publication is drawn further from the collective wisdom of several other pioneering yachtsmen and women, as well as scientific polar research. I am certain that it will prove an essential resource for anyone planning to make a passage in the far North.

The Pilotage Foundation is very grateful to Andrew Wilkes, his wife, Máire Wilkes, and to Willie Wilson and the team at Imray, who have all worked so hard to bring this book to publication.

Jane Russell
Director, RCC Pilotage Foundation
June 2014

There is ever more interest in high latitude sailing. The two years since first publication of Arctic and Northern Waters have seen a number of voyages in the far north. Every such voyage generates more information and better understanding. This continuing feedback of information enables fellow yachtsmen and women to prepare and plan more effectively. If you have any comments or updates from your own voyages I urge you to contact us at info@rccpf.org.uk. This revised first edition incorporates all the supplementary corrections and additional information garnered from the 2014 and 2015 seasons and we are grateful to all who have contributed. Annual supplements and other supporting information are available as free downloads via www.rccpf.org.uk or direct from www.imray.com.

The RCC Pilotage Foundation remains profoundly grateful to Andrew and Máire Wilkes for their ongoing passion and commitment to Arctic waters, both in the sailing and in the writing.

Jane Russell, 2016

Preface

Willy Ker is retired now and tends to stay on his farm in Devon with his wife Veronica. Much of his life, however, has been spent sailing his battered old Contessa 32, *Ascent*, across some of the Atlantic's stormiest seas to Greenland. He spent his summers exploring and recording the pilotage of the Faroe, Iceland and Greenland coasts. He did all this alone. When satellite phones became available, he bought one so that he could talk to Veronica every night. Come the autumn, he would sail back to Devon and haul out his boat onto a home-built trailer. Willy's farm tractor towed *Ascent* across fields to a barn next to his house because the roads in this part of Devon are too narrow to handle the 2·9m beam of a Contessa 32. In the winters, with the help of fellow RCC members such as Christopher Thornhill and his daughter, Katherine Ingram, Willy wrote the RCC's cruising guide to Faroe, Iceland and Greenland. The book became a labour of love for him and this became immediately obvious when one read it. Even more so when it was used to help explore Faroe, Iceland or Greenland. It is their work which forms the basis of the cruising notes for these countries in this book.

My wife, Máire, and I visited Willy and Veronica before our first trip to Greenland. They were most generous with sharing information, encouragement and hospitality. Willy's enthusiasm encouraged us over the next few years to sail to Greenland, Baffin Island, the Faroe Islands and the North West Passage. They are some of the most beautiful and wild cruising areas to be found anywhere.

People like Willy Kerr and Christopher Thornhill have been generous in sharing their knowledge of these remote parts of the world. A trait which they share with many of the hardy souls who sail these waters. This book could not have been written without the help of people such as Paddy Barry, Jarlath Cunnane, Bob Shepton, Eef Willems and many others. It has been a privilege to meet them in remote anchorages and to write this book with them.

Writing *Arctic and Northern Waters* has been a bit like writing a series of passage plans for voyages we have already made or would like to make in the future. It has taken two years to write and, like a long sailing voyage, the support crew have been essential. Two key companions on this endeavour have been Jane Russell, Director of the RCC Pilotage Foundation, and my wife, Máire. They have both given me lots of practical help and encouragement when it was most needed.

Andrew Wilkes, 2014

ACKNOWLEDGEMENTS

The RCC Pilotage Foundation is indebted to the following people who contributed to this book's predecessor *Faroe, Iceland and Greenland*:

Andrew O'Grady and Ulla Norlander,
Rev Bob Shepton, Annie Hill and Trevor Robertson, Brian Black, Noël Marshall, Anthony Browne,
Lady Denise Evans, Henry Clay, Alistair Pratt ,
Richard Haworth, James Nixon, James F. Foley, Icelandic Maritime Service, Icelandic Coast Guard, Carol Smolawa, Knútur Karlsson, Holger Emmel, Andrew Wilkes, Jim Reeves, Mark Hillmann,
Eric Bann, Chris Hamblin, Alan Ker.

In addition, the author would like to thank the following contributors to this first edition of *Arctic and Northern Waters*:

Eric Abadie for pilotage information

Aki Asgeirsson, Brokey (Reykjavik Yacht Club)

John and Linda Andrews for pilotage information

Paddy Barry for his encouragement and information about the North East Passage

Brian Black for Greenland pilotage information

Grenville Byford for pilotage information

Nigel Calder for Faroe pilotage information

Henry Clay who provided most of the photographs in the chapter about Iceland

Jarlath Cunnane for encouragement and information about the North East Passage and the White Sea

Scott and Mary Flanders for pilotage updates concerning Iceland and Greenland

Rodger and Ali Grayson for their pilotage notes about Alaska and the Aleutian Islands

Robert Headland for information about North West Passage transits

Annie Hill for detailed pilotage information about northern Greenland

Phil Hogg and Liz Thompson for their excellent pilotage information about the Aleutian Islands and Alaska

Richard Hudson for North West Passage pilotage information

Ice off Uummannaq, Greenland *Máire Wilkes*

Vladimir Ivankiv for information concerning Russian formalities

Knútur Karlsson for East Greenland pilotage information

Willy Ker who originally wrote the chapters about Faroe, Iceland and Greenland

Egill Kolbeinsson whose help with Icelandic cruising is much appreciated

Angela Lilienthal who contributed very useful pilotage information from the Oxford West Greenland expedition in 2013

Judy Lomax for Norway pilotage information

Dermot O'Riordan who has sailed with the author in the Arctic and contributed photographs to this book

Christine Rapisardi and Clive Shute for North West Passage pilotage information

Trevor Robertson for detailed pilotage information on Greenland and over-wintering

Jane Russell who wrote the RCC Pilotage Foundation's web-guide to the Arctic and Northern Waters on which this book is based

Peter Semotiuk who has helped many of us and kindly proof read the chapter about the North West Passage

John Sharp who has provided valuable information about the northeast American approaches to Greenland and the Arctic

Rev Bob Shepton for his many contributions to Greenland and North West Passage pilotage, and advice about over-wintering in the Arctic

Jonathan and Clarissa Spaeth for West Greenland pilotage information

Roger Swanson for his pilotage notes about Alaska and the North West Passage

Sibéal Turraoin who has sailed with the author on trips to the Arctic and contributed many of the best photographs in this book

Alex Veccia for equipment evaluation and North West Passage pilotage information

Ralph Villiger whose pilotage notes concerning east Greenland are much appreciated

Victor Wejer for information about many North West Passage anchorages

Ed Wheeler for photographs and information about east Greenland and Iceland and for kindly proof reading the final draft of this book

Glenn Williams for Arctic wildlife information

Alex Whitworth for North West Passage pilotage information

Máire Wilkes (née Breathnach) who has sailed with the author for many years and has been a constant support. Máire took the majority of the photographs in this book

Eef Willems who has shared her extensive high latitude experience and proof read the chapters about Arctic navigation and Greenland

Alan Wilson for cruising information about Faroe, Iceland and Greenland

Clive Woodman who contributed very useful pilotage information from the Oxford West Greenland expedition in 2013

Carl Zaniboni for pilotage information

Introduction

This book offers guidance to navigators planning voyages in small vessels in Arctic and northern waters. It does not replace hydrographic office sailing directions and pilots.

The southern areas covered in this book include some of the most stormy waters in the world. Strong winds and big seas can be expected in both the northern Atlantic and Pacific Oceans. Sailing in these waters requires seaworthy vessels and crews able to cope with gale and storm force conditions.

In the Arctic, the presence of ice is the dominant navigation hazard. Although small boats have been sailed by indigenous fishermen throughout the Arctic for hundreds of years, voyages of any distance in these waters have been few. To access these waters, visiting vessels must first pass through the hazardous seas of the approaches. Although climate change is melting much of the ice, this does not necessarily mean that navigation is easier than it has been in the past. High concentrations of ice still close much of the Arctic waters to navigation for all or all but a few weeks of the year.

There is often a lack of wind in Arctic waters so sailing vessels are highly dependent upon their engines. From a practical perspective, a reliable engine and the ability to maintain it is essential. From an environmental point of view, a transit of the North West or North East Passage does nothing to help global warming!

In recent years people have assumed that the North West Passage is likely to be 'open' and yachts will be able to make the transit in one season. The 2013 season, however, proved the lie, with the sea ice cover being 60% greater than the preceding year. A number of yachts which had anticipated completing the transit in the season became trapped, some were escorted to safety by Canadian icebreakers, some retreated to Greenland for the winter and others over-wintered in Cambridge Bay.

Northabout - a boat built for high latitude sailing *Jarlath Cunnane*

Bronze bust of Roald Amundsen, Nome
Sibéal Turraoin

'Victory awaits him who has everything in order – luck we call it. Defeat is definitely due for him who has neglected to take the necessary precautions – bad luck we call it.'

Roald Amundsen
who was inspired by Sir John Franklin to lead
the 1903–1906 expedition in the *Gjøa*,
the first vessel to transit the North West Passage

1. Arctic navigation

Contents

Defining the Arctic and the high latitude day

The Arctic Circle, at 66°34′N, is the latitude at which the sun does not set at the summer solstice nor rise at the winter solstice. The precise latitude will depend upon the sun's maximum declination in a given year. North of that latitude there will be at least one full twenty four hour period with the sun above the horizon at mid summer. The climate varies widely within the Arctic Circle and is not dependent solely on latitude. Effects such as continental land mass and the Gulf Stream mean that limits of permafrost and the extent of sea ice can sometimes be well above or well below 66°34′N. For the purposes of this publication, Arctic waters are defined as sea areas where there is a likelihood of encountering sea ice.

Day length

The long summer day length in the Arctic is useful to navigators as, when passage planning, it makes sense to try to avoid navigating in icy waters during the hours of darkness. Note that Arctic twilight is quite prolonged and that complete darkness does not occur until some time after the sun has set.

The diagrams indicate the hours of daylight (yellow) which can be expected at various latitudes at different times of the year.

Hours of daylight per day at 60·0°N

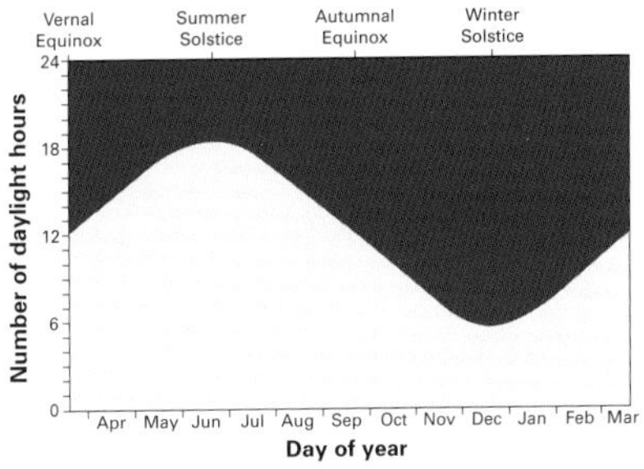

Hours of daylight per day at 65·0°N

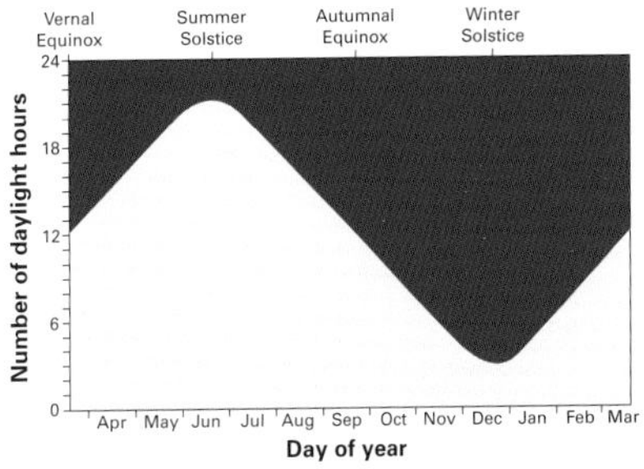

Hours of daylight per day at 66·5°N

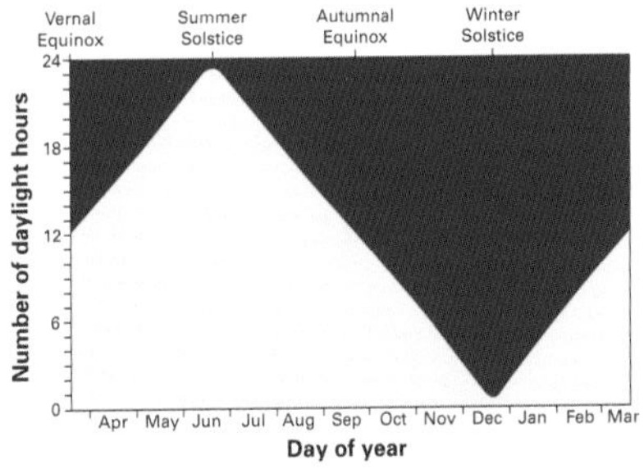

Hours of daylight per day at 70·0°N

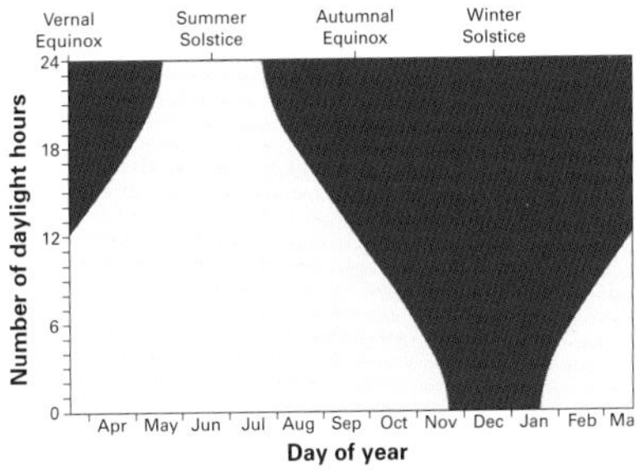

Hours of daylight per day at 75·0°N

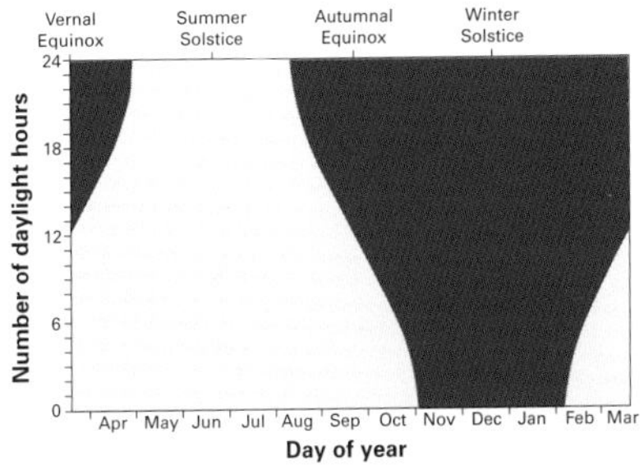

Arctic currents

Warm surface water from the Atlantic Ocean enters the Arctic Ocean between Svalbard and the Norwegian coast. A similar flow of warm water enters through the Bering Strait. Both streams of warm water flow in a predominantly anti-clockwise direction along the Arctic Ocean continental slope. Hence for yachts transiting the North East or North West Passages, the direction of current is predominantly from west to east.

Within the Arctic Ocean there are two main currents:

- **The Beaufort Gyre** is a clockwise ocean and ice circulation pattern in the Beaufort Sea that is fed by a relatively stable high-pressure (anti-cyclonic) system above it. This historically stable pattern meant that any ice forming in or drifting into the Beaufort Gyre then remained circulating for many years, accumulating snow and thickening each winter. However, over the past 20 years ice has begun melting away from the southern parts of the gyre.
- **The Transpolar Drift** runs from the Asian side of the Arctic, across the middle of the Arctic Ocean towards the northern tip of Greenland. Here the majority of the current becomes the East Greenland Current and flows south along the east coast of Greenland. Some of the transpolar drift flows down the west side of northern Greenland and joins the Canadian Current. This flows southwards on the west side of Baffin Bay and becomes the Labrador Current.

Tidal streams vary throughout the region and more information is given in specific chapters.

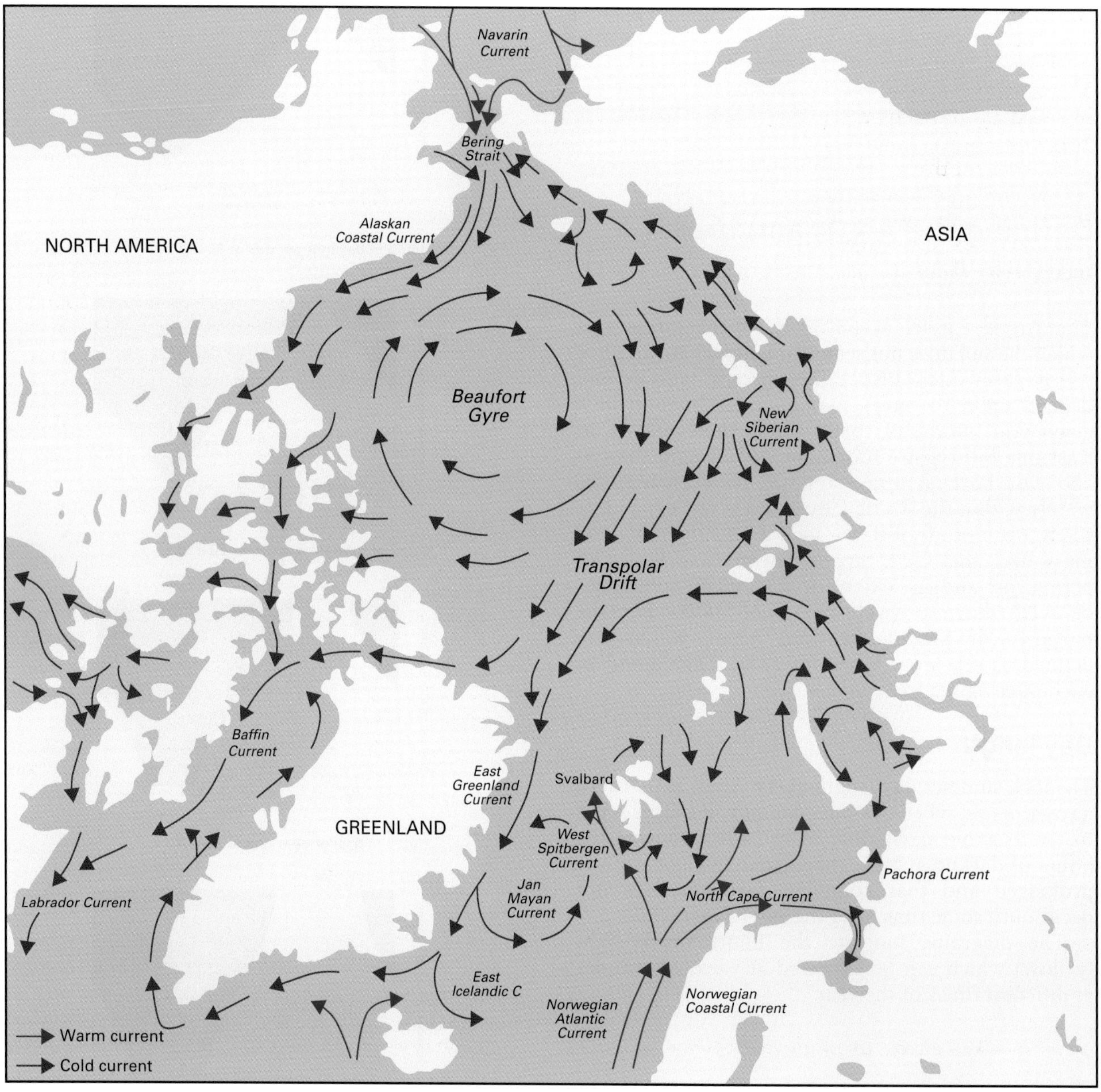

Arctic currents *Image courtesy of Arctic Monitoring and Assessment Programme (AMAP)*

Climate and weather

Climate change

There is an international consensus that the climate of the Arctic is changing, and changing fast. The National Oceanic and Atmospheric Administration (NOAA) reports that 'In recent years, decreasing ocean pack ice, increasing air temperatures, thawing permafrost, and redistribution of plants and animals in the delicately balanced Arctic ecosystem indicate that Arctic climate is changing at an unprecedented rate.' There are many research groups involved in ongoing projects to assess Arctic climate change and some of their websites are listed in this chapter.

The diagram (below) shows a view of the earth looking down on the North Pole. The minimum ice coverage in 2010 (shown in blue) is much less than the minimum ice coverage shown in the early 1980s (shown in orange). In the Eastern Arctic, the sea ice was about 3·25m thick in the 1990s. A decade later, it had reduced to about 1·25m thick.

White ice reflects energy from the sun, whereas blue sea absorbs the sun's energy. As the white ice is replaced by more blue sea the process speeds up. Pollutants from diesel and petrol engines deposit black soot on the ice which also creates a warming effect. There is evidence that the higher temperatures in the lower Arctic atmosphere are shifting the air pressure gradients which drive the winds, causing them to change their general pattern.

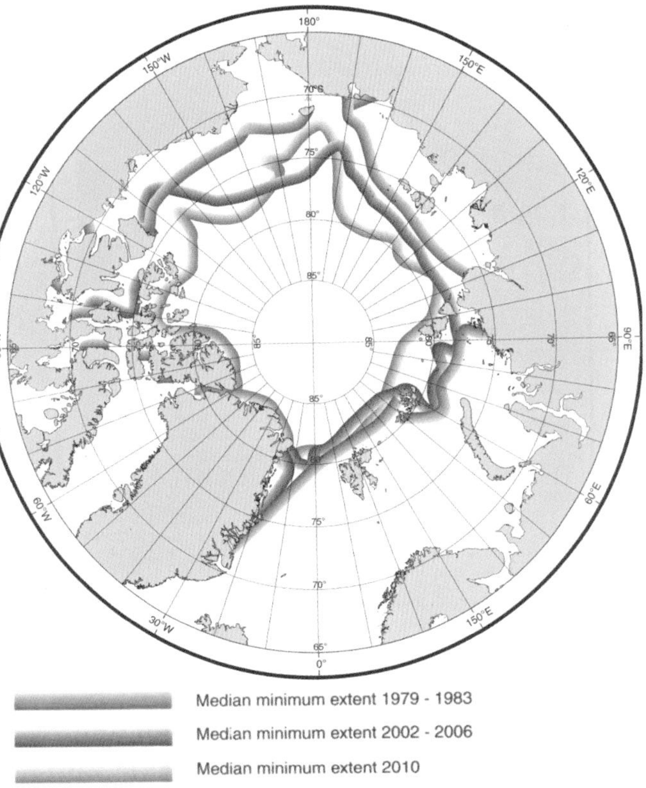

Minimum sea ice extent *UK Hydrographic Office*

Weather patterns

The area of high pressure at the North Pole dominates pressure and wind systems. Summer winds in the high Arctic are often light and localised. Regionally, winds are altered by mountain ranges, and by the great contrasts in the sun heating over forest, tundra, snow, ice and sea surfaces. Prevailing wind patterns are not constant and one should try to receive up-to-date weather information. A shift in wind direction can mean a shift in the ice movement which can make the difference between a passage being navigable or impassable.

Further south, areas of low pressure in latitudes just south of Iceland give strong cyclonic winds.

Frontal systems

A Polar Front is where warm tropical air collides with cold polar air. It is an intermittent front dependent on the temperature gradient. Where the temperature gradient is steep, the front is strong and is a potential site for low pressure system development. Where temperature contrast is small, the polar front is weak.

The Arctic Front occurs north of the Polar Front and is also intermittent at the boundary between air masses of different temperatures. The arctic front can be as strong as the polar front, becoming particularly prominent during summer in northern Eurasia.

Semi-permanent high and low pressure systems

The Icelandic Low lies between Iceland and southern Greenland, and is most intense during the winter months. In the summer it weakens and divides into two areas of low pressure, one near the Davis Strait and the other to the west of Iceland.

The Aleutian Low is centred near the Aleutian Islands in the Gulf of Alaska. It is also strong during the winter and weak in the summer.

Migratory lows tend to slow down and intensify as they enter the areas of semi-permanent low pressure. Easterly winds predominate close to the North Pole on the northern edge of the Icelandic and Aleutian lows.

During the winter months between November and March, high pressure systems, with associated cold temperatures, tend to form over eastern Siberia, the Beaufort Sea and North America.

In April and May pressure gradients decrease. Occasional migratory lows enter the Arctic from northern Eurasia and the north Atlantic, and can persist over the Canadian archipelago. October brings an increase in pressure gradients and a return to the winter systems.

Rain

The amount of water vapour held by the atmosphere decreases with decreasing temperature and is eight times higher in the tropics than in the Arctic. Continental parts of the Arctic receive less than 150mm of precipitation per year. Deserts are defined as areas with an average annual precipitation of less than 250mm (10in) per year. Land masses within the Arctic are therefore technically deserts.

Fog

Fog is common in the Arctic seas. It occurs where there is a temperature and/or moisture differential between water and the air above it. It is often caused when cold air moves over relatively warm water and traps an evaporating layer near the surface. Over sea ice the reverse is true and relatively warm, moist air can condense over the cold ice and give a similar result. Fog can make an enormous difference to navigation in areas of sea ice because detecting leads through the ice requires good visibility. Some reports suggest that as sea ice levels decrease, probability of fog may increase.

Cloud cover

Clouds are important to the Arctic climate because they trap warm air and reflect sunlight in spring and summer. There has been a nearly linear increase in the cloud cover over the central Arctic in the previous two decades. Navigators hoping to rely on celestial navigation to any extent should take this into account.

Sun Dog halo *P. J. Gibbs, National Snow and Ice Data Center*

Arctic environment phenomena

Aurora Borealis The aurora borealis, or northern lights, is centred on the geomagnetic North Pole. It occurs when the solar wind, a stream of electrons and protons coming from the sun, collides with oxygen and nitrogen atoms in the upper atmosphere. It is visible on cold, clear nights, but its appearance is difficult to predict.

Acoustic phenomena Supernormal audibility is caused by the refraction of sound waves downwards due to the relative density of the cold air closer to the ground over Arctic land masses. In some conditions, conversations can be heard up to 3km away.

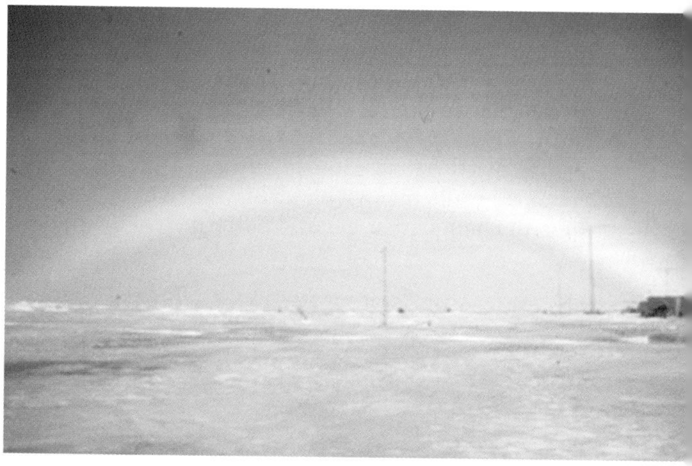

Fogbow *N. Untersteiner, National Snow and Ice Data Center*

Aurora Borealis at Tasiussaq, Greenland *Martin Doble*

Halos Light is refracted as it passes through ice crystals. If there is a thin layer of ice laden cirrostratus cloud between the sun and an observer, a complete or partial halo may be seen around the sun. Different types of halo can be seen, including a phenomenon called 'Sun Dogs' where luminous spots occur within the halo to either side of the sun itself.

Fogbows These occur by light refracting through the water droplets in the fog. Water droplets in fog are much smaller than droplets of rain so, unlike a rainbow, a fogbow has no separate colours but appears simply as a bow of light in the fog.

Coronas A corona is a ring of light that surrounds the sun or the moon. It occurs when light waves are slightly deflected around water droplets in clouds or fog. The anti-corona or 'glory' appears if an observer is looking directly away from the sun and sees one or more coloured rings appearing around their shadow cast in the cloud or fog.

Water sky refers to the dark appearance of the underside of a cloud layer when it is over a surface of open water. It can indicate water beyond the surface horizon of apparently continuous ice.

Ice blink refers to a white glare seen on the underside of low clouds indicating the presence of ice which may be beyond the range of vision. Experienced ice navigators can read 'ice blink' and use it to help find clear water leads. Two or more layers of 'ice blink' on the underside of clouds can indicate corresponding bands of sea ice.

Optical haze Optical haze, or shimmer, occurs in a layer of air next to the ground where small-scale convective currents develop. In this layer, warmer air ascends and colder air descends. Light refracts differently through warm and cold air, so where the two are mixing around each other images can appear undefined. Optical haze occurs quite frequently in the Arctic and makes it difficult to identify details in the landscape. This can make navigation more difficult.

Mirages In the same way that sound waves can be bent or refracted by changing densities of air, so light can be bent in strange ways, depending on the temperatures of the layers of air. Looming mirages are observed when distant objects appear to float above the horizon, and objects that are below the horizon may come in to view. When this occurs it is possible to see a ship or piece of land that is beyond the horizon.

Fata Morgana results in objects appearing to be stretched as well as elevated. In some conditions an inverted image is seen above an object. The fata morgana is a complex mirage in which distant objects are distorted as well as elongated vertically, such that a relatively flat shoreline may appear to have tall cliffs, columns, and pedestals. It is thought that some of the early explorers may have been confused by mirages and seen cliffs where there were none, leading them to believe that some of the passages were dead ends.

Coronas

Water sky *National Snow and Ice Data Center*

Fata Morgana – the icebergs in the background appear to be 'stretched' *Máire Wilkes*

Weather forecasts

Details of where specific regional forecasts can be obtained are given in the following chapters however, if HF radio or internet access is available (see communications later in this section), bespoke weather forecasts can be obtained for any part of the world including the Arctic.

GRIB (GRidded Information in Binary) is the format used by international meteorological institutes to transfer large data sets and is the foundation of modern weather forecasts. GRIB files are available as free downloads from the internet. This enables yachts to view weather data for anywhere in the world including the Arctic. The information includes wind strength, direction, precipitation and pressure. GRIB files can be accessed ashore or on a limited bandwidth connection onboard, either by HF radio or satellite telephone. It is possible to choose and save settings for future use, which can speed up access to relevant data. GRIB files can be downloaded via compression software, which reduces file sizes and minimises the time to download. GRIB files have now largely superseded weather-fax technology.

Useful websites – climate and weather

Athropolis Guide to Arctic Sunset and sunrise	www.athropolis.com/sun-fr.htm
U.S. National Snow and Ice CenterArctic Phenomena	http://nsidc.org/arcticmet/basics/phenomena
NOAA – Arctic This web page has links to a huge amount of information about the Arctic environment	www.arctic.noaa.gov
The Russian-American Long-term Census of the Arctic RUSALCA – a joint project focusing on the Bering and Chukchi Seas	www.arctic.noaa.gov/aro/russian-american
Scott Polar Research Institute SPRI, part of the University of Cambridge, UK, is a centre for research into both polar regions	www.spri.cam.ac.uk
Environment Canada A wealth of information about the Arctic environment	http://ice-glaces.ec.gc.ca

Useful websites – weather forecasts

US Grib A very useful website where GRIB files showing weather in any part of the world can be downloaded	www.grib.us
Passage weather Weather forecasts for most parts of the world without using GRIB software. Poor coverage of the Arctic	http://passageweather.com

Ice

Two basic types of ice are encountered at sea: icebergs and sea ice. Icebergs calve off glaciers, originate on land and are made from fresh water. Sea ice is frozen sea water which forms, grows, and melts in the ocean.

Icebergs

Icebergs are classified both by their shape and size.

Iceberg shapes

Non tabular iceberg
Flat topped iceberg which has been eroded so that it no longer has a flat top. Height to draft ratio typically 1:5
Máire Wilkes

Tabular iceberg
Flat topped, often showing horizontal banding.
Height to draft ratio typically 1:5
Environment Canada

Domed iceberg
Smooth and rounded top. Height to draft ratio typically 1:4
Máire Wilkes

Pinnacle iceberg
A central spire or pyramid with one or more spires.
Height to draft ratio typically 1:2
Sibéal Turraoin

Wedge iceberg
A flat topped iceberg which has partially capsized due to uneven erosion. Height to draft ratio typically 1:5
Máire Wilkes

Blocky iceberg
Flat topped with steep vertical sides
Height to draft ratio typically 1:5
Environment Canada

Dry dock iceberg
Erosion has caused a U shaped 'dry-dock' at or near the water surface with twin columns. Height to draft ratio typically 1:1
Máire Wilkes

Iceberg size

Growler
Height above sea level: less than 1m. Length: less than 5m
Máire Wilkes

Bergy bit
Height above sea level: 1–5m. Length: 5–15m
Máire Wilkes

Small berg
Height above sea level: 5–15m. Length: 15–60m
Máire Wilkes

Medium berg
Height above sea level: 16–45m. Length: 61–120m
Bob Shepton

Large berg
Height above sea level: 46–75m. Length: 121–200m
Sibéal Turraoin

Very large berg
Height above sea level: >75m. Length: >200m
Bob Shepton

An iceberg breaking up with a bang behind an anchored yacht *Brian Black*

Sea ice

Sea ice life cycle

Sea ice has four distinct stages in the sea ice cycle: formation, growth, deformation and disintegration.

Sea ice formation starts when the sea reaches its freezing point. This is always lower than 0°C. The exact temperature at which the seawater freezes is dependent upon the salinity of the water. As the salinity increases, the freezing point becomes lower. The first sign of freezing is an oily appearance to the water caused by the formation of ice crystals. These increase in number until the sea becomes a slushy consistency. Ice forms on the surface in shallow areas first. Water at greater depths may never fully freeze.

Sea ice growth happens when cold air temperatures freeze the lower surface of the ice sheet. The thickness of the ice increases quickly and a thin sheet of ice can thicken to 8–10cm within 24 hours. The rate of growth slows as the thickness, and thus the insulation properties, increase. At first, new fallen snow acts as an insulator and slows down the rate of freezing. Hard compacted snow is, however, a poor insulator.

Initially, it is only fresh water which freezes. Much of the salt water (brine) sinks and some will become trapped in the ice. If the temperature falls further, the brine will freeze creating 'brine cells.' This tends to happen in cold conditions when sea ice forms quickly.

Deformation is the term used to describe the change in shape and size of sea ice as it is affected by temperature, wind and current changes. As the temperature falls below freezing point, the ice will initially expand quite rapidly, then less so until it reaches a point where it will contract slightly. Expanding ice will fill cracks and create pressure ridges in the ice sheet. Contracting ice will open cracks in the ice which can be quite big during a mild spell or at the start of a thawing period.

Disintegration occurs when the ice starts to melt. This is caused by conduction of heat from the air or sea or by by solar radiation.

Movement of sea ice

Sea ice is very susceptible to the effects of bathymetry, wind and current.

Bathymetry the proximity of land and shallow water affect the ice life-cycle. Ice both forms and melts quicker in shallower water. The proximity of land and the contours of the seabed produce current changes and can cause upwelling.

Wind can produce rapid changes in ice conditions. Smaller and higher floes move faster than bigger, lower ones. Therefore greater ice concentrations will be slower moving.

Currents 70–90% of an ice floe is typically under water and heavily influenced by currents. These can be ocean, tidal or coastal run-off currents.

The age of sea ice

Older sea ice is harder than new ice. The age of ice is categorised as follows:

New ice is recently formed ice composed of ice crystals that are only weakly frozen together (if at all) and have a definite form only while they are afloat.

Nilas is a thin elastic crust of ice (up to 10cm in thickness), easily bending on waves and swell and under pressure growing in a pattern of interlocking 'fingers' (finger rafting).

Young ice is ice in the transition stage between nilas and first-year ice, 10–30cm in thickness.

First year ice is sea ice of not more than one winter's growth, developing from young ice, with a thickness of 30cm or greater.

Old or Multi-year ice is sea ice that has survived at least one summer's melt. Its topographic features generally are smoother than first-year ice. It is generally thicker and harder and is therefore less liable to melt.

Pack ice is mostly sea ice, although it may encompass icebergs which have become trapped in it.

Sea ice cover is recorded as 0/10ths to 10/10ths where 0 is no ice and 10 is totally impenetrable.

Sea ice forms

The most common forms of sea ice are:

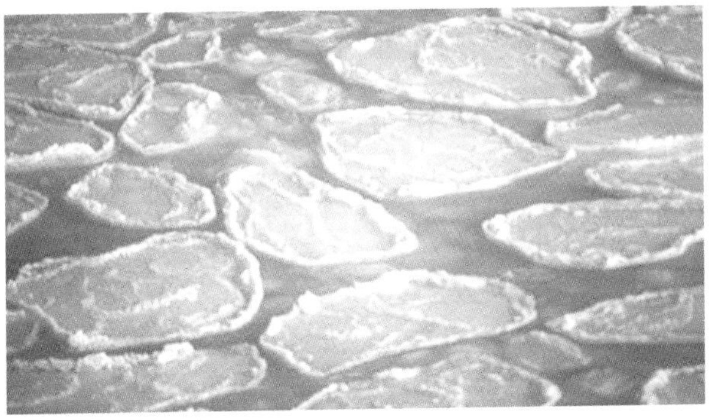

Pancake ice
Circular pieces of ice 30cm to 3m in diameter, up to 10cm in thickness, with raised rims due to the pieces striking against one another

Brash ice
Accumulation of floating ice made up of fragments not more than 2m across, the wreckage of other forms of ice.
Sibéal Turraoin

Ice cake
Any relatively flat piece of ice less than 20m across
Máire Wilkes

Floe
Any relatively flat piece of ice 20m or more across
Máire Wilkes

Fast ice
Ice which forms and remains fast along the coast. Fast ice higher than 2m above sea level is called an ice shelf
Máire Wilkes

The changing extent of sea ice

Satellites have monitored the extent of sea ice coverage since 1979. Ice coverage for March (when the ice is at its maximum extent) and September (when it reaches its annual minimum) show a general trend in Arctic warming. The reduction in the extent of the summer sea ice cover over the past 30 years is particularly concerning to climate change scientists.

The sea ice minimum has been occurring later in recent years because of a longer melting season. Ice growth and melt are subject to local influences. In some areas sea ice will be forming whilst, at the same time, ice will be shrinking in other areas.

Although the area of sea ice in winter remains similar to that recorded 10 years ago, much of the ice is new ice formed within the last 12 months. This is much thinner than the multi-year ice found in the past. Over the past 10 years, the extent of multiyear sea ice has reduced three times faster than the reduction rate during the last thirty years. The thin first year ice breaks up and melts more quickly and more extensively in each subsequent year.

The relevance of this to the passage of yachts is not necessarily straightforward. Even though the ice pack in general may be diminishing, depending on winds, currents and surrounding land masses, any existing remaining ice may still create a total, if only temporary, barrier. Passage through ice of apparently passable density, such as 3/10, is often obstructed where the ice is gathered into areas of greater density. The narrower sections of the North West Passage, such as Peel Sound, Navy Board Inlet and Bellot Strait, are particularly susceptible to becoming blocked when prevailing winds force pack ice into these bottle necks. Conversely, the islands can offer protection to some waters and keep them open. More open expanses, for example in the Beaufort Sea across the top of Alaska, are totally at the mercy of prevailing winds and currents. In prolonged northerly winds, M'Clintock's Channel will deposit a lot of ice into Larsen Sound and James Ross Strait. Similarly, ice from Wellington Channel drifts into the Barrow Straits.

Useful websites

	U.S. National Snow and Ice Centre Monthly sea ice indexes for the Arctic and Antarctic	http://nsidc.org/data/seaice_index
	U.S. National Snow and Ice Centre Quick Facts about Sea ice	http://nsidc.org/quickfacts/seaice.html
	U.S. National Snow and Ice Centre Arctic sea ice news and analysis	http://nsidc.org/arcticseaicenews/index.html

Ice charts

Ice charts are available from a number of sources some of which are mentioned in the following chapters relating to specific areas.

Some charts use colour codes which indicate ice coverage in tenths. 0/10s being ice free and 10/10s being solid ice. A more comprehensive system which can be used in conjunction with colour coded ice charts or with black and white ice charts is the Egg Code.

The Egg Code

The basic data concerning concentrations, stages of development (age) and form (floe size) of ice are contained in an oval symbol. A maximum of three ice types is described within the oval. This oval and the coding associated with it, are referred to as the Egg Code. The code conforms to international conventions and is used in coding all visual sea ice and lake ice observations.

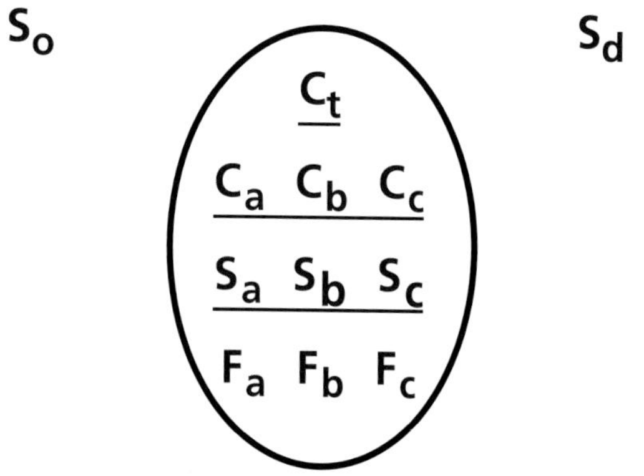

C_t: Total concentration of ice in area, reported in tenths. May be expressed as a single number or as a range, not to exceed two tenths (3–5, 5–7, etc.)

C_a C_b C_c: Partial concentration (C_a, C_b, C_c) are reported in tenths, as a single digit. These are reported in order of decreasing thickness. C_a is the concentration of the thickest ice and C_c is the concentration of the thinnest ice.

S_a S_b S_c: Stages of development (S_a, S_b, S_c) are listed using the code shown in Table 1 below, in decreasing order of thickness. These codes correspond directly with the partial concentrations above. C_a is the concentration of stage S_a, C_b is the concentration of stage S_b, and C_c is the concentration of S_c.

S_o S_d: Development stage (age) of remaining ice types. S_o if reported is a trace of ice type thicker/older than S_a. S_d is a thinner ice type which is reported when there are four or more ice thickness types.

F_a F_b F_c: Predominant form of ice (floe size) corresponding to S_a, S_b and S_c respectively. Table 2 below shows the codes used to express this information.

For example, the ice chart dated 30 December 2012 shows the forecast ice conditions in the Davis Strait for that day. The southern extremity of the seas

Table 1. Egg Codes for stages of ice development (S_x codes)

Stage of development for sea ice	Code figure	Stage of development for fresh water ice
New ice-frazil, grease, slush, shuga (0–10cm)	1	New ice (0–5cm)
Nilas, ice rind (0–10cm)	2	
Young (10–30cm)	3	
Grey (10–15cm)	4	Thin ice (5–15cm)
Grey – white (15–30cm)	5	Medium ice (15–30cm)
First year (30–200cm)	6	
First year thin (30–70cm)	7	Thick ice (30–70cm)
First year thin – first stage (30–70cm)	8	First stage thick ice (30–50cm)
First year thin – second stage (30–70cm)	9	Second stage thick ice (50–70cm)
Medium first year (70–120cm)	1•	Very thick ice (70–120cm)
Thick first year (>120cm)	4•	
Old – survived at least one season's melt (>2m)	7•	
Second year (>2m)	8•	
Multi-year (>2m)	9•	
Ice of land origin	▲•	

Table 2. Egg Codes for forms of ice (F_X codes)

Forms of sea ice	Code figure	Forms of fresh water ice
	~F	Belts and strips symbol followed by ice concentration
New ice (0–10cm)	X	
Pancake ice (30cm–3m)	0	
Brash ice (< 2m)	1	
Ice cake (3–20 m)	2	
Small ice floe (20–100m)	3	
Medium ice floe (100–500m)	4	
Big ice floe (500m–2km)	5	
Vast ice floe (2–10km)	6	
Giant ice floe (>10km)	7	
Fast ice	8	
Ice of land origin	9	
Undetermined or unknown (iceberg, growlers, bergy bits)	/	

covered by the chart (60N 61W) is coloured yellow which the key indicates is an ice concentration of between 4/10 and 6/10. More information can be found by consulting the Egg Code symbol 'K'. This indicates that 6/10 ice is forecast which comprises:

2/10 medium ice 15–30cm thick in medium sized floes
2/10 thin ice 5–15cm thick in small floes
2/10 new ice 0–5cm thick

The arrow to the east of this area indicates that the ice is expected to drift southwards at about 0.6 miles per day.

Most yachts would find difficulty in navigating in ice concentrations greater than 3/10 so a yacht approaching from the east would probably have to travel south to enter the waters coloured blue which indicates ice concentrations of less then 1/10.

K

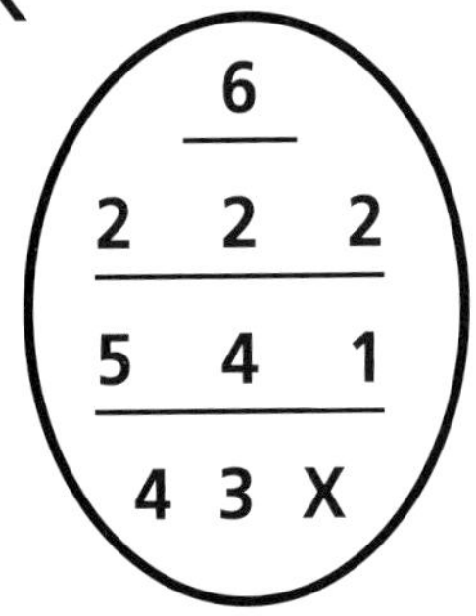

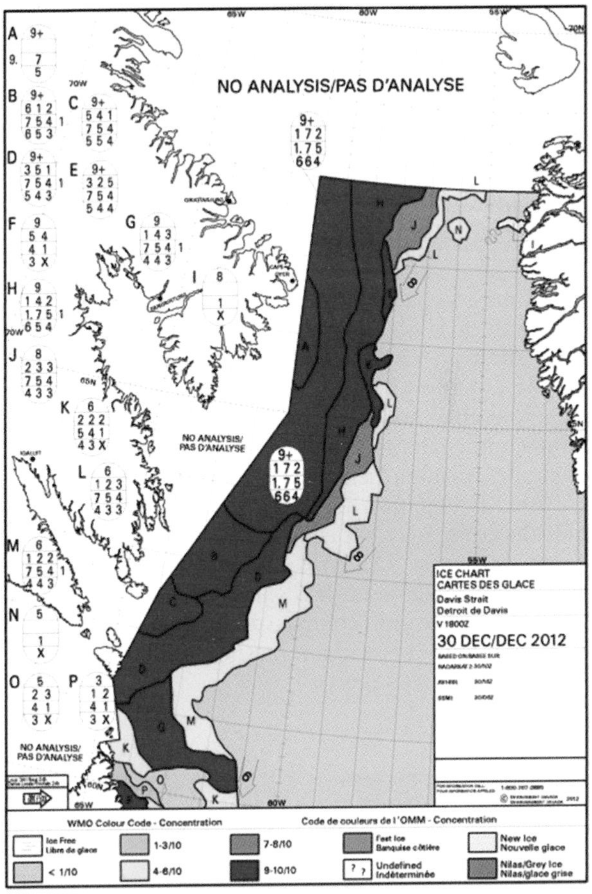

Useful websites

	Environment Canada A detailed explanation of the Egg Code	www.ec.gc.ca/default.asp?lang=En&n=FD9B0E51-1 Enter 'Egg code' in the search box

Ice navigation

Crews planning a transit of the North West Passage or North East Passage are advised to gain experience of navigating in ice in more southern latitudes before planning a transit. *The Mariner's Handbook*, one of the UK Hydrographic Office (UKHO) publications, has a chapter about ice navigation, although older editions of this book have rather more information. This may be a legacy from the whaling industry. The Canadian Coastguard website listed in this section has a lot of valuable information. However these publications are designed primarily for ships and icebreakers. Most small boats will find navigation difficult in ice concentrations greater than 3/10.

The lower the concentration of ice, the easier the navigation, so it is important to monitor ice charts and weather patterns whenever possible. Listening to advice from experts such as Peter Semotiuk, who advises boats transiting the North West Passage, is invaluable. Similarly, Canadian Coastguard personnel are very helpful and will share up to date ice information.

Summer ice is rarely static. Winds and current usually bring about change, for better or worse.

Vessels may have to wait for days, weeks, or even a whole winter to make a transit through an ice bound area and it is sometimes necessary to motor fast to transit an area before it becomes impassible. One has to be prepared to quickly vacate an anchorage if ice forecasts indicate that it will become beset with ice.

Ice leads

Ice leads are the channels of navigable water that open up within areas of sea ice. They can be quite narrow, sometimes less than a boat's beam width, and can open and close within a few minutes. They might vary in length from a few metres to a mile or more.

The opening and closing of leads can be unpredictable and is dependent on the prevailing winds and currents. Small vessels are usually able to navigate through sea ice concentrations of up to 3/10ths. Navigation in areas of sea ice with up to 5/10ths cover may occasionally be possible over very short distances. This will carry a high risk of the vessel becoming beset. It is sometimes useful to have a crew member aloft to help spot any leads.

Individual leads will not be shown on ice charts.

Attempting to manoeuvre in ice off Beechey Island
Andrew Wilkes

In extreme circumstances yachts have found shelter and respite by mooring to the side of a multi-year ice floe, part of which has grounded. This strategy provided *Cloud Nine* with temporary relief from rapidly closing in sea ice as she attempted to reach Resolute in 1995. She managed to find a protected 'harbour' on the edge of an older, thicker, larger and stationary floe. However, when conditions changed the crew of *Cloud Nine* suddenly found themselves in imminent danger as the combined forces of a massive field of sea ice threatened to crush the floe they were moored to. They managed to extract themselves and later witnessed their mooring floe set high up onto the shore.

Useful websites - navigating in ice

	Canada Coastguard Ice Navigation	www.ccg-gcc.gc.ca/Ice_home/Ice_Publications/Ice-Navigation-in-Canadian-Waters
	Environment Canada Manual of Ice – standard procedures for observing and reporting ice	www.ec.gc.ca/default.asp?lang=En&n=FD9B0E51-1 Enter 'Manual of ice-observing and reporting' in the search box

Manoeuvring in sea ice

1. It is always preferable to navigate around ice wherever possible, even if this means taking a longer route. The risk of damage is much higher going through any level of ice. Even if the overall distance is shorter, fuel consumption can be increased because of all the necessary manoeuvring. For this reason it is useful to receive daily ice charts. The chart will show the location of ice to a degree of accuracy which is difficult to describe over an R/T link or written email. This is a good reason for considering a communication system such as Fleet Broadband which has sufficiently high data speeds.
2. Ice blink and fog are useful indicators of ice beyond the horizon.
3. Use the Egg Code on the ice charts to forecast the likely ice type at a given location. Hitting new ice has been compared to hitting solid wood. Hitting old ice is like hitting solid iron. Old ice is well eroded, flatter and much harder than new ice. It is less saline and therefore has a blue tinge to it. Even ice-breakers struggle to break floes of thick old ice. A small boat does not want to hit either type very hard. However, it may be possible to push small floes aside using steady engine power.
4. One or two ice-poles are useful for pushing away small floes.
5. When navigating in thick ice, it should be remembered that floes can move very quickly, either with wind or with current, opening and closing ice leads as they move.
6. Do not get caught between 'a rock and a hard place.' Do not try to navigate between the shore and the leeward side of moving ice. The ice could drift towards the shore and run the boat aground.
7. In shallow water, large floes may run aground and leave sufficient water between them and the shore to allow a small boat to navigate.
8. Pack ice subdues waves. The sea state may worsen when a vessel has cleared an area of pack ice.

Trying to push a floe away from the anchored boat off Beechey Island *Sibéal Turraoin*

Dodo's Delight discovered that ice floes can move into an anchorage very fast *Bob Shepton*

Navigating around glaciers, icebergs and bergy bits

Icebergs are formed by sections of ice breaking away from glaciers (calving). There are no warnings of when this will occur. The breakaway icebergs can be large or small and the calving is often dramatic. For this reason, it is dangerous for a vessel to navigate close to a glacier.

Icebergs are constantly being eroded by wind and sea as well as being melted by the sun. This affects their stability and they are quite likely to capsize without warning. Large pieces of ice can also break off as if they have been exploded making a noise like a loud gun shot.

The action of an iceberg being calved or breaking up often creates a wave called a 'kanele'. These 'mini tsunamis' can be significant and a danger to navigation. Kaneles can propagate into anchorages and refract around headlands.

Icebergs, which usually show up on radar, are deep keeled and are carried by the current. Bergy bits and growlers, which may have calved from the parent iceberg, tend to be wind driven and therefore lie downwind of icebergs. So by passing to windward of the icebergs you should also avoid the growlers. Growlers can be very difficult to spot – they can look like whitecaps in windy conditions.

Currents at varying depths can sometimes move an ice berg in a counterintuitive direction. More than one yacht has reported near collisions when icebergs 'behaved strangely'.

Anchoring in icy waters

An apparently secure anchorage can quickly become untenable if ice encroaches. Ice may be borne in by winds or current. Movement of sea ice can close off the entrance to an apparently protected anchorage, trapping any boats within. It is a common necessity to re-anchor within polar anchorages, sometimes repeatedly over a relatively short time period. This can become tiring for the crew.

Water: it is important to spot and mark your chosen stream or pool before the snows come in earnest, as the terrain then appears altered and can become unrecognisable. An old ski or ski stick has proved useful if there is no drift wood for a marker. Do not be discouraged – keep on digging down at your spot until you can break open the thin ice cover at the bottom and your fresh water will still be there underneath, hopefully! Once you have filled your containers, be careful to recover the water source with a considerable depth of snow blocks to insulate it for the next time.

For short distances such as fetching water, snow shoes can be more user friendly than skis.

It can be difficult getting from the sea ice to the ice foot attached to the land, especially initially when the ice is not so solid. Some sort of gangway can be a help, so it is worth carrying a decent ladder or plank on board.

Perpetual darkness (except for some twilight either side of local midday) can be something of a trial, even for Greenlanders. Humans tend to hibernate as well as animals and sleep for longer. Take plenty of books.

It is all so much better once you are properly iced in, and you can go walk about, or ski about.

'Snow is the best insulator'. You may wish to keep the snow on the decks and cabin roof and even throw some more on top and round the hull to increase the insulation of your vessel.

A tent ashore is a good safeguard against total disaster. It is important, however (lessons learnt from mistakes – too late!), to have it properly stocked already with spare thermorest/karrimat, sleeping bag, stove, food and other emergency supplies.

Some say you should not use a heater, just wear more clothes to save condensation, lighting a stove once in a while to wash clothes. A heater is a great comfort however. But make sure it is properly plumbed in!'

Choose a winter site with care *Trevor Robertson*

Trevor Robertson has over-wintered on two occasions on a small boat in the Arctic and once in the Antarctic. He is probably more qualified than anyone else to write on the subject and advises that 'Having a companion makes a huge difference. The food is better and the bed warmer.' He has kindly written the following notes for Arctic and Northern Waters:

'Probably the best reason to spend a winter on a yacht in the Arctic is to see the full round of seasons, something that a vessel making a short summer dash to the north misses. Another reason is that ice conditions prevent a vessel completing its proposed voyage in a single season and the crew decides to spend the winter aboard and continue on the following year. A yacht that has decided in advance to spend a winter frozen in somewhere remote from a settlement can scout out a good location and perhaps ferry fuel from a settlement to the wintering site. However, if caught by an early freeze-up, the choice of where to spend the winter is going to be limited to finding the safest cove in the vicinity with little chance of getting extra fuel supplies. Either requires complete self-sufficiency for at least eight months. Wintering near a settlement is much simpler as food and fuel are available locally and help is at hand if the vessel is damaged or lost or if medical assistance is required. Having people around provides company through the long winter night, but at the cost of missing the experience of the remote, untouched icescape and its wildlife.

Many of the issues of choosing a site for the winter, preparing the boat, getting through the winter and breaking out of the ice at the end are similar whether near to or remote from a settlement. The rest of this section assumes the wintering site is remote, so some parts can be ignored if near a settlement.

The potential for crew problems when living in a cold, dark vessel through the winter should not be underestimated. Antarctic bases spend a great deal of effort screening numerous applicants for a few winter positions but still have a significant failure rate, and their living conditions are palatial compared to a yacht frozen in a remote bay. A single-hander is not going to have difficulties with crew but has to cope with whatever problems arise alone and may find the long, dark winter's night hard on the mind. A larger crew on a bigger vessel has more comfort in the way of heat and light and people to solve any problems, but with a higher chance of conflict within the group. A couple who have lived and sailed together for long enough to be used to one another's quirks is undoubtedly the best crew for such a venture.

Provisioning for an unsupported Arctic winter is different to provisioning for an ocean passage. The minimum length of time between shopping opportunities will be about eight months and the amount of food required in the coldest months will be nearly double that usual in a warmer climate. Fresh vegetables, including potatoes and onions, turn to mush in the freeze-thaw cycles of autumn and few small boats can store enough refrigerated meat to last a year. This means the menu is going to be heavy on grains, pulses, legumes, rice and pasta and light on steaks, onions and potatoes. Vitamin supplements are a good idea, as is a well-stocked spice locker.

The menu will vary with personal taste, the size of the boat and how the food is stored, but some things are universal. It is going to be cold, requiring as much as 5000 calories a day in mid-winter. A generous ration of carbohydrates and fats will give this. Rice, pasta, flour and oatmeal keep well and are easy to cook. There are many fats to choose from, but vegetable oil, butter and full cream powdered milk are a good start. If the use of tinned food is kept to a minimum but without resorting to dehydrated food, a winter ration will amount to about 1kg per person per day.

Cooking through an Arctic winter takes a lot of fuel as the ingredients are cold and appetites large. The amount of fuel will depend on the boat and on individual practice, but is likely to be about 120 litres of kerosene or the equivalent in propane per person, increased to 200 litres per person if it is necessary to melt ice or snow for water. If using propane, a kerosene backup stove is wise as propane stoves fail at –42°C. Butane is of no use at all as its boiling point is about 0°C. All diesel oil must be winter grade. Any summer grade fuel left in the tanks will gel to an unpumpable sludge during winter.

The pile of gear necessary to survive unsupported through an Arctic winter is considerable when added to food and fuel for cooking. It will include clothes, gloves, mittens and boots, long mooring lines with chain slings to secure to rocks ashore, shovel, pick, crowbar, ice auger, pitons, a sledge, snowshoes, tent, extra sleeping bags, candles and a comprehensive medical kit. Only a large vessel is likely to be able to stow all this and still be able to carry enough fuel to run a heater all winter. Given enough notice, a small vessel may be able to ferry fuel from a settlement to its wintering site, but finding suitable fuel containers in a small settlement can be a problem.

The ideal cove for a wintering site has an entrance only a little deeper than the vessel's draft to keep out the bigger bits of drift ice, is small enough to run lines ashore to moor the vessel securely without aid of anchors and is surrounded by rocks to hold the winter ice in place. It must be deep enough that it does not freeze to bottom as this will cause pressure ridging. The vessel should not be moored directly to a dock or rock face where it may be caught in the shear zone that develops between the floating bay ice and the fixed ice foot attached to the shore. If possible the bay will have interesting wildlife and scenery and a sunny southern outlook. The effects of flash flooding when ice dams up the valley burst in spring needs to be considered if a stream flows into the bay.

Having chosen the winter site, moor with lines ashore so that the vessel is head to the prevailing wind and retrieve the anchors. If an anchor chain is allowed to freeze in, the vessel may be towed out to sea by it when the ice breaks up. The mooring lines need to be kept from freezing in for the same reason. While the ice is thin, the mooring lines can be broken out by hauling a dinghy down them. Once the ice is thick enough to walk on, lifting the lines on top of the snow each day will stop them freezing in. The time between the beginning of freeze-up and being able to walk on the ice is more difficult. All that can be done is to stand on deck and flick the lines clear of the ice for as far as possible and similarly from the shore if it is accessible. The middle section of each line will freeze in and needs to be chipped out as soon as the ice is thick enough to walk on. The rope will be near the bottom of the newly formed ice and will remain there, sinking deeper as the ice thickens, so the sooner it is freed, the easier the job will be. If a rope is left frozen in, it will end up at the bottom of 1.5 or 2m of ice and will have to be cut when the ice breaks out, just when it is most needed.

Once safely moored, the boat can be prepared for the winter. Exactly how the engine is laid up will depend on the installation. A keel-cooled engine with a dry exhaust requires nothing more than an adequate amount of anti-freeze in the coolant and can be run every week or two to keep the batteries full charged. A fully charged battery will not freeze and split its case. An engine with a heat exchanger and wet exhaust cannot be kept in commission once the cooling water inlet freezes and should be winterized by draining the heat exchanger, fogging oil into the cylinders and perhaps draining the block. The body of a seacock should be able to resist the pressure of water freezing in it, but using a dinghy pump to blow air through the line while closing the valve eliminates the problem entirely. Water tanks are best pumped dry before they freeze. Tanks freeze from the outside inwards so there is no problem in the autumn provided there is a small airspace to allow for expansion. However in the spring the tank melts from the outside, leaving in a large ice block surging around in the tank. This is noisy and detrimental to tank baffles and lining.

It is prudent to have a depot ashore to retreat to if the boat is lost, fire being the chief hazard. The cache will need tents, food, stove, fuel and clothes to keep the crew alive for up to eight months, depending on how far the wintering site is from the nearest settlement. The depot needs to be marked by tall spars so it does not become lost under snowdrifts. Tents should not be erected lest they be damaged or lost in winter storms. The food should to be stored in containers strong enough to keep out an Arctic fox. A good quality plastic box will do. By repute, if there are bears or wolverines around, nothing will keep them out for long.

Arctic foxes are common across much of the Arctic. They are inquisitive animals and soon accept a yacht and its crew as part of their landscape, especially if fed occasionally. Arctic foxes are omnivorous and will gratefully accept offerings such as porridge, rice, stew or mouldy eggs (which they always cache). They are timid little creatures that become confiding in time.

A fox may adopt the boat. They are appealing but be cautious as rabies is endemic in the Arctic

1. ARCTIC NAVIGATION

Rabies is endemic in the Arctic and any fox acting aggressively towards humans should be strictly avoided.

If it is not feasible to ferry fuel to the wintering site for some reason such as an early freeze-up, it will be necessary to do without heating for much of the winter. Living in a well insulated but unheated boat is not particularly difficult; certainly easier than it was for the Inuit who until recently spent their winters in relative comfort in snow houses heated by nothing more than a stone lamp burning seal oil. A small vessel with a snow cover is quite habitable even when heated by nothing more than a couple of candles and the intermittent use of the cooking stove. How habitable will depend on insulation, size of the boat and numerous other variables but the temperature will probably rise above freezing once the cooker and candles have been lit for the breakfast and stay there for most of the day.

All portholes and hatches except the main hatch need to be double-glazed. Temporary double-glazing can be made using acrylic sheeting screwed in place or even more simply and equally effectively from cling film plastic stretched across the opening. To conserve heat, decide how much of the boat is going to be lived in through the winter then bulkhead off the rest and let it freeze. The ends of the boat are the obvious areas to isolate. This is best done with purpose-made sheets of foam but an effective insulated barrier can be contrived using cushions from the cabins that are being closed off. The smaller the living area left, the warmer and more comfortable it will be.

Before letting a compartment freeze, open all its locker doors as it is difficult to do this without damage if they are allowed to freeze shut. If possible empty these lockers of everything that is likely to be required during the winter as it will be hard to do so once the locker is encased in ice. Equipment and supplies that will not fit in the warm section of the cabin are better stored ashore than left in the frozen sections of the boat. Cooking and breathing will produce enough condensation for everything in unheated parts of the boat to be thickly encased in hard ice. Anything stored ashore will need to be dug out from under the snow but as it is in a dry environment, will not be frozen into a solid mass as it would be in the frozen ends of the yacht.

As a lead acid battery's capacity drops quickly as the temperature falls, it is essential for the battery compartment to be heated if the domestic electrical system is kept in commission through the winter. Few small vessels can carry enough fuel to do this and also run an engine to generate power, leaving no option except to shut down the domestic electrical system for the winter. Candles and kerosene lamps give safe and reliable light together with some heat. Depending on latitude and thus the length of the polar night, 300 candles or 20 to 30 litres of lamp oil (kerosene) per person should do, varying with individual preference and tolerance to discomfort.

Candles vary dramatically in quality and it is worth trying a couple before buying a large quantity. The best burn all the way to bottom with a steady, nearly smokeless flame that does not vary in height and do not leave a puddle of wax behind. Puddled wax can be recycled by melting it into a shallow tin such as a small tuna can and burned using a wick made from a twist of toilet paper. Candles in proper holders are safer and more convenient than those stuck to a saucer or in a bottle. Even the best candles and most carefully trimmed lamp wicks eventually make the deckhead sooty, something that becomes obvious when the sun returns in the spring. Two candles or an oil lamp with a 25mm wick is usually enough to read by without strain, but eyes need more light as they get older.

Electric pumps and similar paraphernalia will of course be irrelevant for most of the winter so any essential for running the boat must have a manual backup. In fact no pumps except those used to transfer fuel are likely to work in midwinter. All critical systems must be able to run without electricity, which rules out Eberspacher-type heaters and Wabasco or Wallas types of cooking stoves unless they backed up by a system that does not need electric power. Preferred heaters are the drip fed type such as those made by Sigma, Refleks or Dickinson. They require no electricity and, having no electronic components, can usually be repaired if they fail.

Good ventilation is critical. Ideally there will be a dedicated air supply led directly to the heater. In addition the cabin needs a permanent vent that keeps out drifting snow without restricting the flow of fresh air. Dorade vents are not likely to work unless they have cowls at least 60cm high to keep them above the snow.

Great care is needed on the installation of any generator set, especially regarding its air supply and exhaust system. This seems elementary, but has been the cause of a depressing number of incidents of carbon monoxide poisoning on boats in the Arctic. Candles are safer and as they dim and gutter long before the oxygen levels fall to levels critical for humans so giving early warning if the air supply becomes restricted. Unfortunately they do not give warning of accumulating carbon monoxide.

As winter approaches, ice will form around the boat only to break out again in the next strong wind. Ice bumping around the hull is noisy and sometimes alarming, but rarely a serious problem. There is little point in wasting energy fending drifting ice off the boat with an ice pole as anything small enough to push away will not put any significant strain the hull or mooring lines. Ice snagging on the mooring lines is more of an issue as a rope stretching perhaps 100m to the shore can catch a lot of drifting ice, which puts it under great strain. Mooring lines can be partly cleared by flicking them over the drift ice nearest the boat. Ice caught on the mooring lines further from the boat can be cleared from a dinghy but this is difficult in strong winds, just when the problem is most acute. Using masthead halyards to lift the mooring lines above the ice generally causes more trouble than it saves.

Let the ends of the boat freeze!

A snow cover with opening built over the portholes to let in light

As the ice thickens, getting ashore by dinghy becomes more difficult. Hauling a dinghy down a mooring line while chopping with an ice axe works for a while, but there will be a few days where the ice is too thick to break with a dinghy and too thin to walk on. When the ice is 75mm to 100mm thick, it will probably be strong enough to stay in place in a gale and should support a person's weight. For the first few weeks when walking ashore on the ice, the intertidal zone ice will be thin and broken, requiring use of a dinghy either as a bridge or for a short ferry ride to cross it. Care is needed if using an inflatable dinghy for this as some, particularly the PVC type, become brittle and easily damaged at low temperatures.

It is worth building a snow cover over the vessel as soon as the ice will support one. The difference in comfort this makes is dramatic. Shovelling a pile of snow over the decks and around the hull works well, but in much of the Arctic there will not be enough snow on the ice to do this early in the winter. If the snow around the boat is scarce, it can be insulated by building a crude igloo with snow blocks cut from drifts ashore. Not all snowdrifts are sufficiently well packed for the blocks cut from them to be carried or sledded to the boat without crumbling. The Inuit can tell a drift's suitability for building a snow house by plunging a stick into it, but the same information can be had by trial and error. A pruning saw makes a good snow knife and in summer is useful for cutting kelp off anchors. Alternatively a machete or something similar can be used. Building an arch of snow blocks over each porthole to let in light makes the boat a much more cheerful place.

By mid winter all openings in the hull will be frozen shut rendering the toilet and galley sink useless. A stout bucket in the cockpit makes a good toilet with a similar one in the galley for slops. The contents of the toilet bucket will freeze solid in a very short time and can be emptied in down a tide crack, preferably a good distance from the boat. The best buckets for this are made of high density polyethylene (they have HDPE in the recycling information on the bucket's bottom) as they do not become brittle at low temperatures.

Streams continue flowing below the snow for a considerable part of the winter and getting water from them is simply matter of digging through the overlying snow towards the sound of the trickling water. HDPE buckets with clip-on lids are by far the best for collecting and carrying water. Jerry cans are slow to fill, allowing ice to build up around the top and preventing the cap from being screwed on. In cold weather, ice will completely block the neck before the can is full. Water buckets must of course be stored in the cabin to prevent them freezing solid.

After the streams freeze completely, probably in January, it will be necessary to dig a water hole in a lake. In midwinter a lake will have a variable thickness of snow over one to two metres of hard ice. The snow cover is no problem but digging a hole through the ice is hard, slow work. The minimum tools required are a shovel and pick, with a heavy crowbar and an ice auger highly desirable. A lanyard attached to an eye welded to the crowbar allows the crowbar to be retrieved if it slips through icy mittens into deep water. A water hole can be preserved for a couple of weeks by letting it freeze to a depth of 25mm or so then shovelling about a metre of snow over it for insulation. The next time water is needed, all that is necessary is to shovel the snow off and break through 100 or 150mm of ice. Eventually the bottom of the water hole, which is necessarily smaller than the top opening, will freeze shut and a new hole has to be dug.

Digging for water and hauling it to the boat is hard work but the saving in fuel compared to melting ice or snow is considerable. Cooker fuel usage will nearly double if it is necessary to melt ice for water. The conventional wisdom that melting snow for water takes more fuel than melting ice is incorrect. Ice requires less attention to melt as the pot does not need filling nearly as often, but a pot kept full of compressed snow requires no more of fuel to produce a litre of water.

Dramatic photos like those of the crushing of Shackleton's *Endurance* have led to the expectation that any vessel in ice will be subject to pressure and forced upward. In fact the opposite is true. Provided the yacht is in a sheltered bay and protected from the pressure of drifting ice, it will be dragged down as the ice thickens. If the vessel is moored far enough from the shore to be clear of the shearing pressures of the tide crack and in deep enough water that the sea does not freeze to bottom and cause pressure ridging, there is little lateral pressure on the hull.

The sea ice thickens from the top by freezing seawater-saturated snow lying on the surface of the floe, so the oldest ice is at the bottom. Unless a yacht can emulate the *Fram* and withdraw its rudder, propeller and any other underwater projections, these will become embedded in the first-formed, lowest ice and pull the boat down as the ice thickens. Fortunately it will not be pulled down by the full thickness of the ice. Initially the ice is thin and relatively weak so the vessel's buoyancy will break the ice and it will float near its usual lines. As the ice thickens and envelops the propeller, rudder and other underwater appendages, the vessel will be dragged down until its buoyancy exerts enough pressure on the ice to allow it to rise a limited amount through the ice by pressure solution. Typically a yacht will be drawn down by 30 or 50cm in the course of the winter, depending on the hull shape and depth of appendages.

Keeping the bow and stern clear of ice and turning the propeller regularly may stop the yacht from being drawn down at all, but breaking the ice under the flare of the hull is a miserable job. Ice has to be broken from the bottom of a pool of water while working in a kneeling position using a pick or crowbar and the ice fragments then scooped from the pool. Every stroke with the pick or crowbar sends up a show of water that instantly freezes to clothes, mittens and the boat. It is an exercise best avoided.

Living in winter on a small vessel with marginal heating requires a little fortitude and much patience. The alcohol for preheating the kerosene stove will itself need preheating before it will burn, pens do not write and toothpaste will not squeeze from its tube until warmed in an inner pocket, butane lighters are useless, liquid detergent freezes and rum is a slushy solid. However these are merely time-consuming inconveniences, not real problems.

Thin polypropylene gloves are a great comfort working in a cold cabin and also make a good base under two layers of mittens for working outside. These gloves get grubby when working in the galley and wear out quickly, requiring frequent darning. At least ten pairs per person are a good idea.

A vessel with a pressurized hot water shower will find the system frozen for most of the winter and needs to make other arrangements for the crew to wash themselves. Less mechanized boats will probably already have a system that can be adapted to a cold environment. Simplest of all is to sponge bath in a large plastic tub. Alternatively a shower can be had using a sun shower suspended from the deckhead or using a pressurized garden spray. There must be a method of collecting the wastewater from these manual showers so it does not run into the bilges and freeze there.

Laundry is a nuisance but should not be neglected as dirty clothes quickly lose their insulation properties. It is easiest to carry the laundry to the water source and do it there but this is only possible down to –10°C. Below that clothes freeze to the side of the washing and rinsing buckets almost instantly and tear when pulled free. When that happens there is little option but to carry water to the boat and do the laundry there.

Drying clothes is equally problematic. There is an urban myth that clothes hung out in cold condition will dry by 'shaking the ice out'. Nothing of the sort happens to anything more absorbent or tightly woven than nylon fishing net. At temperatures just below freezing, clothes will dry by sublimation when ice evaporates without going through a liquid phase. Sublimation slows as the temperature falls and is imperceptible below –10°C. At this point clothes have to come inside to dry, to the detriment of the cabin's habitability.

Doing the laundry beside a water hole in a frozen lake. This is only possible when the temperature is above -10°C
Annie Hill

Fortunately only the layers of clothes against the body gets grubby, so the only things that need to be washed on a regular basis are underclothes, gloves, socks and hats. Silk long underwear has much to recommend it as an inner layer, being comfortable and having less odour than polypropylene, but polypropylene is easier to wash and dry. A silk sleeping bag liner to protect the bedding is worthwhile and also saves a lot of washing. A coat dedicated for galley wear (or an apron) will protect other clothes from getting greasy and losing their insulation.

The length of the polar night depends on latitude. In most locations the sun will return before the coldest part of winter, which is usually in February. Despite this, with the return of the sun the hardest part of the winter is over. The joy the first sunlight brings is difficult to explain to anyone who has not spent a polar night isolated on a small vessel in the high latitudes.

After sunrise, the days get quickly longer until the first drips of water on south facing rocks herald the approach of spring. Sometime in May it will be warm enough to clear the snow cover from the boat which shortly afterwards will float free of the ice with a narrow moat all around. The stern may still be held down because the rudder and perhaps the propeller are caught in the ice. This is hard on the rudder pintles and uncomfortable for living aboard. If the propeller can turn, running the engine in gear will send (relatively) warm water across the rudder and should eventually free it. If the propeller is not free or if it is likely to strike fast ice when the boat jumps up to float in its normal lines, the ice will have to be broken away using a crowbar, pick and ice saw.

Once the boat is afloat, the toilet will pump out, the sink will drain and the water tanks can be refilled. As the hull warms up, the condensation frozen to the hull behind the linings and in the unheated bow and stern will begin to melt. The bilge pumps will still be frozen so there will be a period of several weeks during which this meltwater has to be bailed by hand. The amount will depend on the exhaust arrangements that were in place in the cabin and galley during the winter, but about 200 litres per person is likely.

Once the sea ice starts to puddle, the yacht needs to be converted back to being an ocean-going vessel in preparation for breaking out. The shore depot has to be brought aboard, sails bent on and hoisted, rigging checked, anchors and chains overhauled and machinery recommissioned.

Breaking out of the ice is potentially dangerous. Ideally the ice will melt around the boat and gently drift away as small, harmless pans. However a gale may send the ice out with a rush, buffeting the vessel on the way, or the bay ice may break out as a single large floe weighing thousands of tonnes with the boat still embedded in it in. Each situation will require a different solution and it is difficult to know in advance what it will be. All that can be done is have the dinghies ready to go, ice poles and spare lines to hand, anchors ready to run and the engine on standby.

The crew's immune system will take a while to get working again after its winter-long germ-free holiday. Everyone will probably come down with a respiratory infection when they first make contact with the outside world. Not much can be done about that other than to allow a few days for recovery before continuing with the new season's venture.'

Summer: this ice is rotten and about to break out

Sails dug out and hoisted to check them and the running gear prior to breakout

Choosing and preparing a boat for the Arctic

It should be assumed that a yacht and her crew will need to be entirely self-sufficient for the duration of their Arctic voyage. This will include thinking through a variety of worst case scenarios in order to plan for repairs and carry any necessary spares.

It is prudent to have some redundancy in key navigation and communication systems. For example spare portable Iridium 'phone and handheld GPS units, with associated chargers, will serve as replacements in the event of a breakdown and can be used if the vessel has to be abandoned or if a shore party are venturing some distance from the vessel.

Boat suitability

It is probable that would-be Arctic voyagers will want to sail in their existing boats. Personally, I would much prefer a steel or aluminium boat for sailing in waters where serious concentrations of ice can be expected, such as the North West and North East Passages. One might consider the following:

1. Hull material. Steel and aluminium are stronger than fibreglass or wood
2. A strengthened bow
3. Watertight bulkheads
4. Rudder protection, both ahead and astern of the rudder. Some boats designed specifically for operating in ice have skegs astern of a keel mounted rudder. (Note – vane steering may have

Northabout - a boat built by Jarlath Cunnane specifically for sailing in the Arctic *Jarlath Cunnane*

to be removed or placed well above water level to avoid ice damage)

5. Propellor protection. Some boats have rings around the propellor to protect it from ice. However, there is a school of thought which says that ice can become trapped between the 'protection ring' and the propellor
6. Fixed or lifting keel. Some people prefer a lifting keel as many high latitude waters are quite shallow. A lifting keel also allows the boat to navigate in shallow water inshore of grounded ice bergs. Others believe a lifting keel is an unnecessary complication. Ice or small stones may affect its operation. Boats with lifting keels tend to have more exposed propellors which are more easily damaged by ice
7. Protection from the elements for the crew on watch
8. Hull insulation and heating. If planning to over winter, double glazing
9. A means of easily climbing the rigging is useful when searching for leads in the ice
10. Simple systems which can be maintained with relative ease
11. Fuel and water tank capacity
12. Storage capacity
13. Engine. A reliable engine is an absolute necessity. Twin engines offer some redundancy but twin propellers are more prone to one propeller being damaged by ice.

Navigation and communications equipment

Compasses

Magnetic variation near the magnetic North Pole is high (60°) and some Arctic charts are annotated with the words 'magnetic compass useless'. Magnetic compasses, including fluxgate compasses, depend upon the horizontal component of the magnetic field of the earth, which becomes progressively weaker as the magnetic North Pole is approached. The compass behaves very sluggishly in areas close to the magnetic North Pole and doesn't react quickly enough to be effective. Larger vessels are often equipped with gyro compasses, but these also become unstable in polar regions and errors need to be compensated for.

Useful websites – boats specifically designed for high latitudes

	Seal	www.expeditionsail.com/contacts/sailboat-seal.htm
	Pelagic and Pelagic Australis	www.pelagic.co.uk
	Northabout	www.northabout.com
	Polar Bound	http://en.wikipedia.org/wiki/File:Polar_Bound.JPG
	Taonui	www.taonui.com http://members.shaw.ca/taonui/cruising_in_taonui.html

A GPS compass utilises three GPS aerials, often mounted within a single aerial dome, to calculate true north. They are more expensive and bulkier than fluxgate compasses but less so than gyro compasses. It is important to ensure that the antenna unit is installed with a clear view of the sky. The true north output can be used to accurately drive auto-pilots, plotters and radar displays.

The auto-pilot on a vessel underway and being piloted by a standard GPS will function but not as well as an auto-pilot driven by a GPS compass.

Radar

Radar is a highly desirable navigation aid and collision avoidance tool in Arctic waters. Although not all ice will show up on radar, much of it does. Low lying sea ice and growlers present poor radar targets. Icebergs usually present good targets, however this is not always the case. The return echo radar signal can be reflected straight up into the air and no signal received by the radar. In unusually dry atmospheric conditions, radar beams can become bent. This shortens or lengthens target detection ranges, depending on the severity and direction of the bending. Inaccurate surveys, areas of low lying, relatively featureless land, and coastlines obscured by a build up of ice, all further contribute towards many potential errors in the interpretation of radar fixes in Arctic waters. It is good seamanship to cross check a variety of information sources and maintain a good visual watch.

A chart plotter with a radar overlay can be used to check that the plotter chart datum and offset are correct. It should be remembered that the radar picture needs to be interpreted: a rock cliff will give a good return but a low lying beach may give a very poor return.

Using two or more radar ranges (distances off a prominent radar feature) is more accurate than using radar bearings on a small radar set. This is because the accuracy of radar bearings is affected by the heading sensor adjustment and radar definition.

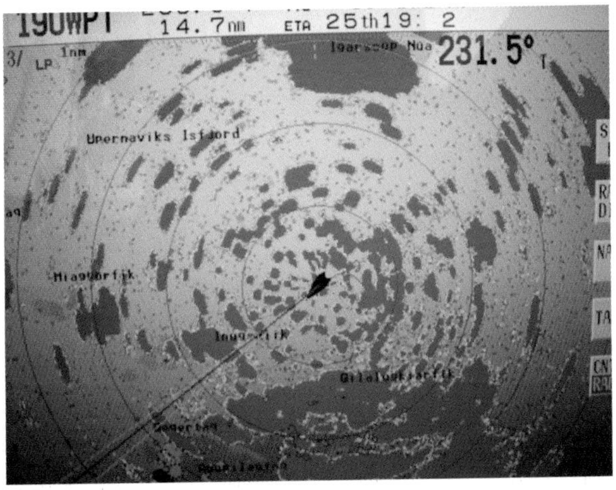

Radar display (three mile range) indicating ice off Upernavik (Greenland) *Máire Wilkes*

Forward looking echo sounders

These are very useful when navigating through poorly charted waters or identifying a suitable anchorage. They are not suitable for detecting ice. The transducer of a forward looking echo sounder protrudes beneath the hull and is therefore vulnerable when manoeuvring in ice. It should therefore be retractable and a conventional echo-sounder retained onboard.

Global Positioning System (GPS)

The reliability of GPS systems has improved polar navigation considerably. Even at the North Pole the orbiting satellites are distributed well enough to create a good fix for vessels navigating these waters. Most of the potential errors due to atmospheric conditions are minimised by automatic compensations made within the GPS receiver. It is good practice to check the chart datum of each chart. WGS84 is virtually equivalent to the North American Datum 1983 (NAD 83). If one were navigating on a NAD 83 chart with GPS using the WGS84 datum there would be no corrections to apply. It is probable, particularly in Arctic waters, that GPS readings may not agree with charted positions. A GPS derived position should be cross checked with other sources of navigational information such as sight, radar and depth readings.

It is prudent for vessels to carry at least one back-up GPS.

HF radio (Single Side-Band)

Radio communications in the Arctic, other than line of sight (VHF), are subject to interference from ionospheric disturbances. Sunspot (auroral) activity can cause difficulties with high frequency (HF) signals in high latitudes and may cause complete communication 'blackouts'. Whenever communications are established, alternative frequencies should be agreed upon before the signal degrades. It may be necessary to use multiple frequencies or relays through other stations.

A laptop computer can be linked to an HF radio to send and receive emails and to receive GRIB files and other information without online charges, although file size is restricted due to limited data speed. Airmail is a radio mail software program (equivalent to Outlook) for sending and receiving messages via a modem over HF radio, either via the ham radio system or participating marine and commercial services. Sailmail is a subscriber SSB email system that uses Airmail. The frequencies used are mostly within the marine bands. Winlink is a free communication system, produced by and for licensed radio amateurs, which also uses Airmail. The various technologies are progressing at such a fast rate that detailed discussion quickly becomes out of date.

Computers can cause radio interference and it is important that on board systems are installed correctly.

Satellite communications

The Iridium system is relatively cheap to buy and is a valuable alternative system in Arctic waters. Handsets transmit to satellites orbiting the globe on a polar orbit so there is global coverage up to the poles. However, sending or receiving lots of data may prove unreliable, slow and expensive. Compression software reduces the data size when sending or receiving emails. A permanent aerial installed above decks is preferable to a mobile aerial as connections are kept dry and the equipment can be used in all weathers.

Inmarsat allows reception of timely and detailed ice charts and is a very useful asset. The Inmarsat system uses geo-stationary satellites stationed over the equator. In the Arctic, the altitude of the Inmarsat system satellites may be as little as 3° above the horizon. Although, in open waters, the system continues to function, it may not be possible to send or receive signals whilst in port or close to high land. When signal strength has diminished below that useable for voice communications, it may still be possible to send data. Mariners should consult the Inmarsat coverage areas to determine if coverage is likely to be available along the intended route of the vessel. In the author's experience, coverage extends beyond the advertised coverage areas. Adequate coverage has been found on the west coast of Greenland up to Upernavik and throughout through the North West Passage, with the exception of about 300 miles on the northwestern coast of Alaska. Vessels have used Inmarsat C successfully for regional weather text but not graphics.

The Fleet Broadband 150, 250 and 500 systems are probably the most suitable for small vessels although they are still relatively expensive. Further information on the system and the coverage areas are available on the Inmarsat website.

The MailASail website gives a good description of the various satphones available and a comparison table of their characteristics. The usage tariffs should be studied carefully when costing the different systems.

A possible alternative is MSAT, a Canadian-owned satellite-based telecommunications network targeted primarily towards mobile users operating in rural and remote areas. According to the Canadian Coastguard website, MSAT Mobile Communicators are compact and have been specifically developed for marine applications and provide excellent coverage over the Arctic.

A satphone is a requirement for transiting the North East Passage.

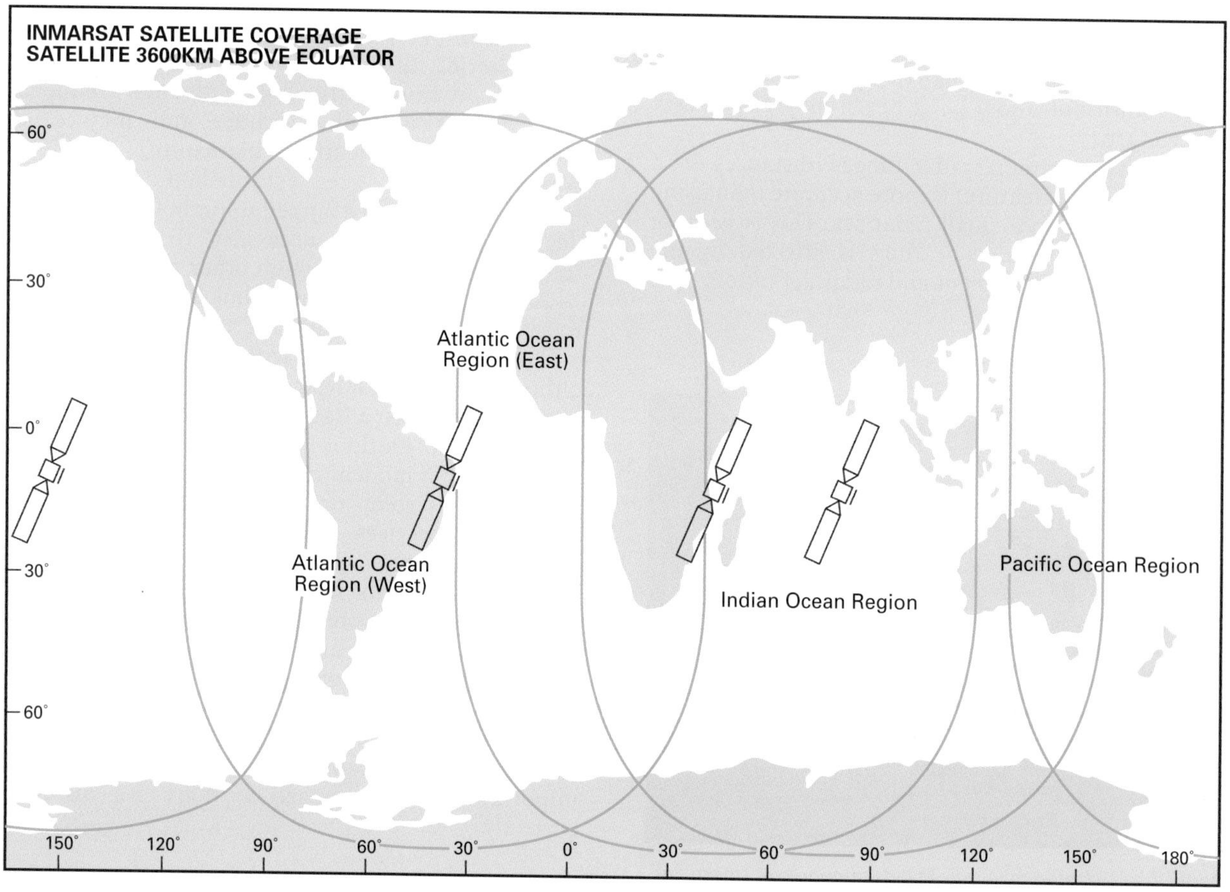

Useful websites – HF and satellite communications

MailASail Ed Wildgoose at MailASail is an excellent source of help and information	www.mailasail.com
Saildocs 'Internet services for the bandwidth-impaired'	www.saildocs.com
Sail Com Marine Marine communications supplier	www.sailcom.co.uk
Sailmail Email service for yachts	www.sailmail.com
Winlink A worldwide system of volunteer sysops, radio stations and network assets supporting email by radio, with non-commercial links to internet email	www.winlink.org
Airmail HF email messaging programme	http://siriuscyber.net/airmail
Mods Modifications repair instructions and improvement of HAM rigs, HAM modems, etc.	www.mods.dk
Icom Communications equipment manufacturer	www.icomuk.co.uk
Pactor Pactor modem supplier for HF data coms	www.pactor.info
Inmarsat Global satellite service provider	www.inmarsat.com

Global Maritime Distress and Safety System (GMDSS)

Sea areas are defined as follows:

Sea Area A1 An area within the radiotelephone coverage of at least one VHF coast station in which continuous digital selective calling (Ch 70 / 156.525MHz) alerting and radiotelephony services are available. Such an area could extend typically 30M (56km) to 40M (74km) from the Coast Station.

Sea Area A2 An area, excluding Sea Area A1, within the radiotelephone coverage of at least one MF coast station in which continuous DSC (2187.5kHz) alerting and radiotelephony services are available. For planning purposes, this area typically extends to up to 180M (330km) offshore during daylight hours, but would exclude any A1 designated areas. In practice, satisfactory coverage may often be achieved out to around 400M (740km) offshore during night time.

Sea Area A3 An area, excluding Sea Areas A1 and A2, within the coverage of an Inmarsat geostationary satellite. This area lies between about latitude 76° North and South, but excludes A1 and/or A2 designated areas. Inmarsat guarantees their system will work between 70 South and 70 North though it will often work to 76° South or North.

Sea Area A4 An area outside Sea Areas A1, A2 and A3 is called Sea Area A4. This is essentially the polar regions, north and south of about 76° of latitude, excluding any A1 or A2 areas.

The limits of the various sea areas for the waters referred to in this book are shown in the diagram. Vessels complying fully with GMDSS and operating in Area 4 (the High Arctic) will require HF DSC (High Frequency Digital Selective Calling) and NBDP (Narrow Band Direct Printing telegraphy) equipment in addition to an EPIRB.

Emergency Position Indicating Beacons (EPIRBs)

EPIRBs are a standard piece of emergency equipment carried on most well found vessels. Their potential importance is never more so than when navigating in the Arctic. Most operate using the Cospas-Sarsat which uses two types of satellite:

1. Satellites in low-altitude Earth orbit (LEO) which form the LEOSAR System
2. Satellites in geostationary Earth orbit (GEO) which form the GEOSAR system

Although GEOSAR satellites provide a quicker response, they do not give coverage over the polar regions. LEOSAR satellites provide coverage in the Arctic but they are not instantaneous.

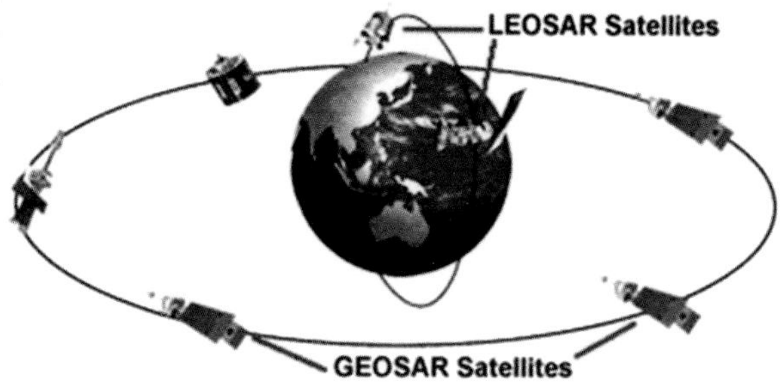

A Refleks diesel burning heater *Andrew Wilkes*

Heating systems

Solid fuel such as coal or wood is unlikely to be available in most Arctic settlements. In some areas of the Arctic, timber is readily available on the shore but tends to be so salt-impregnated that it burns badly. Foraged wood should not be relied on.

A diesel powered heater is practical because the fuel is readily available and is probably already carried onboard. There are two types: hot air blowers and diesel stoves.

1. Hot air blower (fuel drip and fan):
   a. Eberspacher
   b. Webasto
2. Stove type (fuel drip into a bowl with a carburettor similar to an outboard motor):
   a. Dickenson
   b. Refleks

The stove type is quite 'cosy' and some designs can be used as a hot-plate for cooking. A clothes line or rack close to the heater is useful for drying out wet clothing. The stove should be set up correctly and the flue tested before departure. The position of sails in relation to the flue and the boat's angle of heel may affect operation.

Other types of heating include paraffin, gas, electric and engine driven systems. It may be worth considering using the engine cooling water to heat a radiator close to the chart table or watch-keeping position.

Hot water bottles in sleeping bags or clothing are useful. Chemical hand-warmers which are recharged by placing them in hot water have also been used.

Ground tackle

Good heavy duty ground tackle is essential. A variety of anchors to suit different conditions and allow some redundancy should one be lost is recommended. Several long lines (100m or more) may be useful for taking mooring lines ashore. Polyprop rope is cheap and it floats which is an advantage if towing it ashore by dinghy. Polyprop lines should be protected from UV light when not in use.

Dinghies

A good dinghy is essential as there are are very few alongside berths in the Arctic and much time is spent at anchor. It is prudent to carry a spare dinghy. Polar

Dinghy iced up during a gale in Gjoa Haven *Phil Hogg*

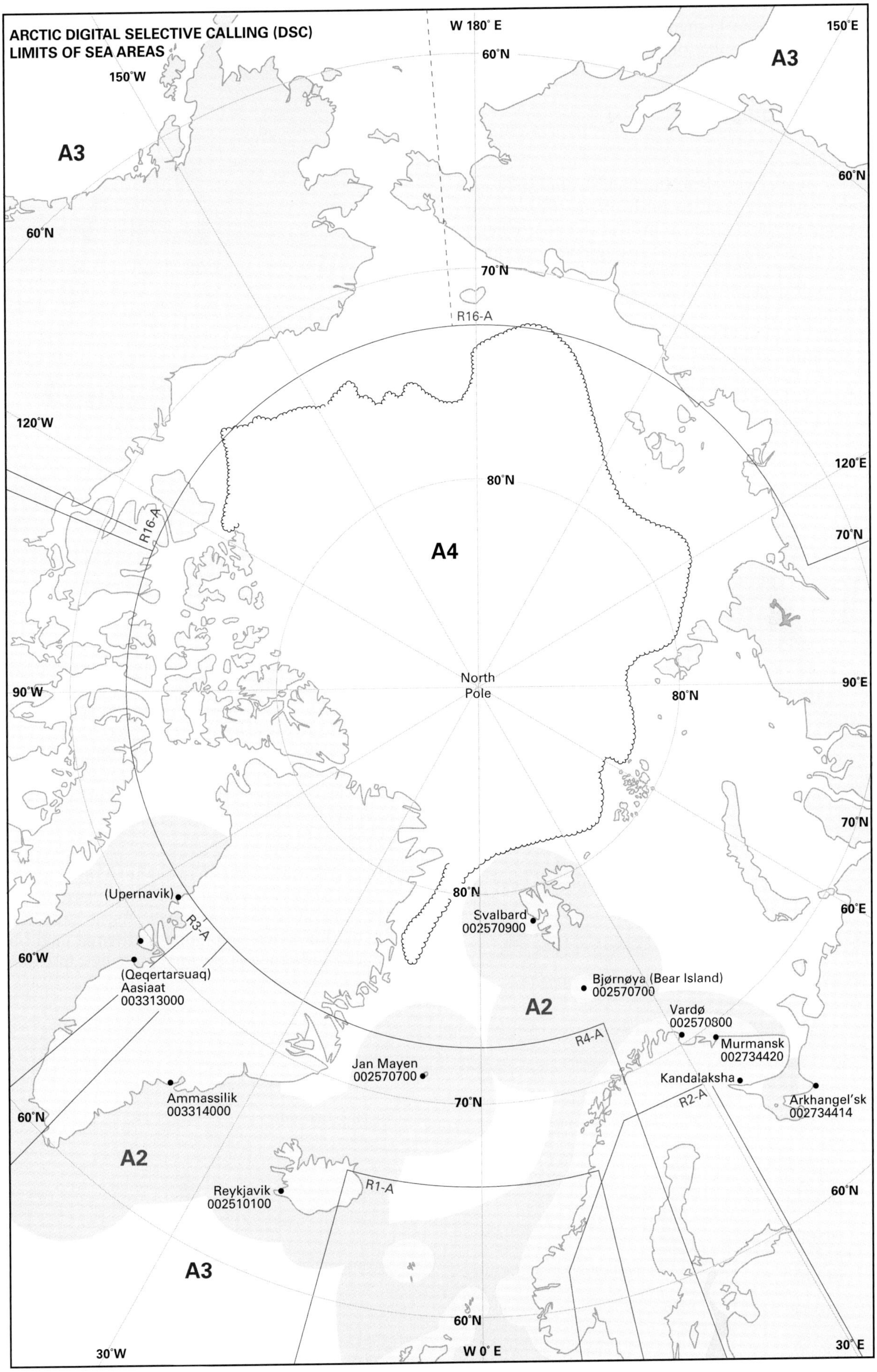

Arctic Digital Selective Calling (DSC) limits of sea areas
Admiralty List of Radio Signals

bears have been known to rip into inflatables and there are any number of other reasons why a dinghy may be lost.

Special equipment

Ice poles

Most smaller vessels in the high Arctic carry an ice pole. They are used to push off ice floes to allow passage of the boat or to protect the boat when it is anchored. They need to be strong poles, ideally with an end that enables a grip into the ice. Length of the pole will depend to some extent on the length and freeboard of the boat, as well as manageability. Yachts have used old windsurfer masts or an aluminium pole about 5m long. The hollow end section does not skid on the ice and the pole is relatively light. Other yachts have used spruce poles with a metal spiked end although timber can be heavy for one person to manoeuvre easily.

Using an ice pole on *Northabout* *Jarlath Cunnane*

Keeping a lookout from the ratlines *Sibéal Turraoin*

Mast steps and ratlines

When navigating in sea ice it is often useful to have a lookout positioned as high as possible to identify leads through the ice or areas of sea where the ice is less concentrated. Mast steps or ratlines rigged in the shrouds give relatively easy access to a higher lookout position. Local fishing boats often have crow's nests, a protective enclosure high up in their rigging, from which a crew member can keep a look out.

Thermal imaging

The navigation equipment manufacturer Raymarine is now owned by the American thermal imaging company Flir Systems Inc. As a consequence, Raymarine offer a handheld thermal night vision camera and range of thermal imaging cameras which

Useful websites

	Eberspacher Hot air blower heating system	www.eberspacher.com
	Webasto Hot air blower heating system	www.webasto-marine.com
	Dickinson Canadian diesel stove manufacturer	www.dickinsonmarine.com
	Refleks Danish diesel stove manufacturer	www.refleks-olieovne.dk/default.asp?pagenumber=1563

Thermal image display of icebergs *Alejandro Veccia*

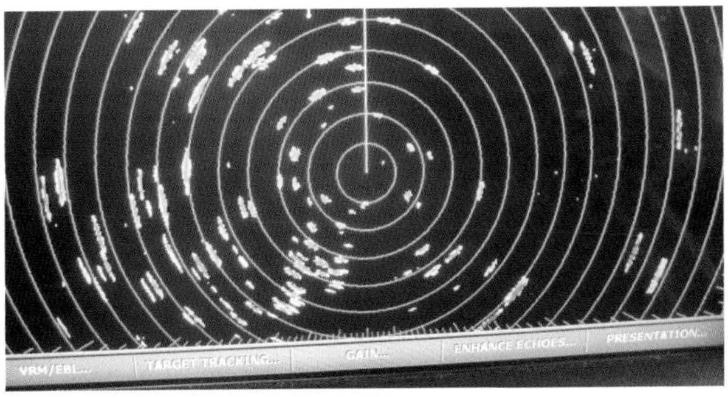

Radar display showing the same icebergs depicted on the thermal image display *Alejandro Veccia*

Photograph of the same icebergs shown in the thermal image *Alejandro Veccia*

Alejandro Veccia the skipper of *Nordwind* reports that:

'The thermal camera in our experience was really good. Our first iceberg was seen through the camera in the middle of the night at the tip of Newfoundland.

In calm waters it was easier to sit inside the dog house looking forward than to be sitting outside with the wind on the face.

One thing important to point out is that the thermal camera doesn't work with fog (and most of the trip was with fog)! The model we have has a low light camera and a thermal camera which can be selected according to conditions. The thermal camera works with NO light and can pick differences in temperature between water and ice.'

integrate with their products. These may be useful for locating ice when navigating in the dark. A thermal imaging camera is also a potentially useful man-overboard recovery aid.

The photographs show the same ice sighted visually, on a thermal imaging camera and on a radar display. Each watch-keeping method has its advantages:

- The thermal imaging camera is viewed from a warm navigation area, it can 'see in the dark' and picks up nearby bergy bits and growlers well
- The radar has a greater range. Its definition is poor and smaller targets are missed
- The 'Mark 1 Eyeball' remains the best anti-collision aid known to man!

It should be noted that thermal imaging cameras do not function well in fog and that sailing at night in areas where there is ice present has been compared to playing Russian roulette.

Wetsuits and scuba gear

Lines caught around propellers, jammed rudders, blocked skin fittings etc, will probably require a crew member to solve the problem from the water. A thick wetsuit, or preferably a drysuit, with gloves, socks and balaclava, together with scuba gear can enable a fit person to spend short periods of time in cold water. Standard breathing apparatus regulators can freeze and cause regulator freeflow. Prolonged diving in cold water is a specialised skill and specialised equipment is used.

Diving equipment can be useful in the Arctic *Máire Wilkes*

Useful websites – thermal imaging

	Safran Long range infrared binoculars	www.safran-group.com/site-safran-en/defense-303/land-defense/portable-optronics/all-models-619
	Raymarine Thermal cameras	www.raymarine.co.uk/view/?id=1147

Chain saws, dynamite and winches

Some yachts have carried a chain saw onboard. The idea of this is that it can be used to cut through the ice around the hull if the hull is threatened.

Dynamite is not recommended! One yacht reportedly carried explosives in order to blast their way through pack ice if necessary, but it proved totally unsuccessful.

Northern Passage (a 31ft Corsair trimaran) developed a 'pegged block and winch' arrangement such that the crew could winch the yacht up onto the shore or ice floes.

Mosquito defences

Mosquitos and biting insects are a part of life in the short Arctic summer. Netting to keep insects out of the cabin and personal nets which hang over hats are useful, as are insect repellents. All of these can be bought in settlements with shops. In Alaska, the mosquito is known as the national bird.

Charts

Before entering Arctic waters, yachts should be equipped with all the relevant charts and other publications appropriate to any planned passages as publications are unlikely to be available locally.

Passage planning should include alternative routes and ports of refuge as passages and harbours may be blocked by ice.

Chart projections

As the meridians converge near the pole, they become more radial and less parallel. As a consequence, Mercator projections suffer considerable distortion in latitude on anything other than large-scale charts of the Arctic. Alternative projections such as Polar Stereographic and Lambert Conformal Conic are sometimes used. It may not be possible to use the latitude scale or compass rose to equate distances and bearings.

Chart accuracy

The value of a chart depends on an understanding of the accuracy and detail of the surveys on which it was based. Chart accuracy varies widely in the Arctic. More visited areas, such as Lancaster Sound and Barrow Strait, are relatively well surveyed. Charts for other areas may be based only on aerial photography. Even apparently new chart editions may be based on information sourced in the early days of Arctic exploration. The dates of the source information should be recorded on each chart and checked by the navigator. Larger scale charts tend to be updated more quickly than smaller scale charts with any new information. Depending on the accuracy of the chart, positioning with GPS can lead to an error of up to four nautical miles. For depth soundings and other detailed information about the seabed, it is estimated by the Canadian Hydrographic Service that less than 25% of the Arctic waters are surveyed to acceptable modern standards.

Every winter the large scale movement of ice re-shapes the sea bed to a greater or lesser extent. Sandbanks are particularly susceptible to being shifted and their charted boundaries are liable to be inaccurate.

Up-to-date chart corrections should be applied whenever possible. In 2010 the passenger ship *Clipper Adventurer* grounded on a rock in Arctic Canada with 128 passengers on board. The rock position was not marked on the chart; however a chart correction advising of its suspected existence had been issued some months earlier.

Russian charts are reported to tie in exactly with GPS positions.

Electronic charts

C-Map accuracy is quite good in both the North West and North East Passages. However, the hard disc on most laptop computers is vulnerable in weather conditions when the motion of small boats is violent. 'Dongles' are also vulnerable to loss or damage. The prudent navigator will not rely solely on electronic charts.

Selecting an anchorage

Many of the historic anchorages referred to in the pilot books were selected by men commanding square-rigged vessels without auxiliary engines. Their criteria for anchorages were very different from today's small vessels and some historic anchorages may be totally unsuitable for a small boat.

Factors to consider when selecting an anchorage include:

- The presence of rivers (including dry beds of Spring run-off channels) tend to provide good holding in relatively shallow water
- A close study of the local topography should give a clue as to whether katabatic winds and/or wind

Useful websites – charts

	Athens University An informative paper about the choice of chart projections in the Arctic	www.iho.int/mtg_docs/rhc/ArHC/ArHC3/ARHC3-3.2.7_Suitable_projections_for_the_Arctic.pdf
	U.S. Geological Survey Detailed explanation of various chart projections	http://egsc.usgs.gov/isb/pubs/MapProjections/projections.html

funnelling are likely to be a problem in the prevailing conditions

- A shoreline which slopes gently down to the water is likely to have a gentle gradient under the water. Steep rocky shorelines often indicate an uneven seabed and deep water which may not be suitable for anchoring
- The distance from the anchorage to open water is correlated to the risk of invading ice
- The absence of soundings should not discourage exploration. Modern yachts, cautiously handled, are manoeuvrable, and a forward looking depth sounder is a handy device.

Anchoring techniques

Normal anchoring techniques apply for most of the time when anchoring in the Arctic, however, it may be necessary to take into account deep water close to the shore or very strong winds. Strong katabatic winds are common close to high land.

It is not ideal to anchor on a seabed which shelves rapidly away from the shore into deep water. An anchorage can sometimes be made more secure by dropping the bow anchor whilst facing offshore and then taking stern lines ashore. The shore-lines (normally 2 triangulated lines) should keep the anchor pulling 'up-hill' and will secure the boat in off-shore winds. Lines can be secured to trees however these are unlikely to be found in the high Arctic. A bight of chain can be placed around a suitable rock and then shackled to the shore-line. This will help minimise chaff. Polypropylene rope is light and floats which makes it relatively easy to tow ashore with a dinghy. Polyprop lines are particularly susceptible to UV degradation so should be stored carefully when not in use.

Shore-lines can also be used to limit swinging room if necessary.

If anchoring on or near a steeply sloping sea bed, another technique is to use a second anchor instead of shore lines. The second anchor is set in shallow water in-shore of the main anchor and, like shore-lines, is deployed to stop the main anchor from dragging 'down-hill' and secure the boat in off-shore winds. The two anchor rodes can be shackled together, then more chain lowered so that the 'join' is lower than the boat's keel.

There is no substitute for a big heavy bower anchor and, as mentioned previously, carrying a variety of heavy anchors is recommended. Two anchors chained together 'in series' can provide additional holding in strong gales and katabatic winds. The shank of the 'first down' (anchor 1) is connected to the crown of the 'second-down' (anchor 2) by, say, 10m of chain. It may ease both the dropping and recovery of anchor 1 if a length of slack polypropylene (floating) line is made semi-permanently fast onto anchor 1 and the other end clipped onto anchor 2. The line can then be unclipped and used, perhaps with a halyard or winch, to lower and recover anchor 1 when anchor 2 is on the bow-roller.

Personal protection and clothing

Polar bears, bear sprays, flares and rifles

Polar bears are an endangered species. The reduction in the summer sea ice has restricted their summer hunting areas to a level that is thought by some to be incompatible with their survival. Killing a polar bear is, therefore, not something that should be considered lightly. On the other hand, they have been known to actively stalk and kill humans and it is wise to be prepared.

Polars bears are immensely strong and are used to climbing out of the water onto high sided ice floes. It is likely that they would be able to climb onto yachts with a low freeboard. When going ashore in areas where polar bears are known to be present, the risk of being attacked is much greater.

Anecdotal evidence is that polar bears will only attack humans if they or their offspring are threatened or if they are very hungry. However, they are often very hungry! The best way to avoid a confrontation is to keep a sharp lookout, especially when walking ashore, and avoid leaving a scent which may attract bears. Polar bears have an acute sense of smell which they use to great effect when hunting. Food and urine leave scents which are attractive to polar bears. Apparently coffee is particularly attractive.

Bear sprays are a type of mace spray which are supposedly effective when sprayed into the bear's face. However, one would have to make sure the wind was blowing towards the bear and away from

A polar bear up close *Jarlath Cunnane*

At NASA's Haughton Mars Camp on Devon Island, in the heart of polar bear territory, no one leaves the camp alone or without at least one gun in the party. Common to many settlements in the Arctic, the scientists live and work with a continual threat from polar bears. Some sources advise a 'shoot to kill' policy when confronted by a polar bear, but this is not policy at the camp.

The crew of *Northabout* had a very close encounter with a Russian polar bear that came close enough to put a paw up on the side deck. Unfortunately their gun was hidden away down below at the critical moment – they were very thankful that banging pots and pans was enough to scare the bear away.

the person! Personally, I think that by the time one was within spraying range, a person would be far too close to the bear for safety.

Flare guns and flares can be used to scare bears away and it is a sensible precaution to carry one or the other when walking ashore. One should ensure that the flare is let off in a location which would drive the bear away from people rather than towards them! When a glacier or iceberg calves, it makes a loud report similar to a gunshot. Polar bears are therefore familiar with this kind of noise and may not be scared by loud bangs.

The recommendation by most Arctic specialists is to carry a rifle onboard and always carry it when going ashore. Rifles should be kept dry, clean and oiled. Ideally they should be stored onboard in a locker which is dry, readily accessible and which can be locked. When travelling ashore in a dinghy one might want to consider placing the rifle in a plastic bag. Some people use a thin layer of masking tape to protect the open end of the barrel from grit and sand. The barrier should not be too thick and it should preferably be removed before shooting the rifle.

Crews would be well advised to discuss polar bear protection and rifle drills before entering areas where bears may be present. One might want to consider when it is necessary to take precautions, who will carry the rifle, their training and 'rules of engagement,' etc. For example, where a rifle holds just three rounds of ammunition, it might be agreed to fire a warning shot in the air when a bear is 100m away leaving two rounds for self defense if the bear is aggressive and closes to within 30m.

It is important for crew to know how to use a gun effectively and safely. The UK National Shooting Centre at Bisley offers a half day 'Polar Bear Protection' course. A Bisley instructor advised that, to stop a polar charging, one should aim at the bear's chest and fire several rounds of ammunition. Do not

Rifles for sale in an Aasiaat supermarket, Greenland *Sibéal Turraoin*

approach the bear until it is absolutely certain that it is dead. Bears are a protected species and the authorities will need to be informed if a bear is killed or wounded.

Skippers may wish to encourage crew to practice safe shooting and additional ammunition will be required for this.

Rifles can be readily bought in Greenland. They can be hired in Norway and Svalbard. See RCCPF *Norway* (Imray). Most countries require a licence to buy a rifle and a permit to carry one. Details about how to obtain permits are given in the following chapters.

Royal Canadian Mounted Police personnel have, in the past, recommended a 12 gauge pump shotgun with heavy predator loads, using slugs for maximum dependability and killing power in case of an emergency encounter with a polar bear.

Fuel

Arctic winds in summer are mostly light, and attempting to sail through ice of density greater than 2/10 is usually unproductive. When calculating fuel needs, one should plan for motoring all the time. Fuel consumption can be higher than normal when navigating in ice because of frequent changes in direction and engine speed. Ice may prevent access to refueling settlements, so it is important to carry plenty of spare fuel. It may be necessary to refuel using jerry cans so these will need to be carried on

Useful websites

	National Rifle Association of the UK The NRA offer polar bear protection lessons at the National Shooting Centre, Bisley	www.nra.org.uk
	Parks Canada This site has several links to brochures about safety in polar bear areas	www.pc.gc.ca/pn-np/nl/torngats/visit/brochures.aspx

Refuelling at Pond Inlet using jerry cans, the dinghy and some local help *Máire Wilkes*

board. One should aim to carry enough fuel to reach the fuel stop after next and then refuel at the next one if possible.

At temperatures below 0°C waxes found in standard grades of diesel begin to form solid particles. Lower temperatures cause these fine particles to grow together into a larger masses which can block fuel filters and pipelines causing the engine to fail due to fuel starvation. Arctic grade winter diesel contains fewer waxes to prevent this happening. It may not be necessary to source winter grade diesel for use during the Arctic summer, however, if it is likely that one may end up overwintering in high latitudes one should fill up with the winter grade diesel.

Butane does not vaporise below 0°C and is useless in the Arctic. Propane must therefore be used at higher latitudes. A butane regulator should not be used with propane. Carrying several smaller bottles of propane rather than one big one will aid the monitoring of gas consumption. Although American and Calor propane connectors appear identical, they are not. An American propane connector can be attached to the female fitting on a Calor bottle and a gas-tight seal can be made. However, it is impossible to get a UK Calor connector into an American female bottle fitting.

Be aware that petroleum products may have different names in different parts of the world. This can cause confusion and has led to accidents with paraffin/kerosene cookers and lamps. Methylated spirit is sometimes called 'denatured alcohol'.

Clothing

One of the factors which enabled Roald Amundsen to succeed in first transiting the North West Passage in 1906 is that he befriended some of the Inuit people and copied many of their survival techniques. He discovered that bear and seal skin clothing was warmer than tweed! The same principle applies today and one would be well advised to copy what the local fishermen are wearing in Greenland, Canada or the Aleutians. Multiple layers of modern clothing work well.

Modern synthetic thermal underwear is designed to wick sweat away from the body to keep the wearer dry. This is particularly useful on a boat where one might be working hard winching a rope or poling ice then be comparatively inactive for some time. The thickness, quality and warmth of thermals vary and it is worthwhile seeking out the best. Merino wool thermals are warm, soft and marketed as 'non-smell,' even if worn for several days at a time.

Mid-layers are typically synthetic and/or fleece lined and it may often be warmer to wear more than one. Jackets and trousers or one-piece suits are available which are fleece lined or insulated with foam.

These days, Eskimo and Inuit fisherman have hung up their seal skin trousers and most wear flotation suits. These are like water-resistant boiler suits with an inner layer of foam. As well as providing flotation, the foam insulates the wearer both in and out of the water. The wrists may have neoprene seals and the leg ends can be 'Velcroed' tight. Flotation suits are not fully waterproof. They are relatively cheap and can be bought in most Arctic settlements of any size. 'Mustang' manufacture high quality flotation suits which can be bought online.

An immersion suit differs from a flotation suit in that it has neoprene seals at the wrists and neck and the feet are enclosed. It acts more like a dry-suit and keeps the wearer dry both in and out of the water. Canadian and U.S. regulations require immersion suits to be carried on board commercial fishing vessels for use in heavy weather or if the vessel has to be abandoned. They are difficult to put on quickly and this should be practised. When approaching the Arctic in the Bering Sea or the approaches to Greenland, it is likely that one will need to work on the foredeck in rough weather. An immersion suit is useful in these conditions. Immersion suits are available from Musto and Mustang.

Boots need to be both waterproof and warm. Consider boots which are insulated or fleece lined. One might want to wear two pairs of thermal socks.

A flotation suit, hat and gloves worn in cold weather *Sibéal Turraoin*

Canadian Coastguards wearing Mustang flotation suits
Máire Wilkes

Like underwear, thermal synthetic socks are warmer than conventional cotton or woollen socks. 'SealSkinz' socks are supposed to be waterproof which is sometimes an advantage if ones' boots fill up with water. It is difficult to dry out socks quickly and several pairs are recommended.

Cold hands are a perennial problem and it is useful to have a variety of gloves. Fishermen often wear thin polyester gloves beneath waterproof rubberised gloves. Ski gloves or mittens can be warm but are not waterproof. Although thick gloves or mittens can help keep hands warm, they are often too bulky to handle ropes effectively. Sometimes one just has to take gloves off and tie off a line quickly before losing all sensation in one's hands!

Like gloves, it is useful to carry several spare hats and 'two-hat days' are common in the high Arctic. A thermal hat can be worn underneath a more weatherproof hat. The outer hat or hood should have a peak to deflect sun and rain. One or both hats need to cover the ears. Hats made from fur are available in Greenland, Canada and Alaska and these are very warm.

A neck-warmer is a useful item to try and plug the gaps! A balaclava might do the same.

A mosquito net hood is useful for land exploration in some areas.

In 1872 a group of 12 seamen were separated from their vessel, the U.S. exploration ship, *Polaris*. Resigned to the ice, the Inuit amongst them soon had igloo shelters built, and they estimated that they had 1,900 pounds (860kg) of food. They also had the ship's two whaleboats, and two kayaks, although one kayak was soon lost during a breakup of the ice.

The Officers reckoned that they were drifting on the Greenland side of the Davis Strait and would soon be within rowing distance of Disko. They were incorrect; the men were actually on the Canadian side of the strait. The error caused the men to reject plans for conserving resources. The seamen broke up one of the whaleboats for firewood, making a safe escape to land very unlikely. One night in November, the men went on an eating binge, consuming a large quantity of the food stores.

The group drifted on the ice floe for the next six months over 1,800 miles (2,900km) before being rescued off the coast of Newfoundland by the sealer *Tigress* on April 30, 1873.

All probably would have perished had the group not included two skilled Inuit hunters who were able to kill seal on a number of occasions. Despite this, scarcely a word was written about the Inuit in either the official reports of the expedition, or the press.

Within the UK a good source of suitable clothing is available in the 'Commercial Fishing and Industry' section of the Guy Cotten website.

Suncream and sun glasses are often useful as the Arctic sun can be surprisingly strong.

Food

Generally food in the Arctic is expensive and the choice of goods is poorer than is normal in more populated areas further south. It is sensible for boats to provision as much as possible before leaving southern climes. Fresh food in the high Arctic may not be available and, if it is, it is often of poor quality and expensive. Tinned and frozen food should be considered.

The stores available in remote settlements are dependent upon supply ships which may visit infrequently.

Useful websites – clothing

	Musto HPX Ocean dry suit	www.musto.com/sailing-clothing/ocean
	SealSkinz Socks and other waterproof garments	www.sealskinz.com
	Guy Cotten Marine and agricultural clothing	www.guycotten.co.uk
	Mustang Survival suits and protective clothing for coastguards and industrial marine uses	www.mustangsurvival.com

Filling with water from a mountain stream near Nuuk *Bob Shepton*

A fisherman in Disko Bay *Máire Wilkes*

Twenty-four hour army ration packs are a useful back-up and could be useful in an emergency.

Water

Water can be obtained from a number of sources:

- An onboard water-maker ensures that water is always on tap, however, alternative methods should be available as spare parts are unlikely to be available in the event of a break down.
- Collecting water from streams can be good fun, if hard work. Water can be collected using jerry cans. Sometimes it is possible to get close enough to a stream or waterfall to pipe or pump water on board.
- Water is often available in harbours and fish stations although the quality may vary.
- Vessels should carry a few jerry cans as these are likely to be used at some stage.

Arctic survival

Older editions of the *Mariner's Handbook*, published by the Hydrographer to the Royal Navy, and the present edition of the *Canadian Sailing Directions for Northern Canada (ARC 400)* give advice about how to survive in an emergency in the Arctic. Much of the information given in this book about communications and clothing is particularly pertinent in an emergency. A correctly registered EPIRB is probably the most effective method of calling for assistance. Satphones and portable VHFs will also be invaluable.

A vessel's grab bag contents should be reviewed with Arctic survival in mind.

If attempting to survive on the water, personal flotation devices, immersion suits, liftrafts/lifeboats need to be considered.

If attempting to survive on land or on the ice it is important to bring as many useful stores from the abandoned vessel as possible. The priorities are:

1. First aid
2. Temporary shelter – this could be in the form of a life-raft
3. Radio contact
4. Campsite and more permanent shelter
5. Hot drinks, food and heat
6. Distress signals
7. Select and mark an emergency airstrip

Personal factors to consider are:

- Frostbite – this appears as a grey or white patch on the skin. Avoidance is the best form of treatment and survivors should look out for signs of frostbite on each other as the victim may not be aware of it.
- Perspiration should be avoided as it soaks into clothing and ruins its insulation properties. Some clothing should be removed before starting arduous work so that working is commenced 'cold'.
- Panting and large intakes of breath can lead to internal frostbite. Rest when required and wear a muffler or scarf on the lower part of the face.
- Dehydration can occur because of the higher rate of water loss when breathing cold dry air.
- Snow blindness is caused by the low sun angles and high amount of reflected ultraviolet light. Protection is afforded by wearing sunglasses or, if not available, a mask with narrow slits to see through.

Shelter

Snow is an excellent insulator and can be effectively used to build some sort of shelter. The best snow for building purposes is found in shallow drifts.

The simplest form of snow shelter is to burrow a cave into a suitable snow bank or drift, providing ventilation near the top and draping the entrance with some material.

An effective shelter for one or two people can be built in shallow drift snow by cutting a trench about 4m long by 1m wide. Cut blocks to build walls around the trench and further blocks to form a roof. Body heat is enough to raise the temperature within such a shelter to 20°C above the outside temperature. Instructions for building igloos are given in the *Mariner's Handbook* and *Canadian Sailing Directions*.

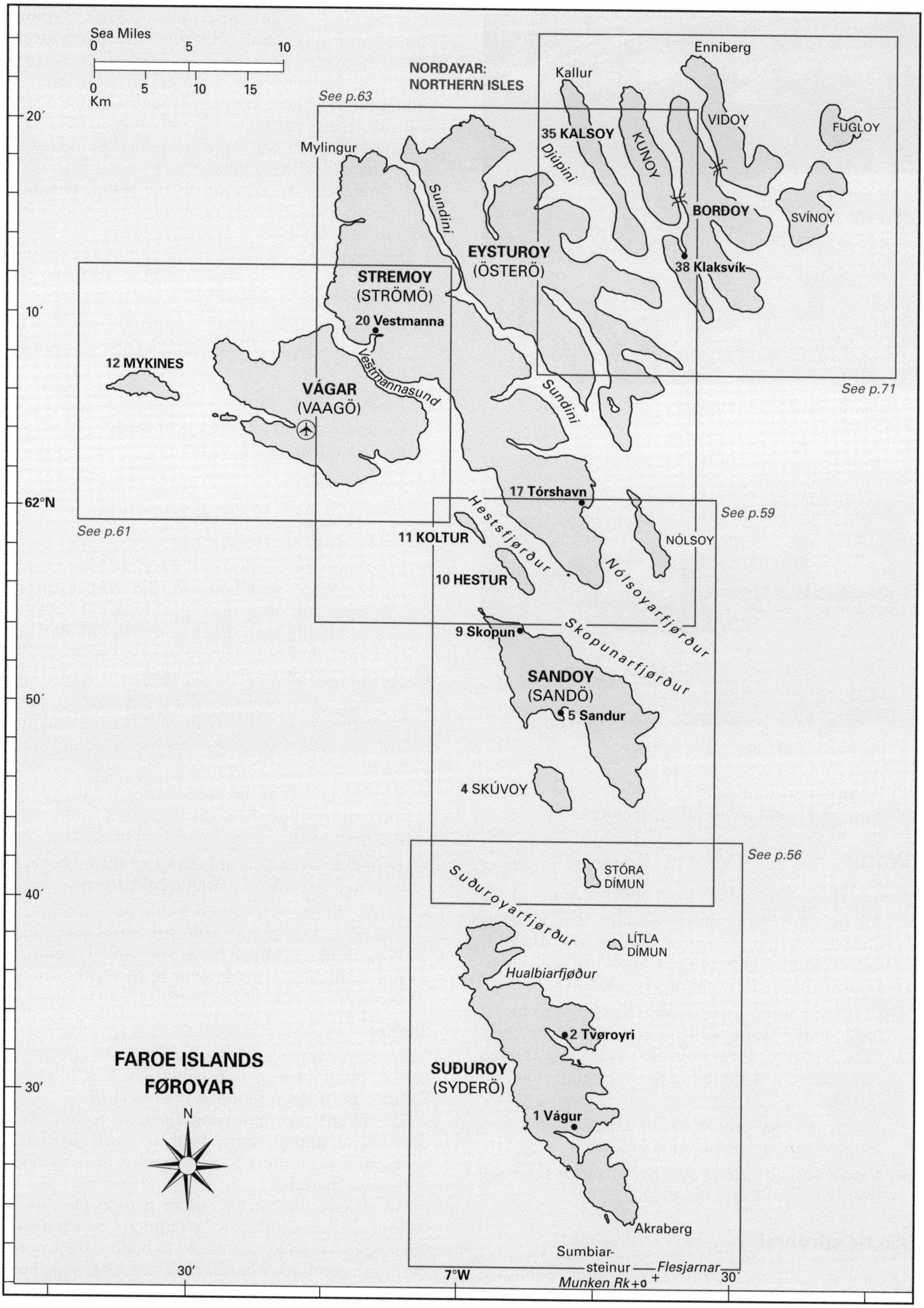
Sea Miles
0
5
10
0
5
10
15
Km
NORÐAYAR:
NORTHERN ISLES
See p.63
Enniberg
Kallur
VIDOY
FUGLOY
35 KALSOY
KUNOY
Djúpini
Mylingur
Sundini
BORÐOY
SVÍNOY
EYSTUROY
(ÖSTERÖ)
38 Klaksvík
STREMOY
(STRÖMÖ)
20 Vestmanna
12 MYKINES
VÁGAR
(VAAGÖ)
Vestmannasund
Sundini
See p.71
17 Tórshavn
See p.59
See p.61
11 KOLTUR
Hestsfjørður
NÓLSOY
10 HESTUR
Nólsoyarfjørður
9 Skopun
Skopunarfjørður
SANDOY
(SANDÖ)
5 Sandur
4 SKÚVOY
See p.56
STÓRA
DÍMUN
Suðuroyarfjørður
LÍTLA
DÍMUN
Hualbiarfjøður
2 Tvøroyri
FAROE ISLANDS
FØROYAR
SUÐUROY
(SYDERÖ)
1 Vágur
N
Akraberg
Sumbiar-
steinur
Flesjarnar
Munken Rk
20′
10′
62°N
50′
40′
30′
30′
7°W
30′

2. Faroe

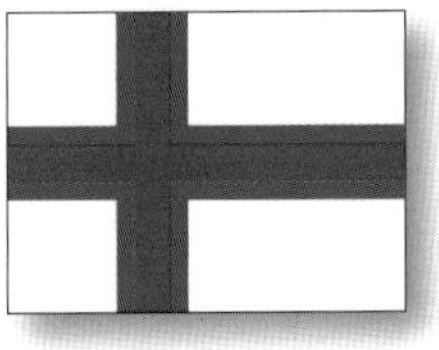

Contents

Introduction

The Faroe Islands, or Føroyar (the islands of sheep), are a group of 18 islands, 17 inhabited, and numerous holms and stacks. They are part of the Kingdom of Denmark with a population of about 49,000. The islands lie across the 62nd parallel, 7°W of Greenwich, between Shetland and Iceland. The group extends about 60M from north to south and 40M from east to west.

The southern tip of the group, Akraberg on Suðuroy is 175M almost due north of the Butt of Lewis and 185M northwest of Sumburgh Head. The capital, Tórshavn, is roughly in the centre of the group, 230M from Stornoway and 365M from Bergen. The islands are 250M from Seyðisfjørður, the nearest port in Iceland.

Many of the cliffs have some of the densest seabird breeding colonies in the world. The sight of these alone is sufficient reason for a cruise to Faroe but the place is also fascinating because of its close connection with the old Norse way of life.

The group of islands is the heavily weathered remainder of a plateau laid down in tertiary times in a series of volcanic eruptions accompanied by floods of lava. The resulting layers of basalt are separated by volcanic ash, tuff and some clays and sandstones. The horizontal strata tilt eastwards and have not been folded but have been eroded by glaciers during the Ice Age and later by frost, wind, rain and the sea. The effect is one of incredibly beautiful green slopes broken by steps, vertical cliffs – impressive when viewed from the sea – flat lands with peat bogs and lakes, and then further steps. There are virtually no trees except in one or two sheltered places. Some cultivation is to be found on the lower levels where small patches of potatoes are grown, and sheep graze on the hills. The erosion of the plateau has also resulted in deep sounds between the islands through which forceful tides stream, with rips and races offshore.

The scenery is some of the most spectacular in northern Europe; most of the land lies between 300m and 800m above the sea, much of it rising as sheer cliffs or very steep hillsides. The more dramatic cliffs are on the west and north coasts and the tremendous ridges and fjords of the Norðoyar (northern islands) are well worth a visit. The eastern coasts of the central and southern islands are gentler and deeply indented by fjords.

History

There is archeological evidence to suggest that people from Ireland, Scotland or Scandinavia settled in the Faroe Islands prior to the arrival of the Norwegians in the 9th century. The inhabitants still speak an old Norse dialect which is similar to Icelandic. In 1380 the kingdoms of Norway and Denmark were united under one crown, a union which ended in the turmoil of the Napoleonic Wars at the Treaty of Kiel in 1814. Norway and Denmark were then separated and Faroe went to Denmark. The Faroe Islands participate in The Nordic Council, The International Maritime Organization and The International Whaling Commission. The islands were staunch allies of Britain in the Second World War and their fishermen showed incredible bravery and persistence in supplying the UK with fish in spite of very heavy losses. The last of the old sailing fishing fleet, *Westward Ho*, which started life in 1884 as a Brixham trawler, and *Johanna*, a smack from Suðuroy, have been restored. The *Norðlysið*, built in 1945, now rigged as a schooner also maintains the sailing tradition and now works on pleasure cruises.

In 1946 Faroe was granted considerable local autonomy; it is economically independent of Denmark but the latter handles defence and foreign affairs. Its parliament (Løgting) consists of 32 elected members plus Denmark's representative, the Rigsombudsmand. Faroe sends two elected representatives to the Danish Folketing (Diet). The relationship is much the same as that between the Isle of Man or the Channel Islands and the United Kingdom. Faroe voted not to join the EC.

Sandavágur, Vágar Island *Máire Wilkes*

People, culture and language

The Faroe Islanders, or Faroese, are of mixed origins including Norse and Gaelic. Most Faroese are Danish citizens.

Faroese music is traditionally vocal accompanied by the fiddle. However the islands now have a wide variety of musicians including Gestir (a rock band), Aldubáran (chamber ensemble) and Tyr (folk metal band).

Føroyskt (Faroese), derived from an old Norse dialect, and Danish are the official languages. Written Føroyskt uses the old Norse letter Ð or ð (called 'eth'), not to be confused with 'd'. It is almost not sounded in speech. 'K' followed by a vowel or a 'j' is pronounced like the English 'ch' (e.g. kirkja (church) sounds 'churcha'). The 'k' in the 'sk' combination – e.g. fisk – is pronounced. A full and clear discourse on pronunciation can be found at the beginning of Lockwood's *Introduction to Modern Faeroese*.

Tórshavn. The *Westward Ho*, a fishing smack built in Grimsby, England 1884 *Máire Wilkes*

Danish is spoken by everyone as a second language. English is now widely spoken in towns and in most shops.

There are considerable differences between the Danish and Faroese spelling of place names, which can lead to confusion. On the whole, Danish charts use the Danish forms. British charts follow the Danish; but the British and Danish Hydrographic Offices are converting to Faroese. The Danish official survey map uses Faroese. The relevant British Hydrographic Office publication, NP52 *North Coast of Scotland Pilot*, uses Faroese with the Danish in brackets, but this rule does not always hold good.

Many of the settlements have clung to apparently untenable sites on the remoter islands for 1,000 years. The typical Faroe boat is closely related to the Viking longship and a visit to the boat museum in Tórshavn demonstrates this well. Post-war road building, general progress and the very successful modern fish-processing and exporting industry are rapidly making the traditional ways of life obsolete. (See Kenneth Williamson's *The Atlantic Islands* for a fund of information on Faroe history and traditions as well as a fascinating glimpse of life as it used to be lived until shortly after the Second World War. *The Faeroe Islands* by Schei and Moberg is worth considering.)

The biggest religious group is Lutheran. The majority of the remaining church goers are Plymouth Brethren but there are small communities of Roman Catholics, Jehovah's Witnesses and others.

Economy

The major industry is fishing and fish processing. The fish is exported fresh, frozen, salted and filleted. There are a number of salmon farming operations. The next largest industry is wool and wool products for export. Agriculture, which was in any case mainly subsistence, is in decline; however, the country is self-sufficient in milk and dairy products. There may be a potential future for the oil industry. Faroe imports fuel, foodstuffs including grain, hardware, etc. The Faroe Islands still have access to the Russian market after the Russian trade embargo on food from the EU. The export of fish to Russia in the first half of 2015 in comparison with 2014 has more than doubled - from 18.6 to 49.7 thousand tonnes. A significant proportion of the exports go to Denmark and the UK and the bulk of the imports come from Denmark and Norway, with some from Iceland.

Wildlife

With an estimated two million pairs of breeding seabirds on the islands there is plenty for birdwatchers to see. Indigenous birds feeding on the sea surface include kittiwakes, fulmars and storm petrels. Gannets and terns dive beneath the surface whilst puffins, razorbills and guillemots can swim 50–80m deep. Elders, shags and black guillemots and foraging skuas can be found on the shoreline.

Puffins and guillemots are historically an important food for the Faroese and they are still

Puffins nesting on a cliff *Ed Wheeler*

eaten regularly today. The traditional method of catching them is by 'fleyging.' This is catching the birds in a 'fleygingarstong' a 3.5m pole with a net attached to it. A 'Fleygises' welds the fleygingarstong from indentations in the cliff-top. Although several hundred puffins can be caught by one person in a single day, bag limits are set to ensure that the harvesting is sustainable.

Grey seals are very common. Several species of whale populate the area, the most common type being short-finned pilot whales. Several hundred pilot whales are killed annually for food. They are hunted in the summer using small boats to herd the whales into shallow bays. They are then killed by cutting their spinal cords, a process which turns the water red with blood.

Climate

Faroe is influenced by the North Atlantic Current, originating in the Gulf Stream, which most of the time (but not invariably) sets NE at about 0.5kn and divides around the group. Daytime temperatures in summer hover around 12–15°C and sea temperatures about 11–12°C. The climate is comparable to the north of Scotland and the Northern Isles but cooler. Take plenty of warm clothes even in mid summer. The main rainfall occurs between October and January but there is no dry season as such; the driest month is May and, even then, on average it manages to rain every other day. Summer gales are rare but strong winds are common. In spring, northerly winds are prominent but, as summer develops, southwesterlies become more frequent; a calm is registered on about one day in four. The incidence of fog in summer is high, about one day in four, and low clouds often obscure the magnificent views.

General information

Formalities

Visas are not required for citizens of EU countries or the Nordic region. On arrival most yachts clear at Tórshavn or at Vágur or Tvøroyri on Suðuroy but other main harbours also have customs offices. Make sure your clearance is stamped and signed as it may be demanded later at Tórshavn. Customs officers are very friendly to visiting yachts and do not seem to be concerned about moderate quantities of alcohol provided you do not take drink ashore. Faroe has strict alcohol laws and visitors who break them are not welcome.

Skippers of vessels arriving at a harbour with no customs office should telephone the Customs ✆ 455 549. Customs officers may drive crew to their offices (usually at Klaksvík or Tórshavn). They are reported to be very helpful and may give permission for crew to go ashore before formalities are completed.

The flag is a narrow red cross on a wider blue cross on a white ground (the Norwegian flag in reverse). The Danish flag should not be worn as a courtesy flag.

British Consulate, Niels Finsensgøta 5, FO-100 Tórshavn ✆ +298 359977 13510

Danish Embassy, London 55 Sloane Street, London SW1X 9SR ✆ +44 (0)20 7333 0200

Tourist information

The Tórshavn Tourist Office (Kunningarstovan) is at Niels Finsensgøta 13 in the town centre.
✆ +298 315788, *Mobile* 227039
Email torsinfo@post.olivant.fo
www.visittorshavn.fo/UK
A mobile version of the Faroe Islands Tourist Guide is available as an app.

Maps

The handy slim booklet *Føroyar, Topografisk Atlas* at 1:100,000, published by the DGA, has details of the scenery and excursions ashore. The islands are also covered by a series at 1:20,000, expensive but ideal for walking.

All are obtainable in the UK from The Map Shop, 15 High Street, Upton-upon-Severn, Worcester WR8 0HJ, *Freephone* 0800 085 40 80, ✆ +44 (0)1684 593146 *Email* themapshop@btinternet.com.

Time

Winter: UT. Summer (from the last Sunday in March until the last Saturday in October): UT+1 hour.

Useful websites – general information

	The Tourist Information Centre in Tórshavn	www.visittorshavn.fo/UK

Tunnel leading to Gasladalur *Máire Wilkes*

Transport and communications

Currently, two airlines serve the Faroes: Atlantic Airways (the national carrier) and Air Iceland. Atlantic Airways fly, in addition, to Reykjavík, London, Aberdeen and Oslo and Air Iceland from Reykjavík only. The airport is on Vágar and transfer to Tórshavn is by bus or taxi.

Relatively cheap helicopter flights link the islands and are centred on the airport on Vágur, which could be useful for a visit to Mykines.

The *Norrønna* car ferry plies between Denmark, Faroe and Iceland and is run by Smyril Line. Inevitably, the services change from year to year and their websites should be visited for up-to-date information.

The inter-island ferry network is well developed and all the main islands can be explored by road in a bus or hired car (taxis are not cheap). In bad weather it is worth considering a visit by ferry to some of the more remote islands where anchoring or berthing is precarious.

The ferry and bus timetable (ferðaætlan) is published by Strandfaraskip Landsins and is available from the tourist information offices, or online.

Cars can be hired and the main islands are linked together by bridges or tunnels.

Telecommunications

International dial code +298 + 6 digit local number.

GSM is the most commonly used mobile network. Local sim cards can be purchased in telecom shops, petrol stations and large supermarkets. Broadband access can be found in Tourist Offices, public libraries, hotels, and cafés.

Money

Since 1940 the currency has been the Faroe Króna which is freely interchangeable with the Danish Krone. Both forms of note circulate, but the coinage is Danish. Credit cards are accepted, Visa and MasterCard outlets being the most common. Many of the main banks have external ATMs.

Shopping

The main towns have comprehensive shopping facilities and well stocked supermarkets with a good selection. Smaller towns and villages have an adequate shop or two but small and remote settlements may have none. Some of the local food is an acquired taste but should be tried: skerpikjot (wind-dried mutton), turrurfis (dried fish), spik (whale blubber soaked in brine), grind (dried whale meat, very hard).

Guillemots and puffins are commonly eaten in various forms. Lately havhestur (fulmar) has been added to the diet – after being slowly stewed for some four hours, it is said to have a strong gamey flavour.

Except in the capital, Tórshavn, restaurants and bars are not numerous.

Alcohol

The local beers Føroyar Bjór and Restorffs come in various strengths. Light beer can be purchased in food shops and stronger beer directly from the brewery's outlets. Wines and spirits can only be bought at the official liquor stores (rúsdrekkasølan) in the main towns.

Useful websites – transport

	Airlines Atlantic Airways	www.atlantic.fo/en
	Airlines Air Iceland	www.airiceland.is
	Ferry services Smyril Line	www.smyrilline.com
	Ferry and bus times Strandfaraskip Landsins	www.ssl.fo

Useful books

The Atlantic Islands Kenneth Williamson. (Routledge & Kegan Paul). Now out of print but possibly available through second-hand bookshops. A very well informed and interesting book on all aspects of life in the islands as it used to be – invaluable background for a visit.

The Faeroe Islands Liv Kjørjvik Schei and Gunnie Moberg (John Murray 1991).

An Introduction to Modern Faeroese WB Lockwood (Munksgaard, København 1965). Clearly written and a great help if you are interested in the language.

The Faroe Islands: Interpretations of History J Wylie (Lexington 1987).

The Faroese Saga (Føroyingasøga) translated by GCV Young and CR Clewer (Century Services Ltd, 51/59 Donegal Street, Belfast. 1973). The Old Norse saga of the 10th and 11th-century politics and feuds of the islands.

Faroe Islands (Bradt Travel Guides) by James Proctor. This is the only English language guide to the Faroes and has been updated for 2016.

Drangarnir is the collective name for two sea stacks between the islet Tindholmur and the island Vágar *Andrea Ricordi*

Cruising information

The yachtsman must have his wits about him. Tides and races are fierce and dangerous; fog is often dense and sudden; most anchorages are exposed to at least one direction and are subject to strong, irregular katabatic winds off the high and precipitous land. There are, however, a number of recently built, completely sheltered harbours. In the right weather, beautiful and impressive anchorages can be found, although beware the numerous fish farms. A few days of fine weather and visibility amply repay the effort of sailing to the Faroe Islands.

Charts

The Danish chart coverage is at a larger scale than the British and includes many more harbour and anchorage plans. Reference to the relevant Danish chart appears at each entry in this text and it is strongly recommended that Danish charts are used. An index of charts can be found on the Danish hydrographic office website and they can be obtained through Imray, Laurie, Norie & Wilson Ltd, Wych House, St Ives, Cambridgeshire PE27 5BT, ✆ +44 (0)1480 462114.

Alternatively in Denmark: from Iver C Weilbach and Co a/s, Toldbodgade 35, DK 1253 København, ✆ +45 33 135927.

They can also be bought in Tórshavn at Jacobsens Bókahandil.

British Admiralty charts

117 Føroyar Islands 1:189,000.
Shows the whole group

3557 Plans in Føroyar.
Shows plans of 12 harbours and fjords at scales of 1:25,000 to 1:6,000

Danish charts

81 Færøerne 1:200,000 is almost identical to British Chart 117

82 Færøerne (N Part) 1:100,000

83 Færøerne (S Part) 1:100,000

84 Harbour and Anchorage Plans (N Part) between 1:40,000 and 1:2,000

85 Harbour and Anchorage Plans (S Part) between 1:20,000 and 1:2,000

(*Note* The datum of the latest editions of Charts 84 and 85 is WGS 84).

Useful websites – charts

Danish Hydrographic Office Danish chart index	www.danskehavnelods.dk/indexkort_faeroerne/faeroskesoekort.html
Imray UK chart and pilot book distributor	www.imray.com
Jacobsens Bókahandil Faroe bookshop and chart distributor	www.bokhandil.fo

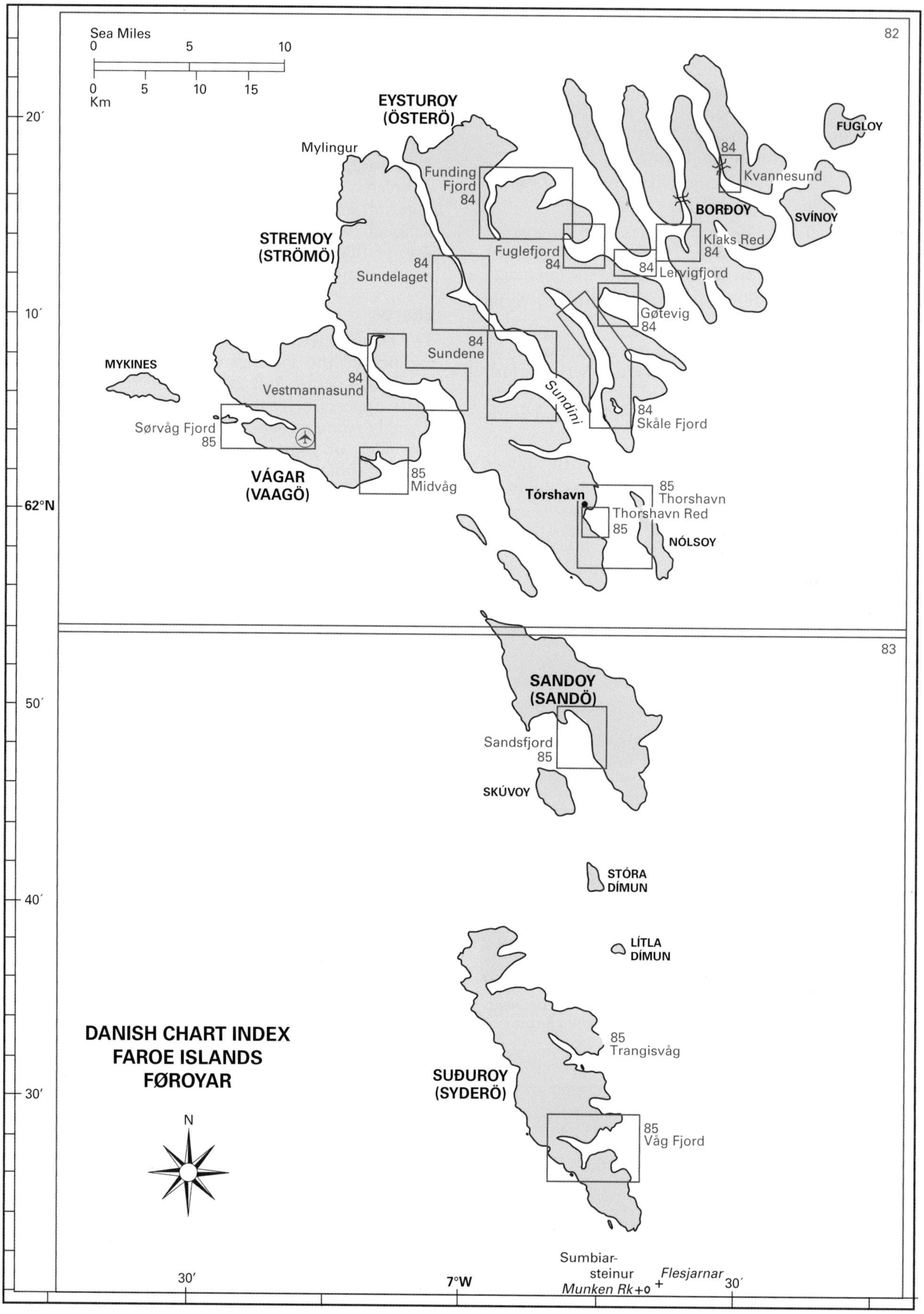
Sea Miles
0 5 10
0 5 10 15
Km
82
83
20′
10′
62°N
50′
40′
30′
30′
7°W
30′
EYSTUROY
(ÖSTERÖ)
Mylingur
Funding Fjord 84
STREMOY
(STRÖMÖ)
84 Sundelaget
Fuglefjord 84
84 Lervigfjord
Kvannesund
84
BORÐOY
Klaks Red 84
Gøtevig 84
FUGLOY
SVÍNOY
MYKINES
84 Sundene
84 Vestmannasund
Sundini
84 Skåle Fjord
Sørvåg Fjord 85
VÁGAR
(VAAGÖ)
85 Midvåg
Tórshavn
85 Thorshavn
Thorshavn Red 85
NÓLSOY
SANDOY
(SANDÖ)
Sandsfjord 85
SKÚVOY
STÓRA
DÍMUN
LÍTLA
DÍMUN
DANISH CHART INDEX
FAROE ISLANDS
FØROYAR
N
85 Trangisvåg
SUÐUROY
(SYDERÖ)
85 Våg Fjord
Sumbiar-
steinur
Munken Rk
Flesjarnar

Both Navionics and CMap electronic charts cover the area.

GPS derived positions should be used with caution as errors of 250m have been reported.

Harbour plans

The information on Charts 84 and 85, which cover all the main harbours, is supplemented by an invaluable little book in Danish, *Havneoplysninger for Færøerne*, published by the Danish Farvandsvæsenet. With its latest supplement it contains plans of nearly every harbour and quay throughout the islands and is recommended. Obtainable from Jacobsens Bókahandil. The relevant plan number appears at each entry in this text.

Pilotage books

The British Admiralty Pilot *North Coast of Scotland* (NP52) includes the Faroes. It is very comprehensive and should be carried on board. The section on ports and anchorages in Chapter 1 is valuable. Chapter 2 has 20 pages of clear pilotage information, nearly all of it highly relevant to a yachtsman. The latest edition is essential because of the rapid programme of harbour construction.

There is a tidal stream atlas, but no indication of the potentially dangerous races: the port of reference for tides in this publication is Reykjavík (see also under Tidal Streams).

Den færøske Lods is the Danish official pilot book, in Danish. It has a number of useful views but may not be worthwhile for a non-Danish speaker. It can be obtained from Jacobsens Bókahandil in Tórshavn.

Yacht services and chandlery

Specialised yacht equipment is in very limited supply but services and chandlery for fishing boats of all sizes are plentiful. There are large repair yards at Tórshavn, Klaksvík (also a sailmaker), Vestmanna and Tvøroyri. Other harbours may have facilities.

Buoyage

There are no navigation buoys in the approaches but there are usually four wave recorders approximately N, E, S and W of the islands. Their position is changed from time to time (Charts: British 117 and Danish 81).

Lights

Powerful lighthouses mark the extremities of the group of islands and the approaches to harbours are generally well lit with plentiful sectored and leading lights. There are no lights on the northwest coasts from Kalsoy to Slættanes on Vágar. During much of the sailing season, lights are extinguished, in some cases from May 20 to July 20, in others from June 1 to July 15. Some harbour lights are extinguished as early as April 20.

Details of lights are given in the *Admiralty List of Lights and Fog Signals, Vol L* and in *Almanakki* under the heading Vitar í Føroyum (Lights in Faroe).

There are no Racons in the Faroe Islands.

Radio

There is good VHF coverage of the islands, maintaining 24-hour watch on Ch 16, working channels and DSC on Ch 70. The call for all stations is Tórshavn Radio. Call on the working channel stating the channel used or use DSC MMSI 002311000.

Tórshavn Radio also gives 24-hour MF coverage listening on 2182KHz and DSC 2187.5KHz.

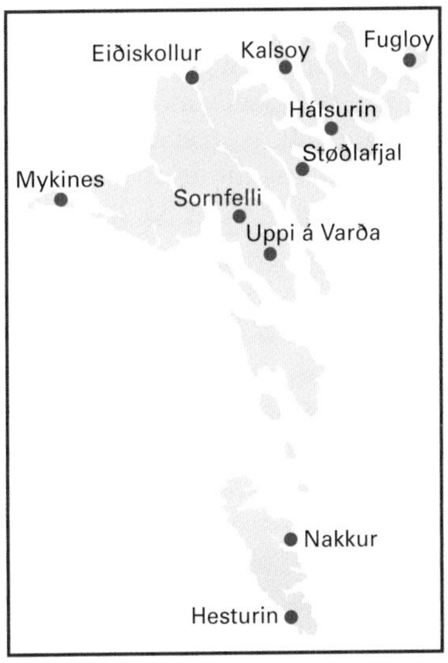

Tórshavn radio VHF transmitters

Weather forecasts

The local forecasts in Faroese are very difficult to understand because they use the old Norse points of the compass.

Useful websites – weather forecasts

	Danish Meteorological Institute Faroe Weather Forecasts	www.dmi.dk
	MRCC Tórshavn Weather and navigation warnings available in English on the Navtex link	www.mrcc.fo

Marine forecasts in English may be obtainable from the Airport Met. Office ✆ +298 333365 or control tower ✆ +298 332092.

Tourist information offices can usually obtain weather forecasts; or visit the Danish Meteorological Institute website.

The UK shipping forecast for sea area Faroes bears little relationship to weather patterns among the islands, where local conditions can vary dramatically over short distances.

A brief, but useful forecast is broadcast in English by the National Radio Station on FM 89.8/87.5MHz and on MW 531kHz at 0845 on weekdays

NAVTEX radio station Føroyar/Tórshavn [D] 62°01'N 06°48'W. (ALRS Vol.5). NAVTEX [D] reported excellent, with weather forecasts at 0030z and 1230z, weather warnings and outlook for the next 24 hrs for the four adjacent sea areas. The Outer banks (Ytri) lie to the SW of the Faroe Islands, Iceland Ridge to the NW, Fugloy bank to the NE and Munkagrund to the SE.

Forecasts and navigation warnings can be obtained on the web on the MRCC Tórshavn website under the sub-menu 'NAVTEX' where there is an English language option.

Safety, emergency help, Search and Rescue

Search and Rescue operations are controlled by MRCC Tórshavn which is based at the same location as Tórshavn-Radio. It is responsible for SAR operations within 200M of the islands. Their emergency telephone number is ✆ +298 35 13 00. A rescue helicopter, back-up helicopter and five rescue boats are based on the islands. Fixed winged SAR aircraft can be requested from Iceland, Denmark or Norway if required.

Lifeboat, Klaksvik *Máire Wilkes*

Navigation warnings can be obtained from Navtex or on the MRCC Tórshavn website under the sub-menu 'NAVTEX' where there is an English language option.

Tidal information

The tidal range varies from 2·0m in the north and west of the islands to about 0·5m in the east and is negligible in Tórshavn, Skálafjørður and in Sundini, SE of the Sundelagið bridge. The tidal range, where known, is shown against harbours; the first figure being the range in metres at neaps and the second at springs. Time of HW at Eiði is approximately +0215 Reykjavík (–0215 Dover) and at Klaksvík +0255 Reykjavík (–0135 Dover). See Admiralty Tide Tables or *Tidevandstabeller for Færøerne* for more detail, but neither are absolutely essential.

Tidal streams among and close to the islands are very strong and there are numerous severe and very severe races, which should be treated with great respect in all but the calmest weather. They pose the greatest problem for an approach in bad visibility.

NP52 and *Den Færøeske Lods* include a tidal stream atlas, but no indication of the tide rips; the port of reference is Reykjavík.

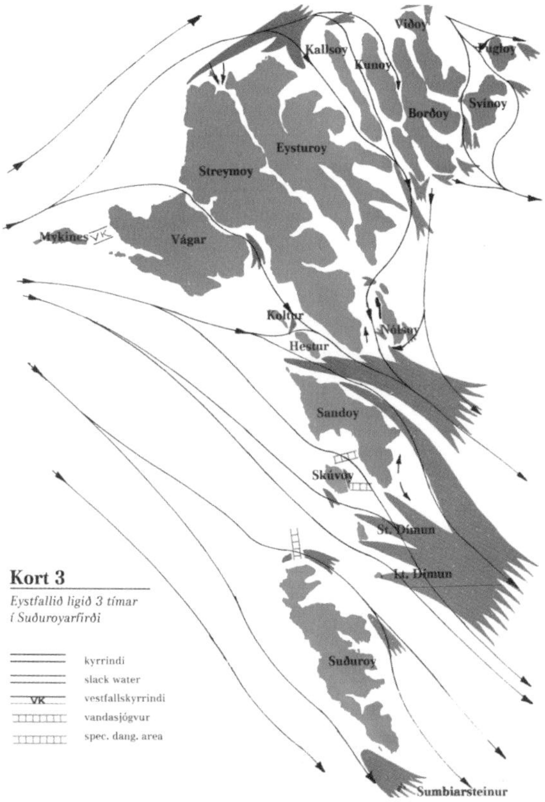

Extract from *Faroes Tidal Atlas* – note overfalls shown in red

Useful websites – tides

	Streymkort Online Tide Atlas	www.mid.fo/streymkort.htm Click 'Streymkort', then click 'Streymkort at printa for charts'

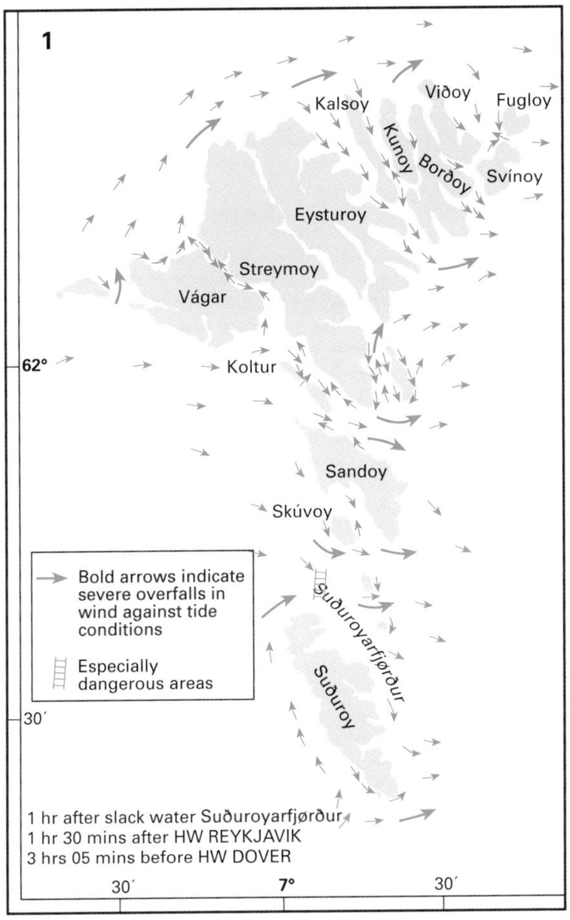
1
Kalsoy
Viðoy
Fugloy
Kunoy
Borðoy
Svínoy
Eysturoy
Streymoy
Vágar
62°
Koltur
Sandoy
Skúvoy
Bold arrows indicate severe overfalls in wind against tide conditions
Especially dangerous areas
Suðuroyarfjørður
Suðuroy
30´
1 hr after slack water Suðuroyarfjørður
1 hr 30 mins after HW REYKJAVIK
3 hrs 05 mins before HW DOVER
30´
7°
30´

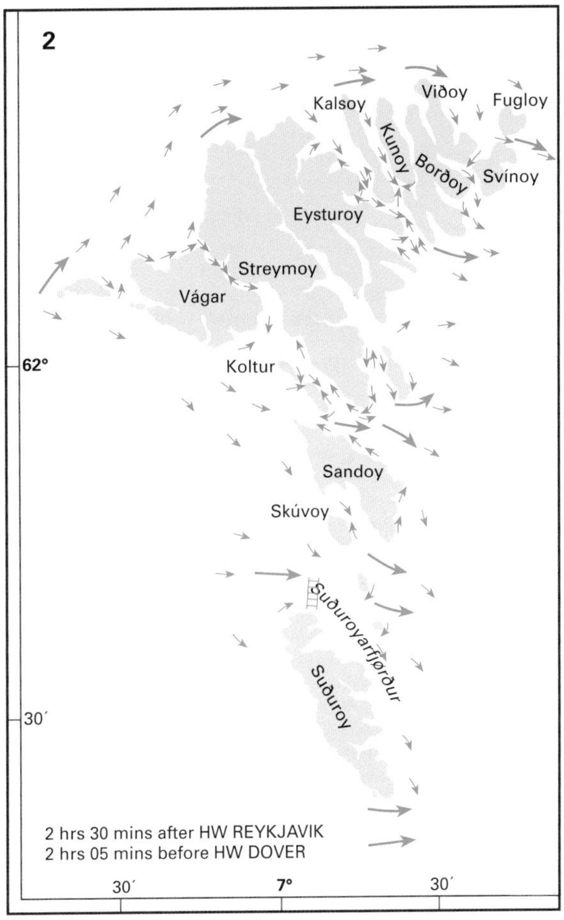
2
Kalsoy
Viðoy
Fugloy
Kunoy
Borðoy
Svínoy
Eysturoy
Streymoy
Vágar
62°
Koltur
Sandoy
Skúvoy
Suðuroyarfjørður
Suðuroy
30´
2 hrs 30 mins after HW REYKJAVIK
2 hrs 05 mins before HW DOVER
30´
7°
30´

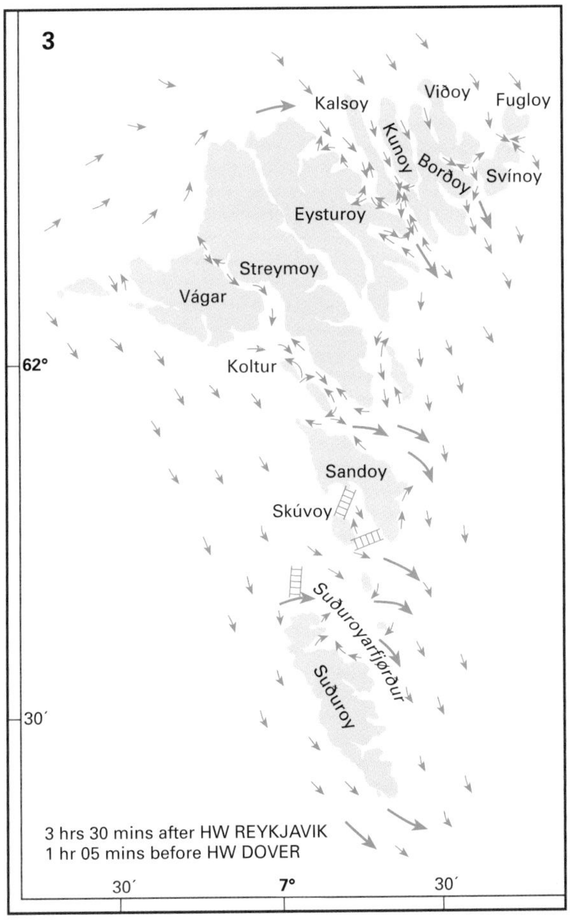
3
Kalsoy
Viðoy
Fugloy
Kunoy
Borðoy
Svínoy
Eysturoy
Streymoy
Vágar
62°
Koltur
Sandoy
Skúvoy
Suðuroyarfjørður
Suðuroy
30´
3 hrs 30 mins after HW REYKJAVIK
1 hr 05 mins before HW DOVER
30´
7°
30´

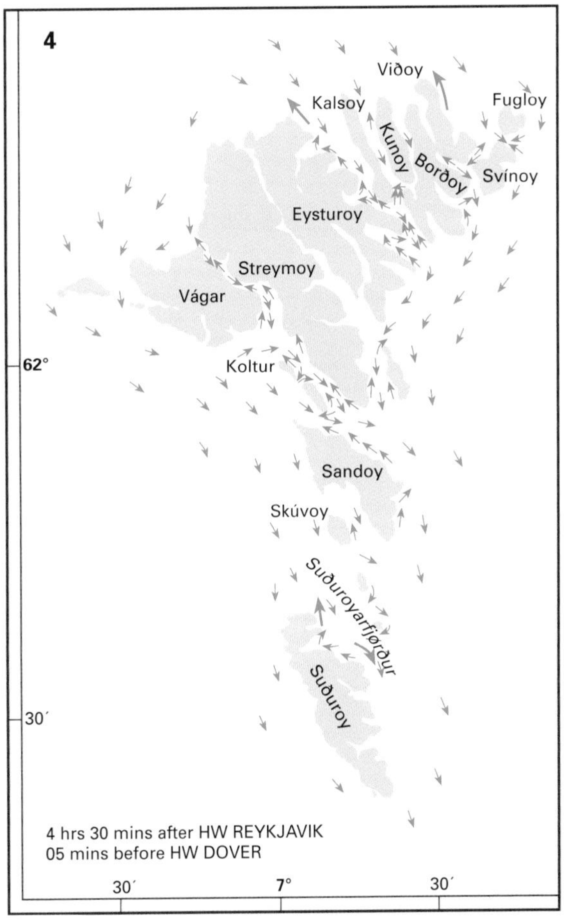
4
Viðoy
Kalsoy
Fugloy
Kunoy
Borðoy
Svínoy
Eysturoy
Streymoy
Vágar
62°
Koltur
Sandoy
Skúvoy
Suðuroyarfjørður
Suðuroy
30´
4 hrs 30 mins after HW REYKJAVIK
05 mins before HW DOVER
30´
7°
30´

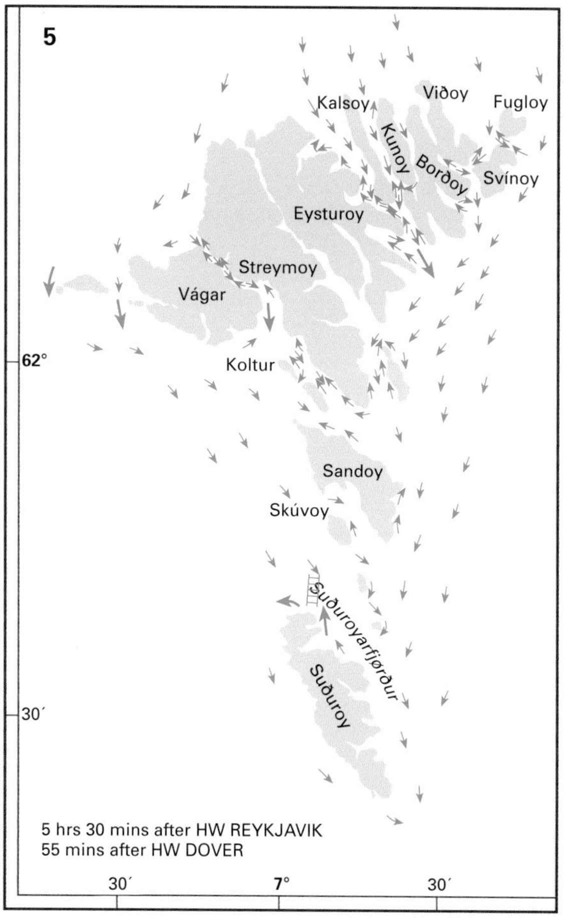
5
Kalsoy
Viðoy
Fugloy
Kunoy
Borðoy
Svínoy
Eysturoy
Streymoy
Vágar
Koltur
Sandoy
Skúvoy
Suðuroyarfjørður
Suðuroy
62°
30´
30´
7°
30´
5 hrs 30 mins after HW REYKJAVIK
55 mins after HW DOVER

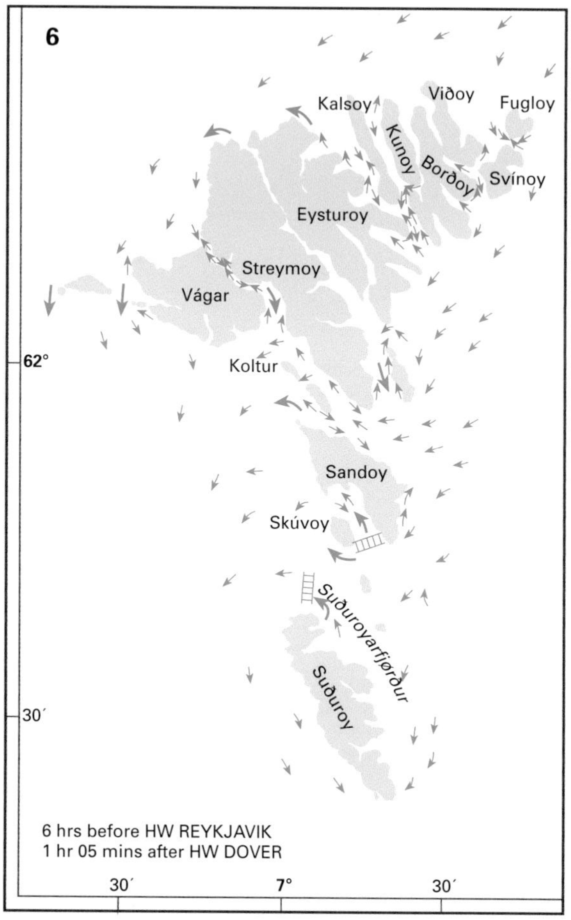
6
Kalsoy
Viðoy
Fugloy
Kunoy
Borðoy
Svínoy
Eysturoy
Streymoy
Vágar
Koltur
Sandoy
Skúvoy
Suðuroyarfjørður
Suðuroy
62°
30´
30´
7°
30´
6 hrs before HW REYKJAVIK
1 hr 05 mins after HW DOVER

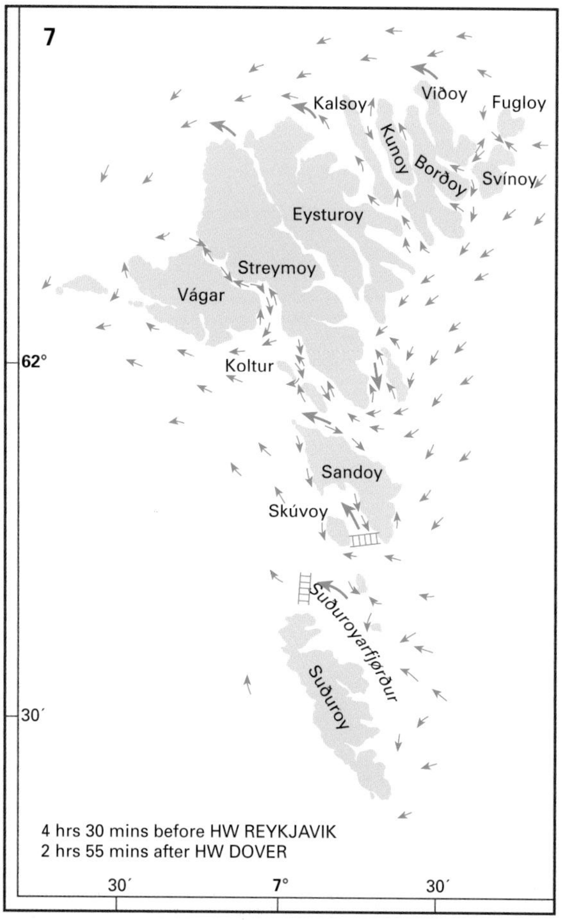
7
Kalsoy
Viðoy
Fugloy
Kunoy
Borðoy
Svínoy
Eysturoy
Streymoy
Vágar
Koltur
Sandoy
Skúvoy
Suðuroyarfjørður
Suðuroy
62°
30´
30´
7°
30´
4 hrs 30 mins before HW REYKJAVIK
2 hrs 55 mins after HW DOVER

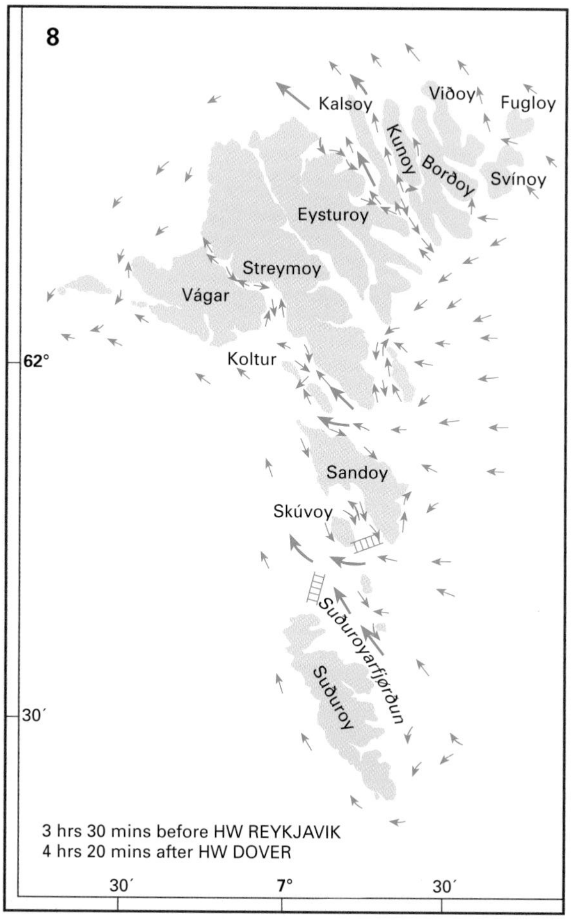
8
Kalsoy
Viðoy
Fugloy
Kunoy
Borðoy
Svínoy
Eysturoy
Streymoy
Vágar
Koltur
Sandoy
Skúvoy
Suðuroyarfjørðun
Suðuroy
62°
30´
30´
7°
30´
3 hrs 30 mins before HW REYKJAVIK
4 hrs 20 mins after HW DOVER

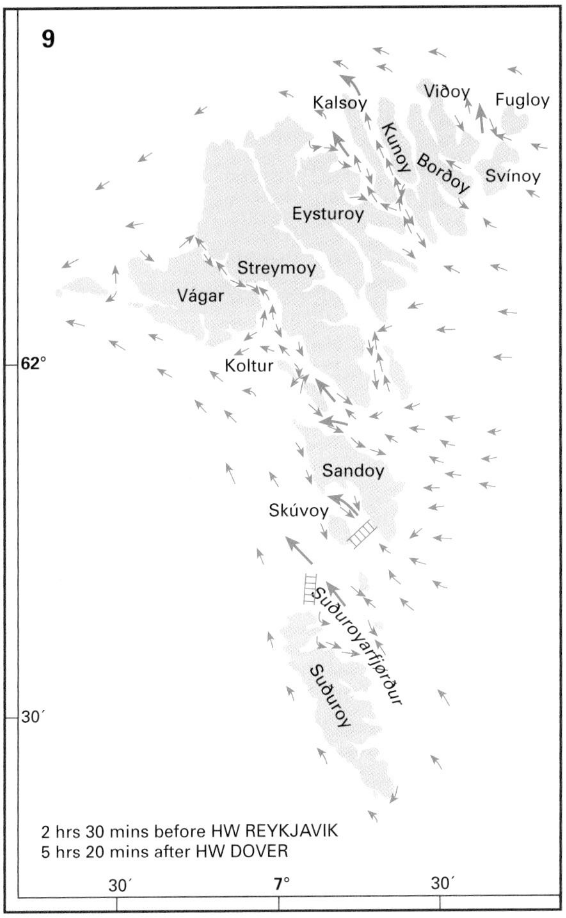

2 hrs 30 mins before HW REYKJAVIK
5 hrs 20 mins after HW DOVER

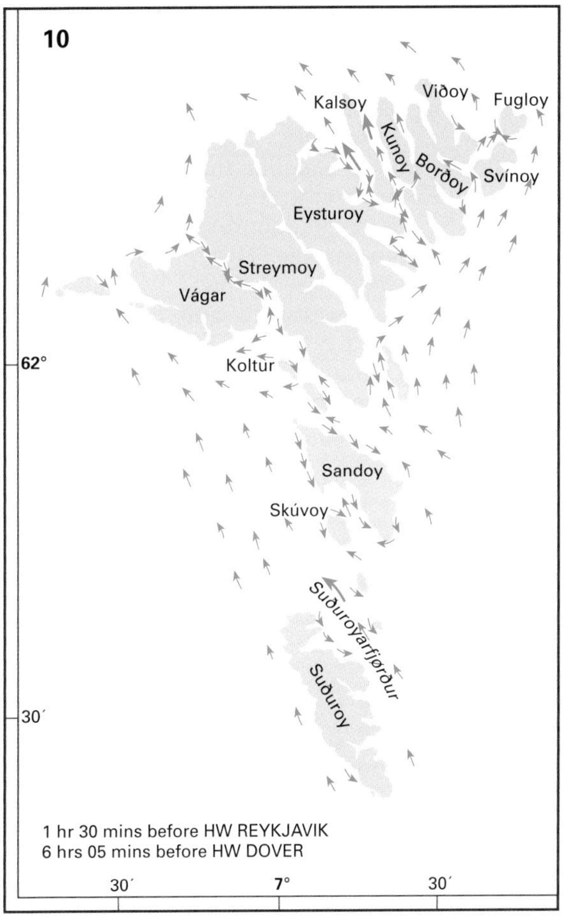

1 hr 30 mins before HW REYKJAVIK
6 hrs 05 mins before HW DOVER

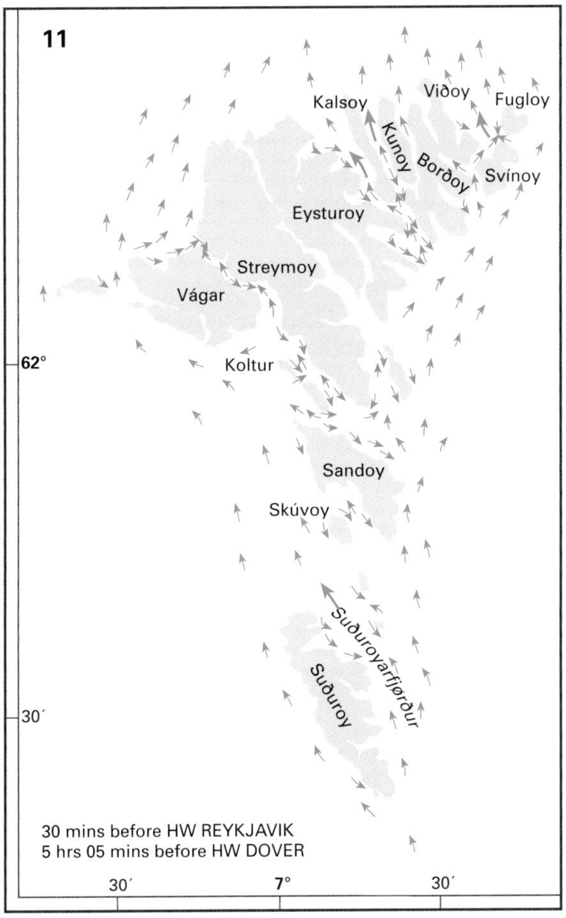

30 mins before HW REYKJAVIK
5 hrs 05 mins before HW DOVER

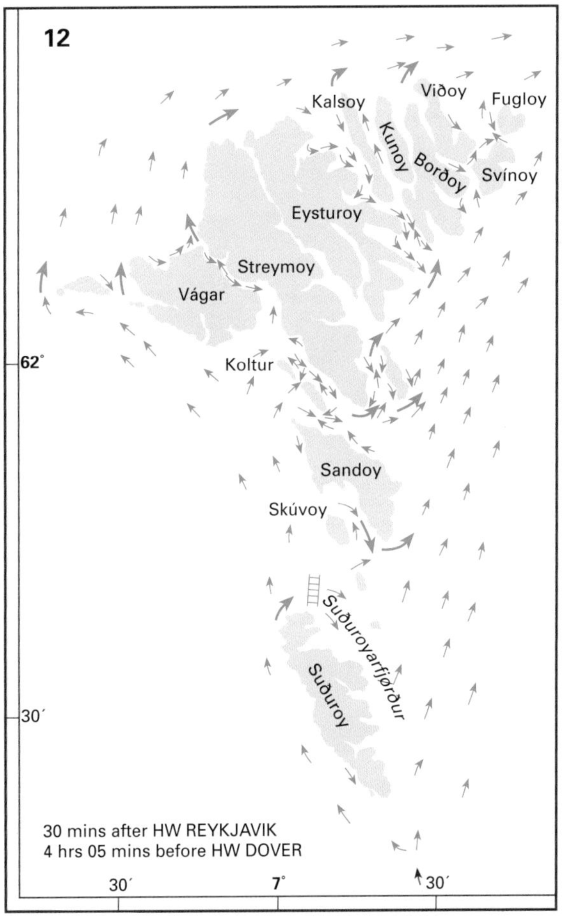

30 mins after HW REYKJAVIK
4 hrs 05 mins before HW DOVER

2. FAROE

The best tidal information is in *Streymkort fyri Føroyar* (tidal stream atlas for Faroe) edited by Fischer Heinesen. It has a frighteningly graphic way of describing the strength of the races and is a good guide to their ferocity. The Faroese preface is difficult to understand but the graphics are awe-inspiring. To interpret it, it is necessary to know the time of slack water in Suðuroyarfjørður and/or the moon's meridian passage. This information is given in the *Almanakki* (see below). 'Vestfalskyrrindi' means the flood westward and 'eystfalskyrrindi' means the ebb eastwards. 'EK' and 'VK' on the charts are slack water. The yellow and black bars indicate areas where heavy overfalls can be expected when wind is against tide. The hatched areas are tidal races.

There is a more detailed tidal stream atlas for the waters near Tórshavn, the Nólsoyarfjørður and Hestsfjørður. This book is interesting because it shows in detail the great value of the eddies and counter-currents, and this also applies in many other places. Both tidal stream atlases can be obtained from Jacobsens Bókahandil.

Almanakki, a comprehensive local almanac, is published by Jacobsens Bókahandil, Tórshavn. It includes the vital table for slack water in Suðuroyarfjørður and moon's meridian passage for use with the Streymkort (it will probably be adjusted for summer time) and a wealth of information on harbour approaches, lights, radiobeacons, VHF and MF radio, courses and distances from headland to headland, distances by land, and a calendar for the islands. It has a register of local ships and boats and even lists the members of the government and the local authorities. The tables are all fairly easy to follow after a bit of thought, but a smattering of a Scandinavian language would uncover a mine of further information.

Almanakki and all the other publications can be obtained by post from HN Jacobsens Bókahandil, Box 55, 110 Tórshavn, ✆ +298 311036,
Email hnj-bokh@post.olivant.fo

Excellent and detailed tidal stream charts are reported to be available on the Streymkort website however some knowledge of Danish is helpful!

Approach

It is quite likely that landfall will be made in poor visibility and bad weather. Approximately 3M south of Suðuroy are the unmarked rocks Sumbiarsteinur (Munken and Flesjarnar) 11m (37ft) and 5m (16ft) high, lying right on the course from Lewis and the Minch. They lie in the green and red sectors respectively of the Akraberg light but this may be invisible (or extinguished in mid summer). They should be given a wide berth by passing well to the E. Using GPS this should not be a problem but otherwise a constant check on the bearing of Akraberg is essential. Tides set very strongly in the area of these rocks, and between them and Suðuroy, and under certain conditions there are dangerous overfalls. Apart from this, the seas round Faroe are free from off-lying dangers and there should be no problems until the local tide is felt.

A village on the island of Vágar
© Ole Kristian Valle | Dreamstime.com

Harbours and anchorages

Chart and plan numbers

Note Chart numbers refer to Danish charts. Plan numbers refer to the relevant plan in the Danish book of harbour plans *Havneoplysninger for Færøerne*

Trøllkonufingur (the troll-wife's finger), Vágar (see page 60)
Christopher Thornhill

The principal anchorages in Faroe are traditionally described either as winter harbours (safe in all conditions – only six are so described in the islands) or as summer harbours (unsafe from some directions in bad weather). Most of these now have a concrete harbour that gives complete safety, but the old designation is worth noting.

Faroe has undergone an intensive harbour improvement and building programme. Nearly all major settlements have a sheltered harbour of concrete quays and rock moles, and many minor settlements have at least a well-sited mole or breakwater. These harbours may, however, be full of fishing boats and very busy with fishing and ferries.

Ferries come and go very smartly in many harbours and it would be a mistake to be on the ferry berth at the wrong time. However, sometimes it is the only place for a yacht to lie alongside and the inter-island ferry timetable (ferðaætlan) is very useful as a warning of when to vacate the berth.

A bit of quay or a resting fishing boat can always be found, but assume a fishing boat may be about to put to sea unless there is evidence to the contrary. Buoys are laid in some harbours and can often be used for short periods.

Take a good plank to act as a fender board, since most harbours walls have large lorry tyres on their walls and pontoons tend to be steel-rimmed. Many harbours have marina pontoons for small craft. These are exclusively for local small fishing boats and there is seldom room even for a small yacht.

Harbourmasters are friendly and helpful, as are the inhabitants. Apart from customs and passport requirements for some nationals, no formalities are insisted on and, except in Tórshavn, no dues demanded.

In general, open anchorages should be treated with caution. Good holding in shallow water can be found but some anchorages recommended in NP52 have been found to suffer from weed. With few exceptions, open anchorages are for good weather only and nearly all are subject to violent, largely unpredictable gusts, even in moderate weather. Some otherwise attractive anchorages may have a rocky and boulder-strewn bottom or be occupied by a fish farm.

NP52 gives comprehensive, detailed information on the coast of all the islands and all anchorages.

This section is a review of the principal harbours, anchorages and fjords. The number against each harbour also appears on the area plans for ease of location. The *Admiralty North Coast of Scotland Pilot (NP52)* has a wealth of further information. The review is arranged by island and then by fjord. Fuel, water and other shore facilities are mentioned only when they are known to have been used by yachtsmen, but it is likely that they can be found in most harbours.

Suðuroy

Charts 83

Suðuroy is the most southerly of the islands and, likely to be the landfall from the British Isles. The unmarked rocks Sumbiarsteinur (Munken and Flesjarnar), approximately 3M south of Suðuroy, are hazardous in the southern approaches. Akraberg lighthouse is on the south tip of the island, off which a dangerous race extends at least 5M south. The west coast consists entirely of precipitous cliffs, very beautiful but devoid of harbours.

On the east coast there are two deep, sheltered fjords, Vágsfjørður and Trongisvágsfjørður. Both are designated as winter harbours and have substantial towns and man-made harbours.

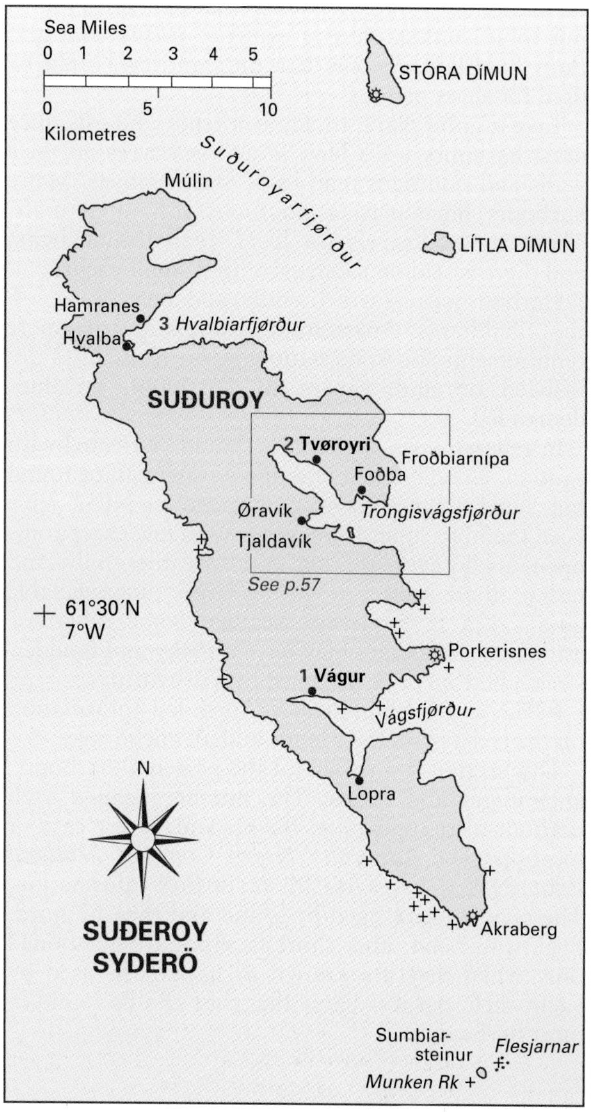

Vágsfjørður

Charts 85 (1:20,000)

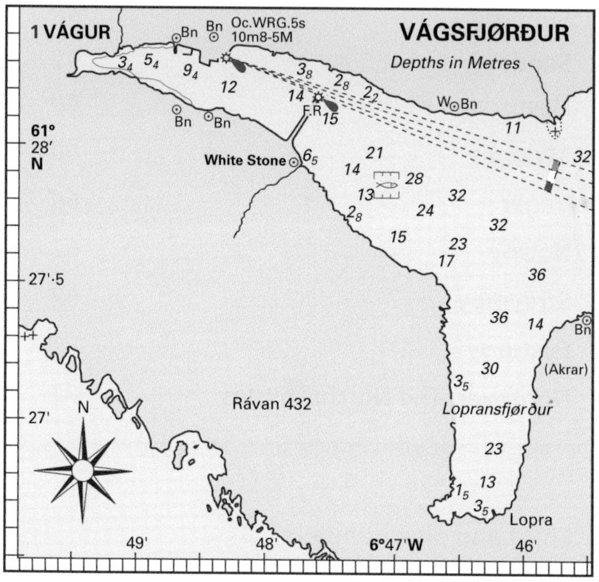

There are two possible harbours in Vágsfjørður: Vágur and Lopra.

1 Vágur (Vaag) 61°28'N 6°49'W

Tide 0·3, 0·8 **Charts** Plan 65

The settlement of Vágur (Vaag), on the island of Suðuroy is not to be confused with the island of Vágar (Vaagö), further north in Faroe.

Approach

The coast between Akraberg and Vágsfjørður is clean and the passage up the fjord straightforward.

Berthing

There is a substantial harbour at Vágur, classed as a winter harbour. Berth as convenient in the harbour: the inter-island ferry berths are on the outside of the outer quay. A rock breakwater extends from the south shore, east of all the quays, and forms a large protected harbour within.

The anchorage at the head of the fjord is subject to strong winds and the holding is badly affected by weed.

Vágur (Vaag), Suðuroy *Máire Wilkes*

Vágur quayside and the sailing trawler *Johanna Máire Wilkes*

Formalities

Customs.

Facilities

Slip up to 150 tons. Water on main quay. Fuel can be ordered via Statoil station between the harbour and the fish factory or Shell depot across the fjord, and arrives in a tanker. There is a good range of food shops. Resident doctor. A small hotel by the harbour provides showers.

Showers, washing machine with tumble drier available on weekdays at Suðuroyar Heimavirki.

There is a spectacular walk, marked by cairns, from Vágur along the west coast of Suðuroy to Famjin from where there is a bus to Tvøroyri.

⚓ Lopra 61°27′N 6°46′W

Charts Plan 28

Lopra, a seemingly snug anchorage on the south arm of the fjord, is reported to be squally and unsatisfactory in south winds. The harbour is protected by a mole. Beware of the many fish cages in this fjord.

Trongisvágsfjørður

Charts 85 (1:20,000)

Trongisvágsfjørður and the town of Tvøroyri may be preferable to Vágsfjørður as a point of arrival because of better facilities at Tvøroyri and the anchorages at Tjaldavík and Øravík which are good places to recuperate quietly after a passage. Tvøroyri is halfway up the northern side of Trongisvágsfjørður. It is the main town on Suðuroy and the third largest in Faroe.

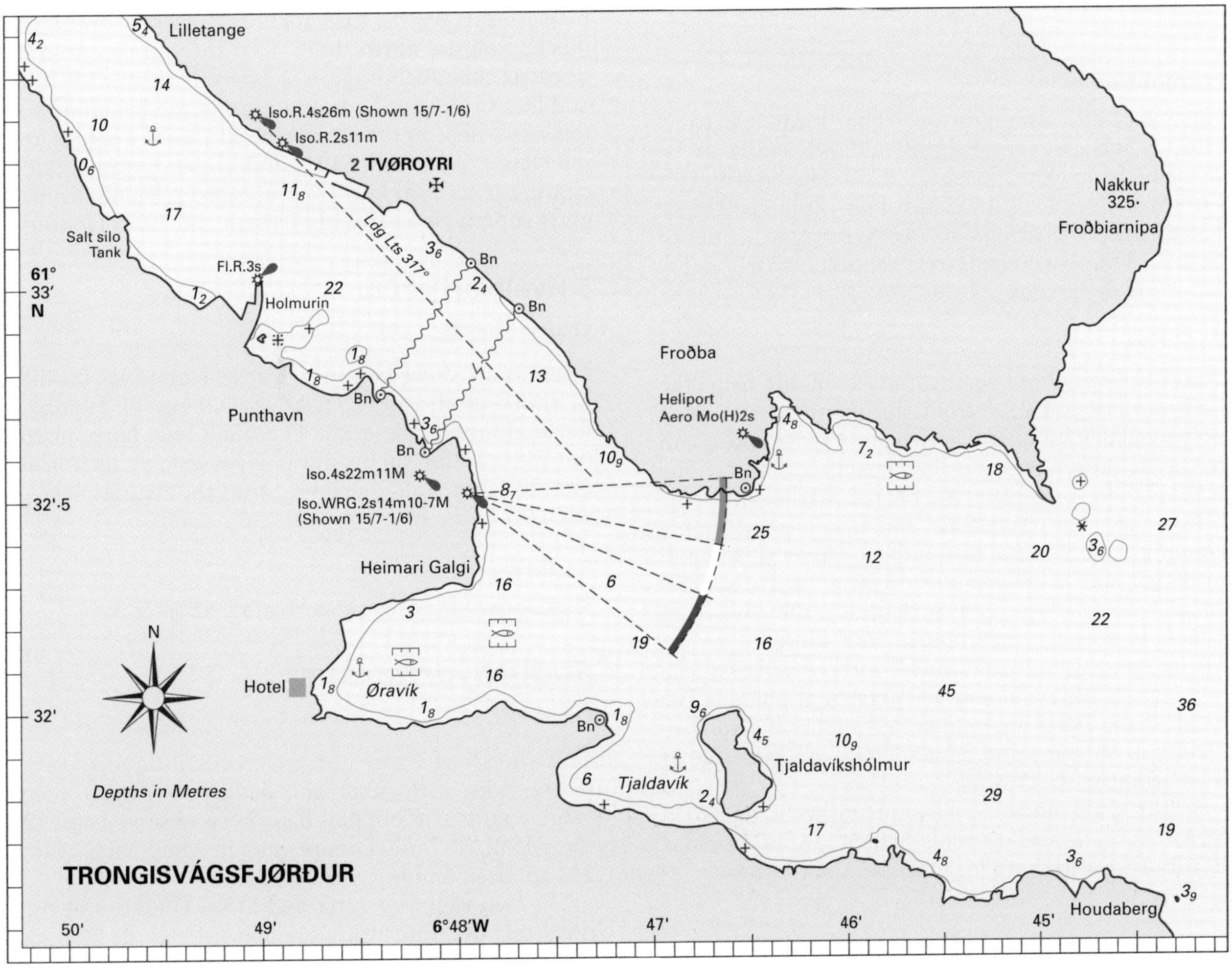

2 Tvøroyri 61°33'N 6°48'W

Tide 0·4, 1·3 **Charts** Plan 64

Approach

The approach is straightforward but vessels should keep well clear of the shoal patches on the south side of the upper fjord, off Punthavn. The first set of leading marks and lights (Iso.4s and Iso.WRG.2s) on 289° are clearly visible both day and night. The second set of leading lights on 317° (Iso.R.2s) are clearly visible at night and dusk. The day marks are not so easily identifiable but this does not matter. Contact the harbourmaster on Ch 16 on entering the fjord. He needs to be contacted whether going alongside or anchoring.

Berthing

The main harbour has been filled in and developed for commercial shipping only. Yachts may go alongside the wooden jetty, labelled 'Hvidenaes' on Chart 85, to the west of the fishing boat harbour. The jetty is 21m long and has about 3m of water. There is water for one yacht only on the inside of the jetty as the depth decreases rapidly. Yachts less than 8m LOA may berth alongside the NW hammerhead. There is a water hose close to the jetty. Alternatively, anchor to the west of Hvidenaes in about 10m, mud. Vessels may anchor off Trangisvaag at the head of the fjord. The holding is good in thick mud. The small fishing boat harbour is unsuitable for yachts greater than 7·5m (26ft) LOA.

Formalities

Customs and immigration. The local Customs Officer, who is very helpful and relaxed, can be contacted on ✆ +298 222 925. Harbourmaster Ch 16 or ✆ +298 371055 (*Mobile* +298 210055 or +298 222509, *Email* havn@tvoroyri.fo) out of hours. The harbourmaster requests that yachts report on departure.

Facilities

Water on pier; hose for hydrant available from the harbourmaster. Diesel from the pump at the quay only available by special licence; otherwise take a can to the chandlers. Supermarket, bakery and cafés. The Kgl. Handíi bar, 50m W of the harbourmaster's office, has an interesting ambiance, good home cooking and is very hospitable. There is a small museum and a tourist information office, several smaller food shops and a chandler, the owner of which is friendly, entertaining and knowledgeable; his influence is valuable for all sorts of repairs. The fish factory is helpful and will arrange slipping at the head of the fjord for long-keeled yachts if required. Hospital. Showers and a launderette are available at the harbourmaster's office.

A 2M walk north to Hvannhagi takes one to a series of spectacular pools which are a popular beauty-spot with both local people and tourists.

⚓ Tjaldavík 61°32'N 6°47'W

A sheltered anchorage in 5–8m sand in the bight west of Tjaldavíkshólmur on the south side of the fjord. The holm is a soft, gentle, island – unusual in Faroe – and has a wealth of wild flowers and ducks. In reasonable weather it is a good place for a quiet night after a passage but it is exposed to the fetch of the fjord and is not suitable when the wind, as it frequently does, funnels down the fjord from the NW or the WNW; however, in a strong easterly, close in to the holm, the anchorage was found to be quiet with no swell. There is a small salmon farm but it leaves space for anchoring.

⚓ Øravik 61°32'N 6°48'W

Charts Plan 68

NP52 reports good shelter and holding in Øravík, one mile to the west of Tjaldavíkshólmur, but holding has been found to be poor, it shoals at the head and is exposed to winds from the NE. A large fish farm leaves little room for anchoring. It is reported that it is possible to anchor in a large area inshore of the fish farm, which offers it some protection. Enter from the S. There is a small hotel which will serve a meal and beer. It is possible to walk to it from Tjaldavík.

⚓ Froðba 61°33'N 6°45'W

In W to NE winds, safe anchorage can be found in this bay on the north shore, near the entrance to the fjord. If this anchorage is a bit rolly, better shelter and less swell may be found around the headland to the west, close in off the northeast shore. There is an interesting waterfall half a mile inland, and a stiff climb up to Nakkur (325m) above Froðbiarnípa gives superb views of Lítla Dímun and Stóra Dímun.

3 Hvalbiarfjørður 61°36'N 6°56'W

Charts Plan 10

There is a fishing boat harbour at Hamranes on the N shore of the fjord, near the village of Hvalba. Berth alongside the quay. The small boat harbour to the W is not for yachts but it is possible to anchor in 6m between this harbour and the lighthouse – exposed to the E.

Facilities

Shop, post office, bank at Hvalba. Shop at Nes.

Suðuroyarfjørður

Charts Plan 83

This stretch of water northeast of Suðuroy has very strong tides with fierce and dangerous races. Some local magnetic anomalies have been observed east of the island of Lítla Dímun and in Dímunarfjørður, 2M south of Sandoy (see NP52).

The two islands – Lítla and Stóra Dímun – to the northeast of Suðuroy are precipitous and the landing place on Stóra Dímun is completely exposed.

Skúvoy

4 Skúvoy 61°46′N 6°47′W (village)

Charts Plan 52

Skúvoy, southwest of Sandoy, is 2M long and 1M wide. It is a dramatic island rising 390m from the village on the east to sheer cliffs on the west. Anchor in fair weather off the village on the east side.

The very small harbour has a narrow entrance and is subject to surge.

Sandoy

Charts 82, 83

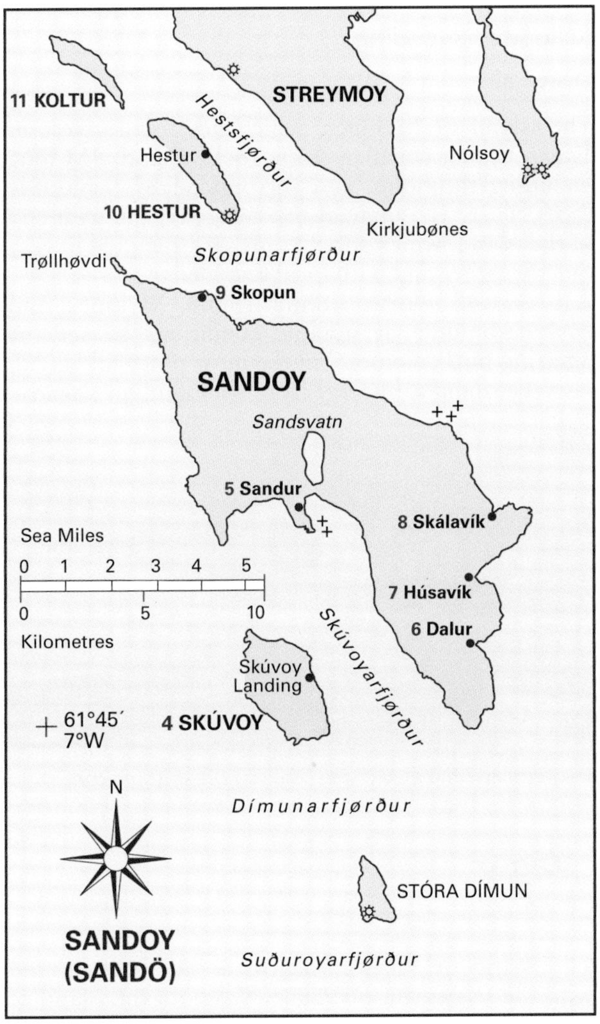

5 Sandur

Tide 0·6, 1·4 **Charts** 85 (1:20,000) Plan 43

The harbour is well sheltered by a long breakwater. It is used by fishing boats and the ferry to Skúvoy. In suitable weather, there is a pleasant anchorage with good holding off the extensive sandy beach at the head of the bay. The small boat landing almost below the church has been extended and improved. There is a shop in the village. Water and showers available in the harbour. Good walks, lakes and interesting diving birds. The small turf-roofed church, with its waxed pine interior, is one of the most attractive in Faroe and is well worth a visit.

6 Dalur 61°47′N 6°40′W

A fair anchorage in suitable weather.

7 Húsavík 61°48′N 6°40′W

Charts Plan 17

Anchor off the village in fair weather only. The pretty little village includes a ruin called 'Heimi a Garði' which was occupied by a colourful and wealthy lady, 'the lady of the house in Húsavík,' in the 14th century. She is reputed to have buried two servants alive.

8 Skálavík 61°50′N 6°40′W

Charts Plan 49

Although the approach is exposed to the E, it is reported that the inner harbour provides shelter under all conditions, with a minimum depth of 3m. Yachtsmen are encouraged to use the community house, with hot water, cooking facilities and toilets. Shop, post office and off-licence.

9 Skopun 61°54′N 6°52′W

Tide 0·6, 1·8 **Charts** Plan 51

Skopun is a busy harbour, well sheltered from south through west to north. It is very tight with narrow entrances leading to outer, middle and inner basins. The ferry uses the outer basin and the middle basin has a fish-processing plant and fishing boat quay but there is usually room for a yacht. The inner basin is very narrow with inshore fishing boats moored bows-on to the east side but, if full, the quay on the west side may be available. Watch the strong surge which may occur at each of the narrow gates. Skopun is a large village with adequate shops. Water on the quay. The ferry runs from here to Gamlarætt on Stremoy.

Island of Skúvoy *Eydfinnur*

Hestsfjørður and Skopunarfjørður

Charts 82

Hestsfjørður and Skopunarfjørður lie between Sandoy and Stremoy, either side of Hestur and Koltur. There are strong tides and races in the fjords and the currents between the islands can be strong and tricky. Details of the tides and counter-currents are shown in the local tide atlas (see Tidal Information on page 50). There is a legend of a lover who swam from Koltur to Hestur with the tide for forbidden assignations. One day the girl's irate father prevented him from landing and, unable to swim back against the tide, he was drowned.

Hestur and Koltur

Charts 82

The Horse and the Colt are a magnificent pair of islands separating Skopunarfjørður from Hestsfjørður. Koltur has a huge hump at its northwest end and Hestur has magnificent cliffs and stacks on its southwest side.

10 Hestur 61°57'N 6°52'W (village)

Charts Plan 12

There is a substantial harbour at the village of Hestur which lies to the east of the island of the same name. Local advice emphasises the danger of being swept on to the harbour wall by strong tides across the entrance. Berth alongside the quay but be prepared to move temporarily when the ferry arrives. A track leads towards the north of the island and others up the slope towards the cliff top. There is a fine modern painting over the altar in the church. There are spectacular caves on the S side of the island, which could be visited by dinghy on a calm day.

Hestur with Koltur behind, looking NW from Streymoy
Máire Wilkes

11 Koltur 61°59'N 6°57'W

Charts Plan 25

Koltur consists of a single farm with some very old and picturesque buildings. It is private, occupied in summer, and permission to land should be obtained. This can be done via the Kunningarstovan in Tórshavn. There is a small quay (dinghy landing only) on the northeast side of the island with a sandy bay for anchoring to the southeast of it. There is also a buoy close to the quay which might be used if unoccupied.

Mykines

Charts 82

12 Mykines 62°06'N 7°38'W (village and landing)

Charts 82

The island of Mykines, which lies to the west of Vagar, is a spectacular, steep, rocky island, 4M long including the holm, and surrounded by fierce tide races. There is a quay at the village on the west end of the island, which should only be attempted in very quiet weather and with local knowledge.

It is well worth sailing round Mykines and Mykineshólmur in suitable conditions to see the amazing bird colonies, but the most practical way to visit the island is by ferry from Sørvágur, on Vagar.

The ferry arriving at Mykines *Isselee / Dreamstime.com*

Vágar

Charts 82

The island of Vágar (Vaagö), not to be confused with the settlement of Vágur (Vaag) on the island of Suðuroy, lies to the northwest of Koltur. The main airport for Faroe is on Vágar.

The E and NE coasts bordering Vestmannasund have no harbours. With the completion of the road tunnel under Vestmannasund, the slip and landing place for the ferry to Vestmanna at Oyragjógv, 62°07'N 7°10'W, is no longer used. There is no shelter on the north coast which consists entirely of high cliffs. The remarkable pinnacle Trøllkonufingur marks the north side of the approach to Miðvágur and Sandavágur. (See photo page 55.)

13 Sørvágur 62°04'N 7°19'W

Tide 0·9, 1·9
Charts 85 (1:20,000) Plan 60

Approach

Sørvágur is at the head of the long Sørvágsfjørður in southwest Vágar. The approach to the fjord from north or south is beset with strong races and should not be attempted in poor weather. Coming from the south, pass west of Gáshólmur (local advice is that it is unwise to attempt to pass through Gáshólmssund). The north shore of the fjord has magnificent waterfalls. The pretty village of Bøur and the remote settlement of Gásadalur were until recently almost the last in Faroe with no road; however they are now connected to 'the outside world' by tunnel. Once in the fjord there are some fish farms that are unlit.

Torrent at Bøur, Sørvagsfjørður, Vágar *Christopher Thornhill*

Nest, Sørvágur *Máire Wilkes*

Anchorage

The best berth is on the pontoon by the entrance of the small boat harbour, just in front of the salmon processing plant a mile west of the main village. The head of the fjord dries. The tidal range at Sørvágur is 2·5m, the biggest in the islands.

Facilities

Shops, banks, etc. Water on quay. The harbour office is at the western end of the salmon plant and may be able to supply weather and tidal information. Gas bottles from the chandler behind the harbourmaster's office. The airport and airport hotel are 1·5M from the village, an uphill walk. Ferry to Mykines.

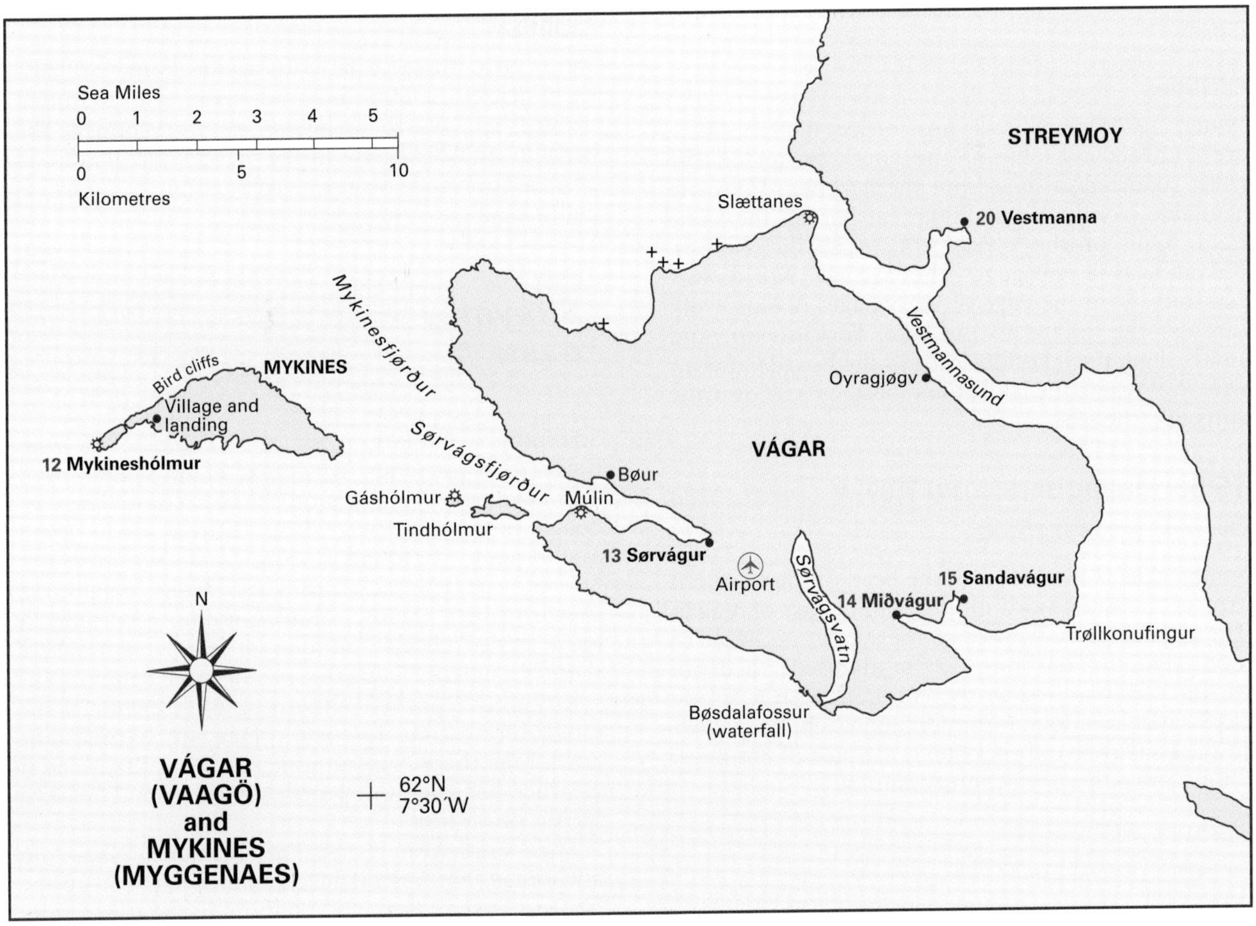

Gasholmur from Bøur *Máire Wilkes*

14 Miðvágur 62°03'N 7°11'W

Tide 0·8, 1·7
Charts 85 (1:20,000) Plan 29

Miðvágur, a substantial village, lies at the head of the western arm of the fjord on the south coast of Vágar. A mole, 350m long, extends from the north shore across the entrance to this arm, almost closing it and giving excellent shelter from all directions.

Berth

Berth alongside one of the quays, or tie up alongside a fishing boat on the port side immediately before the small boat harbour. Alternatively anchor off the village.

Facilities

Water, fuel, shops, bank, post office, doctor. There are showers available at the youth hostel on the coast road half a mile from the harbour. Taxis are available from a house 300m further on the same road. One of the oldest houses in the Islands, Kálvalið, is a museum. The Second World War cemetery is on the edge of the village. A 6km walk through the village to the lake, Sørvágsvatn, and south along the lakeside, leads to the Bøsadalafossur waterfall where the lake pours spectacularly over the cliffs into the sea.

15 Sandavágur 62°03'N 7°09'W

Charts 85 (1:20,000) Plan 42

Sandavágur is the village at the head of the northern arm of the same fjord on the south coast of Vágar. The anchorage is exposed to the south and liable to swell. The tiny harbour has 3m alongside. A depth of 4m was reported in the entrance with a spring tidal range of about 1·7m. On approach, keep close to the quay to avoid rocks on north side of entrance. Shops and a fine 19th-century church.

Nólsoy

Charts 82, 85 (1:20,000)

16 Nólsoy 62°00'N 6°41'W (Harbour)

Charts 82, 85 (1:20,000)

The harbour on Nólsoy, across the fjord from Tórshavn, is a quiet alternative to the berth in Tórshavn.

Nólsoy is a long, thin island, 4¾M long and 1¼M wide, lying parallel to the southeast coast of Streymoy about 3M off. It shelters Tórshavn from the worst of the easterly weather. At the southeast corner is the powerful Nólsoy lighthouse and at the southwest tip is the lighthouse of Borðan that leads into the sound towards Tórshavn.

The small, peaceful harbour with a whale jaw archway and a pretty village are on the isthmus towards the north of the island, just under 3M due east from Tórshavn. It is well worth a visit to escape from the bustle of the capital and to climb Eggjarklettur (372m) for a magnificent view of the Norðoyar on a clear day.

Berthing

Berth inside the northern breakwater, leaving room for the ferry at the outer end; however, ferry berthing seems to vary. Take local advice. If no space here, berth at the fish quays on the S side of the harbour.

Facilities

Shop, post office, café. This is the home of Jens-Kjeld Jensen, a famous taxidermist, whose stuffed seabirds are worth seeing in his workshop at the harbour and his house in the village. He also takes parties to watch storm petrels coming ashore at night.

Streymoy

Charts 82

Streymoy is the largest island of Faroe, 25M from north to south and 7M across at its widest part. Tórshavn, the capital, is on the east coast. The east coast also has two deep fjords with good anchorages, Kaldbaksfjørður and Kollafjørður. Streymoy is separated from its eastern neighbour, Eysturoy, by a narrow sound, Sundini, 15M long. A road bridge crosses Sundini at Sundalagið where there is a narrow navigable passage (see below).

Kirkjubøur, at the southern tip of Streymoy, is the most interesting historic place in Faroe. The anchorage there is unsuitable in all but the quietest weather but it is well worth a visit from Tórshavn by bus or on foot.

The southwest coast of Streymoy has no anchorage, but Vestmanna, a winter harbour up the Vestmannasund, is the best natural harbour in Faroe.

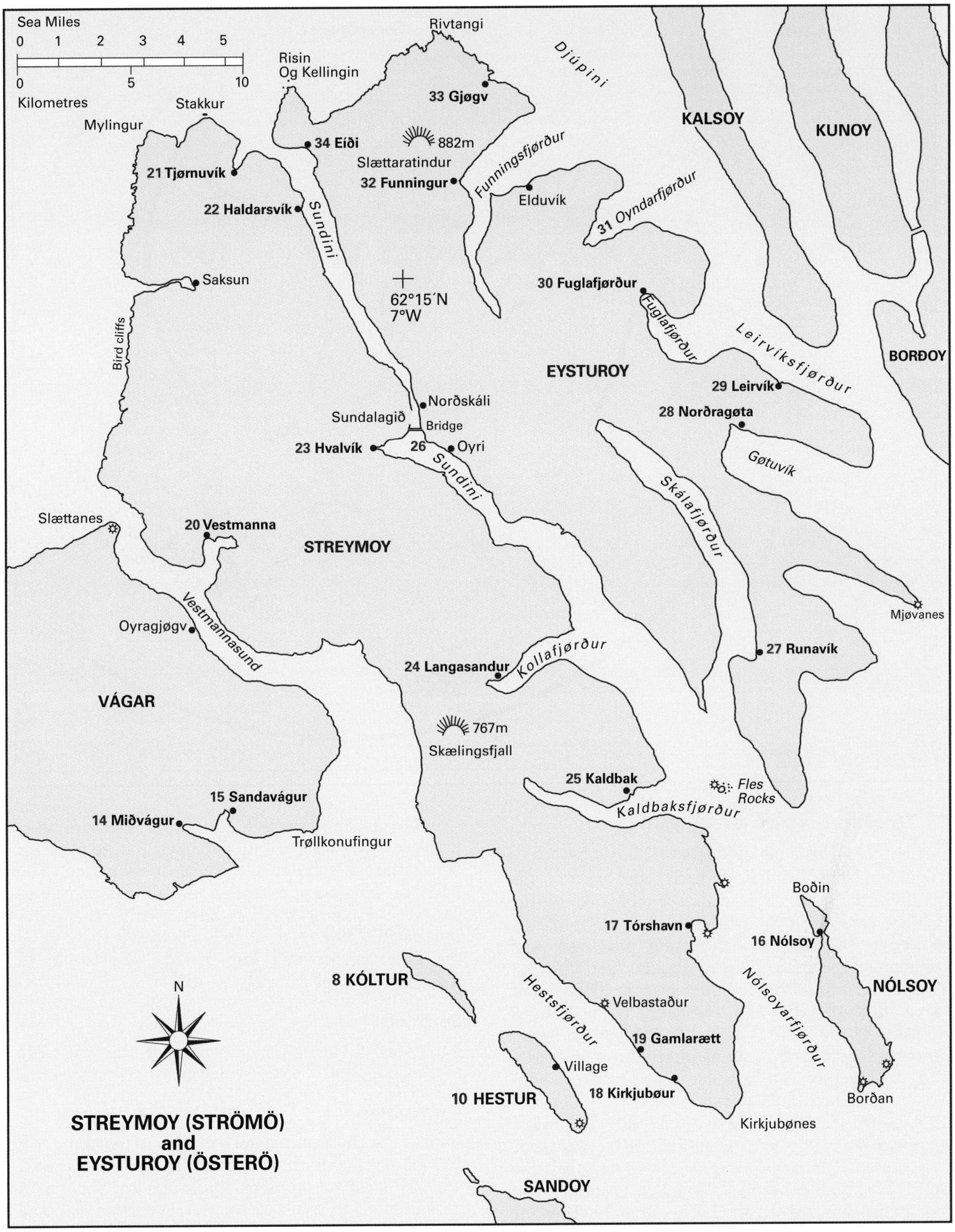

The fuglabjørg (bird cliffs and stacks) of the northwest coast should not be missed. Mylingur, the northwest tip, has fantastic rock pinnacles and several anchorages can be found at the N end of Sundini.

Saksun, an inlet on the west coast, offers an attractive temporary anchorage in offshore winds. It appears to be clean and, in suitable conditions, it is possible to anchor at the head just off the sandy beach in 4–6m. The sea trout fishing is good.

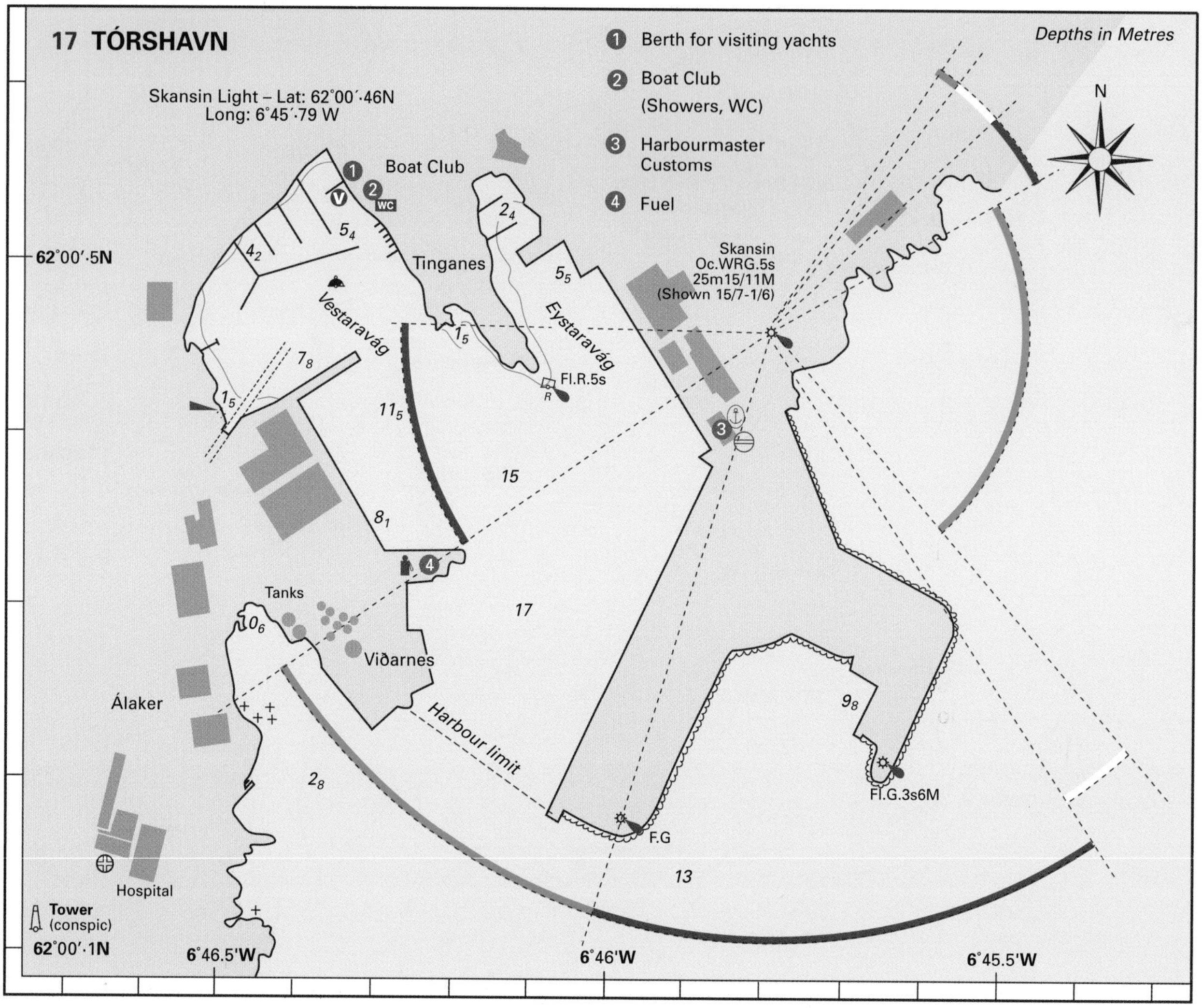

17 Tórshavn 62°00'N 6°45'W

Tide 0·1, 0·3 **Charts** 85 (1:20,000), 85 (1:5,000) Plan 62

Tórshavn is the capital of Faroe and seat of the Løgting (parliament). It claims to be one of the smallest capitals in the world and has a population of about 18,000. It is the main passenger and commercial harbour of the islands. The *Port of Tórshavn Handbook* is available from Tórshavnar Havn, Box 103, FO-110 Tórshavn, Faroe Islands, ✆ +298 311762 (*Mobile* +298 211762), *Email* port@torshavn.fo. It contains information on ferries and air travel as well as general information about Tórshavn's restaurants and shops, etc.

Ólavsøka (St Olav's Day) on 29 July is Faroese National Day and the main festival of the year. The festivities in Tórshavn spread over three days, starting on 27 July, with concerts, sporting competitions and much revelry in the streets. The main highlight is the series of rowing races between teams from all the islands in traditional Faroese boats.

Approach

Approach is straightforward via Nólsoyarfjørður, passing north or south of Nólsoy which is clean on the west side and at both ends. There are no submarine dangers off the cliffs of Streymoy between Kirkjubønes and Tórshavn but be alert for fish farms, if following them close-to in fog. The harbour has been extended on the east side to provide a container facility with an outer breakwater. Enter the harbour between the end of the inner breakwater and a red buoy 300m to the SW.

Berthing

Yachts should lie on the quay in the Vestaravág close to the boat club. There is a charge for visiting yachts.

Formalities

Inform the harbourmaster of arrival (working Ch 12) or at the harbour office (Havnarskrivstova), which is in a modern building in the main commercial port past the ferry terminals. The harbourmaster requests that yachts report departure and destination so that he can inform enquirers of their whereabouts. If this is the first port of call, report to customs in the building behind harbourmaster's office.

Tørshavn looking east towards Nólsoy *David Lomax*

Facilities

Tórshavn has all the facilities of a large town. Details of the Tórshavn and the Faroe Islands Tourist Offices are given under Tourist Information (see Introduction). Both are worth a visit for local information; the staff are pleasant and helpful and can usually provide a local weather forecast. A swimming pool and sauna are located one mile from the harbour. Power available on the quay (payment at the blue hut). If a diver is needed, contact Atlantic Diving ✆ 316979.

Streymoy looking NW to Hestur and Koltur *Máire Wilkes*

All shops, banks, postal, telephone and other facilities expected of a major town can be found. The main supermarket, SMS, which is excellent, is 800m inland – follow Tinghusvegur uphill from the town centre.

Showers and laundry facilities are available at the Marine Club (Bátafelagiðð). Tokens are available from Hotel Tórshavn, close to the yacht harbour.

There are several other restaurants and cafés. The Føroyar Hotel, a grand new building, is rather a long way inland.

The shipyard, Tórshavnar Skipasmiðja, is on the west side of Vestaravág and has every sort of repair facility. There is also a chandlery just up from the harbour, two marine electronic shops and a Yanmar dealership.

Water and electrical power are available in Vestaravág on the quay.

The fuel berth is to port on entry, on the S side of the pier just E of the Shell and Statoil storage tanks

Propane is available at a depot, which is a taxi ride from the town.

Jacobsens Bókahandil, with its old turf roof, will provide the almanac and tidal stream atlas as well as charts and harbour plans. Tourist office with internet access is here too.

The Havnarkirkja (harbour church), on Tinganes, just above the yacht berth, is one of the most beautiful in Faroe. It is open in the afternoons and well worth a visit, as is the fine modern Vesturkirkja. The Historical Museum (Føroya Fornminnissavn) is also worth a visit, particularly for its collection of old Faroese boats.

18 Kirkjubøur 61°57'N 6°48'W

Tide 0·3, 1·0 **Charts** 82

A mile and a half northwest of Kirkjubønes, the southern tip of Streymoy, Kirkjubøur is the most interesting historic site in Faroe and is well worth a visit by boat, road or on foot over the hills from Tórshavn. The settlement is said to date back to

Kirkjubøur is the most interesting historic site in Faroe
Máire Wilkes

Roykstovan, Kirkjubøur *Máire Wilkes*

pre-Norse Celtic monks and it has been a centre of learning, seat of bishops and one of the largest farms in the islands. There is a 12th-century church (the oldest in Faroe), an unfinished 13th-century cathedral and the farmhouse itself, said to be 900 years old and the oldest log house in Europe. The timbers came originally from Norway. It is said that they were floated across and they do indeed have a salt taste. This is not as surprising as it sounds because there are numerous references in the sagas to voyages from Iceland to Norway to obtain building timber for important houses and stave churches as far back as the 10th century. The Patursson family have lived there for 17 generations; Tróndur Patursson, the well known artist, was one of Tim Severin's crew in the currach *Brendan* and on his other voyages. Part of the house, the Roykstovan, is open daily to the public. The old name for Kirkjubøur is Brandarsvík.

Gamlarætt ferryport *Máire Wilkes*

Approach

The tides in this part of the fjord run very fiercely and set over the reef which extends S and SE from Kirkjubøurhólmur. Great care is needed, approaching from east or west, to avoid being set on to the tail of the reef. A course keeping outside the 50m contour is safe.

Anchorage

In suitable weather there is reported to be a good anchorage, sand and weed, close in to the shore. Avoiding the reefs, approach about 80m W of the wall on the shore and anchor as appropriate in 4–6m. Exposed from SE to W. There is a big iron cleat on the rocks that was used by the boats delivering to the farm.

There is a small, rock-girt quay below the house which can be approached by dinghy through a gap in the reef NE of the holm. It should not be attempted in a yacht.

19 Gamlarætt 61°58'N 6°49'W

Gamlarætt is the only harbour on the SW coast of Streymoy. It is dedicated solely to the large ferry which runs to Hestur and Skopun and is not suitable for yachts, although it might be used as a temporary refuge. There is water on the quay and buses to Tórshavn.

20 Vestmanna 62°09'N 7°10'W

Tide 0·8, 2·0 **Charts** 84 (1:20,000) Plan 67

Vestmanna lies at the head of a deep, sheltered bay on the N side of the Vestmannasund, which runs between Streymoy and Vágar. It is rated a winter harbour and is one of the best in the islands.

A road tunnel now connects Streymoy to Vágar.

Approach

The approach through the Vestmannasund from north or south is deep and straightforward but can be squally, with very strong tides and rips at the northern entrance.

Berthing

The main fishing harbour for smaller boats is on the W side behind a stone wall. It is busy, but space has been found. The quay at Hoygarnes is also busy and has a shipyard. The small boat harbour in the northeast corner of the bay is not suitable for yachts. Some heavy fishing boat moorings in the E bight might be used with permission: or anchor in good holding, sand and shell, off the shingle beach close west of the small boat harbour.

The harbourmaster's office is a prominent modern building at the W harbour (VHF Ch 16, working Ch 12).

Facilities

Water and diesel. Showers in the harbourmaster's building. Shops, restaurant, café, banks and PO. Buses to Tórshavn. Bar close to the fish factory. Repairs should be possible at the shipyard. The church is worth a visit.

21 Tjørnuvík 62°17'N 7°08'W

Tjørnuvík is an interesting village with old houses set in a magnificent amphitheatre with many waterfalls pouring down the hillside behind. It has an ancient Viking burial ground and is the place where Tim Severin came to anchor in *Brendan*, after being swept N through Mykines Sound. Anchor towards the middle of the bay, opposite the quay in good holding, sand. Landing on the quay on the NE side of the bay can be difficult in any swell. It is exposed to the E and can be rolly, but is a good alternative to Eiði in a southerly. Probably the best anchorage in the islands, with a splendid view of the Risin og Kellingin.

22 Haldarsvík

A small harbour 5M N of the narrows.

23 Hvalvík 62°11'N 7°01'W

Tide Tide not appreciable **Charts** 84 Plan 18

A village in the wide bay 1·5M south of the Strømmen bridge. There is a shallow harbour on the south side of the bay, 0·5M from the village. It is a convenient place to wait for the tide through the narrows or to catch a bus across the island to visit the ancient farm at Saksun on the west coast (two buses a day in the high season).

24 Kollafjørður

Tide Tide not appreciable **Charts** 84

Kollafjørður is a long, deep inlet 7·5M north of Tórshavn which is subject to bad squalls. At the head of Kollafjørður, Langasandur there are three small quays with 6m alongside and a fine-weather anchorage; it is a good place from which to climb the Skælingsfjall, the highest point in southern Streymoy (767m). The other villages along the shore offer fine-weather anchorages and at Sjógv (near Kollafjørður village a mile W of the entrance, on the N side of the fjord), it is possible to lie alongside the jetty.

Hvalvik church *Christopher Thornhill*

25 Kaldbaksfjørður

Tide Tide not appreciable **Charts** 84

Kaldbaksfjørður is a long, deep inlet 3·5M north of Tórshavn. Fles rocks, awash in the middle of the Sundini sound, 1M off the entrance to Kaldbaksfjørður, have a beacon; the shoal to the NE is reported to have less than the 3·8m shown on Chart 82. Kaldbaksfjørður is subject to bad squalls. In fine weather, anchorage can be had at Kaldbak village, on the N side of the fjord, close E of the church.

Eysturoy

Charts 82 and 84

Eysturoy (Eastern Island) is separated from Stremoy by Sundini, a narrow channel with a bridge connecting the two islands. A long fjord, Skálafjørður, cuts up into the island from its southwestern corner. There are five main fjords and bays on the E coast giving varying degrees of shelter, and a harbour, Leirvík, halfway up the east coast. The N coast consists of steep cliffs and impressive stacks, Risin og Kellingin (the Giant and the Hag), who were trying to tow the islands to Iceland when the rising sun caught them at it and petrified them. The highest point of Faroe, Slættaratindur (882m), is two miles from the N point of the island.

Beware of heavy overfalls near the SE point, Mjóvanes, and off the N coast, as well as very strong tides in Leirvíksfjørður.

26 Sundini and the Sundalagið Narrows

Charts 84 (1:20,000)

Sundini, the channel between Streymoy and Eysturoy, provides an interesting route to or from the NW coast for a yacht with a mast less than 17m high. 180m wide at its narrowest point, the narrows (Sundalagið) are spanned by a road bridge with 15·8–18m clearance. The overhead cable to the N has a clearance of 23m. The dredged channel is 25m wide and has a minimum depth of 3m; the shoal shown on the chart 800m to the S of the bridge is reported to have not less than 3m.

At maximum spring rate the stream through the narrows can attain 12kns in both directions. With careful timing it is possible for a yacht to pass through close to slack water (which occurs at approximately mean tide level) giving a clearance of 17m under the centre of the arch. At low water springs the clearance may be over 18m but the tide runs so strongly that a passage is out of the question. The same applies at high water when the clearance is less then 16m. If nervous about the height of the mast, it is wise to approach the bridge against a slight adverse stream – it might be impossible to stop or turn around in a favourable stream.

Timing of the passage is complicated by the tidal curiosity that, on the SE side of the narrows, there is no tidal range whatsoever whereas, at Norðskáli, 0·5M northwest of the bridge, the spring range is 2m. You should not assume that slack water in the narrows coincides with HW or LW Norðskáli.

S-going stream begins –0045 Vestfalskyrrindi i Suðuroyarfirði.
N-going stream about 6 hours later (for times see the *Almanakki*).

Alternatively:
S-going stream begins at about –0015 HW Reykjavík (approximately –0450 HW Dover).
N-going stream begins at about +0600 HW Reykjavík (approximately +0125 HW Dover).

However, these predictions are approximate and slack water has been observed up to 50 minutes earlier.

⚓ Norðskáli

Small village and quay 5M N of the bridge.

⚓ Oyri

There is a small quay 1M S of the bridge.

Skálafjørður

Skálafjørður, on the southwestern corner of Eysturoy, is the longest inlet in the islands, 7·5M from Raktangi to the head. It has several small harbours and quays and is being rapidly developed as a base for oil exploration. The main harbour is Runavík.

27 Runavík 62°07'N 6°43'W

Tide Tide not appreciable **Charts** 84 (1:20,000) Plan 41

Runavík is in the SE corner of Skálafjørður, 2M from the entrance. It is comparatively free from squalls because it is not as close as most harbours to high hills.

Runavík is the third largest town in the Faroe Islands and a supply base for the North Sea offshore industry as well as a trans-shipment port for freight to and from Europe. An 11km long tunnel to Tórshavn should be complete in 2016. It has a wide range of facilities including banks, hotels, supermarkets, chandlery and a very well-run Seaman's Mission Hotel (Sjómansheim) near the harbour, that will provide meals and rooms; showers may be possible. As part of the development, it is planned to build a boat club about 1M N of Runavík harbour, where there will be facilities for visiting yachts, showers etc. Some old fishing boats (one of them built in Rye, Sussex, in 1887) have been restored to form an embryonic boat museum.

28 Norðragøta 62°12'N 6°44'W

Tide 0·3, 1·0 **Charts** 82, 84 (1:20,000) Plan 34

Heading anti-clockwise around Eysturoy from Skálafjørður, Norðragøta is a substantial village at the head of Gøtuvík, the wide inlet at the SE of Eysturoy. The village centre is a very attractive cluster of old black and turf houses and a pretty church. Historically this is the home of Tróndur í Gøtu, bloodthirsty 10th-century chieftain and anti-hero of the Føroyngasøga.

Round the head of the bay at Gøtugjøgv is a beautiful modern church with all its interior fittings in stained glass by Tróndur Patursson.

The harbour is sheltered behind a long breakwater. There are several fish cages in the bay and the harbour is busy with salmon boats, but space can be found for a yacht in the outer harbour. The inner, small boat harbour is shallow.

Shop. Water on quay.

Djupini & Leirvíksfjørður

Djupini is the wide sound between Eysturoy and Kalsoy. The narrow, southern entrance is the Leirvíksfjørður where tidal streams can reach 11kns at springs. Strong eddies form round the Gøtunes peninsula and off the SW coast of Kalsoy but effective progress can be made against the main tidal stream with local knowledge.

The turn of the tide in Leirvíksfjørður coincides roughly with the turn in Suðuroyarfjørður. (Vestfalls and Eystfallskyrrindi, see *Streymkort fyri Føroyar.*)

In the N part of Djupini, the SE stream begins an hour earlier and the NW stream an hour later.

29 Leirvík 62°13'N 6°42'W

Tide 0·6, 1·1 **Charts** 82, 84 (1:20,000) Plan 27

A secure harbour and a useful small town at the SE of Eysturoy, dominated by the 612m Sigatindur. The harbour is busy with a large fish factory. There is a shop and a Føroyar Bjór store close to the quay.

30 Fuglafjørður 62°14'N 6°48'W

Tide 0·3, 1·7 **Charts** 82, 84 (1:20,000) Plan 5

The head of the fjord has very good holding and is traditionally rated a winter harbour, one of the best in the N part of the islands. The harbour at the village is very snug and secure. Berth on the N of the outer wall, or if this is too busy with fishing boats there is just room for a 32' yacht to lie on one of the fingers in the small boat marina or anchor off. Diesel is available from a pump close by, by arrangement with the small boatyard there. Stores, water.

There is a hot spring S of the village.

Funningur, Eysturoy *Máire Wilkes*

Gjøgv *Máire Wilkes*

31 Oyndarfjørður 62°17'N 6°51'W

Tide 0·3, 1·7 Charts 82, 84 (1:40,000) Plan 36

There is a small harbour at the village and shallow anchorage at the head of the fjord but open to swell and the holding is reported as mediocre. Beware of the shoal that extends E of the breakwater.

32 Funningsfjørður 62°14'N 6°55'W

Charts 82, 84 (1:40,000) Plan 6

The outer part of the fjord is not recommended as an anchorage, being subject to wind and swell. There is, however, anchorage at the villages of Funningur and Elduvík in quiet weather.

The narrow head of the fjord provides good holding, free from swell, but is subject to squalls off the surrounding mountains and in strong northerlies the wind funnels down the narrow fjord.

33 Gjøgv 62°20'N 6°56'W

Charts 82

A very narrow inlet between steep cliffs, suitable only for small boats. It is picturesque but deep water and rocks at the entrance make anchoring off impractical.

Eiði, Sundini, Eysturoy *Máire Wilkes*

34 Eiði 62°18'N 7°05'W

Tide 0·8, 1·6 **Charts** 82 Plan 4

A small town with a large harbour at the N end of Sundini. It is the only secure harbour in the N of the islands and serves as a refuge if caught out off the N coast and as a place to wait for a passage SE through Sundini.

There is a pontoon at the E side of the harbour: it is for small local boats, but there may be room for one or two yachts alongside. Water and electricity are available, but an 80m electricity cable and 120m water hose are needed. Alternatively berth against the quay in the NW of the harbour, against large tyres (fender board essential): water is available, but again a long hose is needed. Diesel is currently only available to fishermen using a special card, but the possibility of providing diesel to visitors is under discussion (2013).

There is an hotel and a supermarket close to the harbour. The 19th-century church with lovely ship models is worth visiting. There is a pleasant 1-hour walk along the cliffs to the north (walk north along the road, past the shop and out of the village. Where the road bends sharp right, take the narrow winding path to the left. Stop when the path peters out at the landslips: further progress is by a hard scramble along steeply sloping rock and is eventually blocked by a fence). A longer and more energetic walk may be made past the reservoir Eiðisvatn to Slættaratindur, Faroe's highest mountain (882m).

Eiði church. Note the hanging ship model *Máire Wilkes*

Norðoyar: The Northern Isles

On the chart these look like imaginary islands in a children's book and the reality is not much different, with huge cliffs and absurdly symmetrical cones of mountains in all directions. The fjords and sounds are difficult to sail, subject to squalls, fitful catspaws and complete wind shadow. There are few good harbours and fewer anchorages, but the views of cliffs, mountains and crags piled on top of each other, of eerie steep-sided sounds and the remoteness of the furthest islands are well worth a day or two's cruising. The great mountain amphitheatre of Villingadalsfjall at the N of Viðoy ends in Enniberg and is said to be the highest sheer headland in the world, falling directly into the sea from 750m.

The largest of these northern isles, Borðoy, is joined to its neighbours east and west – Viðoy and Kunoy – by causeways that block the sounds; but the substantial land mass thus created would still be largely inaccessible were it not for nearly 7kms of road tunnels through the mountains.

35 Kalsoy Island

Charts 82 Plan 16, 30, 57

The westernmost island of the group, Kalsoy is 10M long and less than 1M wide. Most of its spine is over 500m high and rises over 700m at the N and S ends.

There are small jetties at Syðradalur, where the ferry from Klaksvík berths, and also at Húsar, and a landing at Mikladalur.

The tiny population of 80 in the N settlements is served by an amazing series of tunnels totalling over 5km.

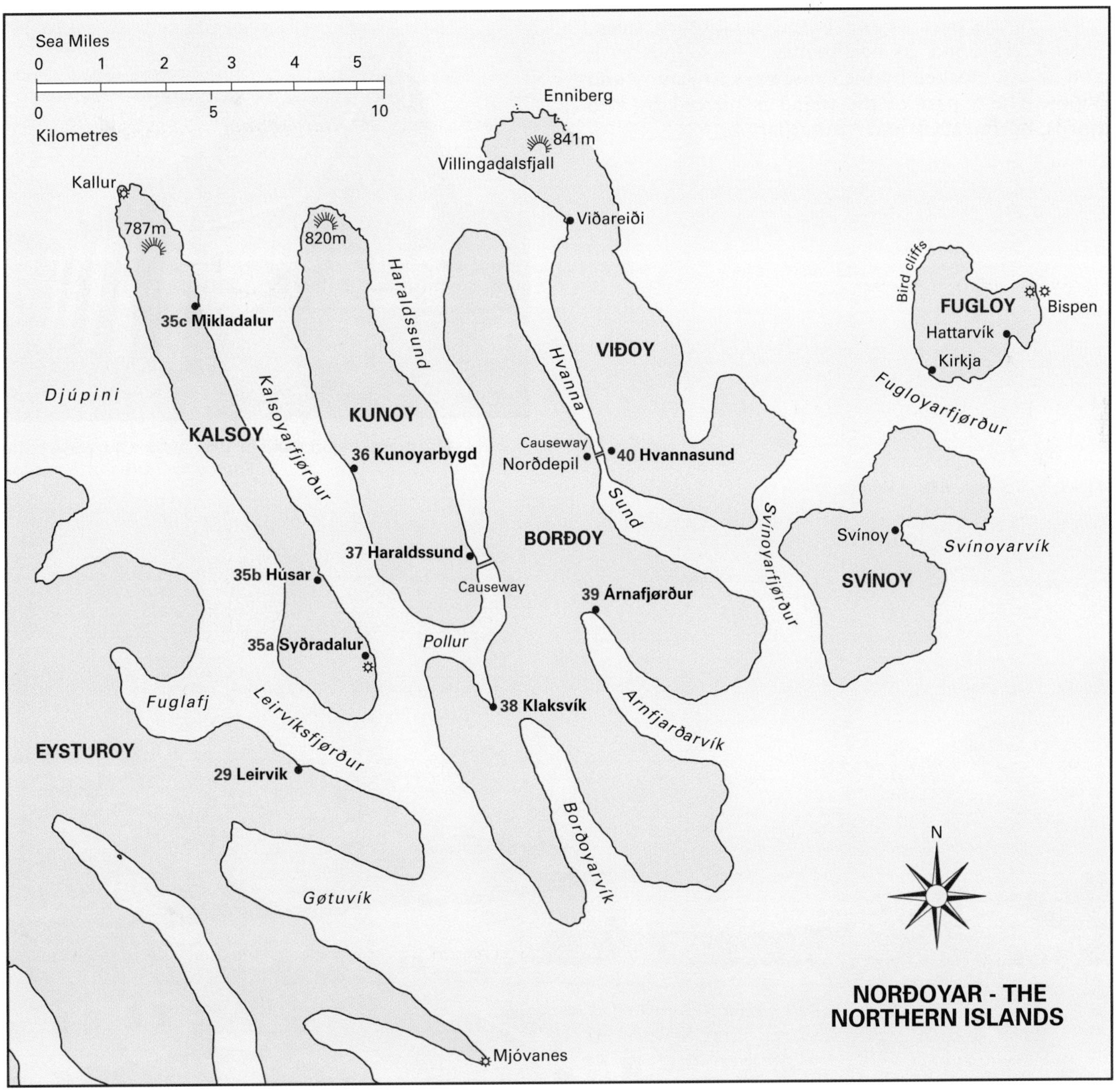

Kunoy Island

Charts 82 Plan 26

Kunoy is a bit shorter and wider than Kalsoy but even higher – a series of craggy ridges joining peaks of over 800m.

36 Kunoyarbygd

The only settlement on the west coast, Kunoyarbygd has a small jetty out of the tide where a yacht can berth on either side, although the S side is more accessible. Pretty church and houses in the village and fine walks along the mountainside. One of the very few tree plantations in the Faroes is just to the S of the village.

37 Haraldssund

The only settlement on the E of Kunoy, where the sound is blocked by the causeway to Borðoy. There is a small quay on the N side of the causeway. Skarð, further up the coast, is now abandoned.

The north part of the island is another steep, narrow ridge like its neighbours. The sounds to E and W are blocked by the causeways to Kunoy and Viðoy. The S part of the island is pierced by two fjords, Borðoyarvík and Arnfjarðarvík.

Borðoy Island

Charts 82

38 Klaksvík 62°14'N 6°35'W

Tide 0·5, 0·9 Charts 84 (1:20,000) Plan 23

Klaksvík is the second-largest town in Faroe, a busy commercial harbour and a centre for ship-building and brewing (Föroya Bjór). The designated winter harbour is excellent. The whole of the harbour shore is occupied by quays and jetties.

Approach

Straightforward.

Berthing

The harbourmaster's office is on the W side of the harbour but the quays here are busy and it is best to call the harbourmaster on Ch 16 and get his advice.

Christianskirkjan, built in 1963 in the Old Norse style
Spumador / Dreamstime.com

Klaksvík, Borðoy *Máire Wilkes*

The area to the S of the ferry pier near the Tourist Information Centre on the E side (easily identified as a modern building with a row of flag poles) is usually very crowded but it may be possible to lie there.

Facilities

Shops and all facilities of a substantial town. Early closing on Saturday. Public swimming pool. The Sjómansheim (Seaman's Mission Hotel) on the SW side of the harbour offers meals and showers. There is a sailmaker in the town (Torbjørn Gaard ✆ +298 455018).

The Christianskirkjan is a very fine modern church with an outstanding altar piece. There is a fine organ and an historic full size attamannfar (traditional eight-oared boat) hanging high in the nave, originally used by the priest for visiting his parishioners on the outer islands. Well worth a visit.

39 Árnafjørður 62°15'N 6°32'W

Charts 82 Plan 34

The village at the head of Arnfjarðavik with a small harbour behind a wall, with just room for a yacht alongside fishing boats.

Norðdepil

(See Hvannasund, Viðoy Island)

Viðoy Island

Viðoy is another long, craggy island like its neighbour to the W. The only harbour is at Hvannasund where the causeway crosses from Norðdepil on Borðoy, blocking the sound and forming harbours N and S – the only secure harbours when cruising these NE islands. The island is almost cut through near the N by the isthmus of Viðareiði. The huge bulk of Villingadalsfjall (841m) rears up to the north, falling sheer into the sea at Enniberg, the highest headland in the world.

40 Hvannasund & Norðdepil 62°18'N 6°31'W

Charts 82, 84 (1:10,000) Plan 19

The harbours formed N and S of the causeway are very useful as a refuge or overnight stop when cruising the NE isles. Both are easy to get into and free from tidal stream. The only alternative secure harbour in the Norðoyar is Klaksvík.

The main quays are S of the causeway and form a harbour with Norðdepil on the opposite bank. A quiet anchorage can be found about 600m SE of the church near a stone jetty alongside which it may be possible to lie. To the N of the causeway is a small boat harbour with a substantial jetty where a yacht can berth, subject to the movement of local boats.

There are some shops and the bus service from Klaksvík to Viðareiði runs through the village.

Viðareiði 62°22'N 6°32'W

Charts 82

Viðareiði is the village on the isthmus at the N end of Viðoy. It is a picturesque collection of houses with a white church at the foot of the mighty Villingadalsfjall, the northernmost peak in the Faroe Islands. There is no quay or harbour. The anchorage shown in the bay west of the village is exposed, rocky and too deep for a yacht. The alternative landing at Eiðsvík to the east is no more satisfactory and, unfortunately, it is not practical to stop here to climb the mountain. There is a possible temporary berth at a small quay 1·5M up the Hvannasund but the best way to get to Viðareiði and to climb the Villingadalsfjall is to walk or take a bus from Hvannasund.

Svínoy and Fugloy Islands

Charts 82

The two most eastern islands of the Faroes, are both magnificent and it is well worth the trouble to sail round them in good visibility; but the only practical way to land on Fugloy is to take the ferry from Hvannasund.

Both islands are steep-to except for a few rocks close under the cliffs and the tide runs strongly in the fjords between them. Navigation has not always been as easy as it is now. Legend states that both islands used to drift about in the banks of mist and could only be anchored firmly if iron could be landed on them; the trouble was that the trolls threw the iron back into the sea. However, a Bible and a pig with iron tied to his tail outwitted the trolls and the islands are now firmly in their charted position.

Svínoy is an island of dramatic cliffs divided by a sweeping valley that almost cuts the island in two. The village is in Svinoyarvík, the bay on the E side of the island, with a new, very small, boat harbour in amongst the rocks in the SW corner. It is too small to use, except in an emergency. In reasonable conditions and offshore winds there is good anchorage in <9m, in the SW corner, about 100m off the harbour. The village has been inhabited since Svínoyar-Bjarni ruled the Norðoyar from here in the 9th century and is a pretty jumble of old houses running down to the water. There is a pier on the other side of the isthmus, where the ferry from Hvannasund berths; but even on the calmest of days, it is subject to swell from the tide races in the sounds.

The two villages of Kirkja and Hattarvík on Fugloy are second to none as inaccessible settlements. There is no harbour and no anchorage and yet people have lived here continuously for over 1,000 years. Even on a calm day it is not practical to take a yacht alongside the tiny quay at either of the villages. Skarðsvík, to the N, looks on the chart to be a possible anchorage but it is cliff-girt, full of rocks, the survey stops at the 45m line and it is quite inhospitable. The cliffs are magnificent, with clouds of puffins in summer.

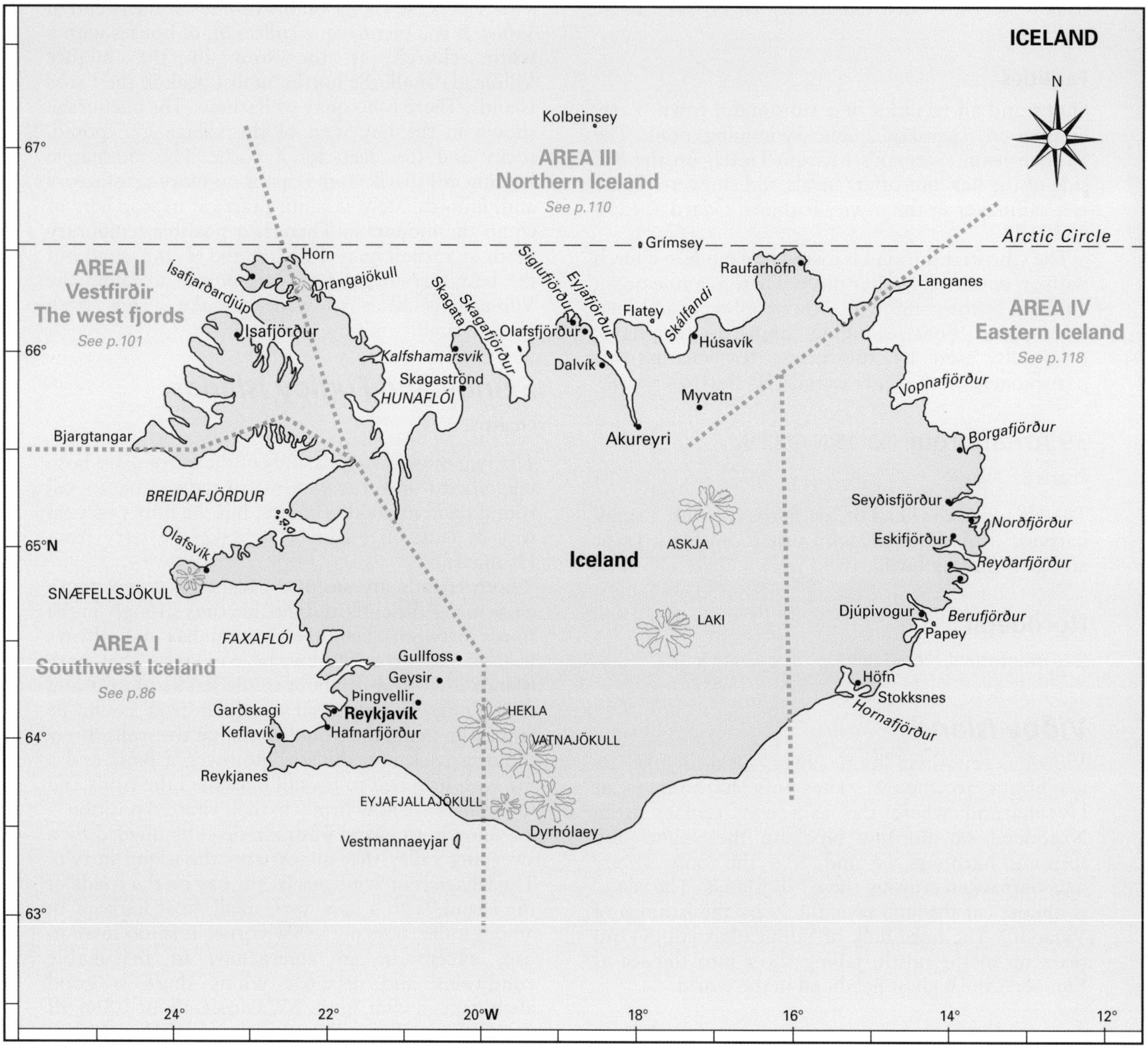
ICELAND
N
Kolbeinsey
AREA III
Northern Iceland
See p.110
Arctic Circle
Grímsey
Raufarhöfn
Langanes
AREA IV
Eastern Iceland
See p.118
AREA II
Vestfirðir
The west fjords
See p.101
Horn
Ísafjarðardjúp
Drangajökull
Ísafjörður
Skagata
Skagafjörður
Siglufjörður
Eyjafjörður
Olafsfjörður
Flatey
Skálfandi
Húsavík
Dalvík
Kalfshamarsvik
Skagaströnd
HUNAFLÓI
Vopnafjörður
Myvatn
Akureyri
Borgafjörður
Bjargtangar
BREIDAFJÖRDUR
Seyðisfjörður
Norðfjörður
Eskifjörður
Reyðarfjörður
ASKJA
Olafsvík
Iceland
SNÆFELLSJÖKUL
LAKI
Djúpivogur
Berufjörður
Papey
AREA I
Southwest Iceland
See p.86
FAXAFLÓI
Gullfoss
Geysir
Þingvellir
Reykjavík
Garðskagi
Keflavík
Hafnarfjörður
Höfn
Stokksnes
Hornafjörður
HEKLA
VATNAJÖKULL
Reykjanes
EYJAFJALLAJÖKULL
Dyrhólaey
Vestmannaeyjar
67°
66°
65°N
64°
63°
24°
22°
20°W
18°
16°
14°
12°

3. Iceland

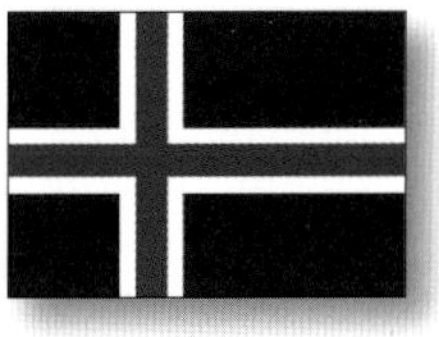

Contents

Introduction

Iceland, which was formerly a Danish possession, has been an independent republic since 1944. It has a population of about 334,000. It is about 500km (310 miles) from east to west and 350km (217 miles) from north to south, an area of 103,000km^2 (40,000km^2), considerably larger than Ireland. The capital is Reykjavík. The coastline is almost 6,000km (3,720 miles) long, with all its indentations. Seyðisfjörður, a possible first port of call, is 250 miles from the Faroe Islands. The Vestmannaeyjar are about 500 miles from the Butt of Lewis, 700 miles from SW Ireland, 600 miles from Norway and 180 miles from Greenland.

The country

The bulk of the interior is a high, uninhabited plateau of volcanic rock with permanent icecaps, of which the Vatnajökull, over 2,000m high and about 6000km^2 in area, is by far the largest in Europe. Much of the area is volcanically active and there are several hot springs and geysers, of which Geysir (the Great Geyser) is the best known. Hekla in the south (once regarded by some as the mouth of Hell); Laki and Askja also have formidable reputations. In 1963, a new island, Surtsey was formed and in 1973 Helgafell in the Vestmannæyja erupted. The 2010 eruption of Eyjafjallajökull was not particularly big but its clouds of volcanic ash caused, for a period of six days, the highest level of disruption to European air travel since the Second World War. Periodic eruptions of Icelandic volcanos continue to disrupt national air travel.

While much of the scenery is stark and exciting, many parts are incredibly green and beautiful. The rivers, which are famous for their salmon, have impressive waterfalls. Of the population of 334,000, roughly half live in Reykjavík and its suburbs; the rest live in scattered communities around the coastline. Reykjavík, the largest urban development, is a busy port and a modern city established on the sites of many very old settlements. A major reason for cruising to Iceland is to visit the country that produced its own significant medieval culture, which had close links with the British Isles as well as Scandinavia, and to see the dramatic countryside in which it flourished.

History

Iceland was settled in the late 9th century by Norwegians from western Norway, motivated partly by a feeling of oppression within their own regime and by Norwegian settlements in the British Isles. It was an independent republic, which early on developed a system of government through discussion and by AD930 had established a parliament – the Alþing. The original settlers were pagan, looking to Thor and abandoning the idea of Odin (who was considered more martial) to the Norwegians. Icelanders were considerable travellers and there are many traces of their connection with the British Isles, particularly in monastic establishments, which were then the seats of learning. Contact with Britain helped to introduce the idea of Christianity. Under pressure from Ólaf Tryggvason, the Norwegian King, conversion was agreed by the Alþing in AD1000, partly because of a need to solve problems arising from quarrels within the island. Christianity was then adopted by the population as a whole. But dissension continued and led to the 'Old Treaty' of 1263 in which Iceland recognised the rule of the King of Norway. The 'Old Treaty' contained a provision that Norwegian ships would sail to Iceland each year with a cargo of timber – an essential supply for Iceland's boat building industry which could not be sourced locally. During this troublesome time the Sagas were composed, reflecting an image of the previous, perhaps more noble, epoch. A good account of that period and of the importance of the Sagas is given in the introduction by Magnus Magnusson and Hermann Pálsson to the Penguin editions of the *Sagas* (Penguin Classics). Suzeranity of Iceland passed to the Danish kings after the union of Norway with Denmark in 1381. There followed a pretty unpleasant tale of economic neglect by the suzerain power, of epidemics and starvation, of dissension and conflict between the leading families. The Lutheran church of today was established by Christian III in 1550 after he executed Jón Arason, the Bishop who had campaigned for national independence. Although there is complete religious freedom, a nominal 77% of today's Icelanders are Lutheran and the church is endowed by the state.

In the 17th and 18th century, trade was controlled by Danish companies and trade with other European countries forbidden. Even when that restriction was removed, trade was confined to Denmark. At the Treaty of Kiel in 1814, when the Kingdoms of Norway and Denmark were separated, Iceland, like Faroe, remained with the Danes. It was recognised as a sovereign state in 1918, tied to Denmark only through a common sovereign. In May 1944, by referendum, Iceland decided to sever its link with the crown and ever since then has been recognised as completely independent. In 1972 Iceland decided to protect its major natural resource, fish, and extended its fishery limits first to 12 and then to 50M. This was disputed by the UK and three 'Cod Wars' ensued, during which the Icelanders followed up their claim through international channels and made strenuous, often dangerous, efforts to cut the trawls from offending UK boats. These episodes are well remembered in Iceland (in one unrecorded incident, the coastguard vessel *Þor*, which earlier had rammed HMS *Palliser*, bombarded the foredeck crew of Palliser with mini Dutch Edam cheeses; *Palliser* responded with a broadside of potatoes). The UK conceded the point in 1976, relations between the two countries were restored and a limit of 200 miles established.

Climate

The Irminger Current, a branch of the Gulf Stream, flows clockwise round the west, north and east coasts, producing a climate that is warm for its latitude just below the Arctic Circle but, due to the proximity of the cold East Greenland Current to the northwest, the climate in summer can be very variable. Summer temperatures are usually cool, hovering around 10°–16°C. One day you can be sunbathing in temperatures up to 21°C in a sheltered fjord, while on another, a cold northerly can bring low temperatures and perhaps occasional snow showers to the north coast, even in July. Summer rain falls about one day in three in the west and about one day in two in the east. In general, winds in June and July are not strong; sudden squalls can occur near the coast, although these do not usually last long. Gales are more common in the east, averaging two days in the months of July and August. Fog may be a hazard but is very variable; again, the east coast fares worst, with fog occurring on average in eight days of each of the summer months. In some years a certain amount of ice breaks away from the pack in the East Greenland Current. In the past, drift ice has frequently come close to the north coast of Iceland and occasionally invades the fjords. In recent years, however, this has become a rare event although one or two large icebergs may be encountered. If sailing in the north and west it is advisable to check the ice situation with the Icelandic Met Office (✆ +354 522 6000) or contact a Coast Radio Station, which will have up-to-date information. Reports of iceberg sightings are included in NAVTEX navigational warnings. New sightings should be reported. All in all, the summer climate is not inclement; it can be very summery and the nights are short – but take heavy weather, thermal gear and a cabin heater.

Language

Icelandic (Islenska) is spoken, but many Icelanders speak excellent English and language seldom presents a problem. Islenska is very close to the old Norse spoken by the original settlers and is much less changed than other Scandinavian languages, retaining its complex grammar. Written Icelandic uses the consonant Þ (lower case þ), called 'thorn', an unvoiced 'th' as in Þór (Thor), þing (thing or council); and Ð (in lower case ð), called 'eth', a voiced 'th' as in English 'the'. Both these letters are Anglo-Saxon in origin, not Nordic, and demonstrate the influence of the Celtic monastic culture on medieval Iceland. These letters are used in this section.

Economy

Iceland's economy has historically been based on their fishing industry but its importance has diminished from an export share of 90% in the 1960s to 40% in 2006. Other significant exports are aluminium and ferro-silicon (used in the casting of bronze, copper and steel).

Agriculture, although less important, ensures that the country is self-sufficient in meat and dairy products. Under 2% of the land is cultivated, the main crops being potatoes and turnips. Grass is now conserved for winter feed mainly as silage rather than hay, and white, plastic wrapped, round bales of silage will be seen in summer dotting the fields close to the farmsteads. Livestock predominately consist of sheep, horses and cattle with some pigs and poultry. Agriculture accounts for 5·4% of GDP.

Iceland had a financial crisis in 2008 when its banking system failed. The government used emergency legislation to take over the operation of Iceland's three largest banks. An IMF loan resulted in interest rates being hiked to 18% which, by 2010 had reduced to 7%. By June 2012, half of the Icesave debt had been repaid. This was aided by diversification into manufacturing and service industries particularly within the fields of software production, biotechnology and tourism. Despite Iceland's troubles, Iceland has, according to the Economist Intelligence Index of 2011, the second highest quality of life in the world. In 2010, the unemployment rate was 8.1% which had reduced to 2·9% in 2015.

Eighty percent of Iceland's total energy requirements is met through geothermal and hydropower sources. Geothermal heated greenhouses produce a significant quantity of tomatoes and other vegetables, although most have to be imported, particularly in the winter months. Heitur pottur – 'hot pots' (geothermal hot tubs or jacuzzis) are common and every sizeable community has its heated swimming pool, sometimes out of doors.

General information

Travel

External

The international airport is 44km (30 miles) west of Reykjavík at Keflavík, on the Reykjanes peninsula. Iceland Air offer direct flights from London Heathrow and, in summer, Glasgow, and many scheduled flights from elsewhere in Europe, Greenland, the Faroe Islands and North America.

Low cost airlines periodically run services to UK and mainland Europe and are worth investigating. Wow Air operates a daily service (except Saturdays) to London Gatwick.

The car ferry *Norröna*, run by Smyril Line, Tórshavn, Faroe, provides a service to Seyðisfjörður in East Iceland from Denmark and Norway, calling at Faroe.

Internal

The internal air network, Flugfélag Íslands (Air Iceland), operates from Reykjavík airport, not Keflavík, and links all the major towns and some quite minor ones. Visit the website or ✆ +354 570 3030.

Roads are being improved, but many country roads, apart from the main coast roads, are rough and unsurfaced. Good bus services cover the whole of Iceland. Reykjavik Excursions operate many one day tour selections.

Taxis are easy to get. Cars may be hired but are expensive. Cheaper hire can probably be arranged in advance.

Formalities

Passports are required although visas are not necessary for citizens of most EU countries. All major ports have customs facilities and yachts must clear on arrival in Iceland and before departure. Customs can be contacted via the Coastguard (Ch 16) or call Reykjavik Customs (24 hours) on ✆ +354 898 8493. An Officer will probably visit the vessel. Customs work closely with Border Control and it is likely that the Customs Officer will perform the border control functions. Customs Officers may check on visiting boats whilst they are cruising in Icelandic waters and it is helpful if the yellow customs form is left in a window when the boat is unattended. Customs should be given 2 hours notice of departure. As in other Scandinavian countries, alcohol laws are strict. Generally no harbour dues are demanded, with the exception of Reykjavík and possibly in Keflavík.

The Icelandic national flag is a red, white bordered Scandinavian cross on a blue background, a permutation of the Norwegian and Faroese flags.

Useful websites – travel

	Iceland Air	www.icelandair.co.uk
	Iceland Express	www.icelandexpress.is
	Air Iceland	www.airiceland.is
	Wow Air	www.wowair.com
	Ferries to Faroe, Norway and Denmark Smyriil Line	www.smyrilline.fo

Useful websites – formalities

	Iceland Customs	www.customs.is
	Iceland Border Control	www.innanrikisraduneyti.is/raduneyti/starfssvid/utlendingamal/upplysingar/nr/860
	Iceland Maritime Administration	http://sigling.is

British Embassy and Consulate, Laufásvegur 31, 101 Reykjavík ✆ +354 550 5100 or *Email* info@britishembassy.is
Postal address: PO Box 460, 121 Reykjavík.

Telecommunications

International dial code: 354 + 7 digit local number.

Mobile telephone systems are GSM and NMT. GSM coverage is very good in the SW of the country and around all the major harbours and is being progressively extended.

The emergency number is ✆ 112.

Time

UT(GMT) is used all year round; thus in summer Iceland is one hour behind UK.

Tourist information

Keflavík Airport – Leifsstöð:
Tourist Information Centre, Leifsstöð – IS-235 Keflavík ✆ +354 425 0330, 421 6760, *Email* touristinfo@gi.is

Tourist Information Centre, Reykjavík Aðalstræti 2, IS-101 Reykjavík ✆ +354 590 1500, *Email* info@visitreykjavik.is

Maps

The Icelandic Topographical Survey (Landmælingar Íslands) produces a series of nine maps covering the whole country at 1:250,000.

Parts of Iceland are covered by a series at 1:50,000 and at 1:100,000. These are all available in the UK from The Map Shop, 15 High Street, Upton-upon-Severn, Worcester WR8 0HJ ✆ +44 (0)1684 593 146.

Useful books

Iceland Saga Magnus Magnusson (The Bodley Head).
Iceland. A handbook for expeditions (Iceland Information Centre, London).
Iceland. Nature's meeting place (Iceland Review, Reykjavík).
Iceland (Lonely Planet Publications 2015).
Vinland Sagas (Penguin Classics)
Walking and Treking in Iceland (Cicerone Walking Guide 2015) by Paddy Dillon

Supplies and services

Yacht services and chandlery

Some chandlery is available in Reykjavík, where there is a keen sailing club. Elsewhere, wherever there are facilities for fishing craft, repairs in steel or wood will be willingly carried out, but chandlery specific to sailing yachts will not be found. GRP is widely used and there are yards producing excellent inshore GRP fishing boats, so major repairs should not pose a problem; however, it would be wise to take sufficient mat and resin to carry out emergency repairs. Every fishing harbour has an engineering workshop, with helpful and competent mechanics, as well as first class electronic workshops in the larger ports.

The cheapest and most practical warm clothes can often be found in stores catering for fishermen.

There are no sail lofts but the tent and tarpaulin manufacturers in Reykjavík, Seglargerðin Ægir, Eyjarslóð 7, may be able to carry out repairs (also see details under Ísafjörður).

Petrol (benzin) paraffin/kerosene (steinolía) and diesel (gasolía or bátaolía) are easily obtainable. Some diesel pumps require a fisherman's co-operative card before fuel is dispensed.

Water, usually of excellent quality, is laid on to landing stages. For Calor (Butane) gas, it is essential to carry sufficient for the trip. Propane gas cylinders and appropriate pressure regulators can be bought in most towns.

Money

The Icelandic Króna (ISK) is divided into 100 aurar (singular: eyrir). The rate of exchange (2016) is about ISK180 to £1.00.

ATMs are found in every town and credit cards as well as travellers cheques are widely accepted in the shops and restaurants. Tipping is not expected.

Useful websites – maps

	The Map Shop	www.themapshop.co.uk

Useful websites – tourism

	Reykjanes Tourist Information	www.visitreykjavik.is
	Visit Iceland	www.visiticeland.com
	'Gateway' to Iceland General information about Iceland	www.iceland.is

Stores

All the usual items can be bought in the well-stocked supermarkets found at most harbours and villages. Fish, lamb and dairy products are of a very high quality and plentiful. Although there is a thriving greenhouse industry, most fruit and vegetables have to be imported. Local specialities are skyr and súrmjólk, which are similar to yogurt. Smoked and dried lamb (hangikjot) is also excellent and there are various forms of dried fish. You have to be a Viking or very brave to try hákarl: this is shark, which has been buried for some time; it is an acquired taste.

Low alcohol beer is widely available in the shops, but spirits, wines and strong beer can only be bought at government controlled outlets, Vínbúðin, which will be found in the larger towns. Alcohol is heavily taxed. Imports are strictly controlled by customs. The normal duty-free allowance on entry is one litre of spirits, plus one litre of wine, or the equivalent amount of alcohol in beer (12x 500ml cans), per person.

Cruising information

Timing

The best months for a sailing cruise to Iceland are June, July and August. It is wise to leave the area by the middle of September, before the weather deteriorates.

Pilotage books

The British Admiralty publication *The Arctic Pilot Vol II (NP11)* covers the whole of Iceland. It is a mine of useful and detailed information and should be used. However, much of the information applies to the winter months and, since the Cod Wars, the constant input from British fishermen has not been available and information on unfrequented areas tends to be out of date. Throughout this section, it is referred to as *NP11*.

The Icelandic Hydrographic office (Sjómælingar Íslands), has produced an excellent pilot book *Leiðsögubók fyrir sjómenn við Ísland*. It is in Icelandic but the text is short and the plans and aerial photographs are plentiful. It is an invaluable book to have on board (obtainable as charts – see Charts and publications below).

Almanac

The Sjómanna Almanak published by Skerpla, Reykjavík, each year, contains a vast amount of information on tides, lights, radio beacons and radio frequencies, as well as a section containing excellent aerial photographs in colour of all the major harbours, together with small plans. It is in Icelandic.

Charts and publications

The Icelandic Hydrographic Service (Sjómælingar Íslands) Seljavegur 32, 101 Reykjavík, ✆ +354 545 2000) produce three excellent series of charts covering the whole coast: The Yfirsiglingakort series covers the entire coast in seven charts with a scale of 1:300,000. More detailed is given in the Strandsiglingakort series which numbers 19 charts at a scale of 1:100,000. Finally, four chart books, Hafnarkort, are produced which contain large scale, 1:10,000 charts and harbour plans of various Icelandic harbours. Icelandic chart corrections are available on the coastguard website.

Plans of the principal harbours at larger scales and the numbers are shown in the text. Some of the remoter fjords have not been fully surveyed; so there is some scope for interesting exploration.

Older Icelandic charts use the Hjörsey datum which is 0°02′N and 0°02′W off WGS 84 and have been converted to WGS 84 as they are reissued.

Useful websites – charts

	Chart corrections and notices to mariners Iceland Coastguard	www.lhg.is/english/hydrographic_department
	Iceland Chart Agent Viking Barbúnaður jörgun	www.viking-life.is
	Faroe Chart Agent HN Jacobsens Bókhandil	www.bokhandil.fo/include/main.asp
	Danish Chart Agent Weilbach	www.weilbach.dk
	UK Chart Agent Imray	www.imray.com
	Northern Ireland Chart Agency Todd Chart Agency	www.toddchart.com

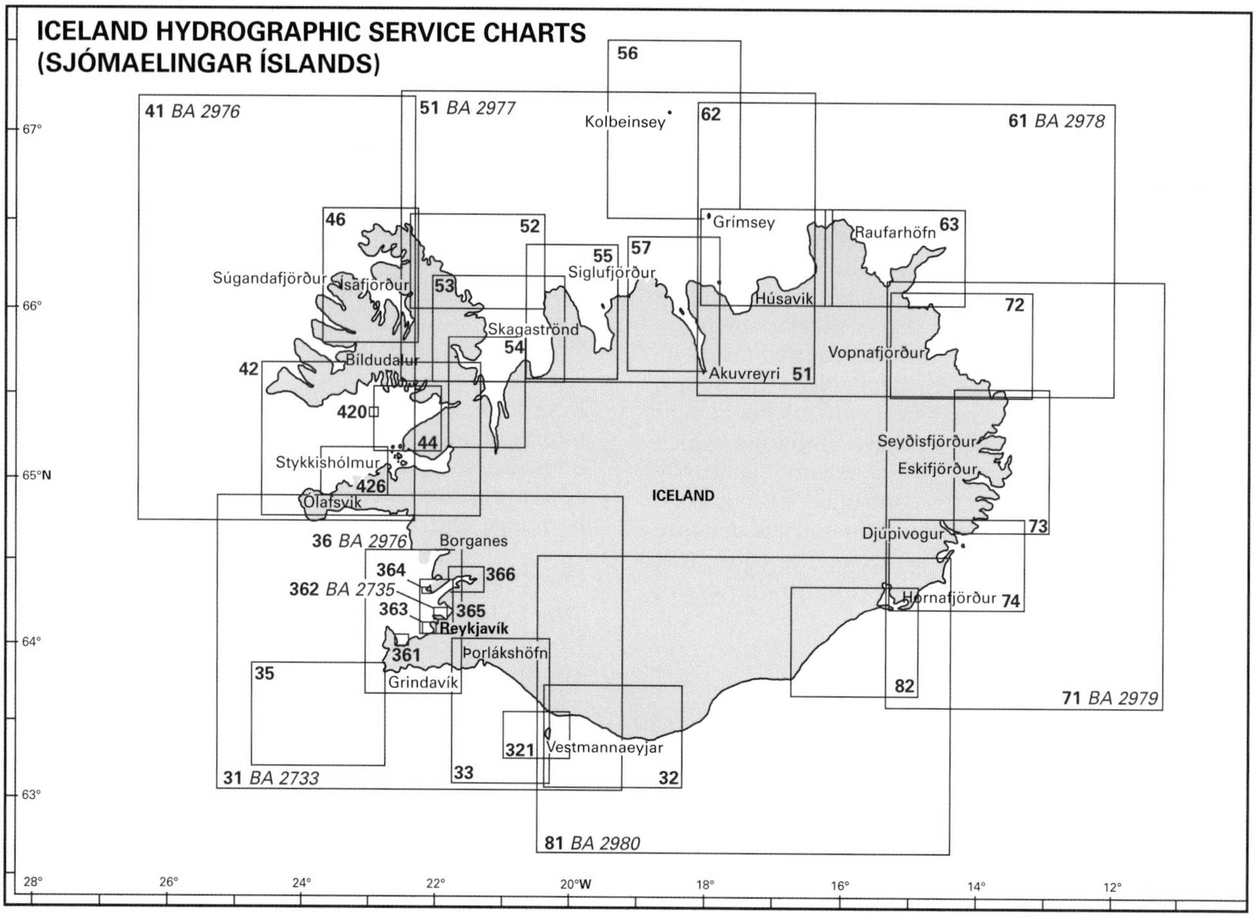

References to the relevant Icelandic charts appear at each entry in the text. Charts are referred to by the Icelandic Hydrographic Service number.

British Admiralty charts of Iceland cover the whole coast at 1:300,000, plus two larger-scale charts of Reykjavík and approach.

Chart agents

In Iceland

Charts, as well as the Icelandic tide tables (Sjávarföll við Ísland) and list of lights (Vitar og Sjómerki), can be obtained in Reykjavík from Raför.

Limited stocks are also held by chart agents in Grundarfjörður, Stykkishólmur, Ísafjörður, Akureyri, Húsavík, Seyðisfjörður, Neskaupstaður, Hornafjörður, Vestmannaeyjar and Keflavík.

In Faroe

HN Jacobsens Bókahandil, Box 55, 110 Tórshavn, ✆ +298 311036, *Email* hnj@hnj.fo

In Denmark

Iver C Weilbach and Co a/s, Toldbodgade 35, DK1253 København ✆ +45 33 13 59 27, *Email* nautical@weilbach.dk

Other charts not shown above:

1001	Iceland	1:1,000,000
1003	Seas around Iceland (East Greenland and Jan Mayen to Scotland and Shetland)	1:5,000,000
20	Iceland to Jan Mayen	1:200,000
25	East Iceland	1:750,000
26	West Iceland	1:750,000
BA565	Iceland	1:750,000

In the United Kingdom

Todd Chart Agency, Navigation House, 85 High Street, Bangor, Co. Down, N Ireland BT20 5BD, who specialise in Icelandic charts
✆ +44(0)28 9146 6640, *Email* info@toddchart.com
or from Imray Laurie Norie & Wilson Ltd, Wych House, St Ives, Cambridgeshire PE27 5BT
✆ +44(0)1480462114, *Email* ilnw@imray.com

Buoyage

There are few buoys except in the approach to major ports. Iceland follows IALA Maritime Buoyage System A.

Useful websites

	List of lights from Iceland Coastguard	www.lhg.is/starfsemi/sjomaelingasvid/vitaskra

Lights

During the sailing season there is almost continuous daylight and most lights are extinguished. Lights S of 65°30′N are extinguished between 1 June and 15 July. Lights N of this latitude are extinguished between 15 May and 15 August. Light details are given in either *Admiralty List of Lights and Fog Signals Vol L (NP84)*, or *Vitaskra* which is published by the Icelandic Hydrographic Service every two years. *Vitaskra* is written in both Icelandic and English. It is also available, free to download, from the Icelandic Coastguard website.

Magnetic anomalies are common and should be noted on charts.

Radio

With the exception of certain fjords, Iceland has complete VHF coverage around the coast. Operators are efficient and friendly and speak excellent English. Weather forecasts in English can be obtained easily. All fishing vessels are equipped with VHF, but CB is also used on small boats.

See the VHF transmitter location and frequency diagram which also gives the MF and SW frequencies.

Currents and tides

The northern branch of the North Atlantic Drift splits off the S of Iceland. The eastern part curves E and SE back into the Atlantic toward Faroe. The western part, known as the Irminger Current, flows N along the W coast: a part turns back southwestwards, but the inshore part flows around Horn and eastwards along the N coast, where it is called the North Iceland Current. Off the NE of Iceland this joins with the East Iceland Current, a cold current flowing from an eddy of the East Greenland Current near Jan Mayen. The resulting current flows S along the E coast.

Off the inhospitable SE coast, an inshore counter-current runs westwards towards Vestmannaeyjar.

The tidal wave runs clockwise round Iceland starting in the SW and advances about 80M every hour. At new and full moon, high water occurs about 0530 on the S coast, 0630 in Faxaflói and an hour later in the Vestfirðir. It rounds the Horn about 0900 and reaches Langanes, in the northeast, about 1230. The rise varies from place to place, reaching 4m at springs in Faxaflói and Breiðafjörður but only 1m in the east. The neap and spring range (in metres) is given for each entry in the text.

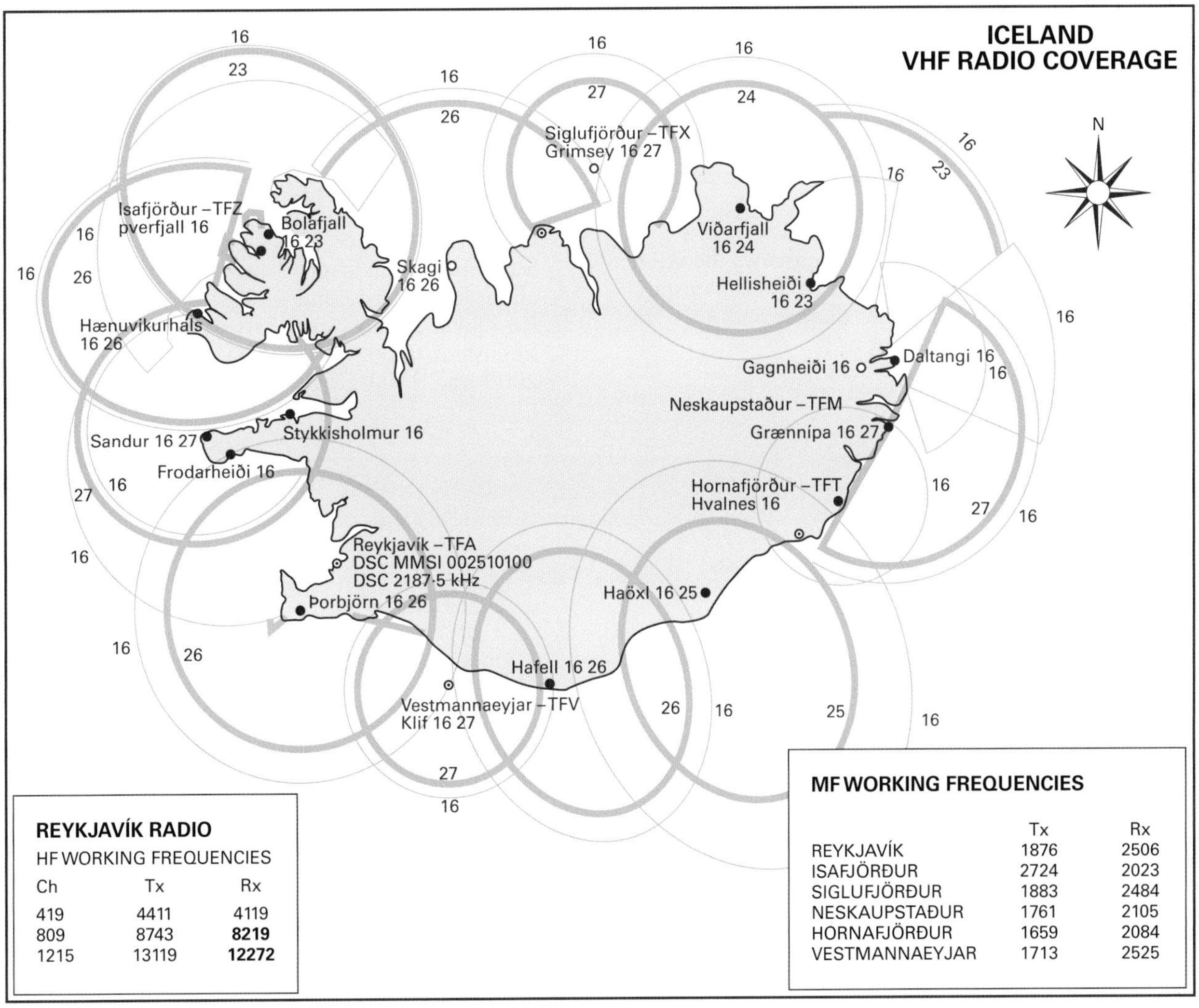

REYKJAVÍK RADIO

HF WORKING FREQUENCIES

Ch	Tx	Rx
419	4411	4119
809	8743	**8219**
1215	13119	**12272**

MF WORKING FREQUENCIES

	Tx	Rx
REYKJAVÍK	1876	2506
ISAFJÖRÐUR	2724	2023
SIGLUFJÖRÐUR	1883	2484
NESKAUPSTAÐUR	1761	2105
HORNAFJÖRÐUR	1659	2084
VESTMANNAEYJAR	1713	2525

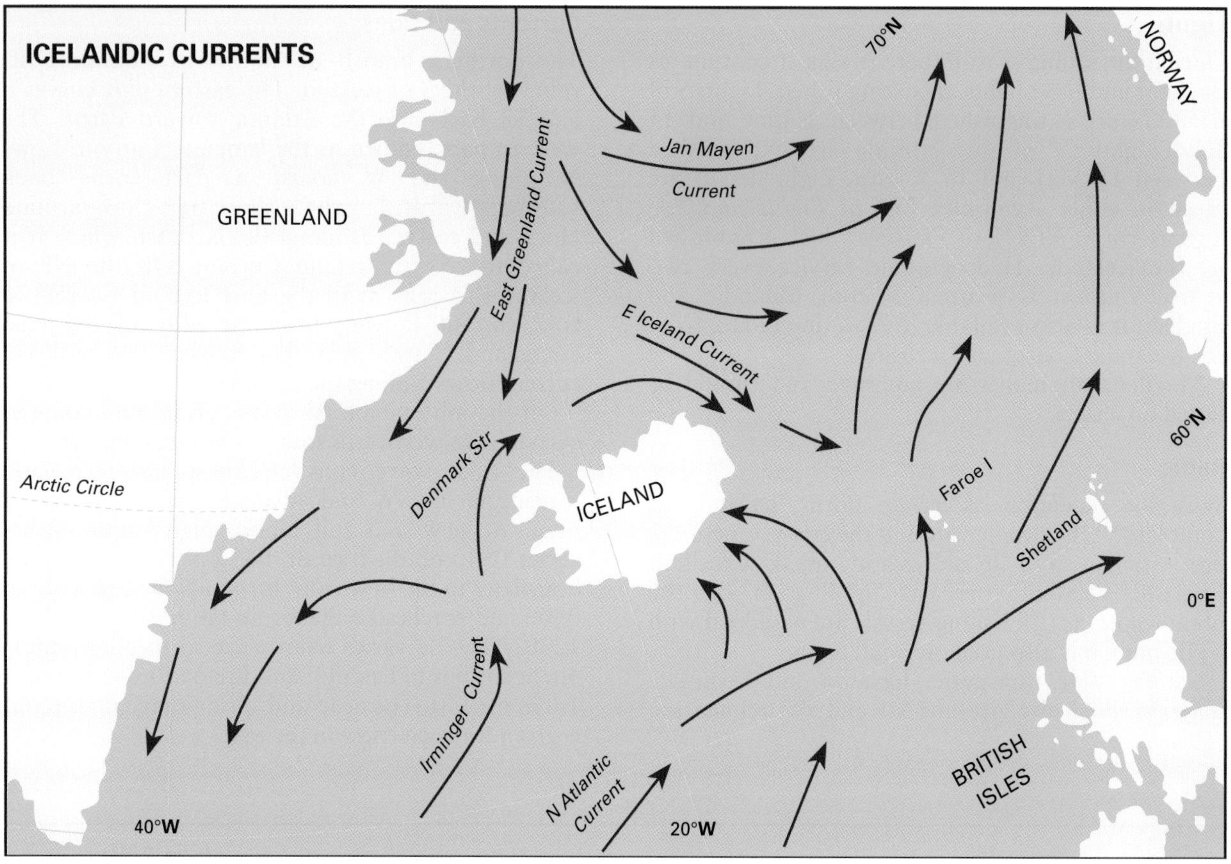

The resulting tidal streams also run clockwise, flooding from one direction and ebbing in the other, but are of course complicated by the huge indentations of the fjords and often disrupted by weather conditions.

In general the tidal stream reaches speeds of 1–3kns but off headlands and in narrows between banks it can reach local speeds of 5–7kns at springs, producing very nasty and dangerous seas in unfavourable weather conditions.

Weather forecasts

1. The British weather forecast on Radio 4 (repeated by Stornoway and Portpatrick coast radio stations at 0703 and 1903 GMT) only extends to sea area SE Iceland, i.e. 65°N and 15°W. It is relevant to the passage from Britain or Scandinavia but it gives little or no information about Icelandic coastal waters.
2. Reykjavík Radio broadcasts weather forecasts in English at 0200, 0500, 0800, 1100, 1400, 1700, 2000 and 2300 UTC, or as close as possible to

Useful websites

	Danish weather and ice forecasts - eastern Greenland DMI	www.dmi.dk/vejr/
	Icelandic weather forecasts IMO	http://m.en.vedur.is/m
	Icelandic shipping forecast IMO	http://en.vedur.is/weather/shipping/text
	Wave height prediction & weather	http://sigling.is/vs/ArealKort.aspx

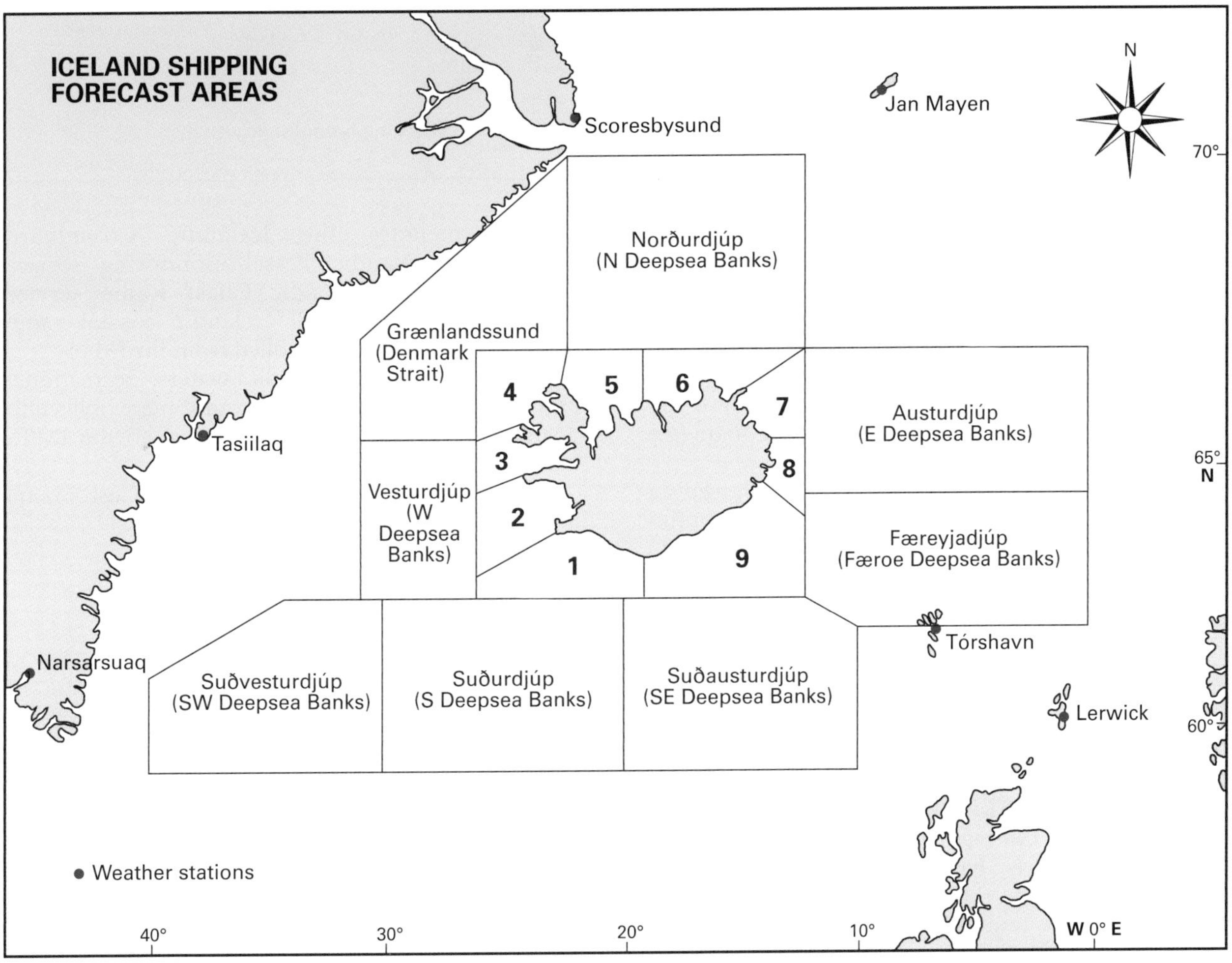

those times and weather warnings as required, after a preliminary call on Ch 16.

3. The Icelandic shipping forecast (in Icelandic) is broadcast on Long Wave (207kHz and 189kHz) and on FM on a number of frequencies round the coast (93·5kHz from Reykjavík). Broadcast times are 0130, 0430, 0730, 1045*, 1245*, 1630*, 1930*, 2230. Those marked with an asterisk include a three day forecast. The land forecast is given first, followed by the forecast for nine coastal and seven offshore sea areas (see diagram).
4. Armed with the name of the sea area you are concerned with, and listening carefully, it is quite possible to pick up the wind speed (m/sec) and direction at least, and quite a lot more with a little tuition and practice.
5. Icelandic coast radio stations are very helpful and are usually able to give a weather forecast.
6. A useful daytime facility is the Weather Telephone Service (in English) of the Icelandic Met Office ✆ 902 0600.
7. Reykjavík Radio 'R' transmits Navtex messages in English on 518kHz at 0250, 0650, 1050, 1450, 1850 and 2250 UTC. Note that Reykjavík Radio 'X' covers the East Greenland coast and transmits Navtex messages one hour later.
8. NAVTEX radio station Føroyar/Tórshavn [D], 62°01'N 06°48'W is now operational

ICELAND SHIPPING FORECAST AREAS

1. Suðvesturmið (SW Banks)
2. Faxaflóamið (W Banks, S part)
3. Breiðafjarðarmið (W Banks, N part)
4. Vestfjarðamið (NW Banks)
5. Norðvesturmið (N Banks, W part)
6. Norðausturmið (N Banks, E part)
7. Austurmið (E Banks, N part)
8. Austfjarðamið (E Banks, S part)
9. Suðausturmið (SE Banks)

Ice

Whether or not ice comes close to Iceland depends on three factors: The quantity of ice in Denmark Strait, the conditions in the ocean near Iceland (i.e. temperature, salinity and layering) and the overall air circulation in the northern hemisphere (i.e. lows and highs) especially the development of static high pressure over either Greenland or the Atlantic Ocean.

It is most likely to be encountered in the waters northwest of Iceland and is forecast on the Danish ice forecasts for SW Greenland.

Search & Rescue (SAR)

Search and rescue is the primary responsibility of the Iceland Coastguard (ICG). They operate three helicopters, a surveillance aircraft and three patrol vessels.

Useful websites – SAR

	Iceland Coastguard	www.lhg.is/english/icg

The national life-saving association, ICESAR, maintains about 10 lifeboats around the coast, as well as a number of orange painted refuge huts on uninhabited stretches of the coast. These are marked on Icelandic charts with the symbol 'S-S' or 'Ref' (on new charts) but do not always appear on British Admiralty charts. They are also marked by a red triangle on the 1:250,000 topographical map (see Maps).

The Icelandic Coastguard (Landhelgisgæsla Íslands) are responsible for the MRCC and operates four helicopters, one fixed wing aircraft and two ocean going vessels. Two SAR helicopters, with maximum ranges of 150M and 270M are on call at all times. Normal response times are 30 minutes from dispatch.

In an emergency, call on Ch 16 or 2182kHz. DSC MMSI 0025 10100 MRCC ✆ +354 511 3333.

Iceland – Ship Reporting System

For full details see *ALRS Vol 6(2)*.

Note that the full reporting system is required for commercial vessels. However the following is the minimum required for recreational craft.

All vessels are required to report to the Icelandic Maritime Traffic Service (IMTS), either direct or through a Coast Radio Station, at least 24 hours before sailing into Icelandic territorial waters (12M limit), giving the following information.

1. Ship's name
2. Registration details
3. Nationality
4. Radio call sign
5. Present position
6. Draught
7. Total number of persons on board
8. Last port of call before arrival in Iceland.
9. Destination and ETA
10. Live animals, weapons and ammunition
11. Crew list (including nationality, surname, first name, date of birth and passport number)

Note that much of this information could be sent by email or fax from the last port of call before sailing to Iceland, so that the final report by MF, VHF or SATCOM etc, can be brief. *Email* sar@lhg.is

The telephone number for the Icelandic Maritime Traffic Service, (IMTS) is ✆ +354 545 2100. (IMTS includes the Icelandic Coastguard operations, Icelandic Vessel monitoring service (VMS) and the Icelandic Coast Radio service (✆ +354 551 1030). All Icelandic coastal radio stations are remotely controlled from the IMTS).

IMTS includes the Icelandic Coastguard operations, Icelandic Vessel monitoring service (VMS) and the Icelandic Coast Radio service (✆ +354 551 1030). All Icelandic coastal radio stations are remotely controlled from the IMTS.

Whilst sailing in Icelandic waters, recreational craft not transmitting AIS information are obliged to give their position every three hours to the IMTS when in transit.

All vessels are required to report to Customs on arrival and just before departure.

Cruising areas and approach

See plan page 74

Landfalls

Iceland may be approached safely from almost any direction, since there are few dangerous outliers. However, the S coast from Hornafjörður to the Vestmannaeyjar should be given a wide berth. There are no harbours and no shelter for nearly 150M and the coast is low lying, shallow and dangerous. For a full description, see *NP11*.

Approach from the E

The shortest sea crossing is about 240M from the Faroe Islands to one of the harbours on the E coast. For those unfamiliar with the coast, the major ferry port of Seyðisfjörður is the easiest to approach and safe in bad weather or poor visibility. Hvalbakur (64°36'N 13°17'W) is an isolated, dangerous rock with radar reflector and lies about 25M E of Djúpivogur (Berufjörður).

Approach from the SE

From the direction of NW Scotland, the choice lies between the E coast fjords, including Seyðisfjörður, a distance of about 440M, or the safe harbour of Vestmannaeyjar off the SW coast, about 500M from Stornoway in the Outer Hebrides.

Approach from the S and SW

From SW Ireland it is about 750M to Vestmannaeyjar or another 50M to the passage inside the Fuglasker off Reykjanes and thence around the peninsula to the capital Reykjavík. If approaching from the SW it is important to keep clear of rocks and skerries, which extend up to 40M in a SW direction from the Fuglasker.

Circumnavigation

The Irminger Current flows clockwise around Iceland and is aided by the tidal stream. Streams are strong off major headlands but weaker offshore. This would indicate a cruise in a clockwise direction; however, in summer the prevailing wind is easterly to the N of Iceland and westerly to the S, so that the decision about which direction to sail is as likely to be determined by the first landfall.

Off the W coast in the Denmark Strait (or the Greenland Strait, as the Icelanders prefer to call it), the opposing East Greenland Current may not be far away. In summer, the occasional iceberg diverts and drifts towards the NW coast, to be picked up by the current and carried along the N coast until it melts. Smaller ice floes may sometimes be blown onto the NW and N coasts, where they can accumulate in the vicinity of Hornstrandir and sometimes further E, but in recent years these have not been a problem.

AREA I — South and southwest Iceland including Faxaflói and Breiðafjörður

The S coast, between Höfn in the SE and Vestmannaeyjar, is inhospitable, shallow and dangerous. There is a set onto the coast and, in bad weather, tidal streams are strong and irregular. In Saga times this coast was settled and farmed, but cataclysmic eruptions in the 17th century covered the coastal strip with lava, which poured into the sea. The resulting reefs are low lying, invisible to radar, and often to the eye, especially in fog. There is no shelter at all on this coast and the navigator is advised to give it a wide berth.

The Vestmannaeyjar, off the S coast, is a fascinating volcanic archipelago. It is well worth a visit to see the new island of Surtsey, which started to emerge from the sea in 1963, and the new mountain, Eldfell, on Heimaey, which grew in the 1973 eruption and is still smoking. The lava flow actually improved the shelter in Vestmannaeyjar harbour on the island of Heimaey, which is the best port of call along the whole S coast.

From Vestmannaeyjar westwards to Reykjanes, there are two harbours, but they are not safe to approach in all weathers.

The W coast, 110M from Reykjanes to Bjargartangar, consists of two large bays, Faxaflói and Breiðafjörður. The bays are separated by the Snæfellsness peninsula, which is topped by the spectacular Snæfellsjökul icecap.

The north part of Faxaflói has little to offer a yacht; but Reykjavík in the SE corner and Keflavík with its airport in the SW are both easy to access. There are also some good fjords to explore N of Reykjavík. Crew changes are easiest at the international airport at Keflavík, although internal flights connect Reykjavík city airport with the main coastal settlements. Geysir (the Great Geyser), Þingvellir and the dramatic Gullfoss waterfall, can all be seen on a day trip from Reykjavík.

In Breiðafjörður, there is some interesting but tricky cruising among a mass of islands and rocks in the NE and some interesting harbours and anchorages along the S shore. Some of the most famous Sagas are set in this part of Iceland.

AREA II – Vestfirðir (the west fjords)

The NW coast, 100M from Bjargtangar to Horn looks like a hand stretching towards Greenland and consists of many long, steep fjords – the Vestfirðir (West Fjords). The southern fjords are austere, each with its fishing village on the eyri (old glacier moraine) where a spit of land and shallow water provides a good harbour.

Ísafjörður, on the S side of the Ísafjarðardjúp, is a major town with good facilities and an airport with daily flights to Reykjavík.

The northernmost of these fjords, now largely uninhabited, are a paradise of flowers and birds in summer and provide fascinating cruising.

AREA III – The north coast from Horn to Langanes

The N coast from Horn in the NW to Langanes in the NE, is approximately 200M. Hornstrandir, in the NW, is an inhospitable rocky coast, occasionally beset with ice and along with the 50M long inlet of Húnaflói, is little frequented by yachts, but would be worth investigating in fair weather. Further E there are a number of good harbours, notably Siglufjörður and the deep inlet of Eyjafjörður – with Ólafsfjörður and Dalvík near its mouth and the major port of Akureyri at its head. The island of Grímsey is an interesting place to visit, not least because it lies on the Arctic Circle and has a panoramic view of the mountains of N Iceland on a clear day.

AREA IV – The east coast from Langanes to Hornafjörður

The East Fjords make an excellent cruising ground of their own with a number of good harbours, particularly between Seyðisfjörður and Djúpivogur in Berufjörður. The difficult harbour of Hornafjörður should only be approached in good weather and with the large-scale chart.

Below left Killer whales, west Iceland *Brian Black*

Below right Surtsey – formed in 1963 by volcanic action *Máire Wilkes*

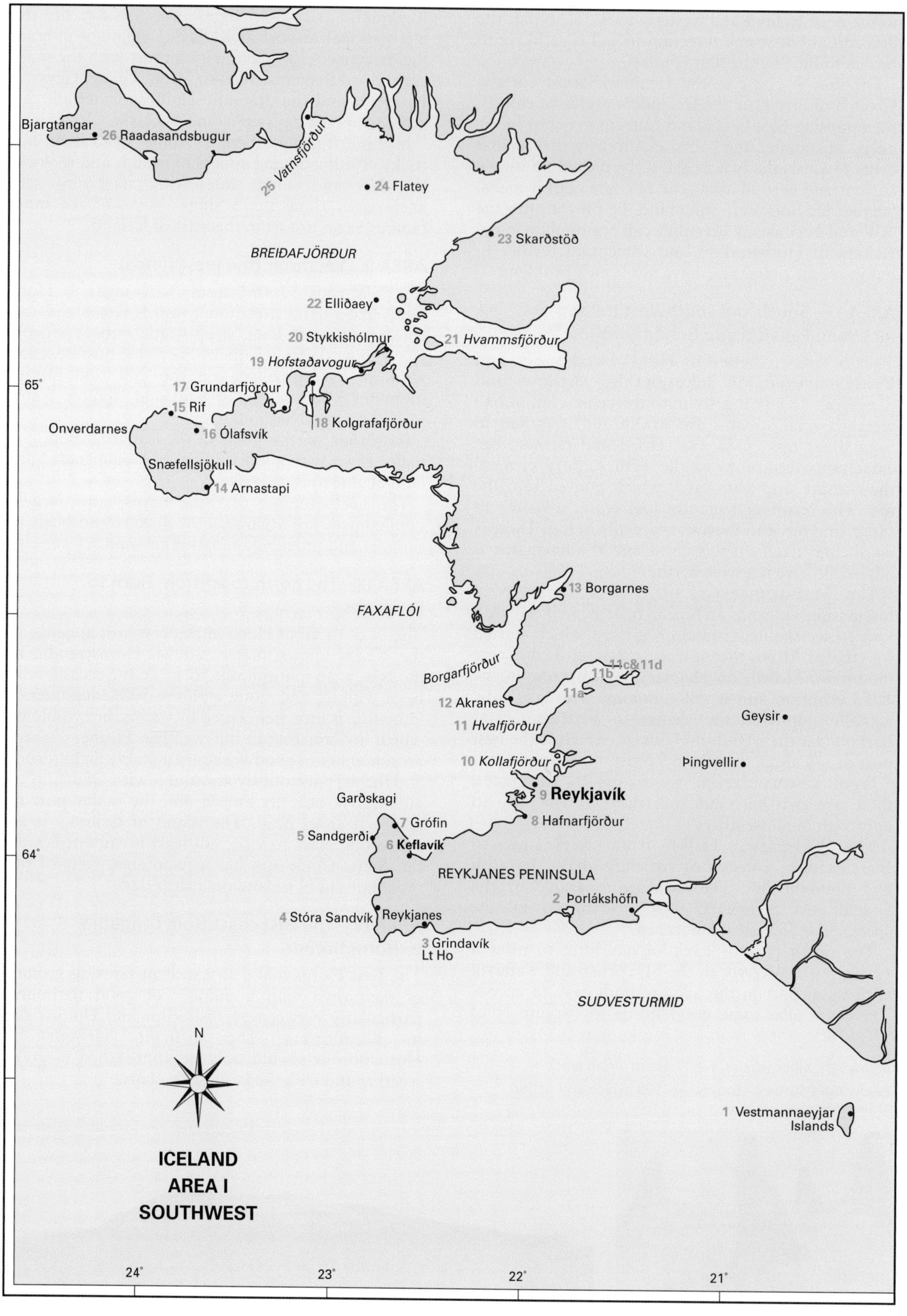
Bjargtangar
26 Raadasandsbugur
25 Vatnsfjörður
24 Flatey
23 Skarðstöð
BREIÐAFJÖRÐUR
22 Elliðaey
20 Stykkishólmur
21 Hvammsfjörður
19 Hofstaðavogur
65°
17 Grundarfjörður
15 Rif
Onverdarnes
16 Ólafsvík
18 Kolgrafafjörður
Snæfellsjökull
14 Arnastapi
13 Borgarnes
FAXAFLÓI
Borgarfjörður
11c&11d
11b
11a
12 Akranes
11 Hvalfjörður
Geysir
10 Kollafjörður
Þingvellir
9 Reykjavík
Garðskagi
7 Grófin
8 Hafnarfjörður
5 Sandgerði
6 Keflavík
64°
REYKJANES PENINSULA
2 Þorlákshöfn
4 Stóra Sandvík
Reykjanes
3 Grindavík
Lt Ho
SUDVESTURMID
N
1 Vestmannaeyjar
Islands
ICELAND
AREA I
SOUTHWEST
24°
23°
22°
21°

Harbours and anchorages

There are innumerable fishing harbours around the coast. It is usually best to obtain permission to tie up alongside a fishing boat or alongside the quay. A stout plank, 3 or 4m long, such as a builders' scaffolding plank, to double as fender or gangplank, is an asset. There are few completely sheltered anchorages; any anchorage with reasonable shelter will have a settlement and the trick is to find the settlement.

AREA I
Southwest Iceland including Faxaflói and Breiðafjörður

The south coast

There are very few good harbours on the S coast of Iceland from Djúpivogur in the SE to the Reykjanes peninsula in the SW – a distance of 250M. In the whole of this distance, the only good harbour of refuge is Heimaey in the Vestmannaeyjar (1). Þorlákshöfn (2) and Grindavík (3), on the mainland, are only useful in certain weather conditions.

The coast between Höfn in Hornafjörður (86) and Vestmannaeyjar (1) is thoroughly inhospitable, with no shelter, no anchorage and no help. It is furthermore difficult to identify in thick weather – radar does not show the low-lying sandy beaches and the set can push a boat shorewards. Keep very well offshore.

There are a few other fishing harbours between Vestmannaeyjar and Reykjanes (Eyrabakki and Stokkseyri, for example) but the approach to all of them is rocky, shallow and exposed.

Vestmannaeyjar Islands to Garðskagi

Charts 31, 32, 33, 81, 310, 321

The Vestmannaeyjar are a group of volcanic islands, rocks and reefs lying between 5M and 10M off the S coast of Iceland. They are named after Irish thralls (slaves) who were put to death by Ingólfur, one of the original Norse settlers in AD874, because they had murdered his blood-brother, Hjorleifur. Heimaey is the only inhabited island and has the only harbour.

The islands are very active volcanically. In 1973 an eruption on Heimaey caused havoc in the town and produced a new conical mountain. In 1963 an underwater eruption produced the new island of Surtsey, the most southerly of the group, named after Surtur, an evil spirit. Landing on this island is strictly forbidden and it is kept almost free from humans, so that scientists can study nature's colonisation of a virgin piece of land. But it is fascinating to sail close around the island and see how the lava cliffs have flowed into the sea and cooled and how the tufa (volcanic dust) has been sculpted by the wind into shapes that, in a more weathered version, are repeated throughout the group and elsewhere.

The chain of small islands extending from Surtsey towards Heimaey are clearly the remains of similar eruptions in the past that have weathered into dramatic cliffs and crags and are now home to vast colonies of seabirds. Sailing among these islands in fine weather is worthwhile but, in any weather, beware the area of rocks and shoals that stretch 8M west of Heimaey.

The approach to the group from the E is straightforward. Heimaey and its northern outliers, Elliðaey (145m) and Bjarnarey (164m) show up well. Approaching from the W, either keep to the S of Surtsey or sail to the N of Pridrangur (Lt Mo(N)30s) (the northernmost of the Drangasker – a group of skerries and rocks which lie 5M WNW of Heimaey). Between the islands and the mainland there is a clear passage 3M wide. Do not venture among the islands, shoals and skerries without *Chart 321* (1:50,000).

Approaches to Vestmannaeyjar (looking east) *Henry Clay*

Vestmannaeyjar Harbour looking east with the Nausthamarsbryggja basin with visitors' berths seen to the right of the incoming vessel *Brian Black*

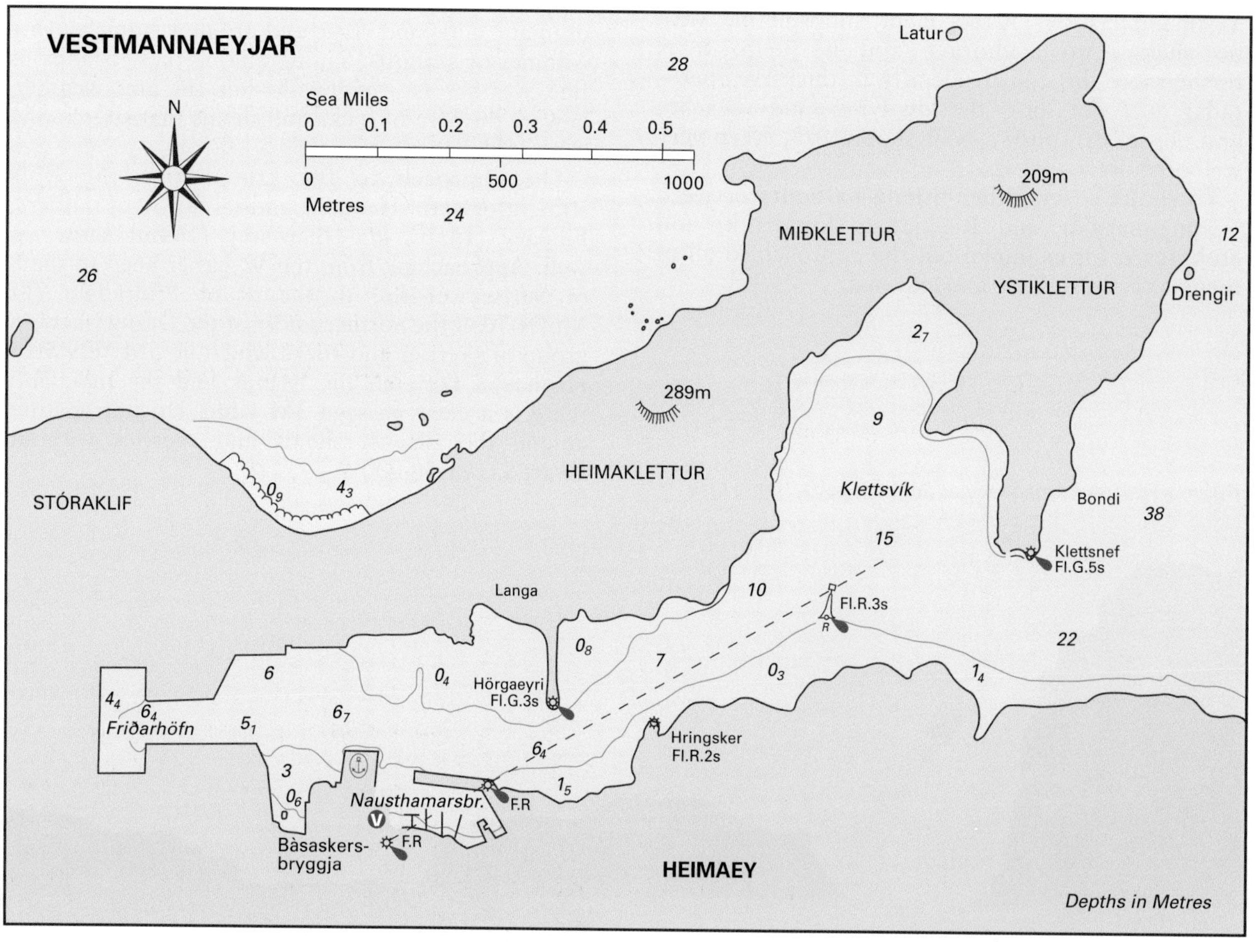

1 Vestmannaeyjar (Harbour)

63°26'N 20°16'W

Tide 1·1, 2·5 **Charts** 31, 310, 321

Vestmannaeyjar Harbour lies on the N side of Heimaey, the principal island of the group and the only inhabited one. It has a substantial town and an airport. The harbour is very sheltered and is one of the most important fishing harbours in Iceland, accounting for over 10% of the total landings. The first weekend of August is the annual festival when the harbour becomes very crowded with fishing boats.

In 1973 there was a major eruption behind the town, which was successfully evacuated with no loss of life. The lava flowed northwards and eastwards, destroying a part of the town, extending the island to the east and almost closing the harbour entrance. Luckily the flow stopped in time, leaving a narrow entrance just over 100m wide. A new mountain was formed (a twin to Helgafell) and it was named Eldfell (fire mountain).

Heimaey is the only port of refuge in bad weather on the whole of the S coast of Iceland, from Djúpivogur in the SE until Reykjanes and Garðskagi have been rounded.

Approach

Straightforward from the E once the twin cones of Helgafell and Eldfell and the islands of Bjarnarey and Elliðaey have been identified. From the W, pass through Faxasund. The approach to Klettsnef is clean, as is the passage past Klettsvík and its curious twisted lava cliffs. The red buoy (Fl.R.3s) opposite Klettsvík marks the edge of the new lava flow and must be left to port, when entering.

Contact harbourmaster on VHF Ch 12 on arrival to check shipping movements (it is a narrow channel) and arrange berthing.

Berthing

Enter the Nausthamarsbryggja (the first basin on the port hand) and go alongside the outer side of the new pontoon on S side of the harbour, which is intended for visiting yachts. This is close to shops. The best berth for a yacht is on the third pontoon. Electricity and water available – contact harbourmaster.

Visitors' berths on pontoons on the southern side of the Nausthamarsbryggja basin in Vestmannaeyjar Harbour *Henry Clay*

Facilities

Water is available on the pontoon. Fuel: either from the end of the second pontoon, a bowser, or from a fuel point at the E end of the basin; but check the depth. Arrangements should be made with the harbourmaster on the central quay (Básaskersbryggja) or the Shell office, which is at the N end of the Friðarhöfn, where payment should be made. All normal requirements can be met; the shops are well stocked and there is an excellent swimming pool on the far side of town. A Ro-Ro ferry goes to Þorlákshöfn on the mainland and there are frequent flights from the airport.

Suðvesturmid

2 Þorlákshöfn 63°51'N 21°22'W

Tide 1·3, 2·8 **Charts** 31, 33, 313

The harbour is the terminal for the ferry to Heimaey and lies about 40M NW of Vestmannaeyjar. The harbour is well sheltered once inside, but it is exposed to the SE and not recommended in heavy weather; however, it may be useful as a passage port in strong westerlies.

Approach

Open to the E through to the S. Follow the leading marks (297°, Oc.R.3s) until you can turn to port into the harbour. The church spire to the west of the port is conspicuous.

Berthing

The main harbour is divided into two parts by an L-shaped pier. In both parts it is possible to berth on a tyre wall or alongside a fishing boat. The southern part (behind the pier) is well sheltered but subject to effluent from the fish factory. The northern part is less sheltered and subject to ferry wash.

Facilities

Water is available on the central pier. Supermarket, bank, bakery and hardware shop.

Reykjanes Peninsula

3 Grindavík 63°50'N 22°26'W

Tide 1·5, 3·3 **Charts** 31, 36, 314

The approach to this harbour, which had a very dangerous reputation, has been much improved by blasting a straight channel and constructing new breakwaters on either side. It is a useful harbour if strong northerlies make rounding Reykjanes unpleasant. It should still be avoided in strong southerly winds.

Vestmannaeyjar Harbour looking southwest from Heimaklettur *Alistair Scott*

Approach

From the S, follow the leading line (003°, Oc.G.5s) straight up the channel, leaving the two red beacons to port. The channel is dredged and there is shallow water either side.

Berthing

There is a small boat harbour at the E end of the main harbour, opposite the lifeboat berth. Approaching the small boat harbour at the E end, note that the S part of the harbour is shallow – keep on the leading line (068°, Oc.R.3s) until near the end of the jetty (Eyjabakki) before turning to starboard into the small boat harbour, which now has a depth of 2–4m.

Facilities

From the small boat harbour the main town is about a 10-minute walk and has all the usual facilities. Regular buses (or an interesting signposted walk) to the Blue Lagoon (Bláa Lónið) – about 8km away.

Reykjanes

Rounding the SW point of the Reykjanes Peninsula, the recommended course is close in – less than 1M – although with wind against tide there will be broken water. Note there are some rocks two cables off the shore at Rejkjanesta lighthouse.

4 Stóra Sandvík 63°51′N 22°43′W

2·5M N of Reykjanes Lt is an excellent sheltered anchorage in strong easterlies.

5 Sandgerði 64°02′N 22°43′W

Tide 1·6, 3·5 **Charts** 31, 316

Sandgerði is a busy commercial fishing port, with a difficult and sometimes dangerous approach; particularly in strong NW winds, but which is rather better protected from the SW by the Bæjarskerseyri reef than would at first appear. Not very attractive but, being close to Keflavík airport, it could be useful.

Approach

The approach is by a narrow dredged channel with below-water rocks on either side. (*Chart 316* is virtually essential.) First identify Sandgerði Light (conspicuous yellow tower) and approach on a bearing of 110·7° until close S of a port-hand buoy, which is half a mile NW of the harbour entrance. Alter course to 139°, with two beacons in transit, which are located half a mile SE of the entrance.

Berthing

The harbour is divided in two by a central pier. Moor alongside the northern breakwater, either alongside a fishing boat or on the tyre wall. The southern part of the harbour is shallow and full of small boat pontoons and moorings. Trawlers lie on the central pier.

Facilities

Water is available on the pier. Normal facilities of a small town.

Faxaflói

Faxaflói is the wide bay NE of Garðskagi and the Reykjanes peninsula. The modern conurbation of Reykjavík and its suburbs is in the SE corner. The whole of the S shore is accessible, as are Borgarfjörður and Hvalfjörður; but N of Þormóðssker lighthouse (64°26'N 22°18'W) the coast is shoal and beset with rocks and reefs.

Coming from the S or W, keep at least 1M off when rounding Garðskagi, which has off-lying rocks and a race under certain conditions.

6 Keflavík 64°00'N 22°33'W

Tide 1·6, 3·6 **Charts** 36, 361

The international airport is only five minutes by taxi from the harbour. This makes it a good place for a crew change, if short of time. The harbour and town are rather uninspiring and it may be preferable to sail the 20M or so up the bay to Reykjavík and use the 'Flybus', which connects with all international flights. The harbour can be uncomfortable in strong easterlies and northeasterlies, which are not uncommon. If obliged to wait in Keflavík, it is possible to get a bus to Bláa Lónið and swim in the famous Blue Lagoon, fed by the water from the Svartsengi geothermal power station. There is a regular bus service to Reykjavík and it is perfectly practical to visit the city and tour the sights of SW Iceland from Keflavík.

Approach

Approaching Keflavík Harbour; a white oil storage tank at the head of the harbour is visible from a distance. This distinguishes it from nearby Njarðvík, 1M to the S, which is a commercial harbour, much further from the shops and not recommended for a yacht.

Berthing

As convenient or as directed by the harbourmaster. The extreme NE corner is shallow and the inner harbour will not float a yacht. The harbour office (hafnarskrifstofa) is in a prominent building. Nominal dues may be charged.

Facilities

Water on the quay. Fuel to order by bowser. Good engineering workshop. There are good supermarkets, some of which open late and at weekends. Car hire or taxis from the airport or the Keflavík Hotel. Bus station at the far end of the main street. Swimming pool, 'hot pot', etc.

7 Grófin 64°00'N 22°33'W

Tide 1·6, 3·6 **Charts** 361

There is a small private marina at Grófin, 1·5M north of the main Keflavík harbour. It has a depth of 3m throughout and is one of the most sheltered in the country. The marina is kept locked and there is limited space; however, it may be possible to leave a yacht there during a temporary return home – boat club members would keep an eye on a vessel left there. However, the entrance is quite narrow and awkward and it is not recommended for a brief stop. The Keflavík harbourmaster is responsible for Grófin and you must contact him before going in.

Facilities

All the facilities of Keflavík are accessible from Grófin, but it is a long walk to the shops. There is a bus terminal, a diving school and a small model boat museum.

8 Hafnarfjörður 64°04'N 21°58'W

Tide 1·7, 3·8 **Charts** 363, 365

Hafnarfjörður combines the attributes of a busy commercial and fishing harbour and an attractive seaside suburb of Reykjavík. It has a snug but crowded inner harbour and is an alternative to Reykjavík for smaller yachts, and is in some respects preferable. The commercial harbour is being developed and extended, relieving some of the pressure on the inner harbour, where there is a thriving sailing club.

Approach

From a point 0·5M S of the Valhússagrun buoy (Fl.R.3s) (approx. 64°05'N 22°05'W), enter on the leading line 98° which passes very close N of the small starboard hand buoy marking the end of the new outer breakwater. The leading marks are not clear and the fixed lights indistinguishable from the surrounding lights: however, the harbour entrance is wide and this is not a problem until late in the season.

Berthing

The inner harbour is mainly filled with private finger pontoons, but a berth may be found on the sailing club pontoon (2m draft) or lie alongside a fishing boat under repair. Total shelter and quiet. There is also a small floating jetty on the E side of the harbour off the Viking-style Fjörukráin restaurant, where it is possible to lie with permission from the harbourmaster.

Facilities

There is a small supermarket close by the inner harbour and diesel is easily obtained from pontoons in one of three locations in the harbour. Most supplies are available in the shopping mall in the town centre, about 10 minutes' walk from the inner harbour.

There are two or three good restaurants in town and, it is said, 'the most attractive swimming pool in all Iceland', a quarter of a mile S of the harbour. Hot water and showers are also available in the sailing club. There are regular buses to Reykjavík from the bus terminal outside the shopping mall ('Firði') and the Flybus to Keflavík airport also stops opposite the Fjörukráin restaurant, but it is wise to book ahead (✆ 565 1213).

Hafnarfjörður is an important ship repair harbour and there is a factory producing GRP fishing boats, so repairs should not pose a problem.

9 Reykjavík 64°09'N 21°56'W

Tide 1·7, 3·8 **Charts** 362, 365

Reykjavík is a modern city with a vibrant nightlife and is also a busy commercial port. Over half the population of Iceland live in the city and its suburbs. It is a good place from which to make a tour inland by bus or hired car. Places of interest within easy reach are Þingvellir (the site of the oldest parliament in the world), Geysir and the famous falls of Gullfoss.

Reykjavík *Henry Clay*

Approach

Straightforward from the N and W using *Charts 362* and *365*.

Berthing

Vessels may contact Harbour Control (Call *Pilot* on Ch 12) on arrival. Visiting vessels should proceed to the Brokey (Reykjavík Yacht Club, ✆+354 5528272) in the SE part of the harbour close to the new Harpa concert hall.

The club's pontoons have both water and electric power. Larger yachts may use the south side of the two 40m pontoons to the west of the Ingólfsgarður hammerhead. The northern side of the W pontoon is used by whale-watching boats. Tuesday is club racing night – the club house is in the SE corner of the harbour and visiting yachtsmen are made very welcome. The club house is made from white painted containers and visitors may use the club's shower. There is water, a laundry and WiFi. The nearby concert hall and conference centre is a massive steel and multicoloured glass structure which was designed by the Danish architects Henning Larsen and Icelandic artist Olafur Eliasson. Construction stopped during the financial crisis but was recommenced in 2008 and it opened in 2011. Customs officers visit the pontoons every day.

Brokey Sailing Club with Mount Esja in the background
Egill Kolbeinsson

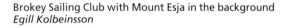

Facilities

WiFi at the marina. There are excellent shops in the town and all provisions can be obtained; but inevitably the bigger supermarkets are some distance from the harbour.

The harbourmaster (locally referred to as the 'pilot') has his office on the fourth floor of a building off Tryggvagata and is very helpful. Diesel is delivered by road tanker and can be arranged by phoning ✆ +354 5509933 between 0700 and 1700 on working days. There are numerous engineering and electronic workshops near the harbour, offering agency support for most well-known makes of engine and electronic equipment. No sail loft, but the tent and awning maker, Seglargerðin Ægar, Eyjarsloð 7, may be able to carry out repairs. There are a couple of chandleries, but these only stock items for motor vessels as yet.

Brokey Reykjavík Yacht Club seen in SE corner of Reykjavík Harbour beneath the new concert hall Harpa
Egill Kolbeinsson

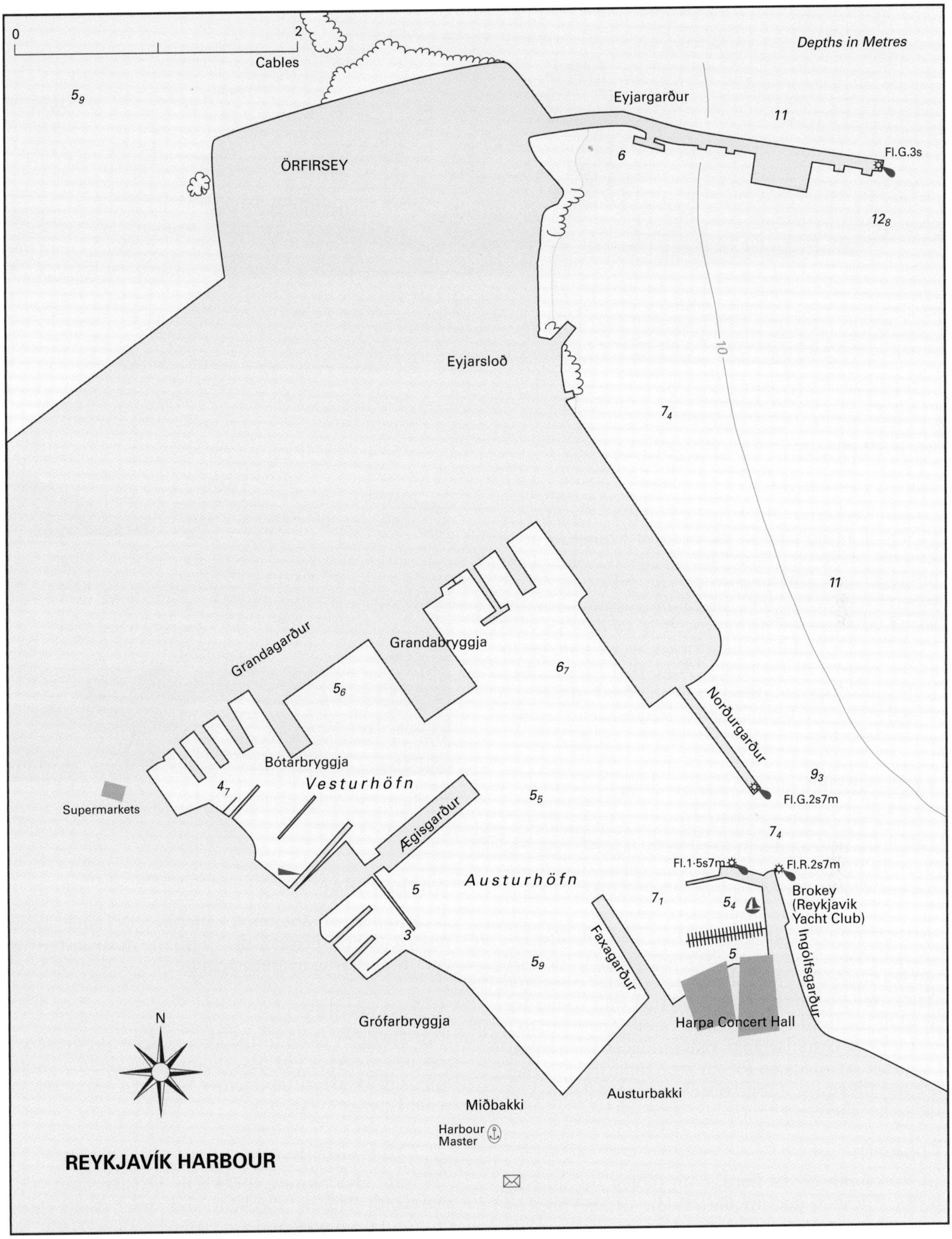

Useful websites

[QR code]	Brokey (Reykjavík Yacht Club)	www.brokey.is

Reykjavík city *Henry Clay*

10 Kollafjörður 64°11′N 21°46′W

Tide 1·7, 3·8 **Charts** 365

NE of Reykjavík, there are a number of relatively sheltered anchorages at the head of Kollafjörður in Eiðsvík, Leirvogur and Þerneyjarsund. Excellent holding and shelter (except in NW winds) is reported between the village of Álfsnes and the island of Þerney. The approach is straightforward from W or N and there is sufficient water for a yacht in the passage E of Þerney. Note that the head of Leirvogur dries and the voe to the N of Álfsnes is closed to yachts beyond, inlet, Helgusker by an 8m overhead cable.

11 Hvalfjörður 64°17′N 21°55′W

Tide 1·7, 3·8 **Charts** 365, 366

This is the nearest major fjord to Reykjavík. It is 7M N of the harbour and runs NE for about 7M. In the Second World War it was used by the Royal Navy for assembling the Murmansk convoys and the remains of the naval shore station, HMS *Baldur III*, are still in evidence. With the completion of the 6km tunnel under the fjord it is much quieter now, and traffic noise from the coast road that runs round the head of the fjord has virtually ceased. There are two factories at Grundartangi; one produces aluminium, the other ferro-silicon for the steel industry, but they are not obtrusive. Large vessels periodically dock at the jetties there.

Approach

At the mouth of the fjord, both shores are beset by rocks. Clear water up the middle of the fjord is marked by two starboard-hand buoys, Brekkuboði (Fl.G.3s) (64°16′·3N 21°57′·2W) and Hnausasker (Fl.G.5s), 2·5M NE. Thereafter the N shore is clean, but the S shore remains foul almost to Hvaleyri. There are no dangers in the narrows N of Hvammsey.

Hvalfjörd anchorage behind Hvamsey *Henry Clay*

Anchorages

A number of sheltered anchorages have been reported at the head of the fjord; the most easterly is cut off by a 10m overhead cable.

⚓ 11a Hvaleyri

E of Hvaleyri close to the shore, clear of two shoal patches 0·6M E of the point. On the N shore opposite Hvaleyri the factory jetty at Grundartangi would give some shelter.

⚓ 11b Hvammsey

SW of Hvammsey, between Selsker and the mainland. This is excellent and quiet. Eider-duck nest on Hvammsey and are farmed commercially for their down. The island is covered with scarecrows to deter seabirds from stealing the ducks' eggs. It is better not to land on Hvammsey and definitely not during the nesting season (up to mid July). There is a 'hot pot' on the beach to the W of the anchorage.

Hvammsey hot pot *Henry Clay*

⚓ 11c Miðsandur

Off Miðsandur on the N shore passing between the Prætusker shoal (S cardinal) and Geirshólmi, or in Helguvík. There are two jetties and oil storage tanks ashore.

⚓ 11d Hvitanes

Off the S shore E of Hvitanes.

12 Akranes 64°19'N 22°05'W

Tide 1·7, 3·8 **Charts** 364, 365

This is a clean and quite pleasant harbour, rather dominated by a cement factory. Shell sand dredged from the Sydra Hraun bank 10M SW of the harbour is used to produce the cement, since there is no chalk or limestone in Iceland. The Garðar Folk Museum near the town could be worth a visit.

Approach

The SE leading line (345°, Oc.R.3s) should only be used in good visibility and quiet conditions, since it passes close to shoals which break. The best approach is from the SW on 051° (Oc.G.5s), which passes close SE of buoy No.11 (Fl.R.3s) two miles out. The leading marks are not clear in daylight, but the line is half a mile to the SE of the cement works, which are conspicuous.

Berthing

Visiting yachts should berth alongside a new concrete pontoon, which runs across the harbour from the central jetty. Friendly harbourmaster. Usual facilities of a small town.

13 Borgarnes (Borgarfjörður)

64°32'N 21°56'W

Tide 1·7, 3·8 **Charts** 36, H-01

Borgarnes town lies at the tip of a narrow volcanic peninsula at the head of a shallow fjord, 20M north of Reykjavík. At one time it was a busy harbour with a regular ferry service to Reykjavík, but due to considerable silting, both in the approach and in the harbour, it has been virtually abandoned. With the construction of the road tunnel under Hvalfjörður it has become a busy transport hub. Saga buffs will find much of interest in the district. Egil Skallagrímsson's father and later his son are buried in a mound in the centre.

Approach

Borgarfjörður is the estuary of a large glacial river and tidal streams can be considerable. Pilotage is interesting and there is a good chance of running aground, particularly near the harbour, but without serious consequences. *Chart H-01* is essential.

Head for Pjófaklettar between 044° and 048° (which is the white sector); Pjófaklettar is a low black cliff clearly visible to the left of Hafnarfjall. Then go for Rauðanes between 003·5° and 008·5° (again, the white sector of Rauðanes). The final line to the harbour is towards the leading marks with small yellow triangles (059°); however, the best course is now somewhat to the N of this line, due to silting.

Berthing

It is possible to anchor just off the harbour in 2–3m. The harbour probably now has less than 1m alongside at low water.

Facilities

Large supermarket, bank, hotels and swimming pool, but a longish walk from the harbour.

14 Arnarstapi 64°46'N 23°38'W

Charts 41

A spectacular anchorage under the SE flank of the Snæfellsjökull, with a very small harbour. It is protected from the W and N and could be useful if head winds cause problems rounding Öndverðarnes.

Approach

Approach is straightforward from the SE, but there are rocks off the point to the S of the harbour to be avoided.

Anchorage

Anchor off in Breiðavik in a suitable depth, good holding.

Harbour

The harbour is entered between the rubble breakwater and a green pole, marking the end of a rock which restricts the harbour entrance.

A shoal area stretches from the green pole to the second innermost ladder on the harbour wall. Inside this line, depths are less than 1·5m at LW. Under the right conditions, this is a most attractive harbour and has been used by a 40ft yacht drawing 2m; but is subject to surge and should not be used if there is swell running in from a southerly direction. Water and shore power available.

Breiðafjörður

Charts 41, 42, 44, 420

Breiðafjörður lies to the NE of Snæfellsnes – dominated by the Snæfellsjökull icecap – and is entered between Öndverðarnes (64°53′N 24°03′W) and Bjargtangar (65°30′·1N 24°31′W), 40M to the N. An area of considerable historical interest, going back to the early days of the Norse settlement and featured in many of the Sagas. Eirikur Rauði (Erik the Red) lived here, before being banished and setting forth from Hvammsfjörður to settle in SW Greenland. The S shore has several useful harbours and anchorages within easy access; but rocks and shoals to the E make pilotage increasingly challenging as one penetrates further in. The NE half is a fascinating area, with over two thousand islands and skerries separated by intricate channels. Most of the islands were at one time settled, but now virtually all are deserted and given over to eider-duck, which are 'farmed' for their down – an important local industry. As recently as the early part of the last century, trading stations like Flatey and Skarðsstöð were still visited by trading vessels from Europe. Along the SE shore, scattered farms raise beef cattle and sheep, along with a few small dairies. By contrast, the N shore is indented with numerous steep sided fjords, which are difficult to access. There is some evidence that the land is rising and depths may be less than shown on the charts of this area, first published in 1915, but the difference is likely to be small.

15 Rif 64°55′N 23°49′W

Tide 1·7, 3·8 **Charts** 42, 421

A modern fishing harbour, 2M from the nearest town of Hellissandur and the first stop after rounding Snæfellsjökull from the south. It is rather a bleak place, but a useful passage port. Huge numbers of arctic terns nest here (wear a hat if going inland) as well as wading birds, dunlins, etc. There is a fine waterfall about a mile south of the harbour. Very strong winds may be experienced blowing off the Snæfellsjökull ice cap.

Navigation

The harbour is about 2M east of Hellissandur, 3M ENE of the tall radio masts (approximately 64°54′N 23°56′W) and 4M WNW of Ólafsvík light. Clear the reef by sailing close to the RW buoy (LFl.10s) and then double back westwards, leaving the large green beacon (Fl.G.3s) close to starboard. The harbour leading marks appear to lead through the reefs, but do not risk this without local advice.

Berthing

The small boat harbour is shallow, but there is sufficient depth at the end of the wooden quay at its entrance. Alternatively, lie alongside a convenient fishing boat, with permission.

Facilities

Very little habitation; but there is a small supermarket and a hardware shop near the harbour. Arn Jóns engineering workshop is helpful and efficient.

16 Ólafsvík 64°54′N 23°42′W

Tide 1·6, 3·7 **Charts** 42, 422, 426

A busy commercial and fishing harbour 3M ESE of Rif. There is a track leading to the foot of the Snæfellsjökull about 3M to the south. The glacier may be dangerous to visit in hot weather. An early Icelandic farm on the nearby Fróðá river is the site of the dramatic 10th-century hauntings in the Eyrbyggja Saga.

Navigation

Keep at least 0·5M offshore until the harbour entrance bears 190°; then enter, leaving the small E cardinal buoy (Q(3)10s) to starboard.

Berthing

The harbour has been dredged and substantially enlarged. Berth on the main pontoon to port as you enter the small boat harbour, by arrangement with the Harbourmaster. If space is not available, berth temporarily at the fuel pontoon on the starboard

View of Breiðafjörður from Ellidaey *Henry Clay*

Ólafsvík. View NE towards Breiðafjörður *Alistair Scott*

side. The Harbourmaster's office has a blue anchor on the wall. Water and electricity available. Fuel on the inner pontoon.

Facilities

All stores are available.

17 Grundarfjörður 64°55'N 23°15'W

Tide 1·8, 3·9 **Charts** 42, 426

A fishing port in attractive surroundings at the head of Grundarfjörður. There are two quays within the breakwatered harbour. The NW quay has a busy commercial fish processing plant. There is a small boat harbour and wooden quay in the SE corner.

It is a worthwhile port of call, with varied and splendid scenery and excellent walking country.

Navigation

From the W, Krossnes lighthouse (Fl(4)WRG.20s) and the low-lying islet of Melrakkaey are useful for locating the Vesturboði buoy (Fl.R.5s) that marks the pass through extensive outlying shoals – however, in reasonable conditions it is possible to enter in the white sector of Krossnes Light between 97° and 128·5°. Note also that a reef extends to the NW of Melrakkaey and it is therefore preferable to leave the island to starboard, when entering from the N. From the N, leave Melrakkaey three cables to port and aim for the E flank of Kirkjufell before heading for the harbour.

Berthing

1. Anchor in peace and quiet off the E end of the beach in the SE corner of the fjord or off the S shore to the E of the harbour.
2. Berth on the wharf opposite the fish landing point with permission from the harbourmaster, or alongside a fishing boat in either of the harbours, or on the wooden quay in the SE corner.

Facilities

All normal facilities. Shops are rather better than those found in most ports of a similar size. Horses can be hired from Kverná, the farm at the head of the fjord.

18 Kolgrafafjörður 65°N 23°03'W

Charts 41

This large bay lies to the W of the famous Berserkjahraun. The narrows to the W of Berserkseyraroddi have been closed by a road bridge, denying the anchorages in the inner bay.

Approach

From the NW, using *Chart 426*, there should be no problems following the deep-water route in.

Berthing

Either anchor in 3m in the SE corner, off Berserkseyri Farm, or for better protection, enter Hraunsfjörður leaving the gravel bank of Seljaoddi close to port – the channel carries 4–5m and there is sufficient water just inside to anchor in perfect shelter in 3–4m mud.

Remarks

From the anchorage, it is a 4km walk to the Berserkjahraun.

19 Hofstaðavogur 65°01'N 22°50'W

Charts 42, 426

Hofstaðavogur is a landlocked bay in gentle green surroundings. The present farm at Hofstaðir is the site of the original 9th-century settlement of the Norwegian Þórófur Mostur-beard, whose son, Þorsteinn Cod-biter, founded the nearby farm near Helgafell. Originally a holy place of Þór, it was a prominent early Christian site after the conversion in AD1000. When Þorsteinn was drowned, the basalt cliff of Helgafell opened and he was seen feasting with his ancestors inside the mountain. Helgafell is a short walk from the head of the bay and the view from the top of the hill SE up Alftafjörður encompasses many of the sites featured in Eyrbyggja Saga.

Three miles to the SW is Bjarnarhöfn, a big farm on the site of the 9th-century settlement of Björn the Easterner. Close by is the lava field Berserkjahraun, where two berserks had to level a path in a labour of Hercules to win a maiden. They completed the task but were cheated out of the maiden and killed.

Approach

It can be approached with care using *Chart 42*, but *Chart 426* is better. The bay is shallow and depending on draught it will be necessary to anchor up to a mile and a half from the head, although it may be possible to sail to the head of the bay in a shoal-draught yacht. Helgafell can be visited from Stykkishólmur.

20 Stykkishólmur 65°05'N 22°44'W

Tide 1·8, 3·9 **Charts** 42, 424, 426

This is an historic trading centre and fishing harbour with access to the 'Saga' country inland. (See above under Hofstaðavogur.) The church is a sight not to be missed.

Stykkishólmur approaches *Henry Clay*

Approach

In good weather the approach to the harbour is relatively straightforward using *Chart 426*, but requires care (see *NP11 4.43*). The leading marks for the approach channel are clear.

Berthing

1. The harbour is very crowded. The outer part (Hafskipabrygga) is full of fishing boats and the small boat harbour has very little space and seems shallow. Berth if possible alongside a pontoon occupied by local boats, immediately to starboard of the ferry, in the central part of the harbour. The pontoon is short, but sufficient for a short stay in quiet weather.
2 Alternatively, a quiet anchorage can be found in the Skipavik, close SW of the town.

There is a channel inside Landey, but it shoals and if coming from the main harbour, it is better to sail around Landey and the off-lying rocks and enter on the leading line (132°, Oc.R.5s) and then leave Bænhúshólmi to starboard. Anchor in 8m, beyond the big ship jetty, with room to swing, but note rocks which cover, on the N side of the harbour. It was reported that this anchorage becomes uncomfortable in strong southwesterlies.

Stykkishólmur *Henry Clay*

Stykkishólmur church *Henry Clay*

Facilities

There is water available on the pontoon in the main harbour. The town has good shops and a museum. The boat yard appears to be excellent and capable of repairs in steel, wood and GRP, to a high standard.

21 Hvammsfjörður 65°05'N 22°04'W

Charts 426 (1:20,000) and 42 (1:50,000) are essential to pass into Hvammsfjörður

Strong tides are experienced and the entrance is all but blocked by rocks, but the passage through (Röst – meaning Race) is shown as an insert on *Chart 42*. This fjord is the area of the wanderings and settlement of the great settler matriarch, Auður Ketilsdóttir the Deep-minded, sister of Björn of Bjarnarhöfn. From these two, and Þórólf of Hofstad, are descended all the main protagonists of the Laxdæla Saga and Eyrbyggja Saga, including the tragic heroine, Gudrún Ósvífursdóttir, who ended her days as an anchorite at Helgafell.

22 Elliðae 65°08'N 22°49'W

Charts 42, 426

Elliðaey is a small island, with a lighthouse (Fl.WRG.10s47m12–7M) on the NW corner. There is a useful anchorage in a bay on the S side which is the remains of a small volcanic crater about 500m in diameter. Anchor in 5–6m, fair holding in the bay, with good shelter.

This island is privately owned, with a derelict farmhouse. Puffins and fulmars nest here.

23 Skarðstöð 65°17'N 22°21'W

Charts 42, 44

It is hard to believe that this harbour was once an important trading centre for this agricultural area, which has been occupied since the very beginning of the 'Settlement' 1,000 years ago. The main farm at Skarð is still owned by the same family and they can trace their family tree back to a remarkable woman, Ólöf Loftsdóttir. In 1467, in revenge for a piratical attack by English privateers, when her husband was killed at Rif, she captured some English sailors and imprisoned them in a cave where she subjected them to slave labour and then killed them.

It is now a collecting centre for eider-down, harvested by local farmers, who own the many islands in this fascinating area. After quite laborious cleaning by hand, the down is exported to Japan. It takes about 60 nests to produce a kilo of raw down.

Approach

Chart 44 shows the leading line. Clear visibility is absolutely essential, since the leading line passes less than 0·2M from shoals and drying rocks.

Berthing

There is just room in the tiny harbour for two yachts to lie alongside a new float; but there is probably less than 2m at MLWS. In calm conditions it is possible to anchor off in 3–4m.

24 Flatey 65°22'N 22°56'W

Charts 42, 420

Flatey, like Skarð, was once an important trading centre for all the smallholdings on the many islands in Breiðafjörður, now mostly deserted; it was also a centre of learning. Trading vessels from England once visited here. The island has an interesting church and library and an old village, now alas mostly summer cottages. Well worth a visit.

Approach

The approach from the SW is straightforward using *Chart 42*.

Flatey, Breiðafjörður *Henry Clay*

Flatey village, Breiðafjörður *Henry Clay*

Berthing

It is not possible to lie alongside. The anchorage is opposite the village on the S side of Hafnarey, in an old volcanic crater about 150m in diameter. There are moorings occupied by local boats, but there is just room to anchor clear in 2–3m. In strong W to SW winds there is modest protection, but at HW waves would break over the lip, which is low on that side.

It is also possible to lie on the jetties at the SW end of the island, clear of the ferry berth.

Facilities

There is a small shop with limited supplies (the locals order from the mainland). There is also a post office near the ferry dock at the SW end of the island, which is open for about an hour around lunchtime.

25 Vatnsfjörður 65°31'N 23°09'W

Charts 42

It was from the head of this fjord, in about AD860, that Flóki Vilgerðarson (Ravns Flóki) – after a very cold winter, when the first settlers nearly died – climbed up to Lónfell and, looking down into Arnarfjörður and seeing it packed with ice floes, decided to call the land Ísland (Iceland).

Approach

Approach with care as this fjord is only charted as far as the fishing harbour/ferry terminal at Brjánslækur on *Chart 42*. Approaching the anchorage at the head of the fjord, keep mid-channel between the island and the E shore, carrying 5–6m, but beware reef projecting from the E side of the island.

Berthing

There appears to be a reasonable anchorage at about 65°34'N 23°09'W, behind the island towards the head of the fjord. There are rocks to the west of the island, but the passage to the E is clear. Depths to the N of the island at the head are relatively shallow, but it is possible to find >2m and the island provides some protection.

Remarks

Not far from the anchorage, on the NW shore, Hótel Flókelundur has a restaurant and a thermal swimming pool.

26 Rauðasandsbugur

Rauðasandsbugur is a large bay, which lies to the SE of Bjargtangar and is protected from the N. If the combination of strong northerlies and tides make progress northward difficult, anchorage can be found in a small bay 7M E of Bjargtangar called Keflavik (65°30'N 24°14'W). Anchor off a small stream and a refuge hut in 6–8m, sand and boulders. Open to swell from the S, but protected to a degree from swells from the W by a small headland which forms the W side of Keflavik Bay.

AREA II

Northwest Iceland: *Vestfirðir (the west fjords) from Bjargtangar to Horn*

Charts 41, 42, 46

The NW peninsula of Iceland, known as the Vestfirðir, spreads like an open hand towards the Denmark Strait – or the Grænlands Sund, as the Icelanders prefer to call it. It is a high plateau, roughly 60M across, deeply indented with fjords, and is a fascinating area to visit. The principal fjord is the Ísafjarðardjúp, which penetrates 40M inland. It is flanked by mountains running up to 1,000m high and by the Drangajökull icecap.

North of a line through the Drangajökull the peninsula is now uninhabited, except for a few old farmhouses used in the summer, notably at Hesteyri.

As it lies so near the Arctic Circle and to the cold East Greenland Current, the snow tends to remain

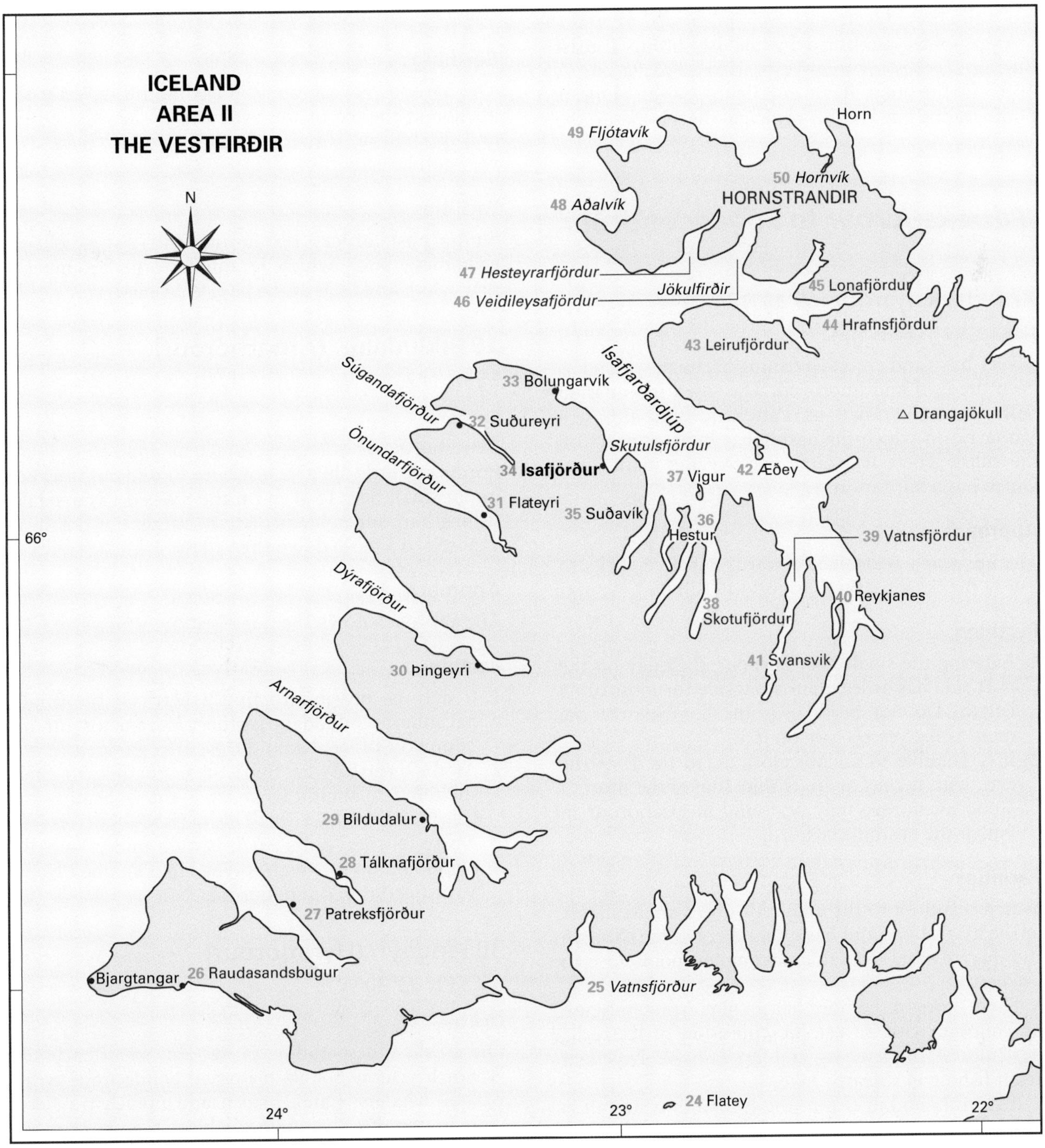

on the mountains until late in the season, in places down to sea level. The sheltered old meadows, however, are a riot of wild flowers in mid-summer – now that there are no livestock to graze them; and there are numerous birds.

Ísafjörður on the S side of the Ísafjarðardjúp is the principal centre with an excellent harbour and good communications. There are also a number of busy fishing harbours in the fjords to the SW.

In many of the fjords, moraines left by the retreating glaciers form the base of a stony bank behind which there may be a sheltered harbour. These are the eyri, which are so characteristic of this area.

In one or two cases the eyri does not rise above the surface and the sudden reduction in depth may be a hazard to navigation, especially to those exploring less well-charted waters.

A pamphlet published by the Ísafjörður Tourist Bureau (Ferðaskrifstofa Vestfjarðar), Aðalstræti 7, 400 Ísafjörður, has excellent aerial colour photographs of all the principal harbours in the Vestfirðir.

Patreksfjörður to Súgandafjörður

27 Patreksfjörður 65°36'N 24°00'W

Tide 1·3, 3·1 **Charts** 41, 42

A very busy and crowded fishing harbour, which has been dredged and improved. The town (population 650) is now known as Patreksfjörður; although Vatneyri, on which the harbour is built, appears on the chart. There is a large fish-freezing plant here, which has a big export trade.

Approach

The approach is straightforward, but note rocks to SW of Blakksnes, as well as just off Tálkni.

Berthing

1. Entering the small boat harbour, the quay on the port side has at least 3m alongside for most of its length. Do not berth near the 'knuckle' of the quay as big vessels turn on it.
2. It is possible to anchor close in, to the E of the eyri, with depths of 4m within 20m of the shore.
3. Good anchorage may be found in Ósafjörður in 9m, at the head of the fjord.

Facilities

Water is laid on to the quay. All stores are available at the local shops and basic chandlery at the shop on the quay. Diesel available. Swimming pool close to the berth.

The S shore of the fjord has an interesting museum at Hnjótur, with an eclectic collection of Icelandic agricultural implements and bric-a-brac. Excellent trout fishing in a nearby lake.

If stormbound, a trip to the Dynjandi waterfall is much recommended.

28 Tálknafjörður 65°38'N 23°50'W

Charts 41

A very sheltered anchorage and small fishing harbour behind Sveinseyri.

Approach

Sail up Tálknafjörður, leaving a derelict whaling station with a prominent chimney to starboard. Sveinseyri appears as a strip of yellow sand, which reaches almost to the S shore, leaving a deep water channel little more than 100m wide. The leading line (121°, Q and Fl.3s) is on the S shore just beyond the gap and is hard to distinguish; but once past the small red port-hand buoy, about 300m S of the tip of the *eyri*, turn to port into the bay. The approach could be difficult in poor visibility.

Berthing

The harbour is very small indeed and it is better to anchor in the lee of the eyri, but it shelves steeply and the bottom is hard. Holding is good, once set; very good shelter.

Facilities

Shop, post office, restaurant and an excellent swimming pool, which is amongst the prominent new white buildings at the base of Sveinseyri.

29 Bíldudalur (Arnarfjörður)
65°41'N 23°35'W

Charts 41

Arnarfjörður is a large, spectacular and rather long fjord with little shelter; however Bíldudalur, tucked into a small bay, 15M in on the SW side, is a small fishing harbour in an attractive setting; but possibly exposed to S gusts down the valley.

Approach

The approach down the fjord is straightforward.

Berthing

1. It may be possible to find a berth in the small harbour at Bíldudalur; otherwise anchor off in 10m. Post office, bank, shops, café, garage.
2. At the head of the fjord, it is possible to find sheltered anchorage at the head of Geirþjófsfjörður in 7m. This may be of interest to Norse History 'buffs', as it is right under Lónfell, the mountain to which Ravns Flóki climbed from Vatnsfjörður in Breiðafjörður.

30 Þingeyri (Dyrafjörður)
65°53'N 23°30'W

Charts 41, 46

One of the oldest trading posts. This small harbour is worth visiting for its historical connections with Basque whalers. Later, British and French trawlers were drawn there by a remarkable old engineer, who was reputed to able to fix anything in his foundry and workshop. It is said that some trawlers left Britain with broken gear and made for Dyrafjörður, knowing that they would be able to get it fixed there. The old man has died but his extraordinary workshop is the oldest functioning mechanical workshop in Iceland.

Approach

Dyrafjörður is now covered on the latest edition of *Chart 46*, but surveys are not complete; however, it is easy to enter.

Berthing

The small harbour is adequate for yachts under 40ft LOA, with 4–6m alongside the outer quays. The inner part on the SW side is shallow and the small boat harbour is also very shallow.

It is possible to find secure anchorage in the fjord further in.

Facilities

Shop, swimming pool, etc.

31 Flateyri (Önundarfjörður)

66°03'N 23°31'W

Tide 1·0, 2·3 **Charts** 41, 46

A fishing village and busy harbour, which has recently been extended and is sheltered from seaward by the *eyri*. In 1996 an avalanche killed 22 people. The population declined for a while, but this now seems to be a vibrant community. It is hoped that any future avalanches will be diverted by two large banks, which have been constructed on the hillside above the village.

Approach

Although very few soundings are shown on *Chart 46*, there appear to be no dangers in Önundarfjörður. On occasions, fierce and unexpected squalls come down off the mountains.

Berthing

Alongside the quay to port as you enter. The NW part of the harbour is very shallow, but there is at least 4m alongside the small boat float, if required.

Facilities

Water, petrol, diesel. Two village stores, post office, bookshop and swimming pool.

32 Suðureyri (Súgandafjörður)

66°08'N 23°32'W

Tide 1·0, 2·2 **Charts** 41, 46

An attractive and very convenient passage port, since it is only 2M from the mouth of Súgandafjörður. The population is particularly friendly.

Approach

The leading line has been removed. To enter, leave the stone jetty about half a cable on the starboard hand and steer approximately 100° towards three spar buoys – one red and two green, which lead into the harbour. Do not sail beyond the harbour, since there are rocks and a drying shoal lying right across the fjord towards Norðureyri. Enter the harbour close to the W breakwater.

Berthing

Berth on the west quay.
There is also a concrete pier 0·5M W of the harbour, which is not recommended but could be used in emergency. Berth on the E face, which has at least 4m at the outer end.

Facilities

One shop, post office, bank, internet café and an excellent swimming pool.

Convenient new WC and hot showers under the harbour office – open 24hrs. Hotel VEG Gisting has internet access and are very helpful.
Road tunnel link to Ísafjörður.

Approach to Suðereyri
Henry Clay

Ísafjarðardjúp and fjords east of Skutulsfjörður

Charts 41, 46

Of the six fjords to the east of Skutulsfjörður (Harpoon Fjord) in Ísafjarðardjúp, only Hestfjörður is reported to be dangerously encumbered with rocks at its entrance. All the others are navigable with deep water on the centre line. The whole area is an attractive cruising ground with crags, waterfalls and many abandoned farms in a wilderness setting; although the shore road which loops round several of the fjords does carry the occasional car. The two islands of Æðey and Vigur are particularly recommended.

33 Bolungarvík 66°10'N 23°15'W

Tide 0·9, 2·0 **Charts** 41, 46

A busy fishing port with a sheltered inner harbour. Recent harbour improvements include a breakwater extending NE from the shore.

Approach

A straightforward approach.

Berthing

In the inner basin, as convenient in about 4m.

34 Ísafjörður (Skutulsfjörður) 66°04'N 23°07'W

Tide 1·0, 2·1 **Charts** 46, 417

Ísafjörður is the principal trading and administrative centre for the Vestfirðir, with excellent facilities and communications, including an airport with flights to Reykjavík. It is ideal for a crew change.

Approach

The approach down Skutulsfjörður to the outer harbour, which lies to the E of the town, is straightforward. To enter the inner harbour (Pollur) follow the narrow buoyed channel SW. The first transit, yellow huts with black vertical stripes (211° F), leads in.

Berthing

The outer harbour is not recommended, since it is very crowded. One or two local sailing craft are berthed on a float there, but this is gated and private. Visiting yachts are recommended to go around into the inner harbour (Pollur) and berth in the NE corner alongside the tyre wall or a fishing boat, with permission.

Note that the harbourmaster's office is at the outer end of the large building to SW of this berth.

It is possible to anchor anywhere in Pollur clear of shipping.

Facilities

New facilities including a lounge, laundry and Wi-Fi should be open for the 2014 season.

Diesel is available by tanker, but unless a large quantity is required, it is probably better to go around to the floating fuel jetty in the outer harbour. The harbour office will advise. Propane is available from the sports shop. Water on the quay. There are very good workshops, (mechanical, electrical and electronic, etc).

There are two or three hotels, a hospital, a swimming pool, museum, good shops and an excellent supermarket. Shops are open on Sunday afternoon. There is a pleasant internet café and also internet access in the library. There is a very helpful tourist office close to the recommended berth, where it is hoped in the near future to provide washing and shower facilities, as well as a visitors pontoon.

The airport is on the E side of the fjord – the 'Flybus' runs from the Hótel Ísafjörður.

Ísafjörður fishing harbour *William Ker*

35 Súðavík (Álftafjörður)

66°02'N 22°59'W

There is a small fishing harbour. In January 1995 an avalanche killed 14 and destroyed six houses in the village.

Berthing

Moor alongside the fish processing plant or alternatively anchor in 5m by the remains of the old Norwegian whaling plant at Langeyri one mile S.

Facilities

Water on the quay, post office, café, bank, shop and garage.

36 Seyðisfjörður (Ísafjarðardjúp)

66°01'N 22°55'W

The fjord has spectacular views of Hestur. There is deep water on the centre line of the fjord.

Berthing

Anchor in 5m behind eyri on the W shore, where there is a church and several summer houses.

37 Vigur 66°03'N 22°49'W

An interesting island at the junction of the three central fjords. The small dairy farm at the S end supports two families, who have survived by diversifying into tourism and live here all year round. In the season, tourist launches from Ísafjörður land parties of visitors at the jetty at the S end. However, there is usually room for a yacht to lie alongside, by arrangement. On the shore there is an impressive longboat, which was once the only transport to the mainland. Iceland's only windmill, as well as many sea birds and spectacular views. Recommended in settled weather.

Approach

From the W head for the mid-point of the gap between Vigur and Folafótur (N end of Hestur). Leave the small green buoy close aboard on either hand and head for the jetty, borrowing to starboard to avoid a rock which lies midway between the buoy and the jetty. (The green buoy has moved from its original position!)

From the E do not close the island until a small red buoy about 500m S of the jetty is sighted. This marks the end of a reef. After leaving the buoy to starboard, head for the houses near the jetty.

Facilities

Permission to land should be obtained from the owner. Tourist shop, café and PO.

38 Skötufjörður 65°56'N 22°49'W

Skötufjörður is a long deep fjord surrounded by high cliffs and there are summer houses at the *eyri*. A rare white-tailed eagle was seen here in 2000.

Berthing

Anchor in 5m off the eyri on W shore.

39 Vatnsfjörður 65°57'N 22°29'W

This is a small shallow fjord with a gently shelving bottom. It is possible to carry 2–3m as far as the pier head. Ashore there are restored fish drying racks and an old church, which is served by a retired priest.

40 Reykjanes 65°56'N 22°25'W

On the E side of the peninsula between Ísafjörður and Reykjarfjörður, S of Borgarey Island, there is a small friendly hotel, with a swimming pool fed by an historic mineral hot spring.

Approach

Approach either side of Borgarey. A small ferry landing stage at Reykjanes with two yellow beacons in line marks the approach (approx SSW). This leads between two rocks. There is 2m alongside at MLWS, but it is only suitable for a short stop, in settled weather. There is a better anchorage at Svansvík, about two miles S.

41 Svansvík 65°53'N 22°25'W

Anchor in 3–5m, gravel and weed, in a small bay overlooked by a farm. It is a 3M walk to Reykjanes along a dirt road by the shore.

42 Æðey 66°06'N 22°39'W

Æðey (Eider Island) is a rocky island on the north shore of Ísafjarðardjúp. One family lives here in the summer rearing sheep, cattle and geese and harvesting the eider-down. The farmhouse overlooks a small rocky pool half way along the eastern shore. The owner prefers yachts to anchor off, rather than attempt to enter the pool; but do not anchor over the power cable, which runs to the entrance to the pool and not as shown on the chart.

If sailing around the N of the island keep N of the islet off the N point since the passage between is obstructed by an alkathene water pipe. There is no longer the overhead power line mentioned in *NP11*. The old ferry jetty may be approached from the NW and has at least 2m on the end.

Approach

Beware an isolated rock awash at MLWS, approx 200m SE of the lighthouse. At half tide, the bay can be entered by a yacht with a draught of 2m or less. Bottom is soft mud. Anchor off in 4–5m or ask permission to use the mooring buoy. The disused ferry jetty at the N end of the island is not recommended.

Jökulfirðir

Charts 41, 46

The clutch of five fjords branching northwards off the Ísafjarðardjúp are known collectively as the Jökulfirðir (the glacier fjords) because of the Drangajökull glacier to the east. Very strong winds off the glacier can affect the anchorages in these fjords, while conditions in the Ísafjarðardjúp may be moderate.

43 Leirufjörður 66°15'N 22°35'W

Charts 41, 46

An interesting fjord giving access to the Drangajökull. The foot of the glacier is visible from the fjord and the glacier meltwater looks milky. Good walking and views of the retreating glacier. There are a few summer houses along the shore.

Approach

There is a bar across the entrance, formed by the old terminal moraine, and care is needed. Midway between the two rocks shown on *Chart 46*, there is a rocky patch with less than 2m over it. Just to the E, the following route may be used – a back transit of the spot height 656m northeast of Kjarfjall and the waterfall below, in line with the westernmost vertical cliff of the Lónanúpur headland leads through in 4m. An alternative route, used by local boats coming

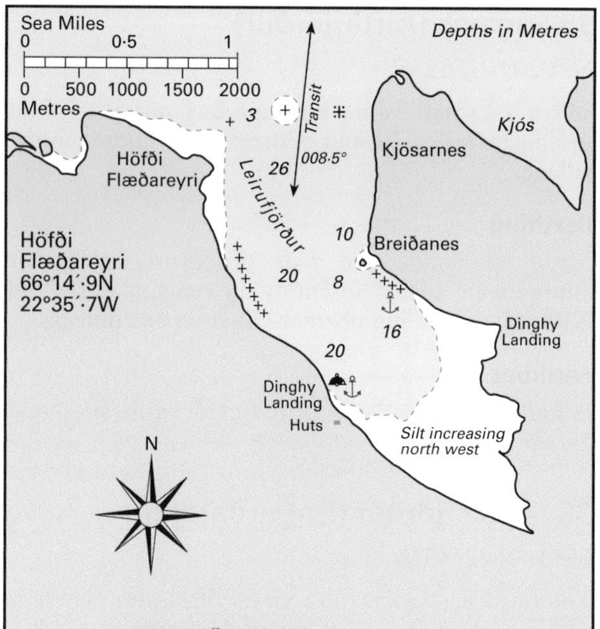

43 LEIRUFJÖRÐUR

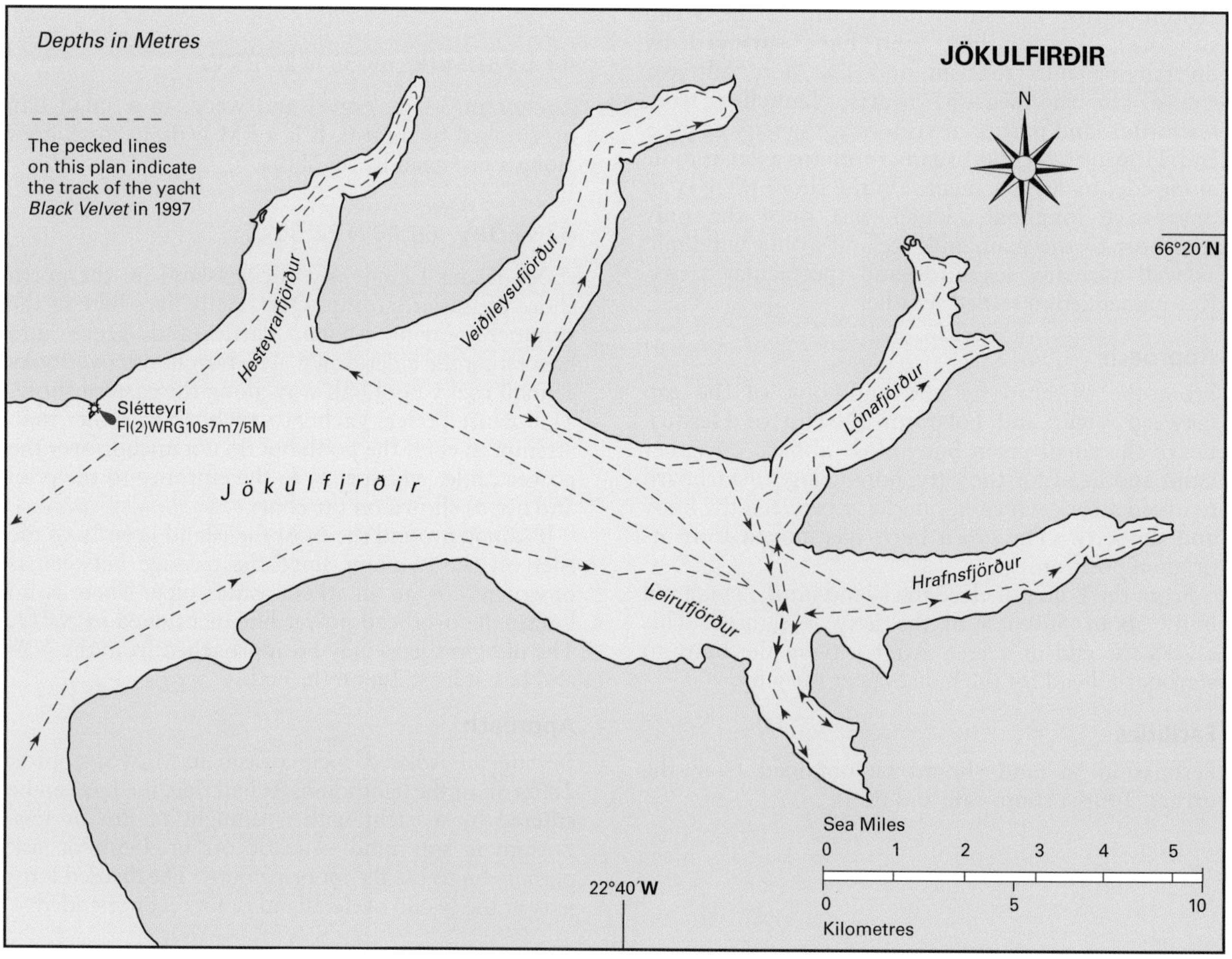

JÖKULFIRÐIR

from the W and steering 90°, is as follows: with the toe of the glacier in view, there is a low ridge visible below it and behind the ridge a summer cottage, whose red roof is just visible. When the red roof is just shut out, steer about 170° until within the fjord – depths increase rapidly to about 20m. Note that this route passes E of a reef, which projects approx. 0·1M from Höfði in an ENE direction.

Anchorage

The head is very shallow, but close to the outwash there are depths of 10–16m. Anchor either in the SW corner near the foot of the stream, where it is possible to get fairly close to the shore, or on the E side, but keep an eye out for a reef to the N of this point. For exploring the glacier the E anchorage gives the better access, but it is necessary to anchor some distance off. There are very strong gusts off the mountains in certain conditions. Holding in the deep glacial mud is satisfactory with a CQR, Bruce or similar anchor. The mooring buoys on either side of the fjord are private and should not be used.

44 Hrafnsfjörður 66°15'N 22°33'W

Apart from the entrance off Lónanúpur, no soundings or details are shown on *Chart 46*. This fjord was examined by Black Velvet in 1997. After passing Meleyri, clear, deep water was found on a line a little S of the centre of the fjord. Skipseyri may extend further to the N than indicated on *Chart 46*.

Anchorage

1. E of Skipseyri, close to the shore in 7·5m.
2. At the head of the fjord, keeping clear of the point on the N shore where submerged rocks were observed. There are two mooring buoys in 6–7m, the seaward of which might hold a medium sized cruising yacht. Good holding. There is a rescue hut on the shore.

45 Lónafjörður 66°17'N 22°32'W

No soundings are shown on *Chart 46*. Safe depths have been reported for a yacht drawing a moderate draught within 0·5M of the S shore up to the entrance to Sópandi and close to the NW shore between Borðeyri and Snoðseyri. Subject to downdraughts in strong winds.

Anchorage

1. NE of Borðeyri. The eyri may extend a bit further than shown on *Chart 46*. It is steep-to on its E side. Anchor in 6m off the root of the eyri.
2. Rangali, the NW extremity of the fjord, in 6m – shoals suddenly.
3. Miðkjós, the NE extremity of the fjord, in 6m. An outcrop of rocks cluttering part of this anchorage is quite easily identified.
4. Sópandi, the E extremity of the fjord, in 8m.

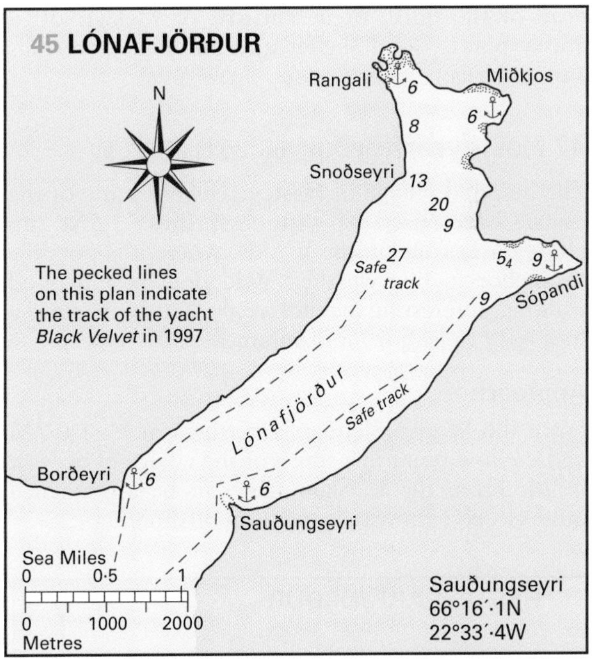

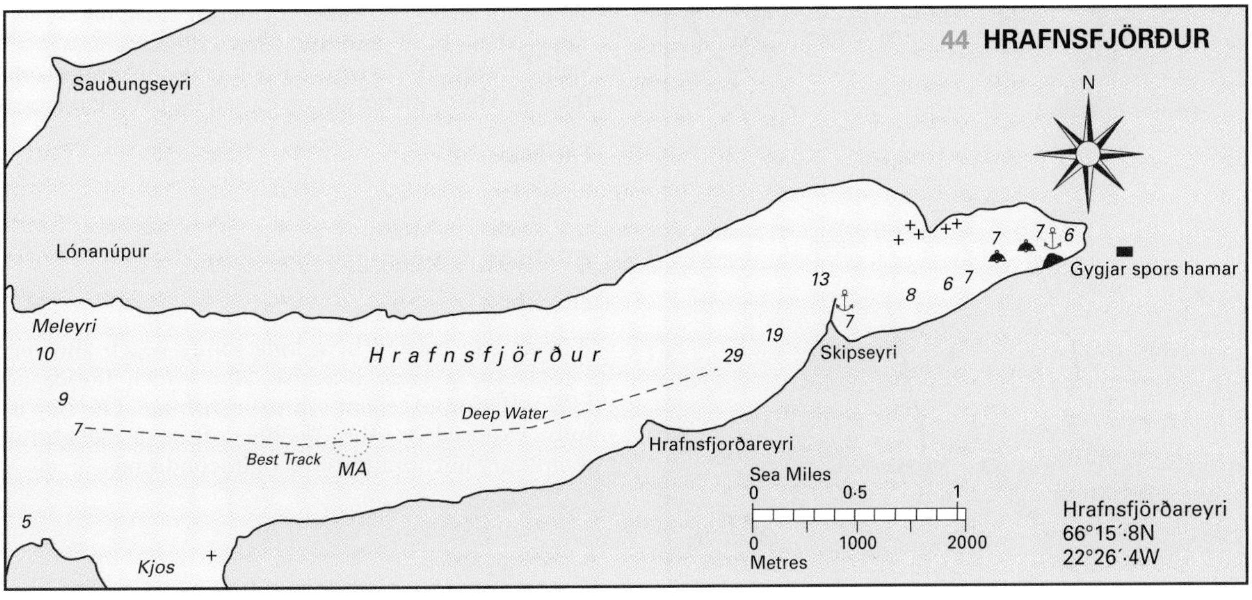

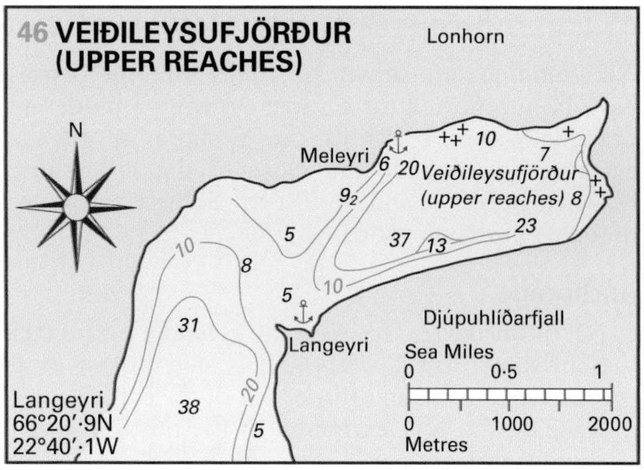

46 Veiðileysufjörður 66°21′N 22°41′W

A quieter alternative to Hesteyri, in some conditions. Anchor in 6m behind the Langeyri spit 1M from the head of the fjord, or in 9m east of Meleyri off a grassy plain. Good shelter and holding. Waterfalls and seabirds.

47 Hesteyrarfjörður 66°20′N 22°51′W

The deserted village of Hesteyri, where some of the houses are used in summer, lies 1·5M up Hesteyrarfjörður on the W side, where it is possible to anchor in fine weather. Wild flowers and good walking. Interesting derelict whale factory. There is a foot ferry to Ísafjörður in summer.

Approach

From the W give Sletteyri a berth of at least 0·2M and the low point just south of the village of at least 0·7M. From the E, Skaufanes can be approached quite closely; 3m was found 30m offshore.

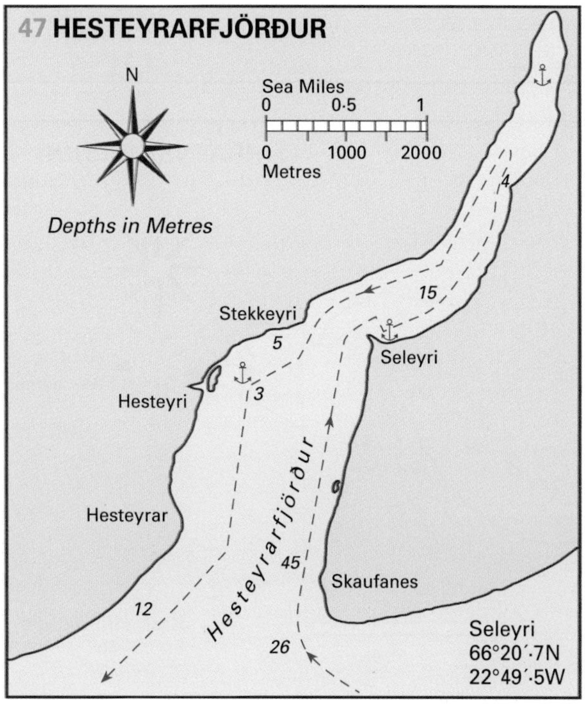

Anchorage

1. Anchor 0·2M off Hesteyri in 3–4m, fine sand, good holding but exposed.
2. NE of Seleyri with more shelter in S winds. The eyri runs about 0·1M further than shown on *Chart 46* and dries at springs. The anchorage close behind the eyri is too steep-to for swinging room and is not recommended
3. There is a good anchorage at the head of the fjord. It shoals suddenly but it is possible to anchor in 6m about 0·2M from the end. Perfect peace, with whooper swans and ducks.

Hornstrandir – west and north coasts

Charts 41, 46

Hornstrandir's rugged country and vast colonies of fulmars, guillemots, kittiwakes, puffins and razorbills have led to it being designated as a Nature Reserve.

48 Aðalvík 66°23′N 23°02′W

Charts 46

The settlement at Látravík has been abandoned, but there are some holiday houses and an airstrip built by the US during the Cold War. Excellent walking ashore – waterfalls, easily accessible snow, masses of flowers, whooper swans, golden plovers, snow buntings and red-necked phalaropes.

Approach

A yellow sand dune climbing up a cliff in the centre of the bay is conspicuous.

Anchorage

The anchorage is in the NE corner of a wide, sandy bay between Ritur and Straumnes. Anchor as close as practical to the shore in gently shelving sand. Exposed to the W and SW. Alternative anchorage at Sæból in the SE corner of the bay is sheltered from the SW. These anchorages are used by fishing boats.

Facilities

None.

49 Fljótavík 66°27′N 22°56′W

Charts 41, 46

A wide bay backed by a long sandy beach and the Fljótavatn, a large brackish lake which floods at HW, offering excellent sea trout fishing. The bay is fully exposed to the W but offers a delightful temporary anchorage in the right conditions.

Hornvík headland *Henry Clay*

Anchorage

Anchor in 5–8m sand, in the NE corner near the rescue hut (which is under the slope of Kögur – not as shown on *Chart 46*).

50 Hornvík 66°26'N 22°29'W

Charts 41, 46

An attractive anchorage with striking scenery. On the NE shore, Hornvík Farm is occupied in summer and there is a refuge hut and a campsite used by backpackers near the S anchorage; otherwise nothing but the birds and the flowers! The cliffs around have one of the largest colonies of guillemots in Iceland. Look out also for the red-necked phalarope. Good cod fishing off the headland.

Anchorage

Anchor off Höfn at the head of the bay, in the SW corner. Exposed to the N; however, just to the N of the anchor shown on *Chart 46* is a submerged reef to be avoided, but which offers some protection. In N or NE winds it is better to anchor as close in as possible under Hornvík Farm. Off Hornvík Farm, the bottom is round boulders. Trip line may be advisable.

Facilities

None.

Hornvík anchorage *Henry Clay*

AREA III

The north coast from Horn to Langanes

Charts 51, 61, 56

Hornstrandir – east coast

Charts 52

The coast running SE from Horn, known as Hornstrandir, is a mass of shoals, but in quiet weather and good visibility a yacht can be piloted fairly close inshore along this dramatic coast. Icebergs sometimes break away in summer from the East Greenland Current and drift slowly eastwards off-shore and their associated bergy bits and floes very occasionally come down onto the shore. There are numerous fjords but also numerous rocks and *NP11* goes so far as to describe the approaches to the fjords between Straumnes and Seljanes as 'encumbered with dangerous rocks and open to onshore winds'.

A large undefined magnetic anomaly has been reported 4M north of Horn.

51 Ingólfsfjörður (Hornstrandir)

66°02'N 21°38'W

Charts 52, 53

Described by the *NP11* as 'the westernmost safe shelter on the north coast of Iceland'. It is a deep, narrow fjord tucked away behind Krossnesfjall. There is good shelter, but the place is almost deserted.

Approach

Identify the light on Selsker (Mo(N)30s, Racon (O)) and give a good berth to the long line of rocks and islets running 1M NNW from Munaðarnes. Once round this obstruction, the fjord is clear. Beware of possible katabatic winds from the Drangajökull ice cap.

Berthing

Anchor on the E shore, just S of the derelict factory, in 10–13m. The quays and jetties are in ruins and unusable.

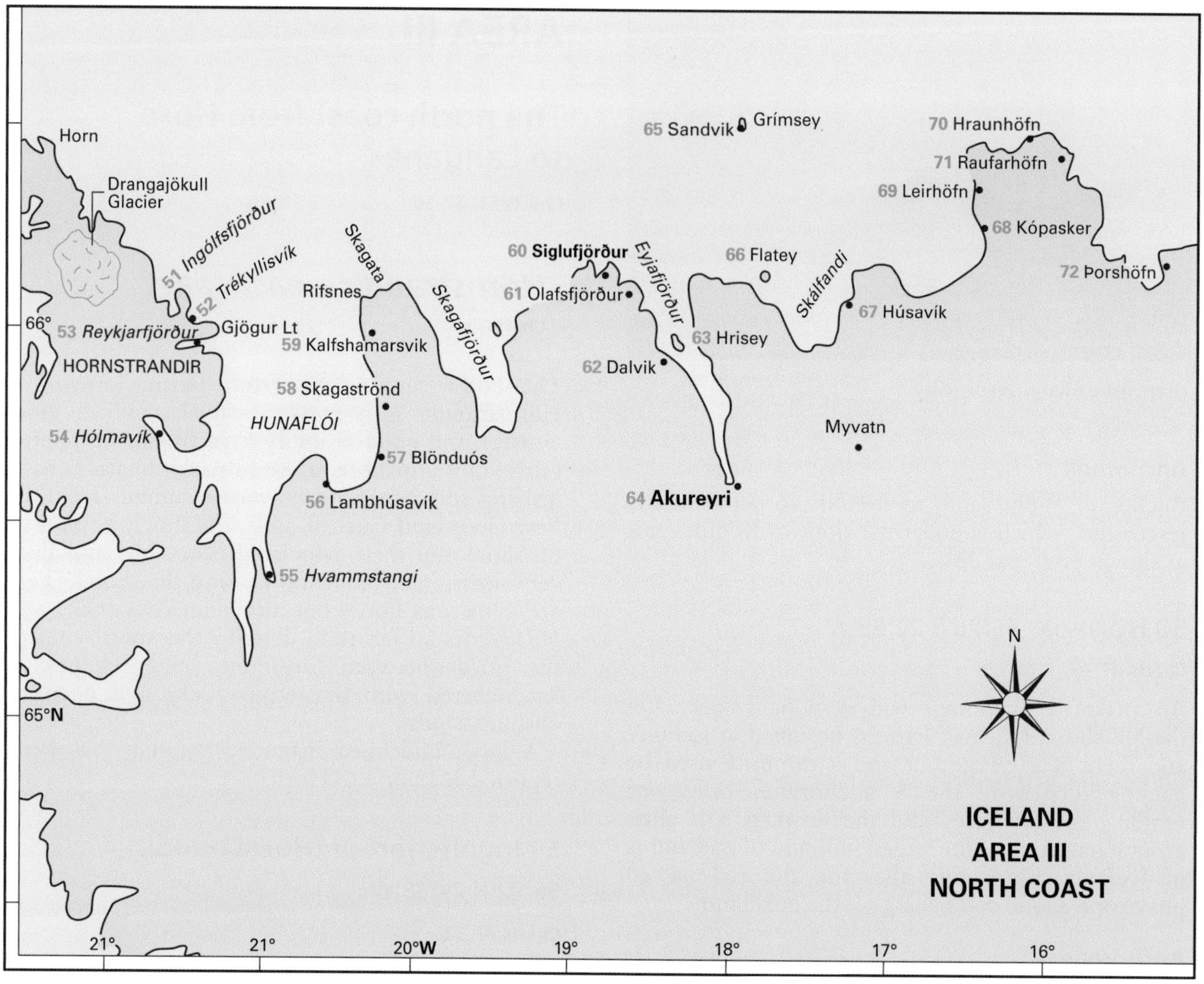

Húnaflói

Charts 51

Húnaflói is a wide bay extending 50M to the SE of the Hornstrandir and to the W of the Skagi peninsula and is fully described in *NP11 6.95 et seq.* There are few good harbours and it lies off the circumnavigation route; however, in suitable weather it would be well worth exploring. The area is noted for its agriculture, in particular horse breeding, as well as excellent salmon rivers.

52 Trékyllisvík 66°02'N 21°30'W

Charts 52, 53

Trekyllisvík is an open bay 4M northwest of Gjogur. There is an anchorage amongst islets SW of Árnesey, the island off Árnes. The island is covered with hundreds of scarecrows and is a dense ternery with phalaropes and redshanks.

Approach

A spit, with a shoal patch at its N end, extends 1·5M north from Reykjaneshyrna. Otherwise the approach to the bay is straightforward.

Anchorage

To approach the anchorage SW of Árnesey, clear the shoal 0·2M N of the island and sound in between the islets to the anchor symbol on old *Chart 53*. Anchor in 8m with the big rock bearing 100°, 200m. It is exposed to the NE.

There is an attractive anchorage with much better shelter in Norðurfjörður, the NW corner of the bay. Either anchor at the head of the fjord, or tucked in behind the stone jetty at Krossnes.

Facilities

Farm and church. Geothermal pool. No shops.

53 Reykjarfjörður 65°58'N 21°22'W

Charts 53

A deep fjord 5M long, 4M S of Trékyllisvík, offering good protection. Near the head, there is a former herring oil factory and the friendly Hótel Djúpavík.

Approach

The fjord is entered to the S of Gjögur Lt – Fl(4)WRG.30s – on the Reykjanes Peninsula. Detatched reefs lie 2M E of the Lt and are covered by the green sector, but the approach from the ESE is clean.

Berthing

Either anchor in sand just off the hotel, avoiding the ruins of the old wooden jetties in front of the factory, or go around into the next bay to the W, where better protection may be had close in. There is a small private jetty about 200m E of the hotel with 2m alongside, which might be used with permission.

Facilities

Showers and good meals at the hotel. The old factory is being developed as a small herring museum.

54 Hólmavík 65°42'N 21°41'W

Charts 53, 54

A small fishing harbour lying 7M up the broad Steingrímsfjörður, with easy access.

Approach

Shoals lie to the NE of Grímsey Lt to be avoided, thereafter the fjord is 2M wide and clean. The harbour entrance faces SE and note that rocks extend a short distance from the rubble breakwater on the E side.

Berthing

Berth on the S quay. Note that the small boat float is shoal.

Facilities

Bar and restaurants in the old village by the harbour. Supermarket, bank with ATM and petrol station 10 minute walk up the hill, in a new development. Contact the harbourmaster for diesel and water.

55 Hvammstangi 65°24'N 20°57'W

Charts 54

Small harbour on the E side of Miðfjörður, in an attractive agricultural area, with very easy access.

Berthing

The harbour entrance faces SW. Berth alongside the S quay.

Facilities

Small supermarket with Vin Búð liquor store. Diesel and water available.

56 Lambhúsavík 65°37'N 20°37'W

In suitable weather there is an attractive anchorage in the SW corner of Húnafjörður, 8M WSW of Blönduós (*NP11*). It is reported that, at the head of the fjord, the mouths of the rivers have silted up due to hydro' schemes and can not now be entered.

57 Blönduós 65°40'N 20°18'W

Charts 53

An important town and centre for the horse breeding area, as well a base for salmon fishermen; the nearby Laxá river reputedly the best in Iceland. There is a large hotel, banks, supermarket, etc; however the very small harbour is some distance from the town and poorly protected. Unless there are particular reasons for visiting by yacht, it is better to berth at Skagaströnd, 10M to the N and visit by road.

58 Skagaströnd 65°49'N 20°20'W

Charts 53, 55, 518

Previously known as Höfðakaupstaður; it is a developing port on the W side of the Skagi peninsula. Useful if exploring Húnaflói.

Approach

Straightforward. Oil tanks on the headland are conspicuous.

Berthing

As available.

Facilities

Fuel and water at quays. The usual facilities of a small fishing port.

59 Kálfshamarsvík 66°01'N 20°26'W

Tide 0·7, 1·3 **Charts** 55

A convenient passage anchorage on the W side of the Skagi peninsula, 5M S of Rifsnes.

There is a columnar basalt cave below the lighthouse with remarkably regular formations. In the hills to the E of the road are ptarmigan, snow bunting and golden plovers and the lake close by has all sorts of waders.

Navigation

If rounding Skagi from the E, give the nasty shoals off Rifsnes a wide berth. Otherwise straightforward.

Berthing

Anchor in the bay SE of the lighthouse. The bottom is sand with kelp, which was reported in 2006 to be sparse enough to give good holding. No facilities.

60 Siglufjörður 66°09'N 18°54'W

Tide 0·6, 1·3 **Charts** 51, 57, 522

Its strategic position and easy access makes this an excellent stop on passage. It was once the 'herring capital of the world', but since the collapse of herring stocks in 1967, it has lost its importance. A visit to the Herring Museum (Síldarminjasafn) is fascinating and strongly recommended.

Siglufjörður harbour *Henry Clay*

Siglufjörður herring industry museum *Henry Clay*

The harbour is said to be liable to sudden squalls off the mountains. It is an important ski centre in the spring.

Approach

The approach is straightforward, but the Helluboðar reefs projecting 1M NW of Siglunes should be given a wide berth.

Berthing

There is a new small boat harbour in the NW corner of the main harbour. Visiting yachts should berth on the outside of the first pontoon in 4m.

Facilities

Water and diesel are available close to the berth. WC and showers 100m N of the berth. Good shops, post office, banks and swimming pool. Washing machine and drier in the shower/WC building. Key from the Herring Museum office – small charge. Folk Music Centre worth a visit.

Eyjafjörður

Charts 57

This magnificent fjord penetrates 30M south to the busy port of Akureyri. The facilities in the port for visiting yachts are not good and unless there are particular reasons for sailing down the long fjord – often against the wind – it is better to stop at Ólafsfjördur, or preferably Dalvík and go to Akureyri by road.

61 Ólafsfjörður (Eyjafjörður)

66°05′N 18°39′W

Tide 0·6, 1·3 **Charts** 57

Ólafsfjörður is a small town at the head of a fjord of the same name, on the W side of Eyjafjörður. The town is in an attractive setting and is of some antiquity. It is worth visiting.

Approach

Straightforward, but the E side in the approach is shallow near the harbour.

Berthing

In 5m in the Vesturhöfn, the basin on W side of harbour. The wooden quays in the SE corner offer the best chance of a quiet berth. The sheet-piled, tyre-fendered quays on the E side of the harbour are used by cargo vessels and large fishing boats.

Facilities

As expected from a small town in Iceland; swimming pool. The bird museum is worth a visit.

62 Dalvík (Eyjafjörður)

65°58′N 18°31′W

Tide 0·6, 1·3 **Charts** 57

An artificial harbour 8M down Eyjafjörður, on the W side, with excellent protection, thanks to a new breakwater N of the harbour entrance. Helgi the Lean, the first settler, who claimed ownership of the whole of Eyjafjörður, spent his first winter here in around AD880. Straightforward approach.

Berthing

Berth alongside the SE mole. Do not use the pier in the middle, except for fuel. The bottom shoals very quickly to <1m beyond the fuel berth – the deeper water is on the E side.

Facilities

Supermarket, good DIY shop, restaurants etc. Fuel arranged through Olis Garage on the outskirts of the town. Superb open-air swimming pool, 15 minutes'

Dalvík Harbour and visiting yachts *Henry Clay*

walk. If you are there in January, you could lie in a 40°C 'hot pot' and watch the skiers on the hill under floodlights! Even in September it is pretty scenic with snow on the hills down to 500m. Two buses a day to Akureyri (50 minutes).

63 Hrísey (Eyjafjörður)

65°59'N 18°24'W

Charts 57

An attractive small island E of Dalvik in the mouth of Eyjafjörður. Research farm with herd of Galloway cattle. Bird Sanctuary.

Navigation

The harbour is at S end of the island. The approach is straightforward.

Berthing

For a short stay berth alongside a fishing boat on the W side of the harbour; however, watch the depth, as it may be shallow. Alternatively berth in 5m alongside the E or S wall.

Facilities

Shop, café, post office, small swimming pool.

Hrísey *Henry Clay*

Hrísey bird sanctuary *Henry Clay*

Akureyri *Henry Clay*

64 Akureyri (Eyjafjörður)

65°41'N 18°05'W

Tide 0·6, 1·3 **Charts** 57, 530

Akureyri is the most important port and trading centre in the N of Iceland. It lies in an attractive, fertile agricultural area, surrounded by striking mountains and is an important ski centre in the spring. The modern cathedral has a fine stained glass window, made in part from glass obtained from Coventry Cathedral.

Excursions can be made to Myvatn, which is one of the national beauty spots and a paradise for birdwatchers.

Approach

The harbour is 30M from the open sea, at the head of Eyjafjörður. The fjord is approximately 2M wide over much of its length and there are few dangers.

Berthing

Visiting yachts should sail past the main commercial docks into the Pollurinn. The recommended berth is on a floating pontoon on the N side of the Torfunesbryggja. There are no facilities there, but it is close to the post office, banks and the very helpful tourist office.

Facilities

All stores available. Ship repair facilities. Airport. Hotels. Excellent heated swimming pool, with hot showers, etc., to the W of the cathedral. Well-equipped hospital.

Grímsey

65 Sandvík 66°32'N 18°02'W

Tide 0·6, 1·2 **Charts** 56, 62

A rather barren but historically interesting island, with a lively fishing population. Its main claim to fame is its position on the Arctic Circle as well as its inhabitants' traditional skill at chess. In 1857 an American named Daniel Willard Fiske, the reigning chess champion of the United States, glimpsed Grímsey as he passed in a steamship and he decided to take its local population under his wing, although he never visited the island. He sent a gift of 11 marble chess sets, one for each of the farms on the island, and this was followed by a gift of money to finance the island's first school and library and a generous bequest in his will. Sadly, Grímsey is no longer a chess centre, but a number of the male islanders sport the name Willard. The pillar at the end of the airstrip claims to mark the Arctic Circle, but the pillar is in fact about half a mile south of it. The tiny wooden church is well worth a visit, as is the N tip of the island with its puffins, terns, golden plovers and an extraordinary number of kittiwakes on the E cliffs. Little auks are said to breed among the boulders.

Approach

There are no dangers in the approach to Sandvík from the SW.

Grímsey Harbour *Ed Wheeler*

Grímsey - playing chess *Henry Clay*

Flatey *Henry Clay*

Berthing

The breakwater at Sandvík has been extended and concreted to form a jetty, with a least depth of 4m alongside, on the E face. This gives protection from the WNW and probably around to winds from WSW. The inner harbour is completely protected, but full of small fishing boats; however, a berth could no doubt be found in bad weather from the southwest.

Facilities

Water and diesel on the quay, by arrangement with the fishermen. There is a shop, post office and the guesthouse at the airstrip provides simple meals and showers. Daily flights to Akureyri.

66 Flatey 66°09'N 17°51'W

Tide 0·6, 1·2 **Charts** 62

An abandoned island with about 30 summer cottages, community hall, church and a lighthouse. Meadow hay and wild flowers. Highly recommended. The quay on the south side of the island is useable in settled weather. 200m to the E is the entrance to a small inner pool with leading marks giving at least 3m.

There is about 2m MLWS at the wooden quay inside.

Berthing

In 2006 the inner harbour was choked with weed and there was <1m alongside the wooden quay on the S side, however it was possible to lie in about 2m at the end of the new floating pontoon. Dredging is carried out, once in a while; but it is wise to anchor off, or lie alongside the stone jetty outside, to check the situation before entering.

67 Húsavík 66°03'N 17°21'W

Tide 0·6, 1·2 **Charts** 62, 534

A prosperous town with a new inner harbour and Iceland's leading whale-watching centre, with four large wooden ex-fishing boats operating during the season. It is a good starting point for a visit by car or bus to Myvatn and the spectacular Dettifoss waterfall.

Approach

The approach is straightforward, but if coming from Tjörnes, note that Lundeyjarbreki is a good mile and a half NW of Lundey, a small island 41m high with a lighthouse (Fl.5s).

Berthing

As available in the inner harbour.

Facilities

Water is available on the quays and fuel on the end of the central pier (contact the operator through the harbourmaster to arrange a time). Excellent whale museum, art gallery and maritime museum. Supermarkets, bank, post office, swimming pool and cinema. This is an active fishing port and also a busy tourist centre.

Húsavík *Henry Clay*

Húsavík sailing vessels *Henry Clay*

68 Kópasker 66°18'N 16°27'W

Tide 0·5, 1·1 **Charts** 62

A small fishing village. It is more sheltered than it may appear to be at first sight and has been used to shelter from a SE–NW Force 9–10. However, there is very little room and it is somewhat exposed.

Approach

A reef extends 300m W of the village, NW of the harbour. There is a shoal patch (1·6m) 100m S of the breakwater, with a port-hand buoy (Q.R) inshore of it, marking the deeper passage to the quay. There are three sets of leading marks. The first (068° 2F.R) lead clear S of the shallows. The second (006° 2F.G) around the buoy and the third (331° 2F.R) to the quay.

Berthing

Berth on the E side of the main pier, where there is >2·5m alongside, as far as the white oil tank. For better shelter, the small inner harbour is now protected by a breakwater running W-E from the main breakwater and has a pontoon for small craft. Towards the end of the main pier on the W side, there are depths of 3m alongside and >2m on the E side of the pontoon near the S end – the W side is shallow.

Leirhöfn skerries *Henry Clay*

Facilities

Water and electricity are available on the pier. Small supermarket, service station, bank and post office.

69 Leirhöfn 66°25'N 16°30'W

Charts 62

This ancient anchorage behind a protecting screen of reefs, which cover at HW, was once a hive of activity with many houses around the bay. Now there are only one or two farms left. Leirhöfn is of interest, because it has been in use since Viking times. This has proved to be an excellent anchorage in a SE Force 5 gusting 6 but would not have been possible without the plan in the Leiðsögubók.

Approach

It would be unwise to attempt entry, except in clear visibility, an offshore wind and with no sea running. Approaching from the W, just N of Lat 66°27'N, a 'beacon' consisting of a large fuel tank painted yellow lies on the beach, just N of Kílsnes and leads on to the first leading line. The route is clearly shown on page 162 of the Leiðsögubók, but it takes a vessel to within 'a biscuit toss' of the beach, before passing over a 'bridge', with barely a foot under the keel, before entering the pool. The stone beacons (varða) are well maintained and reasonably clear.

Berthing

Anchor in 3m in the SW corner.

70 Hraunhöfn 66°32'N 16°02'W

Charts 62, 63

This ancient Viking anchorage lies just SW of Hraunhafnartangi – light Mo(N)WR.30s. This is the northernmost point of Iceland and just S of the Arctic Circle. Protected from the NE through S to WSW and to a certain extent from swell by a shallow bar, which runs SW from the Lt Ho across the bay.

Approach

Approach from the NW. Care is needed entering the bay, but there appears to be about 3m over the bar, which lies between the Lt Ho and the 3·9m sounding on the chart. Depths increase inside the bay.

Berthing

Anchor in 7m close to the shore S of the Lt Ho, good holding.

Remarks

The area appears to be deserted, but the coast road runs close S of the anchorage and it is, no doubt, busy at the Summer Solstice.

71 Raufarhöfn 66°27'N 15°56'W

Tide 0·6, 1·3 **Charts** 63, 610

The most northerly port on the mainland of Iceland, 3M south of the Arctic Circle, with a small harbour which has an inner basin providing excellent shelter. Yachts crews visiting in summer over the years have reported air temperatures between zero and 23°C.

The local delicacy is lake trout smoked over smouldering sheep manure, which is highly recommended!

Navigation

The coastline is very low to the N of Melrakkanes Point, but the mountains on the W side of the peninsula can be seen. Enter, leaving Baka green buoy (Fl.G.3s), to stbd. This is 0·3M S of Raufarhöfn light (Fl(3)WRG.20s).

Berthing

The best berth is on the pontoon in the small boat harbour, on the starboard side opposite the church and the lifeboat. Alternatively, it may be possible to lie alongside the quay in front of the fish factory, on the other side of the harbour.

Facilities

Water on the pier. Petrol and diesel obtainable. Hotels, bank, supermarket, post office and swimming pool. Showers and meals are available in the Hótel Norðurljós.

72 Þorshöfn 66°12'N 15°20'W

Charts 63, 611

This small harbour is somewhat off the beaten track, but is interesting because it is the only harbour in Iceland processing clams for export to the US. The harbour is being extended and dredged. Friendly people. Good walking country.

Approach

Approaching from the W, the leading line (036°, Oc.G.5s) brings you onto the main pier. The large area to starboard, which is protected by a new breakwater on the S side, was shallow; but dredging will improve and deepen the small boat 'marina'.

Facilities

Water and diesel on the dock. Restaurant and bar close by. Shops. There is a very nice covered swimming pool about 10 minutes up the road.

Raufarhöfn harbour *Ed Wheeler*

Raufarhöfn *Henry Clay*

3. ICELAND

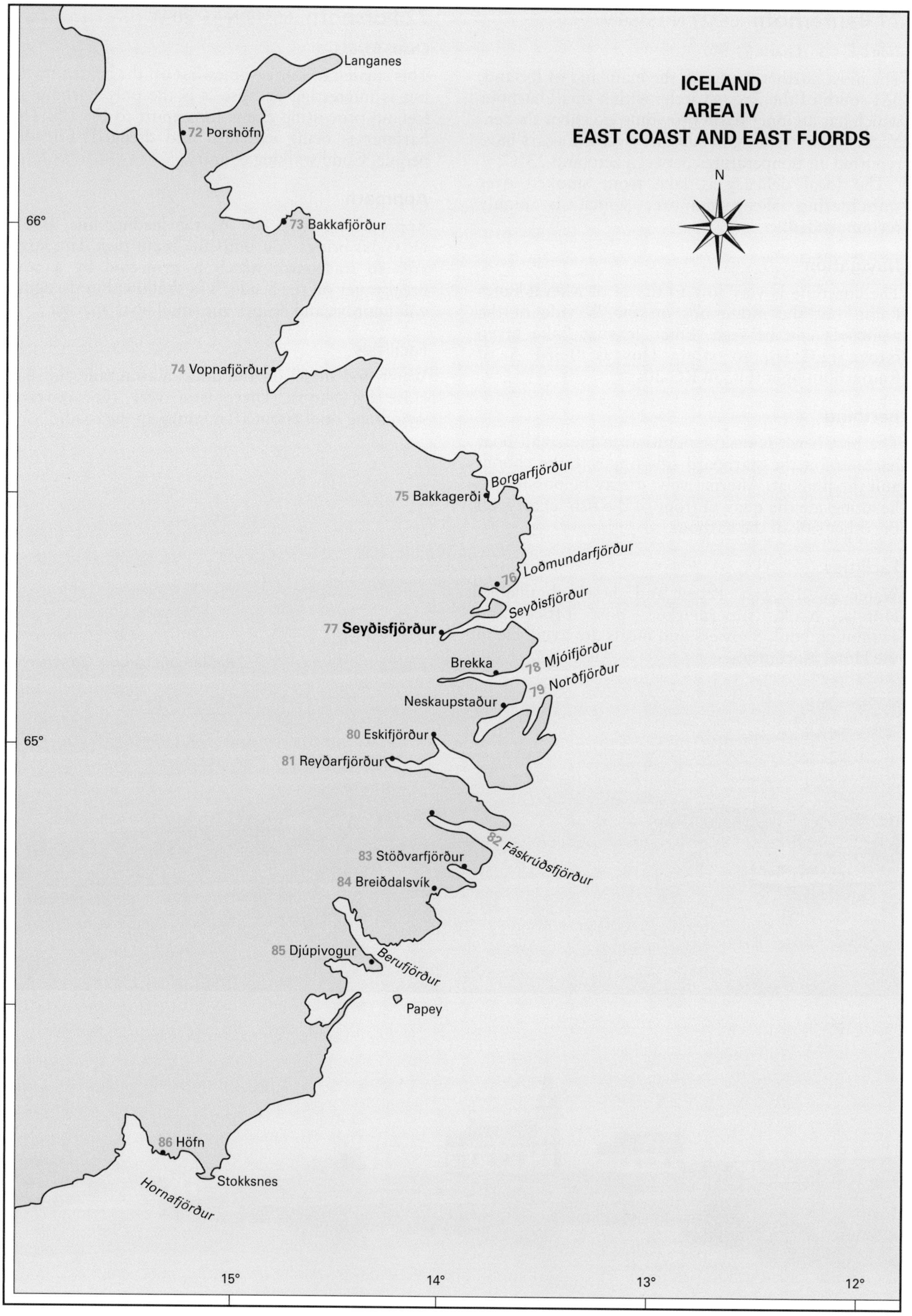
ICELAND
AREA IV
EAST COAST AND EAST FJORDS
N
Langanes
72 Þorshöfn
66°
73 Bakkafjörður
74 Vopnafjörður
Borgarfjörður
75 Bakkagerði
76 Loðmundarfjörður
Seyðisfjörður
77 Seyðisfjörður
Brekka
78 Mjóifjörður
79 Norðfjörður
Neskaupstaður
65°
80 Eskifjörður
81 Reyðarfjörður
82 Fáskrúðsfjörður
83 Stöðvarfjörður
84 Breiðdalsvík
85 Djúpivogur
Berufjörður
Papey
86 Höfn
Stokksnes
Hornafjörður
15°
14°
13°
12°

AREA IV

The east coast and the east fjords from Langanes to Hornafjörður

Charts 63, 71, 72, 73, 74, 82

Langanes

66°23′N 14°32′W
Charts 63

Langanes is the NE tip of Iceland and has a poor reputation because of fogs and the Langanesröst (overfalls), which may extend far out to sea. It deserves respect (see *NP11*); however, it is steep-to, with no off-lying dangers and if rounded close in at slack water seldom poses a problem in settled weather. On *Chart 63*, there are three or four anchorages in Bakkaflói, which would offer temporary shelter in off-shore winds – look for the anchor symbol.

Höfn (Bakkafjörður) entrance *Henry Clay*

73 Bakkafjörður 66°02′N 14°50′W

Charts 72

Bakkafjörður is an open bay, exposed to the N, but could be of interest in settled weather. There is an exposed jetty at Höfn on the E shore. Following further improvements, the small fishing harbour, 1M SSW of the village of Höfn, is now very snug and well protected. The village has a small shop, post office and bank, all in the same building, with limited opening hours and a 20 minute walk from the dinghy landing.

Berthing

There is a substantial wooden quay on the N side of the harbour with >2m alongside. This is used for unloading fish, but it should be possible to lie alongside with permission.

Left Langanes *Henry Clay*
Below Höfn (Bakkafjörður) harbour *Henry Clay*

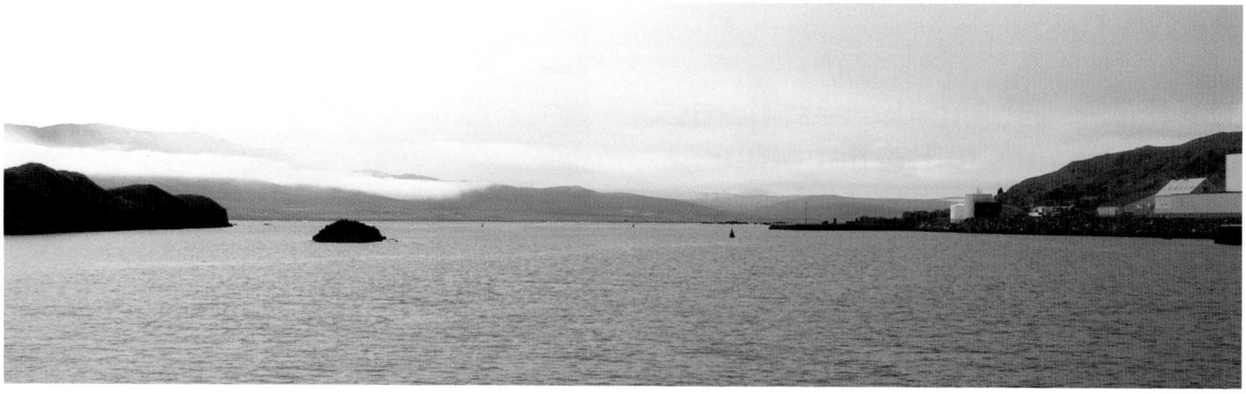

Vopnafjörður from the north *Henry Clay*

74 Vopnafjörður 65°45'N 14°49'W

Tide 0·6, 1·2 **Charts** 72, 613

Vopnafjörður is the only sheltered harbour between Seyðisfjörður and Þorshöfn (W of the Langanes headland), 70M to the N. The harbour is near the head of the fjord, on the W side, behind a barrier of skerries. Its main claim to fame, perhaps, is that it has bred two Miss Worlds!

Approach

The gap between Miðhólmi and Skiphólmi has been closed by a substantial breakwater (see *Chart 613*). Approach about half a mile S of Skiphólmi and enter on the first leading line bearing 323° Occ.G.5s.

The second leading line bears 10°30' Occ.R.5s and passes between two port and starboard lit buoys into the harbour.

The harbour entrance is at first difficult to make out; but it should be clear with the new harbour plan (*Chart 613*) The leading line (341·5° Oc.G.6s) leads between two skerries marked by pole beacons, Krossvikurlending (which covers) to port (Fl.R.3s) and Húkkasker to starboard (Fl.G.3s). Both pole beacons are small and hard to see. The leading line should be visible over the end of the main quay (Ásgarður), which is at the N end of the town.

Berthing

There is a new small boat harbour to the N of the Ásgarður, but it is full of local boats. The best berth for a yacht is at the inner end of the Ásgarður, on the N side. This is a substantial wooden quay with >3m MLWS alongside and clear of the big ships.

Facilities

Fuel and water is available on the quay. The hotel and telephone are near the harbour. Good supermarket.

75 Bakkagerði (Borgarfjörður)

65°32'N 13°48'W

Tide 0·7, 1·4 **Charts** 72

Bakkagerði village is at the head of Borgarfjörður, backed by a magnificant panorama of mountains. It is, however, notorious for squalls coming off the mountains and is open to the N.

Berthing

The quay is rather exposed and only suitable for a yacht in settled weather. Approach until the quay bears just S of W, then turn towards it. Half way along the E side of the fjord, a small boat harbour has been constructed under Hafnarhólmi, which is connected to the shore by a causeway. It is crowded and too small to be useful for yachts and is some distance from the village.

In E to SE winds, good anchorage can be found close in, in the SE corner, with some protection from NE, good holding.

It is reported that the small boat harbour under Hafnarhólmi has been dredged to 3m and that there is usually room for a 12m yacht to lie on the inside of the S pier.

Facilities

Restaurant, supermarket, diesel from the service station. There is an interesting turf house.

76 Loðmundarfjörður 65°23'N 13°46'W

Tide 0·6, 1·4 **Charts** 73, 712

A spectacular unspoilt anchorage just N of Seydisfjordur, ¾M wide and 3M long. Open to the E; sheltered from other directions by mountains. Subject to strong katabatic winds funnelling down the mountainsides, but this effect is lessened by the width of the fjord. Subject to swell; use in fairly settled weather but not with winds from NE to SE. There are no facilities.

Approach

No outlying dangers; sides are reasonably steep-to.

Anchorage

Anchor at the head of the fjord, in the middle (to reduce wind funnelling): good holding, in 5–15m of (volcanic) sand.

77 Seyðisfjörður 65°16'N 14°00'W

Tide 0·6, 1·4 **Charts** 73, 712

An important port and the main passenger and car ferry terminal with connections to Europe. The *Norröna*, the car ferry that plies between Faroe and Denmark, now runs throughout the year and calls once a week on Thursdays. The big new ferry terminal has been completed, but this does not affect yachts. The approach up the fjord is spectacular. It is undoubtedly the best first port of call for a yacht arriving on the E coast, with good shops and good facilities for boat and crew.

Approach

Seyðisfjörður harbour can be approached under virtually any conditions, including dense fog – the sides of the 8M long fjord are steep-to and show up well on radar. The only off-shore danger is Hvalbakur (64°36'N 13°17'W), which is 40M SSE.

Berthing

Contact the Harbourmaster by phone or on VHF Ch 12 for advice on the best berth. If the harbourmaster is not in his office, he may be contacted by telephone (✆ 470 2360/ 8621424).

Fuel is now available about 400m NE, on the Shellbryggja (✆ 840 3172), close to the Harbourmaster's office. Originally called the Porshammarbryggja, it is named the Essobryggja on *Chart 712* and has fuel available. Do not go beyond the small boat harbour as the fjord shoals, and do not approach the dredged channel to the ferry quay, which is used by the *Norröna*.

Formalities

If this is the first port of call, report to customs.

Facilities

Water on the quays. Fuel is available from a pump on the Essobryggja (ask at the petrol station just down the road). Adequate shopping with two supermarkets, bank, post office, swimming pool and hotel. Charts may be obtained from the bookshop, but they only hold a limited stock. Cars can be hired at the petrol station. The nearest airport is at Egilsstaðir, where there is a huge supermarket. A bus runs twice daily from the information office at the ferry terminal. The shipyard and chandlery were closed in 2003. There is Internet access at the Skaftafell Café, two minute walk from the quays.

78 Mjóifjörður 65°12'N 13°51'W

Charts 73

Brekka is a small village on the N shore of this most spectacular fjord, which has sadly been taken over by a large industrial fish farming operation. This occupies virtually the whole width of the fjord. It is difficult to recommend this harbour at present.

Berthing

At Brekka there is a small T-shaped wooden jetty to the E of the church; however, it is now in continual use by the fish farm. It seems likely that the harbour will be developed in the future, so it may be worth finding out the latest situation before going there.

79 Norðfjörður 65°09'N 13°41'W

Tide 0·7, 1·5 **Charts** 73, 714

The harbour for Neskaupstaður, which is the largest community on the E coast and an important fishing centre, is now known as Norðfjörður. Major harbour works have been completed at the end of the fjord to accommodate larger vessels, together with a substantial breakwater. There is excellent protection in the small boat harbour, however this is more than a mile from the town.

Approach

Straightforward. In poor visibility, note that Norðfjarðarhorn is relatively low (250m rising to 600m inland) but both sides of Mjóifjörður are relatively high (800–1000m).

Berthing

In calm conditions it is possible to lie on the wooden 'Old Town Quay' either on the inside (shoal) or on the outside; but note that the facing boards do not reach the water at LW. Otherwise sail down to the new harbour.

Facilities

There is a fuel jetty by the petrol station close to the town. This is approachable at HW, but there is only 1m alongside at MLWS. All stores. Customs, hospital, post office and swimming pool within ¼M of quays. Bus to Egilsstaðir.

80 Eskifjörður 65°04'N 14°01'W

Tide 0·5, 1·3 **Charts** 73, 715, 716

Eskifjörður leads N from the outer part of Reyðarfjörður, which is a highly spectacular fjord surrounded by snow-capped ridges and is the largest fjord on the east coast. Very strong winds can blow from these ridges and peaks. Eskifjörður is the main fishing and container port, but is not very satisfactory for a visiting yacht; however, there are a number of suitable anchorages nearby in Reyðarfjörður (No.81).

Approach

The islet of Skrúður on the S side of the entrance to the fjord is an excellent landmark, but if approaching from the SE should be given a berth of at least 2M. Snæfugl (757m) is the left-hand of two prominent peaks seen to the N of Reyðarfjörður, when approaching from the SE.

Berthing

In Eskifjörður the only sheltered berth is in a small basin at the W end of the main container port. The tyre walls here have only a single row of tyres and it is possible to get trapped as the tide rises. An alternative berth is on the quays at the head of the fjord but these are in frequent use by ships and fishing boats.

Facilities

Eskifjörður has all basic facilities. However, the main shopping centre for the area is 20km away. Showers at the swimming pool.

81 Reyðarfjörður 65°02'N 14°00'W

Charts 73, 716

From the entrance to Eskifjörður, Reyðarfjörður leads off to the W, where there are two or three useful anchorages. At the head of the fjord, there is a small harbour at Búðareyri (now known as Reyðarfjörður). A new aluminium smelter plant was completed in 2008, which is 2M E of Búðareyri on the N shore, with its own dedicated hydro-electric plant and deep-water quays.

Anchorage

1. Stórhólmi. A beautiful anchorage behind the islands to SW of Hólmanes. Anchor, as depth and wind dictate, either side of Leiðarhöfdi. Open to fetch across the fjord. Nature reserve ashore.
2. It is possible to anchor, in offshore winds out of the swell, almost anywhere along the shore to the W of Grima Lt, up to and including the small cove behind Biskupshöfdi.

Facilities

The new aluminium smelter has had a profound affect on this hitherto sleepy place and facilities are changing.

82 Fáskrúðsfjörður 64°55'N 14°00'W

Tide 0·7, 1·7 **Charts** 73, 717

A very small fishing harbour. The village in the northwest corner of the Fáskrúðsfjörður fjord is Búðir.

Navigation

When making a landfall in this area, the easiest point to identify is the islet of Skrúður, at the northern approach of Fáskrúðsfjörður.

Berthing

Near the end of the fuel berth as convenient. All the quays are protected by large tyres which make mooring alongside difficult. Not recommended.

Facilities

Water and fuel available. Stores as expected from a small village, plus barber and restaurant. Bus to Egilsstaðir daily.

83 Stöðvarfjörður 64°50'N 13°54'W

Charts 73

A lively fishing port with a very sheltered harbour on the N shore of the fjord.

Navigation

Straightforward.

Berthing

The large outer harbour is used by the fishing fleet. The smaller breakwater provides a well sheltered but uncomfortable berth alongside the tyres on the quay. It is possible to anchor off, just to the W of the harbour, but it can be rather rolly.

Facilities

As usual for a fishing harbour. Shop (open late at night), café and swimming pool.

84 Breiðdalsvík 64°47'N 14°00'W

Charts 73

This is a delightful harbour, in a broad valley, better protected and easier to approach than first appearances would suggest. Seas entering the bay are broken up by the Rifsker reef on the N side and the skerries and islets around Hafnarey on the S side. The harbour itself is tucked in behind the Selnes peninsula.

Approach

The best approach is directly from seaward, a mile S of the dangerous Lárungar reef. Enter the bay on a bearing of 306°, aiming at the Selnes light (Fl.WRG.8s). It is possible in good visibility and reasonable conditions to follow the inshore route from just off Kambanes shown in the Leiðsögubók pilot book. Iðusker islets and the beacon on the end of the Rifsker are conspicuous.

Berthing

A new L-shaped quay has been constructed to provide a landing for larger fishing boats and is best avoided. The inside face of the old wooden quay provides a safe berth for yachts up to 35ft with about 3m alongside at MLWS.

There is a traditional anchorage under Hafnarey, which might be worth investigating under suitable conditions.

Facilities

Very pleasant village, with shop, small restaurant and bar. New small swimming pool with showers, 'hot pot', etc. Great walking country.

85 Djúpivogur (Berufjörður)

64°40'N 14°17'W

Tide 1·6, 2·0 **Charts** 74, 720

A well sheltered natural harbour with all modern facilities. This fjord is the most southerly on the E Coast with comparatively easy access. Búlandsnes is a low peninsula, very Scottish looking and attractive for walking.

Approach

Papey and its off-lying rocks and shoals should be left to the W and S. Papey is not a good radar target in poor visibility. Hvalbakur (64°36'N 13°17'W) is an isolated, dangerous rock with radar reflector and lies about 20M E of Papey. Karlsstaðatangi lighthouse (Fl(2)WRG.10s) on the N shore may not be conspicuous in some conditions. The channel into the harbour is very tight between shoal and rocks and is marked by two green and one red lit buoys.

In poor visibility, if the leading line (209° Oc.R.6s) or the buoys can not be seen, it is better to sail up the fjord and anchor until conditions improve. It is reported that the buoyage in the approach is unreliable.

Berthing

As convenient, at the S end of the fish quay. The N part is used by large vessels and the head of the harbour is shallow and full of small boat moorings.

There are also two or three useful anchorages 5M or so up Berufjörður, at Gautavík, Skálavík and at the head.

Facilities

Water and fuel is available on the quay. All normal shops. Good open-air heated swimming pool. The 'cultural centre' is in the brown timber building above the harbour and has internet access at a price. Free internet access is available at the hotel, with your own laptop. Also at the hotel; buy tokens for the washing machines, which are at the campsite.

86 Höfn (Hornafjörður)

64°15'N 15°12'W

Tide Harbour 0·5, 1·1, off Hvanney 0·9, 1·9 **Charts** 74, 810

A busy fishing port in a lagoon at the SE corner of Iceland, away from routes normally followed by yachts. The entrance is very tricky, but it is worth a visit because it is the nearest point from which to get onto the Vatnajökull glaciers (accessible by bus).

It is an unremarkable town but the glacier scenery is spectacular. Buses leave from the Höfn Hotel where the latest schedules and tour information are available. In the past a special 4-wheel drive tour bus ran trips to the glacier, 30M up some very rugged roads. This tour goes via the Jökulsárlon, an amazing freshwater lake behind the shore, full of icebergs that calve from the glacier. This lake can be reached by the ordinary coast road bus.

Navigation

This narrow entrance among shifting sandbanks is regarded by the locals as one of the most difficult harbour approaches in Iceland. The tide can run at 8–10kns at springs and turns one hour after high and low water. *Chart 810* is essential and the entrance should be treated with caution – call the harbour on VHF on Ch 12 or try to follow a fishing boat.

Note This is not a landfall to make for in poor weather: the deep fjords further north are infinitely preferable.

Approach

Hvanney lighthouse (Racon (T) can be approached from E or SW, taking care to avoid the Hvanneyarsker shoals. From the E, pass S of the Pinganesskar rocks, visible about 1m high. After passing Hvanney lighthouse, keep close to the Suðurfjörutangi shore, until Hellir light is open of the N shore of Austurfjörutangi. Turn to starboard and keep close to the latter shore, until the leading marks on that shore indicate the channel leading NNW past the E side of Hellir. A further pair of leading marks on Álögarey lead through a narrow channel to the harbour.

Berthing

As convenient at the extreme N end of the quay.

Facilities

All normal facilities of a town. Fuel and water on the quay. Hotel and swimming pool.

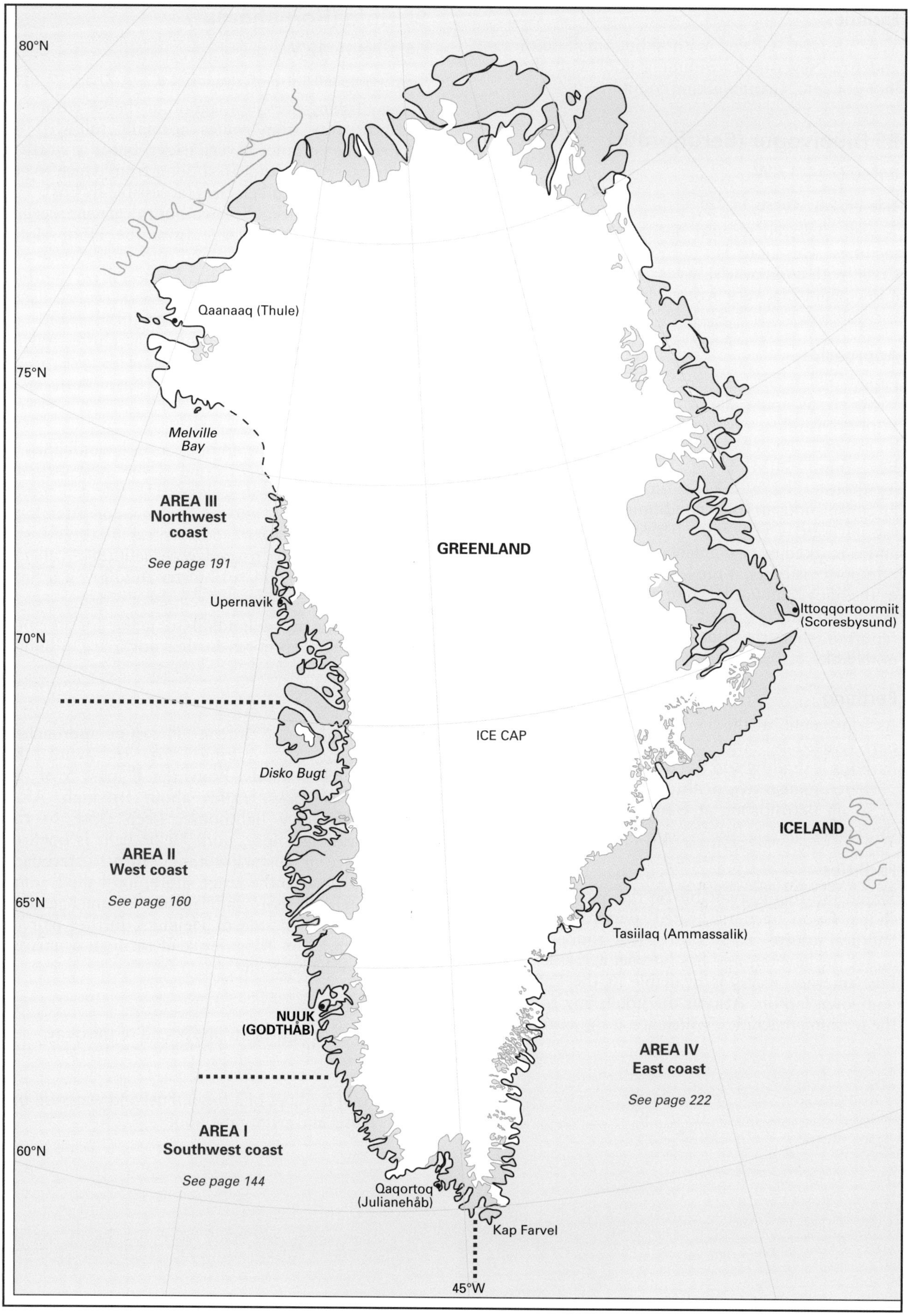
80°N
75°N
70°N
65°N
60°N
45°W
Qaanaaq (Thule)
Melville Bay
AREA III
Northwest coast
See page 191
Upernavik
GREENLAND
Ittoqqortoormiit (Scoresbysund)
ICE CAP
Disko Bugt
ICELAND
AREA II
West coast
See page 160
Tasiilaq (Ammassalik)
NUUK (GODTHÅB)
AREA IV
East coast
See page 222
AREA I
Southwest coast
See page 144
Qaqortoq (Julianehåb)
Kap Farvel

4. Greenland

Contents

Introduction

Greenland (Kalaallit Nunaat or Grønland) is the world's largest island, but 80% of it is permanently covered by ice and it has yet to be circumnavigated, even by an icebreaker. Greenland has a population of about 56,000. The main centres of activity lie along the coast of west Greenland, which is home to the capital, Nuuk (Godthåb). About 3,500 people live in the only two major settlements on the coast of east Greenland and another 850 Greenlanders live in the Thule District of north Greenland.

Over much of the area, sea ice and icebergs present a severe hazard to shipping for part of the year; but in summer this is not a serious problem along the west coast, south of Disko, and there are more than 500 miles of interesting cruising. The fjord area around Qaqortoq (Julianehåb) is particularly attractive, but the approach requires care due to the presence of storis (polar pack ice), often until late summer, particularly around Kap Farvel.

Following the introduction of home rule in 1979, Danish place names have been replaced by Greenlandic names; this process has not yet extended to all Danish or British charts. In this text Greenlandic names are given first, with Danish names and, if necessary, English names in brackets afterwards.

The country

The ice cap covers most of Greenland and, towards its centre, reaches a height of more than 3,000m over a bedrock reckoned to be at about sea level and possibly depressed by the weight of the ice above. In the S where the ice is thinner, coastal mountains up to 2,500m high stretch away NE and NW of Kap Farvel, bounding the ice which forces its way through the cracks in the escarpment forming glaciers, many of which are extremely active and calve into the fjords. Towards Tasiilaq (Ammassalik) (65°37′N 37°30′W) on the east coast and Melville Bay (74°N 54°W) on the west, the ice cap reaches the sea and the mountain tops (*nunataks*) project above the ice.

There is a coastal strip of land, free of glacier ice, along much of the east coast; although storis – heavy pack ice drifting south from the Polar Basin – makes it hazardous for a yacht to reach the coast or cruise along it in most years. It has one of the biggest and most complicated systems of fjords of any coast, including Franz Joseph Fjord and Scoresby Sund (70°N 22°W). The latter is the longest and most magnificent fjord in the world and was discovered and partly mapped by the William Scoresbys, father and son, in 1822. The area was also the scene of some interesting meteorological expeditions mounted by the Germans during the Second World War.

The west coast is not unlike northern Norway. It is mountainous with deep fjords, raised beaches and scores of promontories and islands. In the south, there is a coastal belt of land, anything up to 100 miles wide, which is free of ice. This narrows to less than a mile towards Melville Bay, where the coastline itself is a wall of ice.

Off the ice cap there are heaths and fell fields among the snow patches along the coast, and often a desert further inland. Further south, dwarf scrub, heaths and dwarf birch grow inshore whilst crowberry, willow and alder scrub grow along the coast. In the far south, well inside the fjords, there are willow and birch thickets, which grow up to 3m high in a few sheltered places. There are about 400 species of flowering plants, some expected, such as heaths and alpines, and others, like harebell and dandelion, which seem quite out of place. It is just possible to grow certain vegetables and flowers in private gardens.

Around Narsaq there is a thriving sheep-farming operation with crops of barley and grass grown for hay and silage. Arctic fox and hare live along the coastal strip and reindeer, which were shot almost out of existence, have been re-introduced and are also farmed for meat in the Qaqortoq area. The other land-based polar mammals – polar bear, musk ox, wolf and lemming – are most likely to be found in the far north. In the summer months, polar bear work the drift ice hunting seal. Musk-ox herds have been introduced near the airfield at Kangerlussuaq (Søndre Strømfjord) and also at Kangilinnguit (Grønnedal) in the south. Walrus and narwhals and other seals and whales live and feed offshore, and the Davis Strait is also an important feeding ground for the Atlantic salmon. In the air, the gyr falcon, raven and white-tailed eagle are resident, although many other birds breed here – snow bunting, wheatears, geese and the arctic tern, which makes an annual round trip of 35,000km to the Antarctic.

History

Icelandic sagas attribute the discovery of Greenland in 877 to Gunnbjørn, an Icelander, but it is more reliably known to have been explored by Erik the Red (Eiríkur Rauðe) in 982 while he was exiled from Iceland. In 986, he brought an expedition of colonists from Iceland to settle the west coast and, although only half reached their destination, settlements were successfully established near Julianehåb (Qaqortoq) and Godthåb (Nuuk). The colony flourished and was reinforced from Iceland. Leif the Lucky (Leif Eiríksson), is credited with the introduction of Christianity in AD 1000, at the same time as it was adopted in Iceland.

In 1261 Greenland recognised the King of Norway as Sovereign, chiefly to ensure continued support and supplies, and sovereignty was transferred to Denmark when the two kingdoms merged in 1381. However, the climate deteriorated, growing conditions worsened and Denmark, whose trade was largely handled by German factors concerned with the Baltic, lost interest and the colony declined.

During the 15th century communication between mainland Europe and Greenland stopped, and by about 1500 the Norse element in Greenland had become extinct. Throughout, the Greenlanders appear to have disputed the presence of the foreigners and attacked settlements on more than one occasion. An English expedition led by John Davis in 1585 found only Greenlanders. The Greenlanders were left alone until 1721 when a Norwegian missionary, Hans Egede, supported by Bergen ship owners and Frederick the Fourth of Denmark, landed at Nuuk (Godthåb); trade followed and the development of the west coast began. Both missionary and commercial activities were soon controlled from Copenhagen and when, in 1814, the Danish king renounced the Norwegian crown, the west coast of Greenland as well as Iceland and Faroe were specifically retained by Denmark.

Greenlanders demonstrating the traditional kayak and umiak *Máire Wilkes*

The Danish monopoly, introduced in 1774 to develop resources without their being exploited at the expense of the Greenlanders, lasted until 1951. Foreigners were only allowed access for specific and limited purposes – for instance, anthropological, topographical or meteorological research. But pressures built up. The Danish claim to the whole of Greenland led to a protest from Norway, whose whalers frequented the east coast; this was settled by the International Court in favour of the Danes in 1933.

Greenland became important as a re-fuelling point on transatlantic flights between Europe and America. After the German invasion of Denmark in 1940 Greenland was declared by the US to be a protectorate. Despite this, a little-known series of operations took place between 1940 and 1944 when the Germans sent a number of parties to east Greenland to provide weather information.

After the war, and following the conclusions of a Committee of Greenlanders and Danes which reviewed ways and means of forwarding Greenland's interests, the Royal Greenland Trading Company's monopoly was abolished in 1951, though it was allowed to continue its activities in competition with others. The US base at Thule was established in that year.

In 1953 colonial status was abolished and Greenland was integrated into Denmark. There followed a devolution of authority from Copenhagen to Nuuk and, on 29th June 2009 Greenland changed to self government. Denmark still pays Greenland (in 2016) a grant of DKK 3·6 billion per annum (index linked). Whenever it wishes, Greenland can take control of the remaining agencies dealt with by Denmark which includes foreign policy, police, legal system and surveillance of Greenlandic waters. The official language is now Greenlandic. Greenland is not a member of the European Union.

Landsting, the Greenlandic parliament, is based in Nuuk and governs the four large municipalities which now divide the country. The democracy has four main parties which are: Siumut who promote independence from Denmark, the Democrats who focus on the economy and development, Inuit Ataqatigiit with strong independence policies, and Atassut which would like to see a continued close relationship with Denmark.

Climate

The summer climate is influenced by the arctic high-pressure system (average 1025hPa) and, on the W coast, it is usually dry and sunny. On land the air temperature can be relatively warm, with a mean daily maximum around 15°C in sheltered places and a minimum of 2°C. At sea, however, the air temperature is generally lower, since the sea temperature does not rise above 4°C and the effects of wind chill should be taken seriously. Summer rainfall is light. Fog can be encountered at any time, particularly in association with ice, but is less frequent in the area around Nuuk (Godthåb), 64°N. In an average summer, winds along the coast tend to be light and variable, commonly with a northerly component to them, but the summer winds themselves are variable. Although *NP12* states that 'gales are rare' they can occur even in the summer cruising season. Some fjords are noted for strong katabatic winds which descend off the ice cap and can be severe, but are infrequent in summer; however, *föhn* winds, which are a characteristic of SW Greenland, can be equally severe on occasions.

National costume *i love greenland*

Nordre Sunds ice and weather

Annie Hill and Trevor Robertson over-wintered in in a bay on NE Nako, Nordre Sunds, between September 2004 and June 2005. They wrote the following notes based on their observations made during both the summer and the winter:

Ice

There is very little drift ice in Nordre Sunds in summer, certainly not enough to present any hazard to navigation or to inconvenience a vessel at anchor. In August 2004, there were no more than 10 bergy bits in the 100 miles of channels, in Nordre Sunds and Laksefjorden. At the same time, there was considerable ice in Upernaviks Isfjord and the adjacent parts of NE Nutârmiut, although not enough to hinder navigation. In mid-June 2005, a huge jumble of icebergs at the head of Upernaviks Isfjord, restricted access to the basin in front of the ice face, to one channel only.

In a protected cove on Nako, fast ice formation commenced on 21 September, with the formation of new freshwater ice in the floating freshwater lens, but this was broken up and driven out by any breeze over Force 3. Throughout October, the new ice was thicker and more stable each time it formed, until on 5 November, *Iron Bark* was frozen in for the winter and the ice was thick enough to walk ashore. The outer part of the cove was still open at this time and the sounds around Nako did not appear to have enough ice seriously to impede navigation, until the middle of December. By early January, travel on the sea ice was possible; however turbulence from tidal streams in shallower sections of the sounds, produced open water pools that hampered travel on the ice.

Puddling of the fast ice began in early May, with the final break-up in early June. The ice in 'Winter Cove' broke out on 8 June 2005 and within a week, the Nordre Sunds were largely clear of drift ice.

Local Weather

In summer, Nordre Sunds and Laksefjorden typically experienced a day or two of fine, clear, calm weather, which alternated with three or four days of overcast and drizzle, with light winds. Strong winds and gales are rare and occurred after a fall in the barometer, when it started to rise again. The first snowfall at sea level was on 18 September, but the snow cover was insufficient to make the use of snowshoes or skis worthwhile until the end of October.

The winter was generally calm. October and June were the windiest months, but the wind exceeded Force 7 on only two occasions in each month. Despite the mountainous terrain and the proximity of the icecap, katabatic winds were rarely experienced in Nordre Sunds.

On 12 November, when the sun set at the beginning of the 80-day winter night, there was about seven hours of bright twilight. By mid-winter (22 December) this had decreased to about three hours of twilight in clear weather, and about one hour when overcast. *Iron Bark*'s bilges froze to the extent they could no longer be pumped out on 10 December. The stream flowing into 'Winter Cove' did not freeze to bottom until about 7 January; thereafter water was obtained from a nearby pond. Ice cover on this pond reached its maximum thickness of 0·8m, plus a variable amount of snow on top, in late April. Typically the newly opened water hole froze to a thickness of 3 or 4cm in 24 hours and if insulated by shovelling snow over the newly formed ice, was rarely more than 20cm thick after a week. The sea ice in the open sounds was 20–50cm thick in seal breathing holes, but as the breathing holes are probably sited in areas of thin ice, the main body of the fast ice in the sounds is almost certainly thicker.

Diurnal temperature variation in summer is about 10° in clear weather and considerably less when overcast. In October, as the days become shorter, the diurnal variation decreased and by November it was imperceptible. Temperature in winter varied with changes in cloud cover (and hence radiation), particularly if associated with an intrusion of warm, wet North Atlantic air, displacing the dominant cold, dry polar air. Cold weather was invariably associated with clear conditions and warm weather came with cloudy, unsettled conditions. On two occasions in February when warm, unstable air intruded, the temperature rose by more that 30°C in a 24-hour period, from approximately -30°C to approximately +1°C. On several other occasions under similar conditions, between December and April, the temperature rose by more than 25°C in 24 hours.

Melting of the snow cover started in late April, but was initially very slow. By mid-May warmer weather sent rivulets of water cascading off south-facing rock faces. In late May and early June, ice dams in the streams leading into 'Winter Cove' burst, each releasing a minor flood. The destructive potential of flooding, following the burst of an ice dam, should be considered when choosing a wintering site.

4. GREENLAND

In late 2013, Professor Jens Christian Svenning of Aarhus University published research indicating that climate change would enable 44 species of North American and European trees and bushes to thrive in Greenland in the near future.

People

Of the total population of 56,000 (1940: 17,500), about 50,000 were born in Greenland. The original inhabitants passed through Canada on their way to Greenland and brought an Inuit culture; but their descendants call themselves Kalaalit (pl. Kalaaleq) rather than Inuit. However the name 'Greenlanders' is used throughout this text. Many foreign residents are of long standing and are mostly Danes, some married to Greenlanders.

The state education programme has produced good results and a remarkable transition from a hunting economy to the 21st century has been brought about. Greenlanders are to be found in many skilled jobs and professions and those who still follow the old hunting culture are mainly to be found around Qaanaaq in the NW and on the E coast, although hunting is still very much a way of life for many Greenlanders.

Greenlanders remain proud of their Inuit heritage and language, although few would wish to return to the 'old ways'. The Lutheran Church is the dominant religion.

Hunting

Until the beginning of the 20th century, hunting for seal, whale and other mammals was the primary activity and means of survival for the Greenlandic people. Today, approximately 10% of the workforce is directly or indirectly involved with the hunting industry. The main prey are seal and whale. Hunting for whales is regulated by quotas from the International Whaling Committee (IWC). Hunting equipment has to be approved and the kill is humane.

Sea birds are hunted for the local market as well as grouse, arctic hare, musk ox and reindeer. The most common prey is seal which are killed for their meat and the skins are used for clothing.

Languages

Greenlandic and Danish. English is quite widely understood, particularly in the towns.

Kalaallisut is the main Greenlandic dialect and is the official language of the country. It is a polysynthetic language which allows the creation of long words by stringing together roots and suffixes. For example, the word for 'computer' is *qarasaasiaq* which, directly translated, means 'artificial brain.' The Kalaallisut word for potato is *naatsiliat*, meaning something for which one waits a long time to grow up. The literal translation of the Kalaallisut word for money is 'shiny like the moon.' Other Greenlandic dialects are Inuktun and Tunumiit which is spoken on the east coast.

Economy

Fishing and fish processing remains the key contributor to Greenland's economy. For a time, cod fishing was very important but this has now declined with falling fish stocks. In 2010, Greenland exported DKK 129 million of cod. To some extent, halibut has taken cod's place with an annual catch worth DKK 511 million. Cold water prawn however is the biggest export with a value of DKK 1.2 billion per annum which accounts for 50% of Greenland's exports. Other species caught include catfish, salmon, haddock, lumpfish, dab, crab and whiting. Fish and shellfish accounted for 91% of Greenland's exports in 2015. The majority of the fishing is managed by the Greenlandic company, Royal Greenland A/S and their presence can be seen in most of the bigger ports.

Precious metal extraction accounts for exports of DKK 176 million. Trade is mainly with Denmark and the Danish influence is very strong. The UK is a significant buyer. The main imports are foodstuffs, fuel and machinery. Tourism is being encouraged and there are increasing numbers of cruise liners operating on the west and southern coasts Greenland in the summer. Although, as of Spring 2016, hydrocarbon exploration has been put on hold following the decline in oil prices, the economy as a whole is expected to continue to expand.

In 2014, the total amount of imports was valued at DKK 4.3 billion and the exports were DKK 3 billion. The DKK deficit was made good by a grant from Denmark.

General information

Travel

Air Travel

The main international airport is at Kangerlussuaq (Søndre Strømfjord), with Narsarsuaq serving the SW.

There are also STOL airports at Nuuk (Godthåb), Ilulissat (Jakobshavn), Paamiut, Sisimiut (Holsteinsborg), Aasiaat (Egedesminde), Quaarsut (70°44'N, 58°39'W) for Uummannaq, Maniitsoq (Sukkertoppen), Upernavik, Qaanaaq, Kulusuk for Tassiilaq (Ammassalik) and Nerlerit Inaat for Ittoqqortoormiit (Scoresbysund). Other major settlements are served by helicopter.

Useful websites – tourism

	Greenland Tourist Information Greenland Guide	www.greenland-guide.gl

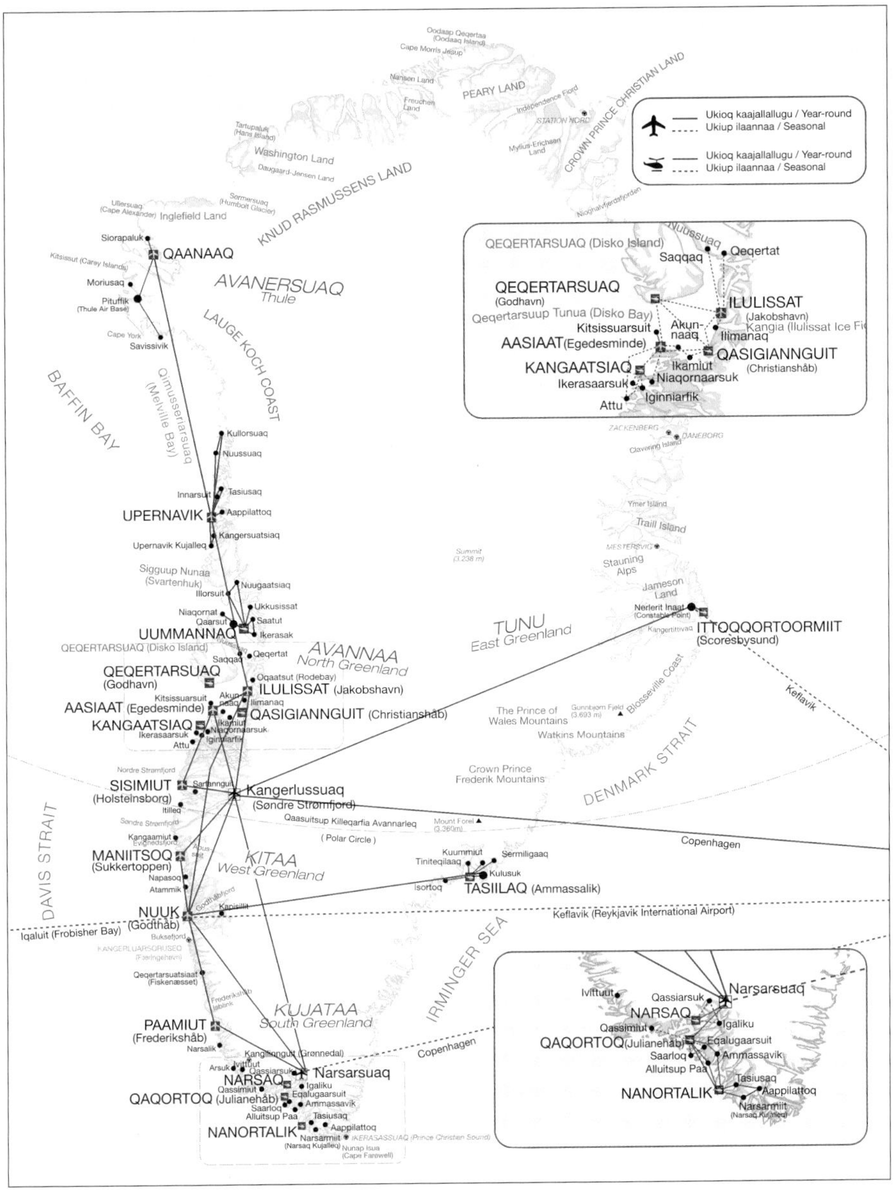

Air Greenland routes
Air Greenland

Useful websites – travel

	Air Greenland International and internal flights	www.airgreenland.com
	First Air	www.firstair.ca
	Air Iceland	www.airiceland.is
	Air Nunavit Canadian Charter Company	airnunavut.ca
	Arctic Umiaq Line Ferry Service	http://aul.gl/en.html
	Disko Line Ferries	http://diskoline.dk

Aasiaat wall murals *Máire Wilkes*

Air Greenland run three to four flights a week from Copenhagen to Kangerlussuaq and to Nuuk. In the summer they also fly to Narsarsuaq several times a week. From April to October there are flights from Keflavik (Iceland) to Nuuk.

Air Iceland operate daily flights from Reykjavik to Kulusuk (E Greenland), Narsarsuaq, Ilulissat and Nuuk.

First Air operate daily flights from Ottawa to Iqaluit (Frobisher Bay on Baffin Island) with onward flights to Greenland possible.

Air Nunavut operate charter flights to Greenland from Iqaluit. Spare seats are sometimes available.

Internal helicopter flights are expensive and they can get heavily booked, but seats are sometimes available on 'standby'.

In S Greenland, Blue Ice Explorer operates four ferries between Narsarsuaq, Narsaq and Qaqortoq.

Arctic Umiaq Line run a regular ferry service to and from the larger settlements on the west coast of Greenland. This can be a useful and scenic method of transport.

Formalities

Greenland is not a member of the European Union nor is it in the Schengen Agreement area. However it is 'integrated' with the Schengen countries which eases border crossings. It has its own customs arrangements. A visiting yacht's skipper should report to the harbourmaster at the first port of call, and he will arrange clearance. This is not onerous.

The importation of firearms is forbidden and a licence is required to lawfully possess a gun. However hunting and wildlife protection firearms are common and widely available.

The Greenland flag is flown as a courtesy by all visiting ships, including Danish-registered vessels.

Those intending to hunt or fish, should check the regulations with the local authorities.

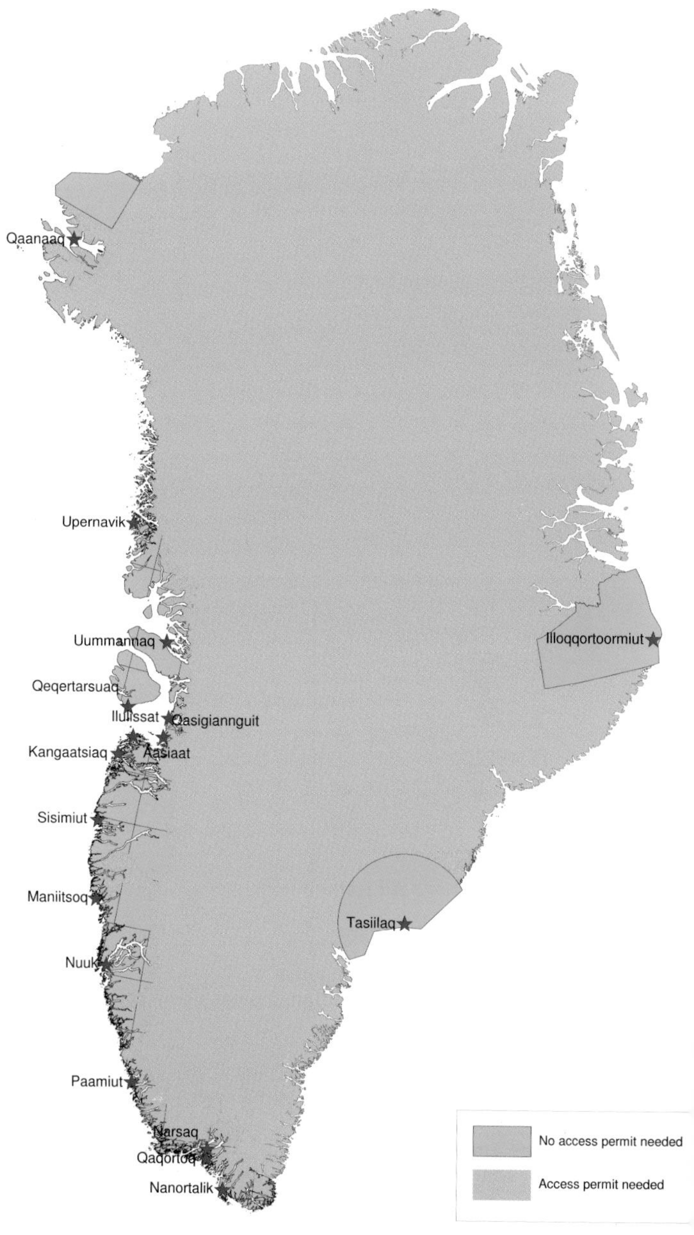

Useful websites – permits

	Naalakkersuisut - the Greenland Government Travel permit requirements	http://naalakkersuisut.gl/en/About-government-of-greenland/Travel-activities-in-remote-parts-of-Greenland
	Official website of Denmark	http://denmark.dk/en/society/greenland-the-faroes-and-the-german-minority/

UK and US diplomatic representatives are based in Copenhagen but there is a British Consulate in Nuuk at Royal Greenland, Vestrevig 45. The postal address is PO Box 1073, 3900 Nuuk, Greenland and ✆ +299 32 44 22.

Permits

Permits are required to access remote areas and special areas such as Ilulissat Icefjord (World Heritage (UNESCO) Site), research, animal welfare projects, archaeological studies, wildlife studies etc. Details of requirements and how to apply for the permits are given on the Naalakkersuisut website. Of particular interest to visiting yachtsmen are the areas which require 'access permits' - these are shown on the map.

Harbourmasters

Harbourmasters are usually located in the Royal Arctic Line offices. They are invariably friendly and helpful with berthing and will get weather and ice forecasts if required. At the first port of entry they can arrange customs clearance.

When berthing in a busy harbour, it is as well to remember that fishing boats move about, so it is best not to leave your yacht unattended. Greenlanders do not give much warning of departure. A fishing boat may look well and permanently tied, but all of a sudden two or three men will arrive on board, start the engines and leave within minutes.

Telecommunications

Whilst all the major settlements on the Greenland west coast have good mobile phone coverage, both making and receiving calls on a UK mobile contract in Greenland is expensive. Free WiFi hotspots and internet cafés are not commonplace. The Seamans' hotels (Sømandshjemmet) and some hotels offer WiFi hotspots for an hourly charge.

It may pay to get a Tele Greenland pre-pay SIM card for telephone and mobile data which can be bought and set up at a Post Office. There are 2 prepay options available (as at 2015):

SIMPLE a data only SIM card suitable for an iPad, tablet, dongle, or laptop with a built in SIM card slot.

TUSASS a combined voice and data SIM card suitable for data enabled smartphones.

In both cases quality is very good with good 3G connection speeds. The voice SIM card allows you to receive international phone calls at no charge, and since it is possible to dial a Greenland mobile number from a European landline for under 50p a minute, this offers a far more cost effective alternative to using a UK mobile.

To activate the service on an iPad or iPhone the following steps are necessary:

- insert the SIM card in the device
- enter the PIN number which comes on the scratch card with the SIM card – go to

Taateraat Sermiaat glacier *William Ker*

Settings/cellular data and turn cellular data on – go to settings/cellular data/APN settings and type in 'internet' in the cellular data APN field. The APN username and password can be left blank
- power off the device and turn back on to apply the new settings.

If outgoing emails are not being sent, it may help to change the SMTP outgoing server on your mail software to smtp.greennet.gl.

Supplies and services

Under home rule, the Royal Greenland Trade Department has been replaced by the Kalaallit Niuerfiat, KNI (pronounced *Koo-en-ee*) which runs supermarkets (called Pisiffik or Pilersuisoq, depending on size), postal services and local shipping. The bigger settlements have supermarkets and bakeries run by independent operators as well, notably Brugsen, which set a high standard. There are also bookshops and fishermen's chandleries. Prices compare with Scandinavia and are similar throughout Greenland; but, of course, any items flown in (flyfresh) like lettuce and tomatoes are expensive. Wines, beers and spirits are readily available but are heavily taxed.

Nearly every harbour has a Brættet (open market), or 'Kalaalimineerniarfik' in Greenlandic, where local fishermen and hunters sell fresh fish, seal and whale meat as well as reindeer and musk ox, depending on locality and season. Eqaluq (Arctic char), either fresh or smoked, are excellent and sometimes salmon are also available.

Diesel (diesel olie), petrol (benzin) and kerosene (petroleum) are available at reasonable prices. Most large settlements have a small boat jetty with delivery by hose; but in the smaller places, cans have to be filled from 40-gallon drums.

BP/Kosangas (propane) cylinders can be bought or exchanged in most major settlements.

Water can usually be obtained from a hose or from clear mountain streams.

Repairs

Most large settlements have boat building and repair facilities, but it would be wise to take a full set of engine spares. GRP is widely used and major repairs can be carried out in Qaqortoq, Nuuk and Aasiaat. As most fishing boats are well equipped – GPS, radar, VHF and echo sounders – there should be no difficulty in getting repairs carried out in the bigger settlements. There are no sail-makers.

Money

Currency is the Danish Krone. There are banks in all the major harbours and most have ATMs where cards can be used to draw cash. Many shops accept Visa, etc.

Mosquitoes

Mosquitoes can be a pest, but are not usually a problem, except early in the season. Anchoring off will help. Mosquito repellent and nets are worth taking, as well as smoke coils.

Accommodation and restaurants

There are hotels in all the bigger towns, some of a high standard, but correspondingly expensive.

There are Seamen's Homes (Sømandshjemmet) in Qaqortoq, Nuuk, Sisimiut and Aasiaat, which are a good place for a shower and an inexpensive meal. They also have accommodation. They are open to anyone and, because they do not serve alcohol, the cafeterias are popular with local families.

Cruising information

The west coast of Greenland between 63°N and 69°N is virtually clear of sea ice as early as June. The days are long and the weather normally good. Although by September and October ice cover is at its minimum, deteriorating weather and longer nights make this an unfavourable time for yachtsmen and, on balance, July and August are the best months for cruising.

It is intended that this guide to Greenland should supplement the Admiralty Sailing Directions, *Arctic Pilots Vol III (NP12)* 9th Ed 2012 and *Vol II (NP11)* 10th Ed 2010; referred to in the following text as *NP12* and *NP11*. Where the information in the pilots is described in sufficient detail for yachts, reference will be made and not usually repeated.

Pilots and charts

In addition to the British Admiralty pilots *NP11* and *NP12*, which are by far the best source for both ice and pilotage information, Den Danske Lods Vols 1 and 2 would really only be of use to Danish readers but have some useful sketch plans. Den Grønlandske Havnelods contains excellent harbour plans although no soundings are shown.

See the International Maritime Organisation (IMO) warning in this chapter about using GPS with paper charts (page 135).

British Admiralty and US charts can be used for planning and approach, but are at too small a scale to be of use for inshore pilotage.

The Danish Geodata Agency (DGA, formerly Kort & Matrikelstyrelsen) publishes excellent charts covering both the E and W coast at 1:400,000 and the W coast at 1:80,000 as far north as Disko Bay. It also publishes larger-scale charts of some areas. The 1:80,000 series is adequate for practically all the inner leads and harbours. Where it is felt that the larger-scale chart would be worth having this is mentioned in the text, otherwise the sheet number is placed within brackets.

Danish charts are well produced and clear but surveys are not complete and GPS should be used with discretion. In many areas, soundings are only

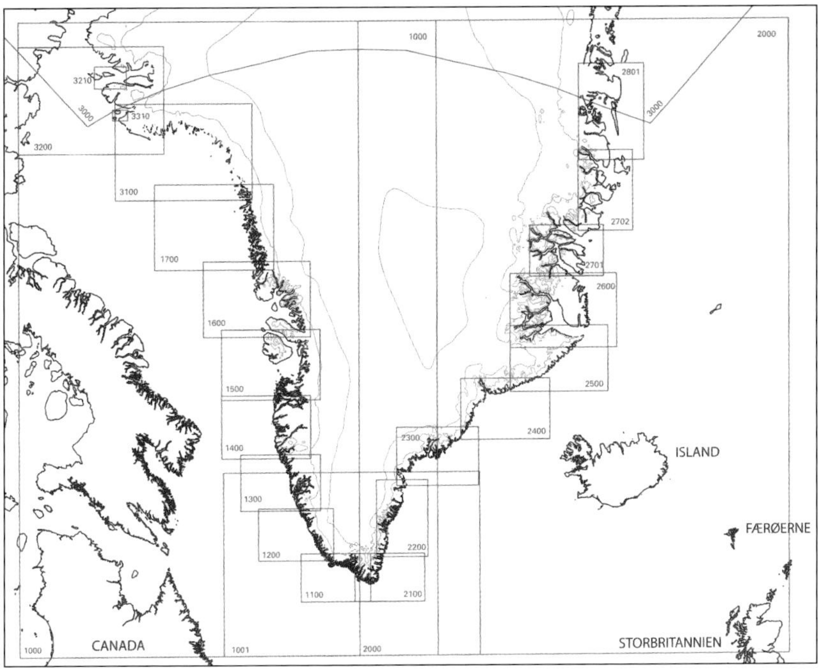

Danish 1:400, 000 series chart index

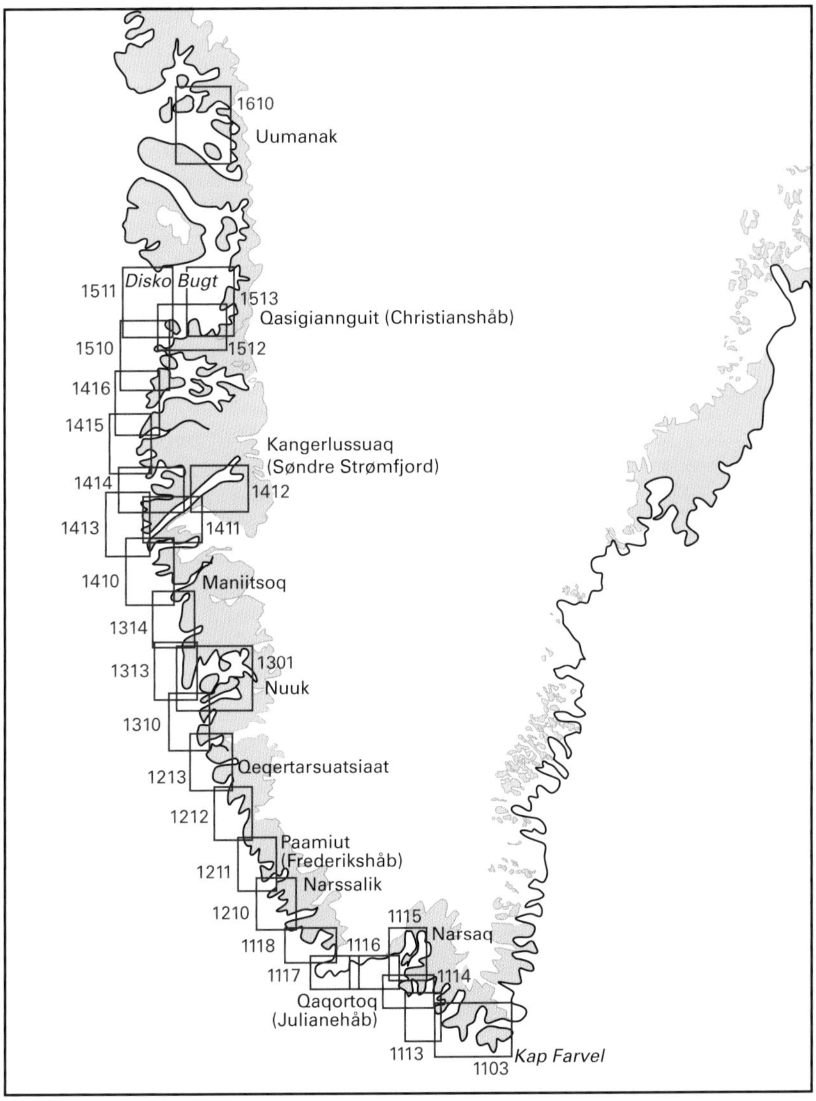

Danish 1:80, 000 series chart index

Useful websites – charts

	Danish Geodata Agency List of current Greenland charts	www.danskehavnelods.dk/indexkort_gronland/gronlandskesoekort.html
	Weilbach Danish chart supplier. Website includes thumbnail pictures of current Greenland charts	www.weilbach.dk/index.asp?l=155
	Imray UK chart distributor	www.imray.com
	The Map Shop, Upton-on-Severn	www.themapshop.co.uk
	Saga Maps Greenland maps	http://sagamaps.dk
	Danish Maritime Authority Several useful links relating to navigation in Greenland waters	www.dma.dk/ships/sider/greenlandwaters.aspx

shown on recognised routes. Areas left blank have not been surveyed and areas marked *urent* (foul) should be avoided. Not all rocks are marked and they may or may not cover. The only rule is to exercise caution. Grounded bergs or ice floes indicate shoals, and by their size, give a measure of the depth – very big bergs can be aground in 120m. Older Danish charts of the west coast are based on the Qornoq 1927 (International) Datum – please see the note in the GPS section (page 135).

A typical navigation mark *Máire Wilkes*

Although Danish charts can be bought in Greenland, only local coverage is normally held. It is safer to obtain all charts needed before departure, either from the chart agents, Iver C Weilbach in Denmark or in the United Kingdom from Imray Norie Laurie & Wilson Ltd.

In the text, numbers are prefixed with BA for British Admiralty, D for Danish.

Electronic charts can be bought from the usual sources and are a great asset for pilotage in the archipelago one should be very cautious when using electronic charts, particularly on inner routes. Errors of 100m are common. They may also be available in Nuuk. Most of the local fisherman with bigger boats use a chart plotter in preference to paper charts. The well found cruising yacht will probably carry both.

Topographical maps covering the coastal regions at 1:250,000 provide much supplementary information, especially north of Disko and more particularly on the east coast. They are published by the Danish Geodata Agency and may be ordered from the Map Shop, Upton-on-Severn or from Stanfords in London.

Saga Maps produces a series using the 1:250,000 topographical maps as a basis, but on convenient sheet lines. 18 sheets cover the west coast from Kap Farvel to Thule and sheets 19 and 20 cover Tasiilaq (Ammassalik) and Ittoqqortoormiit (Scoresbysund). They are widely available in Greenland or in the UK from The Map Shop, Upton-upon-Severn or from Stanfords in London.

There are few navigational buoys because they would be displaced by ice movements. The system of beacons placed on small islands and headlands is reasonably effective, but not always easy to see and a pair of binoculars is almost essential. When sailing N and W through inshore passages on the west coast, leave all beacons with the triangle pointing upwards to starboard. Port hand beacons have now nearly all been changed to 'cans'; in practice these are rectangular boards usually slatted and sometimes outlined in 'day-glo'. The colour is a rather dark red and the yellow base is often easier to see in poor light.

Lighthouses

These are small, inconspicuous, with weak light range and not always reliable. This is not important because of long daylight hours, except late in the season.

Racons

A number of racons have been established and are shown on the relevant charts.

Radar

Radar response from the rocky coast and skerries is excellent. Icebergs also show up quite well, but sometimes may not be seen at more than two miles, if they do not present a good reflecting surface. Large areas of heavy drift ice show up, but isolated bergy bits and 'growlers' may not be seen, particularly in rough water. A powerful spotlight would be useful late in the season at night.

GPS

The International Maritime Organisation (IMO) recommends caution when using GPS derived positions on Greenland paper charts. It states that charts of the west coast are misplaced by 0 to 1,000m and, on the northern and eastern coasts, positions are misplaced by up to 5km. It recommends that radar and terrestrial navigation methods are used.

Vessels with combined radar/chart plotters can use the radar overlay facility to check the accuracy of the plotter.

Older Danish Charts of the west coast are based on the Qornoq 1927 (International) Datum, which may be used if this setting is available. If using the WGS 84 setting, satellite derived positions should be moved 0'·08 northward and 0'·28 westward to agree with the chart. This figure may not be true for all of the west coast and should be checked. New charts are being converted to WGS 84 as they come up for revision.

Compass variation increases rapidly N of Disko Bay and the magnetic compass becomes unreliable W of Melville Bay.

Marine Telecommunications

All coastal radio traffic is now controlled by Aasiaat Radio which has remote stations providing VHF, MF and HF coverage for the areas covered in this publication. The northwest, north and northeast coasts are not covered.

Aasiaat Radio's contact details are ✆ +299 130 000 / +299 893 126, *Email* oyr@telepost.gl

Frequencies are given but should be checked. Full information is available in the Greenland Tele website and also in the *Admiralty List of Radio Signals, Volume 1 part 2 (NP281(2))*.

Distress, Search & Rescue

Aasiaat Radio listens for voice distress calls on channel 16. It does not operate DSC on VHF.

The Greenland coast is designated in the GMDSS system as an Area 2 area which means SAR communications are primarily MF. That is, using DSC on 2187.5 KHz and 2182 KHz.

SAR Authority: MRCC Nuuk

Aasiaat Radio: frequencies as above

Email mrcc-nuuk@mil.dk

Primary contact number: ✆ +299 364 010

Aasiaat Radio does not operate distress frequencies in the HF (short wave) range.

Marine safety information

Warnings of storm, gale or icing are announced on 2182 kHz and channel 16 before they are broadcast on working frequencies, including HF, in English, Greenlandic and Danish at 06.05, 11.05, 16.05 and 21.05 local time. The weather forecast areas are listed later in this chapter.

Warnings received outside the above mentioned fixed times are announced on MF DSC, the MF emergency channel and channel 16 before they are broadcast on the working frequencies including HF. Warnings are repeated following the next silence period.

Navigational warnings are transmitted by Aasiaat Radio following the first silence period after receipt from MRCC Nuuk. The transmissions are announced on MF DSC, 2182 kHz and channel 16.

VHF

VHF cover is comprehensive from Kap Farvel to just N of Upernavik. All the Aasiaat sub-stations monitor channel 16 and their working channels are shown on the diagram.

There are blank spots due to topography and MF may have to be used on these occasions, as well as when beyond VHF range. Radio operators are friendly and helpful and most speak good English. Link calls are accepted with your call sign and accounting code.

Further information is available in the Greenland Tele website and also in the *Admiralty List of Radio Signals, Volume 1 part 2 (NP281(2))*.

MF

As part of the Global Maritime Distress and Safety System (GMDSS), Aasiaat Radio provides a service on MF for emergency and safety, using DSC on 2187·5kHz. They do not now maintain a listening watch on 2182 kHz, but do listen on their principal MF working channels (see table).

VHF

East/West Coast	Channel	Position
East Coast	25	Pingels Fjeld
	26	Sermiligaaq
	27	Kap Tycho Brahe
West Coast	01	Ikerasassuaq
	03	Top 775
	04	Nanortalik
	28	Tretopfjeld
	02–25	Qaqortoq
	24	Narsaq
	23	Narsarsuaq
	26	Simiutaq
	27	Arsuk Ø
	23	Paamiut
	28	Kangaarsuk
	03	Qingaaq
	26	Telegraføen
	25	Maniitsoq
	24	Kangaamiut
	26	Dye One
	01	Sisimiut
	28	Rifkol
	27	Aasiaat
	23	Lyngmarksfjeld
	25	Ilulissat
	24	Pingo
	02	Niaqornaq
	03	Uummannaq
	63	Uviq
	04	Sanderson's Hope
	60	Tinu

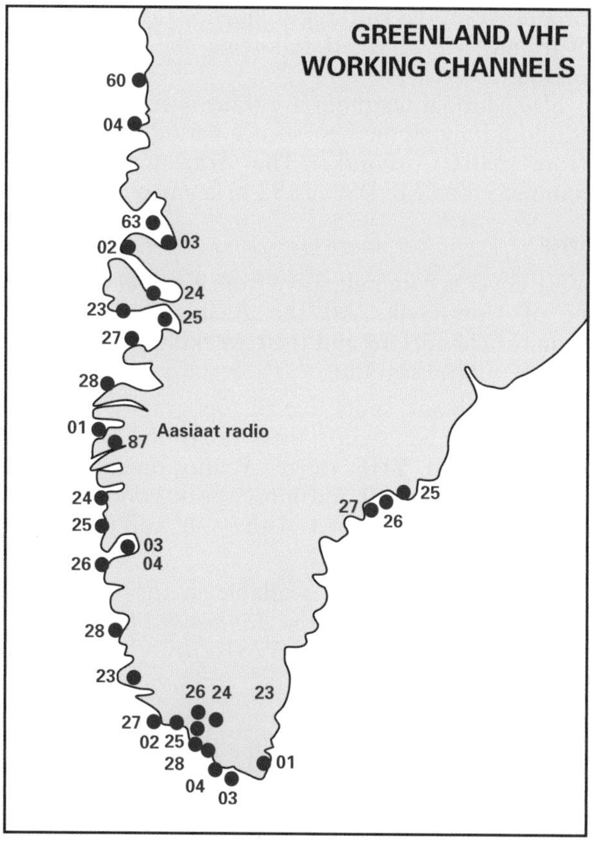

Aasiaat Radio station *Máire Wilkes*

DSC facilities are located as follows:

MMSI 003313000 – Upernavik, Qeqertarsuaq, Sisimiut and Nuuk (Kookøerne, TX ; Skinderhvalen, RX)

MMSI 003311000 – Paamiut, Simiutaq and Ikerasassuaq

MMSI 003314000 – Ammassalik

Aasiaat Radio has a number of remote MF radio stations which provides GMDSS A2 coverage for areas A, B, C, and D referred to in this publication. Coverage extends approximately 300 nautical miles from the coast. The northwest, north and northeast coasts are not covered.

Aasiaat Radio

Shore transmit frequency (kHz)	Station	Ship transmit Frequency (kHz) – primary & supplimentary
3276	Upernavik	**2310**, 2045
3280	Uummannaq	**1665**, 2045
2304	Qeqertarsuaq	**1995**, 2045
3125	Sisimiut	**1868**, 2045
2400	Manitsoq	**1895**, 2045
2116	Nuuk	**1933**, 2045
2225	Paamiut	**1638**, 2045
2129	Qaqortoq	**2630**, 2045
2265	Ikerasassuaq	**2090**, 2045
2250	Tasiilaq	**2090**, 2045

HF

Aasiaat Radio HF frequencies

HF Channel	Ship Frequency	Coast Station Frequency
409	4089.0kHz	4381.0kHz
608	6221.0kHz	6522.0kHz
811	8225.0kHz	8749.0kHz
1217	12278.0kHz	13125.0kHz
1603	16366.0kHz	17248.0kHz

Traffic lists and navigation warnings are transmitted on the 4 and 6 MHz bands.

There is no monitoring of HF distress frequencies.

Weather information

The sea area forecast is broadcast, in Danish and Greenlandic only, by Greenland Radio (KNR) at 0635, 0845, 1630 and 2145, local time. An alternative is to ask the radio operator for a translation of the sea area forecast (see area map, in which the areas are numbered as well as named).

KNR transmit on medium wave on 570kHz from Nuuk (Godthåb), 650kHz from Qeqertarsuaq (Godhavn), 720kHz from Simiutaq near Qaqortoq (Julianehåb), 810kHz from Upernavik and 900kHz from Uummannaq, as well as FM near towns and villages. Gale warnings are broadcast by Coast Radio Stations in Danish, Greenlandic and in English when received and repeated after subsequent silent periods, on VHF Ch 16, 2182kHz and DSC 2187·5kHz.

Weather information can be obtained by phoning the duty Met. forecaster at Kangerlussuaq (Søndre Strømfjord) Airfield (✆ +299 84 10 22, or via Aasiaat Radio.

The officers of the Royal Arctic Line are usually very helpful.

Weather forecasts are broadcast twice a day by the Canadian Coast Guard Radio Station from Iqaluit on Baffin Island and from Resolute, on 2582kHz and 4363kHz. The broadcasts from Iqaluit at 1340 and 2235 UTC include the western Davis Strait and from Resolute at 1240 and 2310 UTC include western Baffin Bay.

Labrador Coast Guard Radio broadcasts weather forecasts for the Labrador Sea on 2598kHz at 0137, 1007, 1437 and 2037 UTC. The forecasts cover the sea areas to within 50 miles of the Greenland coast and can be helpful.

Radio facsimile weather charts are broadcast on 3253 & 7710kHz from Iqaluit at 1000 & 2100 UTC and Resolute at 1100 & 2330 UTC. The weather charts cover the whole of the area to 70°N including W Greenland. See ALRS Vol 3 Part 2 NP283(2), or the Canadian Coast Guard Radio Aids to Marine Navigation, available on their website.

A weather forecast for tourists on the W coast of Greenland is broadcast on local FM radio in English at 0910 from Monday to Friday and at 0815 on Saturday between 15th June and 15th September. Times may vary with locality and the broadcast is not always every day.

Navtex

Two Navtex stations covering S Greenland broadcast Weather Bulletins and Navigational Warnings, including Ice Reports. The broadcasts do not include weather forecasts except storm warnings.

In SW Greenland, the met forecasts from Cartwright (Labrador [X]) are helpful, in particular 'East Labrador Sea'.

Kookøerne [W] 64°04'N 52°01'W, is near Nuuk (Godthåb) and covers W Greenland from Kap Farvel to N of Disko.

Broadcasts are on 518kHz at 0340, 0740, 1140, 1540, 1940 & 2340 UTC.

Useful websites – weather and ice forecasts

	DMI Weather and ice forecasts for Greenland	www.dmi.dk/vejr/
	Environment Canada Canadian Arctic marine weather forecasts	www.weatheroffice.gc.ca/marine/index_e.html
	Canadian Coastguard Canadian Arctic weather and ice broadcasting information: VHF, HF, Navtex and fax	www.ccg-gcc.gc.ca/eng/CCG/Home
	Greenland Tele	www.tele.gl
	Aasiaat Radio	www.telepost.gl Select 'English', then 'Coastal Radio'

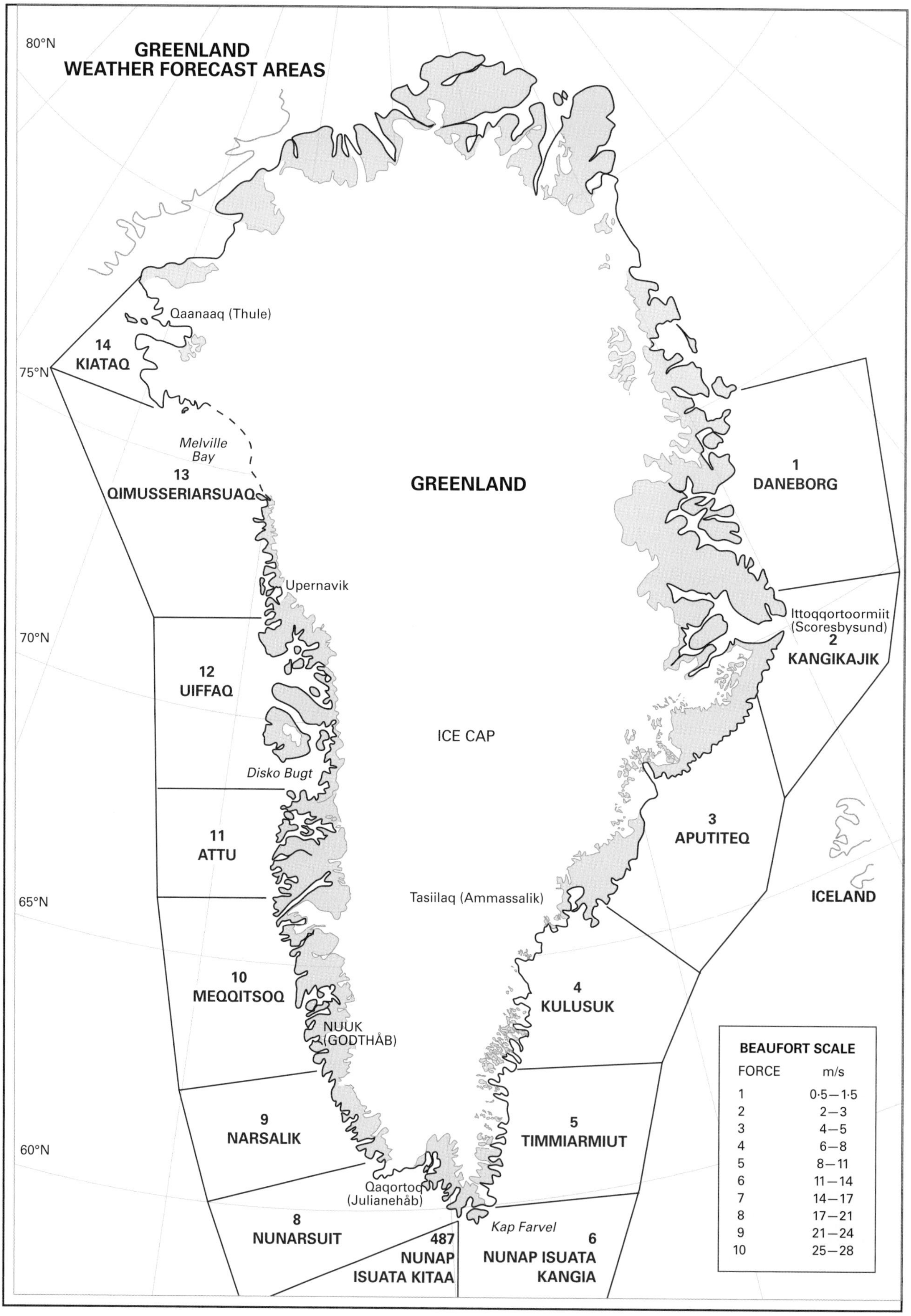
80°N
GREENLAND
WEATHER FORECAST AREAS
Qaanaaq (Thule)
14
KIATAQ
75°N
Melville
Bay
13
QIMUSSERIARSUAQ
GREENLAND
1
DANEBORG
Upernavik
Ittoqqortoormiit
(Scoresbysund)
2
KANGIKAJIK
70°N
12
UIFFAQ
ICE CAP
Disko Bugt
3
APUTITEQ
11
ATTU
65°N
Tasiilaq (Ammassalik)
ICELAND
10
MEQQITSOQ
4
KULUSUK
NUUK
(GODTHÅB)
BEAUFORT SCALE
FORCE m/s
1 0·5–1·5
2 2–3
3 4–5
4 6–8
5 8–11
6 11–14
7 14–17
8 17–21
9 21–24
10 25–28
9
NARSALIK
5
TIMMIARMIUT
60°N
Qaqortoq
(Julianehåb)
8
NUNARSUIT
Kap Farvel
487
NUNAP
ISUATA KITAA
6
NUNAP ISUATA
KANGIA

Reykjavík Radio [X] 64°05′N 21°51′W. This station covers E Greenland and broadcasts on 518kHz at 0350, 0750, 1150, 1550, 1950 & 2350 UTC.
Note that Reykjavík Radio [R] covers Iceland waters and broadcasts on 518kHz at 0250, 0650, 1050, 1450, 1850 & 2250 UTC.

Simiutaq (M) 60°41'N, 046°35'W (near Qaqortoq). Broadcasts at 0200, 0600, 1000, 1400, 1800, 2200 UTC (518 Khz).

Ship reporting systems in Greenland waters

There are two reporting systems in operation in Greenland waters:

- Greenpos which is managed by the Joint Arctic Command at Nuuk, Grønlands Kommando. It applies to all vessels approaching or leaving Greenland waters.
- Coastal Control which is mandatory for all vessels greater than 20 GRT navigating in Greenland coastal waters, and is managed by Aasiaat Radio.

GREENPOS REPORTS

Four types of report are used:

1. Sailing Plan

This is the first report made when joining the system about 250M off the coast. The report is preceded by the indicator 'SP' and comprises:

A. Ship Name/Callsign
B. Date and time (UTC)
C. Present Position
D. Course
E. Speed
F. Destination and ETA
L. Route
S. Actual weather and ice information
X. Persons on board (POB)

2. Position Report

These should be made every six hours (0600, 1200, 1800 and 0000 UTC). The report is preceded by the indicator 'PR' and comprises:

A. Ship Name/Callsign
B. Date and time (UTC)
C. Present Position
D. Course
E. Speed
S. Actual weather and ice information

Landing fish in Nuuk *Máire Breathnach*

3. Final report

This is made on reaching the vessel's destination in Greenland or leaving the Greenpos reporting area. The report is preceded by the indicator 'FR' and comprises:

A. Ship Name/Callsign
B. Date and time (UTC)
C. Present Position
S. Actual weather and ice information

4. Deviation report

This should be made if the vessel changes its route or if the vessel's arrival is likely to be differ from its ETA by more than an hour. The prefix is 'DR' and it comprises:

A. Ship name/Callsign
B. Date and time (UTC)
C. Present position
L. Short description of new route

Greenpos reports should be made to COMMCEN NUUK by one of the following methods:

- HF, MF or VHF radio via Aasiaat Radio
- INMARSAT C: 433 116 710
- *Email* ako-commcen@mil.dk
- ✆ +299 364 023, *Fax* +299 364 099

If a report is more than 30 minutes over due, they will try to contact the vessel. If they cannot do so, SAR operations may commence.

More details of the scheme can be found in *ALRS Vol 6 (NP 286)* Ship Reporting Systems.

Aasiaat Radio is responsible for Kystcontrol (Coastal Control) for vessels making coastal passages.

Details in *ALRS Vol 6 (NP 286)* Ship Reporting Systems.

Coastal control reports

Coastal Control Reports, also known as 'Kystcontrol,' are mandatory for vessels of more than 20 GRT. They may also be used by smaller vessels wishing to be more visible to the Greenlandic SAR authorities. The format is similar to the Greenpos reporting system and comprises four types of report.

The four types of report used are:

1. Sailing plan

This is the first report made when joining the system. The report is preceded by the indicator 'SP' and comprises:

To: Coastal Control

SP

A. Ship name/Callsign

B. Date and time (UTC)

D. Present position or port

I. Destination and ETA

L. Route

X. Persons on board (POB)

2. Position report

Made every 24 hours whilst on passage

To: Coastal Control

PR

A. Ship Name/Callsign

B. Date and time (UTC)

D. Present Position or port

E. Course

F. Speed

3. Final report

This is made on reaching the vessel's destination and should be made immediately on arrival. The report is preceded by the indicator 'FR' and comprises:

To: Coastal Control

FR

A. Ship name/Callsign

B. Date and time (UTC)

D. Position or geographical location

4. Deviation report

This should be made if the vessel changes it's route or if the vessel's arrival is likely to be differ from its ETA by more than an hour. The prefix is 'DR' and it comprises:

To: Coastal Control

DR

A. Ship name/Callsign

B. Date and time (UTC)

C. Present position or geographical location

L. Intentions or cause of deviation

Coastal Control Reports should be made to Aasiaat Radio by one of the following methods:

- HF, MF or VHF radio direct to Aasiaat Radio. MMSI: 003313000
- *Email* oyr@telepost.gl
- ✆ +299 893 126
- ✆ +299 130 000

If a report is more than 30 minutes over due, Grønlands Kommando will try to contact the vessel. If they cannot do so, SAR operations may commence.

More details of the scheme can be found in ALRS Vol 6 (NP 286) Ship Reporting Systems.

Medical advice

Aasiaat Radio will give free medical advice in an emergency.

Tides and Tidal Streams

West coast

The mean spring range on the W coast decreases from about 2·5m at Kap Farvel and Qaqortoq to about 1·9m at Aasiaat and 1·0m at Uummanaq; however, the range at Nuuk is somewhat higher at 3·5m.

Tidal streams are not well documented and are much influenced by wind conditions. Except in one or two locations, which are mentioned in the text, they are not strong.

East coast

The mean spring range on the E coast decreases similarly from about 2·5m at Kap Farvel to less than 1m at Kap Tobin, at the entrance to Scoresby Sund. The range at Tasiilaq is about 2·8m.

Tidal streams are probably less than 1 knot except in long narrow fjords.

Tide Tables

Tide Tables (Tidevandstabeller for Grønland) are published by Danish Geodata Agency, København and may be obtained from chart agents.

The *Admiralty Tide Tables Vol 2 (NP 202)* give information about Greenlandic tides as well as Iceland and Faroe.

Tide tables are also available on the DMI Website.

Currents

The East Greenland Current sets southwards along the east coast of the country. It is the major outflow of cold water from the Arctic basin and carries much storis ice with it (see diagram below).

The relatively warm West Greenland Current sets northwards from Kap Farvel along the west coast at a rate of up to 3 knots inshore, and about 1 knot offshore. In the northern part of Baffin Bay it circulates anticlockwise and is joined by the south setting Canadian Current formed by polar waters setting south from Lancaster, Jones and Smith Sounds. The cold Canadian Current sets southwards from Baffin Bay along the east coast of Baffin Island.

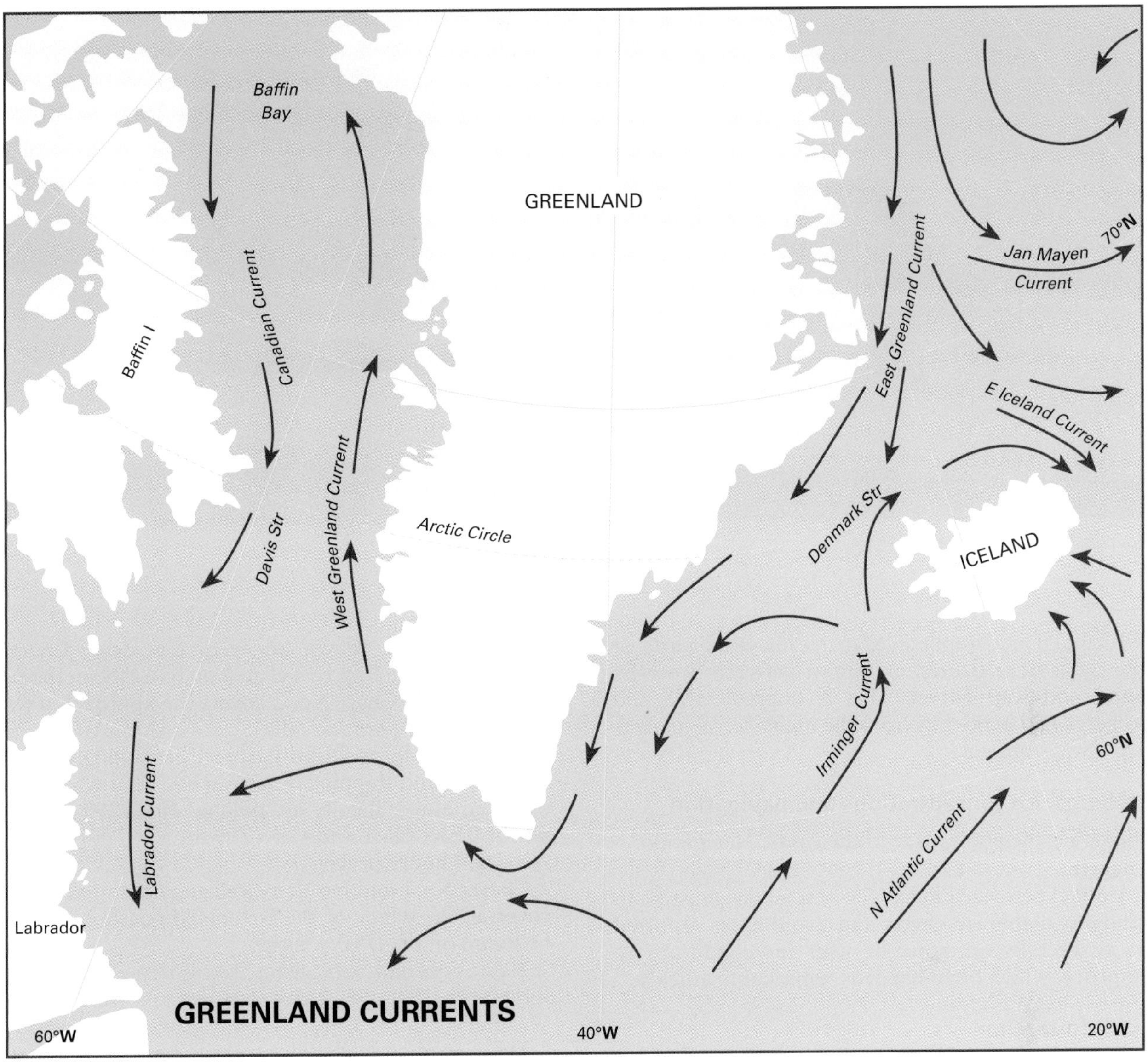

Ice

The presence of icebergs and sea ice is the main limitation to successful cruising in Greenland waters.

Sea ice cover varies considerably from season to season. It is governed partly by winter temperatures and the carry-over from the previous season, but mainly by the effect of wind and the warm and cold currents.

The *Admiralty Arctic Pilots Volumes II* and *III* (*NP11* and *12*) have detailed explanations of the ice regime; a summary of which is given below. For a glossary of ice terms see the Arctic Navigation chapter.

West Greenland coast

Each winter, sea ice fills the whole of Davis Strait and Baffin Bay from Labrador to Thule, leaving a strip of navigable water along the W coast of Greenland which is kept open by the West Greenland Current.

In the summer, navigable water extends northwards along the coast beyond Disko to Upernavik and then around Melville Bay to join up with the 'North Water', a polynya, which opens up early in the season between Greenland and Arctic Canada.

In a very good year the whole of Davis Strait and Baffin Bay are almost clear of drift ice, but icebergs are always present. The icebergs in the south derive mainly from the East Greenland glaciers and thin out considerably north of 62°N on the West Coast. North of Disko the concentration of icebergs calved from the huge glaciers in Disko Bay and further N increases again, until in Melville Bay they can be so dense in places as to appear to fill the horizon.

East Greenland coast

All year round, the cold East Greenland Current carries icebergs as well as heavy polar pack ice (storis) southwards in a belt 50–100M wide, close to the East Greenland shore. From Kap Farvel the ice is carried up the southwest coast to Kap Desolation and on to Paamiut, sometimes reaching its greatest extent as late as July. In most years the presence of storis makes access for yachts to the East Coast

An iceberg at sunset *Máire Wilkes*

difficult, if not impossible; in recent years parts of the coast have cleared in August between Scoresby Sund and Kap Farvel. This is unpredictable and icebergs and bergy bits from the many active glaciers are always present.

Icebergs, ice concentrations and navigation

Please see the notes made in the Arctic Navigation chapter.

Until experienced in ice, the best advice must be to study available ice charts and avoid areas reported as two-tenths or more, or wait for conditions to improve, which often happens remarkably quickly.

Ice information

Obtaining ice information is much easier if the vessel has an internet connection in which case the DMI website should be used.

Iscentralen (Ice Patrol) Danish Meteorological Institute is located in the airport terminal buildings at Narsarsuaq and provides an ice advisory service for shipping, as well as ice charts. Postal address: Iscentralen, Postbox 505, 3923 Narsarsuaq, Greenland. *Email* isc@greennet.gl

The office is staffed by merchant marine officers with experience in ice; they speak excellent English and may be contacted through Aasiaat Radio, or ✆ +299 66 52 44, weekdays 0800–1200 and 1300–1600 local time. Their Iridium number is +881 631 420 563.

When approaching SW Greenland, ice can extend beyond VHF range and it is therefore advisable to make contact on MF through Aasiaat Radio or by satellite communications. The Ice Patrol staff will give the ice limits and advise on the best course to take.

Ice charts are drawn up every few days. Chart No. 1 covers the Kap Farvel area up to 62°N on the E and W coasts. Chart No. 2 covers the approaches to Tassiilaq (Ammassalik), Ittoqqortoormiit (Scoresbysund), or Disko Bay, etc. depending on ice conditions and shipping requirements. Charts may be obtained automatically by 'polling' *Fax* +299 66 52 44 for Chart No.1 and *Fax* +299 66 52 47 for Chart No. 2 (24 hour service).

Charts No. 1 and No. 2, as well as a chart (ugekort) covering the whole of the Greenland coast, can also be found on the DMI website.

Navtex broadcasts from Kookøerne [W] and Reykjavík [X] also carry ice reports (see under Weather).

The Canadian Ice Service website has excellent ice charts which extend to Baffin Bay and the Davis Straits. Ice charts are also broadcast by radio facsimile on 3253kHz & 7710kHz from Iqaluit at 0500 & 2125 UTC and Resolute at 0100 and 0700 UTC (see *ALRS Vol 3 Part 2* or the Canadian Coast Guard *Radio Aids to Marine Navigation*).

Note Ice information can get out of date very quickly and should be treated with caution, especially when there are strong winds.

Cruising areas and approach

AREA I – Southwest coast

60°N – 63°N

Narsaq Kujalleq (Frederiksdal) to just south of Qeqertarsuatsiaq (Fiskenæsset)

This area is affected by off-lying polar pack ice (storis) coming around Kap Farvel, making access difficult and sometimes hazardous until late July.

Approaches to the southwest coast (Area I)

Access to the coast and the fjord area around Qaqortoq (Julianehåb) is complicated by the presence offshore of storis, often until August. The initial approach to Greenland, particularly earlier in the season, may therefore be made further north (Area II). There is serious danger in attempting to penetrate the storis and at least three yachts have been lost for this reason. Approaching from the northwest, there is frequently a shore lead north of Nunarsuit (Kap Desolation), so that an approach is possible through Torsukataq and Knækket (see Inner Lead north of Nunarsuit, below, and *NP12*). Seek advice on the radio from Ice Central, Narsarsuaq (see Ice Information). Late in the season it is normally possible to enter from the east through Ikerasassuaq (Prins Christians Sund), but having negotiated the storis, the channel itself is very often choked with ice.

AREA II – West coast

63°N – 70°N

Qeqertarsuatsiaq (Fiskenæsset) to Disko Bay

This area is accessible to shipping for most of the year and to yachts early in the season, although somewhat later in Disko Bay.

Approaches to the west coast (Area II)

If aiming to cruise the west coast of Greenland in June or July from the direction of Iceland and Northern Europe, a course should be laid to pass to the south of latitude 58°30'N until on the meridian of Kap Farvel (Cape Farewell) (i.e. at least 75 miles to the south). Severe weather conditions are often experienced off Kap Farvel, and in late June 2000 a yacht was lost in a storm in Lat 58°32'N. For this reason, if there is a forecast of strong winds it would be prudent to give Kap Farvel a berth of at least 120M. In a bad year storis can also extend as far as 120M south of Kap Farvel (see *NP11* and *12*). Depending on the ice situation it may be possible to approach the West Coast at Paamiut (Frederikshåb) in 62°N; but if not, it is probably better to make for Nuuk (Godthåb), 64°N.

Approaching from North America it should be noted that, between the iceberg belt off Labrador and the storis and icebergs off the SW coast of Greenland, there is a large area of virtually ice-free water that leads northwards towards Davis Strait. It may, therefore, be better to make an easterly course from Halifax or St Johns, rather than take the route through the Strait of Belle Isle, which is normally foggy and encumbered with icebergs.

Disko Bay *Máire Wilkes*

AREA III – Northwest coast

70°N – 78N

Disko Bay to Smith Sound

This area opens progressively northwards from Disko in July, but drift ice nearly always causes problems in Melville Bay.

Approaches to the northwest coast (Area III)

There should be no problem in sailing to Upernavik by mid to late July. Progress northwards will depend on the ice situation at the time.

Areas I, II and III are covered by *NP12*.

AREA IV – East coast

Heavy polar pack ice (storis) makes access to this coast hazardous, if not impossible, until late in the season in most years.

Approaches to the east coast (Area IV)

The normal approach is from Iceland, where up-to-date ice information can be obtained and departure delayed, if necessary, until conditions have improved. In an exceptionally mild ice year, it may be possible to approach the coast south of Tasiilaq (Ammassalik) in early July or even sometimes in June; however, August offers the best chance in an average year. The difficulty of cruising in this area should not be underestimated and, in some years, heavy polar pack ice bars access to the coast throughout the summer, except to ice-strengthened vessels. Icebergs and bergy bits produced by the numerous tide-water glaciers are always present.

This area is covered by *NP11*.

AREA I

The southwest coast from Narsaq Kujalleq (Frederiksdal) to 63°N

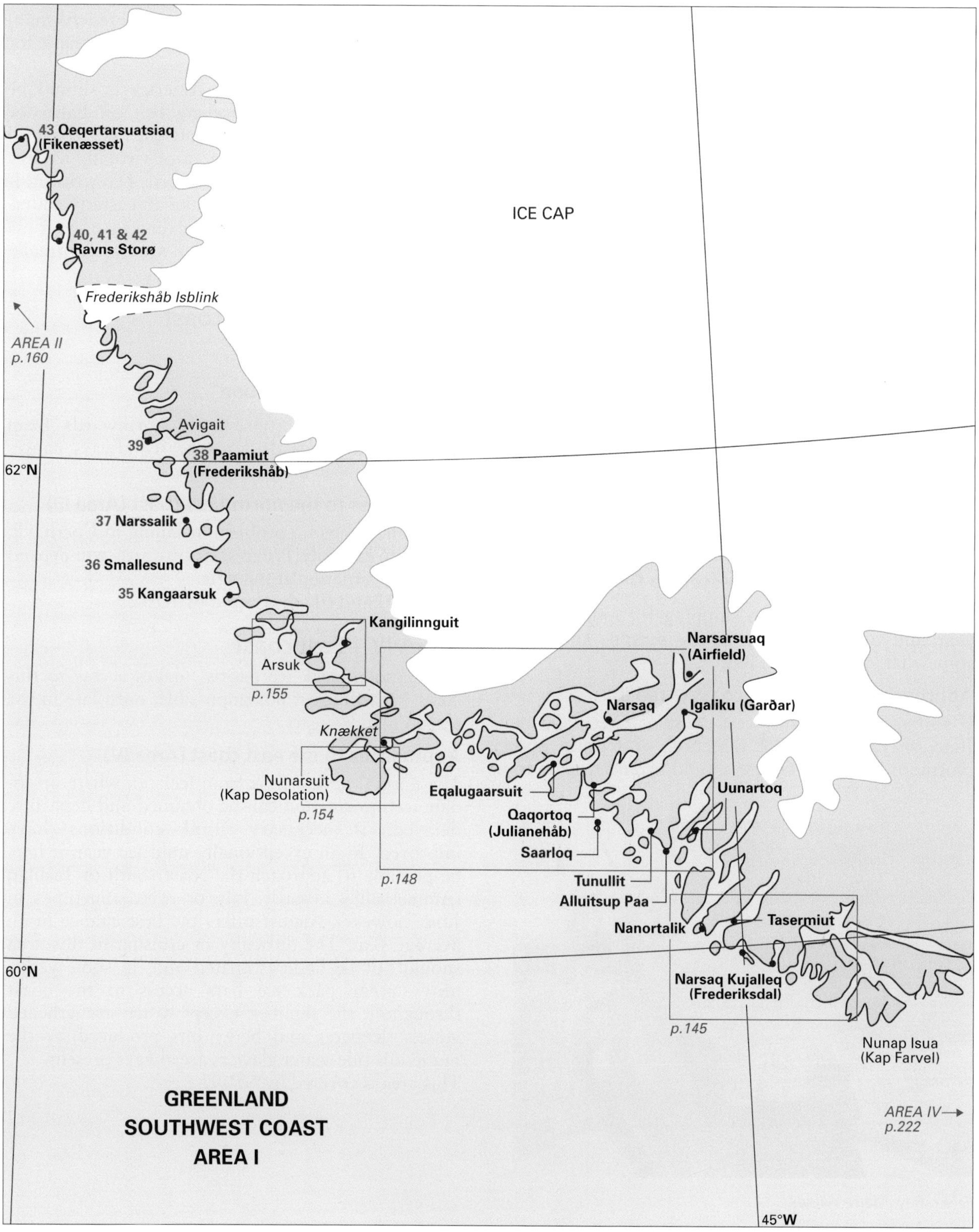

General

Much of this area was settled by the Norse from Iceland in the 10th century. This was the Eystribygð (Eastern Settlement) which lasted until the late 15th century, when it died out for reasons not fully understood. There are a number of interesting archeological sites remaining from that period, the best preserved of which is Hvalsey Church, near Qaqortoq, whose walls and one window still stand after more than six centuries. Sheep farms have been re-established on many of the old farm sites and upwards of 20,000 lambs are produced every year. Reindeer are also grazed on the less productive land.

Approach

Caution The presence of heavy polar pack ice (storis) which comes around Kap Farvel, often as late as July, makes access to this area difficult and demands care.

1 Narsaq Kujalleq (Frederiksdal)

60°00'N 44°40'W

Charts D 1103 (1130)

A small fishing port with KNI store, post office and fuel. There is a small jetty; anchoring in the harbour is possible but could be uncomfortable. The historic Norse settlement of Herjólfsnes (Ikigait), with its ruined church, lies 2M to the SW.

Approach

Follow the instructions in *NP12. Chart D 1130* would be useful but is not essential.

Anchorages

2 Ikigait (Herjólfsnes) 60°00'N 44°43'W

This is well worth a visit and the attractive anchorage in a small bay facing NE offers shelter under most conditions. There is a below-water rock, not marked on the chart, just N of the anchorage.

Herjólf Báðarson was one of the Icelanders who accompanied Eirik the Red and settled here in 986. His son, Bjarni Herjólfsson, is credited with being the first European to sight America, having been blown off course on a voyage from Iceland to join his father the following summer. Archaeological digs have shown that there was European occupation here until at least the middle of the 15th century – the last real evidence of Norse settlement in Greenland.

Ikigait (Herjolfsnes) small bay opposite Frederiksdal
Máire Wilkes

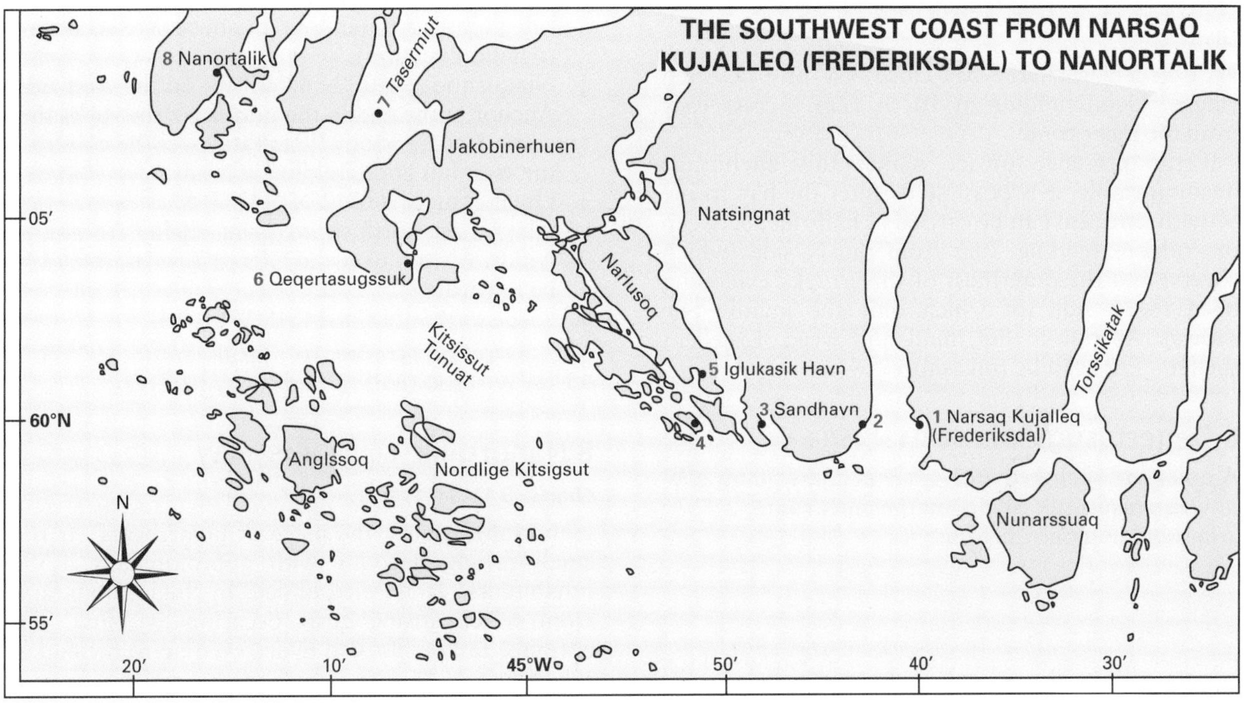

3 Sandhavn (Māukarneq)

60°00′N 44°48′W

Charts 1103

A shallow sandy bay, 2M to the W of Ikigait (Herjólfsnes), which was an important harbour and trading centre during the Norse period. There is reported to be good anchorage in the NW corner.

4 Inner lead route from Narsaq Kujalleq (Frederiksdal) to Nanortalik

60°00′N 44°51′W

Charts D 1113 (1130, 1131)

If ice is bad in the Kitsissut Tunuat, the inner route between the islands of Illukasik and Narlusoq provides a sheltered alternative (see *NP12*) with a couple of good anchorages.

The below-water rock in mid channel (60°02'·3N 44°55'W), mentioned in *NP12*, uncovers at low water and appears to be closer to the beacon than indicated. The SW side of the channel is steep-to and if the rock cannot be seen, it would be advisable to proceed with care within a boat's length or so of the SW side.

Approach

See *NP12*.

Anchorages

5 Iglukasik Havn 60°01′N 44°51′W

Charts 1103

An excellent sheltered bay close NW of a deserted village. Good holding in 10 to 12m. Access easy from the inner route.

If the presence of ice makes this anchorage uncomfortable, it is possible to enter the bay to the W with care. 2m can be carried at half-tide, between the ridge extending 20m from the N side (which covers) and the outermost of three rocks extending from the S side (of which only the middle one shows). Anchor in 8m, mud and weed. Excellent shelter – lines can be run ashore.

6 Qeqertasugssuk 60°04′N 45°06′W

A quiet and sheltered anchorage in a bay 600m NW of Qeqertasugssuk island, on the inner route.

Fair holding only in 15m.

Tasermiut *Adam Lugiewicz*

7 Tasermiut (Ketils Fjord)

60°07′N 45°08′W

Charts D 1113 (1131) Map 60 V 2

A highly spectacular fjord, which is entered just SE of Nanortalik and runs 30M NE to a tide-water glacier. A 'mecca' for serious rock climbers but also an important area during the Norse settlement. The remains of the Augustinian Monastery at Klosterdal (Uiluit kuua) (60°27′N 44°33′W) can still be seen.

Anchorages

Although only the lower section of the fjord is on the chart, the fjord is deep without dangers and can probably be navigated up to the glacier face. Anchorage can be found at Tasiussaq and also on the S side of the bay where the stream debouches from Tasersuaq Lake. There are almost certainly anchorages off the old Norse farmsteads marked on the map, which could be investigated.
Some of which are:

1. Jacobinerhuen (60°06′N 45°04′W) on the east side going north (choose an anchorage according to wind direction)
2. Niaqornoq (60°09′N 45°07′W) on the west side. Anchor at the end in the pool after the rocks that cover. Can be windy (katabatic over the col) from the west but good holding in mud
3. Quvnerssuaq (60°12′N 44°54′W) – a pleasant inlet on the north shore giving shelter from most winds. A walk over the hills to Tasuissarssuk can be rewarding
4. Tasuissoq (60°12′N 44°48′W).

The narrow entrance to Tasuissarssuk 60°11′N 45°04′W is too shallow and rocky for entry.

8 Nanortalik 60°08′N 45°14′W

Charts D 1113 (1131)

Nanortalik means 'the place of polar bears'. It is a small fishing harbour with approximately 1,500 inhabitants. It is surrounded by high mountains from which strong gusts occasionally blow. The entrance can be blocked by ice even up to the end of

Nanortalik *Máire Wilkes*

July, particularly in S winds. The harbour is exposed to the SE; but alternative shelter is available close by, in the bay NE of the town.

Approach

Follow the instructions in *NP12* if approaching from the S, or alternatively, approach can be made from the N through the Ikerasarssuq (see *NP12* & *Chart D 1131*).

Anchorage

Vessels can anchor or lie alongside. The fish jetty has two usable faces, the northernmost rebuilt in 2013. There is also a second short jetty to the west past the fuel storage area in mid harbour. Both sides have space for yachts up to about 50′. The face dock has more room. The small boat harbour is attractive and sheltered, but very shallow and not suitable for a boat with a deep keel.

Alternative secluded anchorages can be found in the circular fjord just NE of Nanortalik in position 60°09′N 45°10′W and at Quagssuo Tuna, the bay just to the north the town, where care is required in the approaches. *Chart D 1161* is helpful but not essential.

Young girl, Nanortalik *Máire Wilkes*

Facilities

There are two small hotels, the Kap Farvel and the Tupalik, where it is possible to get meals and showers. There are two supermarkets with all the usual foodstuffs and hardware. Diesel is available at the jetty next to the small boat harbour where a depth of 2.0m has been reported at low water. Containers are required to take on fresh water. There is a good boatyard and machine shop. The town has a post office, an attractive church, as well as some interesting old buildings around the old harbour and a small hospital. There is a heliport with regular flights to Narsarsuaq. The tourist office is helpful and the museums interesting. WiFi at tourist office and restaurant.

9 Uunartoq 60°30′N 45°20′W

Charts D 1113, 1114

Uunartoq island lies 7M ENE of Alluitsup Paa (Sydprøven). A hot spring, well known to the Norsemen and mentioned in the Sagas, is now something of a tourist attraction. It lies just SW of the isthmus at the N end. Well worth a visit and a bathe, with the fjord a mass of small icebergs by way of contrast.

Approach

Beware the dangerous rock (60°29′·8N 45°22′·8W) off the W tip of the island, not marked on older charts.

Anchorage

Anchor in sand either side of the isthmus, depending on wind. The spring is closer to the W anchorage, which is also protected by a gravel spit.

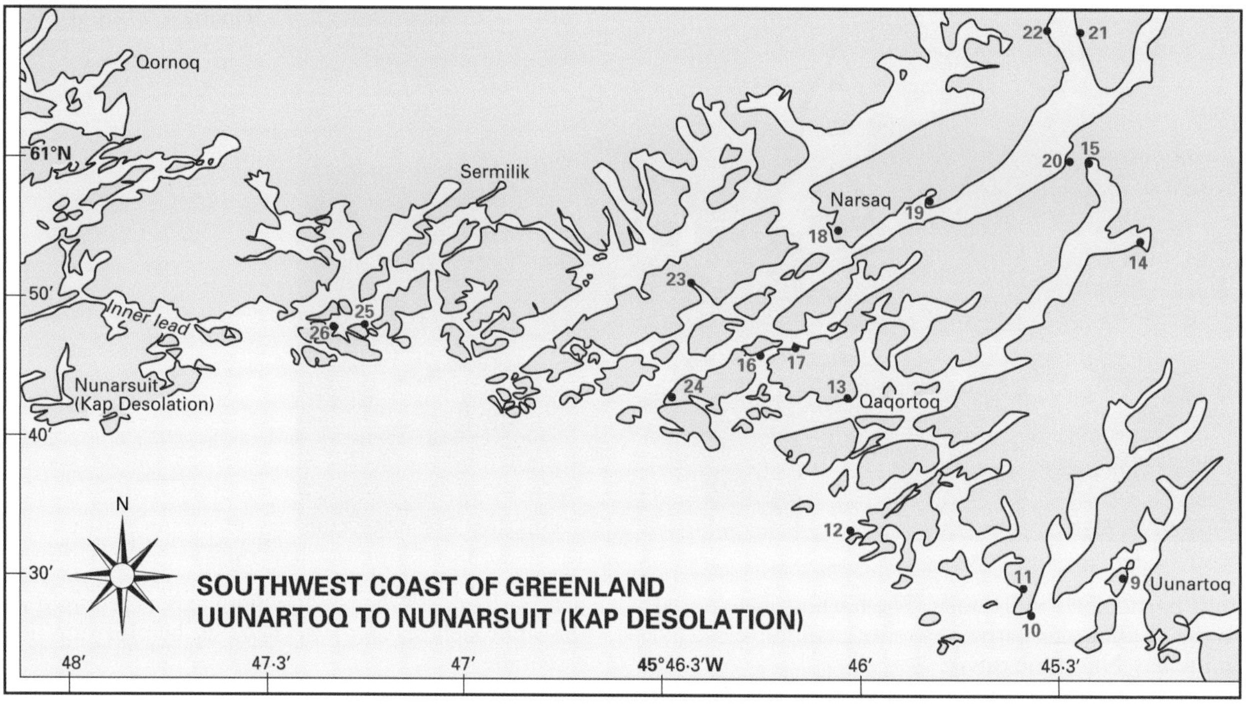

Uunartoq viking hot tub *M Hillman*

Channel NE of Simiultaq on inner lead between Qaqortoq and Sydprøven *Máire Wilkes*

10 Alluitsup Paa (Sydprøven)

60°28′N 45°33′W

Charts D 1113, 1114 (1150)

A small and basic settlement with a population of about 500, comprising a fishing harbour on the N side and a boat harbour on the S side. Alluitsup Paa is exposed to severe gusts from the mountains. It is also subject to swell. If conditions are unsuitable, shelter can be found in the anchorage at Tunullit (Zakarias Havn), see below.

Approach

At times between January and July the seaward passage between Nanortalik and Qaqortoq (Julianehåb) is blocked by ice, while the inland passage of Sermer-suup Saqqaa and Kanajormiut Ikerasaat to Alluitsup Paa (Sydprøven) is frequently open. The route is dramatic and scenically beautiful. The approaches to Alluitsup Paa are straightforward (see *NP12*).

Anchorage

The N fishing harbour is located in a creek named Quarsorat, beside the main settlement. There is a fishery jetty with 2·5m MLWS where it is possible to tie alongside. There is little traffic in this harbour but there is a harbour manager. A passenger ferry from Qaqortoq is a fairly regular visitor. The S boat harbour has depths of 4m MLWS. Both harbours can, at times, be blocked by ice between January and July.

Facilities

There are two hotels and a supermarket which is fairly well stocked with food supplies. It is possible to get diesel by arrangement with the fish factory but Qaqortoq (Julianehåb) or Nanortalik are better fuelling ports.

Alluitsup Paa (Sydprøven) *Máire Wilkes*

11 Tunullit (Zakarias Havn)

60°29'N 45°35'W

Zakarias Havn, which is entered 1·75M NNW of Sydprøven, is a really good anchorage (see *NP12*). When entering, keep mid-channel between the S point with the beacon and the two small islands NW of this. Anchor in the middle in 10 to 14m, good holding; better shelter from the E, in less water, can be found further in. Excellent water from the stream on the N side of the anchorage, but there are some underwater rocks to be avoided.

12 Sadrloq 60°32'N 46°01'W

Charts D 1114, 1150

A small settlement of about 44 inhabitants which is about half the 1990 levels, who emigrated from East Greenland. It is worth visiting if you want to see a small and isolated Greenlandic settlement. In SE winds this harbour can be subject to severe mountain gusts. Between January and July, Sadrloq can be blocked by ice.

Approach

Sadrloq is on the inner route from Alluitsup Paa to Qaqortoq (see *NP12*).

Anchorage

There is a jetty alongside the settlement with timber facing and a depth of 2m MLWS where it is possible to tie up. If anchoring, do not do so in the main Ikerasak Channel, as it is much used by vessels going to Qaqortoq. Anchor in Torssukaatáraq between Saarloq Island and Inugsuk.

Facilities

Drinking water from the de-salination plant. Weekly helicopter flights.

13 Qaqortoq (Julianehåb)

60°43'N 46°02'W

Charts D 1114, 1115, 1116 (1132, 1151)

Qaqortoq is an attractive place and the largest town in SW Greenland, with a population of about 3,200. This is an excellent centre from which to explore the Eystribygð, the Norse East Settlement, now a sheep-farming area with one or two reindeer ranches as well. The harbour caters for small container ships as well as the coastal passenger vessels. The fjord is often blocked by an incursion of storis between January and July and ice (though not large icebergs) may enter the harbour.

The harbour is open to the S but has a stone breakwater running E from the W shore. Strong winds from the S are not frequent, but when they occur they are dangerous because they set up high waves and swell in the harbour, at times washing straight over the breakwater. When this happens it may be necessary to leave the harbour and seek shelter under Akia or in the nearby passages (see below). With strong winds between E and NE it can be squally.

Approach

Straightforward (see *NP12*).

Harbour

The harbour is extremely crowded and it is not feasible to anchor. The Atlantic pier is reserved for large commercial vessels, while the schooner pier is usually lined with fishing vessels and local passenger boats; it may be possible to tie up at the root of the new container quay. The small fishery jetty is kept busy by many small craft and is not suitable for yachts, nor is the 'marina' in the area behind the breakwater, which is filled with small local craft. There are moorings in the inlet NE of the Atlantic pier to the W of the ship-repair yard. Take advice from the harbourmaster, whose office is in the Royal Arctic building. Try calling on VHF Ch 16 or 12 during working hours.

Qaqortoq *Máire Wilkes*

Alternative anchorages

Alternative anchorages can be found in Qaqortoq Fjord, about 12nm ENE of Qaqortoq, at Hvalsey Church (Qaqortoq Kirkeruin) (60°49'N 45°47'W). If strong southerly winds should make this a lee shore, shelter can be found in coves on the south shore of the inlet beyond the sheep farm (60°49'N 45°45'W), the second (east) of the two together having fewer underwater rocks.

A sheltered cove on the south side of Qernertup nua (60°48'N 45°47'W) also offers protection from southerly winds.

Qaqortoq *Máire Wilkes*

Facilities

There is one hotel and one or two bars and restaurants of varying quality. Restaurant Napparsivik has been recommended. Showers, clothes washing, and WiFi may be available in the high school/hostel at the far side of town. Maps at the Tourist Office.

Fuel at the pontoon on the west side of harbour, but access can be narrow as it is restricted by local boat moorings. Water by hose on the third pontoon from the west shore of the small boat harbour. Propane from Polaroil.

The two main supermarkets, KNI and Brugsen, have everything you want and there are one or two other butiks as well as bakeries, bookshops, banks and a post office. There is a hospital and full medical facilities.

There is a ship-repair yard, which can handle most work, including engine repairs and GRP (fibreglass) repairs, with a fully enclosed and heated shed. There are also a couple of well-equipped electronic workshops.

There is a heliport with frequent flights to the main airfield at Narsarsuaq.

Remarks

A visit to the Museum and the Old Stone House is rewarding; there are many artefacts illustrating the 'old ways' of the Kalaaleq.

Qaqortoq (Julianhab) *Máire Wilkes*

The 14th century Norse church at Hvalsey *Bob Shepton*

In September each year, the Greenland Adventure Race is held. This is a guelling five-day event which includes running, mountain biking and kayaking in the fjords between Qaqortoq and Narsaq.

Chart *D 1115* shows the magnificent cruising grounds around Qaqortoq. An excursion to the best-preserved ruined church in Greenland, at Hvalsey, is worthwhile. If visiting Hvalsey, 10M NE of Qaqortoq, it is possible to anchor off in 10m, mud. Another is a visit to Igaliku, the site of the old Norse cathedral, palace and farm of Garðar. The ruins of the church, the farm and stables are still visible. Several sheep farmers now live there.

Instead of sailing up Igaliku fjord, you can visit Garðar on the way to Narsarsuaq. The two fjords are only separated by a narrow isthmus and it is a pleasant walk along the Kongevejen (Kings Way) from Tunugdliarfik (Eriks Fjord) – see under Narsarsuaq.

View from hotel, Qaqortoq *Máire Wilkes*

14 Søndre Igaliku 60°54′N 45°17′W

Charts 1115

A temporary anchorage, subject to katabatic winds.

Farm and interesting Norse church ruin. This attractive area was settled by the Norse and known as the Vatnaverfi. From Søndre Igaliku, a track leads 10M SW past sheep farms and lakes to a useful anchorage in a bay facing NW at Qanisartuut (60°50′N 45°29′W).

15 Igaliku 61°00′N 45°25′W

Charts 1115

It is possible to anchor in the bay just N of the settlement.

See also 20 Ittileq

16 Mato Løb Passage 60°46′N 46°15′W

Charts D 1116, 1132 (1151)

This is a convenient short-cut from Qaqortoq to Narsaq; but, if in doubt, check with Iscentralen, Narsarsuaq before going through. If there is much storis offshore there is a better chance of getting through the Mato Løb than going out to sea.

Route

The passage is straightforward and D 1116 is adequate. The only danger in the approach from the SE, is a pair of rocks awash half a mile ESE of Kilagtoq light structure – even local boats have been known to hit these!

Anchorage

There are bays for anchoring in the Mato Løb, close to the shore. This waterway will provide shelter from all winds and weather, but is rather open. Better shelter can be found in Eqalugaarsuit (see below).

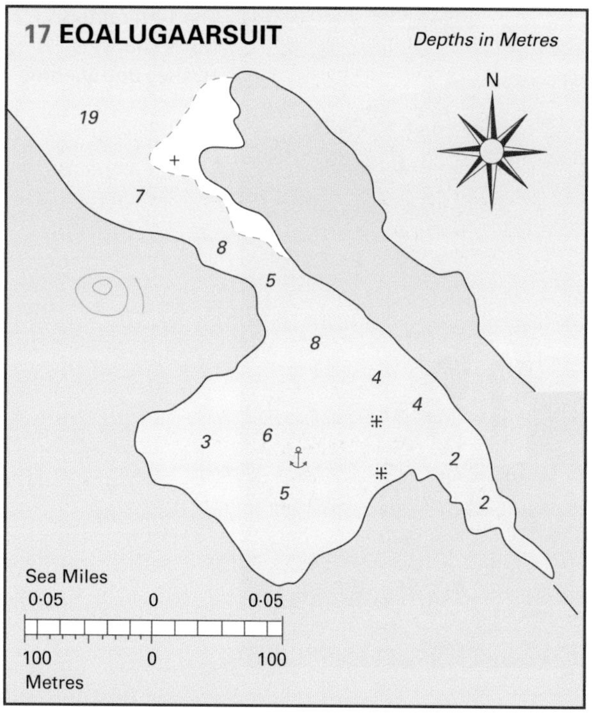

Narsaq *E. Grodel*

17 Eqalugaarsuit 60°46'N 46°10'W

Charts 1115

This is the site of an abandoned settlement in a small creek at the northern entrance to the Mato Løb, providing perfect shelter. This should not be confused with the fishing harbour of Eqalugaarsuit, which is 6M NE of Saarloq.

Entrance

The entrance is just under 1M due E of Nupiluk point (see *NP12*) and can be identified by the prominent hillock on the SW side. The channel, though narrow, is clean and carries 5m.

Anchorage

Anchor in the middle of the small bay just inside the entrance to starboard in 5 to 8m. Holding is good and there is adequate swinging room. There is a rock 50m N of the SE point of the bay; this dries at springs but remains covered at LW neaps. Additional anchorage in Tunulliarfik (Skovfjorden or Eiriksfjord)

18 Narsaq 60°55'N 46°03'W

Charts D 1115, 1116 (1151)

Narsaq means 'the plain'. It is a picturesque little town situated under a high mountain with a population of about 2,000. The approach can be quite dramatic when the glacier at the head of Sermilik (Bredefjord) is calving.

The fish plant doubles as a slaughterhouse in the autumn for the 18,000 lambs raised on the sheep farms in this district, which are brought to the harbour in a converted landing craft.

Approach

From seaward, Simiutaq at the entrance to Skovfjord is easily identified by the tall radio mast. Straightforward thereafter, but ice may cause problems.

It is also possible to approach Narsaq up Bredefjord by steering to pass just N of Inugsugtût light. Once abeam of this light the passage in Bredefjord is clear. Frequently, however, Bredefjord is impassable because of huge quantities of ice and bergs drifting down from a busy glacier at its head. Consequently the Skovfjord approach is safer unless you have clearance for Bredefjord from Ice Central.

Harbour

In the East Harbour, there is a new L-shaped concrete quay with an arm 90m long and a minimum of 4m alongside on the inner face. This should provide much better shelter than hitherto.

Facilities

Most supplies are available at the supermarkets and there is an excellent bakery. There are two small hotels, as well as a couple of restaurants and bars. Showers are available at Hotel Narsaq or the Youth Hostel. There is an ATM at the post office. Water is available in the harbour and fuel is delivered by tanker, but for small quantities it may be more convenient to sail into the shallow West Harbour. There are diesel and petrol pumps by the roadside 200m away from the float, which has about 1m alongside at LW.

Narsaq is a port of call for the Arctic Umiaq Line ferry service.

19 Karra 60°56′N 45°50′W

Charts 1115

Good anchorage can be found inside the point NE of Karra island in a small bay facing NW. Anchor in 5m, mud, with lines ashore if necessary.

20 Ittileq 61°00′N 45°28′W

Charts 1115

It is a pleasant walk along the ancient Kongevejen, a track which goes from Ittileq a couple of miles across the isthmus to Igaliku. There, the remains of the old Norse cathedral and farm at Garðar are well worth a visit. There is a small village and a few sheep farms in the area.

There is a jetty on the S side of the peninsula at Ittileq; but this is exposed to the full fetch of the Tunugdliarfik. There is better anchorage on the N side of the peninsula in 10m, sand. If there is much ice coming out of Qooroq, it may be carried into the bay by an eddy at certain states of the tide, making the anchorage untenable.

21 Narsarsuaq 61°09′N 45°26′W

Charts D 1115 (1151)

Narsarsuaq ('the large plain') is the main airport for SW Greenland and was built by the US in 1941, as a staging post for military aircraft flying to Europe. It was decommissioned in 1958. The following year, the passenger ship *Hans Hedtoft*, on her maiden voyage, was lost in the ice off Kap Farvel. There were no survivors and, as a result, the Danish government set up the ice advisory service with reconnaissance aircraft – now called Iscentralen (Ice Patrol) – and the airfield was brought back into use. It has a permanent population of 200 people, greatly increased during the summer months by passengers in transit and by tour groups.

Approach

The approach to Narsarsuaq is clear, but when approaching the mouth of Qooroq it is best to keep to the W side of Tunulliarfik (Eiriks Fjord), to avoid glacier ice coming out of Qooroq.

Harbour

The harbour consists of a 140m pier with 6–11m on the outside and 5–8m on the inside at MLWS. The W side (outside) of the pier is reserved for larger ships. Yachts and small vessels should moor on the E side, where there is better shelter. If the ice boom is in place, there may be insufficient clearance above the wire for a deep-keel yacht to go beyond the boom. With prolonged southerly winds the harbour can become blocked with ice.

Facilities

There is a large hotel with a café and a good but expensive dining room; showers are available. There is a small supermarket at the back of the accommodation block with adequate supplies. There is no bank. Water and fuel are available in the harbour. At the airport, the duty-free shop is available to incoming passengers and prices are very reasonable. It is worthwhile making contact with Iscentralen; all the up-to-date ice information is there, ice charts are available and it is pleasant to see the faces of those people to whom you have been talking on the radio.

22 Qassiarsuk (Brattahlíð)

61°09′N 45°31′W

Charts 1115

Brattahlið lies just across the fjord from Narsarsuaq. This is where Eirik the Red settled and farmed in 986 and the remains of his longhouse and other ruins are still to be seen. There is a small museum and a reconstruction of a Viking longhouse as well as one or two other reconstructions and is well worth a visit. There are a number of sheep farms in and around the village.

The small pier is in constant use, but temporary anchorage can be found anywhere along the shore.

23 Sildefiord (Tugtutoq Island)

60°51′N 46°25′W

Charts 1116

There is an excellent anchorage 11M WSW of Narsaq, on the SE side of Tugtutoq Island. Complete shelter at the head of a long, narrow fjord. Anchor in a pool below an old Norse farm site in 12m. A most attractive spot and very secluded. Good walks and reindeer on the hill.

24 Motzfeld Havn 60°43′N 46°28′W

Charts 1116

A small bay on the N side of Ikerasarssuk, between Hollænderø and Kingitoq. Just inside the entrance, there is a rock almost awash at HW, which should be left to port. Anchor in 5m.

25 Tunulliatsiaap Nunaa

60°48′N 47°15′W

Charts 1116

An almost landlocked bay, offering perfect shelter, in the Nordlige Mågeløb opposite Pinguiarneq Island. The entrance carries 3·5m; anchor in 5·5m.

26 Nunakajaat 60°48′N 47°20′W

Charts 1116

A narrow creek on Nunakajaat Island, which is on the S side of the Nordlige Mågeløb. The entrance to the creek is marked by two beacons. Anchor in 10m.

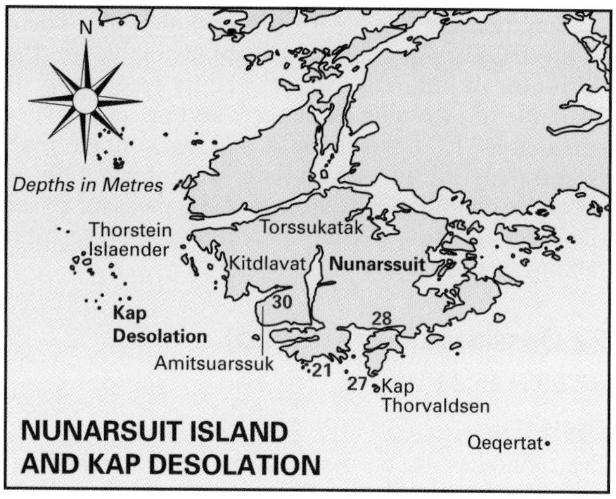

27 Nunarsuit Island and Kap Desolation

60°45′N 48°00′W

Nunarsuit is a large island 130M NW of Kap Farvel. Kap Desolation, named by Davis in 1585, is at the southwestern extremity of the Island and 9M WNW of Kap Thorvaldsen. The scenery is magnificent. The Thorstein Isænder group of islets lie 4M off Nunarsuit. From here, the coastline follows a more northerly direction. Storis ice originating on the east coast of Greenland rounds Kap Farvel and is borne northwards on the West Greenland Current. Much of it runs aground in the Kap Desolation area and there is often enough ice present for it to be a navigation hazard. There are a number of good anchorages in the area, some of which are mentioned in *NP12*. Bob Shepton has cruised in the area several times and reports interesting pilotage, scenically impressive peaks, reindeer herds, sea eagles, good hiking and dramatic climbing. Some of the anchorages he has used are given below.

27a Kap Thorvaldsen 60°40′N 47°54′W

A rather unique anchorage, protected except perhaps from the east, in the channel between the cliff of Kap Thorvaldsen and the line of islands at its foot.

The entrance on the east side is wider. Beware rocks to the north side when entering. Anchor in the NW corner of the channel. It may be possible to take lines ashore. Any ice within the bay tends to move west on the flooding tide and east on the ebb. There are usually fewer icebergs inside the anchorage than out.

27b West Kap Thorvaldsen

Anchor in 60°41′N 47°55′W where it is possible to find shelter in the north east corner in north winds.

Nunarsuit (Kap Desolation) Approach to inner lead from northwest *Máire Wilkes*

Kap Thorsvalden - inside channel *Bob Shepton*

28 Saningardlak

Saningardlak is the waterway 2·5M north of Kap Thorvaldsen running from west to east along the parallel 60°42′N. Anchorages, all of which need careful pilotage, have been reported at:

- 60°42′N 47°54′W – a pleasant cove which is protected except from the northwest
- 60°42′N 47°56′W
- 60°42′N 47°57′W

29 Kangerdluluk

Three anchorages are reported on the southern shore of Kangerdluluk promontory on the south of Nunarsuit and west of Kap Thorvaldsen. These are:

- 60°41′N 48°00′W Coming south down the west side of the fjord. A long fjord, surprisingly ice free. Anchor at the far end just before the final narrows (too shallow within) or in an inlet just after the first narrows (60°41′N 49°59′W) on the north side.
- 60°41′N 48°01′W The inlet to the north of the prominent spire shaped peak on the shoreline (the ‘Thumb’) or at the end of the inlet which is protected but often subject to ice.
- 60°41′N 48°03′W (Kangerdluluk) Convenient when approaching from the north or west. Anchorages can be found in bays and slots especially on the north side beyond the mid-island and the rock which covers.

30 West Nunarsuit

30a Hvibdjørnens Havn 60°44'N 48°06'W

A sheltered anchorage can be found in the channel between the island and mainland on the north side, preferably with lines ashore. The harbour to the north here can be prone to big icebergs. The zawn (a deep and narrow sea-inlet cut by erosion into sea cliffs with steep or vertical side-walls) on the southern side opposite might be possible but looked unfriendly.

30b Head of Hvibdjørnens Fjord

60°44'N 48°05'W

A pleasant anchorage past the dramatic rock scenery in the fjord to the east of Kap Desolation. It is on the northern side between two islands. Anchor at the start of the channel. A reef bars entry into the inner pool. Lines ashore can be rigged. Eagles and reindeer can be seen above and ashore.

The 6m sounding on the chart in the main fjord appeared to be mythical. The fjord can be guarded by big icebergs.

The longer narrow channel on the north side at the end of the fjord is shallow and rock strewn.

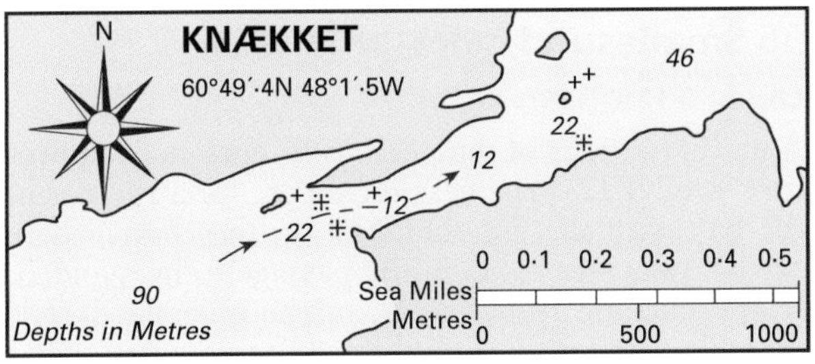

Inner lead north of Nunarsuit (Kap Desolation)

60°50'N 48°00'W

Charts D 1116, 1117 (1167, 1168)

Charts 1116 and *1117* are adequate for the passage, although Knækket appears obstructed by rocks at the smaller scale. It is used by quite large craft and carries at least 10m in mid-channel.

The inner lead runs E–W from Inugsugtût Light through either the Sydlige Mågeløb or the Nordlige Mågeløb and thence through Ikerasassuaq, Knækket and Torsukattak. The route is useful if there is storis to be avoided around Nunarsuit (Kap Desolation).

If entering Torsukattak from seawards, there are a number of off-lying islets and rocks in the approach, so good visibility or radar are essential, since there are no navigational aids. The routes are adequately marked with beacons. (See *NP12*.)

Note that the flood tide makes strongly westwards through the Ikerasassuaq and out to sea through the Knækket.

31 Kangilinnguit (Grønnedal)

61°14'N 48°06'W

Charts D 1146

Grønnedal, near the head of Arsuk Fjord, was the site of the Royal Danish Navy HQ of the Admiral, Island Commander Greenland. The base was originally established to protect the important cryolite mine at Ivittuut (Ivigtut), now worked out.

The base has now moved to Nuuk and the buildings abandoned.

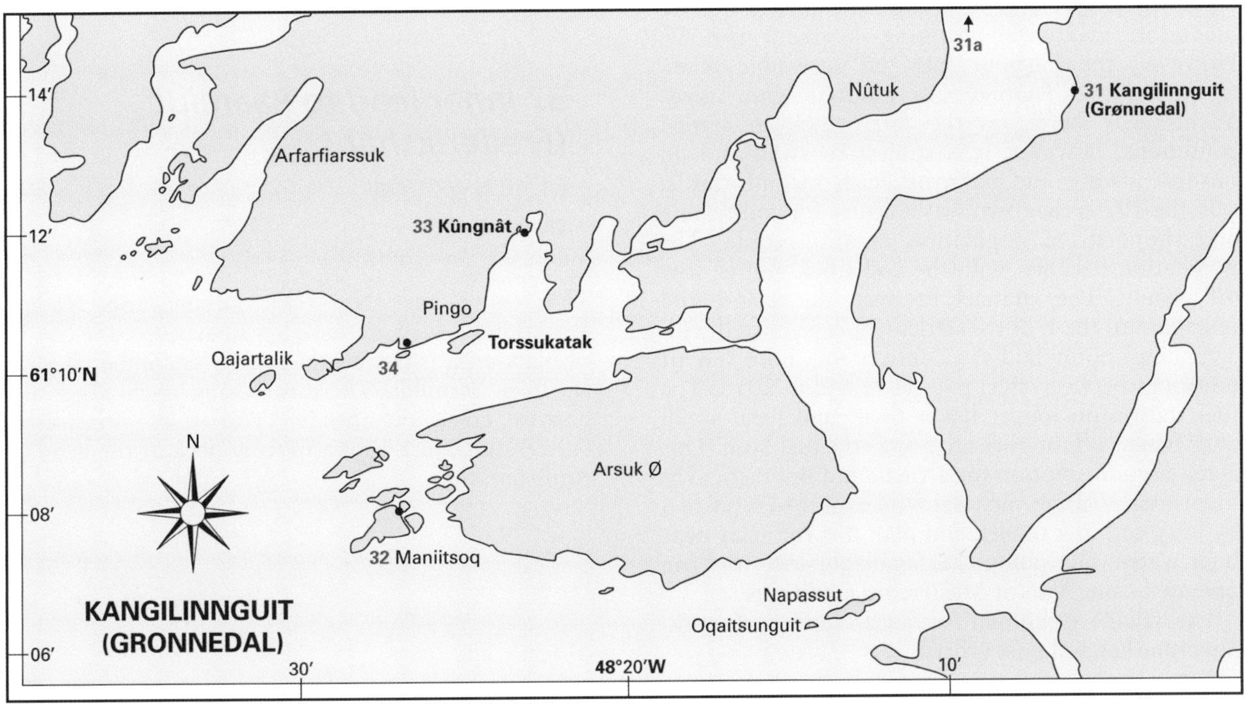

Approach

Approach either through the Søndre Løb or through the Karsakken, which, though narrow, is straightforward (see *NP12*).

Harbour

The main jetty is reported to be dilapidated and unusable.

31a Ellerslie Havn, Arsukfjord

61°18'N 48°08'W

Charts D 1146

An almost landlocked and very attractive anchorage NW of Kangilinnguit. Anchor in 8m, thick mud, beneath a waterfall.

Anchorages in the approaches

32 Maniitsoq 61°08'N 48°27'W

Charts 1118

There is a useful protected anchorage off Isberg Sund, in the S of two bays on the NE side of Maniitsoq. Anchor in 5m, good holding. Lines could be taken ashore if necessary.

33 Kûngnât Bugt 61°12'N 48°23'W

Charts 1118

Anchor near the head in 5m about 1 cable SW of the beacon, good holding. The inner bay at the outflow of the river is shoal.

34 Arsuk village 61°10'N 48°27'W

Charts 1118

Small pretty village and harbour. Prone to ice incursion and swell running in from the W. However, the harbour may be accessible when Qaqortoq and Paamiut are blocked with storis. Yachts may berth on the ferry dock in settled conditions, however, it is subject to swell and an onshore wind would make this berth uncomfortable.

In the 1970s the town was a centre for cod fishing and supported a population of 400 people. The population declined with the cod stock and is now 90 people. The channel between the island and mainland to the E of the settlement is protected with a chain ice-boom laid at a depth of 4m. Fore and aft moorings between steel piles were laid in 2015. The fuel station no longer has a float, and local small craft fender off the rocks to access the fuel hose. This is not a good solution for a yacht and impractical at low water. Visiting yachts should expect to ferry fuel by jerry can in a tender, and plan this for at or near high water. The pumps are available 24/7 and are operated using Visa or Mastercard credit cards.

The village is known for its art and craftwork. Supermarket and post office.

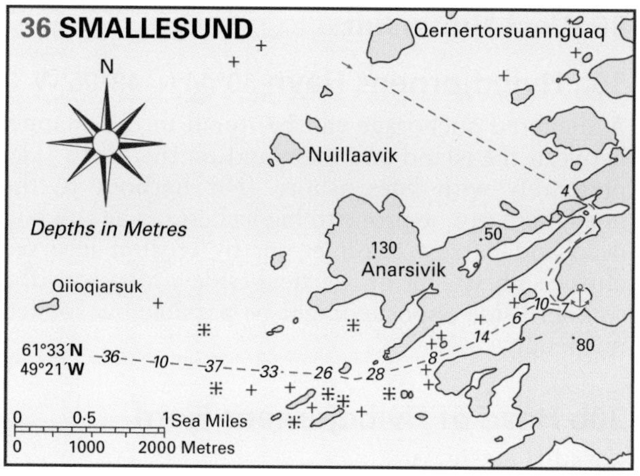

Anchorages on the coast between Arsuk Island and Paamiut

35 Kangaarssuk 61°28'N 49°00'W

Charts D 1210 (1251)

Easier to access than Smallesund and sheltered by a group of small islands. Anchor off an abandoned settlement in the NE corner of the bay or in a small inlet in the SW corner in 9m.

36 Smallesund 61°33'N 49°16'W

Charts D 1210 (1251)

A useful harbour of refuge, but the entrance requires care (see *NP12*). The best anchorage for a yacht is in the bay with the 7m sounding on the chart. There are below-water rocks in the passage to be avoided. If approaching from the N, in the inner lead, it is possible to enter through the very narrow passage at the NE end of Anarsivik, carrying 4m.

37 Inner lead to Paamiut (Frederikshåb)

61°40'N 49°19'W

Charts D 1210

This route past Narssalik village and NE of Vesterland is well marked; but Imartuneq, the bay N of Narssalik, is frequently heavily encumbered with ice from Sermilik. There is a snug anchorage in a narrow creek on the NE corner of Anarnitsoq (Vesterland), just N of a narrow neck at the head of Amitsuarssuk.

Narssalikhavn *Máire Wilkes*

Narssalik village *Máire Wilkes*

38 Paamiut (Frederikshåb)

62°00'N 49°40'W

Charts D 1211

Paamiut ('those who live by the mouth') is a small harbour with a population of 1,620. Its main attraction is that it is very sheltered. Rather drab blocks of flats and high unemployment detract from the beauty of the place and it is said to be the most expensive town in Greenland to reach by air. However, it does provide a starting point for an interesting inner lead to the N, which passes close to the Frederikshåbs Isblink. It can be blocked by ice as late as July.

Approach

Although it is sometimes possible to approach Paamiut, when storis precludes closing the Greenland coast further S, Paamiut has the reputation of being one of the more difficult harbours to approach because of ice brought round

Paamiut quay *Máire Wilkes*

Paamiut landfall *Bob Shepton*

on the East Greenland Current, even as late as August. The harbour is a little 'coy' and does not make itself obvious; but the burnt-out wreck of the Greenland Star on the rocks in the entrance is a useful landmark.

Berth

It should be possible to lie alongside one of the quays. The narrow creek, where a lot of small craft are on marina-type floats, is shallow and not suitable for a yacht.

Facilities

Good supermarket. Convenient diesel hose from fuel station to boats. Helpful tourist office. Showers at the large sports hall. Washing machines under the community flats with tokens from the post office. Fuel and water. Expensive helicopter connection to Narsarsuaq and airport. Paamiut is known for its soapstone artists. It is a port of call for the Arctic Umiaq ferry service.

Paamiut shop
Máire Wilkes

Alternative anchorages

Alternative anchorages in the SE approaches to Paamiut can be found at:

- **Ikerasak** 61°54'N 49°26'W
  Open roadstead but a convenient anchorage by two pebble beaches on the western shore near the start of the inner channel to the south and east of Paamiut, a little before the narrows leading to or from Kuanersoq (Kvanerfjord)

Paamiut - mooring warps to allow for a big tidal range *Bob Shepton*

- **Ikergsasarssuk** 61°55'N 49°25'W
  South and east of Paamiut. A short fjord with a right angled off-shoot giving an intriguing hurricane hole with protection from all winds. It can be found just west of the narrows marking the start of the inner passage leading to Kuanersoq (Kvanefjord). Anchor in the east inlet or pool, or in the south cove – beware of a rock which covers on east side. Possible to pass either side of the rock island.

Frederikshåb Isblink to Qeqertarsuatsiaat (Fiskenæsset)

62°30'N 50°20'W

Charts D 1211, 1212

Inner lead route

An interesting inner lead route from Paamiut to Qeqertarsuatsiaat (Fiskenæsset) (see *NP12*). The route is marked by rather indistinct beacons. Reasonably good visibility and binoculars are needed; but it is not difficult to keep to the surveyed track with its line of soundings. The route passes close to the Frederikshåb Isblink, an impressive but rather grubby 'piedmont' fan of ice, with a 10M foot fronted with sand flats and dunes and what might pass for an attractive sandy bathing beach in warmer climes. There are two or three useful anchorages on or near Ravns Storø, 12M N of the glacier.

Note This route should not be attempted if there is a strong onshore wind or heavy swell, as part of the route is exposed to the open sea and it becomes a lee shore.

Pilotage

Depths are mostly more than 2m, but NW of Ravns Storø there is an exceedingly narrow passage on Kangaatsiaup-Timaa with 2m shown on the chart. This is clean, but needs care and is less intimidating at high water. It is possible to avoid this by going out to sea from Ravns Storø.

From the narrows at Kangaatsiaup-Timaa, however, the route is interesting and straightforward, passing to the east of Qeqertarsuatsiaat.

Anchorages

39 Avigait 62°13'N 049° 51'W

There is a convenient passage anchorage at Avigait (NW of Niaqornaq), which is an abandoned settlement but with well kept houses used in the summer. The bay is well protected from all directions, but the northern half is rock strewn and shoal. Anchor in 10m with good holding in mud and weed.

40 Ravns Storø, North Harbour

62°44'N 50°25'W

Chart 1212

An abandoned Faroese fishing camp with a dilapidated wooden quay tucked in to the SE corner which has now collapsed and is dangerous. Holding in the harbour is very unreliable, due to heavy weed; but lines could be run ashore. The mooring buoy in the middle is in use by local fishing boats. A convenient and very sheltered harbour disturbed only by the croak of ravens.

There is an alternative anchorage in the entrance to a narrow bay 200m W of the quay. Anchor in 4·5m, mud. The head is shoal.

41 Ravns Storø, South Harbour

62°43'N 50°23'W

Chart 1212

Although somewhat exposed to the SW, it is protected from all other directions and is a useful passage anchorage. Access is straightforward. The entrance is marked by a well maintained beacon on the SW point. Anchor near the head in 10m, good holding.

42 Teisten Havn 62°41'N 50°20'W

Chart 1212

NP12 mentions Teisten Havn, the northernmost of two bays on the W side of Umiarssuakulup nuna. It is not very attractive and Ravns Storø North Harbour is preferable for yachts.

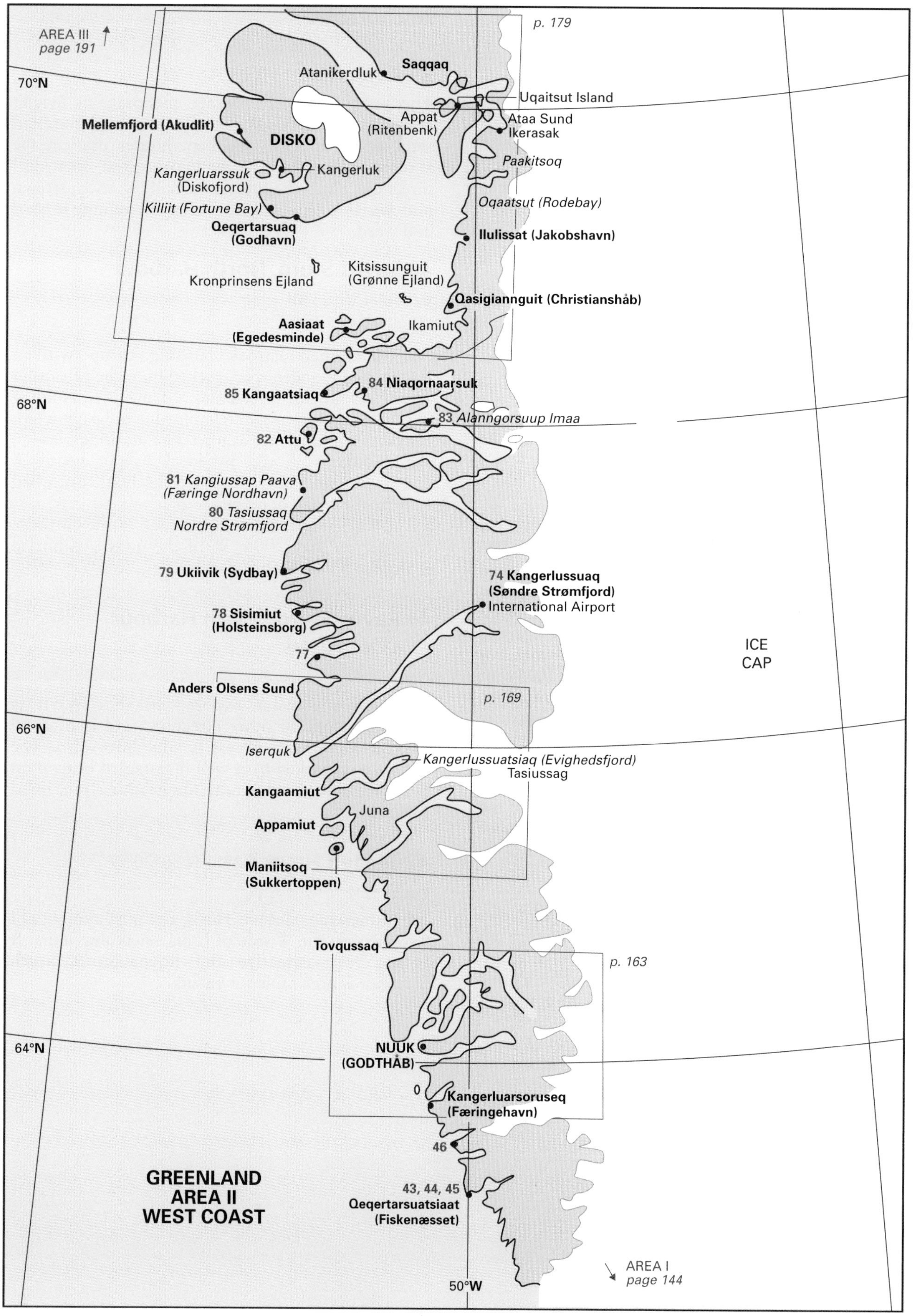
AREA III
page 191
p. 179
70°N
Atanikerdluk
Saqqaq
Uqaitsut Island
Appat
(Ritenbenk)
Ataa Sund
Ikerasak
Mellemfjord (Akudlit)
DISKO
Kangerluarssuk
(Diskofjord)
Kangerluk
Paakitsoq
Killiit (Fortune Bay)
Oqaatsut (Rodebay)
Qeqertarsuaq
(Godhavn)
Ilulissat (Jakobshavn)
Kitsissunguit
(Grønne Ejland)
Kronprinsens Ejland
Qasigiannguit (Christianshåb)
Aasiaat
(Egedesminde)
Ikamiut
84 Niaqornaarsuk
85 Kangaatsiaq
68°N
83 Alanngorsuup Imaa
82 Attu
81 Kangiussap Paava
(Færinge Nordhavn)
80 Tasiussaq
Nordre Strømfjord
79 Ukiivik (Sydbay)
74 Kangerlussuaq
(Søndre Strømfjord)
International Airport
78 Sisimiut
(Holsteinsborg)
ICE
CAP
77
Anders Olsens Sund
p. 169
66°N
Iserquk
Kangerlussuatsiaq (Evighedsfjord)
Tasiussag
Kangaamiut
Juna
Appamiut
Maniitsoq
(Sukkertoppen)
Tovqussaq
p. 163
64°N
NUUK
(GODTHÅB)
Kangerluarsoruseq
(Færingehavn)
46
GREENLAND
AREA II
WEST COAST
43, 44, 45
Qeqertarsuatsiaat
(Fiskenæsset)
AREA I
page 144
50°W

AREA II

The west coast between 63°N and Disko Bay

This area is open to shipping for most of the year and to yachts early in the season.

Inner lead passage from Qeqertarsuatsiaat (Fiskenaesset) to Kangerluarsoruseq (Faeringehavn)

The last 8 miles of the inner lead route south of Kangerluarsoruseq is very open and exposed, littered with rocks awash, relatively shallow in places, and probably best not attempted if there is any significant onshore wind or swell.

However, the inner lead route can be safely used at Evqitsut, just to the north of marker post 508, and thereafter southwards it is well sheltered from offshore swell all the way from Qeqertarsuatsiaat. This part of the route is generally wide and easily followed even in poor visibility (provided you have radar, since GPS positions cannot be relied upon), with no depths of less than 10m encountered.

Although not officially part of the marked inner lead route, if time permits an interesting and very scenic diversion can be taken to reach Qeqertarsuatsiaat by the 'back door'. Just south of marker 504 head NE up the Ugarsiorfiup Svudlua for 2M before turning SE down Tuno for a further 2M. Turn NE up Aniggoq and continue for 6M before once again turning SE for a further 6M to reach Qeqertarsuatsiaat.

43 Qeqertarsuatsiaat (Fiskenæsset)

63°05'N 50°41'W

Charts D 1212, 1213, (1251)

Qeqertarsuatsiaat means 'the great islands'. Qeqertarsuatsiaat is a small attractive fishing village of about 230 inhabitants. The harbour lies to the W of the promontory and there is a landing stage. Small store, water and diesel. Obviously a popular port of call in old days – Inglefield, Kane and Prince Napoleon (son of Napoleon III) all called here – and now the Umiaq Line ferry stops here.

Shelter in the small western harbour bight is excellent. Although the chart shows an anchorage in this bight, the depths in general seem to be significantly greater than charted and in most places are over 20m. The tides also swirl strongly into the bight setting up a circulatory flow, adding to the difficulties of anchoring.

However, there are 2 sturdy quays in the bight, one wooden, one stone, on which it is possible to safely berth with 3m depth at LWS. The 2 smaller floating pontoons in the harbour are only suitable for small motor boats and are filled with local craft.

The Royal Denmark fish factory also has a substantial wooden quay on the northern side of the village in the main sound where one could temporarily berth with permission. However, this berth is susceptible to swell in strong southwesterly winds.

Qeqertarsuatsiaq (Fiskenæsset) harbour *William Ker*

24 hour fuel from credit card operated pumps on the wooden pier. Good store and bakery.

Water from stand pipes in village.

The surrounding area could offer some attractive cruising and an interesting inner lead route S to Ravns Storø is entered from E of Qeqertarsuatsiaq (see Fredrikshåb Isblink inner lead route).

44 Lichtenfels 63°03'N 50°45'W

Chart 1212

Lichtenfels stands on the S side of a cove situated 3M NE of Fiskenæs Fjord (Avalleq) Lt (63°01'·7N 50°49'·9W). On chart 1212, it is labelled 'Akunnaat'. There are shallow and kelpy creeks either side of the old Moravian mission at Lichtenfels which offer temporary anchorage. Interesting and historic old buildings and burial ground.

45 Irkenshavn 63°04'N 50°47'W

Chart 1212

Lies one mile NW of Lichtenfels (see *NP12*). On chart 1212, it is called 'Eqalugissat'. The anchorage is in the NW arm where it widens out into a pool. A largish anchor is needed to bite through the weed, but lines can be run ashore if necessary. Note that the channel beyond the pool is encumbered with below water rocks and is impassable by a yacht.

A useful anchorage with good shelter, which it is easy to approach.

46 Marraq 63°26'N 51°11'W

Approach from the south is fairly straightforward but from the north and west requires careful pilotage through rocks and islands.

Two fine bays can be found north or south of the peninsula, anchoring in sand, with the shore a unique feature of huge sand dunes obviously the remains of some ancient outflow. Highly recommended.

Kangerluarsoruseq (Færingehavn)

63°42'N 51°33'W

Charts D 1310, 1350

Færingehavn is an abandoned Faroese fishing harbour on the N side of Kangerluarsoruseq. The big Polaroil depot is on the S side of the fjord and, further up on the N side at Nordafar, is a large abandoned fish plant. Færingehavn harbour itself is encumbered with islets and rocks and would be difficult to enter without Danish Chart 1350. However, the main fjord of the Kangerluarsoruseq provides good shelter in certain winds and is not difficult to access.

Approach

Approaching the area from the S the great whale back of the Skinderhvalen is a good landmark. Saatút light structure is indistinct. The sea breaks on Sankta Maria Skaer and Sorteskaer; but once the light on Den Smukke Ø and the leading lights have been picked up, the entrance is straightforward.

Although the anchorages in Kangaluarsorusek (47 Nordafar, 48 Orsivik and 49 Faeringehavn) make perfectly good passage anchorages in normal conditions, they do not have sufficiently good holding and shelter to be considered as comfortable places to sit out a gale. If a gale is expected then either (54) Nuuk to the north or (43) Qeqertarsuatsiaat (Fiskenaesset) to the south are more protected and secure bolt holes.

47 Kangerluarsoruseq

Charts D 1350 desirable

The anchorage just to the NNE of the abandoned fish plant provides excellent shelter in all but fresh south westerly winds when an uncomfortable fetch penetrates the anchorage. Holding is reasonably good in 7-8m in weed on stiff clay.

The Nordafar fish plant, built by the Norwegians and originally operated by a Norwegian, Danish, Faroese consortium (from which the name derives) although abandoned is still largely intact and an excellent example of Norwegian plants from that era, bearing a remarkable similarity to the whaling stations the Norwegians built and operated in South Georgia. Although the buildings are still largely intact the jetties are in a dangerous state of disrepair and are not suitable for berthing alongside.

48 Orsiivik (Polaroil) 63°41'N 51°30'W

Charts D 1350 desirable

The bay immediately to the W of Orsivik, shown on the charts as Qasigiaqarfa or Sydhavn, has a number of anchoring possibilities in the mini bays around the edges depending on wind direction. Shelter is reasonably good provided the wind is blowing from a southerly sector but if there is any northerly element to the wind then the anchorage a mile further in the fjord, just to the NNE of Nordafar, provides much better shelter. Moderately good holding in very thick kelp and matted weed on mud in about 10m.

If no tankers are expected, it may also be possible to go alongside the well maintained and fendered main quay of the Polaroil depot (6m approx at LWS). The small depot staff of 5 or 6 people maintain a listening watch on VHF Channel 6 and are very helpful and friendly.

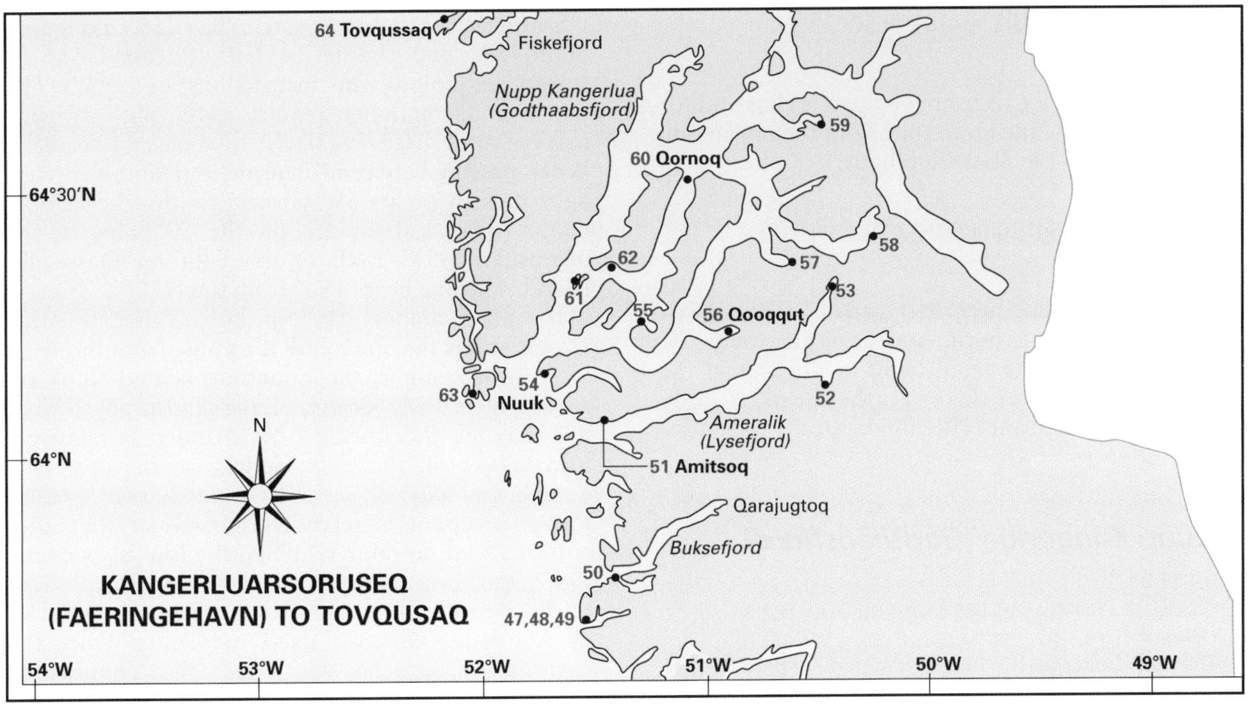

49 Færingehavn (old harbour)

63°41'N 51°32'N

Charts D 1350 desirable

This harbour has been abandoned, but one or two of the houses are occupied by local fishermen and the old hospital building is used as a summer camp for a special school. There are now no facilities.

Approach

Having entered Kangerluarsoruseq, the old harbour with its buildings will be apparent to the N. There are two entrances: using the first, leave the island with the red rectangular beacon (Baakeø) to port; for the second, pass beyond Den Smukke Ø and turn to port between the two leading lights for the main entrance. Note that the buoys inside the harbour have been withdrawn and there are underwater rocks to be avoided. The marker posts shown on the chart are not maintained and some are missing. In view of the large number of unmarked rocks, entry and anchoring can now only be recommended in the most settled of conditions with good visibility and taking all precautions.

Anchorage

Either anchor off the old settlement or preferably about 200m to the N in 8m. The holding is poor in heavy weed, but there are ring-bolts to which lines could be taken if necessary. There is a better yacht anchorage about 6M to the NNE in Buksefjord.

50 Buksefjord 63°47'N 51°25'W

Chart 1310

Just inside the fjord, 6M NE of Saatut, there is an excellent sheltered anchorage. Entrance is straightforward, but note two underwater rocks N of the line. The anchorage is in a small sandy bay close to the isthmus SE of Qornoq. The sandy bay, while attractive in moderate weather, is somewhat exposed in strong westerlies and the holding suspect in weed. Better shelter in these conditions may be found in the small bay just to the E in the main fjord.

Ameralik (Lysefjord)

64°04'N 51°30'W

The entrance to Ameralik lies 10M SE of Nuuk and runs 40M ENE to the head of Ameragdlia. It is deep throughout its length with no dangers, but is shoal at the head.

During the period of the Norse Western Settlement (circa AD1000–1350) there were a number of farms in the area, of which the largest at Sandnæs with its church (now Kilaarsarfik on the map), has been subject of considerable archaeological interest. The first crossing of the Greenland Ice Cap by Fridtjof Nansen in 1888, finished close by.

51 Amitsoq 64°05'N 51°28'W

Charts 1310, 1301

A useful anchorage at the entrance to Ameralik, on the N side, with moderate shelter from the S. Beware shallows when approaching from the E. Anchor in 5m.

52 Eqaluit Ilordlit 64°09'N 50°29'W

Charts 1301

Popular with the locals fishing for arctic char and for hunting reindeer. Anchor in the SW of the bay in 8m, sand; or pick up the Boat Club buoy.

53 Itivdleq 64°20'N 50°27'W

Charts 1301

There is a Boat Club mooring just N of the islet 3M from the head of the fjord. Anchor in 5m, mud, 1M N of the islet, in the small bight to port, or at the head. The seawater lake at the head is only accessible by dinghy at HW.

Nuup Kangerlua (Godthåbsfjord)

64°N 51°W

Charts D 1301 at 1:200,000 covers the area, but is rather sketchy.

The Nuuk boat club (Godthåb Bådeforening) produces an information folder showing sketch charts of a number of anchorages in the fjord.

The fjord area behind Nuuk stretches 50M inland and is a fascinating maze of deep fjords and mountainous islands running up to 1600m. Two large glaciers calve into the head, producing a considerable number of bergs. This was the Norse Western Settlement and the area is dotted with old sites.

54 Nuuk (Godthåb) 64°10'N 51°44'W

Charts D 1310 (1331, 1351, 1353)

Nuuk is the capital of Greenland and 16,500 of the 56,000 inhabitants live here. It is worth visiting, not only because it is the capital, but also because there is excellent cruising in the surrounding fjords. Storis very occasionally comes up from Kap Farvel and can cause problems, but this is most unusual.

Information can be obtained from the harbourmaster's office, which operates a 24-hour service on Ch 16.

Approaches

There are two approaches to Nuuk (Godthåb): the Narssaq Løb and the Nordløb.

The southern approach through the Narssaq Løb has the merit that the entrance is over two miles wide and is more easily recognised; the route is sheltered, and for the most part wide, free of dangers and less subject to ice. Tidal streams run strongly in the Narrsaq Lob and reach up to 5 knots at springs in the narrows, and 1-2 knots elsewhere. If heading south, leaving Nuuk around HW Nuuk should ensure a fair tide is carried to Faeringehavn. Heading north, the ideal time to arrive at Saatut would appear to be around LW Faeringehavn.

Saatut Island (light and racon) has a reef extending 800m SW and should be left at least 0·5M to starboard. Follow the instructions in *NP12*. The narrows at Simiutaa require care, but are well marked and used regularly by coastal steamers. When passing between Kingittoq and Simiutaa (with light beacon on its SW corner) follow the leading marks. The beacons are on the W point of the peninsula, 1·5M ENE of the light on Qassisallit Island. The line bears 184° from the N.

The main channel, the Nordløb, is used by large vessels and is the one to use if coming from the W or N. In good visibility the mountains behind Nuuk are readily identified, because all the land to the NW of the channel, the so-called Nordlandet, is relatively low. Closer in, the radio aerials on the low-lying Kookøerne may be seen. Its disadvantage is that, though deep, it is relatively narrow at the outer entrance and, in poor visibility, the low islets of the Kookøerne and the navigation marks are very hard to distinguish. The radio mast on Radioø, 1·8M SE of Agtorsuit, has two fixed red lights. Once the entrance has been identified the channel is straightforward (see *NP12*). The harbour lies to the E of the town, with its huge blocks of flats.

There are always a number of small icebergs and growlers in the Nordløb from the glaciers above Nuuk and, for this reason, entering in the dark is not to be recommended (although this really only applies late in the season at this latitude).

Chart D 1331, although at a larger scale, does not show more detail than *D 1310* and the latter is quite adequate.

Nuuk Harbour

Although yachts do anchor in the harbour, this cannot be recommended, since there is a good deal of rubbish on the bottom. The best plan is to go alongside one of the boats lying on the Kutterkaj, a timber quay on the west side of the Vestre Vig, in 2 to 4m at MLWS. The 'marina' pontoons in the Vestre Vig are filled with small craft and are not suitable for yachts. A large orange mooring buoy in the Skipshavn, just N of the Kutterkaj, is owned by a member of the Nuuk Boat Club and has been used to moor a 20 ton yacht. Request permission from the Boat Club before use.

The Nuuk Boat Club (Godthåb Bådeforening) now has a marina off the suburb of Nuussuaq, where it welcomes visiting yachtsmen. A visit to the Boat Club to get information about the numerous anchorages in the area is recommended. Permission may be given to use the nine ton mooring buoys which have been laid in many of the anchorages. The marina has a full-time manager, some facilities, however there are few spare berths. Yachts up to 38' have been offered berths. It is possible to arrange to lay up a yacht ashore here. The harbourmaster can advise. ✆ +299 32 38 33.

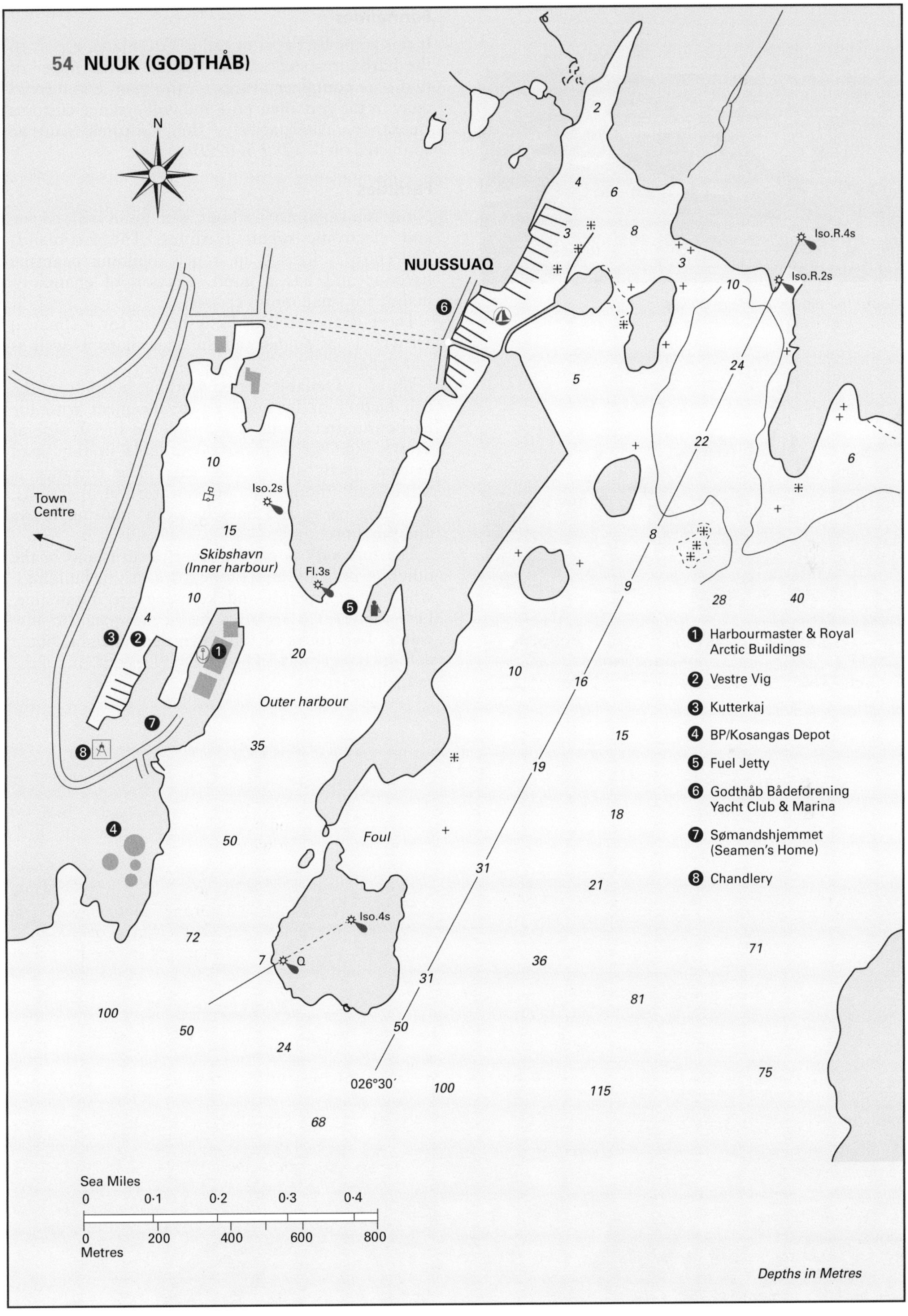
54 NUUK (GODTHÅB)
N
NUUSSUAQ
Town Centre
Skibshavn (Inner harbour)
Outer harbour
Foul
Iso.2s
Fl.3s
Iso.4s
Q
Iso.R.4s
Iso.R.2s
026°30´
1 Harbourmaster & Royal Arctic Buildings
2 Vestre Vig
3 Kutterkaj
4 BP/Kosangas Depot
5 Fuel Jetty
6 Godthåb Bådeforening Yacht Club & Marina
7 Sømandshjemmet (Seamen's Home)
8 Chandlery
Sea Miles
0 0·1 0·2 0·3 0·4
0 200 400 600 800
Metres
Depths in Metres

Nuuk - the old town *Máire Wilkes*

Nuuk inner harbour *Máire Wilkes*

Formalities

If this is the first port of call in Greenland, report to the harbourmaster who is located in the upper of two blue container offices on the main commercial quay in the container port and will arrange customs clearance. Alternatively, the Customs can be contacted on ✆ +299 560220.

Facilities

Nuuk is a very busy harbour, with good hull, engine and electronic repair facilities. The Grønlands Bådcentre is located in a new building near the harbour and has a good selection of chandlery, mainly for small motor cruisers.

There is an excellent bookshop in town (Imaneq 1), which has guides and the Saga maps as well as some charts.

Water is available during working hours from the fish factory or by hose, by arrangement with the harbourmaster. None is available on the W side of Vestre Vig, but it may be available in the small marina north of the fuel jetty. The entrance is tidal and there are underwater obstructions, including rocks and lines between mooring buoys and the shore.

The fuel jetty is on the point of an island in the outer harbour, 300m E of the Royal Arctic buildings, where diesel, petrol and kerosene are obtainable. Less than 2m is reported in the approach at low water. Two rocks of unknown depth/height, but a definite danger to keel boats, lie off the far end of the re-fuelling jetty.

Nuuk viewed from the east *Sofia Rossen*

Nuuk. The Danish-style buildings have an imposing backdrop *Sibéal Turraoin*

Nuuk swimming pool *Máire Wilkes*

Nuuk fuel jetty in the outer harbour *Máire Wilkes*

The Orsivik store associated with the fuel station has a good selection of rifles which may be useful for a cruising yacht heading into northern waters where polar bears can be a threat. It also supplies/ exchanges Kosangas cylinders. BP/Kosangas is available in cans, which are shipped in, since there are no facilities at present in Greenland for filling cans. The depot is about 200m S of the Seamen's Home. Kosangas fittings can be bought at the KNI store.

There are a number of well stocked supermarkets, a shopping mall and all the services one would expect in the capital. The swimming pool, which is in the Nuusuaq area, is worth visiting. There is a chandlery (Qalut Vonin) close to the Seaman's Hotel which has a good stock of equipment aimed at the local fishing market. A more comprehensive chandlery can be found at the 'Bådcentre' in Nuusuaq in the industrial estate behind the incinerator building with a tall rust coloured chimney. The Bådcentre can import spares efficiently. There is a Volvo agent at the small boat marina. Laundry can be taken to the Seaman's Hotel. An alternative, and cheaper, option is to buy a laundry card (Vaskemashine kort) at the main Brugsen supermarket in town. The laundromat is a red building on the left side of Kongevej Road which is passed on the right when walking into town. The Hotel Hans Egede serves good quality food.

Just above the harbour is an excellent Seamen's Home (sømandshjemmet) which provides showers, accommodation and good food at reasonable prices. Taxis operate all night and take credit cards.

The museum close to the old harbour is well worth a visit as is the cultural centre, Katuaq.

Alternative anchorage

Qasigianguit (64°11'N 51°43'W) is a well protected anchorage just to the north of the town, useful for escaping from the hurly burly of the city. A favoured fishing cove for the locals. Good holding.

55 Itissoq 64°15'N 51°14'W

Two fjords, Itissoq to the south and Ikatut to the north, giving pleasant anchorages at their heads in clear water. Good fishing. Good streams for filling with water to save trying to find it in Nuuk.

56 Qooqqut 64°15'N 50°55'W

Chart 1312, 1301

Site of an abandoned sheep-rearing station. A popular spot at the weekend. Anchor off in 5–10m, good holding. Some good walking and scrambling in the area.

Under certain conditions, winds in this anchorage can be severe. A reasonably secure anchorage in 6–10m, with better shelter, can then be found 7M NW, behind the islet under the SE flank of Qeqertarsuaq (Storø) (64°18'N, 51°08'W).

Itissoq fjord, Nuuk *Robert Beddow*

A pleasant anchorage in favourable winds is also possible in the tuck of the coastline on the southern shore (Tingmianguit). Saves going the extra 2·5M to the end of the fjord. Several local holiday homes ashore.

57 Sulussugutip Kangerlua

64°23′N 50°38′W

Chart 1301

Approach straightforward with no dangers. Anchor in 5m, mud, in the NW of the bay below dense greenery, which marks an old Norse farmstead. There is a Boat Club buoy about 1M W, just inside a small islet.

58 Kapisillit 64°26′N 50°16′W

Chart 1301

Kapisillit means 'the salmon'. It is a small fishing village with a population of about 86. It is close to the only stream where salmon spawn in Greenland. Arctic char are also plentiful. It is a good 2M walk across to the very spectacular Kangersuneq Isfjord. Either anchor in the bay to the E of the settlement in 8m or go across with care to the foot of the salmon stream, 1M E of the village. It is about 50M from Nuuk but well worth the effort.

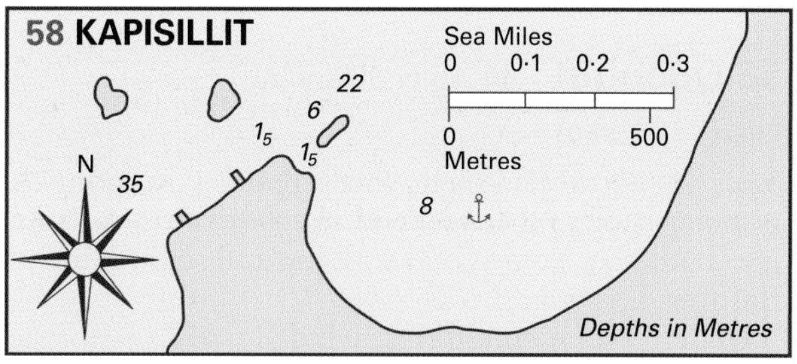

59 Kangiussaq 64°38′N 50°30′W

Chart 1301

An interesting anchorage, close to the Nuup Kangerlua Isfjord, with excellent shelter. Old Norse farmstead with stone store house ruin. Two drying rocks lie off the E side of the narrows in the approach. Anchor in 4–6m, sand, off the river outflow.

60 Qornoq 64°32′N 51°06′W

Chart 1301, 1312

A small settlement, where a big fête is held during the first weekend in July. This was the base from which the geodetic survey of W Greenland was started in 1927.

Either anchor in the small bay to the SE of the island, 5m sand and kelp, but beware obstructions at the S end; or in the inlet to the W of the island, 5m mud and kelp. There is a Boat Club mooring in the latter.

61 Qeqertaq 64°20′N 51°34′W

Anchorages can be found for every wind direction around these two islands, and in the inner channel between them.

62 Qarasuk 64°22′N 51°22′W

Site of an old settlement. Anchor inside the line of the two rock islands, choosing your cove according to wind direction. Good holding.

63 Håbets Ø Havn 64°08′N 52°03′W

Charts D 1331 , 1351, 1313

A useful sheltered anchorage on the N side of the Nordløb.

The entrance through the Ikerasak is about 5M NE of Agtorsuit (Lt and Racon). Anchor in 5 to 10m, mud, as convenient.

Inner lead route to the west of Akia (Nordlandet)

This route, although intricate, is well marked and protected. It has been followed by a yacht drawing 2m, with attention to tides, however, there are a number of unmarked rocks and the route cannot be recommended for most cruising yachts. There are a number of anchorages *en route*.

64 Tovqussaq 64°52′N 52°12′W

Charts D 1314, 1352

An abandoned fishing harbour 35M SE of Maniitsoq, with secure anchorage in a sheltered landlocked bay (Inderhavn) with easy access from seawards (see *NP12*).

Approach

Approach from the W, either to the S of Langø and N through Qaersup Ilua or through the relatively narrow passage to the N of Langø, which carries 12m. The 'rock awash' on the N side of this channel appears closer to Hestenæs and dries 3m.

Anchorage

Secure anchorage can be found in the Ankerbugt in 5m, mud, on the N side of the Inderhavn. In strong southerlies it is possible to anchor close off the SE shore.

Inner lead route, Tovqussaq to Maniitsoq

Charts D 1314

The route is described in *NP12*. There are several possible anchorages en route. A sheltered anchorage is reported in Kuulik (65°09'N 52°20'W), a landlocked bay in Ingiata Nuna, 20M NNW of Tovqussaq; however, the entrance is shallow.

65 Ikerasak 65°11'N 52°16'W

Site of an old settlement. Best approach is from the east of the island guarding the bay. A well protected anchorage can be found inside on the western side.

The next bay to the east is shallow and is not recommended. It has a rock in the middle that covers.

66 Maniitsoq (Sukkertoppen)

65°25'N 52°54'W

Charts D 1314, 1410, 1352

The area around Maniitsoq was well known to Dutch, German and British whalers of the 17th and 18th centuries. The 'sugar loaves' (sukkertoppen) were probably the hillocks around Old Sukkertoppen, now called Kangaamiut. A steep-sided island, Kin of Sal, is a remarkable landmark approaching Maniitsoq with a name given to it by British whalers.

Maniitsoq itself is a large, attractive and busy fishing settlement on the island of Maniitsoq, with a good, protected harbour.

Maniitsoq - a typical Greenlandic settlement perched on the side of a mountain *Sibéal Turraoin*

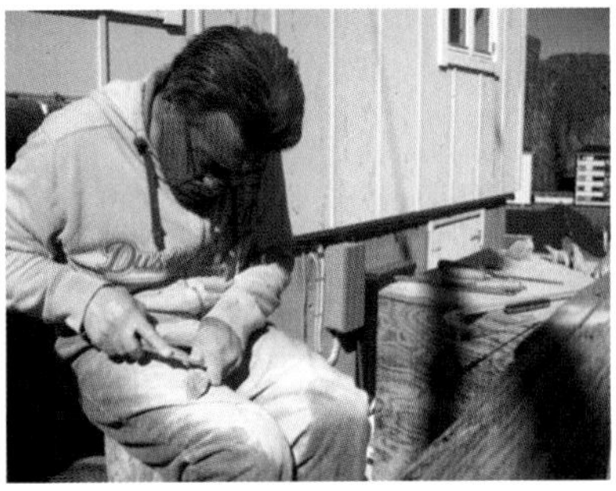

Maniitsoq carver *Sibéal Turraoin*

Approach

The approach from the S is moderately straightforward (see *NP12*).

Berth

Moor on the outer pontoon of the marina in front of the hotel. Keys for the marina are obtainable from the hotel. A charge is made for berthing and a deposit taken for the keys. Possible to alongside the quay just beyond the fuel point in the NE corner but this is very crowded, or at the new fish factory wharf, with permission.

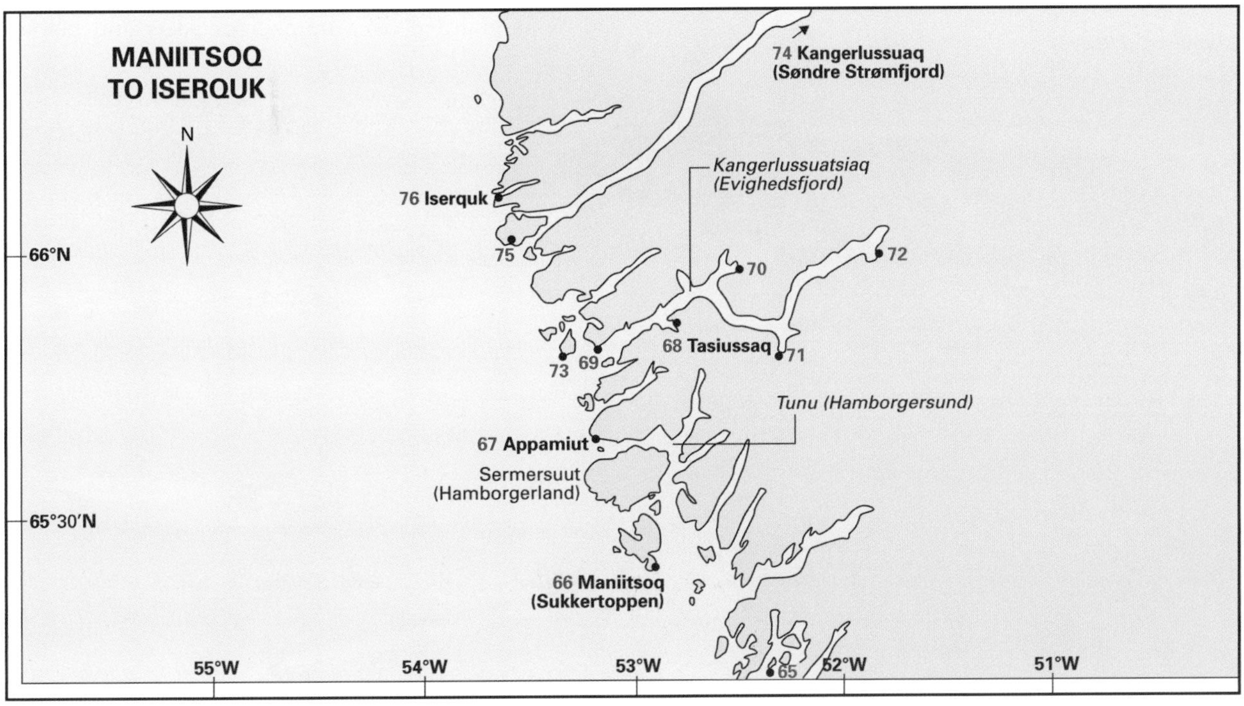

Maniitsoq pontoon berth *Sibéal Turraoin*

Facilities

There are two supermarkets and a hotel. Fuel and water. Marine and electronic workshops. WiFi at the marina. Mobile phone and 3G coverage.

There are daily flights from the STOL airport to Kangerlussuaq (Søndre Strømfjord).

Alternative anchorages

An alternative anchorage can be found at 'Kin of Sal' (Uummannassuaq), an island W of Maniitsoq. The Inuit name means 'Great Heart'. Gunk-holing through the islands and channels on the southwest side of Maniitsoq Island can be rewarding; but probably best at low water as it is uncharted and there are rocks that cover. A good echosounder is required. The anchorage in the channel immediately to the south of the island (65°26′N 53°04′W) gives surprisingly good protection in most winds. Anchor deep, in mid-channel. Dramatic rock climbing.

Tunu (Hamborgersund)

The passage E of Sermersuut (Hamborgerland) is spectacular and leads to a good anchorage at Appamiut.

There is also a wide and clean passage between Maniitsoq and Sermersuut (Hamborgerland) leading into Tunu (Hamborgersund).

If the weather is fine then a side trip up the 6 mile long Sermilinguaq offers views which are at least the equal of those in Hamborgersund and possibly even better. At the head of the fjord the ice cap descends almost to sea level, whilst the north facing shore sports a splendid collection of hanging glaciers and waterfalls, and the south facing one sheer cliffs teeming with Guillemot and Fulmar colonies.

Although unsurveyed, the mid-line of the Sermilinguaq carries depths greater than 50m up to within a mile of the head of the fjord. It might be possible to anchor off the terminal moraine at the head of the fjord, but since the water is extremely milky with glacial silt at this point it would be unwise to approach too closely without either the aid of a forward looking echo sounder or taking soundings in a dinghy.

67 Appamiut 65°40′N 53°11′W

Charts D 1410

A delightful anchorage off a deserted settlement, with splendid views of the mountains and glaciers of Sermersuut (Hamborgerland).

Approach

Very easy from Tunu (Hamborgersund). Coming S, the inner lead route from Kangaamiut is intricate, but well marked; however, the approach from the NW is guarded by a number of islets and below-

Maniitsoq *J Reeves*

Tunu (Hamborgersund) *Máire Wilkes*

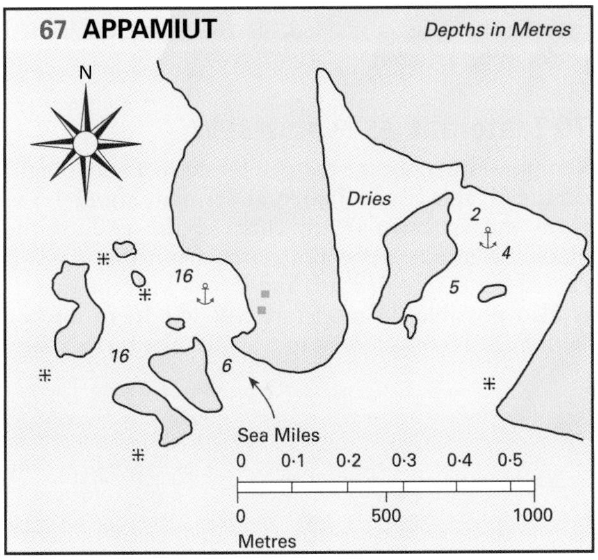

water rocks. In good visibility, a 095° course to pass between Skildpadderne, 2M west of Appamiut, and an islet 0·25M to the S, leads into the sound.

Anchorage

Good holding and protected by a ring of islets and skerries. A weak tidal stream runs through this anchorage. Better protection can be had in the second of two inlets half a mile to the E. The first inlet dries out; but the second provides excellent shelter in 3 to 4m beyond the central islet, sticky mud and weed. Note the drying rock off the SE point.

Kangerlussuatsiaq (Evighedsfjord) 65°52'N 53°00'W

Charts D 1410 **Maps** 65 V.1, 66 V1

This dramatic fjord provides access to an excellent mountaineering area including 2190m Taterat (Mt Atter). Tilman anchored in 1962 in Tasiussaq, a bay, which opens up to starboard about 10M up the fjord and provides the best shelter. Three other possible anchorages have been used.

68 Tasiussaq 65°53'N 52°48'W

The head of the bay to the SE is shoal, with irregular depths beyond the 26m sounding on the chart. Depending on wind conditions, the following anchorages have been used.

Anchorages

1. Anchor about one cable SE of the 26m sounding, mentioned above under 'General' is reported to provide good shelter and has good holding. About 0·2M E of the anchorage, there is a line of below-water rocks, some of which show at LW, extending SE from the point on the N side, towards a conspicuous loaf-shaped boulder on the opposite shore.
2. Enter Tasiussaq and steer mid-channel for about 1M beyond Nugssuaq, then turn on to 075° to clear the E point of the hammer-headed peninsula

Appamiut *Máire Wilkes*

by 200m. The leading line is the double pinnacle S of the peak of Amaassuak, open to S of the small conical island which leads in, in 16m. Anchor between the conical island and the low island 150m to the SW in 12m. Holding is only moderate but lines can be taken to the two islands. Water from a small stream and a few mussels on the beach, blueberries on the hill.

The channel to the south of the islands gives access to the inner bay where there are even more possible anchorages.

3. Anchor in the small bay NE of the hammer-head peninsula. Beware reef which covers in NW corner.

Other anchorages in Kangerlussuatsiaq (Evighedsfjord)

69 Timerliit 65°50′N 53°11′W

Charts 1410

About 4M ENE of Kangaamiut, there is an anchorage which is relatively sheltered just off the old settlement of Timerliit, or preferably in the blind channel 500m to the W. Good holding in mud and filamentous weed. Allow plenty of swinging room as the wind swirls around in the anchorage.

The only thing that now remains of the old settlement is a single concrete foundation block. Enter from the E between Maniitsorsuaq and the mainland. Care is needed, as there are uncharted rocks to be avoided.

70 Taateraat 65°59′N 52°31′W

Temporary anchorage may be found in a small bight on the SE side of the Taateraat Sermiat, about 1·5M from the spectacular ice cliffs at the end of the glacier. There is some protection from the mass of calved bergs that drift up and down with the tide. It is also possible, in moderate SW winds, to anchor with lines ashore close in to a small inlet further W.

Taateraat Sermiat glacier *William Ker*

71 Kangiussaq 65°50′N 52°18′W

Anchor at head of the fjord just before the silt bank from the moraines. It may be useful to use two anchors to limit swinging room and prevent being blown onto the silt bank if the wind changes.

72 Kangersuata Illu 66°01′N 51°50′W

From the Taateraat Sermiat the fjord winds a further 25M inland, forming a spectacular canyon 1–2M wide between vertical walls of rock and ice, which reach up to peaks 1600 – 2000m on either side. Close to the head of the fjord where it forks, there is an anchorage on the NE side of the Qinngua Kujalleq off Kangersuata Illu. Anchor 200m off the ancient ruins in the centre of the shallow bay in 20m, clay and grit. A place of extraordinary beauty.

73 Kangaamiut (old Sukkertoppen)
65°49′N 53°21′W

Charts D 1410 (1450)

A lively and friendly village with a tiny harbour in a narrow gut between two islands. The wooden jetty is apt to be busy. Stores and fuel. During the salmon-fishing season the area is surrounded by drift nets

Kangaamiut approaches *Máire Wilkes*

Navigation marker *Máire Wilkes*

Kangaamiut, wooden jetty *Máire Wilkes*

Kangaamiut approaches *Máire Wilkes*

Kangaamiut from the anchorage *Máire Wilkes*

and fresh salmon can be bought off the boats. Power lines are reported to cross the harbour from the village to the small centre island, with a clearance of 23m.

Inner lead to Kangerlussuaq

Running north from Kangaamiut, there is an interesting route to Fiskemesterenshavn at the entrance to Kangerlussuaq where there are three or four anchorages, mostly rather deep.

74 Kangerlussuaq (Søndre Strømfjord) 66°58'N 50°57'W

Charts D 1411, 1412

Kangerlussuaq International Airport is the main airport for Greenland with regular flights to Copenhagen and Reykjavik. It is no longer a US Airforce base, all the facilities being handed over to the Greenland authorities in September 1992. It lies at the head of a 100-mile long, narrow fjord, with strong tides in the lower section. Winds tend to follow and are accentuated by the narrow fjord. The scenery is magnificent or forbidding, depending on your viewpoint and the conditions at the time. A powerful engine is desirable and the trip up the fjord is not recommended, unless visiting the airport. It may be preferable to meet a plane at the STOL airports at Sisimiut (Holsteinsborg) or Maniitsoq (Sukkertoppen), providing seats can be booked.

Approach

Follow the directions in NP12. The leading beacons are very visible and there is a racon on the west point of Qeqertasugsuq. Tides are very strong and it is advisable to approach at the slack (which, from observation, occurs about three hours after local low water) and carry the flood up the fjord. If approaching from the S, it is better to enter the inner lead at Kangaamiut and anchor if necessary in Fiskemesterens Havn to wait for the tide.

Anchorage

The harbour for Kangerlussuaq airport (ex-Camp Lloyd, and referred to as such in *NP12*) is reached through a dredged channel with a nominal depth of 3m. It is possible to pick up a buoy or anchor off the mud flats, but it is some distance in to the quay.

At the head of the dredged channel there is a quay with 3m alongside, but there is little room and you may be required to move at short notice.

Facilities

The airport is 9km from the harbour and there is no regular transport, but it is usually possible to get a lift. The airport is a different world, with a hotel, restaurant, bars, souvenir shops, ATM, etc., but no bank. Showers and a washing machine are available in the hotel.

There is a good butik, with a fair selection of groceries and probably the freshest flyfresh vegetables in Greenland. There are tennis courts, a

Kangerlussuaq (Søndre Strømfjord) *media.gl*

bowling alley, golf course, etc., thanks to the US Airforce.

The Met office is above the butik and it is worth going up to meet the duty forecaster, who can also get hold of the latest ice charts.

75 Cruncher Island 66°01'N 53°34'W

A useful anchorage at the start of the long fjord. Follow the leading beacons in and either turn at the eastern end of the island (beware outlying rock), or cut through the obvious gap to port (north) on approach, keeping over to the east side to avoid rocks. Least depth 5 metres. Then select best bay on north side of the inlet.

76 Iserquk 66°08'N 53°40'W

Charts D 1413, 1450 **Map** 66 V1

A deep, narrow fjord, 4M long, running NE about 1½M north of Simiutaq, at the entrance to Søndre Strømfjord, with 3 or 4 useful and sheltered anchorages. *Chart 1450* desirable but not essential.

Approach

The approach in mid channel from the SW is straightforward and clean, but note that rocks lie 300m N of the starboard-hand beacon on Tasilik Is.

Anchorages

1. In a bay guarded by an islet (No.76a), ½M further in (see *NP12*), but rather deep for yachts.
2. At the head of the fjord in either fork in 5m mud (No.76b). Some underwater and drying rocks to be avoided. Fresh water from the streams. Subject to gusts in SE gales.

77 Anders Olsens Sund
66°29'N 53°41'W

Charts D 1413, (1450)

A useful passage anchorage 2M S of Qeqertarssuatsiaq Lt, behind Inugsugtussoq Island (see *NP12*).

Approach

The approach from the W is straightforward to the entrance, which is marked on the N side by a port-hand beacon. Ikardlugssuaq is a small low island, 6M SW of the entrance, which is indistinct and only shows on radar at just over 1M.

Anchorage

Anchor on the W side of the sound, about 1M S of the entrance, in 4–5m.

Sisimiut approaching from the south *Máire Wilkes*

78 Sisimiut (Holsteinsborg)
66°57'N 53°41'W

Charts D 1414, 1415, (1430)

Sisimiut lies just north of the Arctic Circle and is the first settlement on the W coast where sledge dogs are kept. It is Greenland's second-largest town, with 5,500 inhabitants; a pleasant place with a busy fishing harbour and an extensive fjord area which would make interesting cruising. The original settlement was at Sydbay, 20M to the N, but it was moved to its present site in 1764. It was often visited by whalers and, later, by cod fishermen.

The STOL airport has daily flights to Kangerlussuaq (Søndre Strømfjord) International Airport, making this is an excellent place for a crew change.

Approach

The easiest approach is from the W or SW, but there are several unmarked outliers (see *NP12*).

Coming from the N, enter between Inugsulinguaq (67°03'N 53°58'W) and Avangnardlerssuaq, 3M SW, but note the dangerous rock 1M N of Avangnardlerssuaq.

Sisimiut *Sibéal Turraoin*

Sisimiut whale bones *Máire Wilkes*

Over-wintering ashore at Sisimiut boatyard *Bob Shepton*

Anchorage

Sailing yachts cannot enter the Ulkebugt, since the clearance under the bridge, which connects the town with the STOL airport, is only about 5m. The fishing harbour is normally very crowded but it may be possible to lie alongside at the small shipyard with permission. Under settled conditions it is possible to anchor with care near the shore to the W of the harbour.

Good anchorage can be found 500m NW of the new bridge, in the NW corner of the bay, in 3–8m, mud. Some fetch from the SW. It is reported that a fishing boat mooring has now been laid in this position; however it is possible to anchor in 15m with lines to the shore to the E. Good holding.

Facilities

Two supermarkets: the Pisiffik (KNI) and the Brugsen. Banks, post office, hospital and hotels, two or three good bakeries, cafés, chinese restaurant and an excellent bookshop.

Sisimiut inner harbour *Bob Shepton*

Sisimiut has the best Seamen's Home on the coast with spotless accommodation, showers and restaurant. There are two chandlers in the town: one near the shipyard and another (Sirius) which is 2km from the harbour. The small boatyard in the southwest corner of the harbour is friendly and helpful. It is possible to winter ashore here at a reasonable price. The director, Bent Lyberth, can be contacted at bl@ang.gl, ✆+299 86 61 58 or *Mobile* +299 53 15 70.

Fuel is available on a float in the harbour. Laundry can be dealt with at the Seaman's Hotel or, less expensively, by buying a laundry card (Vaskemashine kort) at the Brugsen supermarket in town. The Tuapannguanut laundromat is located to the west of the town centre off Nikkorsuit Road.

Route north of Sisimiut 67°N 54°W

Charts D 1415, 1416 and 1510 (adequate)

Inner lead route

From Sisimiut an inner lead runs north for 10M, but it is quite hard to follow and it is probably easier to go straight out and enter another lead, either at Færinge Nordhavn, or just NW of Kangeq (67°45'N 53°49'W). The latter is interesting, with a number of possible anchorages. Alternatively make direct for the Sydvestløbet into Aasiaat (Egedesminde).

79 Ukiivik (Sydbay) 67°13'N 53°55'W

Charts D 1415, 1450

Originally established as a whaling station in 1756, it became the site of the colony of Holsteinsborg in 1759 until it was moved to near its present site, now called Sisimiut. A pleasant anchorage between the island of Ukiivík and the mainland. Better shelter, if needed, can be found to the NE of the islet N of the main anchorage; but beware drying rock in the channel just N of the islet. There are a few remains of old turf houses and, for exercise, you could take a brisk scramble up to the light structure.

80 Tasiussaq (Nassuttooq) (Nordre Strømfjord) 67°29'N 53°40'W

Charts D 1415

Tasiussaq is a shallow bay 3M within the entrance of Nordre Strømfjord. Good shelter from the N and very easy access. Good holding in 2–3m, sand with weed patches. Some shelter can be obtained from the SW, behind the point on the W side of the entrance, but it is shoal.

Ukiivik *J Reeves*

Ukiivik *J Reeves*

Tasiussaq (Nassuttooq) approaches *Máire Wilkes*

81 Kangiussap Paava (Færinge Nordhavn) 67°39'N 53°39'W

Charts D 1416, 1451

This fjord is easy to access by passing to the N of Simiutanguit and its associated foul ground.

Anchorage

Anchorage can be found in an indentation on the E side of Qeqertarssuaq Island. Anchor in 8m sand and weed. Protection is better than it appears. Better protection can be found by sailing farther up the channel SSW of Qeqertarssuaq and anchoring in 8–10m; but the narrow bay at the end is shoal and rocky and can not be entered.

A pleasant spot, with gulls, duck and guillemots.

Note Do not be tempted to enter Eqalugssuit, the fjord to the S. Although this was the original site of Egedesminde before it was moved to its present location in 1763, the depths are irregular and it is shoal at the head. The largest lake in Greenland, the Gieseckes Sø, drains into the fjord and the Greenlanders have a number of summer fishing camps along the south shore.

Inner lead route from Færinge Nordhavn

67°N 54°W

Charts 1416 (adequate)

The Ikerasarssuk appears to be blocked by a rock 1M N of the southern entrance. Although a 'rapid' is caused by the constriction at certain states of the tide, just over 3m was found here by holding to the western shore. The remainder is straightforward.

From offshore, the inner lead route to Aasiaat is more easily entered W of Kangeq (approximately 67°45'N 53°59'W).

82 Attu (Agto) 67°56'N 53°37'W

Charts D 1416, 1451

A small village, on the inner lead route, in a shallow bay (NP12). Anchor off in 5–8m.

Anchorages nearby

There is a moderately sheltered anchorage just SE of the island of Satue (No.35a) 2M NW of Attu; good holding in 11m. Better protection can be found in a landlocked bay (Tasiusaa Killeq on the 1:250,000 map, 68.V.1) opposite the island of Pikiulersuaq (No35b) 7M NNE of Attu. The entrance channel is shallow – approx. 1·5m at LW in the narrowest part – however, depths increase to 30–40m in the bay. Anchorage is possible in 14m, within the bay near the entrance channel.

Attu (Agto) *Máire Wilkes*

83 Alanngorsuup Imaa

68°10'N 51°34'W

Arfersiorfik is entered N of Alanngorsuup (68°09'N 53°30'W). A reconnaissance of this long fjord has been made as far as the Nordenskjøld Glacier (68°21'N 51°10'W), see *NP12*. Sofiashavn was the base for an abortive attempt by Baron Nordenskjøld to cross the ice cap in 1883. The harbour has now silted up and cannot be entered. The glacier is quite impressive, but the long route there is rather dull. No chart; the 1:250,000 topographical map can be used, but this cannot really be recommended for navigation.

84 Niaqornaarsuk 68°14'N 52°52'W

Charts D 1510 (1550)

Small, out-of-the-way but lively village with numerous dogs. Store and diesel. Water dubious and in short supply (see *NP12*).

Approach

Although there are no soundings on the chart within 1M of the settlement, a direct approach on a bearing of 025° appears to be clean, with depths in excess of 30m until within 400m of the pier. Anchor in 10m close to the fish factory. It is not advisable to go beyond the pier as there are a number of below-water rocks.

Attu (Agto) *J Reeves*

Kangaatsiaq *Máire Wilkes*

85 Kangaatsiaq 68°18′N 53°28′W

Charts D 1510

A clean and friendly little village on the inner lead route to Aasiaat (Egedesminde). Usual fairly basic facilities (see *NP12*).

Many glaciers calve icebergs into Disko Bay and it is a highlight for most boats sailing in Greenland. In the summer months, the Disko Line ferry company operates ferries calling at most of the settlements between Attu, in the south, and Saqqaq, in the north. Disko Line ferry details can be found on the website address given on page 129.

Disko Bay

86 Aasiaat (Egedesminde)

68°43′N 52°53′W

Charts D 1510 (1530, 1550)

This is a large settlement with an excellent, but crowded, harbour. It is now the administrative centre for the Disko area and is of some importance.

The whole of the Disko Bay freezes solid in winter and huge numbers of bergs calve in summer from the Ilulissat (Jakobshavn) Isfjord. There is therefore apt to be a good deal of ice in the Aasiaat area and the channels leading to it, which gradually clear in August. Navigation should, however, be possible in July over most of the area.

Aasiaat Radio, with its chain of subsidiary transmitters, provides radio coverage for the whole of Greenland. There are MF transmitters on Disko Island and at Upernavik, which extend coverage to Kap York. A visit to the coast radio station is very worthwhile and the radio operators are most welcoming.

Approach

Fairly straightforward. Three approaches are described in *NP12*; see *Chart D 1530* but *Chart D 1510* is adequate.

Anchorage

The fishing quay, S of the commercial dock, is suitable for yachts. Use either side, but note that the root is shoal and it may be too crowded to use.

Transitøen Island is no longer used commercially; however the small quay, which is badly maintained, on the W side provides a quiet place for a yacht to lie alongside.

If approaching from Langesund, it is possible to anchor in the channel to the S of the fuel storage tanks, with easy access to the main harbour by dinghy; however it is not possible to pass through in a yacht, since the channel is spanned by a low power cable just to the S of the tanks, with a vertical clearance of about 7m.

In the event that strong northerlies make the harbour uncomfortable; good sheltered anchorage

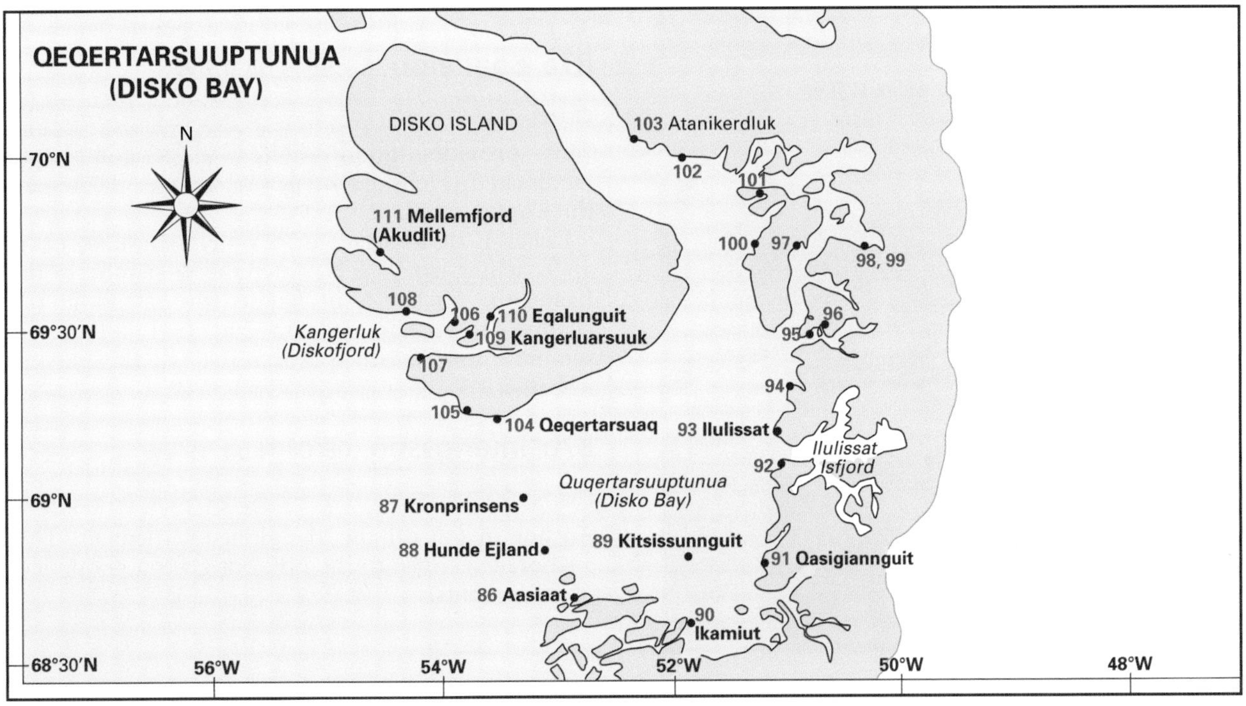

Aasiaat anchorage with the boatyard on the right *Sibéal Turraoin*

Aasiaat boatyard *Sibéal Turraoin*

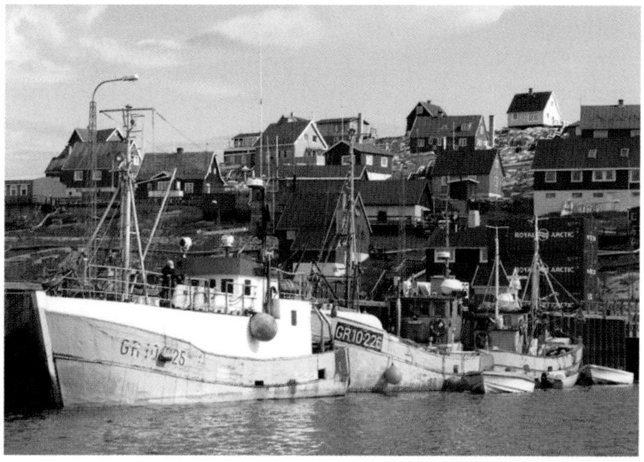

The commercial dock at Aasiaat *Máire Wilkes*

Whale breaching near Aasiaat - Disko Bay *Sibéal Turraoin*

has been found on the S side of Aasiaat Island (on the N side of Langesund /Ikerasassuaq). The anchorage is in the easternmost of three bays. Anchor in 11m, mud, SE of the islet in a small bay on the W side. (68°42′N 52°47′W).

There is an alternative very sheltered anchorage in 10m, in a bay on the NE corner of Aasiaat Island. (68°43′N 52°45′W)

Facilities

Two supermarkets and all other normal facilities – banking, hospital, etc. Good quality fresh water can be obtained from the Royal Arctic Lines jetty. Fuel available. There is an efficient ship-repair yard, where it is possible to lay up a yacht. It would be prudent to check the costs for laying up a vessel before plans are finalised. Good Seamen's Home just W of the ship-repair yard.The shipyard has a chandlery shop and there is also a Qalut Vonin chandlery (near the shipyard). The DIY shop 'Stark', is well stocked.

STOL airport with regular flights to Kangerlussuaq (Søndre Strømfjord) and Ilulissat.

87 Kronprinsens Ejland (Disko Bay) 69°00′N 53°19′W

Charts D 1511 (1550 shows Imerigssoq, but is not essential)

A group of low islands, halfway between Aasiaat and Qeqertarsuaq. They form a natural division in Disko Bay. N of the islands a majestic procession of icebergs moves W past Disko, whereas, to the S, there are only scattered icebergs. There are two possible anchorages.

Approach

This is fairly straightforward (see *NP12*).

Anchorages

87a Baadeløb 68°59′N 53°19′W

Charts D 1511

This provides good shelter in a completely landlocked, Hebridean-type anchorage. There are three approaches.

Either E of Kitsigsut or S of Nunarssuaq; or, if approaching from the N, down the W channel of the Baadeløb. Anchor S of Baadø (the island in the channel) on the W side in 7m good holding. A scramble up Uigordleq will reveal all the passing icebergs.

87b Imerigssoq 69°01′N 53°19′W

Charts D 1511, 1550

Anchor in 6m off the abandoned settlement. This anchorage is open to the NE, but gives a good view of the icebergs.

Disko Bay from Disko Island *Máire Wilkes*

A huge number of icebergs calve from the Ilulissat glaciers *Máire Wilkes*

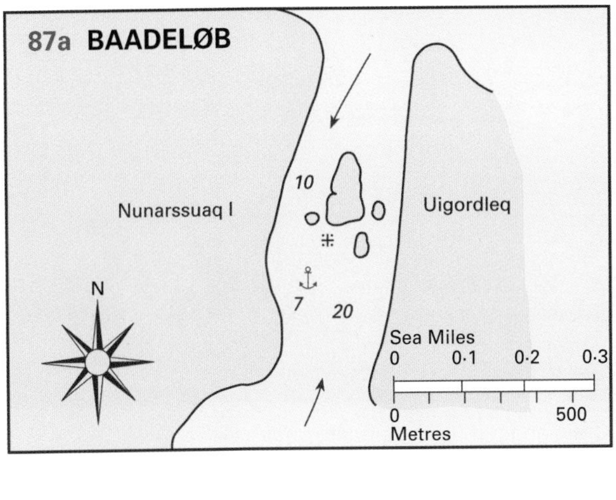

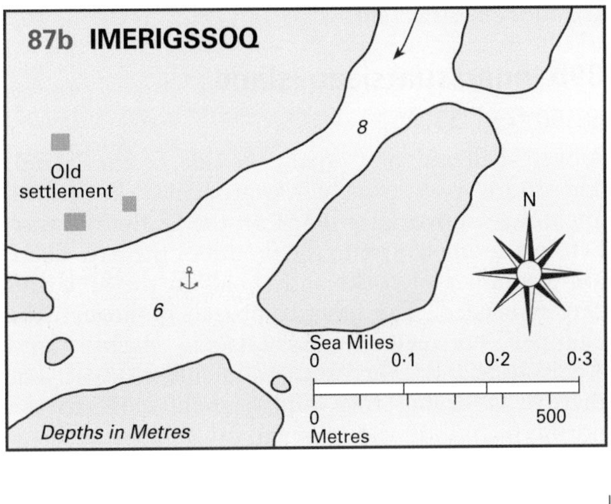

Disko iceberg procession *Máire Wilkes*

88 Hunde Ejland 68°51'N 53°06'W

Anchor in front of the village in 5–7m. Good holding in sand. Swinging room is limited so a stern anchor may be used. A small orange buoy marks a drying rock in the bay which is too shallow for yachts (approx. 1m deep). Approach see *NP12.*

89 Kitsissunnguit (Grønne Ejland) (Disko Bay) 68°50'N 51°55'W

Charts D 1500, 1513

This is a group of low-lying islands in the S of Disko Bay. Grønne Ejland is a nature reserve and landing is not permitted between April and August as this is the breeding time for the island's arctic terns. On Basisø Island there is an old abandoned settlement, with the remains of several sod houses dug into the hillside.

Approach

To the N of the islands is an extensive area of foul ground, making it necessary to approach from the S. Note Racon (M) on S tip of Basisø, W of the anchorage.

Anchorages

There are two anchorages.

89a Kitsissunnguit (Basisø Island) 68°50'N 51°55'W

A cove on the S side of the island open to the SE. Anchor in 9m at the head of the cove off the abandoned settlement.

89b Innarssuatsiaaq Island 68°50'N 51°53'W

A well-sheltered bay on the N side of the island. There are two possible approaches. From the anchorage above, keep 0·5M off the SE tip of Basisø before altering course to the mouth of the bay. There are a number of rocks and shoals in the area and care is needed. The other approach is through the channel between Innarssuatsiaaq Island and Angissat Island. This is clear in mid-channel, but there is a drying rock and a shoal close to the northern end of the channel off Innarssuatsiaaq. From the channel to the entrance to the bay, a clear passage is found by keeping 200m off the island.

Depths in the bay are between 3 and 7m, shoaling at the head. This anchorage allows a perfect view of the midnight sun.

90 Ikamiut 68°38'N 51°50'W

Charts D 1512

A small village on the W side of the Sydostbugten, with a useful and attractive sheltered anchorage in Ilorput, a landlocked bay 1M SW. The entrance is narrow, with a least depth of approx 1·6m at LW. The bottom is uneven and requires care. Anchor in a small cove in the NE corner, off a sandy beach in 4m, with room to swing.

91 Qasigiannguit (Christianshåb) 68°49'N 51°13'W

Charts D 1513, (1551)

An interesting and historic town with an excellent natural harbour, from which it is possible to sail 18M north to get an outstanding view of Kangia (the Ilulissat Isfjord).

Qasigiannguit (Christianshåb) *Máire Wilkes*

Qasigiannguit Museum *Máire Wilkes*

Approach

The approach from the W is straightforward, using Chart *D 1513* (*1551* is not necessary).

Anchorage

The bay to the SE of the town provides an excellent anchorage in 3–10m. Shelter is good except when weather conditions favour föhn winds, for which it has a reputation.

Facilities

Pisiffik supermarket, excellent bakery, etc. Interesting museum of Inuit culture. Fuel from a float. Helicopter connection to Ilulissat during the winter months.

92 Avannarliit (Nordre Huse)

69°08'N 51°06'W

Under suitable conditions, it is possible to sail N up the coast past Ilimanaq (Claushavn) and get close to the formidable Ilulissat Isfjord. From 1M N of Claushavn there are no soundings within 1M of the shore and there are some small islets not shown on the chart, so great care is needed. Temporary anchorage can be found in the small bay off the abandoned site at Nordre Huse. A scramble up to the 85m spot-height gives an incomparable and awesome view of the crowded icebergs forcing their way out to sea. Undoubtedly one of the wonders of the world!

93 Ilulissat (Jakobshavn)

69°13'N 51°06'W

Charts D 1513, 1552

General

Ilulissat and its nearby glacier Sermeq Kujalleq, is a World Heritage Site. Ilulissat is a busy fishing port with some 4,000 inhabitants. The harbour is a very narrow bay, which is open towards the NW. The outer harbour is mainly reserved for larger commercial ships, while the inner harbour is used by fishing vessels and small craft.

Access through the ice may be difficult or impossible early in the season.

It is well worthwhile motoring around the spectacular icebergs outside Ilulissat, but be warned that a boatload of tourists were drowned, when an iceberg overturned. A walk from the harbour across to the Isfjord provides one of the greatest sights in the world.

Many sledge dogs are bred in Ilulissat and constant barking, by the estimated population of 5,000 dogs, is a noticeable feature.

Approach

Kangia, the huge Ilulissat Isfjord, is visible in clear weather from many miles off. Coming from the sea it will often appear as if the entrance to Ilulissat, which is just to the north of the glacier, is closed by ice, but as you approach, openings in the ice front will appear. If the ice is too packed to head towards the harbour, there will often be a passage north of the grounded icebergs. Close the land N of Ilulissat and move S near the coast. There is a Racon (O) on Nordre Ness 1M NW of the harbour.

There are leading lights comprising two red lights, which, if kept in line, will give a course of 119° direct to a second set of green leading lights (143°) just 150m outside the harbour entrance. At times, the entrance is completely blocked by ice and it is not possible to enter or leave.

Anchorage

The harbour is exceedingly crowded with small craft lying to moorings or at anchor. There are marina-type finger pontoons running out from the N shore where a berth may be found. The harbourmaster (in the Royal Arctic building) may be able to help. It is not advisable to tie alongside the quay in the inner harbour, except temporarily, since these berths are used by fishing vessels, which come and go all the time. Apart from the slight danger of being locked into this harbour by ice, another unusual phenomenon is the kanele. Kanelen result in violent oscillations in the water, with a difference of up to two metres, but very well spread, between the highest and lowest levels. These oscillations are caused by icebergs calving from the glacier. Waves rush into the harbour causing severe currents and whirlpools. If berthed in the inner harbour the

Navigating the ice from Ilulissat to Rodebay *Sibéal Turraoin*

New icebergs recently calved from the Ilulissat glaciers *Máire Wilkes*

breakwater will lessen the effect of the kanele; but before the breakwater was built, the inner harbour was a dangerous place when the kanele occurred.

In 2014, a fishing vessel sunk in the middle of what was already an over-crowded harbour. An alternative anchorage can be found at 69°14′N 51°04′W in an inlet locally known as Hollander Havn, from where it is a 2 mile dinghy ride back to the town.

Facilities

Rough drying slip, diesel and water. There is a big supermarket next to the post office half a mile S of the harbour. There is also a smaller store next to the bakery just above the harbour. Doctors, dentists and a hospital. There are hotels and two banks. There is no Seamen's Home but it is possible to get a shower at the Youth Hostel.

There is a STOL airport with two or three flights a day to Kangerlussuaq (Søndre Strømfjord), except Sundays; as well as connecting flights to Aasiaat, Qaarsut for Uummannaq and Upernavik. Relative ease of travel by air from Europe via Kangerlussuaq makes this a good place for a crew change.

Ilulissat (Jakobshavn) *Máire Wilkes*

Oqaatsut - Qeqertaq, Aug Pilagtoq Island *Sibéal Turraoin*

Oqaatsut (Rodebay) *Franziska Mahler*

94 Oqaatsut (Rodebay Disko Bay)

69°21'N 51°00'W

Charts D 1500, 1513 (1551)

This is a well-sheltered bay 8M north of Ilulissat (Jakobshavn). The settlement dates from the 17th century when it was used by Dutch whalers as a trading centre. The Danes imposed their monopoly and drove out the Dutch at a naval battle outside Ilulissat (Jakobshavn).

Approach

There are two approaches to the bay. The narrow channel S of the island of Qeqertaq is the one to take when coming from the S. There are two drying rocks just to the N of the centre of the channel so care should be taken. Stay in the south, close to the shore. A minimum depth of 3m was found in the channel.

It is also possible to approach the bay by passing to the N of Qeqertaq (see *NP12*).

A whale being butchered on the rocks *Sibéal Turraoin*

Anchorage

Anchor off the settlement in 6m, or in the SE corner of the bay where juicy mussels can be found at low water. This bay is protected from the incursion of icebergs by the relatively shallow water east of Qeqertaq.

Facilities

Stores and fuel are available. There is also a post office, communal bathhouse, launderette and restaurant.

95 Paakitsoq (Disko Bay)

69°30'N 50°50'W

Charts 1500

This is a fjord at the southern entrance to Ataa Sund. At the head of the outer fjord, at the NE end, an inlet guarded by a drying reef provides a sheltered anchorage (see Tasersuaq section). From the SE side of the fjord a narrow channel leads into a large tidal lake which reaches almost to the ice cap. Local knowledge suggests that, under favourable circumstances, this may be navigable by small craft at high water when there may be sufficient depth, but tidal streams are very strong.

A narrow creek, just to the W of the channel mentioned above, offers an interesting, if insecure, lunch stop; with a walk to the top of the hill, NE of the inlet, giving a good view of the inner fjord and ice cap.

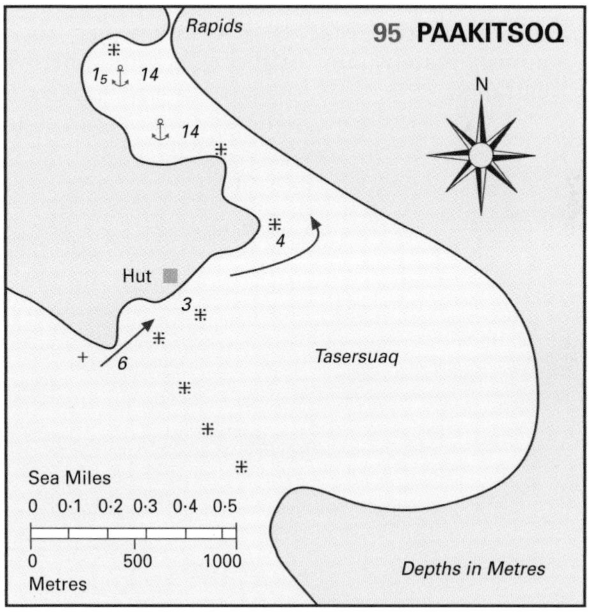

96 Tasersuaq 69°31'N 50°43'W

Charts 1500

An inlet at the NE end of the outer fjord. A drying reef extends most of the way across the entrance, but a channel with a least depth of 3m was found by sailing a 'biscuit's toss' from the NW shore (see plan). It is recommended that the anchorage is entered when the drying rocks, marked on the chartlet, are exposed. However, note that care is necessary at low water, since a shoal appears to extend from the N shore, before entering the channel. The pool in the NW corner is most attractive. It would be wise to sound around, as there are some below-water rocks. The rapids which drain the lake above the bay are obviously submerged at springs, since the water is too brackish to be drinkable.

97 Ataa (Ataa Sund) 69°46'N 50°56'W

Charts 1500

This is an abandoned settlement but occupied in the summer. The lake to the N of the settlement is supposed to have the best trout fishing in Greenland. From the hills above there is a superb view over the inland ice cap.

Anchorage

Anchor in 7–10m just off the settlement. Rather open to the S but protected from big ice by shoal water.

Alternative anchorages can be found at:

- The southwest side of the settlement in a small bay with good holding in sand but open to the east. Depth of more than 2m at low water but care is needed because there might be some below water rocks.
- East of the camp in a well sheltered bay. Care is needed when entering or leaving the bay because on the eastern side is a below water rock approximately 5m offshore in the narrow entrance.

Ataa Sund *Máire Wilkes*

98 Ikerasak (Ataa Sund) 69°46'N 50°17'W

Charts 1500

If ice conditions permit it is possible to sail up to the Eqip Sermia glacier snout. The French expedition hut to the S of the glacier is still used and a marked trail leads up to the inland ice (about 7 hours' walk).

Anchorage

Two good anchorages are reported:

- One in a quite sheltered bay 3M W of the glacier (described above).
- The second is directly E of the bay, where a river flows into the fjord producing a current of approximately 1–1·5 knots. This pushes the ice away. Good holding in fine sand which deepens very slowly and offers a choice of anchorage depth (4m–20m). Care is needed when there is not much wind because the Sund can be filled with small ice pieces within hours.

99 Nuugaarsunnguaq 69°46'N 50°20'W

Charts 1500

Anchorage

Anchor in soft mud in 7m under a rock outcrop about 3M west of the glacier. Exposed to ice.

100 Appat (Ritenbenk) 69°46'N 51°18'W

Charts 1500

The settlement of Ritenbenk is almost completely abandoned (two of the houses may be occupied in summer), with no facilities. Anchor off the cove at the SE end of the island in 8m. An attractive spot. The approach is straightforward (see *NP12*).

101 Oqaitsut Island 69°55'N 51°16'W

Charts D 1500

This little anchorage lies off Smalle Sund. It is not very easy to identify when the sun is low. See *NP 12*.

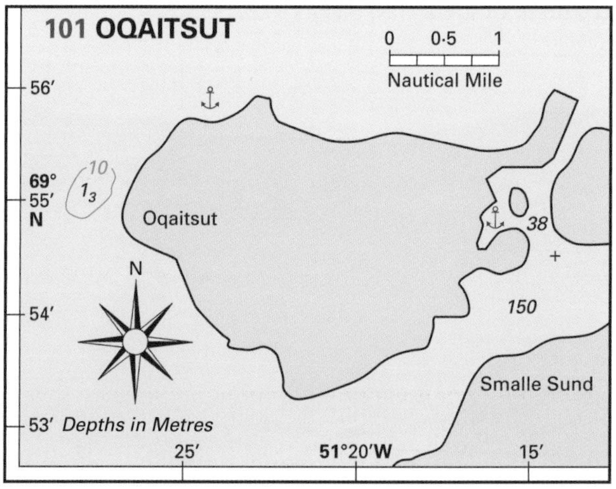

Approach

Approach from SW, along the centre of the channel between Oqaitsut and the land to the SE. When you can identify the passage to the E of the island, close the W shore – there is plenty of water. A rock lies in the middle of the channel, as shown on the sketch chart.

Continue to follow the shore round, passing between a small island and the rocky cliff face.

Anchorage

Vessels can anchor at the S end of the bay in about 10m.

A local fishing boat tied up alongside the cliff on the S shore, just S of the small island.

An alternative recommended anchorage is the little indentation to the WNW of the island.

102 Saqqaq 70°01′N 51°56′W

Charts D 1500 (1552)

A clean and pleasant small settlement with a fish factory. At the back of the settlement, next to a two-storey house, is Hannibal Fencker's Arctic Garden, locally famous and a minor tourist attraction. Unfortunately, since his death, the garden has been somewhat neglected. There is a small shop and fuel is available.

Saqqaq, supply ship and lighter *Sibéal Turraoin*

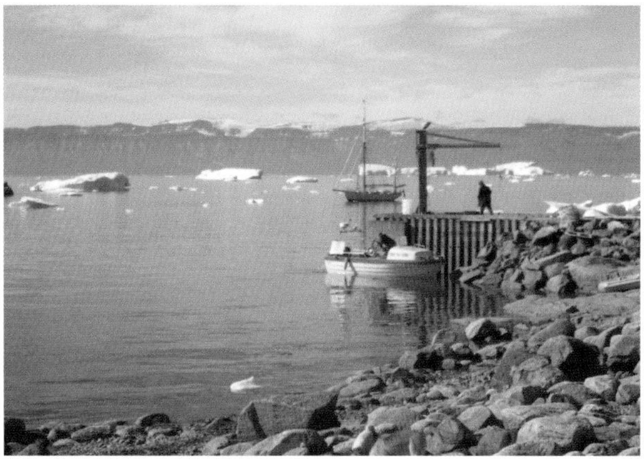

Saqqaq quay *Máire Wilkes*

Approach and anchorage

Approach from the W and anchor as soon as you are between the island and the land, in 3m. The water shoals to less than 1m further in and the SE entrance is normally blocked by grounded icebergs, which provide a degree of shelter. In some seasons, in August, there is a considerable amount of ice along this stretch of coast, close inshore.

103 Atanikerdluk (Iluarâ)

70°04′N 52°22′W

Charts D 1500

The bay to the E of the Nunguaq spit provides good shelter in a W or NW blow, when traversing the Vaigat. The spit does however, cover at High Water Springs, allowing a surge and small pieces of ice into the anchorage. This is easily identified, being adjacent to a large bluff. If N bound around Nuussuaq, this is a useful anchorage to wait for a favourable breeze. See *NP 12*.

The entrance is very open and ice, including sizable bergy bits, finds its way in.

Saqqaq small boat pontoon *Sibéal Turraoin*

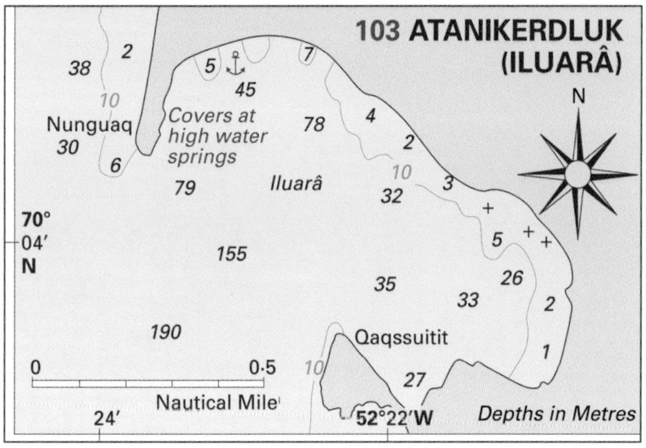

Approach

The approach is straightforward and there are no dangers if you keep a sensible distance from the shore.

Anchorage

Anchor either N or S side of the bay, according to wind direction, and be prepared to move if the wind shifts. Although the chart shows the Nunguaq peninsula as above water, when visited it was observed to be breached at high water. This could not only let in any swell, but also brash.

A S wind will bring an unpleasant swell into this anchorage causing rollers on the beach, which would make anchoring in suitable depths unwise. However, when the wind is in the N, the swell is very moderate and a lee can be obtained under the sand and shingle spit know as Nunguaq, under the N shore in about 10m.

When visited, anchorage was found in the N end in order to shelter from a N breeze. The boat swung between wind and tide. Anchoring on a very narrow shelf, the anchor was in 11m while the boat swung into 30m, lying to 50m of chain. When the wind changed and blew parallel with the coast, the boat swung into 6m.

Although the anchor came up covered in kelp, the holding appeared to be quite good.

When leaving, with a S wind, a fishing boat was observed anchored at the S end of the bay.

Disko Island south and west

104 Qeqertarsuaq (Godhavn) (Disko Island) 69°15'N 53°33'W

Charts BA 276 (from a survey by Sir Edward Belcher 1852); D 1511 (1551)

An excellent and protected harbour. It is a good port of call if going N because of its ease of access, but facilities are better at Aasiaat (*NP12*).

This historic settlement on Disko Island was of some importance, which diminished with the decline of whaling and the move of the administration to Aasiaat. McClintock called here in July 1857 on his way N in the screw yacht *Fox* (177 tons) during the search for the Franklin Expedition. He said of the area, 'I do not know a more enticing spot in Greenland for a week's shooting, fishing and yachting than Disko Fjord.' Certainly the view across Disko Bay, studded with hundreds of drifting icebergs, towards the great Ilulissat Isfjord and the Greenland ice cap, is quite stunning on a clear day.

Qeqertarsuaq, Disko Island *Máire Wilkes*

Qeqertarsuaq (Godhavn) whale bones *J Reeves*

Approach

Straightforward using *NP12* and one of the larger-scale plans, but note that the leading line 061° passes only 50m SE of Lindbergs Skær.

Anchorage

The best anchorage for a yacht is in Eulners Bugt, which is the SW arm of the harbour. However, there have been reports that Eulners Bugt is foul in places and holding variable; care should therefore be taken when anchoring.

The E arm is rather shallow and more exposed. Eulners Bugt is perfectly sheltered, good holding in 11m. Lines could be taken ashore if necessary.

Facilities

Normal for a medium-sized settlement. Heliport with regular flights to Aasiaat and Ilulissat in the winter. Disko Line ferries operate in the summer.

105 Killiit (Fortune Bay) (Disko Island south) 69°15'N 53°45'W

Charts D 1511 is adequate (1550)

Fortune Bay is a ragged bight with many islands and rocks, lying 5M W of Qeqertarsuaq. Many of the islets have sledge dogs stranded on them for the summer. Kangerluarssuk, the inlet at the E end of the bay, provides a landlocked anchorage.

Approach

Two approaches to the inlet are possible. If coming from Qeqertarsuaq, enter through the channel E of Qaqaq. Keep the rock shown awash to starboard; it only covers at high water (see sketch chart).
If coming from the W, pass north of Qaqaq.

Anchorage

There is an anchorage in 10m halfway along the N shore of Kangerluarssuk, off a small stream.

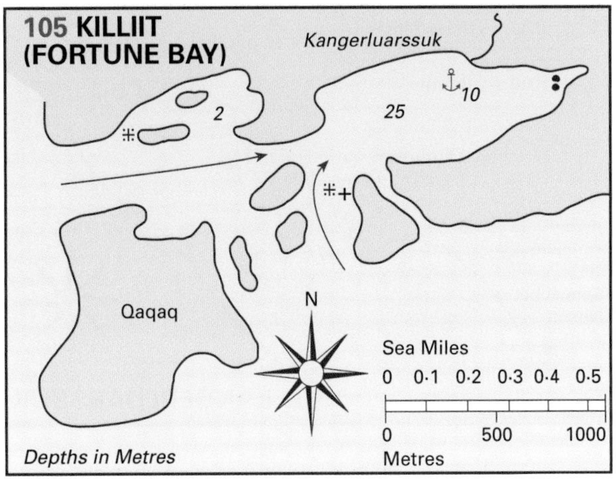

106 *Kangerluk (Diskofjord)* (Disko Island west) 69°30'N 54°00'W

Charts D 1500

This is a fjord on the W coast of Disko Island with many branches leading off from it.

Approach

Straightforward. If coming from the S, it is possible with care to pass inside Saattut (Satoq) Island to the W of Maligiaq, but note that it is fairly shallow with depths of 3 to 10m quite well offshore.

Anchorages

107 Nipisat 69°27'N 54°13'W

Charts D 1500, 1550

Nipisat, which means 'lump fish' and refers to the island's shape, is a small bay just to the E of Maligiaq, the site of an abandoned Loran station. It is a former whaling station and is also noted for its well preserved Saqqaq culture archeological site. There are about 20 buildings still standing. The jetty is now in ruins. Anchor off the jetty to the ENE in about 6m. The inner bay is very shallow.

108 Kuanit 69°34'N 54°20'W

Charts D 1500

A rather bleak spot but giving shelter from the N to the NE, otherwise exposed. Anchor in 5m off the stream.

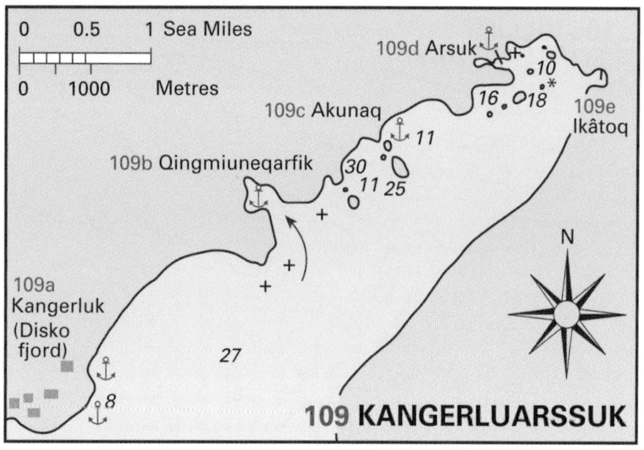

109 Kangerluarssuk 69°30'N 53°50'W

Charts D 1500 (barely adequate) **Map** 69.V.1

General

A 5M-long arm of Disko fjord. A small settlement, Diskofjord, is at the mouth of the inlet. The NW side of the inlet has many bays and islets and a pleasant day could be spent exploring them. In the absence of a detailed chart, the plan shown here should help, but go carefully!

109a Kangerluk (Diskofjord) settlement

Anchor to the E of the settlement in 8m, just outside some small-craft moorings or, alternatively, off the quay by the end of the beach. There is a small, comprehensively stocked shop and fuel is available.

109b Qingmiuneqarfik

A small bay, 2M north of Diskofjord. Anchor a little to the S of the centre of the bay in a depth of 8m. The N side is much deeper at 14m. The inner bays to the SW and north are very shallow. There are a couple of boat moorings in the bay.

109c Akunaq

A reasonable depth for anchoring can be found in the NW corner of this bay. Anchor as soon as you are in 10m as the bottom shoals quickly.

109d Arsuk

This is the best anchorage in Kangerluarssuk. Anchor halfway down the bay in 7m, mud. A stream runs into the bay from a lake. Very beautiful.

109e Ikatoq

A keyhole-shaped bay at the E end of Kangerluarssuk. Unfortunately it is very shallow with a sounding of about 1m just inside the entrance and into the pool. Ideal for shoal draught boats or for vessels which can take the ground.

Disko Island, huskies on the icecap *Máire Wilkes*

110 Eqalunguit 69°33'N 53°35'W

Charts D 1500 **Map** 69 V.1

Excellent anchorage in 6m, thick mud, in the middle of a small bay on the W side of the Kuanersuit suvdluat, where it swings around to the E.
Good walking and fishing.

111 Mellemfjord (Akudlit)
69°44'N 54°35'W

Charts D 1500 **Map** 69 V.1

Useful passage anchorage 5M within Mellemfjord, on the S side, behind the remains of a terminal morraine. This anchorage is marked on the map and offers better shelter than Enoks Havn, 3M to the W, which is marked on the chart. At the point where the fjord turns SE, there is a pronounced spit on the southern shore. The water immediately behind this spit is deep (>20m) until very close to shore.

A more suitable anchorage for smaller boats may be found towards the SE end of the bight created by the spit, opposite a dry river bed and about 100-200 metres behind the spit. The water here is 10-11 metres at high tide or less for those who do not mind being close to shore. There are reports of the anchor being quite difficult to set but, once dug in, holding well. The end of the fjord dries out extensively so vessels are advised not to proceed too far down the fjord in search of an anchorage.

AREA III

The northwest coast north of Disko, 70° to 77°N

The possibilities of cruising N of Disko depend entirely on the ice situation. In a normal season there should be no problem in getting to Upernavik in June or July. North of Upernavik, progress will depend on the season.

Arguments about the best route to the 'North Water' have raged since John Ross' voyage in HMS *Isabella* in 1818 when he named Melville Bay. Whalers and, later, explorers followed him and all had their opinions. Every season is different and the

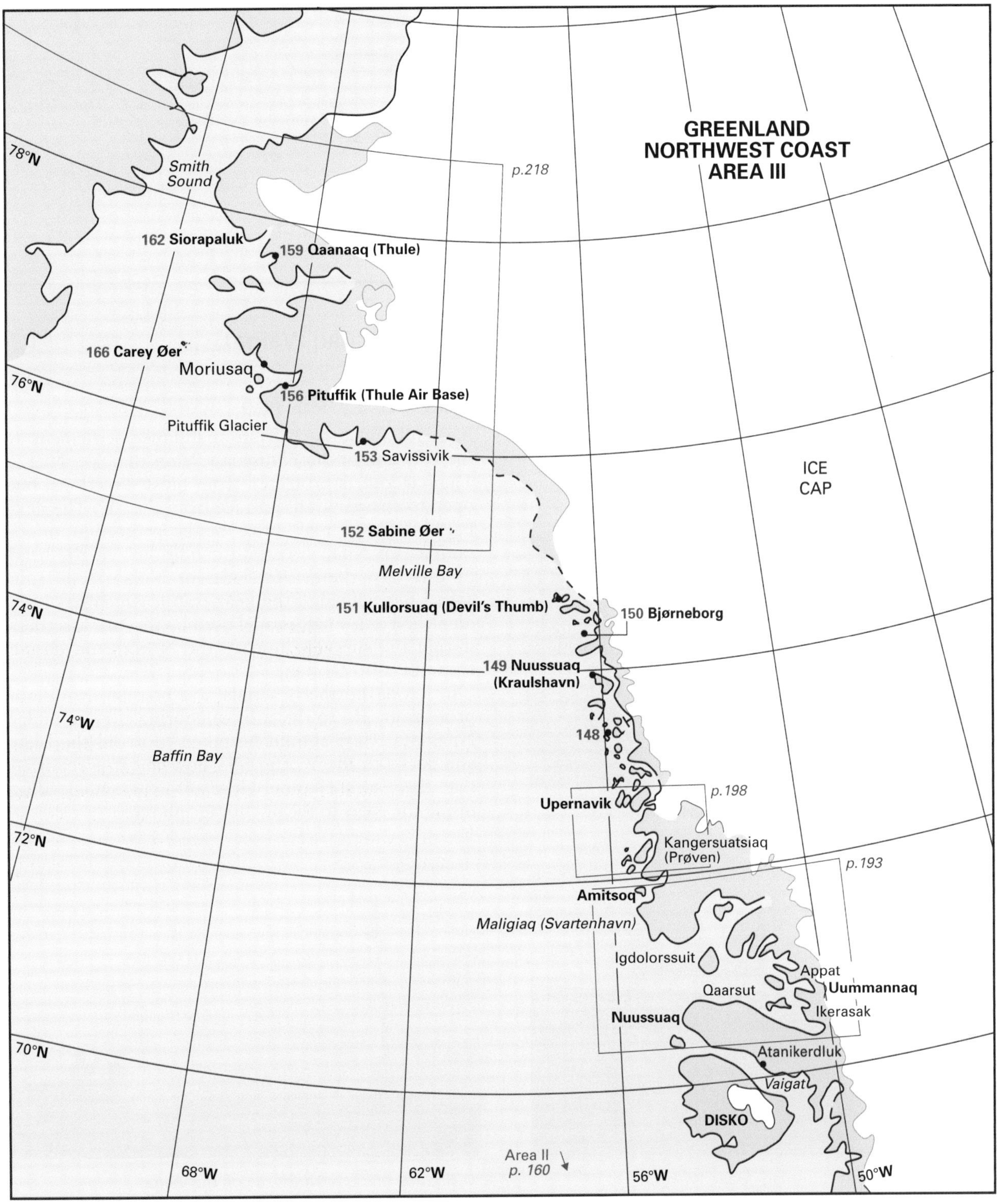

best advice must be to consult with Iscentralen, Narsarsuaq, who will send a fax or email of the ice chart. Skippers of local boats and supply ships are usually very helpful.

Iceberg density increases dramatically north of Upernavik and drift ice may also be met. In most years the 'middle pack' (called vestis or 'west ice' by the Danes) is never very far away and, in strong winds, can move rapidly.

Between Upernavik and Qaanaaq (77°28'N 69°13'W) there are a few very small communities. The big Thule US Air Force Base (Pituffik) is a security area and not available except in an emergency. See under Pituffik (North Star Bay).

Charts

Apart from the two 1:80,000 charts covering the Uummannaq and Upernavik areas, Danish chart coverage is at 1:400,000 and there are few soundings shown inshore. The 1:250,000 topographical maps are useful, as they show many details which do not appear on the smaller-scale charts.

Vaigat 70°N 53°W

Charts D 1500, 1600

Vaigat is the strait between Disko Island and the mainland, along which many of the icebergs which eventually end up on the Grand Banks off Newfoundland start their journey. This being the case, navigation may not be possible in some seasons until late July; however, the W coast of Disko Island may be clear of ice earlier in the season.

Vaigat with a fog back approaching and iceberg *Máire Wilkes*

The burial ground at Nuussuaq *Máire Wilkes*

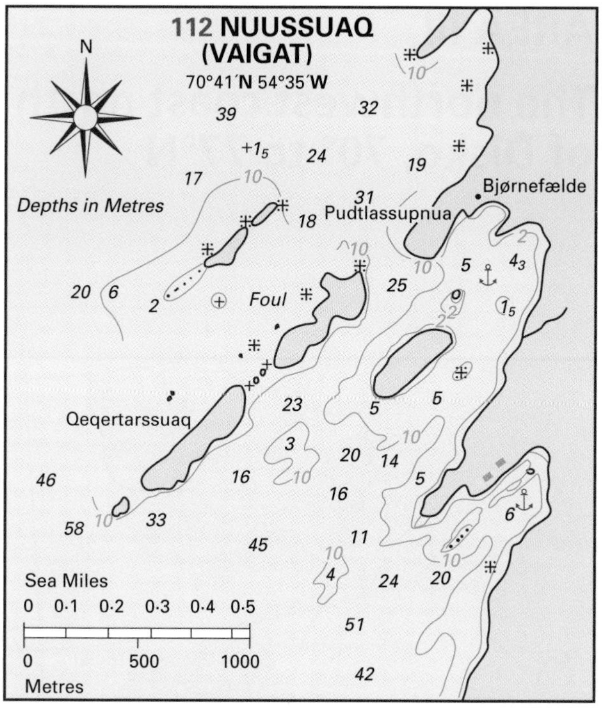

112 Nuussuaq (Vaigat)

70°41'N 54° 35'W

Charts D 1600 **Map** 70 V1

A useful anchorage off an abandoned settlement at the NW end of the Nuussuaq Peninsula. (see *NP12*) The harbour is protected from most directions, but open to strong winds and ice from the SW. The next bay to the N may offer better protection under Pudtlassup Nua, in certain conditions. At the head of this bay, there is an ancient Norse stone ruin called Bjørnefælde ('the bear trap'), which has been identified as a small chapel used by the Norse settlers during the summer hunt in the Norðrsetur, dating from the 13th century.

In strong northerly winds it is possible to obtain protection, 2M to the S, by anchoring close in under Nugssuta. Care should be taken to avoid the islets and rocks to the W and SW, however it is reported that there is a channel close off Nugssuta leading inside the islets to the anchorage above.

Navigation marks at Nuussuaq on the Vaigat *Máire Wilkes*

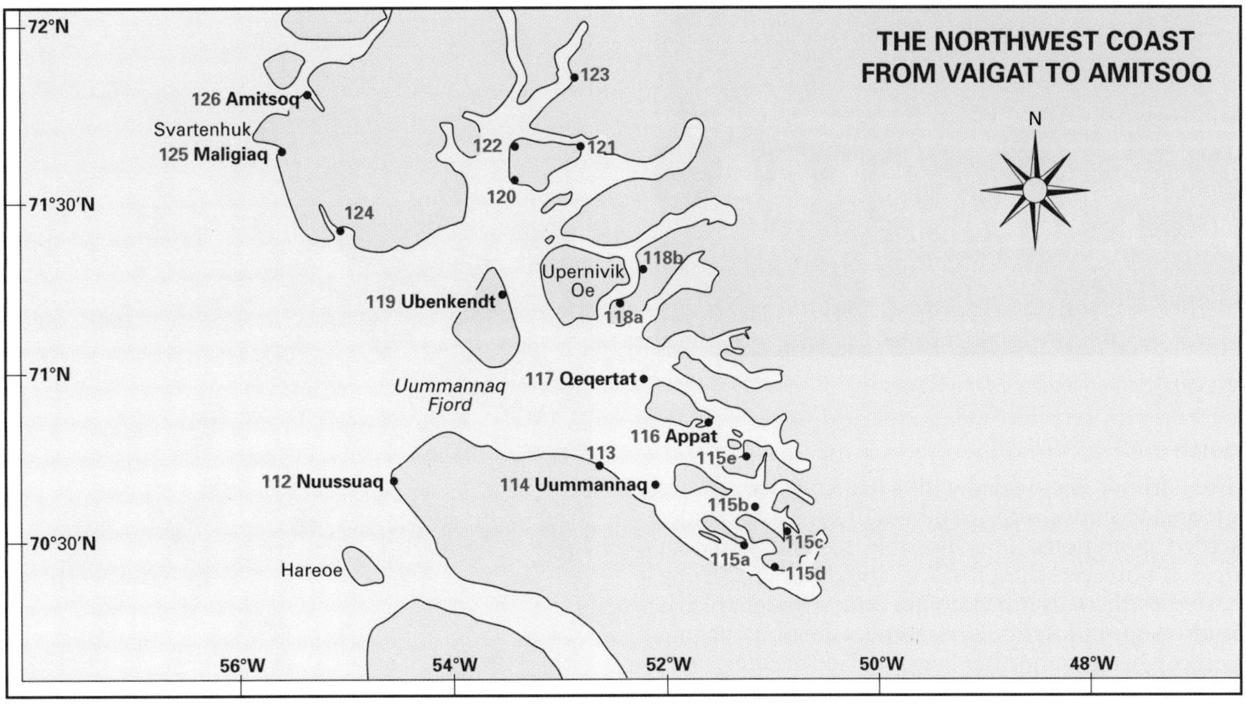

A protected anchorage in easterly winds can be found off the spit at the NW of the Nuussuaq Peninsular (70°49'N 54°11'W). It is open to westerly winds.

Nordost Bugten & Uummannaq Fjord 71°N to 54°W

Charts D 1600, 1610 **Maps** 70 V 1 & 2, 71 V 1 & 2

A large and spectacular area, with heavily glaciated mountains running up to 2200m and a number of very active tide-water glaciers. As a result, a considerable number of bergs and bergy bits will be met at all times. However, there are many useful anchorages, making this an excellent cruising and mountaineering area. Apart from the major settlement on Uummannaq Island, there are a few smaller settlements.

113 Qaarsut 70°44'N 52°39'W

Charts 1600, 1610 **Map** 70 V2

A small settlement 10M W of Uummannaq. This is now the site of a STOL airfield, with a helicopter connection to Uummannaq. Temporary anchorage can be obtained close offshore near the airfield, in settled weather; but it is not recommended (see *NP12*).

114 Uummannaq 70°41'N 52°08'W

Charts D 1610 (1650)

A beautiful town, clinging to the face of the rock at the S end of the island.

Approach

The harbour is sometimes protected by an ice boom consisting of a steel cable suspended 3m below the surface and marked by orange buoys. The boom stretches across the channel between the islands of Kødø and Smedeø. If necessary, it is possible to enter the harbour through the channel between Kødø and the main island, favouring the Kødø side and carrying 4m, but note that there are below-water rocks to be avoided on the main island side of the channel. The channel may be blocked by small craft moorings. If the ice boom is not deployed, ice enters the harbour which can be a concern to vessels anchored there.

Uummannaq Island *Máire Wilkes*

Washday, Uummannaq *Máire Wilkes*

Berth

The harbour is crowded with small craft, which are moored to buoys with stern lines to the shore. Under settled conditions, it is possible to find space to moor; however due to overcrowding, in strong easterlies the harbour becomes almost untenable. It is also subject to growlers and occasional damaging waves when grounded icebergs outside disintegrate.

Visitors' vessels anchor and take stern lines ashore to reduce their sailing room. A safe anchorage, except in strong westerlies, can be found in the Qasigissat (Spraglebugt) on the W side of the island (see NP12). Note also, that there is a totally sheltered anchorage on Qeqertat (No104), 20M to the N.

Facilities

Launderette. Bank. Supermarket and bakery. Heliport with daily connecting flights to the STOL airfield at Qaarsut.

Good quality fresh water is available from the jetty used by local fishing boats or by jerry can from the public standpipes in the town (located in the brightly painted blue huts). There are no public internet facilities ashore, however, the Tele Greenland 3G network is quite fast.

114a Uummannaq, West Bay

70°41'N 52°00'W

A pleasant anchorage in the SW of the island, recommended in contrast to the crowded and ice prone main harbour, though quite a walk to the town. Best approached, and left, by keeping close to the shore on either side because of outlying reefs and rocks guarding the anchorage. Good holding in reasonable depth. Open to the west but some protection even then from rocks and reefs.

115 Uummannaq Fjord, southeast

70°30'N 51°00'W

Charts D 1600 **Map** 70 V.2

Huge numbers of bergs, bergy bits and brash are carried out of the Qarajaqs Isfjord (Ikerasaup Suvdlua), which is virtually impenetrable. The rest of the area, depending on the season, is also much

Uummannaq Fjord *Máire Wilkes*

affected; but the following anchorages have been used and others are possible in good conditions.

115a Ikerasak 70°30'N 51°18'W

A small village at the SE tip of Ikerasak Island with a relatively sheltered anchorage (see *NP12*) A few turf houses are still occupied and one can get a flavour of the 'old ways' with numerous sledge dogs. A short walk out to the tip of the island, provides a splendid view of the Qarajaqs Isfjord.

The anchorage has plenty of swinging room despite the large number of small fishing boats moored in the harbour. The anchorage in the bay to the northwest of the Royal Greenland jetty, and more directly beneath the iconic peak has been recommended. Like all anchorages in the area it is subject to drifting ice floes.

Large quantities of ice are to be found floating up the main channel between Ikerasak and the Drygalskis peninsula, but the prevailing currents seem to keep them clear of the bight in which the anchorage is located. It can be be a far more sheltered and ice free anchorage than Uummannaq, despite the fact that it is some 20M closer to the Qarajaqs Isfjord.

The passage between Ikersak and the 112m high island Qeqertarssuaq is navigable with care and has between 3–4m of water at LW, with the deeper water lying on the Qeqertarssuaq side of the channel. The Ikerasagssuaq passage between Qeqertarssuaq and the Drygalskis peninsula carries far more water. However both of these passages are prone to becoming blocked with ice and under such circumstances the only approach to Ikerasak may be from the NW.

If leaving Ikerasak to the S using the channel between Ikerasak and Qeqertarssuaq care should be taken to avoid two uncharted rocks which are only visible at LW (see picture opposite for approximate locations).

There is a remarkably well stocked store ashore with a surprising array of goods ranging from rifle bullets, international antifouling and anchors at one extreme to freshly baked bread and pastries at the other.

A heliport offers connections to the STOL airfield at Qaarsut.

Fresh water is available by jerry can from the blue hutted standpipes in the settlement and fuel from pumps close to a floating pontoon in the main anchorage (dinghy access only).

115b Niaqornakavsak 70°37′N 51°13′W

Charts 1610

Reasonably secure anchorage in a narrow creek on the NW side of the tip of the peninsula. The entrance may be too narrow to approach in windy conditions. Lines can be taken ashore. Scramble up for a fine view of the ice cap.

115c Sermerdlat Kangerdluat (Drygalskis Halvo) 70°33′N 50°50′W

Charts 1600

Anchorage may be found in the SE corner, in 15m, close inshore by the two streams. It gives shelter from fresh easterly winds, but may be subject to gusts. There is deep water either side of the two islands approaching the anchorage, with a drying rock between them.

An alternative anchorage can be found in the slot to the north of the anchorage referred to above. It is reported to provide good protection from all but west winds. Fresh water lake to southeast.

Another pleasant anchorage can be found at Kujatdlikavsak (70°30′N 0°55′W). It is well protected though a little open to the northwest. Fresh water lake above to the southeast.

There is an abandoned Inuit camp at Niaqornakavsak (70°36′N 51°13′W) on the NW extremity of the peninsula. This is reported to be an open but scenic anchorage with good fishing and a fresh water stream. Underwater reefs necessitate careful navigation.

115d Akuliaruserssuaq 70°27′N 51°00′W

Charts D 1600 **Map** 70 V.2

Anchorage sheltered from wind and ice on the N side of Qarajaqs Isfjord. Anchor in 16m, mud, to the E of two islets or in 12m at the head of the bay. Water from the stream. Good walking, with views of the glacier.

Akuliaruserssuaq *Máire Wilkes*

Appat Island approaching Umiasugssuup Ilua *Máire Wilkes*

115e Qaqugdlugssuit

A number of anchorages have been utilised on the Qaqugdlugssuit peninsula:

- **Qaqugdlugssuit waterfall bank** (70°42′N 51°10′W) An open anchorage close to a waterfall and stream.
- **Qeqertanguaq** (70°45′N 51°18′W). Subject to strong unpredictable katabatic winds but possible to get lines ashore. Not particularly recommended.
- **Anoritup nüa** A potential lunch stop on the north east corner of Qaqugdugssuit, an inlet used occasionally by local dories. Open to the west, and underwater rocks on the north side. A pleasant temporary stop.
- **Augpilagtoq** (70°39′N 51°06′W). On the southern promontory of Itivdliarssup by an old Fanghus. This is the venue for the festival in or around July where three local settlements meet together annually.

116 Appat 70°52′N 51°39′W

Charts D 1610 Map 70 V2

Umiasugssuup Ilua is a deep inlet, which indents the SE end of Appat island, with high cliffs on either side as you enter. At the head of the inlet, anchorage may be found in 15m, very close inshore, off a grassy slope. This was completely free of ice, when visited, despite large quantities outside. There is a handy stream nearby, from which to water. A climb up the steep slope will give you a view towards the Kangerdlua glaciers.

117 Qeqertat 71°00′N 52°15′W

Charts D 1610 **Maps** 70 V2 & 71 V2

There is a totally secure and sheltered anchorage in the pool at the end of a narrow inlet on the S side of the island. A scramble to the top of the hill (164m) is rewarded by panoramic views of the icebergs and mountains.

Approach

If approaching from the W, the shoal and rock awash, 6M NNW of Qeqertat, will be indicated by the large number of icebergs aground on it. Note also the rocks off Qernertuarssuit Island, just S of the entrance to the bay. The channel leading to the pool is narrow and carries 3m through most of its length, but a rock in the middle has less than 2m at MLWS.

Anchorage

Either anchor in 3m at the mouth of the narrow channel leading to the inner pool (which is reported to offer very good holding in sand), or enter the inner pool and anchor in the middle in 3m, soft mud. Lines may be taken ashore, if necessary.

If the channel is blocked by ice, it is possible to anchor on the N side of the bay, in 10m. The thick kelp and rocky bottom here offers a fine weather anchorage only.

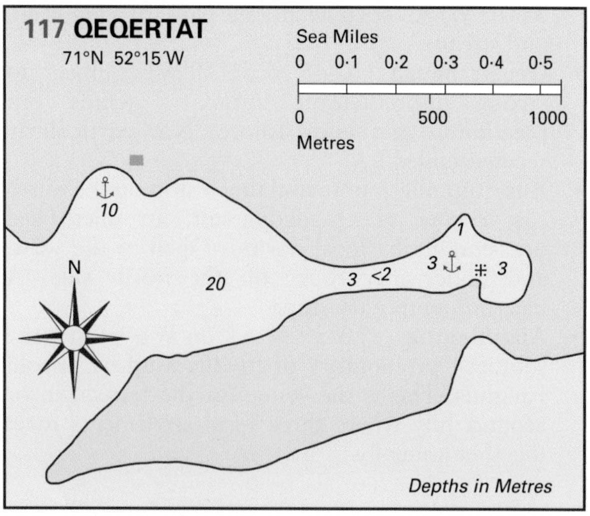

Inukavsait anchorages - a crew member is ashore collecting fresh water *Máire Wilkes*

118 Inukavsait

Charts D 1600 & 1610 **Map** 71 V.2

The deep passage between Upernivik Ø and Qioqe has two useful anchorages on the E side. In an area where suitable depths for anchoring are difficult to find, these are worth noting.

⚓ 71°13′N 52°27′W

Charts D 1610

Anchor in <10m, good holding in mud, SW of the glacial stream and fan.

⚓ 71°19′N 52°15′W

Charts D 1600

Suitable depths can be found on the N side of the glacial fan, but care is necessary in the approach, since the shoal extends out some distance. Tilman spent a difficult nine days here in *Baroque* in 1975.

Nordost Bugten, Karrats Fjord 71°N–72°N

Charts D 1600 **Map** 71 V1 & 71 V2

An outstanding mountaineering area, but with few if any secure anchorages. Amongst other climbers, Bill Tilman visited the area in *Baroque* in 1975. More recently Bob Shepton has used the following anchorages.

119 Igdlorssuit 71°14′N 53°34′W

Charts D 1600

A small settlement (pop. 91) on the NE side of Ubekendt Ejland, where fuel and limited stores are available. Local resident Hans Holm speaks excellent English and is very helpful. Indifferent anchorage, exposed from N through to SE (see *NP12*).

120 Nugatsiaq 71°32′N 53°14′W

Charts D 1600

A very small settlement with limited supplies. Indifferent anchorage, exposed to the S (see *NP12*).

121 Nuugaatsiaup Tunua
71°40'N 52°49'W

Charts D 1600

An excellent anchorage on the NE tip of Qeqertarssuaq Island, with better shelter than is apparent from the chart. This is in an inlet facing W, at the E end of the Nuugaatsiaup Tunua, on the S side. Anchor in 5–8m in the SE corner. The inlet is relatively shallow and large ice appears to be kept out by the current in the main channel. Water from the stream at the head of the inlet.

122 Itsakuarssuq 71°40'N 53°26'W

Charts D 1600

A pleasant anchorage on the NW corner of Qeqertarssuaq Island, between Itsakuarssuq Island and the main island. Staightforward approach from the N. From the S; reefs extend from both points and care is needed.

123 Puatdlarsivik 71°52'N 52°52'W

Charts D 1600

A large bay on the E side of Íngia Fjord. The anchorage is close to the outwash from the braided stream on either side; but ice seems to be less troublesome on the N side. The silt bank comes a fair way out and is inconsistent in shape, so care is needed.

124 Arfertuarssuk 71°25'N 55°05'W

Charts D 1600

A small fjord running NW from Kap Cranstown at the S tip of Svartenhuk Halvo, with several possible anchorages, either in the fjord itself or in the Tasiussap Imaa to the E of the entrance.

125 Maligiaq (Svartenhavn)
71°39'N 55°39'W

Charts D 1600 **Map** 71 V1

A shallow bight SE of Svartenhuk, open to the W. (See *NP12*) Approach from the W, keeping clear of the reef, which extends 4M SW of the entrance and take soundings as you go.

Depending on the wind, protection can be found under the N or S shore, subject to swell. Good holding is reported.There is a rejsehus (traveller's hut) on the S shore near the anchorage. Good Arctic char fishing in the river.

126 Amitsoq 71°49'N 55°23'W

Charts D 1600 **Map** 71 V1

12M NE of Sigguk (Svartenhuk), at the entrance to Amitsup suvdlua, there is an anchorage behind a gravel spit on the SW side. This is probably the remains of a terminal moraine and gives excellent shelter. Even in a SE gale, shelter was found close in

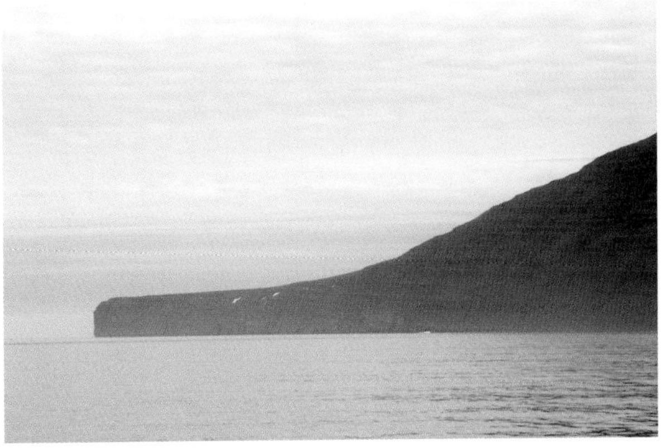

Svartenhuk *Máire Wilkes*

by the *rejsehus*. The spit is shown on the map, but not on the chart. Note that the depths in the approach from the S, are less than charted. Only 6m was found 1M from the shore, all the way from the S end of the peninsula to the anchorage. Water from the stream.

Pilotage notes for the waters near Ikermiup Island and Nutârmiut Island

An uncharted rock lies between Ikermio and Ikermiup Is, in (approx) position 72°38'N 56°01'W (Qornoq 1927).

An uncharted islet is situated off the SE corner of Nutârmiut I in (approx) position 72°35'N 55°20'W (Qornoq 1927).

Existence doubtful

The rock shown at 72°36'N 55°41'W does not appear to exist.

127 Upernavik Kujalleq (Søndre Upernavik) 72°09'N 55°32'W

Charts D 1600 **Map** 72 V1 (See *NP12*)

Small settlement with store. Diesel by hose on pontoon jetty (<1m at LW). A convenient place to refuel, if the jetty is accessible.

Upernavik Kujalleq (Sondre Upernavik) whale hunt spoils
Máire Wilkes

4. GREENLAND

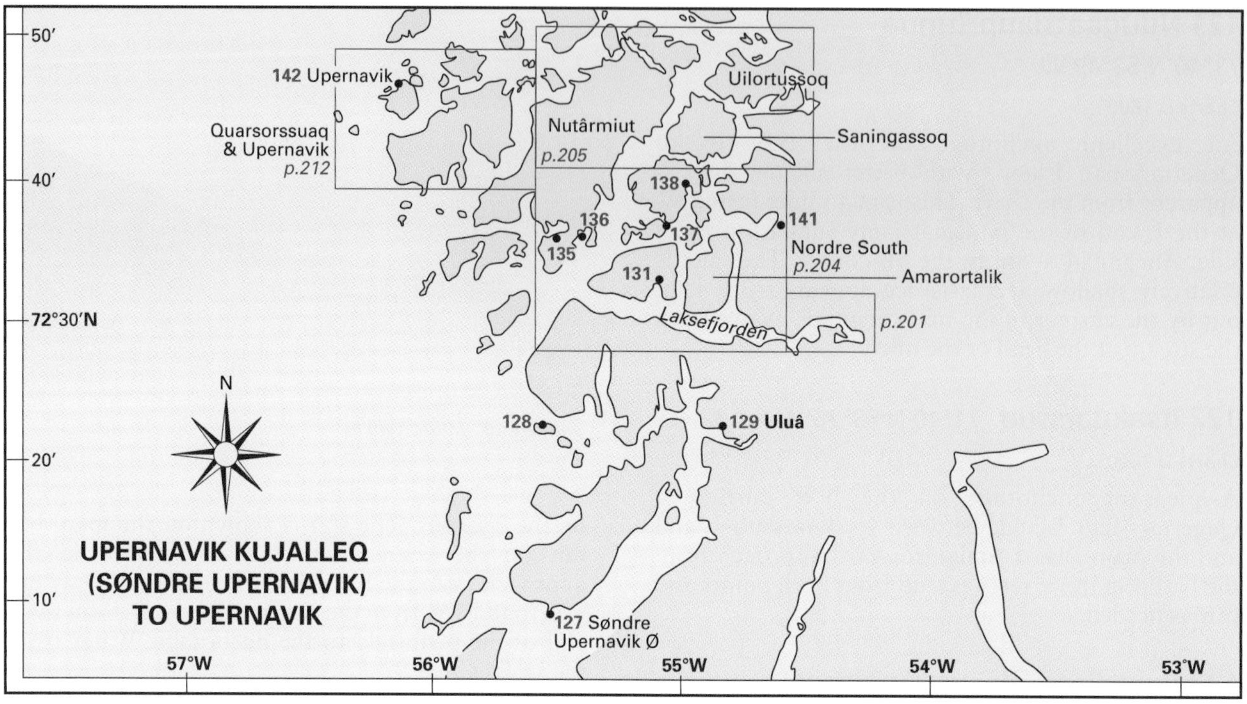

128 Kangersuatsiaq (Prøven)

72°23′N 55°33′W

Charts D 1600, 1650

An attractive village on the inner lead route to Upernavik, with a small crowded harbour (see *NP12*). It is of historical interest, having been visited by a number of explorers, including Kane in 1853, who called here on his way N in the Advance, in order to purchase dogs and complete his stock of fur clothing. Fairly well protected but subject to heavy swell in gales from the SW to NW.

Approach

The approach from the N through the Nordløbet is straightforward. Approaching from the S through the Sydløbet, favour the E side of the passage; this carries 6m and avoids the islets and rocks on the Sandøen side. Anchoring transits for large vessels consisting of two rocks painted red have been placed on Prøvens Ø ½M S of the village. This line, bearing 138°, clears W of the group of rocks, which lie 70m SW of the town jetty. Another pair of marks on Sandøen, which bear 252°, lead into the small craft anchorage on a back bearing and clear S of the rocks mentioned above and N of the rocks in the S part of the cove.

Anchorage

Small boats can anchor amongst the fishing boats in the SE part of the cove with lines ashore to bollards. The leading marks are red marks on the rocks which maybe difficult to spot. It is possible for small vessels to lie temporarily on the town jetty to load stores or fuel, with 2m at LW. When approaching or leaving the dock, beware of the underwater rocks that lie about 70m to the SW and on a direct course to and from the approach channel.

Facilities

Store and Post Office with telephone. Credit cards are not accepted and there is no ATM. Fuel by can from a hut near the store where payment is made. There is no public water supply.

Kangersuatsiaq (Prøven) – the yacht anchored in the deep water anchorage where the two pairs of leading marks intersect *Máire Wilkes*

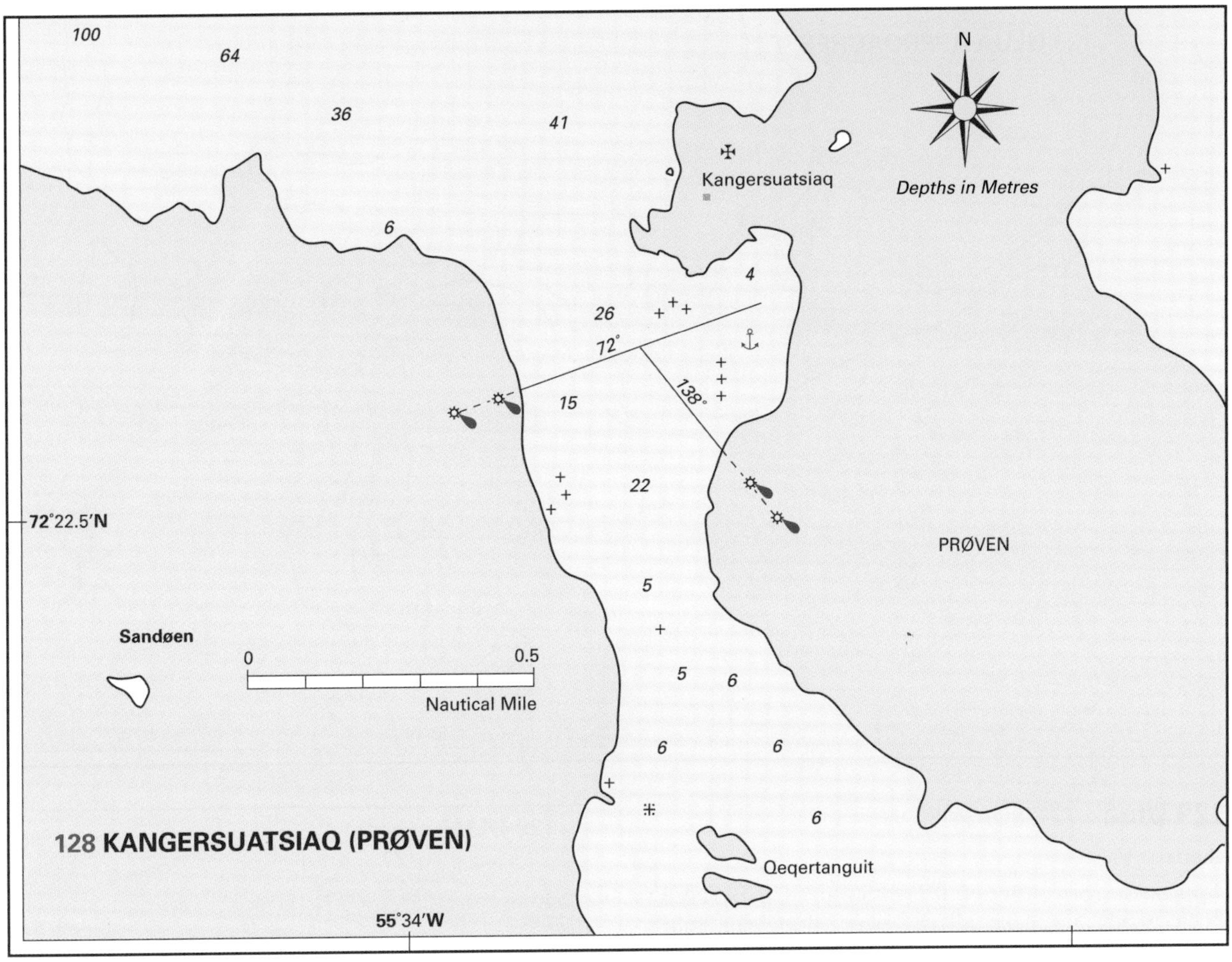

128 KANGERSUATSIAQ (PRØVEN)

Kangersuatsiaq (Prøven) *Bob Shepton*

4. GREENLAND

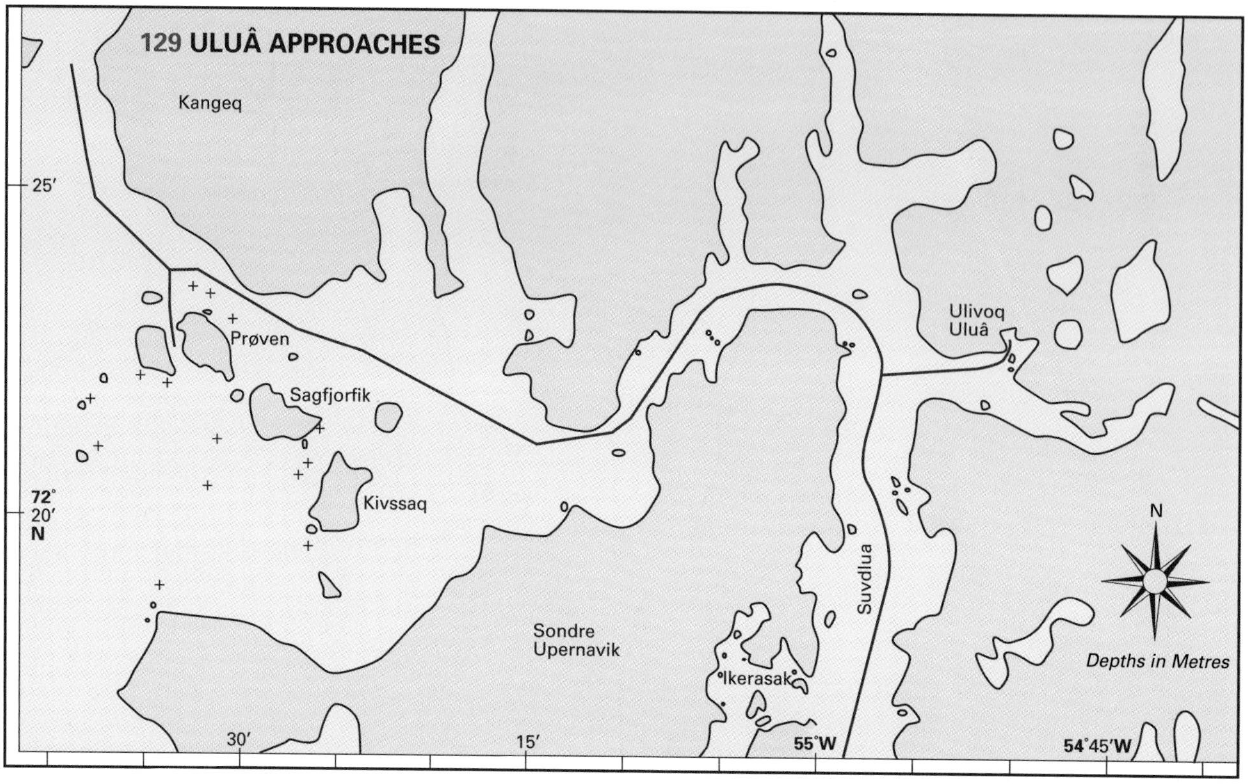

129 Uluâ 72°23′N 54°50′W

Charts D 1600

Approach from either N or E of Sondre Upernavik I. Both fjords are deep all the way, along the mid-channel line. Enter the bay from the SE keeping a reasonable distance off the shore on the port hand side, because most of the promontories have rocks off them.

The best anchorage is towards the N end of the bay, just before you reach the inner pool. This pool is strewn with rocks in its entrance and not suitable for anchoring. Anchor in about 10m, avoiding the rocky shoal that sticks out to the S. Good holding.

The anchorage is well protected and there is a pleasant walk up to the lake.

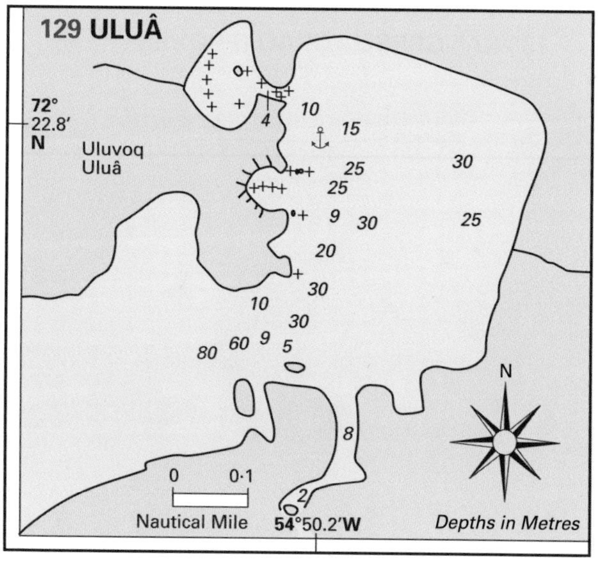

Uluâ anchorage *Annie Hill*

130 Laksefjorden 72°30′N 54°30′W

Charts *NP12* 5.67 D 1700

Lakesefjorden extends from Angmarqua (72°32′N 55°25′W) for 21 miles E into J P Kochs Land. The 14-mile long W section between Angmarqua and the 'First Narrows' (72°29·2′N 54°37·5′W), has the grand, forbidding aspect expected of a Greenland fjord. The inner part of Laksefjorden, E of the 'First Narrows' is surrounded by lower, comparatively fertile land, intersected by a number of rivers. Bilberries, crowberries and several varieties of edible mushroom abound in summer. In several of the river valleys, willow groves reach a height of 1·5–2·0m . Laksefjorden has very little drift ice in the summer.

Salmon are found in a number of the rivers in the inner part of Laksefjorden (which means Salmon Fjord in Danish), most notably near Ekaluarsuit (72°29.9′N 54°27.5′W). In July and August, local fishermen camp nearby in order to net salmon. A permit, obtainable in Upernavik, is required to fish for salmon and there is a closed season enforced by a fisheries patrol.

Ilulialik, a silt-laden river, flows from the icecap into the head of Laksefjorden. Silt from Ilulialik and other rivers has reduced the water depth E of Ekaluarsuit to such an extent that this section is only navigable by a yacht of average draught near high water. The sediment-laden water in the inner part of Laksefjorden is nearly opaque, making pilotage difficult. Rocks covered by as little as 10 cm of water are invisible, even from aloft.

Navigation

Angmarqua to 'First Narrows'

From its junction with Angmarqua to the 'First Narrows', the 14-mile long, W section of Laksefjorden, has mid-channel depths of more than 150m, except for a 10m shoal off the SW end of Amarortalik. This shoal is nearly mid-channel, extends about 400m E-W and less than 200m N-S. It is centred at 72°29·91′N 54°50·55′W (Qornoq 1927 datum). The shoal is steep to, with depths of over 50m in all directions within 200m of its shallowest part. Except in the immediate vicinity of this shoal and very close to shore, no depth of less than 150m was encountered in six traverses along the W part of Laksefjorden.

'First Narrows' to Ekaluarsuit

There is a channel with a least depth of 20m between 'First Narrows' and Ekaluarsuit, but it is narrow and tortuous, with at least one pinnacle rock close to it. None of shoals and underwater rocks close to the channel is shallow enough to be dangerous to a yacht, excepting those S of the islets just beyond the 'Second Narrows'. A vessel with a draught greater than 5m would be advised to send a boat ahead to buoy the channel.

An island in the 'First Narrows' constricts the entrance to the inner part of Laksefjorden. The navigable channel passes S of this island. Favour the S shore at the 'First Narrows' and, once in the pool beyond the narrows, alter course to SE to avoid an underwater rock lying approximately 100m off the N shore. This rock has a minimum depth of 5m and rises abruptly from 70m. Its GPS-derived position is 72°29·126′N 54°35·011′W (Qornoq 1927 datum). Steer ESE to pass between a high, rocky island and a small skerry, almost awash, to the S of the island. There is deep water on both sides of this skerry.

130 EAST LAKSEFJORDEN

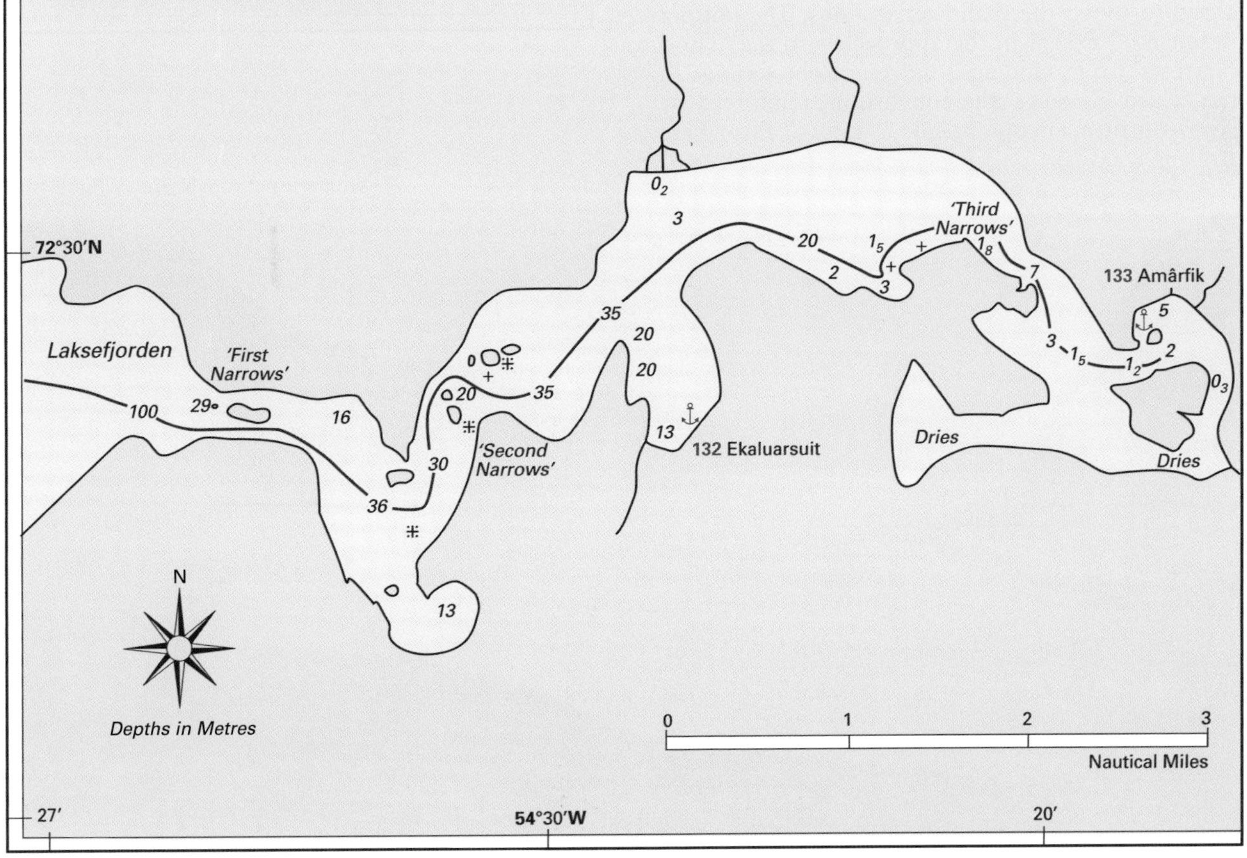

Follow the fjord around to NNE, where an island and several rocks constrict the passage, forming the 'Second Narrows'. Pass N of this island, because its S side is foul, and then steer ENE to pass about 200m S of a string of islets and skerries in mid-fjord. A drying rock and several underwater rocks, with less than 3m, extend up to 150m S of these islets.

Once past the islets, Ekaluarsuit opens up to the S. In summer, there will probably be a number of tents here, which belong to fishermen netting salmon. Ekaluarsuit appears free of dangers and a depth of 20m can be carried close to the head of the bay.

If continuing further E along Laksefjorden, steer to pass 50m off the headland on the NE side of Ekaluarsuit to avoid a bank extending from the delta of a river, which flows into the N side of the fjord. This is the first of the silt banks that fill the head of Laksefjorden. These banks restrict navigation by yachts of average draught to two or three hours either side of high water.

Ekaluarsuit to Orpik

Between Ekaluarsuit and the head of Laksefjorden are extensive silt banks that have been deposited by Ilulialik, a sediment-laden river that flows from the icecap. These form extensive drying flats and shallows, with a few deeper channels and holes scoured by river current and tide. At high water neaps, 2·4m can be carried to the head of Laksefjorden, but pilotage is difficult because the silty water is opaque and depths cannot be gauged by eye.

The sketch chart shows the best channel, but it is probably prudent to anchor and send a dinghy ahead to sound the shallower sections. The bottom is soft mud except in the approaches to the 'Third Narrows', so grounding is unlikely to be serious. In the 'Third Narrows' the ebb stream, reinforced by river outflow, may exceed 3 knots. Elsewhere streams are weak.

131 Akuliaruseq 72°33'N 55°05'W

Charts Sketch chart: Plans in Nordre Sunds South and Laksefjorden (plan on page 204)

This is a pleasant, safe anchorage off Laksefjorden on the S shore of Akuliaruseq. Anchorage is in 13m with ample swinging room, but open to the SW. Better shelter can be found further into the bay in 6m, with restricted swinging room but good all-round shelter. The bottom is mud, with scattered boulders and fine filamentous weed, generally good holding. Shorelines could be used.

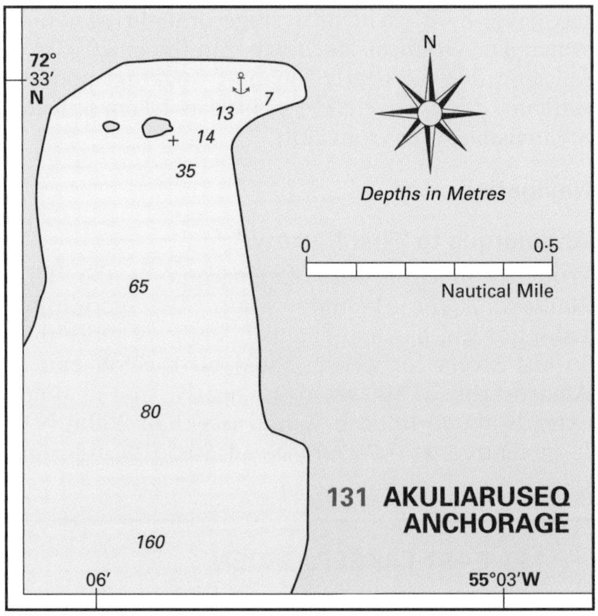

Akuliaruseq from N *Trevor Robertson*

132 Ekaluarsuit 72° 29'N 54°28'W

Charts Sketch chart: Laksefjorden East Part (page 201)

This anchorage is in the inner part of Laksefjorden near the mouth of one of the salmon rivers. Fishermen camp around the bay in summer and set nets extending 20–30m offshore. The nets are usually marked by white floats and are obvious. The best berth for a yacht is in 13m, near the head of the bay with apparently good holding. There are no dangers in the approach.

Beyond Ekaluarsuit, Laksefjorden is very shallow. In settled weather, it is possible to anchor wherever there is enough depth to float at low water. The tidal range is about 1·6m on springs, 1·0m on neaps. A useful anchorage, if waiting on the tide, is ½M SE of the 'Second Narrows' in 9m, mud. This is more protected than it looks because the surroundings are shallow. The tidal stream here is sufficiently strong that a vessel will normally be tide-rode.

133 Amârfik 72°30'N 54°18'W

Charts Sketch chart: Laksefjorden East Part (page 201)

This is a lovely anchorage to the N of the island that nearly fills the head of the fjord. The approach is via a shallow channel winding across silt banks. The sketch chart will help, but it may be prudent to anchor and sound ahead with the dinghy. There is a least depth of about 1m at LW springs in the approach, and about 2·6m at HW springs. The anchorage is in 4–7m, mud, excellent holding and well protected. The surroundings are beautiful, with two good watering streams nearby. These streams are salmon rivers, but note that a permit is required for fishing.

Amârfik anchorage from NE *Annie Hill and Trevor Robertson*

134 Nordre Sunds 72°40'N 55°00'W

Charts NP12 D 1700, D1710

Sketch charts: Nordre Sunds North and South

Nordre Sunds are a series of cross-connected sounds and fjords between Laksefjorden and Upernaviks Isfjord. Nordre Sunds, together with Laksefjorden, form a network of about 100 miles of protected channels with magnificent scenery and many all-weather anchorages. The sounds are nearly ice-free in summer. All the sounds are navigable with care by a yacht, and most are navigable by larger vessels. Chart *D1700*, the only chart available for most of the area, is of limited use because it lacks any soundings, except in the SW entrance to Angmarqua. The outline of the coast on *D1700* appears accurate within the limitations of its scale of 1:400,000, except in the vicinity of Upernaviks Isstrøm where the ice front has retreated 3–5M from its charted position. The sketch charts should help, but as always, need to be used with care.

Angmarqua 72°35'N 55°20'W

Charts NP12 D 1700

Sketch charts: Nordre Sunds North and South

Angmarqua is a long, narrow sound extending miles NNE from Laksefjorden to Upernaviks Isfjord. Nutârmiut forms its NW side and the islands of Akuliaruseq, Nako and Sáningassoq, together with Uilortussoq peninsula, form its SE side. The name Angmarqua appears on Danish and British charts and in NP12, but does not seem to be used by the local inhabitants.

The 9-mile long, SW section of Angmarqua between Kangeq (72°28'N 55°40'W) and the narrow section off SE end of Sáningassoq (72°43'N 55°04'W), is deep and the mid-channel course appears free from dangers, with no depths under 185m encountered during three transits. In the narrow section off SE Sáningassoq, the depths decrease and the bottom is irregular, with a least depth of 37m recorded in two transits. Tidal currents prevented these narrows from freezing over completely in the winter of 2005. A group of rocky islands off the NW corner of Sáningassoq, about 2·5 miles NW of the narrows described above, constricts Angmarqua. The section of Angmarqua opposite Sáningassoq, between the narrows and the islands, is deep and apparently free from dangers, with no sounding less than 100m recorded in two transits. Near these islands the bottom is irregular, with a least depth of 14m on a rocky shoal close S of the most S island of this group. When proceeding N, leave the first large island to port and the remainder of the group to starboard. Between these islands and the NE end of Nutârmiut, where Angmarqua joins Upernaviks Isfjord, the bottom is irregular, but without any obvious hazards to surface navigation. The least depth encountered in two transits was 27m.

The islands off the NW corner of Sáningassoq, and between Sáningassoq and Uilortussoq, keep drift ice in Upernaviks Isfjord from penetrating S into Nordre Sunds; in August 2004 there was considerable drift ice N of the islands, but very little to the S. Tidal streams are generally stronger N of these islands than to the S.

A bay halfway along the NE side of Nutârmiut (72°50′N 55°01′W) looks as if it might offer shelter, but it is too deep for a yacht to anchor conveniently and it may be subject to sufficient drift ice which could make the use of shore lines difficult.

'Akuliaruseq Sound' 72°33′N 55°00′W

Charts NP12 D 1700

Sketch charts: Nordre Sunds North and South

'Akuliaruseq Sound' is an informal name for the unnamed sound that extends N from Laksefjorden for 5M between Akuliaruseq and Amarortalik. The S part of the sound is fjord like, with steep shores, mid-channel depths of over 100m and no obvious dangers. NW of Amarortalik, depths decrease and the bottom is irregular. It is possible to cross this section without encountering anything shallower than 40m, but unless a route is sounded first, a more likely minimum is 20m. In four transits, no depths of less than 16m were encountered, nor were any submerged hazards seen. A 4M long cross channel connects 'Akuliaruseq Sound' with Angmarqua. This cross channel is deep and appears to be free of mid-channel hazards.

'Nako Sound' 72°38′N 54°58′W

Charts NP12 D 1700

Sketch charts: Nordre Sunds North and South

North Nako anchorages (see page 210)

'Nako Sound' is the informal name given to the 5M long, N extension of 'Akuliaruseq Sound' and runs along the E side of Nako, terminating in a 2M long inlet into the island of Nako. There are several islands and above water rocks on the E side of 'Nako Sound'. Provided these visible hazards are given a reasonable berth, there appear to be no submerged hazards near the mid-channel course. The least mid-channel depth encountered was 45m in the inlet forming the N part of the sound. The S part of the sound is deeper. There is an excellent all-weather yacht anchorage on the W side of the inlet, about 700m from the head of the sound (see North Nako anchorages).

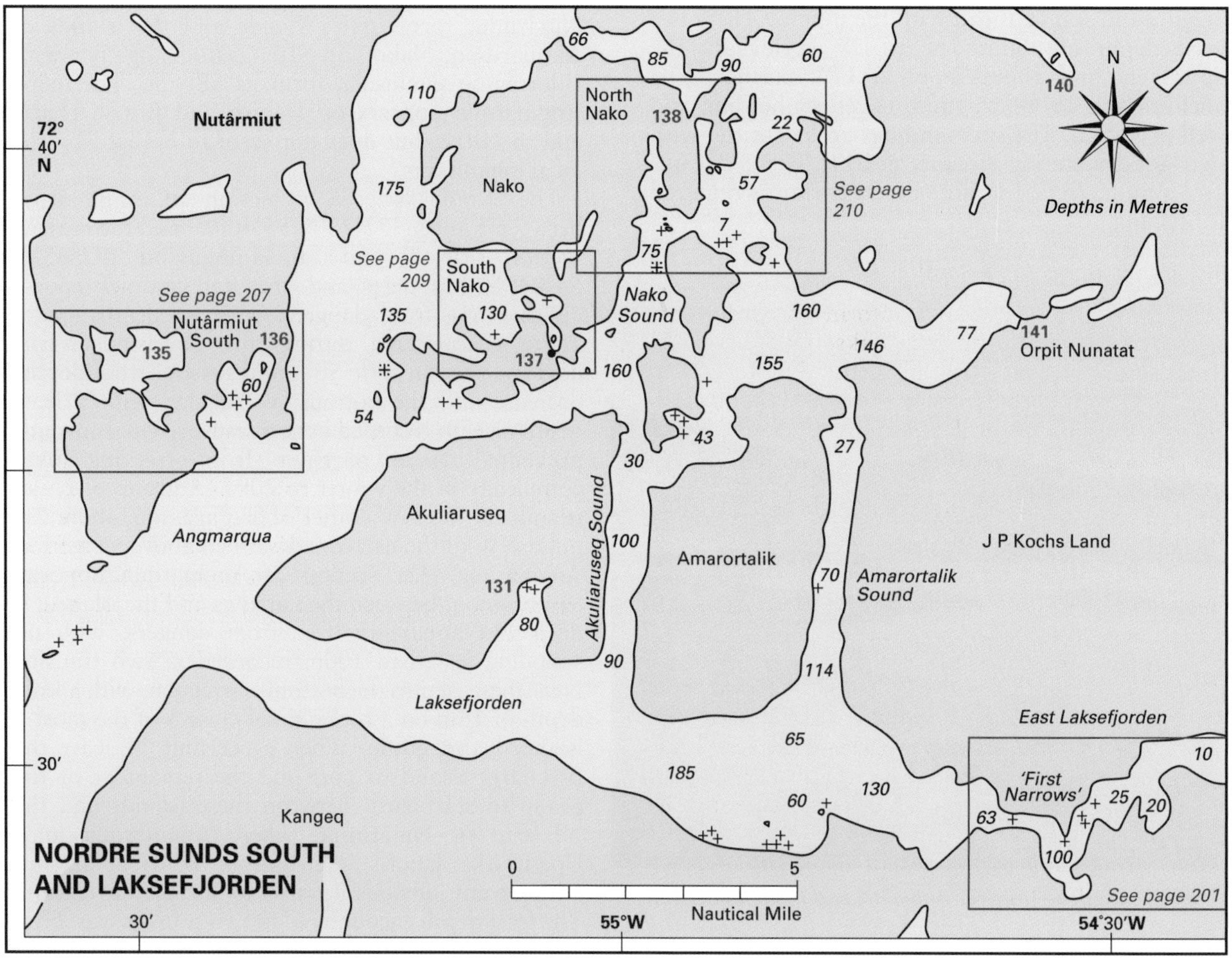

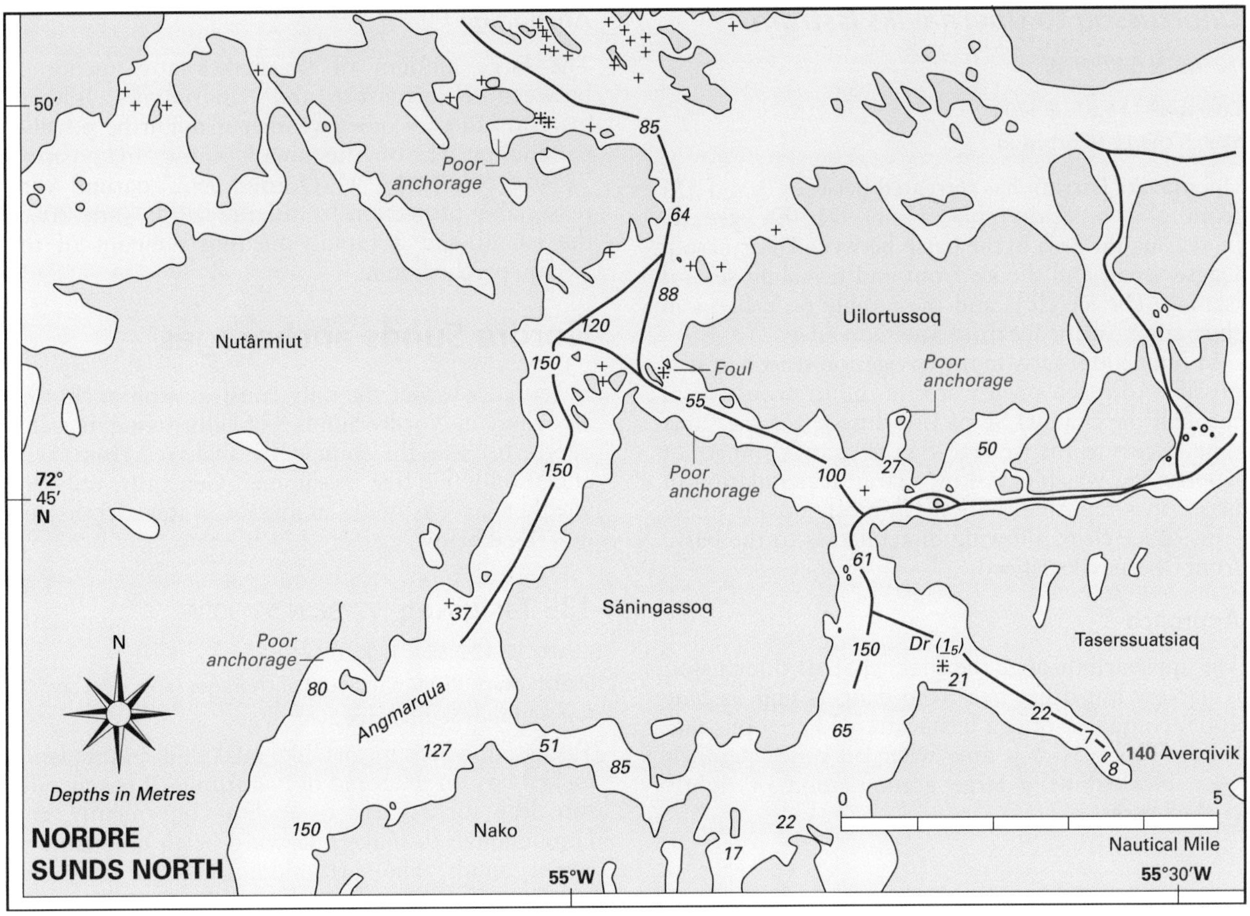

'Amarortalik Sound' 72°35'N 54°46'W

Charts NP12 D 1700

Sketch charts: Nordre Sunds North & South

North Nako anchorage (page 210)

'Amarortalik Sound' is the informal name for the sound extending north from Laksefjorden for 6M, between the mainland to the E and Amarortalik to the W. Depths decrease from about 100m in the S to 10m in the narrows at the N end of the sound. These narrows are about 100m wide and the tidal stream in them is appreciable at times. Below-water rocks extend out from the W shore of the narrows, reducing the navigable channel to about 50m. To avoid these rocks, favour the E side of the narrows. No other dangers were apparent in three transits of this sound.

Cross channels lead W and NW from the N end of 'Amarortalik Sound' to 'Nako Sound'. Depths are in these cross channels are irregular and the navigable channels are tortuous. However, with care, they present no undue difficulty to a yacht (see sketch charts Nordre Sunds South Sheet and North Nako Anchorages). Tidal currents in these cross channels were strong enough to prevent them freezing over completely in the winter of 2005.

'Sáningassoq Sound' 72°43'N 54°43'W

Sketch charts: Nordre Sunds North

'Sáningassoq Sound' is the informal name for the 4M long, N-trending sound, which runs between the E shore of Sáningassoq and the mainland. No depth of less than 55m was encountered in one mid-channel passage through this sound, but the bottom is irregular and shallower water may exist close to the course followed. E–W cross channels connect the N and S ends of 'Sáningassoq Sound' to Angmarqua. These channels are narrow and encumbered with above- and below-water rocks but, with care, are navigable by a yacht (see sketch chart Nordre Sunds North Sheet). In recent winters tidal currents maintained pools of open water and thin ice in the S cross channel.

Uilortussoq to Upernaviks Isstrøm

72°45'N 54°30'W

Charts NP 12 5.67 D 1700
Sketch charts: Uilortussoq

Upernaviks Isstrøm has retreated between 3 and 5M from the position shown on D1700, greatly increasing the area of the basin between Uilortussoq, Qagserssuaq and the ice front and revealing several islands. The ice cliffs and the jumble of icebergs in the basin near the ice front are impressive.

In June 2005, early in the navigation season, it was possible to reach open water in the ice-front basin, through the channel SE of Uilortussoq. At the same time, access to the ice face via the channels north of Uilortussoq was blocked by a large accumulation of bergs. It is reported that late in most seasons, these jams of ice clear, allowing direct access to the basin from Upernaviks Isfjord.

Approach

The approach through the channel SE of Uilortussoq is narrow but deep, free from dangers and in June 2005, contained only a few scattered bergy bits and brash. This was at a time when all other channels were blocked by a large accumulation of tightly packed bergs.

Anchorage

The large amount of ice makes any anchorage between Uilortussoq and Upernaviks Isstrøm insecure. In very quiet weather it might be possible to anchor SE of the small island in position 72°46.5'N 54°22.7'W (Qornoq 1927 datum) with reasonable protection from large ice. In June 2005, the island had a rapidly melting remnant of the icecap, perched on it.

Nordre Sunds anchorages

In settled weather the only constraint on anchoring anywhere in Nordre Sunds S of Uilortussoq, is water depth, because the sounds are sheltered from swell and usually ice free in summer. Generally, only all-weather havens with moderate water depths are described below.

135 Tasiussaq 72°36'N 55°30'W

Charts NP 12 5.68 D 1700, D 1710
Sketch chart: Nutârmiut South anchorages (opposite) and Nordre Sands South (page 204)

Tasiussaq, which means 'like a lake', is a large land-locked bay on the S end of Nutârmiut. It is generally too deep for a yacht to anchor conveniently, and large enough to make a leeward berth untenable in strong winds. The surrounding hills are steep and sombre, and suggest they could generate strong

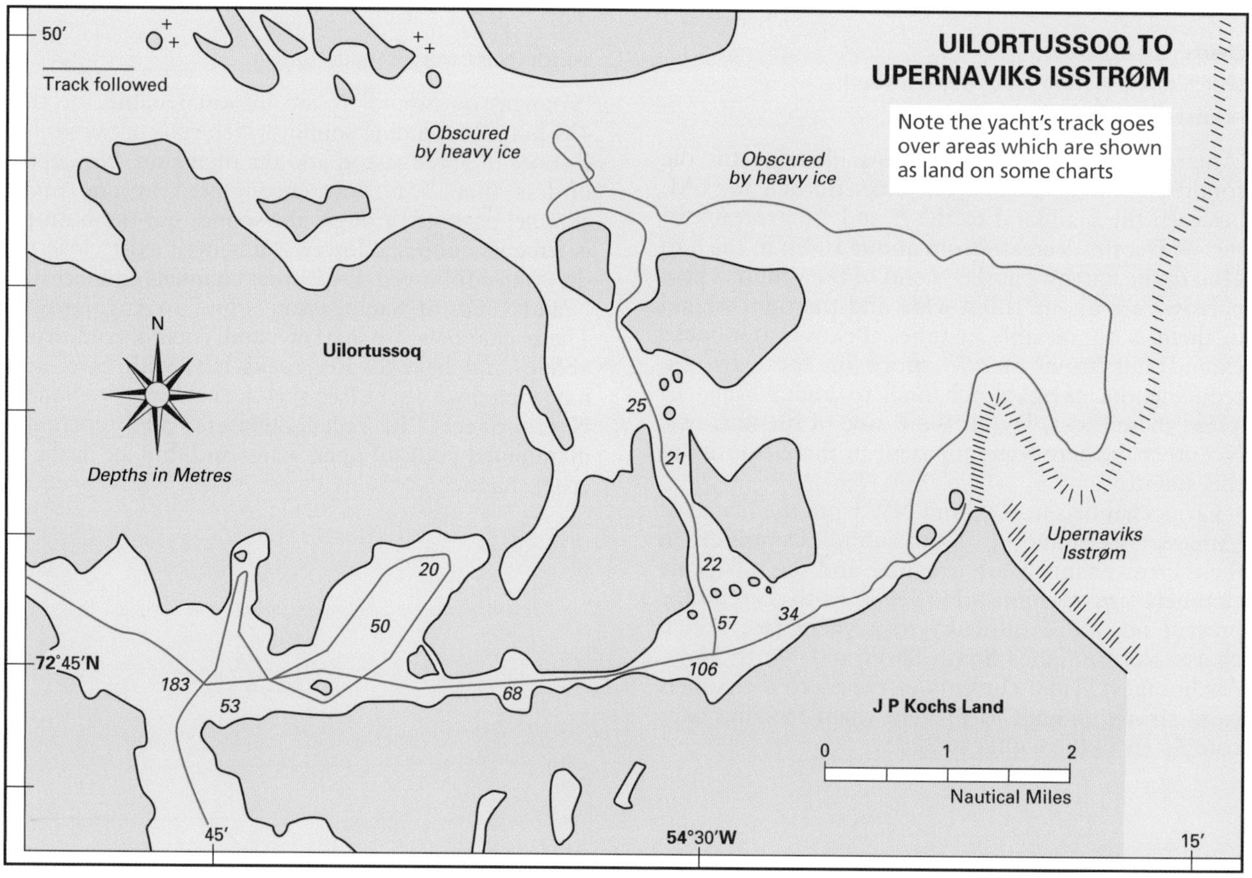

Tasiussaq Inner Pool from SW *Annie Hill*

Tasiussaq *Máire Wilkes*

downdraughts in bad weather. The narrow bay extending SE from the main bay, where the hills are lower, offers a good berth, but the entrance is too shallow for a yacht of average draught to enter at less than half tide.

Approach

The entrance to Tasiussaq is narrow but straightforward. Foul ground extends about 100m NW from a large, low, rounded rock off the S entrance point. The outer end of the foul ground is in the approximate position of the rock shown in the middle of the entrance, on *D1710*. Enter from the NW, keeping between 60 and 80m off the entrance's N shore, with a least depth of 10–13m. The rock shown on *D1710* off the tip of the northern entrance point, is not a danger because it is above water and close to shore.

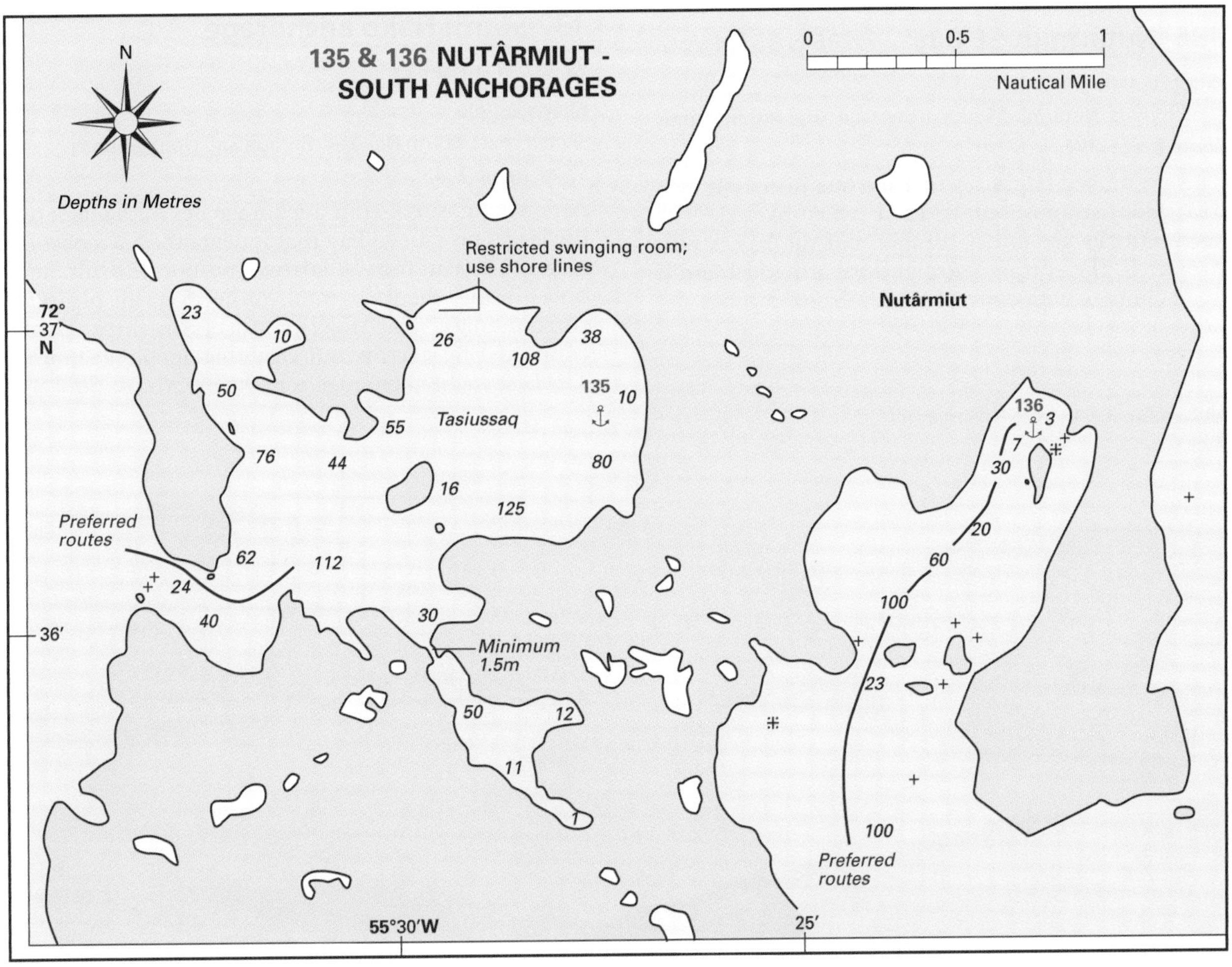

Anchorage

Inside, the depth increases rapidly and most of the inlet is too deep for a yacht to anchor easily. Three likely berths in the main part of the bay are shown on the sketch chart. The best berth for a yacht in the main part of the bay appears to be in the cove on the E side of the NW arm, in depths from 8–12m. A shore line is probably necessary, as there is restricted swinging room. The other two berths are on steeply shelving, rather exposed shores, and are only suitable for use in settled weather.

A cove off the S side of Tasiussaq provides a sheltered berth for a yacht. The entrance is a narrow, shallow, rocky gut about 10m wide and 70m long, with a least depth of about 1·6m at low water and 2·5m at half tide. This is not a place to go aground: the bottom and shores of the gut are boulders and the tide sluices through it at about 3 knots. Sounding from a dinghy is recommended before attempting the passage. Favour the port (NE) side on entry. Once through the narrow section, the depth increases to 50m. There are well-sheltered berths for a yacht in either the E or SE arm of the cove in 10–13m. The berth in the SE arm is probably the better of the two. Holding is good but there is no room to swing to a single anchor in either berth, so a stern line ashore is necessary. Tidal currents are weak in either berth. The pool at the head of the SE arm is shoal.

136 'Nutârmiut SE Bay' 72°36'N 55°24'W

Charts D 1700

Sketch chart: Nutârmiut South anchorages and Nordre Sunds South (page 204)

This un-named bay is separated from Tasiussaq by a 1M wide isthmus but is 12M away by sea. The surroundings are rather sombre, but the bay is well protected, the entrance straightforward and there is an anchorage with convenient depths for a yacht.

Approach

The entrance to the bay is nearly ½M wide, but islets and rocks reduce the navigable channel to approximately 100m. Enter on the W side of the mouth of the bay, leaving all the rocky islets and skerries to starboard along a mid-channel course, between the W headland and the most E islet. Underwater rocks extend a few metres from the W entrance point, leaving a clear channel 50m wide, with a minimum depth of 25m. Once inside the depth increases rapidly to over 150m and there appear to be no dangers apart from a line of rocks and skerries, N of the island in the NE arm of the bay.

Anchorage

The anchorage is behind the high, rocky island in the NE arm of the bay. Approach from the W side of the island, because the E approach is foul. Although the bottom is irregular on this route, it appears to be free from dangers, with a least depth of 7m, found on a mid-channel course. Anchor behind the island, W of the line of rocks and skerries, which extends from the island to the N shore of the cove. There is restricted but adequate swinging room in 12–14m, mud and filamentous weed, with scattered boulders. Good holding, at least with a fisherman anchor. Shore lines could be used.

137 South Nako anchorage

72°37'N 55°04'W

Charts D 1700

Sketch chart: South Nako anchorage and Nordre Sunds South (page 204)

A very snug, small-craft anchorage lies in the inlet off the large, un-named bay that indents the SW coast of Nako. The entrance is narrow, but not difficult, and once inside there is total protection in pleasant surroundings. The inlet consists of three pools connected by narrow but easily navigable channels. The best yacht anchorage is in the innermost pool.

Nutârmiut SE Bay from N *Annie Hill*

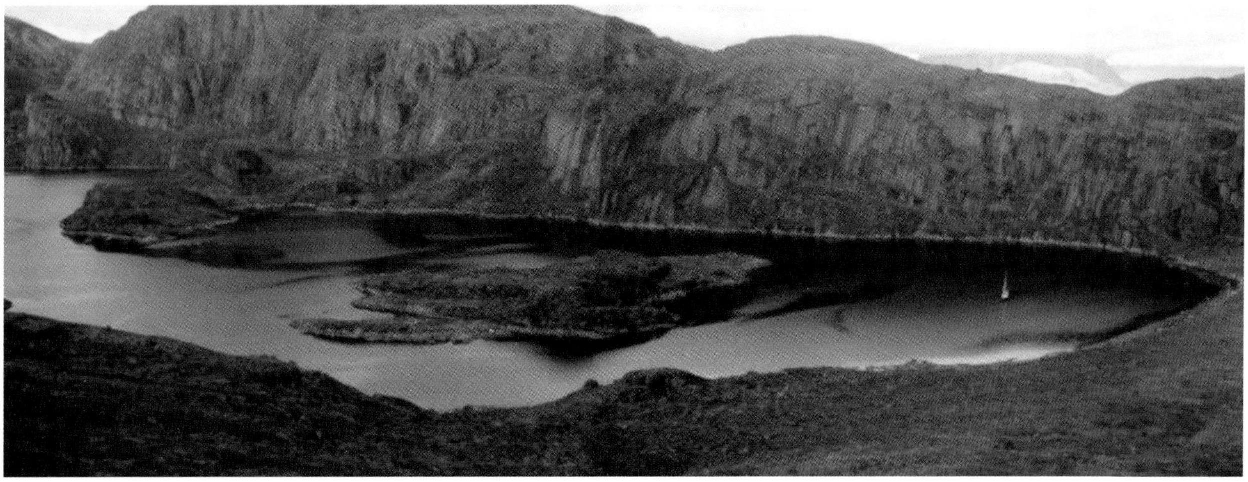

South Nako Anchorage from SW *Bob Shepton*

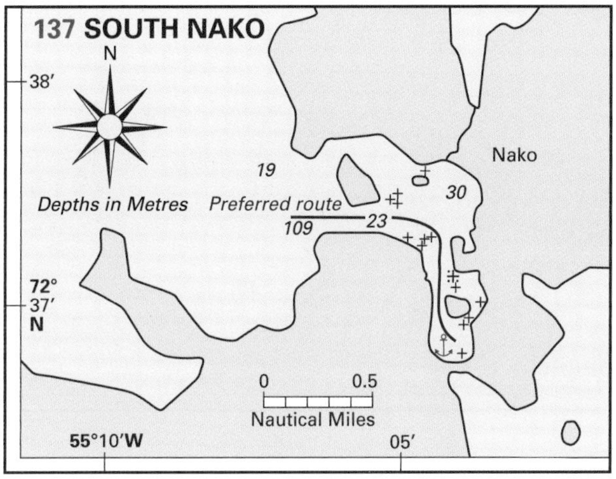

Approach

The approach from Angmarqua across the unnamed outer bay, is deep and free from underwater dangers. Enter the inlet S of the rocky island that almost fills the mouth of the inlet, through a channel with a least width of approximately 80m and least depth of 10m. Once past the island in the entrance, a pool opens up ahead and to port (N). Do not alter course into this pool, until well past the E end of the entrance island: a rocky shoal extends 150m E from that island. This first pool is well protected and has a good watering stream, but depths are generally too great for a yacht conveniently to anchor.

For the second pool, steer E across the first pool until a channel opens up, leading S. Once this is fully open, turn down it, being careful not to cut the corner, which has a rocky ledge, extending 40 or 50m NE from the cliffs on the W side of the channel entrance. This channel, which has a least width of approximately 60m and a least depth of 15m, leads into the small second pool that opens up to port (E), with a rocky island on its S side. The E part of the second pool is encumbered with underwater rocks and although there is room to anchor between them, this is not a good berth.

Continuing S leads into the nearly-circular, third pool, S of the island. Stay on the W side of the second pool, to avoid the abovementioned rocks, and proceed past the rocky island, leaving it to port. The channel here has a least mid-channel depth of 8m and a least width of about 30m. The channel E of the island is foul. There are no underwater dangers in the third (southernmost) pool except for two rocks within 20m of the SW shore of the island, well clear of the obvious berth.

Anchorage

Anchor in 8–12m, mud and weed, good holding, with protection from all directions. Shore lines could be used. A low, narrow gravel bank separates the anchorage from the sound that runs between Nako and Akuliaruseq. There are two huts on this isthmus, one of which is weatherproof and could be used for an emergency refuge.

138 & 139 North Nako anchorages

72°40′N 54°58′W

Charts D 1700 Sketch chart: North Nako anchorages and Nordre Sunds South (page 204)

Two bays indent the NE coast of Nako. The eastern bay is here informally named 'East Nako Anchorage' and the western bay 'Winter Cove'. *Iron Bark*, an 11m cutter, wintered in the western bay in 2004–2005 and in 2012–2013. The bays are separated by a half-mile wide isthmus and are 2M apart by sea. Each bay has a safe, well-protected anchorage, but 'Winter Cove' is more attractive, has a better watering stream and probably better holding. The pond feeding the watering stream, provided water for Iron Bark throughout the winter. It froze to a maximum depth of about 0.8m with a further ½–1m of snow cover.

Nako is less mountainous than the adjacent islands and mainland and there are some pleasant walks inland to the scattered lakes and ponds. In summer,

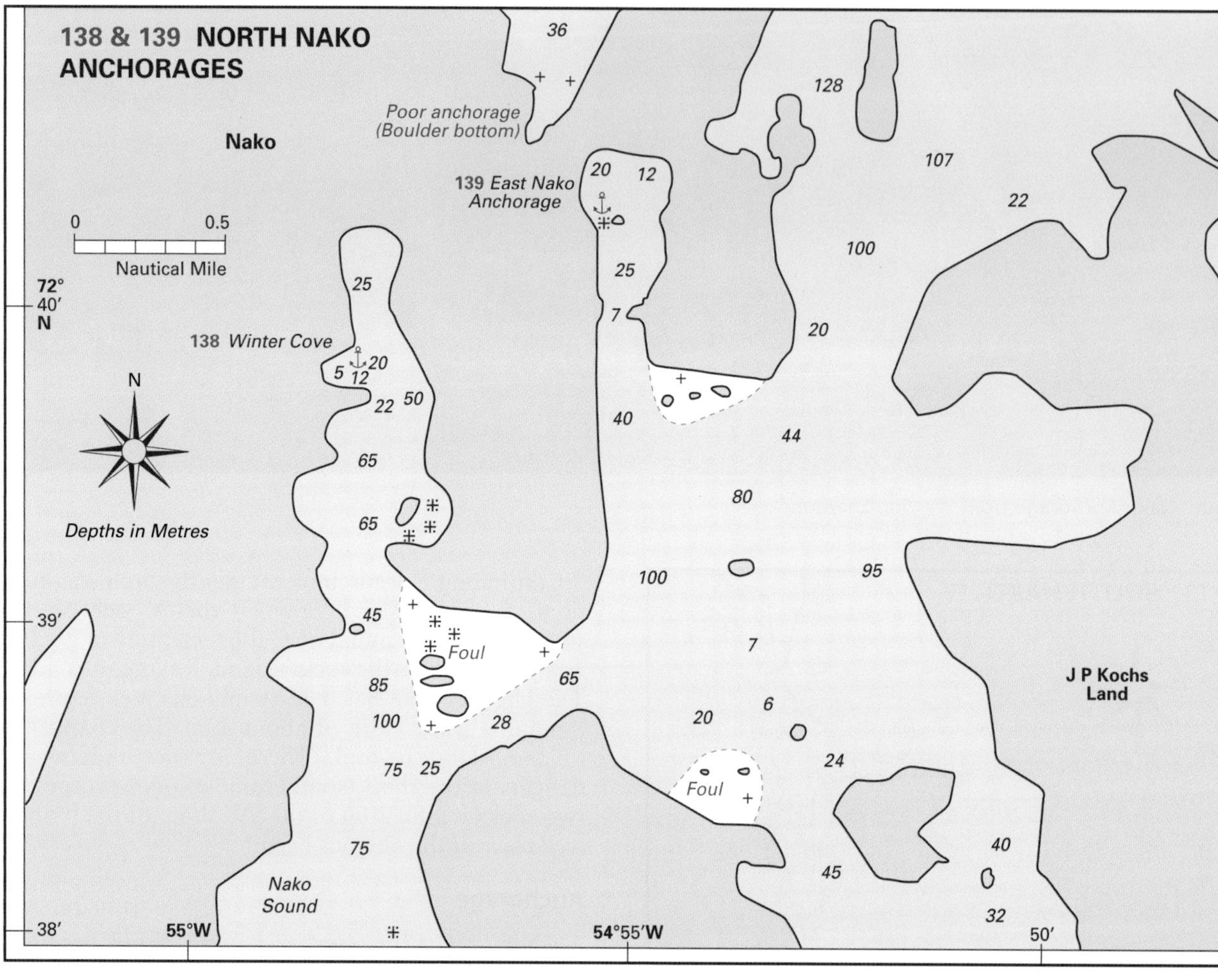

these ponds have loons, Canada geese and ducks on them, with ravens, snow buntings, redpoll and longspurs on the hills. Bilberries and crowberries abound and there is a small dwarf willow thicket along the watering stream. A few very old antlers are all that remains of the caribou that formerly grazed here.

Approach

There are rocks and foul ground in the approaches to both bays but the dangers are apparent and easily avoided (see plan of North Nako Anchorages).

Anchorages

'Winter Cove' (125) is tucked behind a low rocky spit on the W side of the bay, about 700m from its N end. Depths within the cove decrease from 15m in the E to 5m in the W. A number of large boulders encumber the bottom but except very close in to the shore none of them has less than 5m over it. The boulders are large, widely scattered and unlikely to foul an anchor. The anchorage is in 7–15m, sandy mud, good holding. Shore lines can be used

'East Nako Anchorage' (126) is in the inner part of the E bay behind a small, rocky island. Leave this island to port when approaching the anchorage, as there is a drying rock to W of it. The anchorage is in 12–15m, mud, weed and rock.

Winter Cove from NW *Trevor Robertson and Annie Hill*

140 Averqivik 72°41′N 54°33′W

Charts D 1700

Sketch charts: Nordre Sunds North (page 205) and Nordre Sunds South (page 204)

Averqivik is the well-protected pool, lying behind an island at the head of the fjord named Taserssuatsiaq on Saga map 14, running E from Sáningassoq. The island is a flat-topped deposit of glacial till and looks very like a slag heap. The surrounding country is comparatively low, with rolling hills and open views to the icecap, seven miles away. The low land south of the bay is boggy and tussocky, which makes for slow walking, at least early in the season while the snow is still melting.

Approach

A mid-channel rock obstructs the entrance to the fjord, which is shown on chart *D1700*. This rock dries about 1·5m and should be visible at most states of the tide. The channel N of the rock is 600m wide and has a least mid-channel depth of 75m. The channel S of the rock is narrower and has an irregular bottom with a least depth of 21m, encountered in one transit. Beyond the rock, the fjord is deep and apparently free from dangers until about ½M W of the island, where a bar, with depths of 7–13m, crosses the fjord.

The channel leading to the anchorage is on the N side of Averqivik. By favouring the island side of mid channel, the least depth encountered at half tide was 5m, so the channel should have more than 4m at LWS. The passage to the S of the island has a least depth of about 1·5m.

Anchorage

Anchor in 8–9m in mud, good holding, with ample room and excellent protection from all winds.

Averqivik from S *Trevor Robertson and Annie Hill*

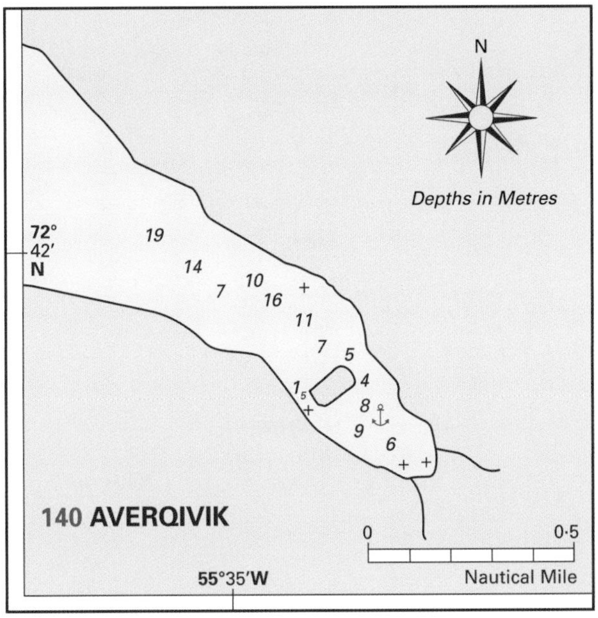

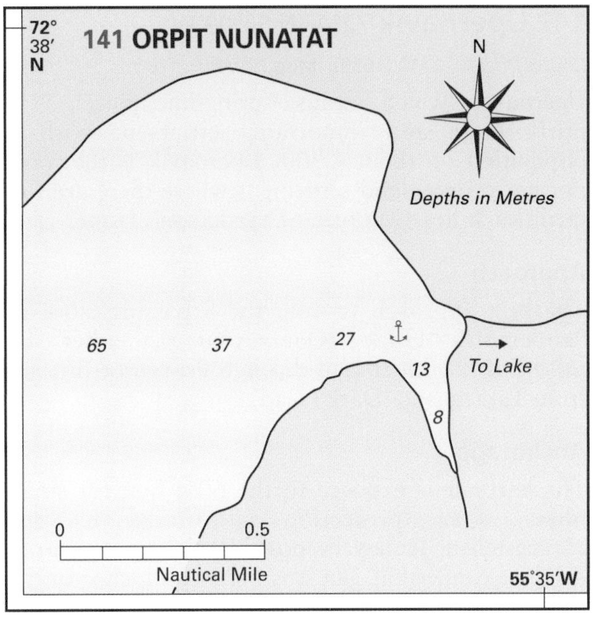

141 Orpit Nunatat 72°37′N 54°36′W

Charts D 1700

Sketch chart: Plans in Nordre Sunds South (page 204)

Orpit Nunatat is the cove at the head of a short fjord named Kangerdluarssuk on Saga map 14, which extends into the mainland, from the N end of Amarortalik. The surroundings are exceptionally attractive and there is an interesting walk up the large stream to a lake, about half a mile inland.

Approach

The approach is straightforward with no apparent off-lying dangers

Anchorage

Anchor off the small stream on the SE side of the bay in 10–13m, good holding but partially open to the SW. Alternatively, anchor further in, with a stern line to shore, protected from all winds.

Orpit Nunatat from S *Trevor Robertson and Annie Hill*

Upernavik in the evening sun *Máire Wilkes*

Alongside in Upernavik *Bob Shepton*

142 Upernavik 72°47′N 56°09′W

Charts D 1700, 1710 (1650) **Map** 72 V1

Upernavik, which means 'springtime place', is a fairly large and important settlement with a population of about 1,200. Upernavik is the most northerly Greenland settlement where there are full facilities. It lies 4M north of Sanderson's Hope.

Approach

The best approach is from the S passing close to Sanderson's Hope (Qaersorssuaq), either by following the inner lead through Prøven or directly from Tukingasoq (Dark Head).

Anchorage

The harbour is exposed to the NW; but, for small boats, some protection is offered by the Havnestenen. It may be possible to lie temporarily on the Skonnertkaj, but it is better to anchor in the SE corner of the harbour if there is room or, in settled weather, lie alongside one of the small 'traders', which are anchored there. A significant surge can develop in strong winds from any direction and an alongside berth may not be tenable for smaller vessels.

Facilities

Supermarket, bakery and fishermen's chandlery. Boat repair yard and engine repair shop. Post office (with ATM, 1000–1500). Hospital. Diesel is obtained from a road tanker brought to the quay.

WiFi is available at the post office. Fuel can be ordered at the Polaroil office (behind the supermarket). Fresh water can be ordered from the Royal Arctic Line office who will arrange delivery by the Nukissiorfit Company (who deliver fresh water to all Upernavik's houses). There is a minimum charge for each delivery of the water truck, so sharing the cost with other boats may make good financial sense. There is no bespoke laundry but it

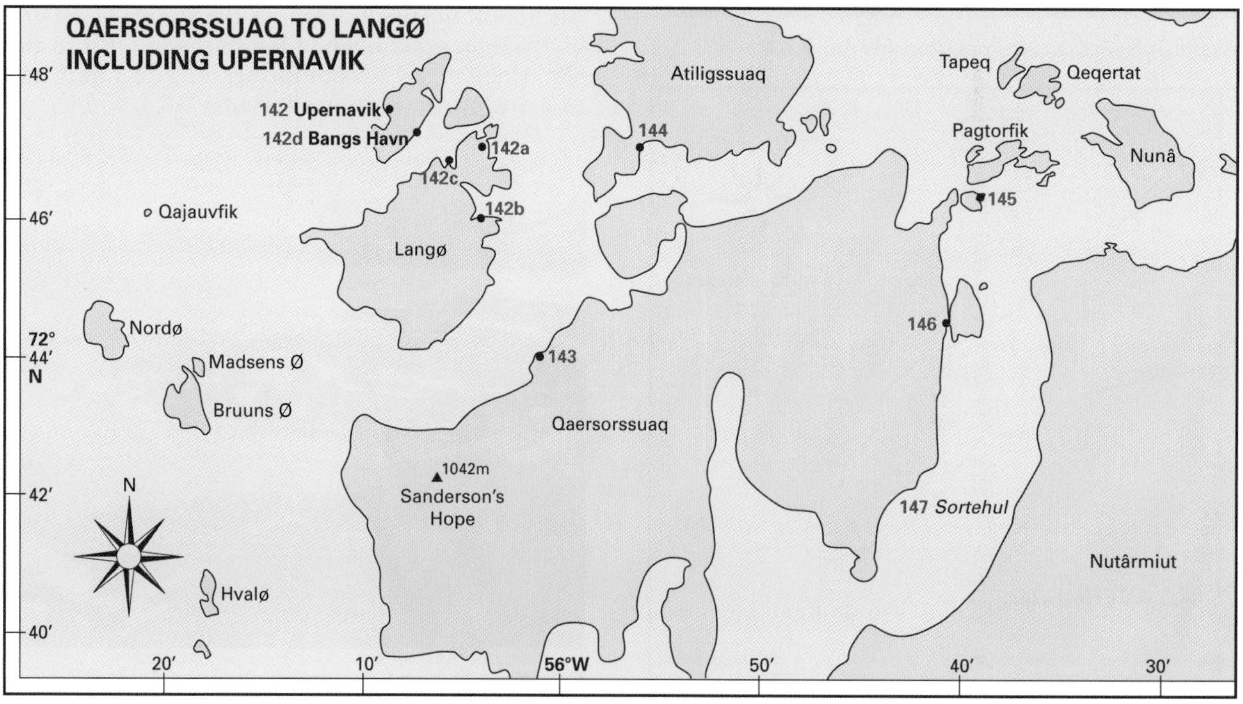

may be possible to make an arrangement with Gina's Guesthouse or the hospital. It may also be possible to arrange for showers at the hospital.

STOL airport with regular flights to Kangerlussuaq (Søndre Strømfjord), via Ilulissat and Qaarsut.

Upernavik, approaching from the south *Máire Wilkes*

The supply ship manoeuvring alongside the quay in Upernavik. Note the yacht anchored on the right of the picture *Máire Wilkes*

Pilotage notes for the waters near Upernavik

An unmarked rock is reported south of Qaesorssuaq (Sanderson's Hope) near the island of Ikermia at approx 72°37'.6N 56°00'.4W

Two groups of rocks are situated between Upernavik Skibshavnen and the SW entrance to Ikerssuaq. If these are visible, it is safe for a shallow draft vessel to pass inshore of them; otherwise stay well to seaward.

The 3m patch charted off Smedeø is reported not to exist.

Anchorages near Upernavik

Charts D 1710, 1650 **Map** 72 V1

There are a number of useful and attractive anchorages in the area, of which the following are recommended.

Aorrussaarssuk inbetween Akutdliarssuk & Laugo *Sibéal Turraoin*

Aorrussaarssuk, preparing for wintering *Bob Shepton*

An ancient navigation mark at Aorrussaarssuk inbetween Akutdliarssuk and Laugo *Sibéal Turraoin*

142a Aorrussaarssuk 72°47'N 56°04'W

Charts D 1710, 1650

This well protected bay lies on the SE side of the channel between the islands of Langø and Akutdliarssuk and is preferable to Bangs Havn or Umiarssuaqarfik for yachts. Bangs Havn, however, offers the possibility of walking overland to Upernavik.

The burnt-out wreck of the yacht *Dodo's Delight* lies on the bottom of the anchorage on the N side and the outline can still be seen. There is room to anchor on the S side well clear of the wreck, but care is needed and a tripping line is advisable. Anchor in 3–6m.

142b Sarpinat 72°46'N 56°04'W

Charts 1710, 1650

A large bay on the E side of Langø, which offers protection in either the NW bay or the smaller bay on the SW side. The merits of each anchorage are hotly contested between two very experienced Arctic skippers. However, it should be noted that the smaller boat's rudder began to dry out on a rock when anchored close to the shore in the NW bay and

Sarpinat *Máire Wilkes*

Sarpinat *Máire Wilkes*

the larger boat ran aground whilst entering the SW bay.The latter can be approached by keeping close to the S shore to the S of the small island (not shown on Chart *D 1650*) which is not clean on its S side. Either anchor in the start of the pool in 5–6m or either side of a reef which lies further in, with lines ashore if necessary. This anchorage was used as the base for the first ascent of the North Wall of Sanderson's Hope in August 2000.

142c Umiarssuaqarfik (Elliot Bight)

72°47'N 56°05'W

Charts 1710, 1650

Umiarssuaqarfik, a bay on the NW side of Langø, has good protection from all directions except N, with moderate depths. A small headland divides the N end of the bay into two coves. The SW cove has ample swinging room for a yacht, in 11m, apparently good holding. Iron Bark rode out a SW gale here lying to a single anchor.

The SE cove is more restricted and shore lines would probably be required in addition to the anchor.

The poor holding mentioned in the Pilot (NP 12), probably applies to the deeper part of the bay, further offshore than a yacht would normally anchor.

142d Bangs Havn 72°47'N 56°07'W

Chart D 1700, 1710, 1650 **Map** 74 V1

Bangs Havn is a small bay on the SE side of Upernavik Ø, fronted by a small islet, on which dogs are sometimes kept. A small barge is moored across the head of the cove between bollards set in the shore. There is reported to be a good anchorage about 100m NNE of the islet in 17m, but this has not been confirmed.

143 Qaarsorsuaq (Sanderson's Hope) N side 72°44'N 56°01'W

Charts 1710

Temporary anchorage, in settled weather, in a small cove at the outlet of a stream, giving access to a walking ascent of Sanderson's Hope from the N side. Tripping line recommended due to boulders on the bottom. This is close to the winter sledging route marked on the map.

144 Torssút 72°47'N 55°56'W

Charts 1710

A pleasant anchorage in sand can be found in position 72°46'N 55°54'W in the bay to the north.

145 Savigssuaq 72°46'N 55°39'W

Charts D 1710 **Map** 72 V1

An interesting anchorage in an inlet on the E side of a small island just to the S of Pagtorfik. Fangsthus (hunter's cabin) and ancient Eskimo graves. Beware of the rocks to the S of the entrance opposite the fangsthus. Open to the E.

One of the ancient Eskimo graves on Savigssuaq *Máire Wilkes*

Savigssuaq anchorage *Máire Wilkes*

4. GREENLAND

Sortehul with sea mist *Bob Shepton*

Ikerasarssuk *Máire Wilkes*

146 Qornoq Kangigdleq

72°45'N 55°40'W

Charts D 1710 **Map** 72 V1

Very snug anchorages, either side of the peninsula with lines ashore.

Scrambling and some rock climbing possibilities.

147 Sortehul 72°44'N 55°40'W

Charts 1710

Sortehul (Akornat) is the passage between the islands of Nutârmuit to the SE and Qaersorssuaq to the NW. There are a number of fair weather anchorages in and around the Sortehul but the only strong wind anchorage is at the northern end, either side of Qornoq kangigleq (72°44'N 55°44'W) depending on wind direction.

A reasonable anchorage can also be made in the bay at Kingigtok (Iterdlagssuaq), at the southern end of Qaersorssuaq, in northern winds, but the bottom is rocky. This was base camp for the first ascent of Sanderson's Hope in 2000.

148 Ikerasaarssuq 73°32'N 56°26'W

Chart D 1700 **Map** 73 V1

A fair weather anchorage in a narrow channel between Nutaarmiut Isl and Ikerasaarssuq Islet (see *NP12*). Anchor in 20m. Holding doubtful and strong tidal stream – subject to ice. Shallow draught vessels may be able to anchor in the 'boat harbour' to the S of the channel.

Sortehul - Qornoq Kangigleq, the only protected anchorage in the area *Bob Shepton*

Ikerasarssuk, overlooking the anchorage *Máire Wilkes*

149 Nuussuaq (Kraulshavn) (Nuussuaq Peninsula, Melville Bay)

74°07'N 57°04'W

Charts D 1700, 1650 **Map** 74 V1

A very small settlement with a few basic necessities, including fuel, phone and post. The village lies on the E side of a large landlocked bay. The approach from the S has few soundings on the chart, but appears to be clean. When entering, leave the island with the beacon on it to starboard. Bergs may block the entrance.

150 Bjørneborg (Melville Bay)

74°24'N 57°03'W

Charts D 1700, 3100 **Map** 74 V1

The emergency hut established here by Knud Rasmussen on Inugsuligssuaq, was moved in 1937, three years after his death, and rebuilt on Blochs Ø (74°43'N 57°50'W). It is the fangsthus close to an anchorage on the N side, marked on the 1:250,000 map (sheet 74 V1).

Kullorsuaq *J Cunnane*

151 Kullorsuaq (Melville Bay)

74°35'N 57°10'W

Chart D 3100 **Map** 74 V1

A small settlement with the Devil's Thumb (Djævelens Tommelfinger) as a backdrop. It is one of the most traditional hunting and fishing villages in Greenland and one of the few settlements which is increasing in population. It has a population of about 430, a store and diesel.

4. GREENLAND

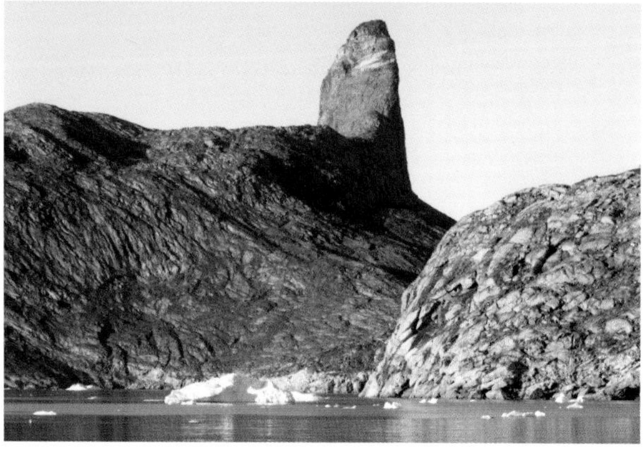

Devil's Thumb,Tommelfinger is a distictive landmark in Melville Bay *Bob Shepton*

152 Sabine Øer (Melville Bay)

75°30'N 60°10'W

Chart D 3100 **Map** 75 V1

A small group of low islands, named after Captain Sabine RA, who served with Ross and Parry and probably took gravitational measurements with a pendulum here in 1822, when with Clavering in HMS *Griper*. The islands mark the SW corner of the Melville Bay Nature Reserve. There is a useful emergency anchorage between the islands, with shoal at each end of the passage, preventing ice of any size encroaching. Approach clean from the SW (see plan).

There is a strong hut, which would provide shelter of a sort, at the W end of the westernmost island. Magnificent views across Melville Bay.

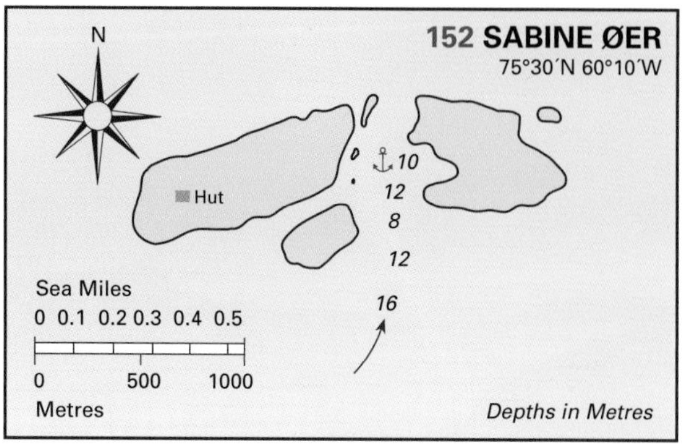

153 Savissivik (Melville Bay)

76°02'N 65°05'W

Chart D 3100

A small trading station with very limited supplies and facilities, within the Qaanaaq commune of Polar Eskimos. There is a temporary, very exposed, anchorage off the settlement with much ice. The settlement lies on Meteorit Ø, which was made famous by Peary's controversial removal of two meteorites in 1895.

Approach

Approaching from the SW, Bushnan Ø (named after John Bushnan, midshipman aboard John Ross' *Isabella*), can be left on either hand, however reefs extend to the W of the island, which should be given a wide berth. The area between Bushnan Ø and Kap York (on which stands the Peary Monument) tends to hold the pack and numerous bergs and is best avoided.

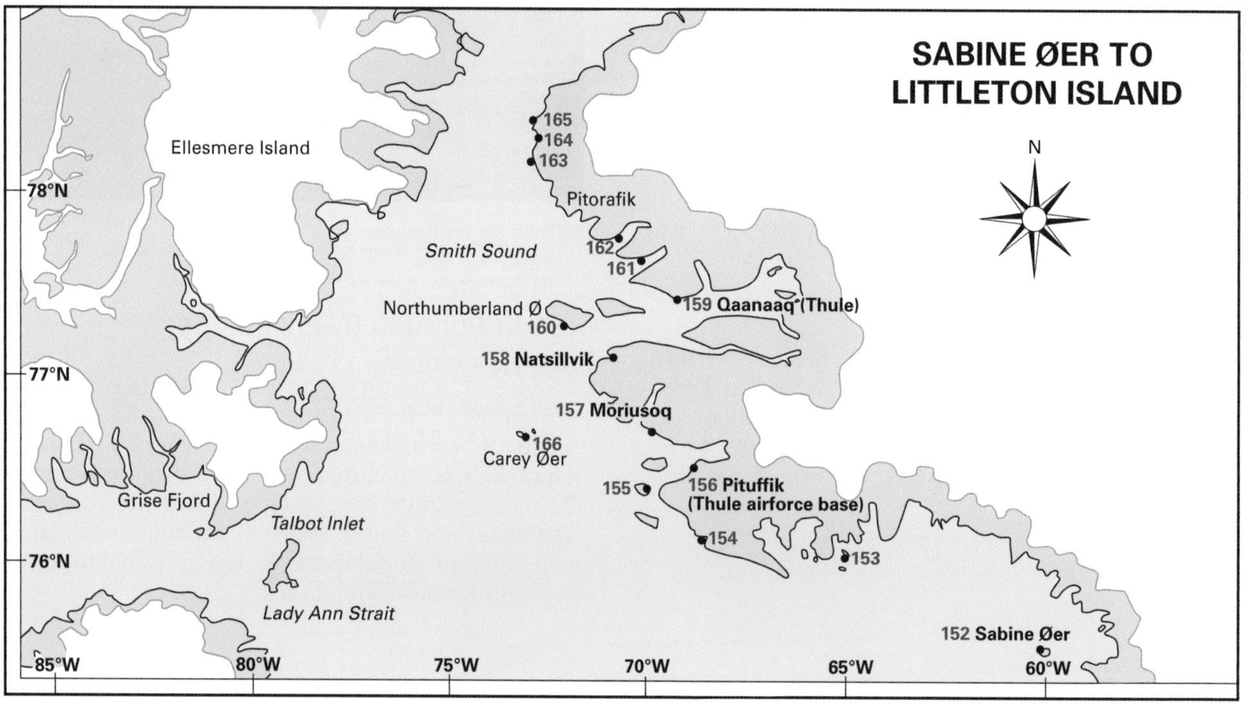

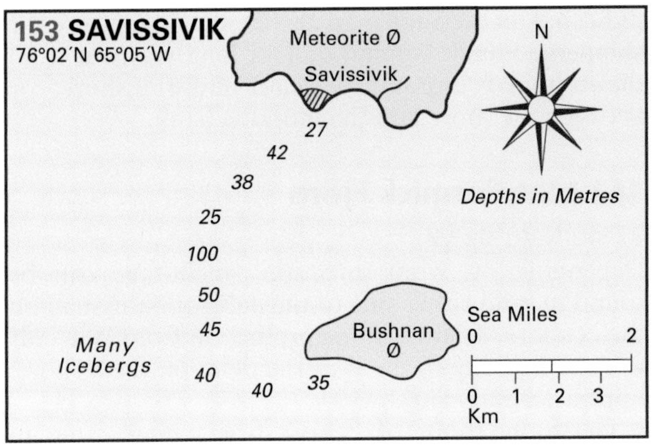

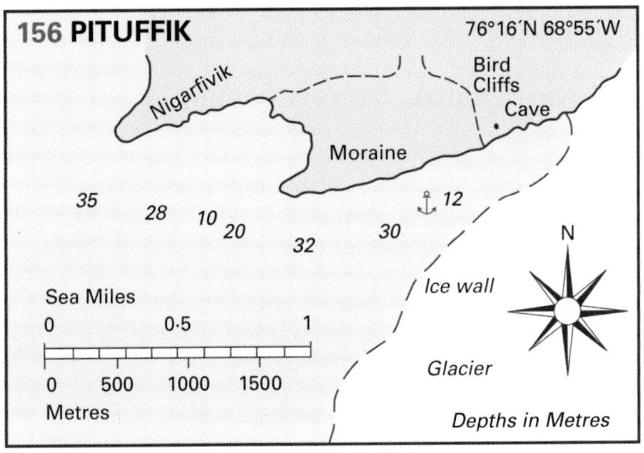

Pituffik Glacier (North Baffin Bay)

76°16′N 68°55′W

Charts D 3100

The glacier toe is over 3M wide and forms a continual ice cliff. Between the N face of the toe and the old lateral moraine there was an excellent and spectacular anchorage but part of the glacier has collapsed and it is not possible to anchor here now. However suitable depths may be found in the next two bays farther N, but there is little shelter. Large number of little auks (dovekies) breed on the cliffs and snow geese nest in the valley.

It was here in the spring of 1855 that the American explorer Dr Elisha Kent Kane and his surviving crew in two boats, rested and fed on dovekies and their eggs. They were on their way S, having abandoned their brig, the *Advance*, in the ice in Rensselaer Bay, in 79°N.

154 Parker Snow Bugt

76°08′N 68°40′W

Charts D 3100 Canadian chart 7302

There is an excellent anchorage at the head of this large bay, in clay.

The bay is NW of the Crimson Cliffs (of John Ross 1818) and under Cape Dudley Digges (of Baffin 1616).

155 Wolstenholme Ø 76°26′N 70°00′W

In strong W or NW winds, it is possible to find shelter and anchor on the E side of the island.

156 Pituffik (North Star Bay) Thule airforce base (Bylot Sund)

76°33′N 68°52′W

Charts D 3100, 3130

Knud Rasmussen established his trading post here among the Polar Eskimos in 1910 and called it Thule. When the US base was established, the community was moved to Qaanaaq 60M further N. The port facilities are operated by the Greenland Government in support of the Thule US Air Force Base and special permission is needed to enter North Star Bay. Application should be made in advance to the Danish Ministry of Foreign Affairs in Copenhagen or Danish Embassies abroad. In Nuuk the harbourmaster may be able to help.

Anchorage

It is possible to anchor off, but it would be preferable to go alongside. The harbour is formed by a causeway and pier extending 800m from the SE point. Immediately S of the pier, there is a sheltered small boat harbour suitable for yachts. Leave the pier head to port and approach with caution, since there are a number of underwater rocks. Call the Thule US Air Force Base, by radio, for permission to anchor off Dundas, at the head of North Star Bay

Facilities

Providing prior permission has been obtained, the Danish Naval Liaison Officer will be helpful, but it is clear that visitors are not welcomed by the US authorities and facilities are unlikely to be made available.

157 Moriusaq (Wolstenholme Fjord)

76°45′N 69°50′W

Charts D 3200

This is a small abandoned settlement 20M NW of Thule Air Force Base, where limited supplies and fuel can be obtained. Exposed anchorage off the beach amongst grounded bergs.

158 Barden Bugt 77°10′N 70°50′W

Depending on wind direction, anchorage can be found close to the N shore by the deserted settlement of Natsilivik, in 4–6 m, or on the S shore in one of the small bays formed by moraines, either side of the Tyndall Gletscher, good holding, or in silt farther to the E.

Qaanaaq *Jarlath Cunnane*

159 Qaanaaq (Thule) 77°28'N 69°14'W

Charts D 3200, 3210 Canadian chart 7302

The community moved to its present location in 1953, when the Thule US Air Force Base was established at Pituffik. It now has a population of about 700.

Anchorage

This is an open roadstead, exposed to the SW and very subject to ice. It is possible to anchor in 6 to 8m close to the drying flats just off the settlement. Any further out and you would be in 'iceberg alley'.

An alternative anchorage can be found in the shallow bay to the west of the drying reef (77°27'·8N 69°17'·0W). Enter through the narrow passage with a least depth of 3·5m.

There is a small hotel, KNI supermarket, post office and telephone. Fuel is available. There is a new STOL airport with regular flights to Kangerlussuaq via Upernavik.

160 Northumberland Ø

77°20'N 72°06'W

There are several useable anchorages around the island, depending on wind direction, particularly at North West Hook 77°26'N 72°18'W and Sandy Beach 77°20'N 72°06'W. If using the anchorage indicated on the Saga map at the NE end, beware the submerged bank coming quite a long way out from the terminal moraine. Anchor close inshore, or between the shore and the moraine bank.

Northumberland Island anchorage *Bob Shepton*

161 Mac Cormick Fjord

77°40'N 70°06'W

Depending on wind direction, anchorage can be found in sand either side of the delta at Nuussuaq on the N shore. There is some protection from W winds in the small bay to the E of the delta on the S shore, opposite Nuussuaq.

The foundations of Peary's first winter camp in 1891–92 may be seen near the entrance to the fjord on the S shore, about 2M from Kap Cleveland.

162 Siorapaluk 77°47'N 70°40'W

Chart D 3200

This is the world's most northern indigenous community, with a population of about 70. The traditional hunting culture is still an important feature.

Anchorage

This is a very exposed anchorage, which drops off steeply. Under certain conditions, it is possible to anchor in 6m to the NE of a sand-bar running SE from the settlement.

Facilities

There is a small shop and post office. Helicopter connection to Qaanaaq.

163 Kap Alexander 78°10'N 73°00'W

It is possible to find shelter on the S side of Kap Alexander in the vicinity of Sutherland Ø. In northerly winds, anchor W of the southern arm of the Dodge Gletscher, in gently shelving sand off the western of two small beaches, (the eastern beach is guarded by rocks which cover) or off another small beach about 1M W. Just to the W of the NE point of Sutherland Ø, there is a sandbank with good holding, giving protection from southerly winds.

164 Foulke Fjord 78°18'N 72°42'W

The abandoned Inuit settlement of Etah lies at the head of the fjord. This is of historical interest, having been visited by a number of explorers, including Inglefield, Kane and Nares as well as Cook and Peary, who used Etah as a base and recruited Inuit and their dogs for their expeditions to the N Pole.

The approach should follow the N shore and N of the prominent island midway. This is reputed to be one of the windiest places in the Arctic and anchoring at the head proved steep-to with poor holding.

165 Littleton Island 78°22′N 72°52′W

(see: NP 12)

Anchor either end of the channel between the main island and its smaller northern subsidiary (Mc Garry Is). The W end is recommended as there is a good beach in the inlet opposite for landing from a dinghy; but beware under water rocks in the approach and in the channel.

The anchorage is subject to floes and growlers brought down the channel by tidal currents, but it is the only feasible anchorage here. Littleton Island was used as a staging post by various expeditions, and the National Museum at Nuuk believes there are the remains of a longhouse from the Dorset culture (c.1000AD) but so far all attempts at finding it have failed.

Littleton Island, Smith Sound *Bob Shepton*

166 Carey Øer (Northern Baffin Bay)

76°43′N 73°04′W

Charts D 3200

A group of islands lying between Greenland and Arctic Canada and part of Greenland territory under the Danish Crown. They were discovered by Baffin in 1616 and named after Alwyn Carey, his ship's husband. There are a number of ancient Inuit ruins and it is a favourite nesting site for guillemots. Although well known to whalers, the islands were not often visited as they were not charted and foul ground surrounds them to the S. Surveys were carried out by J M Wordie during his expedition in 1937 and reported in the RGS Journal in November 1938, with a sketch map.

On the crag on Isbjorneø overlooking the anchorage there is a cairn and flagpole on which there is a Danish flag. This is reportedly visited annually by the Danish Liaison Officer from Thule. Apparently, at one time, sovereignty was in dispute.

There is a protected anchorage between Isbjørneø and Mellemø.

Approach

There are no soundings shown on the Danish Chart but, in 1987, the islands were approached from the E to a point 4M NE of Bordø, course was then altered to the SW using Wordie's sketch. The magnetic compass is too unreliable for bearings to be of any significance, but a course leaving Bordø (which appears to be steep-to) 0·2M to port and aiming at the southern tip of Mellemø leads in depths of more than 80m.

When the sound between Isbjørneø and Mellemø is clearly visible, enter through the channel 0·1M wide between the southern tip of Isbjørneø and a rocky islet, which is 0·2M S and where a least depth of 6m was found. Alternatively leave the islet to starboard, passing 0·1M to the S of the islet, which is not clean.

Anchorage

Anchorage was found in 4m sand and weed close into Isbjørneø. Care is needed however for any deep draft vessels approaching and rounding the rocky island guarding the entrance to the anchorage. Protection can be found from most wind directions, either further into the sound or under the SE flank of Mellemø. Due to the surrounding reefs it is unlikely that ice of any size would penetrate this anchorage, although sometimes there is a fair amount of small ice. However, this area is normally fairly clear of ice, being in the 'North Water'.

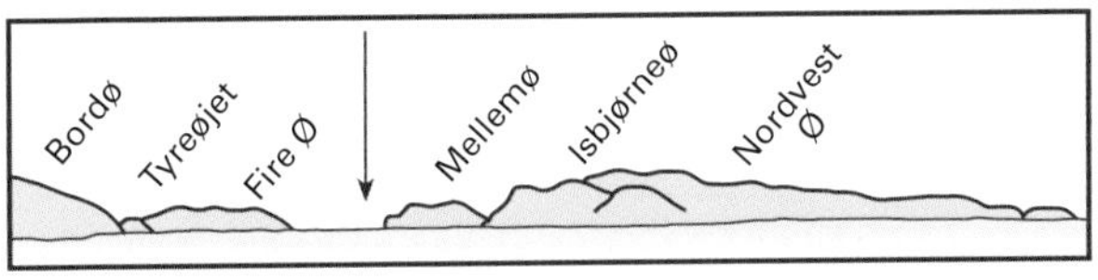

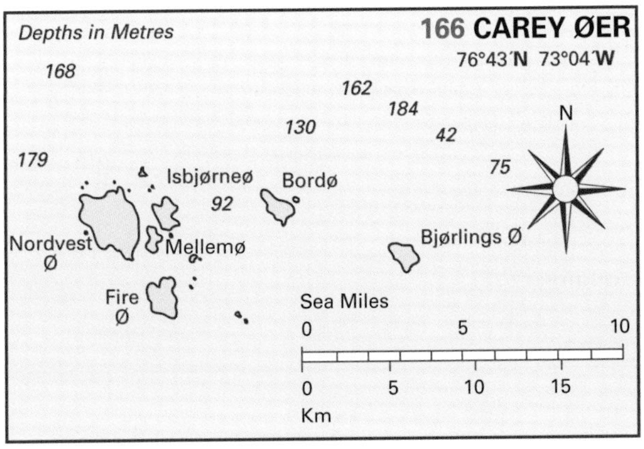

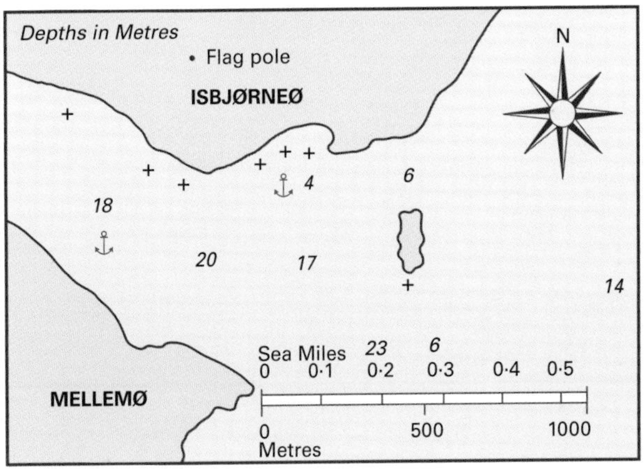

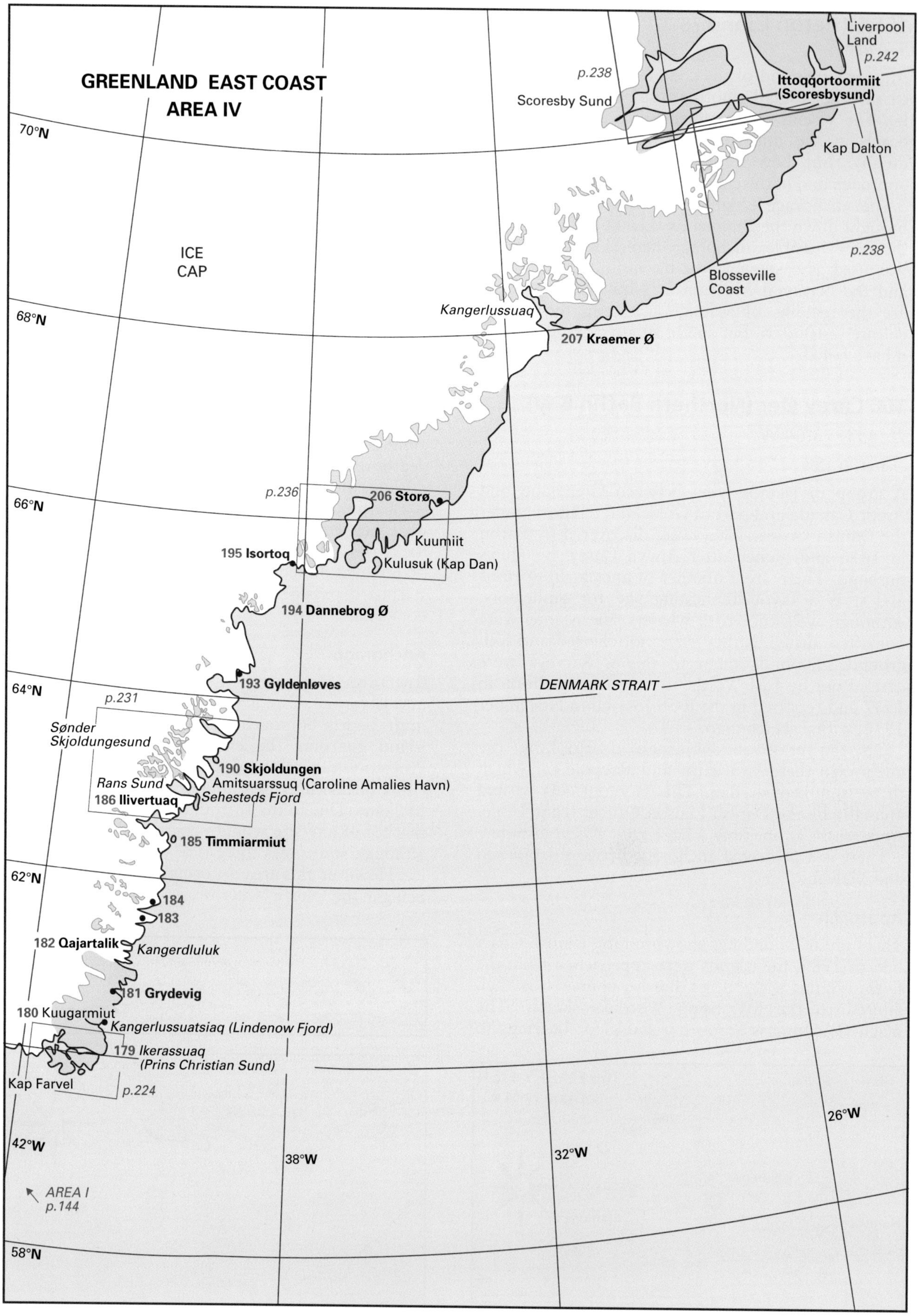
GREENLAND EAST COAST
AREA IV
70°N
68°N
66°N
64°N
62°N
58°N
42°W
38°W
32°W
26°W
ICE
CAP
Liverpool
Land
p.242
p.238
Scoresby Sund
Ittoqqortoormiit
(Scoresbysund)
Kap Dalton
p.238
Blosseville
Coast
Kangerlussuaq
207 Kraemer Ø
p.236
206 Storø
Kuumiit
Kulusuk (Kap Dan)
195 Isortoq
194 Dannebrog Ø
193 Gyldenløves
DENMARK STRAIT
p.231
Sønder
Skjoldungesund
190 Skjoldungen
Amitsuarssuq (Caroline Amalies Havn)
Rans Sund
186 Ilivertuaq
Sehesteds Fjord
185 Timmiarmiut
184
183
182 Qajartalik
Kangerdluluk
181 Grydevig
180 Kuugarmiut
Kangerlussuatsiaq (Lindenow Fjord)
179 Ikerassuaq
(Prins Christian Sund)
Kap Farvel
p.224
AREA I
p.144

AREA IV

The east coast including Ikerasassuaq (Prins Christian Sund)

In most years, storis (heavy polar pack ice) makes access to the east coast of Greenland difficult, if not impossible, until late in the season. In some years, the coast south of 65°N may clear early; however, icebergs are always present and most of the fjords have active tide-water glaciers which produce a lot of icebergs and bergy bits. In some years, the storis clears almost completely from Cap Farvel to Scoresby Sund and beyond. In other years, it clears from the coast north of 68°N, but remains until late in the season around the Ammassalik area and south around Cap Farvel, causing problems in the approach to Qaqortoq. There may well be years when storis prevents access to the east coast, until late in the season.

It is very important to obtain the latest ice information, before making an approach.

There are now no permanent settlements for 300M between Ikerasassuaq (Prins Christian Sund) and Tasiilaq (Ammassalik), but there are some good anchorages which are suitable for yachts if ice conditions permit.

With the exception of the areas around Tasiilaq and Ittoqqortoormiit, the hydrographic charts are at 1:400,000, the topography is somewhat sketchy and there are very few soundings inside the 3M limit. The 1:250,000 topographical maps show much more detail and are almost essential for navigating close to the shore.

Surveys are not complete and GPS should be used with care. Charted positions in some areas differ from GPS (WGS 84) by as much as 4′ in longitude – equivalent to 2M – but this is not consistent. The topographical maps generally appear to be more consistent within a given area. Charted positions of anchorages are shown to the nearest minute, with the GPS (WGS 84) position recorded shown in parentheses, where helpful.

This area is covered by the *Arctic Pilot Vol II (NP 11)*.

Landing climbers at a remote anchorage *Bob Shepton*

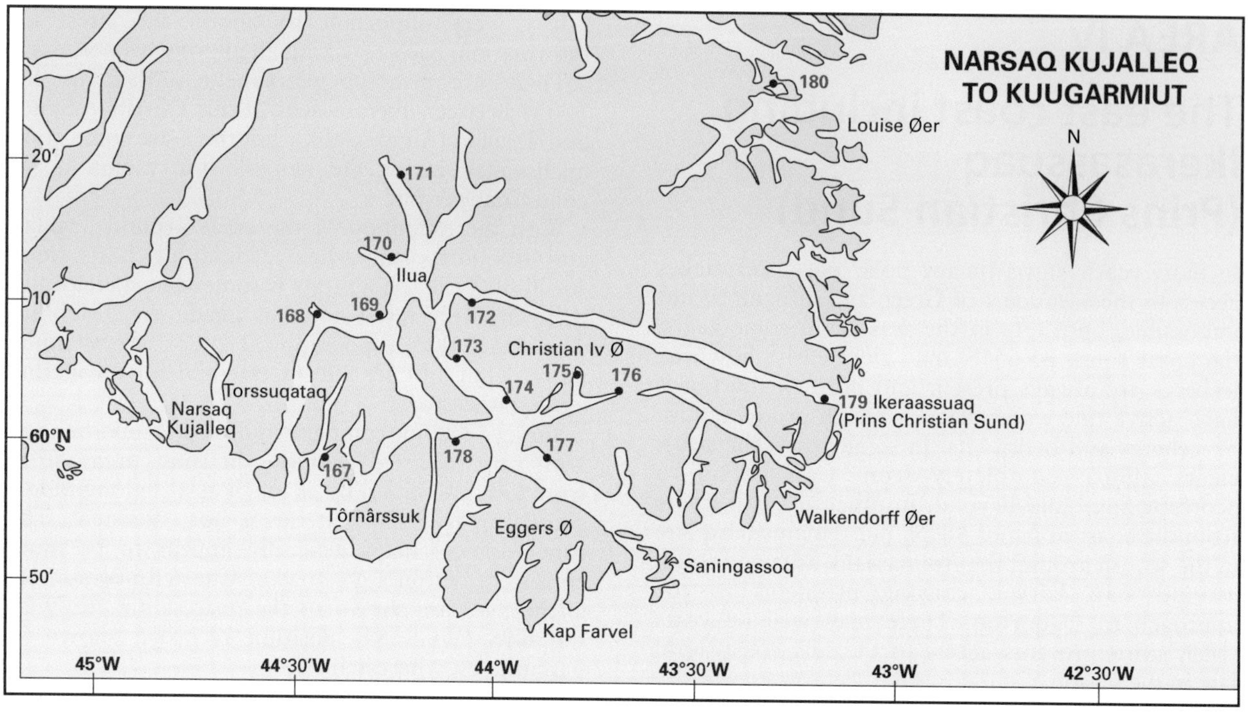

Ikerasassuaq (Prins Christian Sund) and vicinity 60°05′N 43°10′W

Chart D 1103

Ikerasassuaq is a deep, relatively narrow and very spectacular sound which joins Ilua and Ikerasassuaq (166) to provide an east-west passage N of Kap Farvel. It is one of the world's most magnificent passages. Mountains rise between 1200 and 1800m on either side and several glaciers reach down to sea level to add their bergs and bergy bits to the pack ice which blocks it for much of the year. By August, the pack ice has normally cleared. If there is any ice in the E entrance, the sound itself will usually be blocked. Winds are accentuated by the funnelling effect of the narrow passage and tides are strong in the Qornoq narrows. Do not, however, miss the opportunity of visiting Ikerasassuaq, if conditions are at all favourable.

Svardfisken Havn. Ikerassuaq *Máire Wilkes*

Approach from the east

The E approach brings one in to the weather station at Ikerasassuaq, where there is a sectored light, an Aeromarine beacon, a Racon and a MF and VHF transmitter (Ch 01) controlled by Qaqortoq Radio. Heavy storis, sometimes more than 50M offshore, may make this approach hazardous. Study the most recent Ice Charts and seek advice from Icecentralen Narsarsuaq before making the attempt. Icecentralen may be contacted through Aasiaat Radio on MF or directly by phone using Satcom (see sections on Sea Ice and Ice information).

Approach from the west

Torssuqataq is entered from the W near Narsaq Kujalleq (Frederiksdal) (59°59'N 44°40'W) and is fairly straightforward. From Nanortalik (8), use either the main passage through Kitsissut Tunuat or the inner lead route N of Nardlussoq (see page 146). The latter may be useful under certain conditions of wind or ice.

167 Paakitsuarssuaq 59°59′N 44°26′W

Chart 1103

This is a spectacular and almost landlocked bay 3M E of Torssuqataq providing a useful safe anchorage. Approaching from Torssuqataq, pass to the N of Sugdlat. The channel between Pamiugdluk and the islets to the NE of Sugdlaq is clean and carries 5m. The entrance to the bay is partially blocked by underwater rocks extending as far as mid-channel from the N side. A course about 25m N of the islet on the S side, carries 20m. Good anchorage can be found in the second bay on the NW side in 10–15m, mud with some weed. It is unlikely that any ice would intrude.

There are a number of other possible anchorages in the area:

Anchorages in Torssuqataq & Prins Christian Sund

Charts D 2100, 1103

Due to submarine cables, anchoring is prohibited in the sound except where indicated on the chart. Those mentioned in the Admiralty Pilot *NP11* are, in general, unsuitable for yachts.

168 Stordalens Havn 60°09'N 44°27'W

Chart 1103

This is deep and steep-to. It is necessary to anchor in 40m to be clear of the shore; however, holding is good once the anchor has dug in. Liable to incursion of ice under certain conditions, and therefore not recommended.

Stordalens Havn. Cape Farewell. Anchorage on the approach to glacial silt banks *Bob Shepton*

Kangerdluk anchorage *M Hillman*

169 Aappilattoq (Prins Christian Sund) 60°09'N 44°17'W

Charts D 1103

Aappilattoq which means 'sea anemone' is a beautiful natural harbour in a cleft in the rock, with excellent protection. The entrance is about 20m wide. Small fishing village, with a declining population of about 100.

170 Kangerdluk 60°13'N 44°16'W

Chart 1103

If there is much ice in the Nup Kangerdlua this may be carried into the fjord; however, under suitable conditions, anchorage with good holding in sand may be found on the N shore, near the head.

171 Kangikitsoq 60°19'N 44°15'W

Chart 1103

This fjord extends 6·5M NNW from the Ilua and gives access to excellent climbing and walking amongst magnificent scenery: however headnets and repellant are advisable.

According to local information this fjord is frequently free of ice and appears to enjoy some protection, when winds are strong elsewhere. Anchor at the head, in the NW corner, in 20m – good holding in sand. Trout may be caught in the lakes 2–3M up the Tupqusat valley.

Aappilattoq *M. Hillman*

Anchorage

There is little room in the harbour, but yachts up to 20m may lie, for a short while, alongside the small landing stage at the fish factory. It is possible for a yacht drawing 1·8m to enter the shallow bay to the W of the landing stage, with care. Anchor with lines to both shores, fore and aft, as there are below-water rocks and no room to swing.

Facilities

Small store with most essentials. Post office, telephone, fax and internet services. Fuel available in limited quantities. Helicopter service to Narsarsuaq as well as regular ferry to Nanortalik. Note that there are no facilities for 300 miles on the east coast between Prins Christian Sund and the Ammassalik area.

Anchorages south of Prins Christian Sund

Several of the 'Havns' marked on the charts and maps are silted up; however. it may be possible to anchor off the silt banks in depths less than the 40m mentioned in the pilot.

Igdlorssuit Havn, Prins Christian Sund *Máire Wilkes*

172 Igdlorssuit Havn 60°10′N 44°04′W

Chart 1103

Anchor far out (when it is high water) off silt bank.

173 Qasigissat 60°06′N 44°06′W

Chart 1103

Open to the SE but better sheltered than it looks. Good anchorage on a gently shelving beach.

174 Qardlut 60°03′N 43°59′W

Chart 1103

Pleasant inlet. Anchor on the silt bank.

175 Tasiussaq (Christian IV Ø) 60°05′N 43°48′W

Chart 1103

The entrance is very narrow and steep-to. The fjord provides excellent shelter and no ice is likely to intrude. Good anchorage can be found at the N end on a steadily shelving alluvial fan.

176 Tangnera Fjord 60°04′N 43°42′W

Chart 1103

A narrow and spectacular fjord that almost separates Christian IV Ø from Sangmissoq. Anchor at the head with lines ashore. On the other side of the isthmus a likely anchorage was observed 1M to the E in Tunua at the outlet of a lake.

177 Kangerdlutsiaq 59°59′N 43°52′W

Chart 1103

Anchor at the head of the bay, near an old Norse site. Holding is good in 6m, sand over mud on an alluvial fan. Large ice grounds on the shallows.

178 Quvnerit north 60°00′N 44°06′W

Chart 1103

Anchor on silt bank.

Looking down on the Ikerasassuaq Weather Station *Máire Wilkes*

Ikerasassuaq Weather Station jetty *Máire Wilkes*

179 Ikerasassuaq Weather Station (Prins Christian Sund) 60°04′N 43°11′W

Chart 1103

The weather and long range radio station at Ikerasassuaq has a small jetty, relatively exposed to the long fetch down the sound in westerly winds – which are reported to be unusual. Approach with care as rocks lie off the W end. Follow the leading marks till very close in and then turn sharply east for the harbour entrance.

The jetty is not in good condition and limited space leaves little margin for error. Moor alongside the N face. If the harbour is encumbered with ice, it is possible to lie in the small gut to the NE of the fuel tanks, with lines to ring bolts.

The weather station is reported to be going 'un-manned' with effect from 2016. This is a great sadness as the Danish scientists who manned the station have an unbroken record of hospitality and helpfulness to visiting yachtsmen since before Bill Tillman's time.

Anchorages on the southeast coast

180 Kuugarmiut – Kangerlussuatsiaq (Lindenow Fjord) 60°26′N 43°19′W

Charts D 2100 **Map** 60 Ø1

An excellent sheltered anchorage in a landlocked bay between the island of Kuugarmiut Qeqertat and the mainland. It lies 2M NW of Kissarssutalik (Dronning Louise Ø) at the entrance to Kangerlussuatsiaq (Lindenow Fjord).

Approach

Depending on ice conditions, either approach the anchorage by passing S of Dronning Louise Ø and thence through the passage to the W of the island to the S entrance, or through a narrow channel, which is clean and carries 7m, leading from the S side of Lindenow Fjord. The remains of terminal moraines are evident, both across the entrance to Lindenow Fjord and the entrance S of Dronning Louise Ø and care is needed (see plan and track).

Anchorage

Anchor in 8–10m near a house on the mainland shore. This is in good repair and is used periodically by charter groups and local hunters.

Alternative anchorages in Lindenow Fjord

180a Kangerdlorajik

There is also a good anchorage in Kangerdlorajik, a small fjord that leads 1M NE of Lindenow Fjord about 3M N of Kuugarmiut. Anchor at the head in 9m. An attractive place and sheltered from most directions.

180b SW Lindenow Fjord

On the SW side of Lindenow Fjord, opposite the above, a narrow fjord runs SSE to a spectacular bowl. Anchoring is possible on 10m patches near the edge. A ridge leads to a 1000m peak with splendid views over the ice fields.

181 Grydevig 60°35′N 42°57′W

Chart D 2100 Map 60 Ø1

1M N of Kap Walløe, the spectacular narrow fjord of Kangerdluaraq leads W to a fine bowl on the N side. Aptly called the 'saucepan' in Danish.

Approach

A number of rocks are shown in the outer part; however, a course in mid-channel appears to be clean.

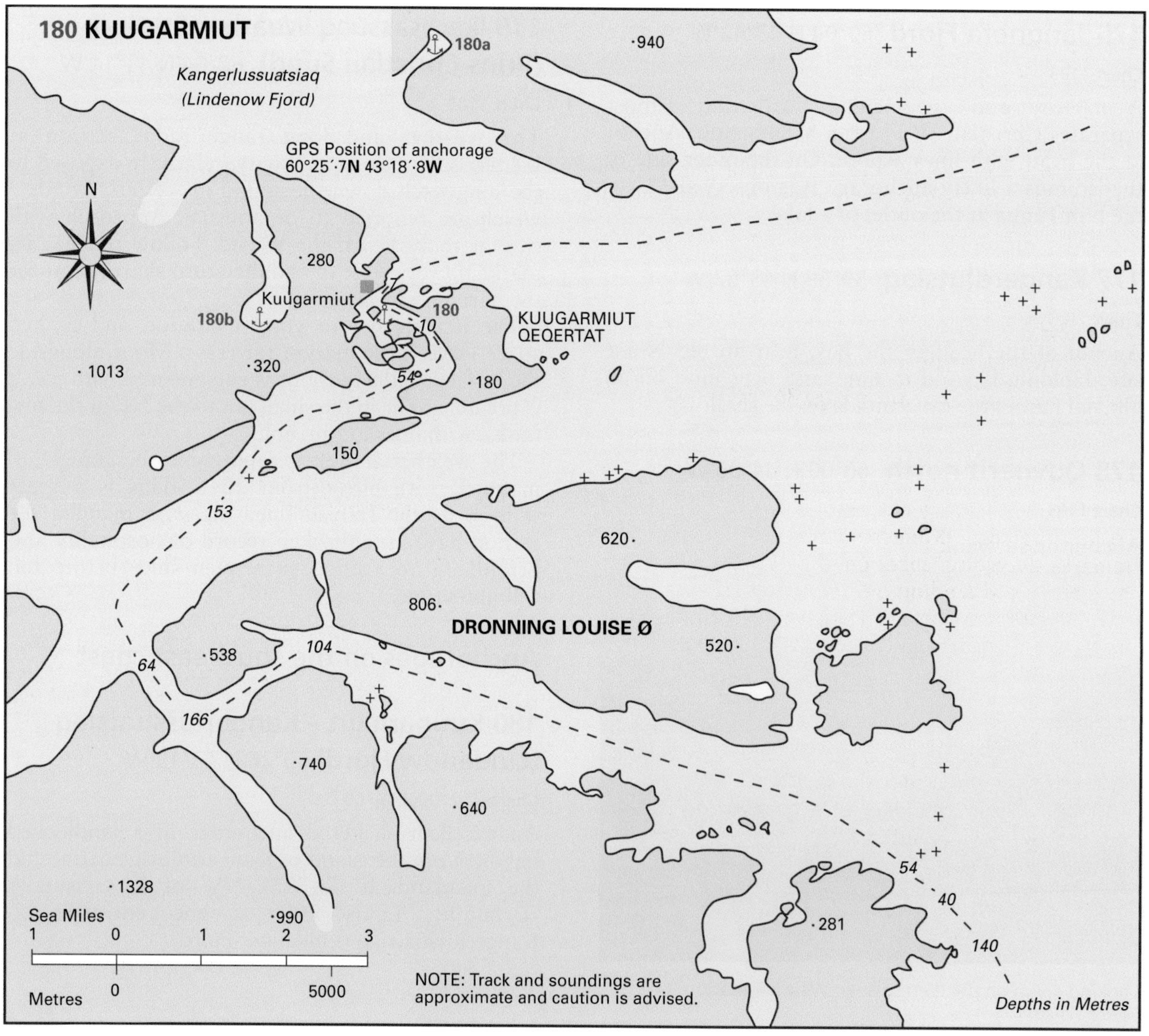

Anchorage

Although there were a number of big bergs in the fjord, they were prevented from entering the bowl by a 5–6m sill. The bowl is deep; but 20m may be found close to some islets in the SW corner and lines run ashore.

182 Qajartalik, Kangerdluluk Fjord

61°03'N 42°44'W

Chart D 2100 **Map** 61 Ø1

A sheltered anchorage in a landlocked bay at the entrance to Kangerdluluk Fjord, 3M SW of Kangingussakasik (Kap Olfert Fischer). The harbour can be encumbered with ice and unusable.

Approach

Through a narrow but deep channel to the S of Qajartalik; which is incorrectly shown as a peninsula on the map. The channel to the S of Qeqertatsiaq and the large bay to the W is shallow, although passable with care and there are below-water rocks to be avoided. When approaching the 'deep channel' from seawards keep clear of the area to the NE of Qeqertatsiaq, where there appear to be rock pinnacles. Qajartalik is an island and it is possible to pass through a narrow channel carrying 10m into Kangerdluluk.

Anchorage

In the inner bay just behind an islet not marked on the map, in 4m. Below-water rocks lie in the inner part of the bay.

183 Qagssidlik, Avarqat Kangerdluat

61°15'N 42°47'W

Chart D 2100 **Map** 61 Ø1

An excellent sheltered anchorage 3M W of Taateraat (see *NP11*).

Approach

Enter Avarqat Kangerdluat 3M N of Kap Herluf Trolle (Taateraat Kangersuatsiat), sailing past the 'remarkable grotto' mentioned by Graah, and enter the short fjord leading SW. Keep initially to the E side, since drying rocks extend from the W entrance point. Depths are irregular, so care is needed.

Anchorage

Secure anchorage can be found in the triangular bay to port in 7–10m, glacial mud. The area to the S and SE of the central island is shoal, but the remainder of the bay is moderately deep. The entrance to the bay carries 10m and is sufficiently shallow to prevent bergs from entering.

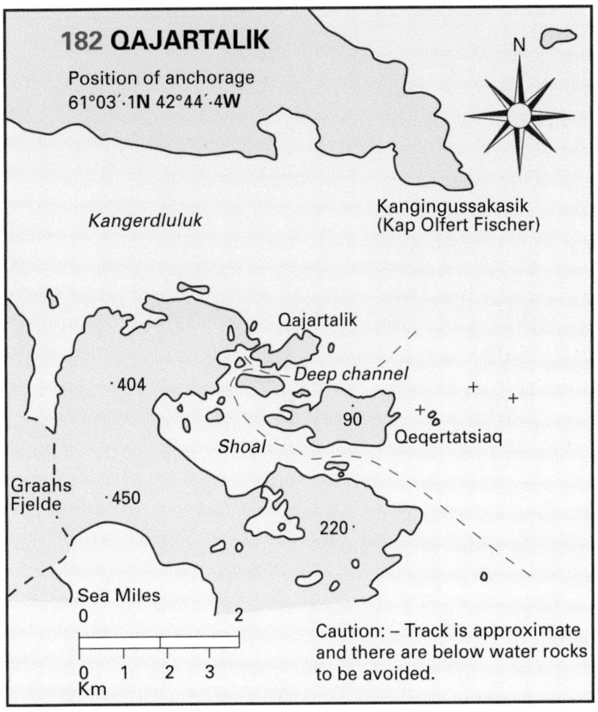

184 Qutdleq 61°32'N 42°17'W

Charts D 2200, 2250 **Map** 61 Ø1

The site of an abandoned Loran station. Moderately sheltered anchorage can be found in 25–30m, either off the old boathouse in the bay on the W side of Qutdleq Island or in the channel between two islands 1M SW. Chart *D 2250* desirable. Although the station was closed in 1973, many of the buildings are still intact and could provide shelter if necessary.

185 Timmiarmiut (Uvtorsiutit Island) 62°32'N 42°10'W

Charts D 2200, (2250) **Map** 62 Ø1

There are secure anchorages off an abandoned weather station, either side of the isthmus in the middle of Uvtorsiutit island.

Approach

The best approach is probably from the E, through a deep, but narrow and tortuous channel. This is the route used by HW Tilman in *Mischief* in 1965. Icebergs may appear to block the channel. When approaching the Nordfjord, note that N of the isthmus, the soundings on Chart *D 2250* appear to be in fathoms, (probably derived from an older chart) and the plan above should be used.

Anchorage

There is a small landing stage in the S harbour. Polar bears have been sighted on the landing stage. It is possible for a small yacht to lie alongside in 2·5m or anchor off in perfect shelter. This harbour is used as an emergency depot for refuelling helicopters. Secure

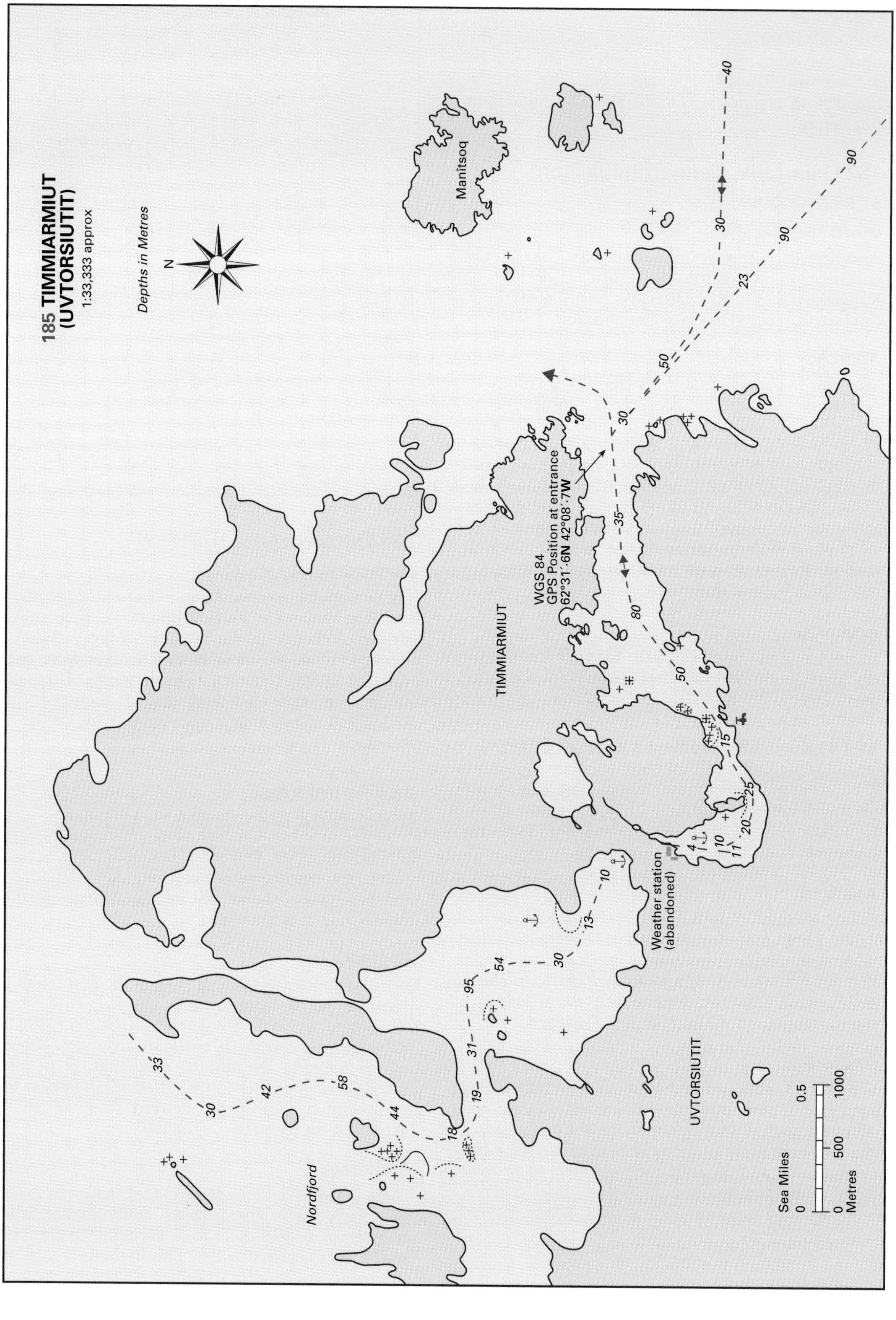
185 TIMMIARMIUT
(UVTORSIUTIT)
1:33,333 approx
Depths in Metres
N
Manîtsoq
TIMMIARMIUT
WGS 84
GPS Position at entrance
62°31´·6N 42°08´·7W
Weather station
(abandoned)
UVTORSIUTIT
Nordfjord
Sea Miles
0
0.5
0
500
1000
Metres

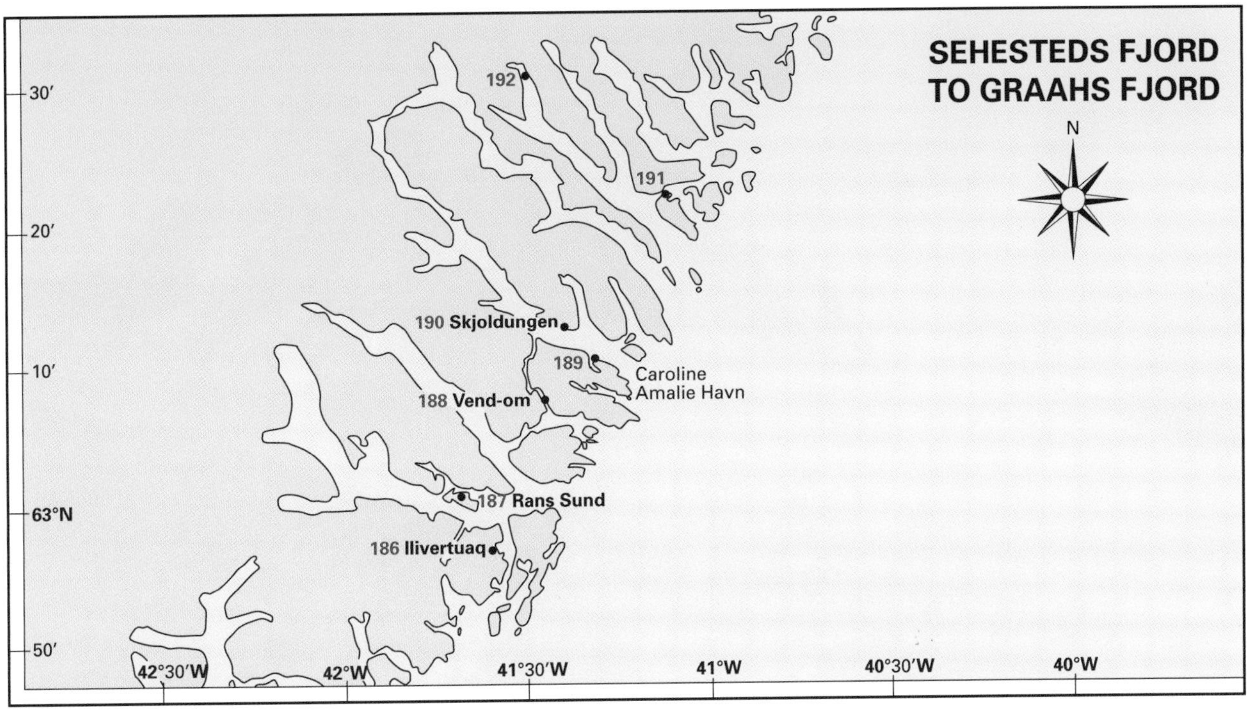

anchorage can also be found in the N harbour in 10m, close to the isthmus, and big ice is prevented from entering by the rocks and shoals in the approach. If inaccessible due to ice an alternative anchorage can be found in a bay on the SW of the island.

Sehesteds Fjord

Charts D 2200 **Maps** 62 Ø1 & 63 Ø1

Approach

The fjord was approached by sailing N through Uumanap tunorqutaria, the deep channel W of Griffenfeld Ø, which was almost clear.

Anchorages

186 Ilivertuaq 62°57′·4N 41°35′·2W

(GPS 62°57′·4N 41°37′·5W)

A useful protected anchorage for small vessels behind an islet in 17m. It is at the head of a V-shaped inlet on the W side of Uumanap tunorqutaria, about 2M N of the narrows.

187 Rans Sund 63°01′·5N 41°41′·5W

(GPS 63°01′·8N 41°41′·7W)

A good anchorage was found in 6m, in a narrow creek at the NW end of Eberlins Ø. Although the E entrance to the sound was blocked, the channel to the W of the island was clear.

188 Vend-om channel to Sønder Skjoldungesund

63°08′N 41°27′W

Chart D 2200 **Map** 63 Ø1

Although this channel is shown as blocked by a glacier on the map, the glacier has now retreated, providing a sheltered route to Skjoldungesund, with an excellent anchorage *en route*.

Approach

The entrance is approximately 6M NE of Griffenfeld Ø. Pass to the N of Uvivaq Island (named Ilugdlermiut on the map) and thence into Vend-om ('turn around' in Danish). The channel is narrow, but appears to be clean and is passable with sufficient tide carrying 3m.

Anchorage

About half a mile up the channel, a 'punch bowl' opens up on the SW side, which provides a beautiful sheltered anchorage in 16m. The next large bay is less satisfactory, as it is rather deep. The channel in front of the glacier is shoal; but carries 4m.

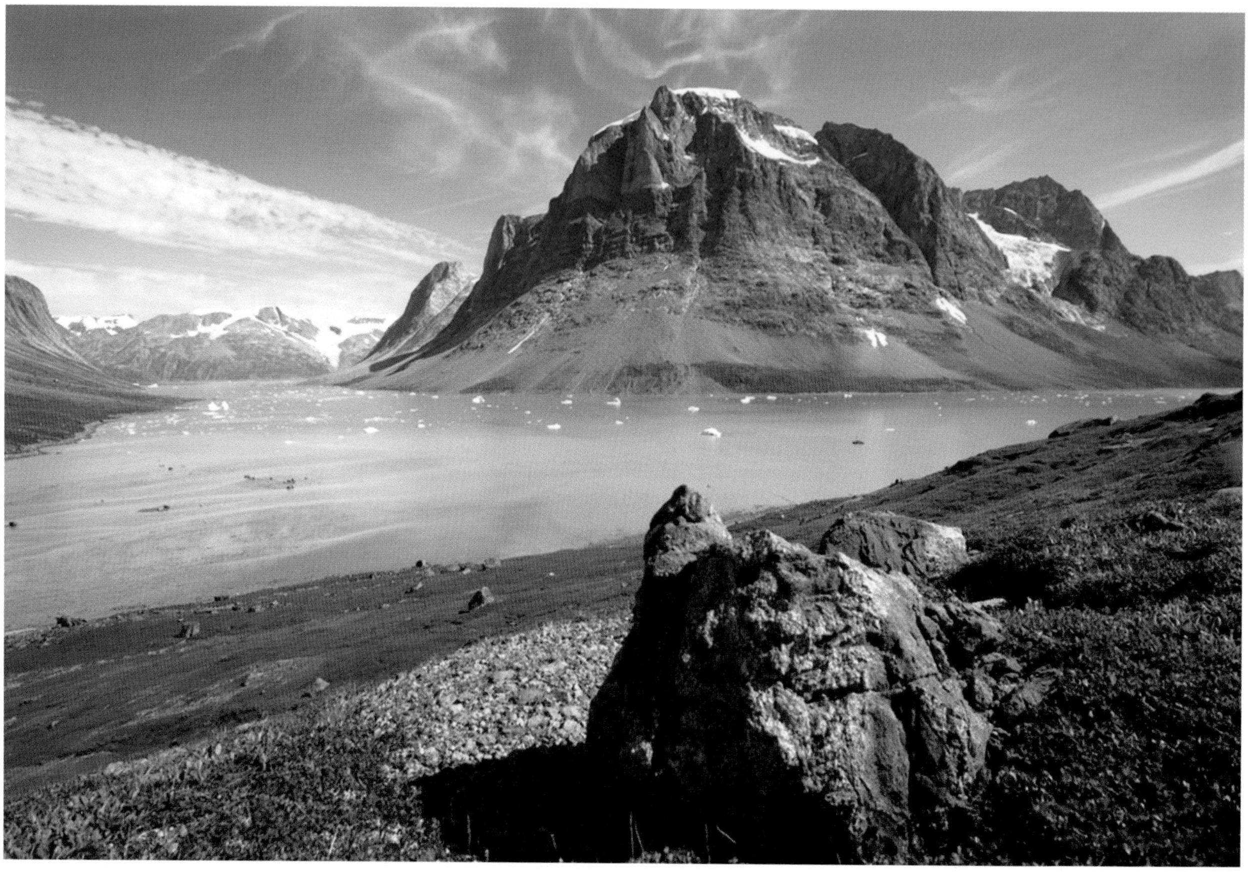

Skjoldungesund *I love Greenland*

Skjoldungen anchorage *William Ker*

Sønder Skjoldungesund

63°10'N 41°18'W

Chart D 2200 **Map** 63 Ø1

Anchorages

189 Amitsuarssuq (Caroline Amalies Havn)

63°11'N 41°19'W

A delightful and sheltered bay on the S side of the sound (see NP11). The bay is guarded by a number of islets and rocks, the entrance being close E of the westernmost high islet and leads in on a bearing of 165°, carrying 20m. The following waypoint in the sound was found useful in poor visibility to locate the entrance: WGS 84 GPS 63°11'·57N 41°19'·98W. Use with discretion.

A very sheltered anchorage in 14m can be found in a bay to port, about half a mile in from the entrance. The entrance to this inner bay carries 6m and is the middle one of three.

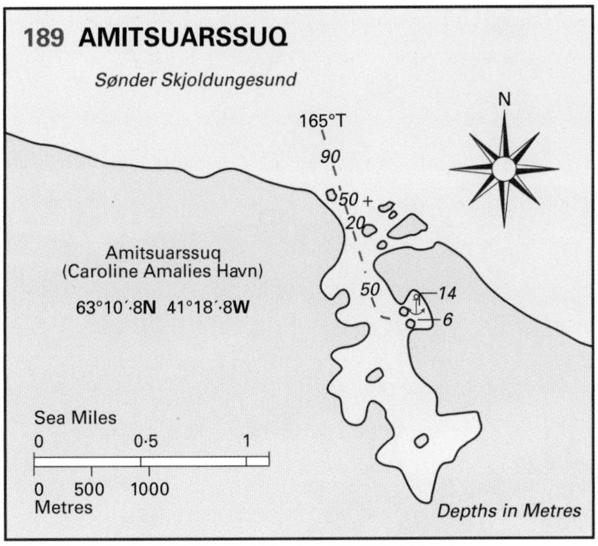

190 Skjoldungen 63°13′N 41°24′W

There is a moderately sheltered anchorage in 8m off the deserted village. Better shelter can be found closer in, by keeping close to the N shore in 3m. Lines can be taken ashore to bolts. The remaining houses are in a poor state of repair, but would offer shelter and are apparently used by hunting parties occasionally.

191 Graahs Havn 63°22′N 41°08′W

Chart D 2200 **Map** 63 Ø1

Capt W A Graah, Royal Danish Navy, returned to winter here during his epic journey by umiaq (an eskimo skin boat) in 1829/30 from Qaqortoq (Julianehåb) to Dannebrog Ø, 120M further N, where he was forced to turn back by ice.

Approach

Enter Graahs Fjord to the SW of Tupikajik or, alternatively, on a westerly course for the SE tip of Imaersivik. Graahs Havn lies at the NW tip of Imaersivik and provides excellent shelter. The narrow entrance is a 'dogleg' and carries 7m (see *NP11*).

Anchorage

The best anchorage appears to be in the second of two small bays in 16m, mud.

Note Finnsbu, 4M to the W of Graahs Havn and mentioned in NP11, is a small, very sheltered bowl, which would be completely protected from winter ice, but access is difficult.

The entrance is hard to locate and is fronted by unmarked rocks; moreover the channel leading to the bowl carries less than 2m. Unless there are special reasons for using it, this harbour cannot be recommended.

192 Anchorage at the head of Graahs Fjord 63°31′N 41°30′W

There is a spectacular anchorage NW of Urds Øer at the head of Lommen Fjord with climbing potential.

193 Anchorage N of Gyldenløves Fjord, W of Nansens Bugt

64°19′N 40°33′W

Providing ice conditions permit, there is a sheltered anchorage in a bay on the S tip of Kiatak. Approach, leaving Qeqertartivik to port. Remarkable views of the ice cap from the 766m hill above.

194 Dannebrog Ø 65°18′N 39°35′W

Chart D 2300 **Map** 65 Ø2

Dannebrog Ø is the largest island in the Graahs Øer group. This was the farthest point reached by Graah in 1829 and where he formally raised the Danish flag. The whole area is seriously encumbered with bergs and bergy bits, which are generated by the glaciers at the head of Ikertivaq and those further N. There is a protected anchorage in a landlocked bay halfway along the SW side of the island (see *NP11*).

Approach

In the absence of drift ice, it may be possible to approach the anchorage on a NW course, from 5–10M offshore, where the iceberg concentration is likely to be less.

Anchorage

The bay is clearly shown on the map. Enter in mid channel on a NE course, until the inner bay opens to starboard. In the middle of the entrance to the inner bay, there is a rock which covers, but there is plenty of room to pass either side. Anchor in 5–10m on either side of the bay, depending on wind direction. Large ice cannot enter the anchorage, but there are likely to be bergy bits to watch out for.

There is a further bay leading to the E, which is shown on the map, but it is shoal and practically dries out.

195 Isortoq 65°32′N 38°58′W

Chart D 2300 **Map** 65 Ø2

This is a very small village 35M from Tasiilaq and the furthest SW in the Ammassalik commune with a population of about 150. It is of interest, because it is possible to get very close to the ice cap and it is from near here that most of the sledge crossings to the West Coast start. A channel leads 3M NE to a shallow bay and to the ice front, which may be approachable at HW.

Tasiilaq Harbour *A. Stenbakken*

Anchorages nearby

195a Isortoq – Kitaq

In the channels to the E of Isortoq (which means 'the foggy sea'), between the island of Kitaq and the mainland, there are completely sheltered anchorages; safe from big ice, thanks to shoals (see *NP11*, but the anchorage mentioned and marked on the map may be subject to large floes).

195b Kap Tycho

Secure anchorage in 5–10m in the narrow fjord leading NE from Isip ilua, behind Kap Tycho Brahe. However, the entrance can be blocked by large icebergs, which are not aground and could prevent departure.

Tasiilaq *A. Stenbakken*

196 Tasiilaq (Ammassalik)

65°37'N 37°30'W

Charts D 2300, 2310, 2351 **Map** 65 Ø1 (see location chart on page 236)

The town and harbour in Kong Oskars Havn on Ammassalik Ø ('a place where capelin are') is now called Tasiilaq. Thanks to the excellent communications by air through Kulusuk airport, it has become popular in the summer with tour groups for walking tours and as a base for climbing expeditions, as well as dog-sled trips in winter. The population of the town is about 1,500, with another 1,500 people living in the half dozen villages in the Tasiilaq Commune. It is one of the fastest growing towns in Greenland.

In most years in the past, it has not been at all easy to get to the Ammassalik area due to storis, but it is worth the effort, if ice conditions allow. There is excellent and scenic cruising in the fjords around, as well as scrambling and serious climbing.

Approach

If approaching from the Kap Dan direction, beware of the dangerous rocks lying SW of Kap Dan and give it a wide berth. Pass Tasiilap nuua in mid-channel and continue around to the harbour on the SW shore – there are no dangers.

Berthing and anchorage

It is possible to lie alongside the quay temporarily, but the coaster supplying the villages is a regular visitor. When the vessel is in harbour, a yacht may lie alongside her. The inner harbour is crowded with small craft on moorings and is shoal. If the weather is calm and settled, it is possible to anchor outside the harbour in 3–6m, to the N of the harbour buildings. The shores shelve steeply, as Bill Tilman found to his cost when *Baroque* dried out, fell and then filled on a rising tide in 1976.

Facilities

There is an excellent bakery by the harbour and a well-stocked KNI/Pilersuisoq store (cards accepted with PIN number). Post office with ATM. The Neriussaq Bookshop has internet access. Diesel on the small fuel dock opposite the quay – pay at the petrol station (which also has kerosene) within walking distance over the bridge. Kosangas available. Public shower and laundry opposite the petrol station. The town water is heavily chlorinated – probably better to fill up from a stream, away from the settlements.

The Hotel Angmagssalik serves set meals. The Red House, run by mountain guide Robert Peroni, is strongly recommended, but book ahead for supper. A visit to the radio station would be worthwhile – they can get weather and ice information.

Helicopter connection to the airfield on Kulusuk Island. See the Lonely Planet guide for more information.

Remarks

When Graah turned back at Dannebrog Ø in 1829, he was unaware that a community existed in the Ammassalik area. It was not until 1883 that Baron Nordenskjöld anchored the Sofia in Kong Oskars Havn; but the population had run away and he did not make contact. Two years later Captain Gustav Holm's expedition, in umiaks, completed Graah's survey of the coast and reached Ammassalik. He found a population of over 400 and in 1894 a trading and mission station was established.

For those who have followed the voyages of the late Bill Tilman, a visit to Erritt Skerries, at the entrance of Sermilik fjord will be of interest. There are three small skerries, the centre having a flat under-water ledge extending from it for about 50m, which Tilman's *Sea Breeze* struck and then sank in 1972.

197 Kulusuk (Kap Dan) 65°34'N 37°11'W

Charts D 2310, 2351 **Map** 65 Ø1
(see location chart on page 236)

Kulusuk has become a popular tourist destination for day trips, since it is only two hours by air from Reykjavík. There are also two or three flights a week to Nuuk (Godthåb) and Kangerlussuaq (Søndre Strømfjord) and a regular helicopter connection with Tassiilaq (Ammassalik). The village, which is about 1M W of the airport, has a post office and store. Fuel is available. If using the airport it is better to go around to the bay closer to the terminal building. There is a small hotel, roughly midway between the village and the airport.

Approach

The approach from the W is straightforward into Torssut, leaving the small island to port; (which is shown on Chart *2310* with triangular beacon, but may not be in position). To sail beyond Kulusuk village, it is almost essential to have the large-scale plan on Chart *2351*, however there are rocks not marked on the plan and care is needed. A rock, which dries, lies on the direct route to the jetty serving the airport, approximately 100m due E of the peninsula guarding the bay.

A course in mid-channel between the peninsula and Akivitse island, before swinging around to approach the jetty on a bearing of 190°, appears to be clean.

Anchorages

197a Kulusuk village jetty

There is a jetty at the village with only 1m alongside at LW. Anchoring off is possible.

197b Kulusuk airport jetty

There is another jetty which is close to the airport, but only has 0·2m MLWS alongside. Anchor off in the bay in 4m.

Kulusuk
I love Greenland

198 Unnamed fjord running SSW from Ikaasak 65°41′N 37°05′W

A reef projects from the SE shore about 1M from the entrance, but there is a clear passage carrying 25m. Anchor near the head in 12m – shoals rapidly. In strong SW winds could be a bit of a wind tunnel.

199 Landlocked bowl 1M E of Qerqikajik Mountain (727m)

65°45′N 37°19′W

Approach either side of Qernertivartivit. The bowl is guarded by rocks and islets. Enter through the narrow passage, in the middle, leaving the islet with the vertical face, close aboard to port. Anchor in the bowl in 10–15m.

200 Tiniteqilaaq 65°53′N 37°47′W

A small village, 17M North of Tasiilaq, overlooking Sermilik Fjord, with magnificent views of the many icebergs calved from the big glaciers at the head. The approach up Ikaasatsivaq, which leads off Ammassalik Fjord, requires care and the entrance to the anchorage close to the village, is shoal. It may be possible for vessels drawing 2·5m or less to transit from Ikâsartivaq to Sermilik at, or shortly before, HW.

201 Marie Havn 65°51′N 37°07′W

There is a useful anchorage about 3M W of Kuumiit, on the S side of Ikerasaalaq, behind Grisøen. The bay shoals to 4m in the inner part and is normally reported to be clear of ice. There are fish in the stream.

202 Kuumiit 65°51′N 37°00′W

Charts D 2310, 2351 Map 65 Ø1

One of the larger settlements in the area with about 360 inhabitants. Said to be comparatively ice free. In strong southerlies it is exposed to the long fetch in Ammassalik Fjord.

Anchorage

The jetty near the village is shallow and foul and it is better to go alongside in 4m at the fish factory, a quarter of a mile W of the village. Limited supplies. Regular boat connection to Tassiilaq (Ammassalik).

Ammassalik Fjord anchorages

Chart D 2310 Maps 65 Ø1

There are a number of possible anchorages close to the fjord, of which the following have been used.

Tasiilaq Fjord 66°00′N 37°05′W

Charts D 2300 Maps 65 Ø1, 66 Ø2

General

Tasiilaq Fjord forks to the NE at the head of Ammassalik Fjord, giving access to a large area of high and dramatic mountains. A hut, which sleeps 10, just N of the top of the first glacier to the E going up the valley. Enquire at the Tourist Office in Tasiilaq and obtain permission and key, before using the hut.

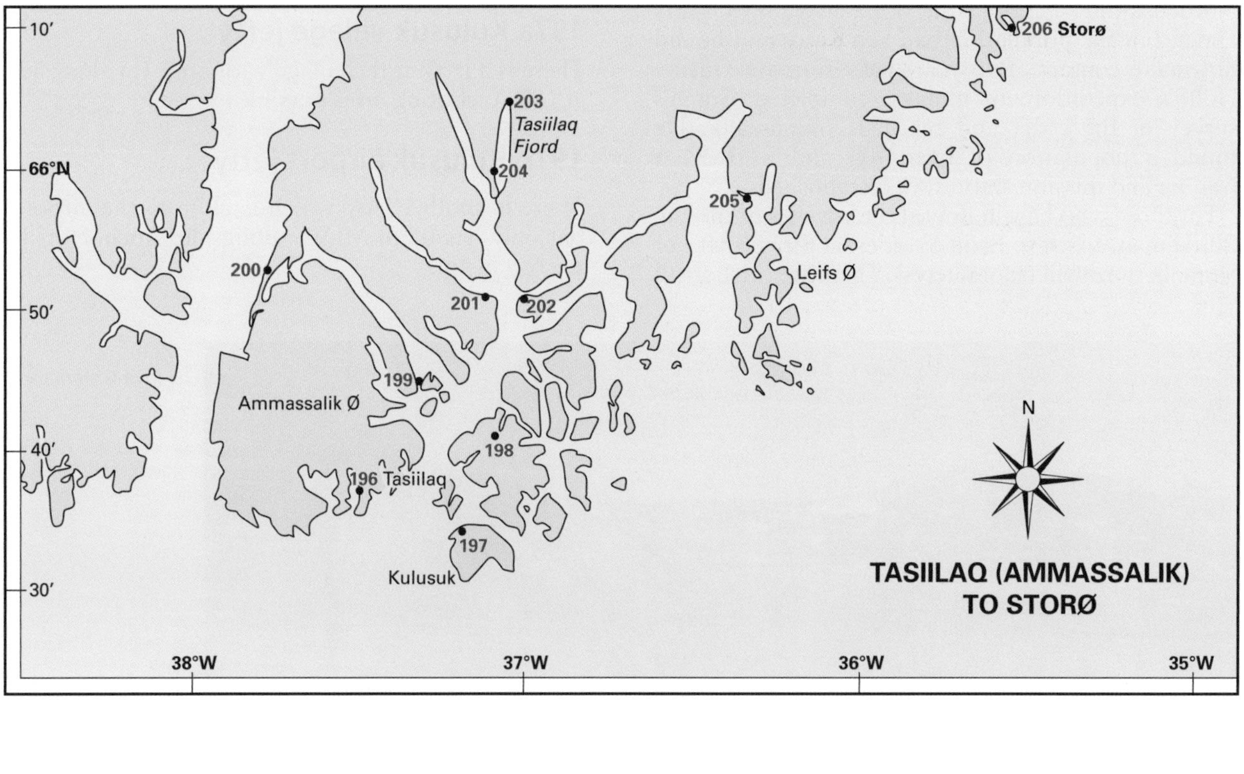

Approach

There are two islands in the approach channel. Leave the first to starboard and the second to port. It is deep inside the fjord; but shoals abruptly at the head.

Anchorages

203 Tasiilaq Head

Anchor in 30–35m, near the head of the fjord. Holding is good, once the anchor is set, but southerly winds have been experienced in the afternoons in July, so this should be considered.

204 W Tasiilaq

There is a sheltered anchorage in 5–8m, good holding, behind a small island near the S end of the fjord, on the W side. Shelter from strong N winds is possible, in the narrow channel S of the island, with lines ashore.

205 N of Leifs Ø

65°58'N 36°20'W

Charts D 2300 Map 65 Ø1

Approach

Approaching the Ammassalik area from the E, it is possible to enter the sheltered fjord system through the channel to the NE of Leifs Ø, if ice permits. The bay to the E of Leifs Ø is without off-lying dangers. Enter in mid-channel through Ikaasak kiateq (Nordre Ikerasaq on the map) between Dobbeltø and Grafitø (which has a rock close off the E tip).

Anchorage

There is a secure anchorage in 5–10m, good holding, in the narrow fjord leading W from Kangertivartikajik towards the abandoned settlement of Ilivtiartik.

206 Storø 66°10'N 35°32'W

Chart D 2300 Map 66 Ø1

There is a landlocked bowl, 2M NNE of Kap Nordenskjöld, on the SW side of Storø, offering complete shelter. The entrance is a dogleg and carries 7m, preventing large ice from entering. The bowl is rather deep, but it is possible to anchor in 20m at the head. It is reported that if there is much ice, Ødesund gets blocked, and the anchorage may not be accessible. Under these conditions it has been possible to moor to the shore, by an old Inuit site on the NE side of Storø.

Kangerlussuaq 68°10'N 32°00'W

Chart D 2400 Map 68 Ø3

Kangerlussuaq is the largest fjord between Tasiilaq (Ammassalik) and Ittoqqortoormiit (Scoresby Sund), giving access to the Frederiksborg Glacier and the Lemon Bjerge range. Several active glaciers feed into the fjord and it is usually heavily congested with ice.

Near the entrance to the fjord, at the SE corner of Kraemer Ø, there is a useful anchorage in a small bay. This was used by the yacht *Suhaili* in 1991, as a base for the Bonnington/Knox-Johnston expedition to climb the Cathedral (2,660m). Several islets and reefs prevent the incursion of large ice.

Approach

The approach to within 2M of the anchorage is adequately described in *NP11*. Turn to starboard when the large conical peak N of Mikis Fjord appears to rise above the saddle formed by the Forbindlsegletscher and bears 83°. Three islets lie between Kraemer Ø and Mellem Ø (see plan). Leave the first two to starboard and the third to port.

207 Kraemer Ø 68°10'N 31°45'W

Anchor in 7–10m in the NE corner of the bay which lies at the SE end of the island. Holding is good and lines can be taken to the shore. The tidal range is about 3m. The area is subject to katabatic winds known as piteraq and precautions should be taken in unsettled weather. Good water can be obtained from the streams.

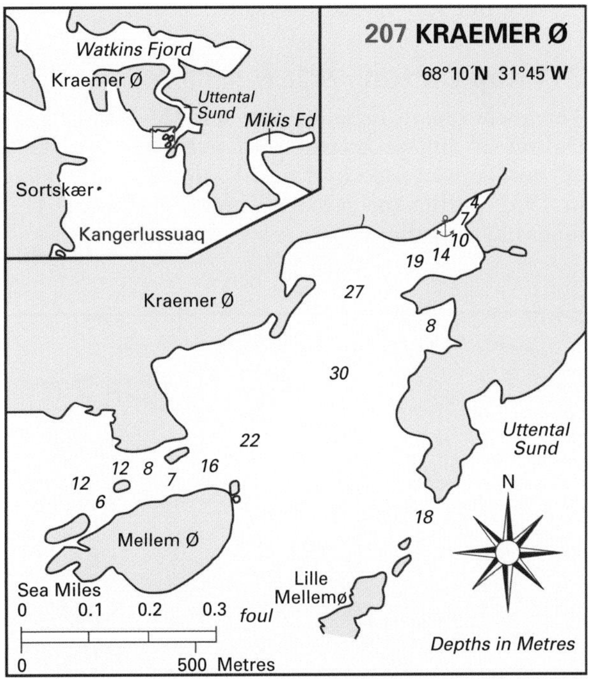

4. GREENLAND

Anchorages on the Blosseville coast N of 69°N

Charts D 2500

There are several useful anchorages between 69°N and 69°45′N, which offer good shelter. If this coast is clear of drift ice, access is easy (see *NP11*). Surveys are incomplete and GPS (WGS 84) should be used with caution. Charted Longitude is 2′ less than GPS over much of the area.

208 D'Aunay Bugt 69°00′N 25°23′W

The anchorage is at the end of the central arm, towards the head of the right fork in 10–15m, mud, which shelves steeply some distance from the head. Subject to bergy bits, but large bergs cannot enter. Good shelter.

209 Høst Havn 69°15′N 24°50′W

The narrow bay leading NE from just inside the entrance to Barclay Bugt, is protected by a bar (moraine) with a least depth of 10m. Anchor at the head in 5–10m, mud.

210 Knighton Fjord 69°22′N 24°32′W

The anchorage is in a bay leading NE off Knighton Fjord, 2M behind Kap Ewart. The bay is protected from ice incursion by a shallow bar with a least depth of 5m. Within the bay, depths increase to >50m, but it is possible to anchor in 5m close behind the moraine spit or near the head.

211 Kap Dalton 69°26′N 24°08′W

The anchorage is behind a low spit 2M NW of Kap Dalton in 3m; protected from swell and ice. This anchorage was used by Knud Rasmussen in Kivioq in 1932 during the seventh Thule Expedition. The inner bay is shallow.

212 Romer Fjord 69° 38′N 23° 30′W

Approach anchorage 69°43′N 23°42′W between Henry Land and Turner Island heading northwest for about 5M. A disused trappers hut is conspicuous on a point of land ahead. Anchor on rocky bottom in 10m off the shore and land by dinghy on gravel beach. Exposed to southeast and area subject to katabatic winds. Hot springs nearby. Better shelter may be had around the point but no information available at this stage.

Scoresby Sund

Chart D 2600

213 Turner Sund 69°45′N 23°28′W

The anchorage is in an inlet running NW from the middle of the sound. Anchor in 10m. Steeply shelving some distance from the head.

214 Ittoqqortoormiit (Scoresby Sund) 70°29′N 21°59′W

Charts D 2600, 2650

Ittoqqortoormiit (a place where there are many houses) is a small settlement with about 450 inhabitants. Another 100 people live in the two villages at Kap Tobin and Kap Hope. The area was settled in 1925 by families moving north from the Ammassalik district. Traditional hunting is the main occupation. With a regular air service from Iceland to the airport 20M NW, at Nerlerit Inaat (Constable Pynt), it has become a base for expeditions to the Stauning Alps and the National Park to the N.

There are some facilities but no harbour – vessels anchor off.

Kangertittivaq (Scoresby Sund) is huge: 200M long and over 20M wide for much of its length, with scope for exploration and climbing, if ice conditions allow.

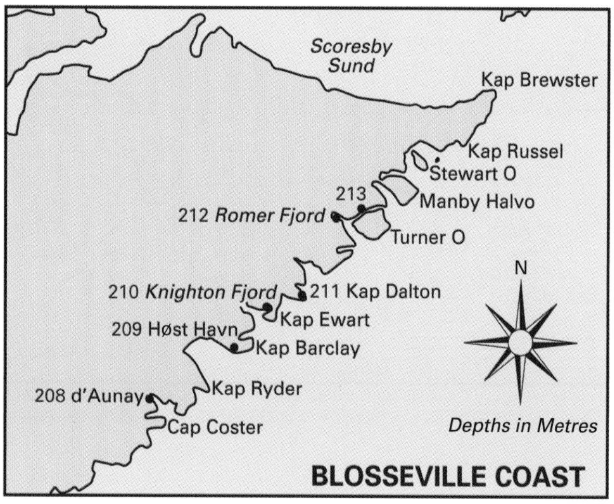

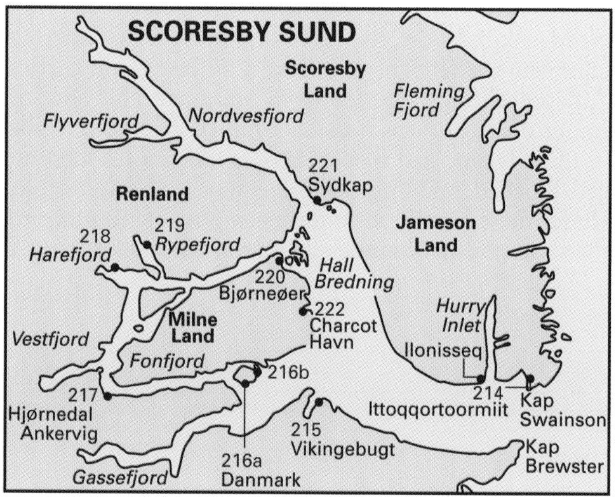

Ittoqqortoormiit *Ingeborg Deppe*

Kap Brewster *Ingeborg Deppe*

Ittoqqortoormiit Roadstead *Ed Wheeler*

Ittoqqortoormiit *I love Greenland*

The National Park Area lies to the N of Scoresby Sund and is a protected area, to which entry is prohibited without permission. Those intending to enter the park, or land on the coast N of latitude 72°N, must obtain prior permission from the Danish Polar Institute, which may take up to three months. For further information visit www.dpc.dk

Approach

Great care is needed in the approach to Scoresby Sund; good information about ice, which can extend up to 70M offshore, and good weather is essential. The entrance, which lies between Kap Brewster (70°09′N 22°03′W) and Kap Tobin (70°24′N 21°57′W), can easily be blocked for long periods, when sea and glacier ice are present, especially if there are onshore winds. There is a 10m patch off Kap Brewster. Call the harbour office on Ch 16 and clear with the harbourmaster.

Berthing and anchorage

The inshore jetty is reserved for commercial vessels. The anchorage recommended (see chart *D 2650*) is in 24m and is for large vessels. Yachts can anchor inshore NW of this in 10m. There is danger from drifting bergs and bergy bits.

Ittoqqortoormiit Scoresbysund *I love Greenland*

Facilities

Store with most provisions. Diesel in cans. Post office with good satellite communications. Small hospital. Laundry and showers in a red building near the shore (tokens from the Kommune).

Helicopter link to Nerlerit Inaat (Constable Pynt) airfield, from which there are flights to Iceland.

214a Amdrup Havn 70°28'N 21°55'W

A less exposed anchorage than that off Scoresby Sund settlement but subject to gusts. The best anchorage is near the S shore, about 0·5M in. Good holding in 5–10m.

Vikingebugt Ingeborg Deppe

Danmark Island *Knútur Karlsson*

215 Vikingebugt 70° 27'N 25° 03'W

South of Kap Stevenson. Good holding in mud 10–15m is reported to the east of the small island near the southern side of Vikingebugt entrance.

216 Danmark Ø 70°30'N 26°15'W

Charts D 2600

Danmark Ø lies 85M W of Scoresby Sund settlement and two sheltered anchorages have been reported.

216a Hekla Havn 70°27'N 26°15'W

This is an excellent sheltered anchorage, where Lt Ryder, Royal Danish Navy, overwintered in Hekla in 1891. There is a cairn on the E point of the entrance; approach on 6° carrying 10m. Anchor in 9m. There is a hunters' cabin at the head.

216b Inlet on N side 70°31'N 26°10'W

There is a spectacular anchorage at the head of the long inlet, which runs SE from Rensund.

Barnacle geese and great northern divers can be seen.

217 Hjörnedal, Ankervig

70° 21'N 28° 08'W

The nearby scientific station carries out research on Narwhales. Good walking with magnificent views of the Scoresby Sund mountains.

Vikingebugt *Ingeborg Deppe*

Hekla Havn

Hekla Havn

Ankervig looking towards Mt. Hermelintop
Knútur Karlsson

Rypefjord *Ingeborg Deppe*

Eielson glacier *Knútur Karlsson*

218 Harefjord, Ternevigerne

70° 57′N 28° 07′W

Good walking. Likelihood of seeing wildlife including muskox and arctic hare. The views of the glacier are beautiful.

219 Rypefjord 71°05′N 27°45′W

The anchorage, being a small shelf of shallower water close to the shore, offers little protection but the Eielson Glacier is well worth seeing.

220 Bjørneøer (Nanut Qeqertait)

71°03′N 25°37′W

Sheltered anchorage was found in Jyttes Havn at the head of the bay. The rock bar (<10m) at the entrance should stop large icebergs from entering the Havn. Holding is poor on rock and stones.

Bjørneøer approaches, Jyttes Havn *Brian Black*

Bjørneøer, Jyttes Havn *Ed Wheeler*

Harefjord Ternevigene anchorage *Knútur Karlsson*

Bjørneøer, Jyttehavn *Knútur Karlsson*

221 Sydkap (Kangerterajiva)

71°18'N 25°04'W

Anchorage was found in the bay 1·5M NW of Sydkap.

222 Charcot Havn 70°47'N 25°25'W

Anchorage was found on the NW side of this large bay in 13m. There are mud banks, which are visible on Google Earth to be avoided.

Sydkap anchorage *Knútur Karlsson*

Charcot Havn, Milneland *Knútur Karlsson*

Liverpool Land & Davy Sund

Chart D 2600 **Map** 70 Ø 1 and 71 Ø 1 or Saga No 20

Liverpool Land is described in *NP11*.

223 Kangertivatsiákajik (Lillefjord)

70°35'N 21°46'W

Good holding found in 10m, gravel, on the E shore of the long inlet 2M W of Spærrebugt. In the approach, give Kap Hodgson a good berth and keep 200m off, until closing the anchorage. Somewhat exposed to the N; glacier at the head may calve, requiring anchor watch.

224 Sandbach Halvø, Kolding Fjord

70°43'N 21°36'W

Good holding found in 10m, gravel, on the S side of the spit linking Kap Hoegh to Sandbach Halvø, off the Fangsthus.

225 Kap Greg 70°56'N 21°40'W

Good holding found in 10m, either in the Hyttebugt on the S side or in the Tangebugt on the N side, off a Fangsthus, with good protection, except from the N. Shallow entrance to the latter protects against big ice. Water from a stream.

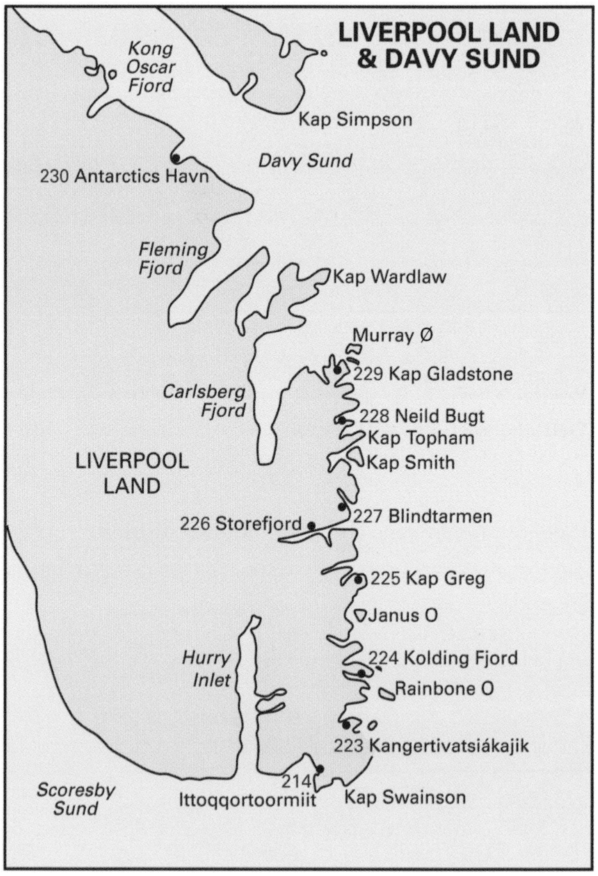

Above and below Warming Island, Liverpool Land
Brian Black

226 Storefjord 71° 06′N 21° 40′W

Between Kap Buddicom and Kap Jones. Long narrow fjord with no apparent anchorage until secondary fjord running north opens after 8 miles. Anchorage found one mile along Norrafjord 71°05′N 22°07′W off stream and small rocky spit on west side in 10m. The spit may give some protection should ice accumulations in upper reaches of fjord break free in strong current bringing it past the anchorage and out to sea. In ice clear conditions it may be possible to find shelter and anchor at the head of fjord but this has not been verified.

227 Blindtarmen 71°09′N 021°51′W

Sidearm of Slien, just north of Storefjord. The shallow water off Cape Jones has been reported to be 18m deep.

Anchor at the head of the bay in front of the sand beach in 6–8m. Excellent holding in sand. Protected on all sides. It is reported that, due to the distance from the icecap, there are few katabatic winds.

The anchorage was used as base camp for the first ascent of Kirken, a conspicuous mountain on the north bank of Storefjord.

228 Neild Bugt 71° 23′N 21° 45′W

From Kap Topham pass next un-named headland and steer 330° towards low cliffs. When close, the entrance will open to sheltered lagoon in magnificent surroundings protected from major bergs. Glacier front appears stable. Water from stream.

229 Kap Gladstone 71°30′N 21°50′W

The glacier which linked Kap Gladstone to the mainland has now melted and collapsed, making it possible with care to pass inside, what has become known as 'Warming Island'. The channel carries 34m but there are remains of a moraine to be avoided. It is possible to anchor off a gravel beach in 10m with good holding.

230 Antarctics Havn, Davy Sund
72° 02′N 23° 05′W

Follow coastline and turn into bay until suitable anchoring spot is found in mud and shingle. Sheltered from all but northerly winds in bleak surroundings.

Above and below Blindtarmen

5. Approaches to the North West and North East Passages

Contents

Passages between Europe to and from the North West Passage and Greenland

Bad weather and heavy seas can be expected

The nearest departure point from central and southern Europe for vessels wishing to transit the North West Passage will be from Ireland. Happily, there are a number of sheltered and convivial departure ports on the south and west coasts of Ireland where one can await a favourable forecast for the passage. Two are Dingle, which has an excellent marina with a lively pub and music scene nearby, and Castletownbere, which is a fishing port with many facilities and good sticky mud in which to anchor.

Vessels making a passage from more northern latitudes may depart from Scotland or Norway. Those departing from Norway may find it useful to sail by way of Iceland, which is conveniently about half of the approximate 1,400M distance to southern Greenland.

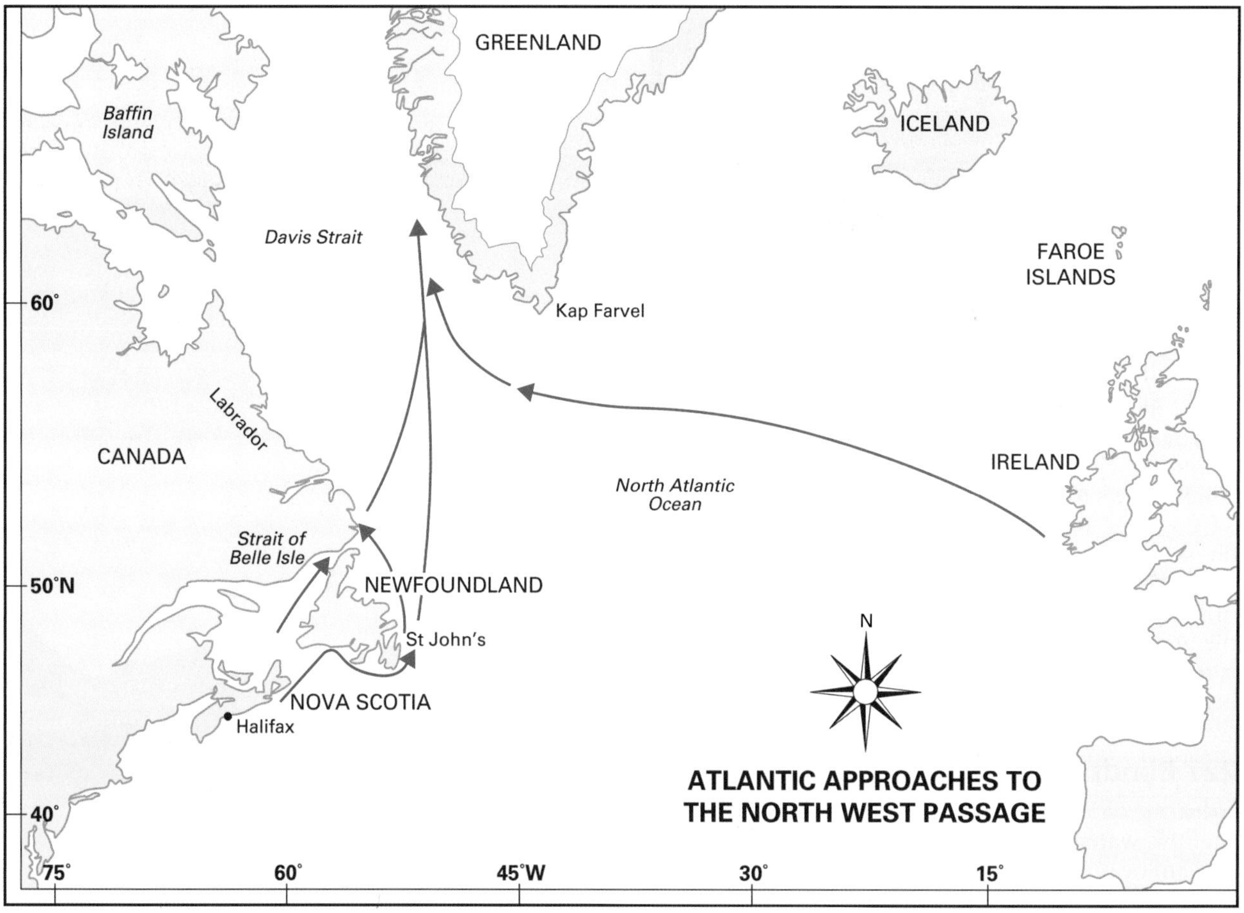

ATLANTIC APPROACHES TO THE NORTH WEST PASSAGE

Dingle has a friendly marina and many pubs with traditional live music *Máire Wilkes*

Castletownbere with its big fishing fleet has a wealth of maritime expertise available *Máire Wilkes*

Vessels departing from southern Ireland for a waypoint 120M south of Cape Farewell will sail about 1,200M if they sail the great circle route or about 1,600M if they sail by way of Iceland. A landfall in Nuuk will add another 450M.

The North Atlantic weather is largely determined by the Azores High area of high pressure and the Iceland Low which is typically to the southwest of Iceland. A series of depressions moving in an easterly or northeasterly direction can be expected over the waters between Europe and southern Greenland. In May the Icelandic Low which, by this time, lies between Iceland and Kap Farvel, will fill. The incidence of winds gale Force 8 or higher during May and June decreases from 11% to 8% in the area south of Kap Farvel. The prevailing wind is from the west. There is an east setting current between Ireland and about longitude 35°W at which point the southerly setting East Greenland Current starts to have an influence. Fog is common on the south and southwest coasts of Greenland.

Vessels planning to transit the North West Passage will want to be in the Lancaster Sound area by early August. The sea ice in the Davis Strait and Baffin Bay is unlikely to have dispersed by July so a route northwards along the western shore of Greenland is preferable.

Kap Farvel, on the southern tip of Greenland, has a very bad reputation for severe weather and vessels are advised to keep at least 120M south of the Cape. Storis ice is also likely to be present near Kap Farvel as it is carried southwards on the East Greenland Current, around the Cape and northwards with the West Greenland Current. The southwest coast of Greenland is subject to sea ice and storis ice until mid summer and, earlier in the year, vessels should make a passage for Paamiut or Nuuk. Icebergs and growlers are present all the time.

Departure times from Europe will depend upon the North Atlantic weather, ice in the Davis Strait and Baffin Bay, the vessel's speed and whether a fast or more leisurely cruise is planned along the Greenland west coast.

Typically, a yacht might be in southern Ireland in early to mid June monitoring the North Atlantic weather forecasts. When a suitable weather window seems likely, a passage is made for a waypoint 120M south of Kap Farvel. A course can then be shaped northwest and north to Nuuk. July can be spent cruising northwards along the west coast of Greenland to the Upernavik region. A passage of about 480M can then be made in late July or early August through the North Water recurring polynya to Lancaster Sound or Pond Inlet. Ice charts will have to be consulted to ensure that a passage is made north of the central pack ice in Baffin Bay.

Passages from the North West Passage to Europe

A vessel transiting the North West Passage from west to east can expect to arrive in Baffin Bay in late August or September. At this time, the sea ice on the east coast of Baffin Island will have decreased significantly and a passage south can be made on either side of Baffin Bay and the Davis Strait. The nights will be dark however, which will make keeping a good lookout for icebergs and growlers, which are more common on the western shores of Baffin Bay and the Davis Strait, difficult.

The frequency of gale and storm force winds increase in September and October from 10% to 17% in the seas south of Kap Farvel, with correspondingly high seas.

Passages between the eastern shores of North America to and from the North West Passage and Greenland

The same timing considerations apply to vessels sailing from North America bound for the North West Passage as apply to those sailing from Europe. The lighter prevailing south and southwest winds should be more favourable to northbound craft than boats travelling from Europe can expect. However, this may be no recompense for the icebergs and growlers born southwards on the cold Labrador Current, and the high incidence of fog.

For the reasons outlined above, an easier more ice-free passage can be expected sailing northwards on the east side of the Davis Strait and Baffin Bay.

In May and June visibility of less than 2M can be expected for 20% or more of the time off the coasts of Newfoundland and Labrador.

Hurricanes and Tropical Storms need to be considered at least as far north as Newfoundland and especially in the months of August, September and October.

Maine, Nova Scotia and Newfoundland are lovely cruising areas which all have fascinating maritime heritages.

South West Harbour in Maine has two major chandleries and a prestigious boatyard. This may be a good opportunity to obtain yacht chandlery or carryout repairs before heading northwards. The Binnacle chandlery in Halifax, Nova Scotia, has an excellent selection of CHS and BA charts and publications as well as general yacht chandlery. Baddeck Marine in Cape Breton Island is also reported as being very helpful for sourcing chandlery, charts, etc.

From Nova Scotia, one can either sail to the west of Newfoundland, through the Strait of Belle Isle or along the Newfoundland east coast. Vessels wishing to reach Labrador or W Greenland, from St John's, Newfoundland could attempt a passage as early as mid April. However, vessels planning to transit the Strait of Belle Isle may find it blocked with ice until late May or early June.

St John's quayside *Máire Wilkes*

West Newfoundland through the Strait of Belle Isle east of Newfoundland

The western route to Labrador is more direct if the Strait of Belle Isle is free of ice. The cruising is, however, more limited and all weather anchorages are few. The coastal scenery is mountainous and two cruising areas are particularly recommended:

- Bay of Islands. A scenic bay entered between towering cliffs forming the inlet to Corner Brook, Newfoundland's second city. Corner Brook has good shops and facilities for refuelling, filling propane, etc. Pleasant anchorages can be found amongst the islands, a short distance from the headlands. The Bay of Islands Yacht Club in Allen's Cove some 6km west of Corner Brook on the south shore of Humber Arm offers great hospitality.
- Gros Morne National Park. A major fjord complex and a UNESCO heritage site offering spectacular scenery and mountain trails around Gros Morne (800+m). At the head of the main fjord, it is possible to weather hurricane force winds in the delta of the main river.

The remainder of the coast has a few good harbours with limited facilities. On the north side of the Strait of Belle Isle is Red Bay which was a major Basque whaling site in the 16th century.

St John's approaches *Máire Wilkes*

East of Newfoundland

The east coast route will avoid any ice in the Strait of Belle Isle. The following cruising options can be considered:

- After crossing the Cabot Strait, cruise eastwards along the spectacular south western coast and its many fjords (inlets) and tiny 'outport' villages. If time permits, the Ramea Islands are worth a detour.
- The French islands of Miquelon (north) and St Pierre (south), have a genuine French culture. Customs formalities have to be observed.
- Passage to St John's for major provisioning and spares with a possible port of call at Trepassey en route. (The passage along the south east and east coasts between Ile St Pierre is exposed and has limited harbours of refuge.)
- Passage via Bonavista, an interesting fishing and trading port with a replica of the *Matthew*, to St Anthony. St Anthony is one of the best natural harbours on the coast and a departure point for Labrador or S Greenland. Not to be missed nearby, is the first known settlement of the Vikings in North America at L'Anse aux Meadows. The provisioning here is somewhat basic and should not be relied upon for a major cruise (use St John's).

Further details of St John's are given in RCCPF *The Atlantic Crossing Guide*. The harbourmaster should be hailed on VHF on arrival and a berth will be allocated. Fuel is delivered by road tanker although the tanker driver may be reluctant to fill jerry cans because of local rules designed to protect the environment. There are good supermarkets and excellent *craic* in the Newfoundland/Irish pubs.

Battle Harbor, in Labrador, is the first major harbour after crossing the Belle Isle Strait. It is a world class historic site comprising an out-island harbour (outport) which serviced the schooners of the Labrador trade. The harbour was established by John Slade from Poole, England in 1775 and became the capital of the Labrador fisheries. Today, it is a heritage site and museum. The communal dining room provides meals and the staff are very friendly. Supplies are limited but it is a memorable and inspiring place; a tribute to the former cod industry which made this area famous.

The Cruising Club of America publishes cruising guides for Newfoundland and Labrador which are a useful addition to the Canadian Hydrographic Services Sailing Directions. Several volumes of CHS Sailing Directions are published which cover the Canadian Atlantic coast.

Environment Canada publishes a useful book called *East Coast Marine Weather Manual*.

Potential harbours where a vessel can be overwintered are:

South West Harbor Maine	Hinckley Yachts	Large undercover storage High capacity lifts All services
Soames Sound, Maine	John Williams Yard Ables Yacht Yard	Smaller yards All services
North East Harbor, Maine	Morris Yachts	Extensive yard and storage possibilities at various locations All services
Chester, Nova Scotia	South Shore Marine	Storage, yard facilities
Baddeck, Nova Scotia	Baddeck Marina Cape Breton Boatyard	Storage, repairs, yard facilities and marina
St John's, Newfoundland	RNYC	Outside storage close to St John's Travelift (50t), Yacht Club
Corner Brook, Newfoundland	Corner Brook Harbor Allen's Cove Marina	Possible storage for yachts up to 35' LOA
Lewisporte, Newfoundland	Lewisporte Marina	Vessels up to 100' LOA. 40t haul-out lift. Repair and maintenance services

Useful websites

	St John's, Newfoundland Local news and information	www.stjohns.ca
	Port of St John's	www.sjpa.com
	Westjet airline	www.westjet.com

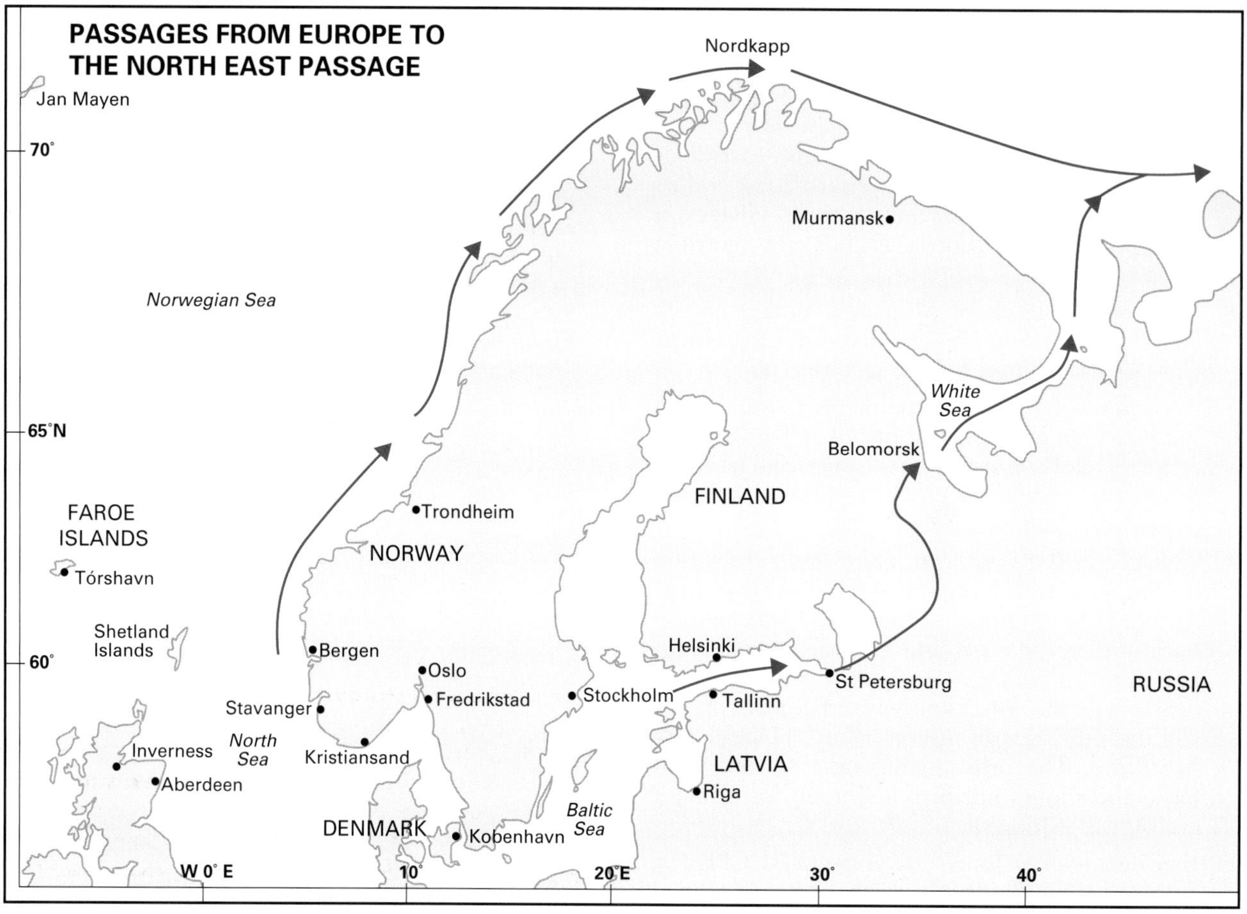

Passages from Europe to the North East Passage

The obvious route from Europe to the North East Passage approaches is to round Nordkapp (North Cape) at the northern extremity of mainland Norway and enter Russian waters off Grense Jakobselv some 80M west of Murmansk. The 1,500M passage from Dover offers spectacular cruising along the Norwegian coast with plenty of opportunities to enter beautiful harbours of refuge if the weather is inclement. The RCCPF Judy Lomax's cruising guide to *Norway* is very informative and covers all aspects of this passage in detail. Note that vessels left unmanned in Norway for more six weeks should obtain prior permission from the Customs authorities, who are normally very helpful, otherwise full import duty may be payable.

An alternative route would be via the Baltic Sea and the Gulf of Finland to St Petersburg. From here, it is possible to navigate north on the Neva River to Lake Ladoga, the Svir River and the White Sea Canal to Belomorsk on the shores of the White Sea. This route was taken by Jarlath Cunnane and the crew of *Northabout* on a 2012 cruise which

Nordkapp *Judy Lomax*

The locks at the northern end of the White Sea Canal
Jarlath Cunnane

circumnavigated Norway by way of Nordkapp, Barents Sea, White Sea, the Russian inland waterways to the Gulf of Finland and the Baltic.

In 2012, the Russian Authorities supposedly dispensed with the need for foreign vessels to carry Russian pilots on their internal waterways. This, however, appears to be open to interpretation and a pilot may be imposed on vessels attempting the transit. The formalities outlined in the North East Passage chapter of this book apply.

Strong currents flow southwards in the Neva and Svir rivers which could be problematic for smaller vessels heading northwards. The route is part of the Volga Inland Waterway network and is a busy shipping route. There are several points of historical interest en route including the 13th-century fortifications at Schlisselburg which are a UNESCO heritage site and, near Lake Onega, the graves of over 9,000 of Stalin's 'enemies of the people.' The White Sea Canal, which was built on Stalin's instigation, is 141 miles long and includes 19 locks and 15 dams. It was built in just 20 months by more than 170,000 gulag prisoners in 1933.

Passages between the Pacific Ocean to and from the North West and North East Passages

United States Coast Pilot 9 gives pilotage directions for the Gulf of Alaska, the Aleutian Islands and the Bering Sea. It can be downloaded, free of charge from the NOAA website.

The Pilot states that the weather over the Bering Sea is generally bad and very changeable. Good weather is the exception and does not last long when it does occur. Wind shifts are both frequent and rapid. The summer season has much fog and considerable rain. There is a slight predominance of winds from the SW however winds can occur from any direction and can be very strong. Seas can be high.

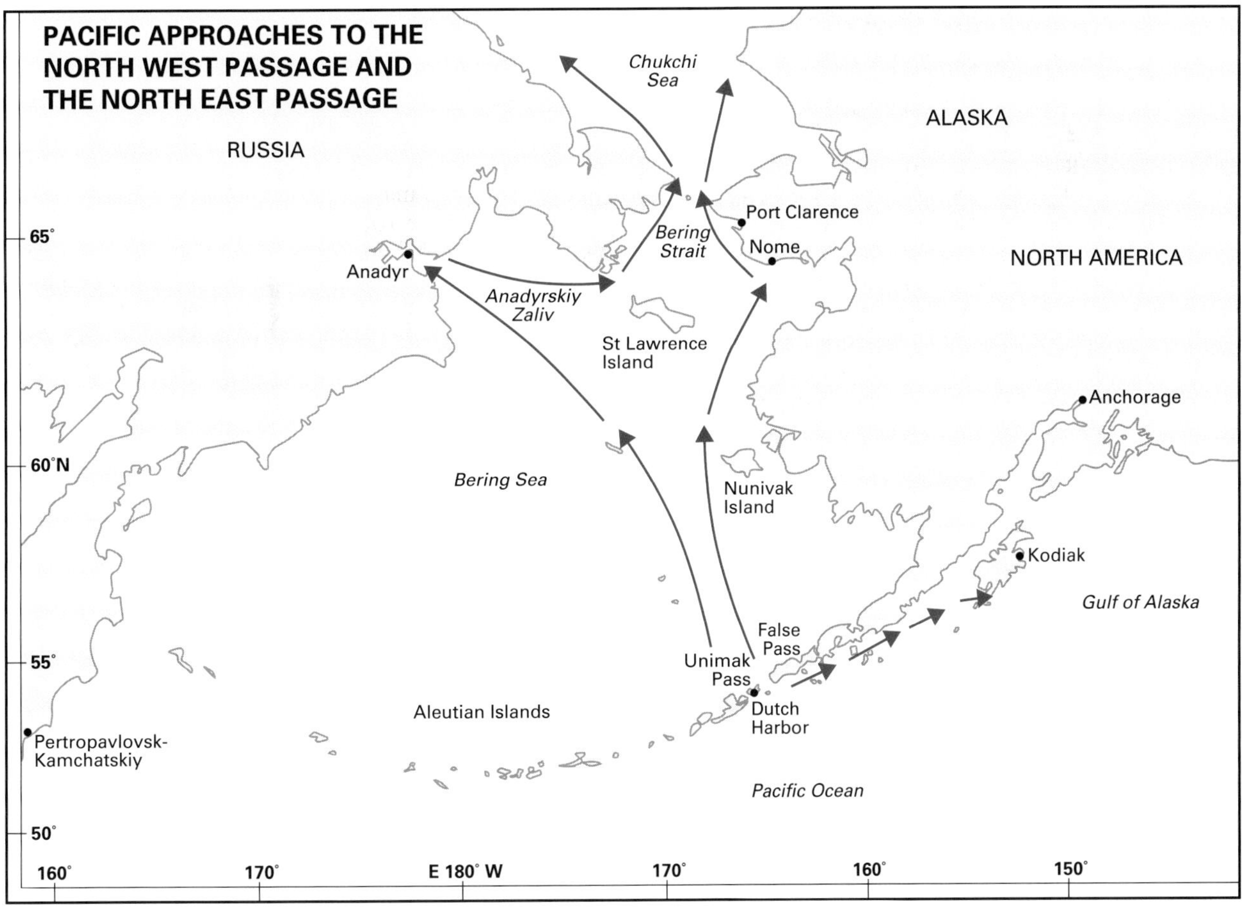

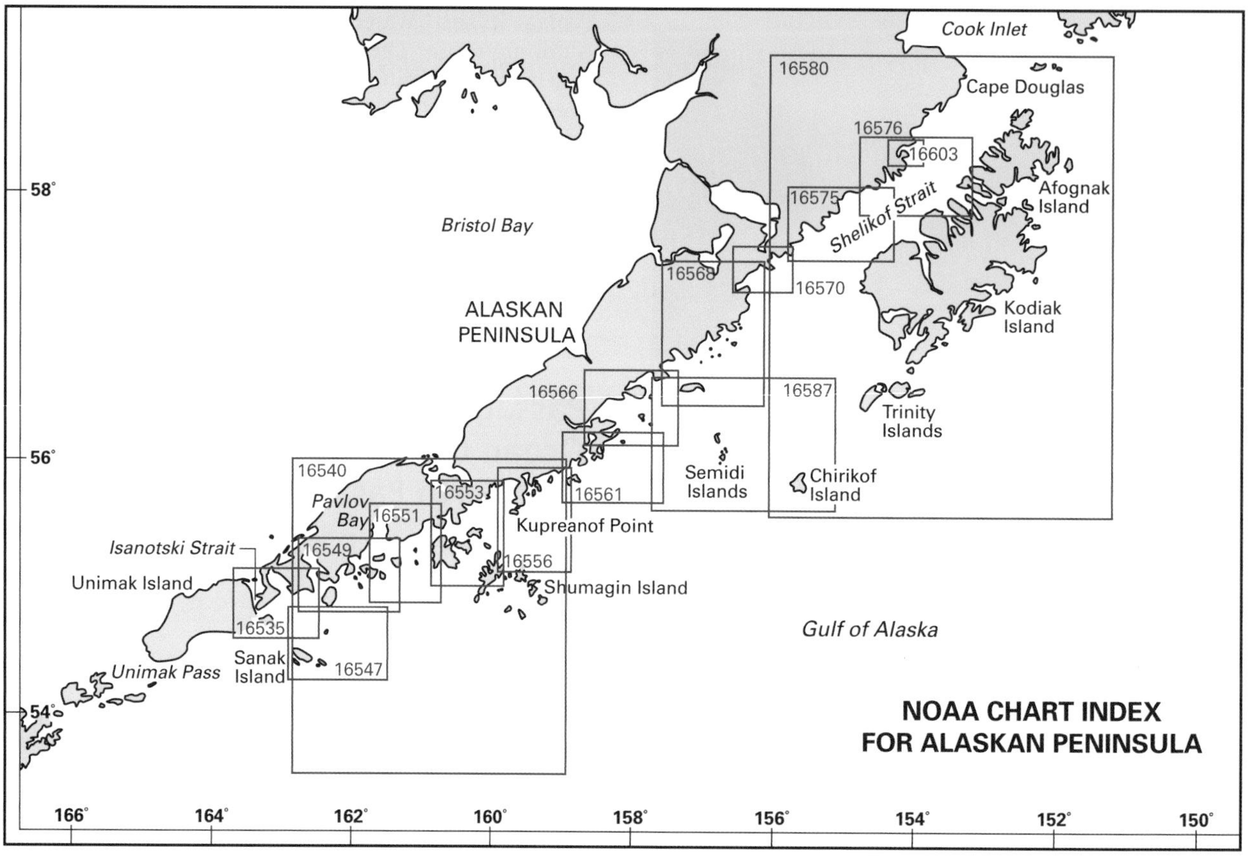
NOAA CHART INDEX
FOR ALASKAN PENINSULA
Cook Inlet
Cape Douglas
Afognak Island
Shelikof Strait
Kodiak Island
Trinity Islands
Chirikof Island
Semidi Islands
Bristol Bay
ALASKAN PENINSULA
Pavlov Bay
Kupreanof Point
Shumagin Island
Isanotski Strait
Unimak Island
Unimak Pass
Sanak Island
Gulf of Alaska
16580
16576
16603
16575
16570
16568
16587
16566
16561
16540
16553
16551
16549
16556
16535
16547
58°
56°
54°
166°
164°
162°
160°
158°
156°
154°
152°
150°

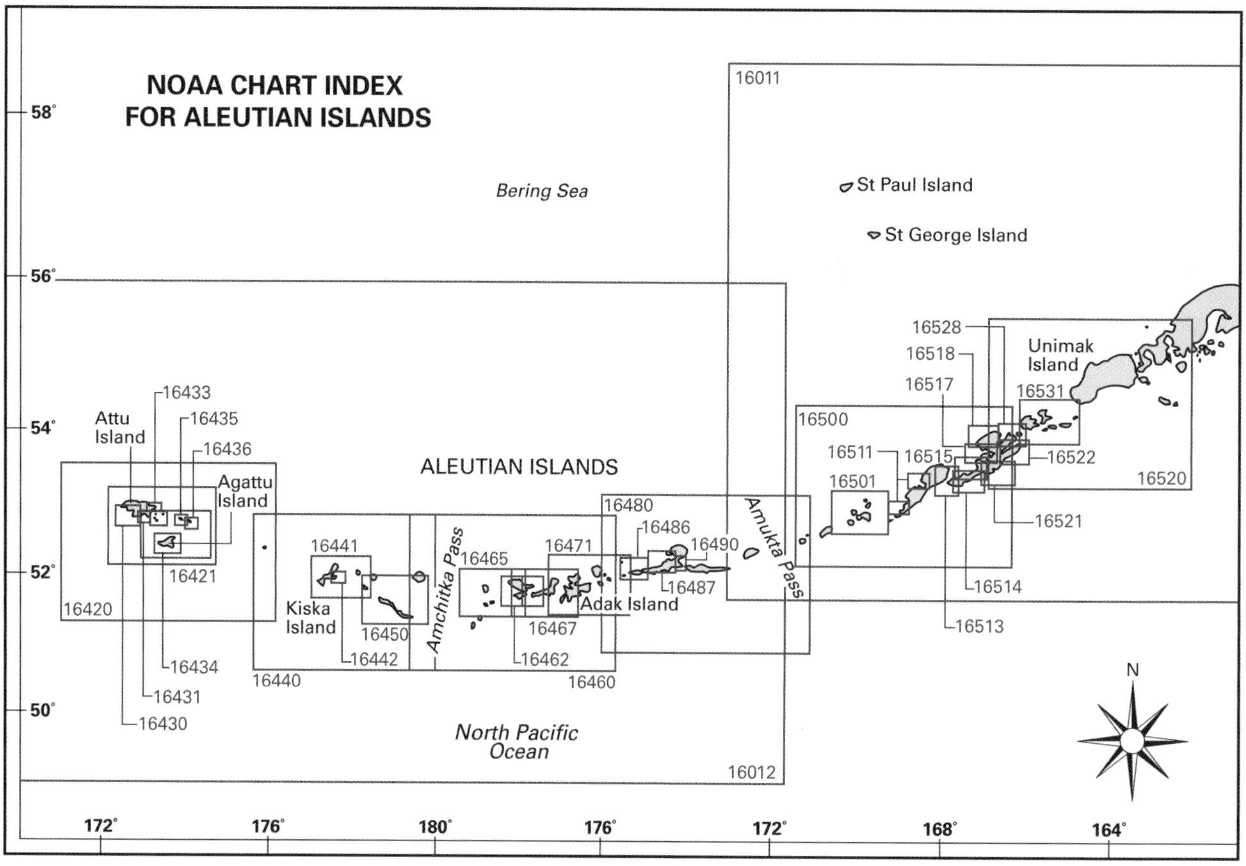
NOAA CHART INDEX
FOR ALEUTIAN ISLANDS
Bering Sea
St Paul Island
St George Island
Unimak Island
ALEUTIAN ISLANDS
Attu Island
Agattu Island
Kiska Island
Amchitka Pass
Adak Island
Amukta Pass
North Pacific Ocean
N
16011
16012
16528
16518
16517
16531
16500
16511
16515
16522
16520
16501
16521
16514
16513
16480
16486
16490
16487
16471
16465
16467
16462
16460
16441
16450
16442
16440
16433
16435
16436
16421
16420
16434
16431
16430
58°
56°
54°
52°
50°
172°
176°
180°
176°
172°
168°
164°

Typical scenery in the Gulf of Alaska *Máire Wilkes*

Many vessels, whether approaching from Alaska in the east or from the Aleutian Islands in the west will want to stop at Dutch Harbor.

Vessels travelling to and from the Bering Sea to southern Alaska will negotiate one of the passes linking the Bering Sea to the Gulf of Alaska. Unimak Pass is commonly used unless vessels are visiting Dutch Harbor when Akutan Pass can be used. They are subject to strong tides and vessels should time their passages accordingly.

The route through False Pass is changeable and is subject to tides of up to 11kns. It should not be attempted without *U.S. Coast Pilot 9*. Transits should be attempted at or near low water slack as the safety factor represented by a rising tide could be necessary.

In the Gulf of Alaska, suitable anchorages can be found, using *U.S. Coast Pilot 9*, to make day passages between the Aleutian Islands and Kodiak Island. Kodiak is one of the USA's largest fishing ports and is a suitable port to lay-up a vessel for the winter.

Vessels approaching the Bering Sea from the west may, in addition to *U.S. Coast Pilot 9*, wish to consult the pilotage notes available on the RCCPF website.

Anadyr, on the northwestern shores of the Bering Sea is a likely Russian port of entry for vessels attempting the North East Passage. It is about 800M from Dutch Harbor.

Vessels voyaging north to attempt the North West Passage may wish to put into Nome which is 700M from Dutch Harbor. A safe anchorage at Barrow, on Alaska's northern shore, cannot be counted upon so Nome could be the last opportunity for crews to buy provisions until they reach Tuktoyaktuk some 1,300M distant.

Dutch Harbor, Unalaska Island

53°54'N 166°30'W

Charts NOAA 16500, NOAA 16520, NOAA 16528, large scale chart NOAA 16528, NOAA 16529 and NOAA 16530

This is the centre of commercial activity in the Aleutian Islands and the only designated port of entry. Although referred to by one and all as 'Dutch Harbor', smaller vessels moor at Iliuliuk Harbor. If approaching from the east then this is the last place to stock up on fresh provisions. It is the commercial fishing capital of the region and regularly the largest US fishing port by weight of catch landed. The nearby town of Unalaska, joined by bridge to Amaknak Is (on which Dutch Harbor is situated) is more like a village elsewhere, with buildings dating back to the time before the US military first began to develop Amaknak Is. Unalaska, to the west of Iliuliuk Harbor, has an excellent library with internet and Wi-Fi access. There several interesting walks, including to the old battlements directly above the small boat harbour.

Approach

There are no off-lying dangers. The entrance is wide and is marked with maintained navigational buoys.

Berthing

There is alongside berthing for smaller vessels in Iliuliuk Harbor but space is at a premium and visiting yachts will probably tie up alongside a fishing vessel in the harbour. There are no facilities in Dutch Harbor for a small vessel to moor other than to take on board fuel. The harbourmaster is available on Ch 16.

Facilities

Alaska Airlines have frequent flights to Anchorage with onward connections to major airports. Repairs are available for electrical, electronic, mechanical and all aspects of commercial boating. Fuel, oil and propane are all available. There are two well stocked supermarkets.

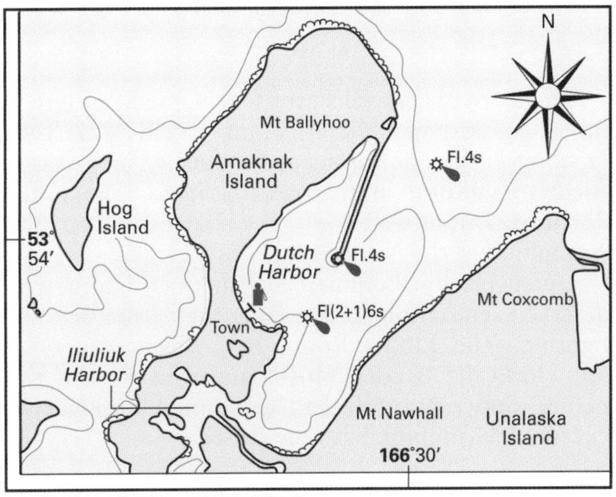

DUTCH HARBOR, UNALASKA

Dutch Harbor. Iliuliuk Harbor is in the foreground *Rodger and Ali Grayson*

Dutch Harbor & Unalaska *Sibéal Turraoin*

There are two excellent museums, the Museum of the Aleutians and the Aleutian World War Two Historic Park. The former has extensive displays of Aleutian cultural and artistic heritage. The latter documents the war with the Japanese and the evacuation of the Aleut people.

Dutch Harbor commercial fishermen had a well deserved reputation for enjoying their drinking and fighting. The Elbow Room bar, which was once known as the 'second most dangerous bar on the planet' and reportedly had an annual turnover in excess of $1 million, has now closed.

Kodiak Harbor, Kodiak Island

57°46'N 152°26'W

Charts NOAA 16580, NOAA 16595

Kodiak is the biggest town in the area and is home to a large fishing fleet. It is an excellent harbour in which to over-winter, whether or not the crew remain onboard, particularly if one is able to secure a berth in the town boat harbour. It is advisable to contact the harbourmaster, who is very helpful, some weeks in advance in order to secure a berth.

The boat harbour next to the town is very convenient for all facilities and supplies which are just a short walk away. The newer harbour, at St Herman Bay on Near Island, is further from town.

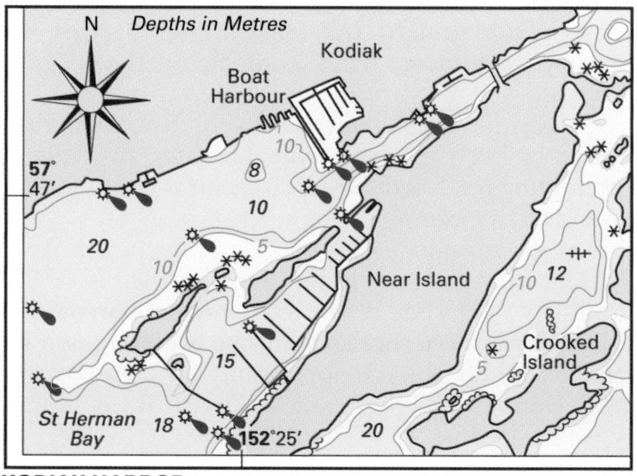

KODIAK HARBOR

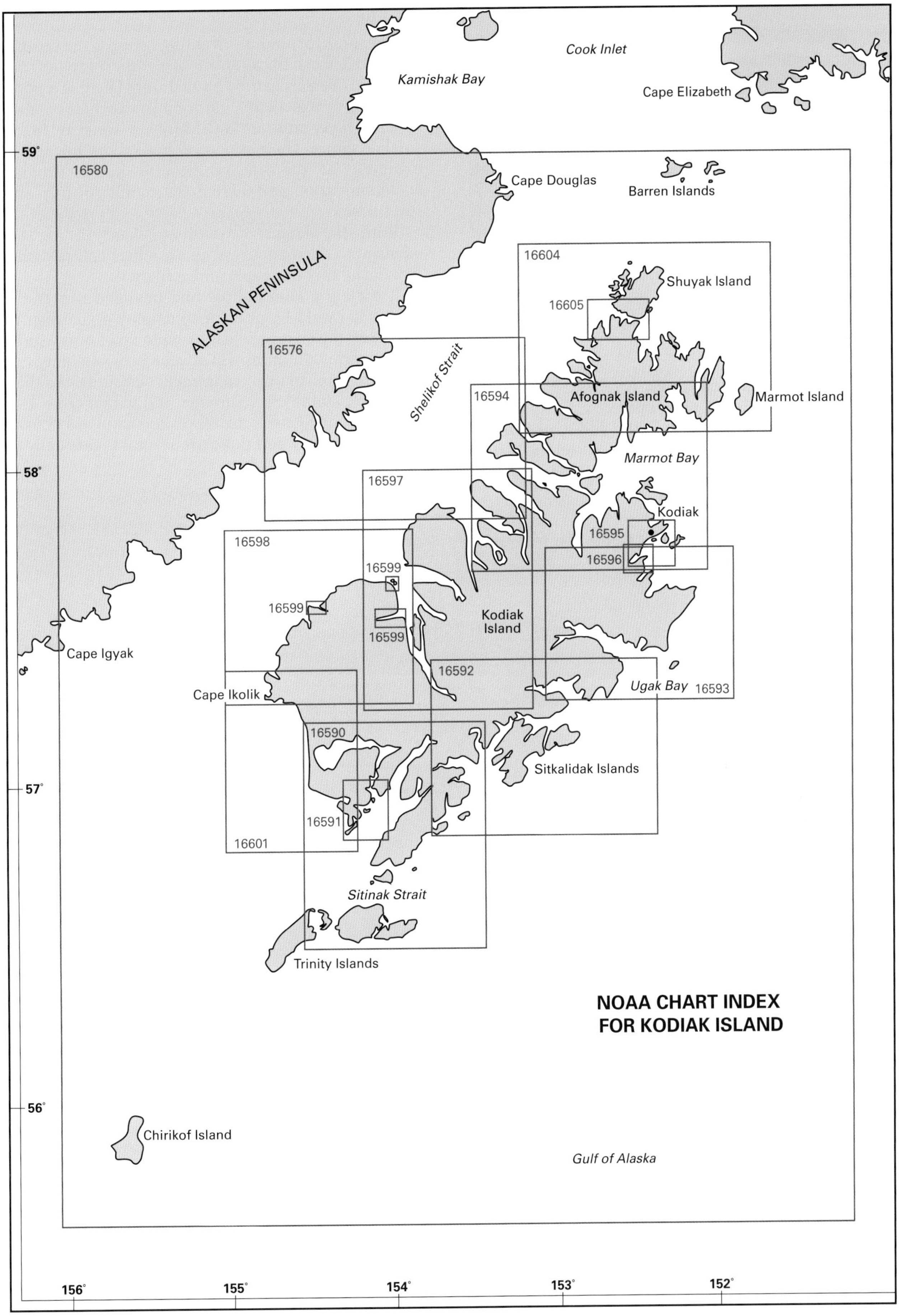
Cook Inlet
Kamishak Bay
Cape Elizabeth
59°
16580
Cape Douglas
Barren Islands
16604
ALASKAN PENINSULA
Shuyak Island
16605
16576
Shelikof Strait
16594
Afognak Island
Marmot Island
Marmot Bay
58°
16597
Kodiak
16595
16598
16596
16599
16599
Kodiak Island
16599
Cape Igyak
16592
Ugak Bay
16593
Cape Ikolik
16590
Sitkalidak Islands
57°
16591
16601
Sitinak Strait
Trinity Islands
NOAA CHART INDEX FOR KODIAK ISLAND
56°
Chirikof Island
Gulf of Alaska
156°
155°
154°
153°
152°

5. ARCTIC APPROACHES

Kodiak as seen from the northeast. The town boat harbour is on the left and St Herman Bay on the right
Roger and Ali Grayson

Approach

There are several obstructions. *US Coast Pilot No.9* and the chart should be studied carefully. The harbourmaster maintains a 24hr radio watch on VHF Ch 16 and vessels should report to him before arrival.

Facilities

Diesel and propane. Welding shops, electronic repairers, mechanics and most other repairs are available. Vessels can be hauled out. There is a good chandler. Excellent shopping includes two supermarkets and a Wal-Mart as well as many smaller shops. There is a good bookshop. Internet is available at the library. Several hotels provide accommodation and there are a number of bars and restaurants.

With the largest Coastguard base in the US adjacent to the main town, this is a lively place with a wonderful mix of people and activities.

If leaving a vessel afloat and unattended over the winter, it would be prudent to employ a guardian to look after the boat regularly. A build up of heavy snow over the winter months will affect a boat's stability.

There are many anchorages close to Kodiak which are suitable for summer and winter trips. It is relatively inexpensive to travel to mainland Alaska on the state ferry and there are several flights daily to Anchorage.

Kodiak Harbor as seen from above St Herman Bay on Near Island *Roger and Ali Grayson*

Useful websites – North East and North West Passage Approaches		
	Canadian Hydrographic Service Atlantic Coast Sailing Directions	www.charts.gc.ca/publications/sd-in/atlanti-eng.asp
	NOAA US Coast Agency	www.nauticalcharts.noaa.gov/nsd/cpdownload.htm
	RCCPF Cruising notes for the Aleutian Islands	www.rccpf.org.uk/publications/264-aleutians-and-alaska
	City of Kodiak Kodiak Harbour Port Information	www.city.kodiak.ak.us Navigate to 'Shipyard'

6. The North West Passage

Contents

Introduction

The North West Passage is the sea route, north of North America, which connects the Atlantic and Pacific Oceans. Professor Robert Headland of the Scott Polar Institute, defines the North West Passage as: 'to or from the Atlantic Ocean (Labrador Sea) in or out of the eastern approaches to the Canadian Arctic archipelago (Lancaster Sound or Foxe Basin) then the western approaches (M'Clure Strait or Amundsen Gulf), across the Beaufort Sea and Chukchi Sea of the Arctic Ocean, from or to the Pacific Ocean (Bering Sea). The Arctic Circle is crossed near the beginning and the end of all transits.'

For most of the time, the North West Passage is blocked by ice and is only navigable for a few weeks, or not at all, each year. Recently there has been much speculation about climate change opening the North West Passage to navigation. However in the spring of 2013, only 134 vessels had transited the complete passage since Amundsen's first transit in 1906. More books have been written about the subject than the number of vessels which have actually transited the passage.

The information in this chapter refers to the central part of the North West Passage between Baffin Bay in the east and Nome, just south of the Bering Strait in the west. An east to west transit is assumed unless otherwise stated. Information about Greenland, Baffin Bay and the seas south of the Bering Straits is given elsewhere in this book.

Most vessels on an east to west transit will touch on the Greenland coast before heading west to the Canadian Arctic. The westerly bound vessel will then sail from Canadian waters into Alaskan waters. Thus, in addition to Greenland, the pilotage, weather forecasts, customs, etc of both Canada and the USA need to be considered. Information about Greenland can be found in Chapter 4. Information about Canada and the USA is given in separate sections within this chapter.

The history of the North West Passage

The North West Passage has a fascinating history which, in many respects, is being added to every year.

The existence of a passage north of North America had been speculated about since the Middle Ages. However it was first seriously considered as a shipping route in the late 15th century when, in 1493, Pope Alexander VI divided much of the world between Spain and Portugal. The division prevented other European trading nations from getting access to the lucrative trading markets in Asia.

In 1497, Henry VII dispatched John Cabot to search for a direct route from the Atlantic to the Pacific oceans and the name the 'North West Passage' was coined by the English. Cabot found the entrance to the St Lawrence via the Cabot Strait that now bears his name. Several subsequent British expeditions explored many of the rivers and straits from the Hudson River northwards. Martin Frobisher reached the southern end of Baffin Island in the mid 16th century.

Although most North West Passage expeditions were westbound from the Atlantic, some expeditions explored from the Pacific. The Russian Great Northern Expeditions in the mid 18th century discovered several of the Aleutian Islands. The Spanish made many voyages northwards up the west coast of North America, searching for a passage as they went. In 1777 Captain James Cook searched north from Nootka Sound as far as 70°N.

Early in the 19th century, significant progress was made by several expeditions, both by ship and over land. These expeditions were led by men such as

70°N
75°N
80°N
85°N
65°N
60°N
55°N
50°N
170° W
160° W
150° W
140° W
130° W
120°W
110°W
100°W
Chukchi Sea
Bering Strait
Point Hope
Cape Prince of Wales
Nome
Barrow
Prudhoe Bay
ALASKA
Beaufort Sea
Demarcation Point
Herschel Island
Tuktoyaktuk
M'Clure Strait
Banks Island
Queen Elizabeth Islands
Parry Islands
Melville Island
Parry Channel
Resolute
Viscount Melville Sound
Amundsen Gulf
NORTHWEST TERRITORIES
Mackenzie River
Victoria Island
Prince of Wales Island
M'Clintock Channel
Larsen Sound
Dolphin & Union Strait
Dease Strait
Cambridge Bay
Victoria Strait
King William Island
Coronation Gulf
Queen Maud Gulf
Simpson Strait
Gulf of Alaska
PACIFIC OCEAN
NUNAVUT
CANADA
THE NORTHWEST PASSAGE

85°N
80°N
75°N
70°N
65°N
10° W
20° W
30° W
40° W
50° W
60°N
55°N
50°N
GREENLAND
ICELAND
Ellesmere Island
s Sound
n Island
Navy Board Inlet
Lancaster Sound
Bylot Island
Pond Inlet
Admiralty Inlet
Baffin Bay
Baffin Island
Fury & Hecla Strait
f of thia
Foxe Basin
Davis Strait
Kap Farvel
Hudson Strait
ATLANTIC OCEAN
Hudson Bay
LABRADOR
55°N
80°W
70°W
60°W

John Ross, William Parry, James Ross, John Franklin, George Back, Peter Dease, Thomas Simpson, Frederick Beechey, Francis McClintock, Robert McClure and John Rae – names which are remembered forever on the charts of the area.

The most famous failure to find a route through was the 1845 expedition led by John Franklin. The two expedition ships, HMS *Terror* and HMS *Erebus*, tragically failed to return. However, the subsequent relief expeditions and search parties resulted in a thorough charting of the region which paved the way for the eventually successful discovery of a route.

One of the Franklin search parties was led by Robert McClure who sailed east from the Pacific on the HMS *Investigator*. This expedition reached Banks Island in 1851 where they were trapped for three winters at the western end of Viscount Melville Sound. They discovered the M'Clure Strait between Banks Island and Melville Island, but the route was permanently ice bound and navigable only by sledge. McClure and his expedition were eventually rescued in 1854 by a search party from HMS *Resolute* who had travelled by sledge over the ice from a ship of Edward Belcher's expedition at the eastern end of Viscount Melville Sound. McClure was celebrated as the discoverer of the North West Passage.

A more properly navigable route between Lancaster Sound and Dolphin and Union Strait was discovered by Orcadian John Rae in 1854. Rae, an employee of the Hudson Bay Company, travelled overland with dog sleds using native techniques. He recorded stories from the Inuit about the fate of Franklin's expedition, including the possibility that some of the crew had resorted to cannibalism. This news was too shocking to be accepted at the time, John Rae was rejected by London society and, during his lifetime, his many discoveries were not given the recognition they deserved.

In 1903, the Norwegian explorer Roald Amundsen approached the North West Passage from the Atlantic side on the converted 47-ton herring boat *Gjøa*. He spent three winters trapped in ice, two in Gjøa Haven, along a route via the Rae Strait. He succeeded in completing the first transit of the North West Passage by water.

Amundsen's vessel, *Gjøa*, in the Norwegian Maritime Museum, Oslo

A picture of Henry Larsen's *St Roch* on the side of a building in Cambridge Bay. The vessel can be seen in the Vancouver Maritime Museum *Sibéal Turraoin*

In 1940, the *St Roch*, a Royal Canadian Mounted Police 'ice-fortified' schooner, captained by Henry Larsen, was the second vessel to transit the passage and the first to transit from west to east. The *St Roch* sailed from Vancouver on the Pacific side to Halifax on the Atlantic and overwintered on the Boothia Peninsula. In 1944, Larsen took only 86 days to return in one season over a more northerly, partially uncharted route.

Subsequent passages have attempted to find a commercially viable formula, but it has only been in the past few years, with the significant recession of the sea ice, that the commercial viability of the route is being taken seriously.

In 1969 the SS *Manhattan*, a U.S. owned 110,000-ton ice strengthened oil tanker, sailed from the Atlantic to Prudhoe Bay in Alaska and returned with a symbolic cargo of one barrel of crude oil. She was escorted by Canadian and U.S. icebreakers and at one point failed to negotiate heavy ice in M'Clure Strait. The transit was controversial as the Canadians believed that the passage went through 'Canadian internal waters' which was disputed by the USA. A dispute which remains unsettled.

In the first seventy years since Amundsen's initial transit in 1906 to 1976 only 14 vessels successfully transited the North West Passage. All of these vessels were coastguard ice breakers, research vessels or vessels escorted by the icebreakers. In 1977, Dutchman, Willy de Roos transited the passage in his 13m steel sloop, *Williwaw*. His transit was the first since Amundsen's to be completed in a sailing vessel and, from Gjoa Haven to the Pacific, he sailed single handedly. A large part of his success was due to meticulous passage planning using records of the few transits made at that time. Canadian, Réal Bouvier, started the transit the year before de Roos but completed it two years after him having wintered in Greenland, Resolute and Tuktoyaktuk.

The first single handed transit was completed by the Japanese sailor Kenichi Horie in 1982. He took three years having wintered in Resolute and Tuktoyaktuk. His yacht, *Mermaid*, was also the first GRP vessel to transit the North West Passage.

American John Bockstoce's 18m yacht, *Belvedere*, became the first eastbound yacht to complete the transit in 1988 and spent five years on the journey.

In 1986, Englishman, David Scott Cowper attempted the second single-handed transit. He sailed in a converted lifeboat, the *Mabel E. Holland*, which he had strengthened considerably. On leaving Resolute, he was beset in ice for 24 hours but managed, by dint of keeping in shallow water close to the shore, to navigate to Fort Ross, an abandoned staging post to the east of Bellot Strait. It was a particularly bad ice year and Cowper planned to follow the *World Discoverer* which had ice breaker assistance. However, he was advised by the Canadian Coastguard that his vessel would be 'crushed within seconds' if he continued. Cowper secured the *Mabel E. Holland* with shorelines and anchors before working his passage back to England at the end of the summer on a merchant ship. He returned the following spring to find that his boat had sunk and spent the rest of that Arctic summer salvaging her and making repairs before dragging her ashore above the high water mark. In 1988, he returned to carry out more repairs and made a passage to Inuvik on the Mackenzie River where the *Mabel E. Holland* was wintered once again. After further repairs in 1989, he continued his voyage by again staying in shallow waters off the Alaskan coast to avoid the more concentrated offshore ice, and thus completed the 38th transit of the North West Passage.

By the end of the 20th century, 75 transits of the North West Passage had been completed. This number had doubled by 2011, many of the passages being completed in small vessels. In 2007, Sébastien Roubinet completed the passage without an engine on *Babouche*, a 7·5m (25ft) ice catamaran designed to sail on water and slide over ice. In 2010, Frenchman, Mathieu Bonnier made a brave attempt to row single-handed from Greenland westwards through the central part of the passage but had to give up after being threatened once too often by polar bears.

The first ice-strengthened passenger ships, the *Frontier Spirit* and *Kapitan Khlebnikov* transited the passage in 1992. An ice-strengthened ship has carried passengers through the North West Passage every year since then.

The original objective in seeking the North West Passage in 1497 was to seek an alternative commercial route from the Atlantic to the Pacific Oceans. This was partially achieved in 2012 by the 53,000 DWT tanker, *Gotland Carolina* which was designed for operating in the ice. She took a cargo from the Pacific Ocean, which was discharged in Tuktoyaktuk and continued in ballast to Baffin Bay and the Atlantic Ocean. Her transit maybe the first of many by cargo ships.

People and culture

The shores of the North West Passage were first populated by nomadic Inuit peoples gradually moving from Siberia eastwards to what is now northern Canada and Greenland. This migration occurred in the last ice age and the people were known as Yup'ik Inuit, Alutiq and Athapaskans. They had extensive trade and cultural networks from Greenland to Siberia and southwards as far afield as Korea, Japan and China.

Inuit women accompanying a traditional dance in Gjoa Haven *Sibéal Turraoin*

A young Inuit boy *Máire Wilkes*

Traditional dance *Sibéal Turraoin*

'Eskimo' or 'Inuit'

The word 'Eskimo' means 'eaters of raw meat' and, although it is widely used outside of the Arctic, most indigenous people in Greenland and Canada prefer the term 'Inuit' which in their own language, Inkitut, means 'the people.' Calling somebody an 'Eskimo' can considered to be offensive in these areas.

The word 'Eskimo' is, however, widely accepted in Alaska although the Alaskan Government uses the term 'Alaskan natives.'

The Alaskan Inuit

The period between 6000 and 4000BC is known as the Northern Archaic period which developed into the 'Arctic Small Tool Tradition' period between 3000 and 2000BC where hunters used a variety of hunting implements made from bone and stone to hunt for caribou and other land based mammals. From 2000BC a maritime culture, known as the Norton Culture, prevailed which focused on the hunting of sea mammals. One of the oldest archaeological sites is at Ipiutak near Cape Hope where the Chukchi Sea meets the Bering Strait. The Ipiutak site comprises more than 600 dwellings and dates from 2000BC.

The Birnirk people co-existed with the Ipiutak for some time before eventually replacing them as the dominant culture in Alaska. Their existence depended on hunting caribou, fish and sea mammals but declining caribou numbers forced them to become more dependent upon the sea. They developed into skilled hunters of both fish and sea mammals including the bowhead whale.

The indigenous peoples now living on the northern coast of Alaska are the Inupiat Inuit. Until the mid-20th century, they specialised in hunting bowhead whales, walrus, seals and polar bears. The most successful hunters were highly acclaimed and both the hunters and their wives were much esteemed.

Further to the south, the Yup'ik Inuit of southwest Alaska focused on hunting land and inshore based animals such as caribou and seals. The Yup'ik are still admired for their traditional ceremonies involving wooden and sealskin masks depicting animal spirits and mythical figures.

In 1741, the Danish explorer, Vitus Bering, 'discovered' Alaska and the exploitation of Alaska's natural resources began. Both the Russians and British traded extensively for seal, otter and land based mammal furs until, by the end of the 19th century, many species were almost extinct. Similarly, American whalers hunted the bowhead whale from the mid 19th century until they became almost extinct. In the 1880s gold was discovered in southern Alaska which prompted an estimated 100,000 prospectors to join the 1896 Klondike Gold Rush. In 1899, gold was discovered at Nome and many prospectors migrated to that area. In the late 20th century, extensive oil reserves were discovered on the Alaskan North Slope.

Contact with whalers, traders, missionaries, miners, oilmen and government administrators forced Yup'ik and Ipiutak Inuit to the fringes of mainstream American culture and their traditional culture has been under threat. To some extent, this has been recognised. In 1966 the Alaskan Federation of Natives (AFN) was formed to represent native Alaskans, including the Inupiat and Yup'ik Inuit. The AFN lobbying of US federal government resulted in the Alaskan Native Lands Settlement Act in 1971 which included a $962 million compensation claim.

Residents of Cambridge Bay *Sibéal Turraoin*

The Canadian Inuit

The Inuit near the Mackenzie River (Tuktoyaktuk) prefer to be known as 'Inuvialuit' whereas else where in the Canadian north people are known simply as 'Inuit.' These people first settled from the west in a continuation of the migration to settle the Alaskan coast.

From 1670 until the early 20th century, economic activity in the area was dominated by the Hudson Bay Company and the fur trade. As in Alaska, the influence of this trade altered the traditional spiritual relationship the Inuit had with the animals they hunted. Western culture, materialism, religion, diseases and alcohol altered their lives for ever. In the mid-20th century, the southern Canadians became aware of the vast mineral and oil wealth in the north and started to exploit it. This provided, and still provides, employment for some Inuit but at the expense of the old hunting culture. In the 1950s the Canadian government believed they would help the Inuit by encouraging them to move to bigger settlements where health and education facilities were available. There was some Inuit resistance to these 'life-style improvements' and the 'taking' of Inuit land. In 1969 the Committee of Original Peoples' Entitlement (COPE) was formed which resulted in agreements for land settlements, financial compensation and mineral rights in the 1970s. In 1992 the Canadian government and the Tungavik Federation signed an agreement which led to the creation of Nunavut in 1999. Nunavut comprises 200,000,000 hectares and covers most of the eastern Canadian Arctic. The population is 80% Inuit and the government is Inuit led. The agreement does not cover the Northwest Territories which lies between Nunavut and Alaska.

The Nunavut flag depicts an Inuksuk - an ancient Inuit stone landmark, cairn or navigation mark

Community and beliefs

Kinship and hunting lie at the core of Inuit community life. In Inuit culture, one's close kin is not necessarily biologically related. For example, two men who hunt together form a close bond and might regard each other as 'kin.' One's kin may include direct family members or may not. 'Kinship' bonds can be closer than family ties.

The Inuit believe that both people and animals have souls. In fact, people have three souls: the personal soul, the free soul and the name soul.

When someone dies, their personal soul might go to the underworld where there they will meet their departed family and kin and the hunting is always good. An unlucky personal soul will travel to the upper world which is cold and the people are starving.

The free soul can leave the body at will, particularly when sleeping. If it wonders too far from it's body, it can become lost and the services of a Shaman, or holy man, may be required to reunite body and free soul.

The name soul determines a person's spirit, physical strength and wellness. When someone dies, the name soul departs the body but returns to another body when a newborn child is named. The qualities associated with the name soul are transferred from generation to generation.

The Shaman is the Inuit holy man. He will have prepared for his calling by spending a long and solitary initiation in the wilderness, much like hermits or some prophets in other religions do. The Shaman has the power to enter the spirit world and communicate with the souls of people and animals. The souls of animals will guide a Shaman through the spirit world on his quest to negotiate with animal spirit guardians for good hunting.

Animals have spirit guardians who will only let their charges be released for human consumption if they are treated with respect. Successful hunting is dependent upon a hunter showing this respect by killing the animal properly and there may be ceremonies to ask the animal's spirit for forgiveness as well as returning its soul to the spirit world.

If an animal is killed without following the proper rituals, the hunter risks offending the spirits which could bring about misfortune, illness, poor hunting and bad weather.

> Sedna, an Inuit girl, refused to marry the man her family had selected so they made her marry a dog. She escaped from her dog husband and married a petrel which had the power to transform itself into a handsome man. Sedna's family rescued her from the petrel but, whilst escaping in a small boat, the jilted petrel discovered his loss and, in his anger, caused a mighty storm to threaten the boat. To save themselves, Sedna's family threw the girl overboard. When she tried to cling on to the boat, her father cut off her fingers one by one. As the dismembered fingers were thrown into the water, they became seals, walruses, whales and narwhales. Sedna sank to the bottom of the sea and became the guardian of the beasts which were once her fingers.

> Inuit tradition says that the aurora borealis, or Northern Lights, are the souls of the dead lighting torches and dancing to guide recently departed souls to the heavens. Another belief is that the aurora are departed souls feasting and playing ball with a walrus skull.

Hunting

When an animal is killed, every part of the body is used. The flesh is eaten, fat and oil is used for fuel, bones are used for tools and utensils, sinews are used for boat or sledge bindings. There is a tradition, which is still followed today, of sharing a catch amongst the community.

Young boys are trained to hunt by their fathers. A boy's first kill is celebrated throughout the community and is an important rite of passage. The kill will often be shared with family and kin in a first-catch celebration.

Today, many Inuit live in wooden houses in settlements. In the summer though, they will gather their family and kin to go hunting. The group may go by boat to a summer camp where they will live in tents, hunting and fishing for weeks or months at a time. Rifles are used extensively and the hunters are superb shots. Modern boats have outboard engines. A hunter will hit a seal's head with a rifle bullet aimed from a small boat several hundred metres away. If necessary, the seal will be finished off with a club – it is cheaper than a second bullet!

In recent years, non-native hunters have visited the Arctic to hunt for sport. A story is told in Pond Inlet about several groups of tourist hunters being dissatisfied with their hunting holidays. They were all wealthy older men who were used to being well looked after by professional hunters and guides. The problem was that local Inuit custom demanded that the hunt be led by the oldest man present. The young Inuit guides were baffled by their guests' ineptitude!

Whaling

The bowhead whale was hunted by the Inuit throughout the North West Passage shores for many hundreds of years. However, commercial whaling by north Americans, Europeans and Asians in the

Preparing for the bowhead whale hunt, Pond Inlet
Maire Wilkes

Granting of a licence to hunt for a bowhead whale, Pond Inlet 2010 *Sibéal Turraoin*

nineteenth and twentieth centuries decimated whale populations. The bowhead whale is part of the Right Whale family (*Balaenidae*). It was 'right' because it yielded good quantities of oil, blubber, meat and baleen (used, amongst other purposes, for ladies' corsets). Also, the dead whale floated which enabled it to be retrieved relatively easily. Commercial hunting for bowhead whales has been banned since 1966 and the number of bowhead whales harvested by subsistence hunters is tightly controlled. In 2010, the community of Pond Inlet in the north of Baffin Island, were granted a licence to hunt for a bowhead whale. The licence was granted at a formal ceremony attended by most of the Pond Inlet population. Spaces on the hunting party were much sought after and the leader of the party was very much respected for his role. The ceremony was followed by a great party. The hunt lasted for several days and resulted in the harvesting of a 42ft long whale. It was one of three bowhead whales allowed to be caught that year in Nunavut.

Inuit life today

In both Canada and Alaska, government policy has been to resettle Inuit in settlements. Although hunting is still very important, the settlements have supermarkets which are stocked with the worst of north american convenience foods. The settlements have schools, police forces and administration centres which provide a certain amount of employment. Tourism is a growing industry. Further employment is provided by defense bases as well as mineral exploration and extraction support services.

Nunavut has the lowest population density in Canada but one of the highest population growth rates. Many Inuit young people leave their native lands for better economic opportunities elsewhere.

Sled dogs are still a common sight throughout the settlements of the Arctic, although their numbers are diminishing due to the widespread use of the skidoo. Visitors should be aware that they are working dogs, not pets, and should not be approached except under the guidance of their handlers. They are a

The stained glass window depicting Arctic life in the Immaculate Heart of Mary Church, Gjoa Havn *Sibéal Turraoin*

Sled dog pup *Sibéal Turraoin*

A chained sledge dog in Gjøa Haven *Sibéal Turrain*

Arctic char drying in Cambridge Bay *Sibéal Turraoin*

Traditional drum dancing at Gjøa Haven
Sibéal Turraoin

particular danger to small children. They are usually kept chained up. In some settlements it is the practice to shoot any dog found on the loose.

Alcoholism is a serious problem in many Arctic communities. In some settlements, the communities have decided to ban alcohol altogether (a 'dry' settlement), in others, alcohol can be imported for personal use but may not be bought or sold (a 'damp' settlement). Visiting yachtsmen are requested to respect these decisions and not use alcohol for gifts or barter. Alcohol should not be taken ashore.

The North West Passage economy

Fur trading, whaling and gold prospecting have been important resources which have been exploited in both the Canadian and Alaskan Arctic. Today, the most valuable commodity is oil.

Prudhoe Bay on Alaska's north slope is the U.S.'s highest yielding oil field producing 400,000 barrels of oil a day. Since 1982, people living in Alaska pay no income tax but receive a 'Permanent Fund Dividend' of between $1,000 and $3,500 per annum. This is financed by oil income from Prudhoe Bay. The biggest non-petroleum Alaskan export is seafood which is mainly caught in the Bering Sea areas.

The Canadian Arctic economy is much smaller than the Alaskan economy. It includes fishing, hunting and tourism. Most of the Canadian oil and mineral activities are further south.

Environmental politics

Many people in Europe and North America are concerned about the environment and a sustainable use of the earth's resources. Organisations such as Greenpeace are vocal about their animal welfare views. The Inuit also feel very strongly about the environment but they are not at one accord with Greenpeace. Commercial fishermen and oilmen have their own views as do scientists working in the area. There is sometimes the opportunity for a lively debate in the few Arctic hotels where these people occasionally meet.

The Inuit believe the threat from air and water borne industrial pollutants in the Arctic is much greater than the subsistence hunting practiced there. In 1977, following the increased oil extraction in Alaska, the Inuit Circumpolar Conference (ICC) was formed. The ICC represents all native people in the Arctic and challenges the policies of governments, multinational companies and environmental movements. It believes that the Arctic environment is best managed by those with local knowledge and should take into account Inuit cultural values. It has NGO status with the United Nations and is a highly respected organisation.

Politics and boundary disputes

The opening up of Arctic seas is having a profound effect on the peoples and politics of the region.

The melting sea ice and potential opening up of new shipping routes has led to disagreements over control of Arctic waters. The Canadian government considers the North Western Passage to be part of Canadian internal waters. However other countries maintain that they are an international strait or transit passage. Under such a regime, Canada would have the right to enact a number of maritime regulations but would not have the right to close the passage. In 2013, Canada was considering increasing its naval presence in the Arctic by commissioning a fleet of patrol vessels.

In north Greenland, Canada and Alaska there is a chain of Defence Early Warning (DEW) stations. These are owned and operated partly by the USA and partly by the host countries. They are designed to warn of missile attacks on North America, but they also mark a presence in the area. Many of the early installations from the 1960s have been abandoned. Others have been brought up to date and are operational.

Under International Law, no country currently owns the North Pole or the Arctic Ocean

The DEW (Defence Early Warning) station at Tuktoyaktuk
Sibéal Turraoin

surrounding it. The five surrounding Arctic states, Russia, the United States (via Alaska), Canada, Norway and Denmark (via Greenland), are limited to an exclusive economic zone (EEZ) of 200M adjacent to their coasts. All five Arctic states have lodged claims that they have exclusive right to certain portions of the Arctic seabed beyond the 200 mile zone and all the way to the North Pole. There is a wealth of minerals and fossil fuels to be fought over and, as the ice recedes, the race is on to exploit these resources. The rights to oil and gas, gold and uranium are fiercely disputed as is the protection of the fragile Arctic environment. Fishing quotas and hunting rights are a part of this discussion and are another emotive topic, not least for the indigenous peoples whose survival has always been dependent upon various forms of hunting.

An extract from the Canadian newspaper *The Star,* 19th February 2012:

The head of the Royal Canadian Navy says Canada needs to bolster its military presence in the Arctic to prepare for a boom in human and economic activity resulting largely from climate change.

Global warming is thought to be occurring faster in the North than anywhere else. The gradual disappearance of sea ice is opening up commercial shipping as well as previously inaccessible areas rich with oil, natural gas and mineral resources.

'From a naval perspective, climate change probably means there will be more open water, so the Arctic will really emerge as the Arctic Ocean,' Vice-Admiral Paul Maddison, Commander of the Royal Canadian Navy, said in a recent interview.

'It also means ... that the circumpolar route will probably open to international shipping from Asia to Europe sometime in this century – probably a lot earlier than most people predicted a few years ago,' he said.

'I know that major shipping companies are planning now to be able to have ships that are first-year ice capable sailing out of Singapore and over the pole into Rotterdam.

Prime Minister Stephen Harper has been vocal about asserting Canada's sovereignty in the region. As part of the government's national shipbuilding strategy, new icebreakers and Arctic off-shore patrol ships are on order. Maddison said the first patrol ship is expected in 2015.

He would like to see even more resources put into improving the navy's surveillance abilities in the North.

'I definitely see room for more investment in surveillance capacity, persistent surveillance capacity in the Arctic ... to provide a more real-time operating picture of what's going on.'

Maddison said that would include space-based assets, unmanned aerial drones, submarines under the ice and a human presence on Canadian ships.

'We will want to know what's happening. The economic activity is attracting a greater human footprint, so that brings greater opportunity. But it also brings risk – risk of pollution incidents, risk of search-and-rescue incidents, risk from a public-health perspective.'

The land

The coast adjacent to the North West Passage is mainly Arctic tundra and, just below the surface, much of it is permanently frozen (permafrost). There are no trees. The low temperatures hinder the decay of organic matter and the formation of humus.

The hardness of the permafrost makes burial and landfill impossible. In many Arctic settlements, human remains are 'buried' above the ground by covering them with stones. A recent concern is that the permafrost might start to melt – this will help with digging but it is also likely to cause subsidence and structural problems to many buildings.

Pingos

In the region around Tuktoyaktuk there are strange mounds that form in the permafrost. These are called pingos, from an Inuvialuk word for small hill, and they can be as high as 70m (230ft). They are a permafrost phenomenon, so the existence of ancient pingos in far flung places such as Norfolk, England, is evidence of conditions in the last ice age. They commonly form in draining lakes or river channels and are created because hydrostatic pressure pushes the inflowing water upwards within the permafrost. The water freezes and expands and, over a very long time under similar conditions, a mound of ice grows up beneath the ground. Because they form very slowly, only a few centimeters per year, the topsoil over the permafrost remains in place and they remain covered in earth and tundra plants. Pingos can also develop on the seabed and, like any growing sea mount, can be a hazard to navigation.

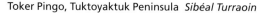

Toker Pingo, Tuktoyaktuk Peninsula *Sibéal Turraoin*

Mountain Avens (*Dryas octopetula*) in Gjøa Haven *Sibeal Turraoin*

Tiny plants found growing on Beechey Island, Erebus and Terror Bay *Sibéal Turraoin*

Plant life

Despite the very harsh environment, a number of Arctic plants survive. Most of them are perennials which go dormant over the winter. They reproduce quickly in the short summer and quickly disperse. Plants include grasses, cotton-grass, arctic poppy, saxifrages, arctic lupine and heathers. Gathering cloudberries to eat is a popular summer pastime. Slightly warmer wetland areas support grasses, sedges and rushes. In the High Arctic, lichens and mosses are often all that can survive.

Fish

A number of freshwater fish survive beneath the ice in inland lakes and rivers.

At sea, the following can be found:
Cod: average weights of less than 2kg
Lamphrey: eel like creatures with no jaws
Arctic char: similar to salmon and found throughout the Arctic. Good eating
Salmon: More common in Alaskan waters
Dolly Varden: similar to salmon and good eating
Sculpin: An ugly fish which is not eaten by humans
Halibut: excellent eating, sadly not very common
Capelin: small silvery fish which live in deep water in the winter and shallow bays in the summer.

Marine mammals

Harbour seal or common seal: brown, tan or grey with a V shaped nostril. They grow to 1·85m and weigh up to 132kg. Found as far north as Ellesmere Island.

Harbour seal *Aqqalu Rosing Asvid*

Ringed seal: commonly encountered seal which lives in the Arctic all year round. It has pale ring like markings on its upper parts. It's single pup is born in the spring in snow dens built on the ice. It feeds on small fish and makes holes in the ice in order to breathe.

Ringed seal *Aqqalu Rosing Asvid*

Harp seal: medium sized, pale grey seal with distinctive harp shaped markings. Regularly seen in Baffin Bay, they go south to Labrador for the winter. Rarely seen in the Western Arctic.

Harp seal pup *Aqqalu Rosing Asvid*

Bearded seal: a large seal with brown colouring and pronounced whiskers. Males can grow to 3m long and weigh 430kg. They are prized by the Inuit because their hide is very tough and is used for harpoon lines. They can be seen throughout the North West Passage waters.

Hooded seal: large dark grey or black seal. It has a very large nose from which it can inflate big red balloon-like sack when angry. They keep to open water and migrate south in the winter. Seen throughout the North West Passage waters.

Hooded seal *Aqqalu Rosing Asvid*

Walrus: a type of very large seal which can grow to 3.4m long and weight up to 1,360kg. They are found throughout the eastern North West Passage waters and are a threatened species.

Walrus *Jarlath Cunnane*

Fur seal (sea lion) *Sibéal Turraoin*

Whales

Bowhead whale: known to the old commercial whalers as the 'Right Whale' because it was relatively easily caught and did not sink when dead. It grows to 18m long and is black. Found throughout the North West Passage waters. It is a threatened species.

Fin whale: a large whale which grows to 24m long. It is grey on top and white beneath. It's right lower jaw and baleen are white. Found in the Davis Straits, it is a threatened species.

Fin whale *Aqqalu Rosing Asvid*

Lesser Rorqual: a smaller thin whale found in the eastern waters of the North West Passage. It is black above and white below. it has a white patch on the upper surface of its front flippers.

Blue whale: the largest of all mammals and can grow to over 30m in length. It is a blue-grey colour on top and has white spots below. It is found on the eastern waters of the North West Passage and is an endangered species.

Humpback whale: commonly seen in the far western and eastern waters of the North West Passage. It has very long flippers. Both the flippers and tail are often covered in barnacles. The body is black on top and white beneath. the baleen is black.

Killer whale or *Orca*: actually a large porpoise with a large black fin. It is black on top and white below with a white patches above the eye and on the flank. Orcas are common in the eastern North West Passage waters but rare in the west.

Beluga whale: a small pure whale which grows to 4m. Found in the central and eastern waters of the North West Passage. It is prized by the Inuit for its tasty muktuk (raw whale meat).

Narwhale: has a long spiral ivory tusk which was once much prized by Victorian gentlemen for walking sticks. It is small and grey growing to about 4·5m in length. More often seen in the eastern Arctic than the west.

Killer whale or Orca *Aqqala Rosing Asvid*

Beluga *Aqqala Rosing Asvid*

Small land mammals

Shrews, voles and lemmings are import creatures in the food chain providing food for larger mammals.

Arctic hares: the largest type of hare and are often a pure white colour. They are not shy and sometimes occur in large groups.

Arctic ground squirrel or *'Siksik'*: lives in the tundra on vegetation and scavenged meat. It caches food in the spring when it emerges from hibernation in a snow den.

Arctic hare *Sibéal Turraoin*

Ground squirrel in Tuktoyaktuk *Sibéal Turraoin*

Polar bear swimming around a yacht at anchor in Beechey Island *Sibéal Turraoin*

Larger mammals

Coyotes: found in the Mackenzie Delta. They are eaters of small game and carrion.

Wolves: travel in packs and hunt large game such as caribou. In the Arctic they are a pure white colour.

Arctic foxes: mostly eat voles and lemmings but will trail larger mammals in the hope of scavenging carrion. They turn white in the winter.

Wolverines: scavengers found throughout the North West Passage waters. They are a type of weasel which grow to the size of bear cubs. Dark brown and solitary. Their fur was sought after for parka linings because it does not freeze readily. They are an endangered species.

Polar bears: seen throughout the North West Passage Arctic waters. They grow to 700kg, can swim at an average speed of 6kns and run at 40kph. They eat seals, walrus, fish, carrion, birds and vegetation. Their only predator is man and sometimes that role is reversed. They are a species of special concern.

Caribou: a member of the deer family and are similar to reindeer. They migrate south in the winter and travel in big herds. In the Arctic they live mainly on lichen. They have always been an important source of food for the Inuit and and larger predatory mammals. They are unusual in that both the male and female have antlers.

Moose: the largest of the deer family. Migrates south in the winter but roams as far as the north coasts of mainland Canada and Alaska in the summer.

Musk-ox: huge hairy oxen which look as if they are throw backs to the last ice age, which indeed they are. They are vegetarians. Their main, non-human, predators are wolves but they can be hunted by polar bears. If attacked, the males form a circle with their horns pointing outwards, the females and young animals being in the middle of the circle. They are not inherently aggressive to humans but, as they can weigh up to 445kg, have horns and charge at 60kph, it is wise to keep one's distance.

Arctic fox *Aqqala Rosing Asvid*

Caribou swimming *Jarlath Cunnane*

Kittiwake *Sibéal Turraoin*

A sandpiper in Gjøa Haven *Sibéal Turraoin*

Ptarmigan *Malik Milfeldt*

Redthroated loon *Aqqual Rosing Asvid*

Bald eagle with a fish *Sibéal Turraoin*

Birds

Most Arctic birds are migratory however the snowy owl, rock ptarmigan, gyrfalcon and raven are resident species. River deltas such as the Mackenzie River delta attract large numbers of waterfowl in the summer. These include greater snow geese, Atlantic brant and Ross's geese, lesser snow geese, common and king eiders.

Fulmars: one of the most widespread sea birds found almost everywhere.

Gulls: include the predatory Arctic skua, kittiwakes, ivory gulls, glaucous gulls, Herring gulls, Sabine's gull and Ross's gull.

Arctic Tern: nests in the Arctic in the summer and flies to the Antarctic, some 20,000 miles, in the Arctic winter.

The *Auk* family is represented by Brunnich's guillemot, the black guillemot, Atlantic puffin and the little auk.

Great Northern diver loon and *common loon*: pelagic in the winter but nest in remote bays and estuaries in the summer.

In Alaska, the *bald eagle* is a fairly common and very impressive sight. Their wing span reaches 1·8m. The body is black or brown except for the head which is white with yellow beak and eyes. They nest in trees, posts and navigation marks. Living for up to 50 years, they feed on fish, ducks and carrion.

Least, *Baird's*, *White Rumped*, *Buff-breasted*, *solitary*, *semipalmated*, *Upland*, *Stilt* and *Pectoral sandpipers* breed on the Arctic shorelines.

General information

Transport and communications

Major settlements are served by sea or air.

Canadian North and First Air fly to the major Canadian Arctic settlements. Their route maps and websites are listed below.

In Alaska, the principal airline is Alaska Airlines who fly the following routes to destinations in the North West Passage:

Barrow:	Flights to Fairbanks and Anchorage
Prudhoe Bay:	Flights to Anchorage
Nome:	Flights to Kotzebue and Anchorage
Kotzebue:	Flights to Anchorage and Nome

An alternative is Frontier Flying and their sister company Era Alaska who fly to the same destinations as well as a few smaller settlements such as Wainwright and Point Hope. Their telephone number is: ✆ (907) 266-8394.

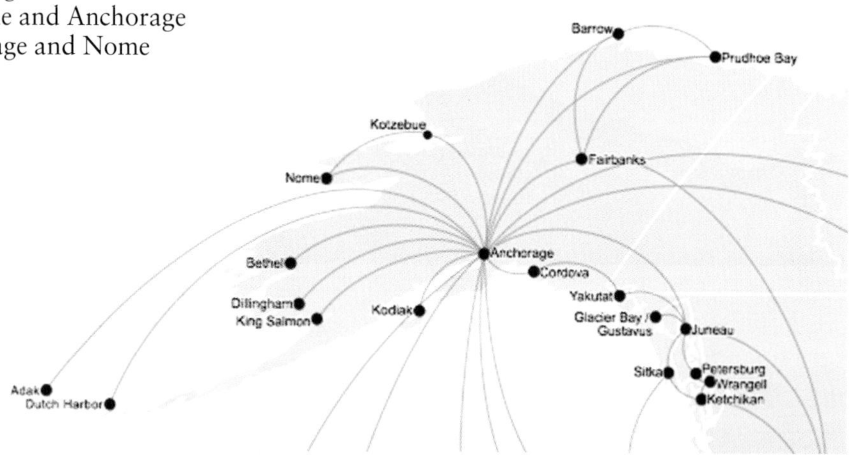

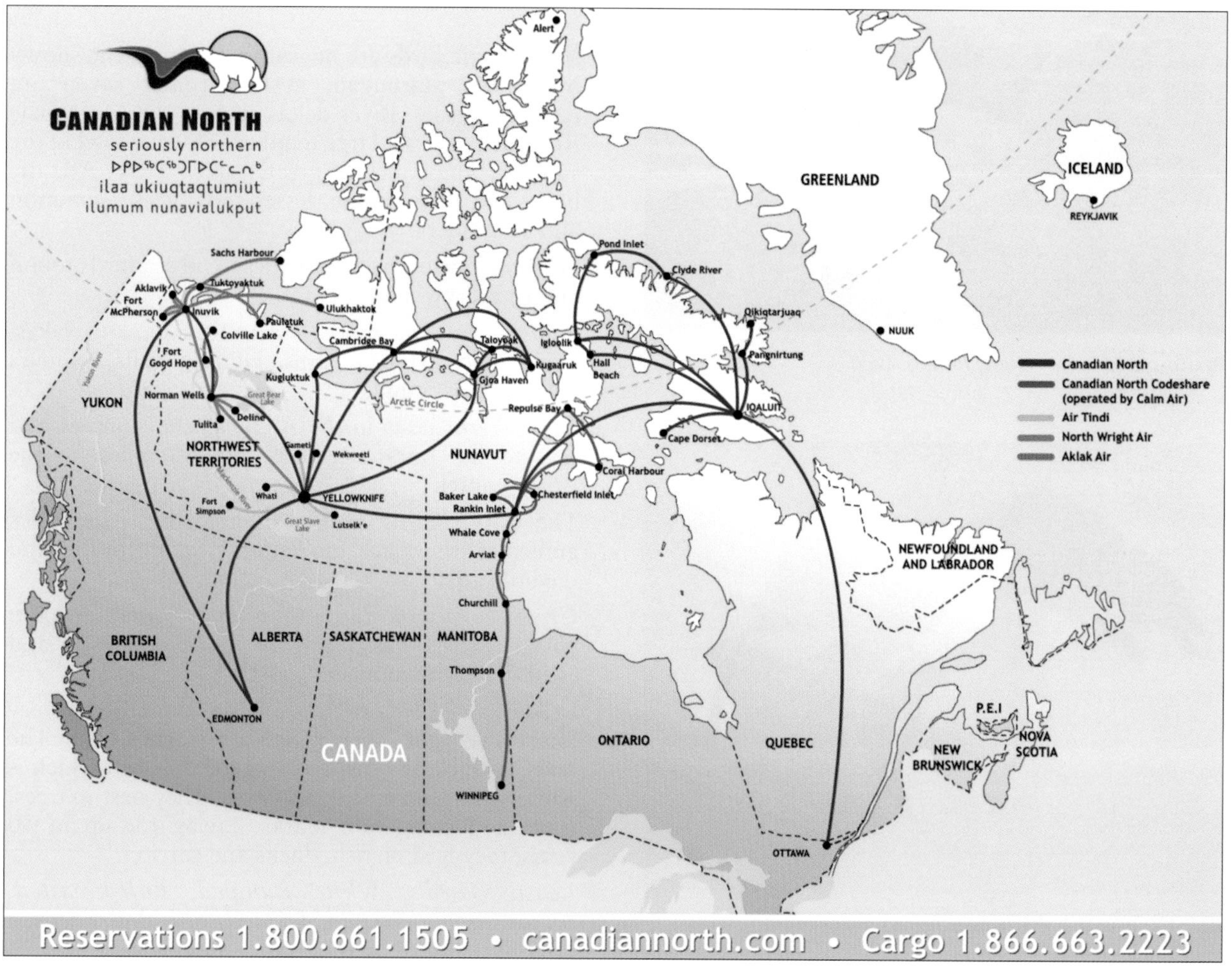

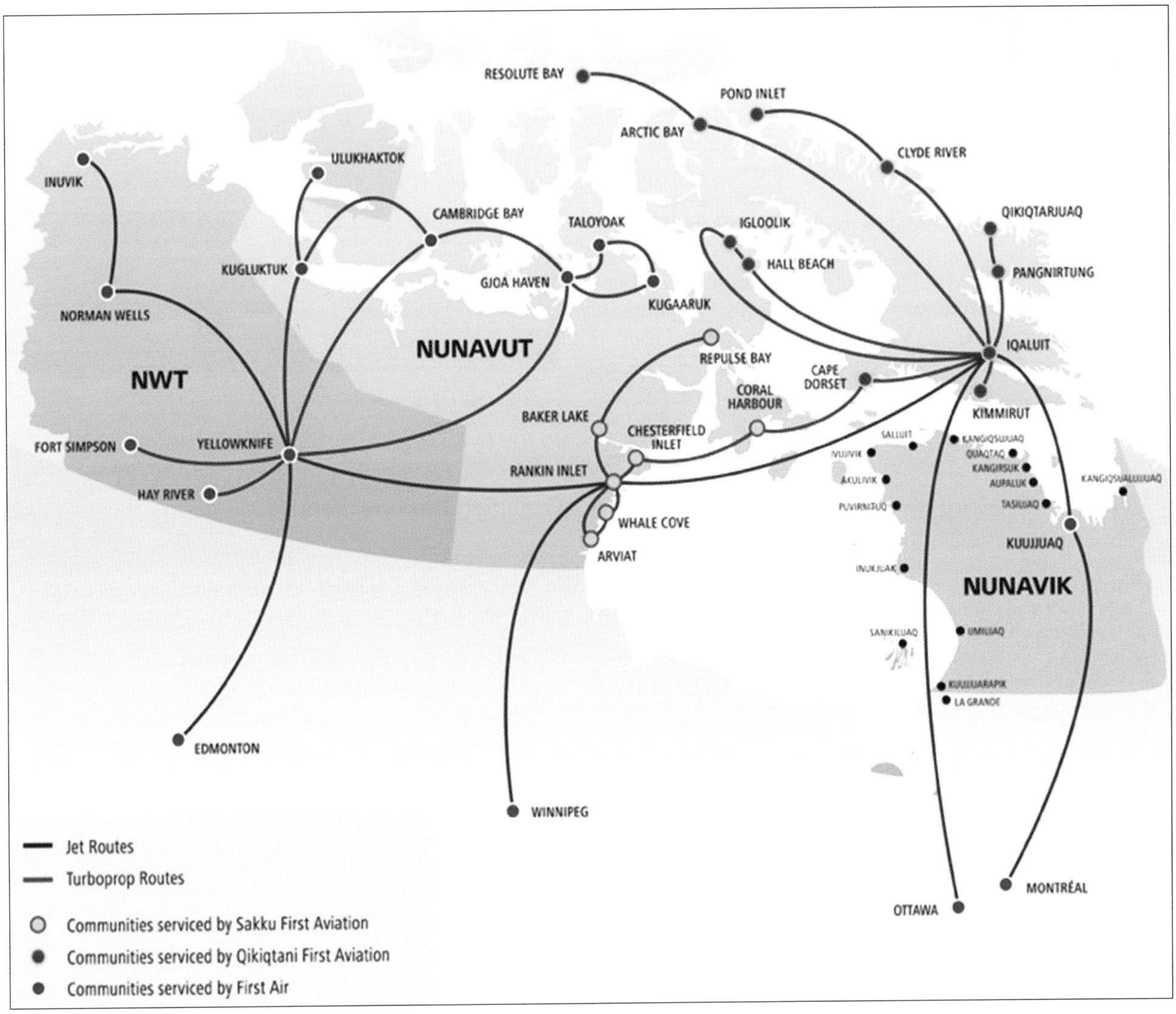

Useful websites – airlines

	First Air Northern Canada Airline	www.firstair.ca
	Canadian North Northern Canada Airline	www.canadiannorth.com
	Alaska Airlines	www.alaskaair.com
	Frontier Flying and Era Scheduled and charter airline	www.flyravn.com
	Ken Borek Air Canadian Aircraft charter company specialising in the Arctic	www.borekair.com
	Aklak Air Western Canada scheduled and charter flights	www.aklakair.ca/scheduled-flights

Climbing and walking

Hiking and trekking opportunities on the shores of the North West Passage and trekking opportunities are continuous, but without the wonderful scenery of Greenland and Baffin Island. The ground tends to be monotonous – a hard mud, with sparse growth.

Bylot Island is at the eastern end of Lancaster Sound. It is one of the gateways to the North West Passage and is now under the control of Canada Parks. There are some challenging ski mountaineering traverses over the island: Tilman's Traverse (repeated by Bob Shepton and Peter Maxwell in 2001), Murray Wright traverse and other traverses have been completed here in the past.

Bylot island *Máire Wilkes*

The following conservation advice is offered by the Canadian National Park:

Hiking

Choose routes on durable terrain such as bedrock, bare hard soil, gravel stream bottoms and snow patches. With such short growing seasons and harsh living conditions, the arctic environment is fragile. Avoid vegetated and soft soil areas, particularly grass-sedge meadows, which are critical feeding habitat for wildlife and are easily damaged by foot traffic.

In steep terrain travel on rock outcrops or snow. Avoid soil-covered surfaces. When descending loose scree, move slowly and cautiously, minimizing the movement of scree and reducing the erosion to the area. Spreading out can also reduce damage.

Camping

Select campsites in durable locations where signs of your occupation will be minimal, especially for base camps or if you are traveling in a large group. Avoid vegetated areas. Wearing soft shoes around camp is not only a great relief after a day spent in heavy hiking boots but also minimizes the impact around your campsite. Avoid camping near sensitive wildlife areas such as sedge-grass meadows. Do not dig trenches around tents or build rock wind breaks. If you use rocks to secure your tent, return them to their original position and location. Do not remove any rocks from any features that look – even remotely – like an archeological site, for example, tent rings, fox traps and food caches.

Cooking

Dish and excess cooking water should be poured into a shallow sump hole away from campsite and bodies of water. Filter food scraps and pack them out with other litter.

Litter and food scraps can be minimized with careful planning and preparation. Food can be packaged in plastic bags instead of cans, bottles, or tin foil. Carefully measured meals should minimize leftovers. Avoid smelly foods.

Personal hygiene

Minimize the use of soaps and, when necessary, use biodegradable soap. Residual soap should not be dumped in lakes or streams. Sponge or 'bird' bath using a pot of water well away from water bodies. This procedure allows the biodegradable soap to break down and filter through the soil before reaching any body of water.

Managing human waste

In Sirmilik National Park, one of the major expenses and challenges is managing human waste along the Akshayuk Pass corridor. Feces decompose very slowly in the Arctic environment and pathogens can survive arctic conditions.

If camping near emergency shelters, use the outhouses for feces. A separate container is located in the outhouse for toilet paper.

Those visitors who use 'Depends', tampons or other sanitary products must also plan for their disposal. Please bring along enough plastic ziploc bags to pack these items out – the same as you pack out all your food garbage. A little powdered bleach in the baggies can reduce the smell. Sanitary items cannot be dealt with in the same manner as toilet paper and should not be left behind at the outhouses with feces or toilet paper.

As a very last resort, feces can be deposited under rocks 50m from camp sites, travel routes and water bodies. Avoid disturbing plant communities.

Urine in healthy people is sterile. Please urinate 50m away from travel routes, camping areas and water bodies. Remember to pack out or burn all toilet paper.

If you are travelling with a large group or using a base camp dig a shallow communal latrine (15cm) at least 50m away from traffic routes, campsites, and bodies of water. Make sure the latrine hole is properly covered after use to hide its presence from those that follow and to discourage animals from digging it up.

If travelling along a body of salt water (i.e. one of the coastal areas of the park) it is acceptable to deposit your feces in a shallow pit below the high water mark.
We suggest to you that packing out your own waste is the last frontier for mountaineers and backpackers! We challenge you to cross it.

Useful websites – hiking

	Parks Canada National Park sites in Northern Canada	www.pc.gc.ca/eng/index.aspx use search facility to find information required

Cruising information

North West Passage ice regime

Davis Strait and Baffin Bay

Factors influencing the sea ice in this region are:

- The warm West Greenland Current sets northwards up the west coast of Greenland. This ensures an early break up of ice on the eastern side of Baffin Bay giving access to the Greenland coast and the 'North Water' polynia when the central and western waters are still ice bound.
- The cold south flowing current flowing from northern Baffin Bay along the coast of Baffin Island causes a delayed break up of the ice on the western shores of Baffin Bay and the Davis Strait.
- The sea ice in northern part of Baffin Bay melts early in the year as a result of the warm West Greenland current. It is pushed southwards by northerly winds and currents forming a recurring polynya known as the 'North Water.' The North Water was well known to the hundreds of European and North American whalers who frequented these waters in the 19th century.

A clear passage from the west coast of Greenland to northern Baffin Island should be possible in late July. Medium range seasonal outlooks and short range ice forecasts are available from the Canadian Coastguard website.

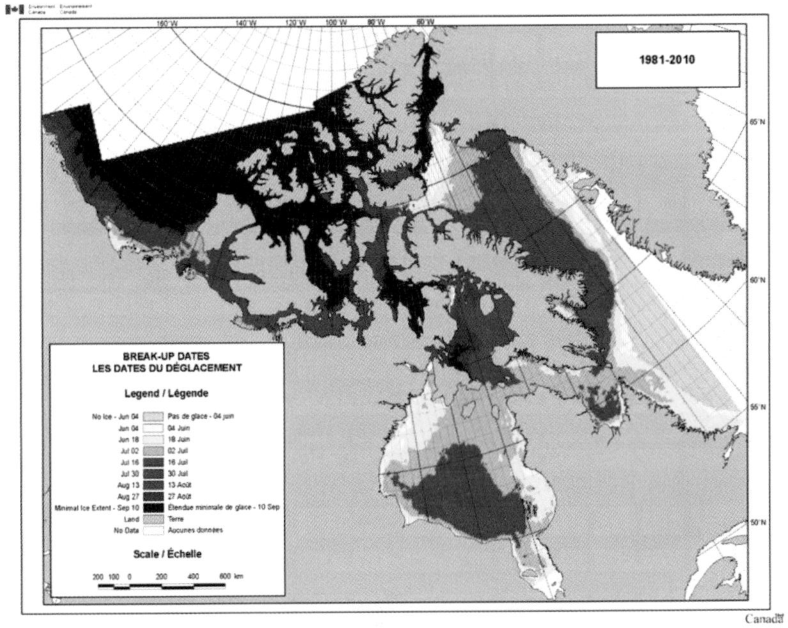

Eastern and Central North West Passage Break up dates in the Eastern Arctic
Canadian Coastguard

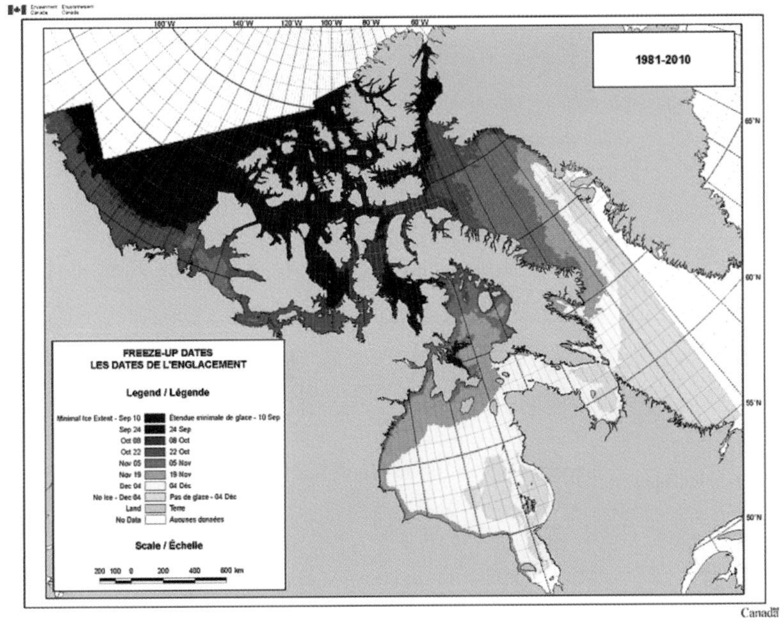

Eastern and central North West Passage freeze-up dates
Canadian Coastguard

Lancaster Sound to the Beaufort Sea ice regime

Break up starts first in Lancaster Sound in the east. This occurs in May and progresses westwards. Lancaster Sound can be expected to be navigable by early July although many of the narrower passages, such as Navy Board Inlet, will take longer to clear. Wind and currents will determine ice concentrations. The waters west and south of Somerset Island will clear in August. The ice in the Queen Elizabeth islands in the north are the last to break up in late August and new sea ice will start to form a few weeks later in early September. The freeze-up spreads southwards and by the end of October the ice in Lancaster Sound will have become consolidated.

Polynya: Any non-linear shaped opening enclosed in ice. Polynyas may contain brash ice and contain or be covered in new ice, milas or young ice; submariners refer to these as skylights. Sometimes the polynya is limited on one side by the coast and is called a shore polynya or by fast ice and is called a flaw polynya. If it reoccurs in the same position every year it is called a recurring polyna.

Ice Glossary: *The Mariner's Handbook*, published by the UK Hydrographic Office

Beaufort Sea

Ice coverage is nearly 100% in the winter and a belt of shore-fast ice lies from Amundsen Gulf to Point Barrow. This becomes mobile by early July but open ice conditions do not occur until the first week of August and open water cannot be expected until the first week of September. The ice location is very dependent upon wind direction, strength and duration.

Break up occurs along the Tuktoyaktuk Peninsula at the end of July and an open water route develops for shallow draft vessels navigating from the Mackenzie delta to Amundsen Gulf.

Freeze up of the Beaufort sea can be expected in late September or early October but it is dependent upon the location of the southern limits of the pack ice as it spreads southwards.

Using an ice pole in an attempt to push an ice floe
Sibéal Turraoin

Western waters of the North West Passage

The Bering Straits, Chukchi Sea, Beaufort Sea and Arctic Ocean all freeze in the winter. Break up starts to occur in the Bering Strait and Kotzebue Sound by early June although there may still be heavy drift ice in the vicinity. East from Point Hope, the pack ice begins to break off from the shore in May however it is moved back and forth by the wind and may return to the shore very quickly. It will, however, move gradually north and west. At Point Barrow, the ice normally moves on and off the shore until July but may remain close to the coast until August or even all summer. Similarly, to the west of Point Barrow, the ice presence is very dependent upon the wind; a northerly wind bringing the ice onshore.

Freeze up begins at Point Barrow in mid-September and in the Bering Strait in late October.

Useful websites – Alaska and Canadian Ice regimes

	Environment Canada A detailed description of Canadian Arctic ice regimes	www.ccg-gcc.gc.ca/Icebreaking/Ice-Navigation-Canadian-Waters/Ice-Climatology-and-Environmental-Conditions#3.7.8
	NOAA US Coastal Pilot No.9 can be downed in its entirety and contains details of the Alaska ice regime	www.nauticalcharts.noaa.gov/nsd/coastpilot_w.php?book=9

Useful websites – North West Passage ice Charts

	Environment Canada Homepage for west and central ice service	www.ec.gc.ca/glaces-ice/default.asp?lang=En&n=D32C361E-1
	NOAA US ice forecasts for Alaska	http://pafc.arh.noaa.gov/ice.php

7/10 sea ice in Peel Sound *Sibéal Turraoin*

Weather and ice forecasts in Canada

Canada has two Arctic Marine Communications and Traffic Services (MCTS) at Inuvik serving the central Arctic and at Iqaluit serving the eastern Arctic. Each station has several remote subsidiary transmitters. Details of their broadcasting schedules are given below.

Inuvik MCTS

Radiotelephony

Inuvik 5803kHz, Hay River 4363kHz, Heart Lake and Parsons Lake VHF Ch 26

0115 UTC/1315 UTC - (Radiotelephony)

- Technical Synopsis for Western Arctic waters (if applicable for Mackenzie River and Great Slave Lake)
- Marine Forecast for Great Slave Lake (Area 180)
- Marine Forecast for Mackenzie River (Area 110)
- Mackenzie Stage Forecast (Mackenzie/Fort Providence, Liard at Fort Liard, Mackenzie at Fort Simpson, Mackenzie at Norman Wells, Mackenzie at Sans Sault, Mackenzie at Fort Good Hope)
- Notice to shipping (Mackenzie Delta, Mackenzie River and Great Slave Lake).

Kugluktuk (Coppermine) 2558.0kHz, Cambridge Bay 4363.0kHz, Inuvik 6218.6kHz

Kugluktuk (Coppermine), Cambridge Bay, Parsons Lake VHF Ch 26

0235 UTC/1435 UTC - (Radiotelephony)

- Technical synopsis for Western Arctic waters
- Forecast for marine areas 111–121 inclusive
- Alaska Marine Forecast
- Notice to Shipping (Canadian waters west of 90°W)

Note: Ice conditions and forecasts available on request.

Radiofacsimile

Modulation: J3C (FM), Index of cooperation: 576, Power: 1KW

Drum Speed: 120rpm, Frequencies: 8456.0kHz, 8457.8kHz (USB)

0200 UTC – (Radio facsimile)

- 1200 UTC aviation prognosis
- Ice analysis Amundsen Gulf to St Roch Basin
- Ice analysis Beaufort Sea/Alaskan Coast
  1630 UTC – (Radio facsimile)
- 1200 UTC surface analysis
- Ice analysis Amundsen Gulf to St Roch Basin
- Ice analysis Beaufort Sea/Alaskan Coast

Broadcast information is available on request for via radiotelephony or radio facsimile.

Useful websites – Canada weather and ice forecasts

	Environment Canada Canadian Arctic marine weather forecasts	www.weatheroffice.gc.ca/marine/index_e.html
	Canadian Coastguard Canadian Arctic weather and ice broadcasting information: VHF, HF, Navtex and fax	www.ccg-gcc.gc.ca/eng/CCG/Home Use website search facility to find 'MCTS'

Iqaluit MCTS

Radiotelephony

Iqaluit site transmits on 2582 kHz, 4363 kHz, 6507kHz and VHF Ch 26 and Killinek site transmits on 2514kHz

At 1410 and 2235, UTC

- Weather synopsis and forecasts for marine areas of West Clyde, East Clyde, West Davis, East Davis, Cumberland, West Brevoort, Central Brevoort, East Brevoort, Frobisher Bay, Resolution, Ungava, North Labrador Coast, Northwest Labrador Sea, East Labrador Sea.
- following areas upon request: Baffin West, Baffin East and Nottingham.
- Notices to Shipping for all NORDREG waters east of 106°W and along the Labrador coast southward to 58°N.

At 0205 and 1705, UTC

- Ice boundary information
- Other bulletins on request

Coral Harbour site using 2514kHz and 6513kHz

At 0110 and 1320, UTC

- Weather synopsis and forecasts for marine areas of Nottingham, Coats, Central, Arviat, Churchill, York, Rankin, Baker, Belcher, Puvirnituq, James Bay.
- Following areas on request Foxe West, Foxe East, Igloolik, Prince Charles, South Central Hudson, South Hudson and Roes Welcome.
- Notices to Shipping for all NORDREG waters east of 106°W and along the Labrador coast southward to 58°N.

At 0205 and 1705, UTC

- Ice boundary information
- Other bulletins on request

Resolute site using 2582kHz and 4363kHz

At 1240 and 2310, UTC

- Weather synopsis and forecasts for marine areas of Barrow, Admiralty, Lancaster, Baffin West and Baffin East.
- Notices to Shipping for all NORDREG waters east of 106°W and along the Labrador coast southward to 58°N.
- Weather forecasts and summaries are available on request for other areas.

At 0205 and 1705, UTC

- Ice boundary information
- Other bulletins on request

Iqalssuit MCTS

Radiofacsimile

Modulation: J3C (FM)
Index of cooperation: 576
Power: 1KW
Drum Speed: 120rpm
Frequencies: 3251.1 kHz, 7708.1 kHz (USB)

Time UTC	Site	Chart
100	Resolute	Surface analysis 1800 UTC, Marine Wind Prognosis 24 hours
100	Iqaluit	Surface analysis 1800 UTC, Marine Wind Prognosis 24 hours
200	Resolute	Ice analysis chart areas [7, 8, 9, 10, 11]
200	Iqaluit	Ice analysis chart areas [1, 2, 3, 4, 5, 6, 7]
600	Resolute	Surface analysis 0000 UTC, Marine Wind Prognosis 24 hours
600	Iqaluit	Surface analysis 0000 UTC, Marine Wind Prognosis 24 hours
700	Resolute	Ice analysis chart areas [7, 8, 9, 10, 11]
700	Iqaluit	Ice analysis chart areas [1, 2, 3, 4, 5, 6, 7]
1000	Resolute	Surface analysis 0600 UTC, Marine Wind Prognosis 24 hours
1000	Iqaluit	Surface analysis 0600 UTC,
1100	Resolute	Ice analysis chart areas [7, 8, 9, 10, 11] Marine Wind Prognosis 24 hours
1100	Iqaluit	Ice analysis chart areas [1, 2, 3, 4, 5, 6, 7]
2100	Resolute	Surface analysis 1800 UTC, Marine Wind Prognosis 24 hours
2100	Iqaluit	Surface analysis 1800 UTC, Marine Wind Prognosis 24 hours
2200	Resolute	Ice analysis chart areas [7, 8, 9, 10, 11]
2200	Iqaluit	Ice analysis chart areas [1, 2, 3, 4, 5, 6, 7]

[1] Hudson Bay South, [2] Hudson Bay North, [3] Hudson Strait, [4] Foxe Basin, [5] Labrador Coast, [6] Davis Strait, [7] Baffin Bay, [8] Approaches to Resolute, [9] Eureka Sound, [10] Parry Channel, [11] Queen Maude - Prince Regent, [12] Amundsen Gulf

For correct reception of this broadcast in WMO standard facsimile recorders requiring 2300Hz for white and 1500Hz for black, 1800Hz centre frequency, radio receivers should be tuned in the Upper Sideband Mode to the given frequencies.

Note The areas included in the chart broadcasts vary with ice conditions and marine activity. All charts available can be transmitted or retransmitted on request.

Navtex

NAVTEX (S) 490kHz (French radioteletype) and NAVTEX (T) 518kHz (English radioteletype)

The Navtex broadcast transmitted by Iqaluit MCTS can be received using a Navtex receiver within the area of Iqaluit.

Schedule for NAVTEX broadcasts in French

Content	Time of Transmission (UTC)
Marine Forecast for areas: 143, 144, 145, 147, 148, 149 and 150	0300, 1100, 1500, 2300
Safety Notices to Shipping and Ice (during ice season)	0700, 1900

Schedule for NAVTEX broadcasts in English

Content	Time of Transmission (UTC)
Marine Forecast for areas: 143, 144, 145, 147, 148, 149 and 150	0310, 1110, 1510, 2310
Safety Notices to Shipping and Ice (during ice season)	0710, 1910

NAVTEX Service is available from various transmitting sites using the frequency 518kHz (English) and 490kHz (French) for the broadcast of the navigational warnings, meteorological warnings, ice bulletins and forecasts, Search and Rescue Information. Additional information on the NAVTEX Service is available in the latest edition of the Canadian annual publication *Radio Aids to Marine Navigation.*

NAVTEX Service is available from the following transmitting sites:

Site	Position
Iqaluit	63°43′N 68°33′W
Prince Rupert	54°17′N 130°25′W
Kodiak Alaska	57°46′N 152°34′W
Kook Island (Nuuk)	64°04′N 052°01′W
Upernavik (Disko Island)	72°50′N 56°09′W
Simiutaq (Cape Farewell area)	60°41′N 46°36′W
Tiksi, SA, Russian Federation	71°38′N 128°50′E

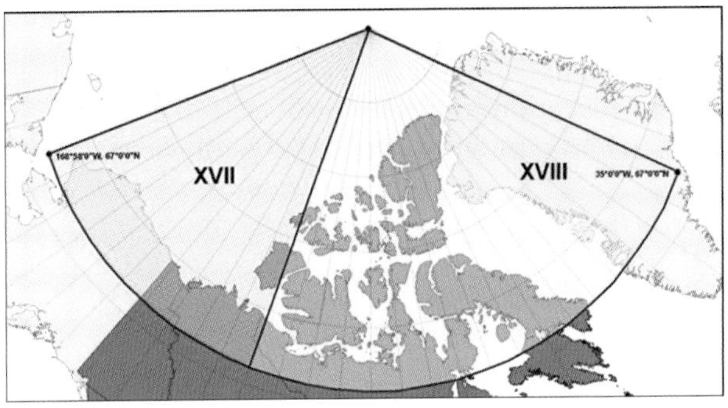

Metareas and Navareas of the North West Passage

Inmarsat

XVII and XVIII south of 75° latitude are broadcast via Inmarsat-C EGC SafetyNET:

METAREA	Satellite Region	Broadcast (UTC)
XVII	(POR)	0300, 1500
XVIII	(AOR-W)	0300, 1500

Navarea warnings for NAVAREAS XVII and XVIII south of 75° latitude will be broadcast via Inmarsat-C EGC SafetyNET:

NAVAREA	Satellite Region	Broadcast (UTC)
XVII	(POR)	1130, 2330
XVIII	(AOR-W)	1100, 2300

High Frequency Narrow Band Direct Printing (HF-NBDP)

In addition, during the navigation season meteorological warnings and forecasts and Navarea warnings for sections of NAVAREAS and METAREAS XVII and XVIII north of 70° latitude will also be broadcast via High Frequency Narrow Band Direct Printing (HF-NBDP):

Frequency	MCTS Centre	Broadcast (UTC)
8416.5 kHz	MCTS Iqaluit	0330, 1530

Weather and ice forecasts in Alaska

HF facsimile broadcasts are made from Kodiak. Their reception in the north will depend upon atmospheric conditions and is probably not reliable.

Kodiak facsimile and broadcast schedule

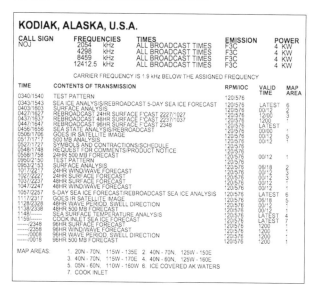

KODIAK, ALASKA, U.S.A.

CALL SIGN	FREQUENCIES	TIMES	EMISSION	POWER
NOJ	2054 kHz	ALL BROADCAST TIMES	F3C	4 KW
	4298 kHz	ALL BROADCAST TIMES	F3C	4 KW
	8459 kHz	ALL BROADCAST TIMES	F3C	4 KW
	12412.5 kHz	ALL BROADCAST TIMES	F3C	4 KW

CARRIER FREQUENCY IS 1.9 kHz BELOW THE ASSIGNED FREQUENCY

TIME	CONTENTS OF TRANSMISSION	RPM/IOC	VALID TIME	MAP AREA
0340/1540	TEST PATTERN	120/576		
0343/1543	SEA ICE ANALYSIS/REBROADCAST 5-DAY SEA ICE FORECAST	120/576	LATEST	6
0403/1603	SURFACE ANALYSIS	120/576	00/12	2
0427/1627	REBROADCAST 24HR SURFACE F'CAST 2227/1027	120/576	12/00	3
0437/1637	REBROADCAST 48HR SURFACE F'CAST 2237/1037	120/576	1200	1
0447/1647	REBROADCAST 96HR SURFACE F'CAST 2348	120/576	LATEST	
0456/1656	SEA STATE ANALYSIS/REBROADCAST	120/576	00/00	1
0506/1706	GOES IR SATELLITE IMAGE	120/576	00/12	5
0517/1717	500 MB ANALYSIS	120/576	00/12	1
0527/1727	SYMBOLS AND CONTRACTIONS/SCHEDULE	120/576		
0548/1748	REQUEST FOR COMMENTS/PRODUCT NOTICE	120/576		
0558/1758	24HR 500 MB FORECAST	120/576	00/12	1
0950/2150	TEST PATTERN	120/576		
0953/2153	SURFACE ANALYSIS	120/576	06/18	2
1017/2217	24HR WIND/WAVE FORECAST	120/576	00/12	3
1027/2227	24HR SURFACE FORECAST	120/576	00/12	3
1037/2237	48HR SURFACE FORECAST	120/576	00/12	1
1047/2247	48HR WIND/WAVE FORECAST	120/576	00/12	1
1057/2257	5-DAY SEA ICE FORECAST/REBROADCAST SEA ICE ANALYSIS	120/576	LATEST	6
1117/2317	GOES IR SATELLITE IMAGE	120/576	06/18	5
1128/2328	48HR WAVE PERIOD, SWELL DIRECTION	120/576	00/12	1
1138/2338	48HR 500 MB FORECAST	120/576	00/12	1
1148/------	SEA SURFACE TEMPERATURE ANALYSIS	120/576	LATEST	4
1159/------	COOK INLET SEA ICE FORECAST	120/576	LATEST	7
------/2348	96HR SURFACE FORECAST	120/576	1200	1
------/2358	96HR WIND/WAVE FORECAST	120/576	1200	1
------/0008	96HR WAVE PERIOD, SWELL DIRECTION	120/576	1200	1
------/0018	96HR 500 MB FORECAST	120/576	1200	1

MAP AREAS:
1. 20N - 70N, 115W - 135E
2. 40N - 70N, 125W - 150E
3. 40N - 70N, 115W - 170E
4. 40N - 60N, 125W - 160E
5. 05N - 60N, 110W - 160W
6. ICE COVERED AK WATERS
7. COOK INLET

HF weather broadcasts

Kodiak (NOJ) transmits weather forecasts for the Gulf of Alaska on 6501 KHz (USB) at 0203z and 1645z.

Kodiak also transmits NAVTEX weather reports 12 times day. It's identifiers are 'J' and 'X'.

NOAA Weather VHF Radio Frequencies

162.400 MHz	(WX2)
162.425 MHz	(WX4)
162.450 MHz	(WX5)
162.475 MHz	(WX3)
162.500 MHz	(WX6)
162.525 MHz	(WX7)
162.550 MHz	(WX1)

Alaskan VHF forecasts

Throughout the U.S.A., the National Oceanic and Atmospheric Administration (NOAA) transmits continuous weather information on dedicated VHF channels. Most modern VHF sets have access to these channels. In the North West Passage areas of Alaska, there are transmitters at Barrow, Kotzebue, Nome, Bethel, Cold Bay and Unalaska. They are, of course, limited to VHF range.

HF radio and email schedules

Peter Semotiuk runs a daily HF radio schedule for yachts transiting the North West Passage. He has been doing this on a voluntary basis for more than 20 years, since sailing through the passage on a friend's boat in 1988. Peter will forward ice and weather reports onto vessels who may have trouble receiving them by other means. He is likely to be in contact with other vessels transiting the North West Passage and can disseminate other useful information. Peter used to live in Cambridge Bay but

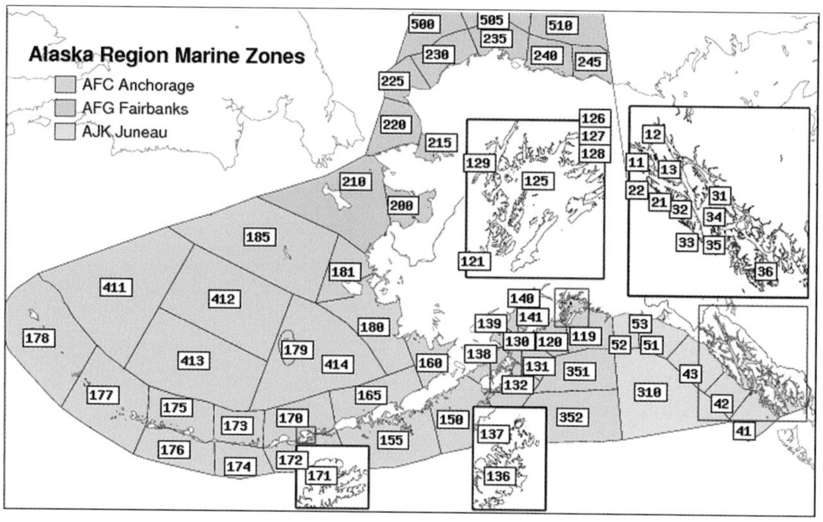

Alaska weather and ice forecast areas

Peter Semotiuk (right) with Alex Whitworth *Alex Whitworth*

Useful websites – Alaska weather and ice forecasts

	NOAA Alaskan weather and ice forecasts	http://pafc.arh.noaa.gov/marfcst.php
	NOAA Alaskan weather and ice forecasts	http://pafc.arh.noaa.gov/index.php?index=alaska

now lives in Winnipeg, in southern Canada, from where he runs the radio sked. Peter is also happy to advise vessels via email.

Peter's callsign is *XNR79*.

Radio schedule is as follows:
8.294 MHz at 0300Z
If necessary, may change to 4.149 or 8.297Mhz.
Other frequencies may include: 4.146, 6.224, 6.227, 6.230, 8.294, 16.628 and 18.825Mhz.
Peter's email is northwestpassage@hotmail.com and his phone number is ✆ +1 204 452 1298. One may wish to contact him before commencing a transit of the North West Passage.

Safety, search and rescue

It is quite likely that small vessels transiting the North West Passage will be aware of similar vessels attempting the same transit. It is prudent to stay in touch with each other so that emergency assistance can be given if possible.

A properly registered EPIRB could be a vital safety aid.

There are no dedicated Search and Rescue (SAR) units in the Canadian or Alaskan waters, however, the Coastguards operating in both countries are responsible for co-ordinating SAR. Both have ice breaking coastguard ships which have a SAR capability and can call upon aircraft.

The Canadian and US Coastguards are very professional and will render assistance whenever they can. However they have limited resources to cover very big sea areas and they have responsibilities other than search and rescue which have to be completed within the short navigation season. Some Coastguard Officers are concerned about ill-prepared 'Adventurers' attempting to transit the North West Passage.

Skippers not 100% confident about their vessel or crew's capabilities might consider consulting experts in high latitude sailing such as High Latitudes Ltd who offer training and consultancy services.

Global Maritime Distress and Safety System

The *Admiralty List of Radio Signals Volume 5 (NP285)* should be consulted for up to date Global Maritime Distress and Safety (GMDSS) information.

Most of the North West Passage waters are designated 'A4'. Which means that vessels are not necessarily within VHF, MF or satellite coverage. EPIRB transmissions will be received and fully compliant GMDSS vessels should also have an HF DSC capability.

The waters south of 70°N are designated as 'A3' GMDSS waters. That is, they should be within Inmarsat coverage.

Satellite communications

The Inmarsat network coverage footprint excludes much of the North West Passage however, in practice, there is coverage in many areas in the east but few in the west.

The Canadian MRCC Land Earth Station is Laurentides and its contact details are:
✆ +1 902 4272102
Telex: +21 1921533 RCC HALIFAX
Inmarsat C: AOR-E 581 493020114,
AOR-W 584 493020115

The USA MRCC Land Earth Station is Southbury and its contact details are:
✆ +1 757 398 6231
Telex: +230 127775 USCG RCC NYK

Although not part of the GMDSS network, Iridium 'phones are relatively affordable and have coverage throughout the North West Passage. It may be prudent to enter MRCC phone numbers and other emergency numbers in the 'phone memory.

HF DSC Stations with MMSI numbers:

Canada: Iqaluit MMSI: 00 31 60023

Alaska: Kodiak MMSI: 00 36 69899

Canadian Coastguard vessel at Erebus and Terror Bay, Beechey Island *Sibéal Turraoin*

Useful websites

	High Latitudes Arctic and antarctic expedition consultancy, training and management	http://highlatitudes.com/index.html
	Canadian Coastguard Canadian Coastguard policy and procedures concerning rendering assistance to disabled vessels and towing	www.ccg-gcc.gc.ca/Publications/Policy-Assistance-Disabled-Vessels

Regulations - Canada

On arrival in Canada, customs should be contacted on ✆ 1-888-226-7277. No person except the skipper may leave the boat until clearance has been granted.

If in doubt where to report, contact a Royal Canadian Mounted Police office. There is one in nearly every settlement.

The skipper will be asked to provide the following information:

- give the full name, date of birth and citizenship for every person on the boat;
- give the destination, purpose of trip and length of stay in Canada for each passenger who is a non-resident of Canada;
- give the length of absence for each passenger who is a returning resident of Canada;
- give the passport and visa information of passengers, if applicable;
- make sure all passengers have photo identification and proof of citizenship documents;
- declare **all** goods being imported, **including firearms and weapons;**
- report **all** currency and monetary instruments of a value equal to or greater than CAN$10,000;
- for returning residents of Canada, declare all repairs or modifications made to goods, including the boat, while these items were outside Canada

The skipper will be given a report number. There is no need to report on departure unless you are exporting goods which need to be documented.

The Nunavut flag flown beneath the Canadian courtesy ensign *Sibéal Turraoin*

Non-Canadian vessels may be left in Canada during the winter only if repair or maintenance work is being undertaken by bona fide marina or service outlet. Details should be given to the Customs who may require proof.

Useful websites – Canadian regulations

	Government of Canada Immigration information for visitors	www.cic.gc.ca/english/visit/index.asp
	Canada Border Services Agency Brochure *Coming into Canada by Small Aircraft or Boat*	www.cbsa-asfc.gc.ca/menu-eng.html Search for 'Coming into Canada by small aircraft or boat'
	Canada Border Services Agency Requirements for entering Canada by small boat	www.cbsa-asfc.gc.ca/menu-eng.html Search for 'Reporting requirements for private boaters'
	Royal Canadian Mounted Police Firearm users visiting Canada	www.rcmp-grc.gc.ca/cfp-pcaf/fs-fd/visit-visite-eng.htm
	Royal Canadian Mounted Police Using a firearm for wilderness protection	www.rcmp-grc.gc.ca/cfp-pcaf/fs-fd/wild-sauvage-eng.htm
	Canadian Coastguard NORDREG regulations	www.ccg-gcc.gc.ca/eng/MCTS/Vtr_Arctic_Canada

Immigration

All nationalities need a valid passport but most do not need a visa. If in doubt, check on the website listed in this chapter. The length of stay is determined by the immigration officer and the maximum stay is six months.

Customs

Firearms must be declared to customs on arrival.

Many souvenirs containing animal or plant products are banned. Examples include sperm whale teeth, fur and ivory products.

Alcohol is limited to 1.14l of spirits or 1.5l wine or 24 x 335 ml cans of beer. Cigarettes limited to 200. For the reasons stated in the last chapter, alcohol is a sensitive issue and should not be taken ashore.

The usual restrictions appertaining to importing meat, diary products, fruit and vegetables apply.

Documents

A certificate of competence is required.

Firearms

Rifles are accepted as a sensible precaution in Nunavut and the Northern Territories. They should be declared to the Customs Officer when checking in to Canada. A non-resident firearm declaration form should be filled in prior to arrival although, if this is not done, the Customs Officer will have the necessary forms. There is a one off fee of $25. The licence granted lasts for 60 days but can be renewed provided that the renewal is requested before the 60 days has expired. The RCMP can perform these duties if a CBP or Customs Officer is not available.

Rifles should be stored under lock and key or disabled when not in use. Ammunition should be stored separately or in a locked locker.

Reporting

Vessels of 300GRT or more are required to comply with the Coastguard NORDREG reporting regulations. See website for details. Reports should be made Iqaluit MCTS ✆ 867-979-5269 or 867-979-5724, *Email* iqaNordreg@innav.gc.ca. Although not required to do so, yachts are also advised to report regularly for potential SAR reasons.

It is good practice to exchange TRs with Coastguard vessels whenever they are passed within the North West Passage. This will help the Coastguard know about vessels in their area which is useful in the event of potential search and rescue operations.

Regulations - Alaska, USA

Clearance

Alaskan ports of entry are: Alcan, Anchorage, Dalton Cache, Fairbanks, Juneau, Ketchikan, Kodiak, Nome, Skagway, Sitka, Valdez, Dutch Harbour and Wrangell. A common port of entry for small vessels transiting the North West Passage will be Nome. Their telephone number is ✆ 907 443 2143. The CBP telephone number for Dutch Harbour is ✆ (907) 581 4114. If a CBP Officer is not available locally, call the Anchorage CBP Office (✆ (907) 271 2675).

US registered vessels should report to Customs and Border Patrol (CBP) within 24 hours of arrival.

Non-US registered vessels should register with the CBP immediately on arrival. Only the skipper is allowed ashore until this has been done. Skipper and crew then have to meet a CBP Officer within 24 hours. This may be in the form of an inspection on the boat. Registration papers, crew lists stores lists and last port clearance will be required.

US Customs and Border Protection (CBP) have a reputation for enforcing regulations strictly. It may be worth noting email addresses and telephone numbers before a passage so that, should it be necessary to land a crew member at a settlement other than a Port of Entry, CBP can be informed by sat phone. CBP do monitor small boat traffic and radio communications and, in recent years, they have followed on-line passage blogs. It is likely that they will be aware of a yacht's movements even if direct contact has not been made. It is prudent to work with them and keep them informed of movements to the best of one's ability.

Useful websites – US clearance

	US CBP Pleasure Boat Reporting Requirements	www.cbp.gov/travel/pleasure-boats-private-flyers/pleasure-boat-overview

Useful websites – US firearms

	Alaska Department of Fish and Game Licences and Permits	www.adfg.alaska.gov/index.cfm?adfg=license.main
	U.S. Department of Justice AFT	www.atf.gov

If a yacht is sailing across the North Pacific from Japan or Russia then the first official port of entry will be Dutch Harbour, which lies at the eastern end of the Aleutians, 1,000 miles from Attu. The official line is that one must clear into Dutch Harbor before going to any of the other islands. In the past officials accepted that this is not practical and were flexible provided the vessel cleared at the first official port of entry, either Dutch Harbor or Kodiak.

Foreign vessels are required to check-in at every US port however this is waived if a Cruising Licence is granted. It is still a requirement of the Cruising Licence for the skipper to telephone the CBP whenever the vessel reaches a new port or harbour. Cruising Licences are available to vessels from the following countries: Argentina, Anguilla, Australia, Austria, Bahamas, Belgium, Bermuda, British Virgin Islands, Canada, Cayman Islands, Denmark, Finland, France, Germany, Great Britain, Greece, Honduras, Ireland, Italy, Jamaica, Liberia, Marshall Islands, Netherlands, New Zealand, Norway, St Vincent and the Grenadines, St Kitts and Nevis, Turks and Caicos, Sweden, Switzerland and Turkey. The list is subject to change and it includes countries with which the USA has reciprocal arrangements.

Immigration

All foreign nationals (except Canadians and Mexicans) entering the U.S. by private yacht must have a visa as the Visa Waiver Programme, used by many nationalities entering the U.S. by 'plane, does not apply. Obtaining a visa is very time consuming. It requires several forms to be completed, money to be paid, finger prints taken and an interview to be conducted in a U.S. Embassy. Expect long queues and little empathy.

All foreigners have to be seen by an Immigration Official on arrival. Visitors will have a form stapled into their passports. This must be returned when leaving the U.S. If it is not, the authorities will assume that the holder is overstaying and future visits to the U.S. may be problematic.

ERIPB Registration

U.S. Authorities require all vessels to have registered EPIRBs and proof of their registration.

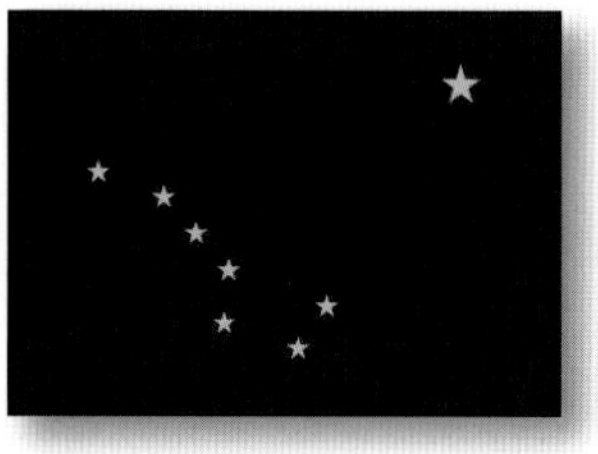

Alaskan flag

Alaskan Pilotage Regulations

Foreign pleasure vessels greater than 65ft are required to carry a pilot. An exemption can be obtained for vessels between 65ft and 174ft. All commercial foreign vessels and all vessels greater than 175ft must carry a pilot. Exemptions must be applied for 30 days before the vessel enters Alaskan waters and last for one year. Exemptions cost $250 + $50 for every foot greater than 65ft.

Firearms

Guns are also an expected precaution in northern Alaska however there is still a significant amount of paperwork required.

A firearm import permit should be obtained from the U.S. Department of Justice/Bureau of Alcohol, Tobacco, Firearms and Explosives (ATF) before the vessel enters U.S. waters. The permit is applied for using ATF form 6NIA, number 5330.3D, which can be obtained from the ATF website. Allow at least 30 days for this form to be processed. The application has to be accompanied by a hunting licence.

If one requires a hunting licence merely in order obtain an import permit for a gun which is to be used solely for wildlife protection, the least expensive hunting license you can purchase is a non-resident small game license for $20. This is easily obtained from the Alaska Department of Fish and Game website.

Both the importation permit and the hunting licence will be required when checking into the U.S.

Charts and pilot books

In Canada, the best charts and pilotage information is produced by the Canadian Hydrographic Office. In Alaska, the best charts and pilotage information is produced by NOAA. C-Map electronic charts cover the North West Passage but their level of detail is not consistent and paper charts are recommended. The British Admiralty pilots are good but not as up to date as the Canadian and American publications.

A good small scale passage planning chart for the North West Passage is Canadian *chart 7000.*

Canada

Charts are produced by the Canadian Hydrographic Service. The CHS *Catalogue 4* covers the northern Canada region. It is available online or free paper copies can be supplied by chart distributers. Extracts from *Catalogue 4* are printed on pages 283–4:

Canadian Sailing Directions ARC 400 is an excellent book with a wealth of information about general navigation, geographic, physiographic and natural conditions in the Arctic and northern Canada in particular.

ARC 402 and *ARC 403* give pilotage directions for the eastern and western Arctic Canadian waters respectively. These publications replace *Vol.I and Vol.II.*

There is a list of charts and publication distributers on the CHS website.

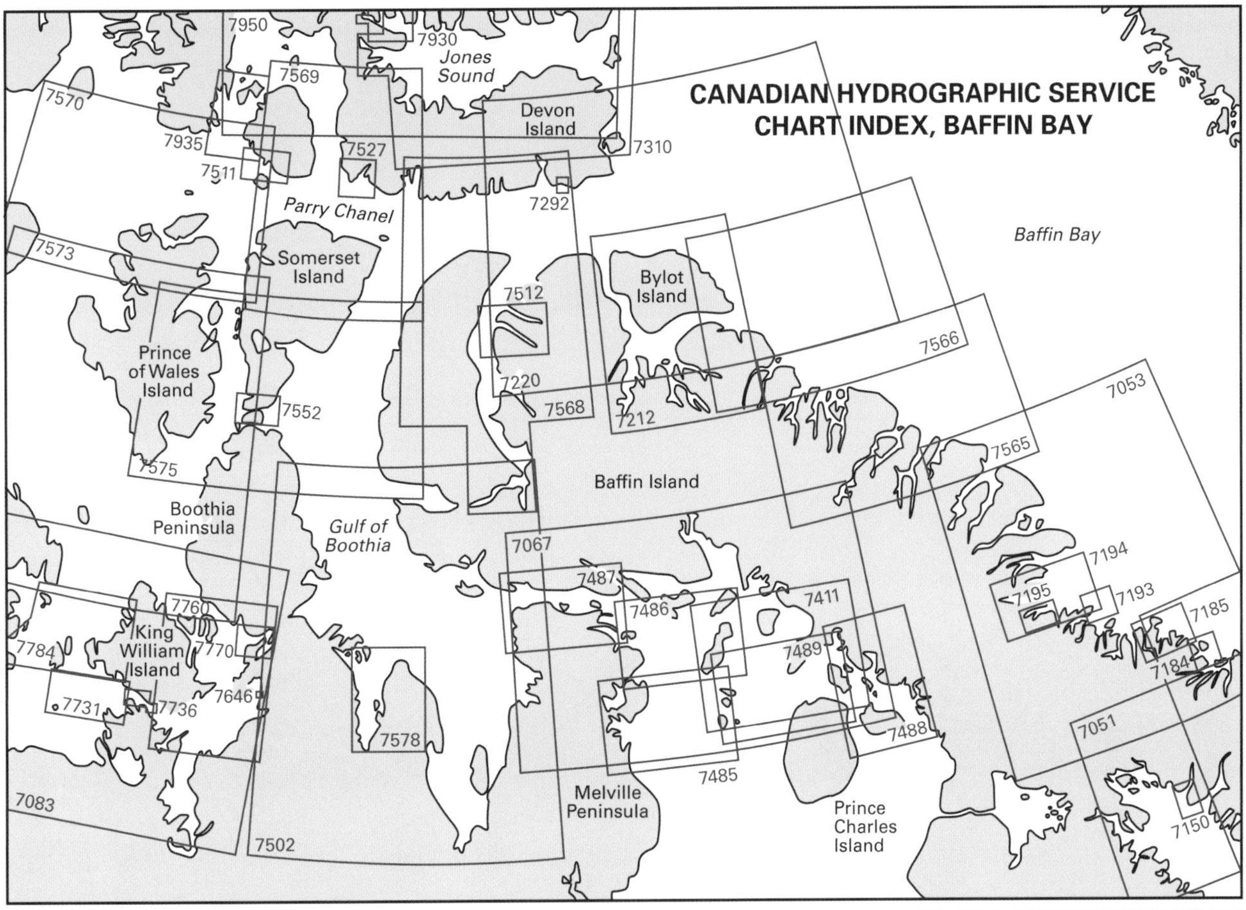
CANADIAN HYDROGRAPHIC SERVICE
CHART INDEX, BAFFIN BAY
Jones Sound
Devon Island
Parry Chanel
Somerset Island
Prince of Wales Island
Bylot Island
Baffin Bay
Baffin Island
Boothia Peninsula
Gulf of Boothia
King William Island
Melville Peninsula
Prince Charles Island
7950
7930
7569
7570
7935
7511
7527
7310
7292
7573
7512
7220
7568
7212
7566
7053
7565
7552
7575
7067
7487
7486
7411
7489
7488
7485
7194
7195
7193
7185
7184
7051
7150
7760
7770
7784
7731
7736
7646
7578
7083
7502

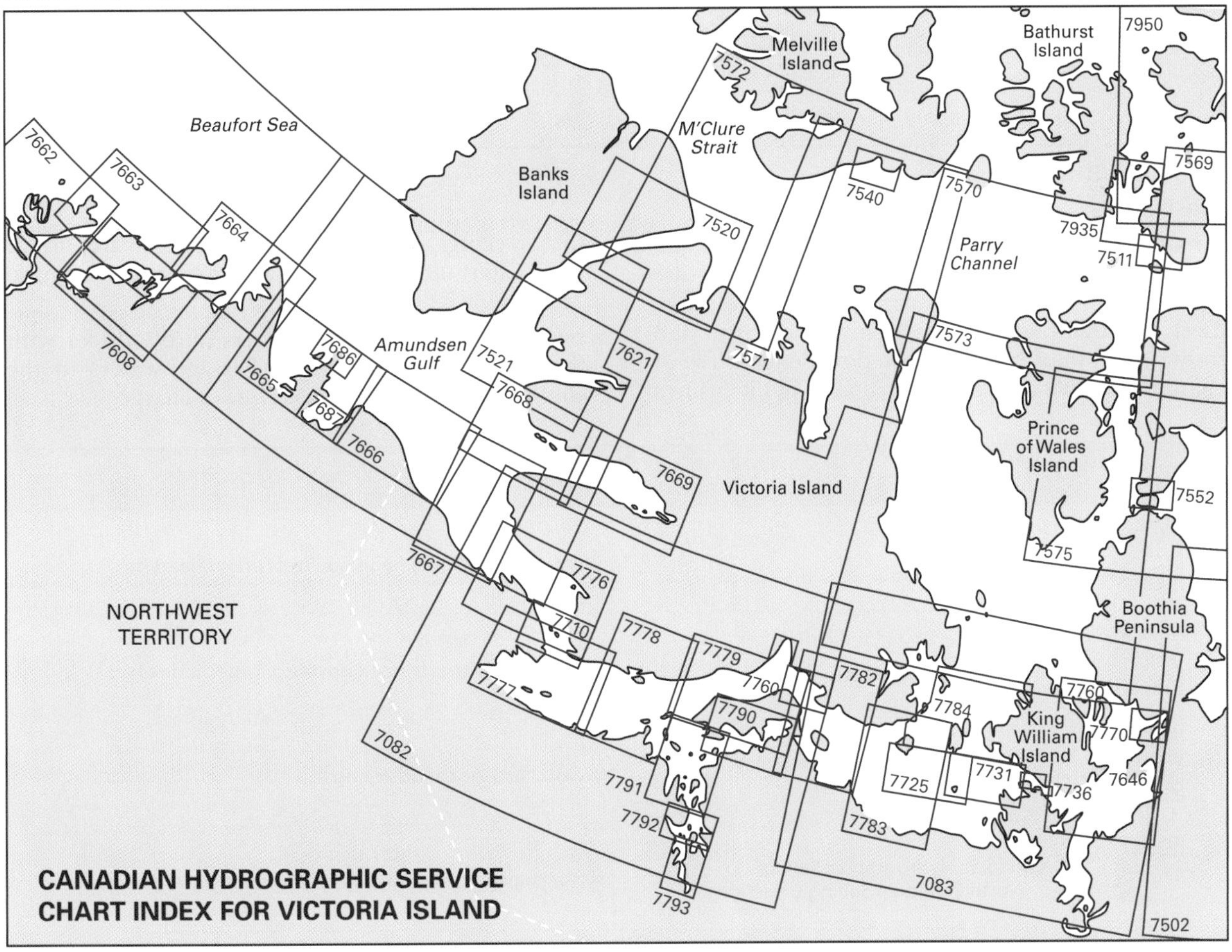
Beaufort Sea
Banks Island
Melville Island
M'Clure Strait
Bathurst Island
Parry Channel
Amundsen Gulf
Victoria Island
Prince of Wales Island
Boothia Peninsula
King William Island
NORTHWEST TERRITORY
CANADIAN HYDROGRAPHIC SERVICE
CHART INDEX FOR VICTORIA ISLAND
7662
7663
7664
7608
7665
7686
7687
7666
7667
7521
7668
7621
7669
7520
7572
7571
7540
7570
7950
7569
7935
7511
7573
7552
7575
7776
7710
7778
7779
7777
7760
7790
7782
7784
7725
7731
7736
7770
7646
7082
7791
7792
7793
7783
7083
7502

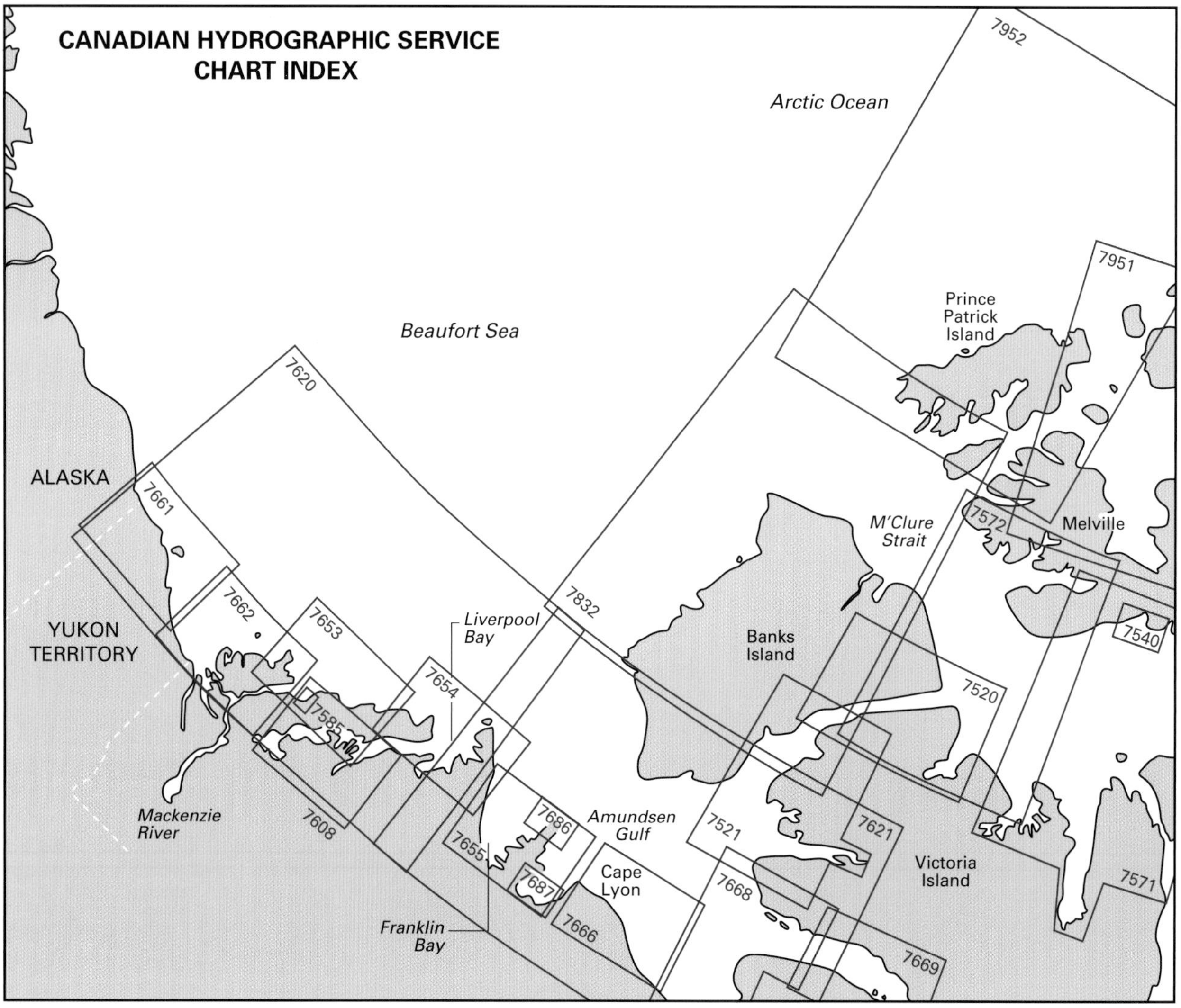

Alaska

US Charts are produced by National Oceanic and Atmospheric Administration (NOAA). NOAA are more generous with their copyright policies than most hydrographic offices. Many charts (in BSB format) and pilot books can be downloaded free of charge. Not only does this save money, but it ensures that recently downloaded publications are up to date. Chart indexes for Alaska are reprinted on page 285–286:

NOAA *Coast Pilot No.9* covers all of Alaska with the exception of the Inside Passage waters to the south. It can be downloaded free of charge.

Useful websites – charts and pilot books

	NOAA U.S. Coast Pilots	www.nauticalcharts.noaa.gov/nsd/cpdownload.htm
	NOAA U.S. Chart downloads	www.nauticalcharts.noaa.gov/mcd/Raster/index.htm
	Canadian Hydrographic Service Canadian Chart Indexes	www.charts.gc.ca/index-eng.asp
	Canadian Hydrographic Service North Canadian Sailing Directions	www.charts.gc.ca/publications/sd-in/north-nord-eng.asp

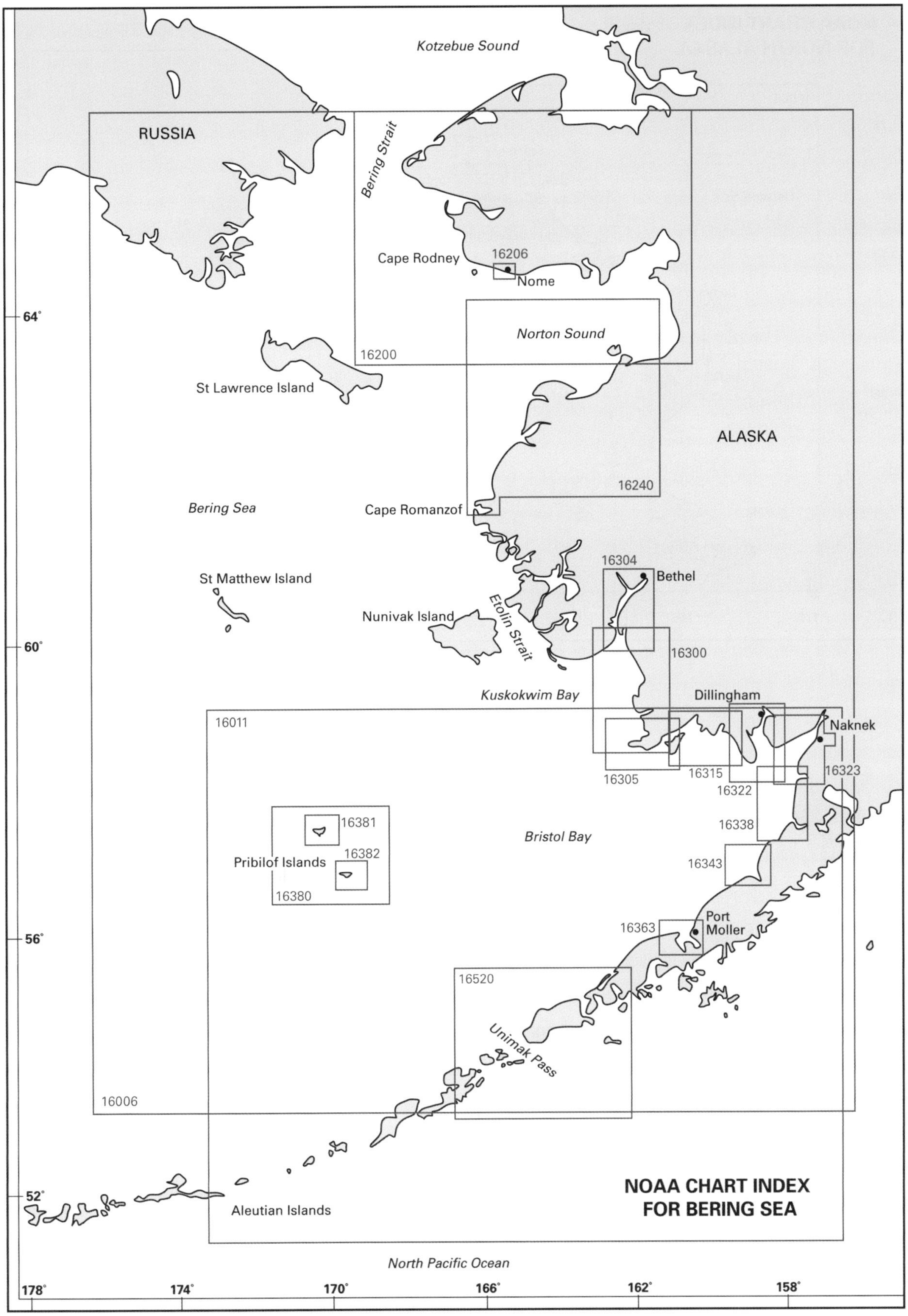
Kotzebue Sound
RUSSIA
Bering Strait
Cape Rodney
16206
Nome
64°
Norton Sound
16200
St Lawrence Island
ALASKA
16240
Bering Sea
Cape Romanzof
16304
Bethel
St Matthew Island
Nunivak Island
Etolin Strait
60°
16300
Kuskokwim Bay
Dillingham
16011
Naknek
16315
16305
16322
16323
16381
16338
Bristol Bay
16382
Pribilof Islands
16343
16380
Port Moller
16363
56°
16520
Unimak Pass
16006
52°
NOAA CHART INDEX FOR BERING SEA
Aleutian Islands
North Pacific Ocean
178°
174°
170°
166°
162°
158°

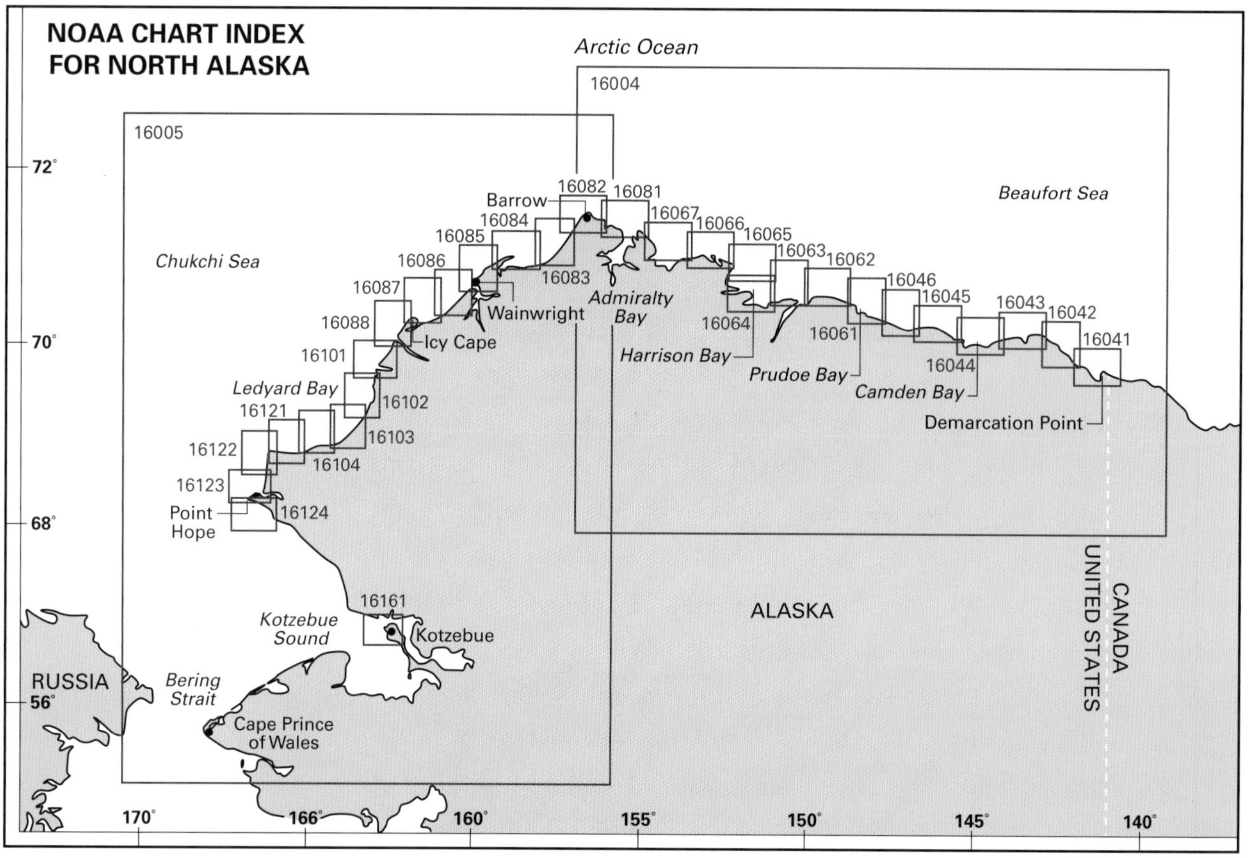

Useful websites – North West Passage notices to shipping

	Canadian Coastguard *Notices to Shipping and Nav Warnings*	www.ccg-gcc.gc.ca/eng/CCG/Notship_Home
	U.S. Coastguard *Notices to Mariners*	www.navcen.uscg.gov/?pageName=lnmDistrict&region=17

Useful websites – North West Passage tides

	Fisheries and Oceans Canada Tide height and current predictions	www.waterlevels.gc.ca/eng Search for 'tide and current prediction'
	Tide Forecast Tides for the Bellot Strait	www.tide-forecast.com/locations/PortKennedy-BellotStrait-Nunavut
	NOAA U.S. Tidal Heights	http://tidesandcurrents.noaa.gov/gmap3

Notices to Shipping

Canadian notices to shipping, *NOTSHIP*, are broadcast by radio and are available on the web.

Alaskan notices to mariners are broadcast by radio and are also available on the web.

Currents and tidal streams

Tides in the Canadian Arctic are, generally, not particularly strong. Narrow straits, such as the Bellot Strait, are the obvious exception to this statement. The Canadian Hydrographic Service *Sailing Directions ARC 400* (ISBN 978-0-660-19855-2) is a good source of information as are the *Canadian Sailing directions ARC 401 and ARC 402 (Arctic Canada Vol.II)*. Online information for tide times can be obtained from the Fisheries and Ocean Canada website.

There are strong currents around the Tasmanian Islands in the Franklin Strait. While not significant in itself, this does mean that ice pressure can build up significantly on one side of the islands (mainly southern) as the passages between the islands let the water through but jam up the ice. This effect can be felt some distance away from the islands.

US Coast Pilot 9 gives information about currents and tides within Alaskan waters.

The north setting currents in the Chukchi Sea are strongest near the coast and are generally greater than one knot when not opposed by the wind. The north setting current in the Bering Straits is strong and can exceed 2·5 knots. The tidal streams flowing in the passes between the Aleutian Islands are very strong and should be approached at the slack water before the tide set changes in the vessel's favour.

The Bellot Strait has a fast tidal flow. On-line information for tide times can be obtained from the Tide Forecast website given on page 286.

Tidal heights

The Canadian Hydrographic Service publish annual *Tide Tables* for the Arctic region. The ISBN number is ISBN 978-0-660-64516-2. An excellent description of arctic tides and their ranges can be found in the *Canadian Hydrographic Service Sailing Directions ARC 400* (ISBN 978-0-660-19855-2). The southern parts of Baffin Island have large tidal ranges (up to 13·1m) but this decreases to a maximum of 2·9m in Lancaster Sound. Along the mainland coast of the Canadian Arctic the range is less than 0·6m. Tidal heights are, however, affected by metrological conditions. In the Beaufort Sea, strong on-shore winds can produce water levels as high as 2·3m above chart datum. Generally, tides are semi-diurnal (two high waters a day). Online tidal data can be found on the Fisheries and Ocean Canada website.

Services, fuel and food supplies

Unsurprisingly, throughout the North West Passage, there are no specialised services for visiting yachts. However, settlements do have small boat and shore-side infrastructure which needs to be maintained. Most local people are happy to help out where they can. The bigger settlements have one or two supermarkets which have good fishing and hardware shelves.

Diesel

Diesel is available in the North West Passage as follows:

Pond Inlet: fill jerry cans and transport by dinghy from beach (good weather only). Arrange delivery at the Co-op supermarket.

Resolute: fill jerry cans and transport by dinghy from beach or pipe from beach to anchorage

Arctic Bay: fuel (by jerry can) probably available

Gjøa Haven: refuel by jerry can (approximately 750 miles from Pond Inlet)

Cambridge Bay: alongside refueling (approximately 260 miles from Gjøa Haven)

Kugluktuk: 67°49'·7N 115°05'·6W. Fuel maybe available by jerry can from the village

Ulukhaktok (Holman): a diesel tanker is stationed here but details of how to buy fuel not known

Sachs Harbour (S coast of Banks Island): fuel probably available by jerry can

Tuktoyaktuk: fill jerry cans and transport by dinghy (approximately 675 miles from Cambridge Bay). Smaller vessels may be able to go alongside.

Barrow: open roadstead. May not be possible to stop in bad weather. It is wise not to rely on Barrow as a refuelling stop. (approximately 500 miles from Tuktoyaktuk)

Nome: alongside berth for main fuel tanks. No jerry cans can be filled at the main marine re-fueling berth for environmental reasons. Jerry cans can be filled at a garage but one would need to hire or borrow a truck or taxi. (1,100M from Tuktoyaktuk)

Diesel may also be available at *Taloyoak/Spence Bay*: a possible refueling point between Resolute and Gjøa Haven, south of Bellot Strait however details not known.

Propane

Propane should be available in the same settlements where diesel is available. However, supplies are totally dependent upon supply barges. In 2010 no propane could be bought in any of the Alaskan or Canadian Arctic settlements.

Pond Inlet settlement fuel truck *Máire Wilkes*

North West Passage routes

The British *Admiralty's Arctic Pilot (Volume III)*, lists four possible routes through the North West Passage. These being:

Route A

From Lancaster Sound through Prince Regent Inlet, Bellot Strait, Franklin Strait, Larsen Sound, Rasmussen Basin, Simpson Strait and Queen Maud Gulf, whence the waters bordering the mainland are followed west through Amundsen Strait into the Beaufort Sea. Route A is restricted to vessels with a draft of not more than 5m. There are difficult currents in the Bellot Strait which is also often blocked with ice. By spring 2013, two west bound vessels had taken this route and 17 east bound vessels. The route gives the opportunity to stop and refuel at Gjøa Haven.

Route B

From Lancaster Sound continuing through Parry Channel as far as the Prince of Wales Strait into Amundsen Gulf and the Beaufort Sea.

Route B is a deep water route but subject to ice drifting southwards down the M'Clure Strait causing severe conditions. It is infrequently used.

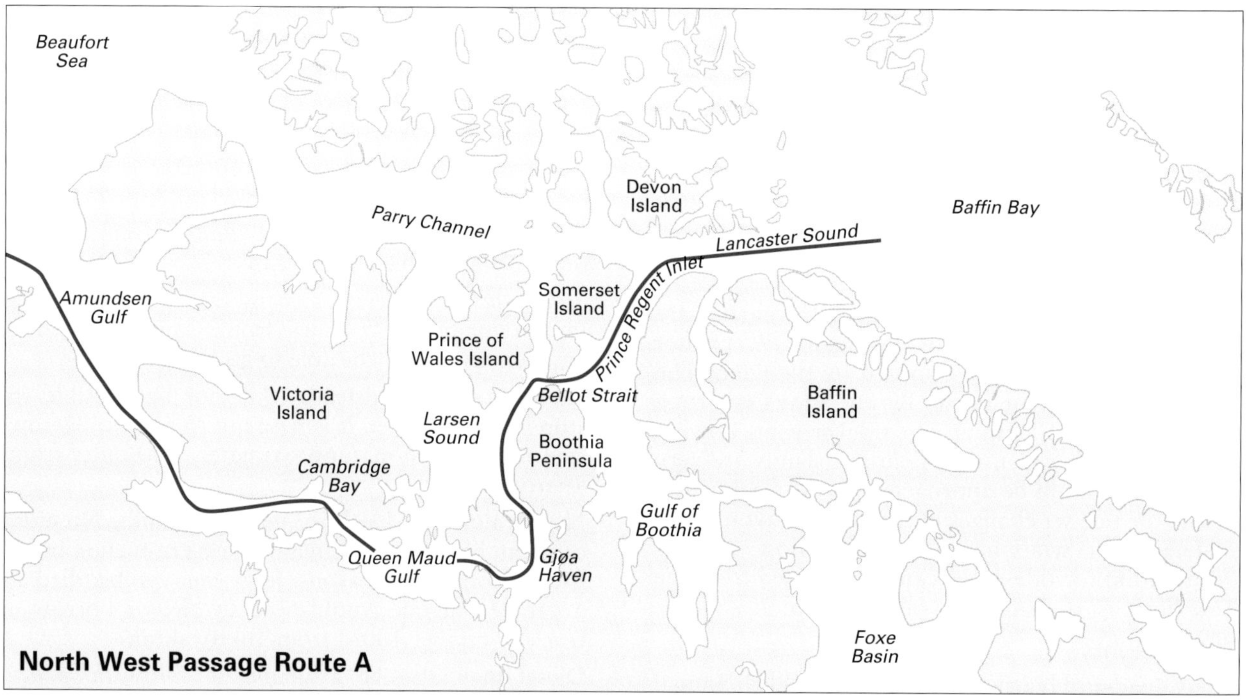

North West Passage Route A

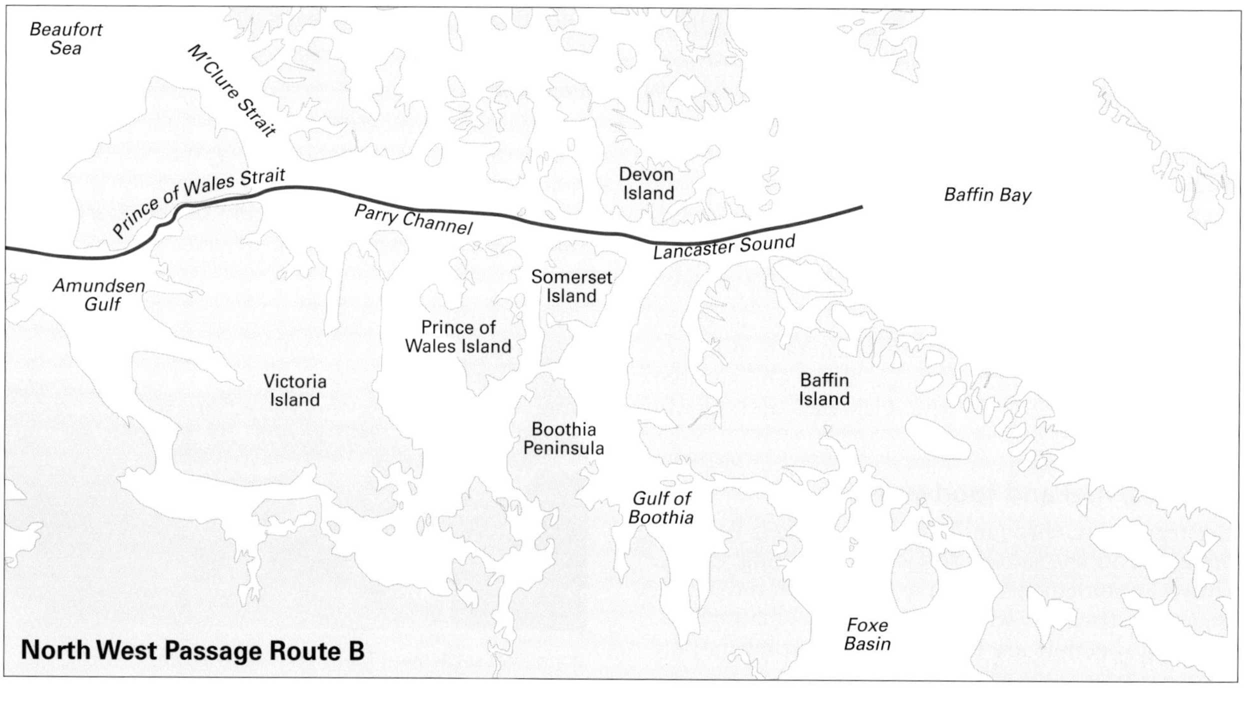

North West Passage Route B

Route C

From Lancaster Sound through the Barrow Strait, Peel Sound, Franklin Sound and Larsen Sound, thence by route (A). Route C is a deep water route and is relatively direct. Ice conditions in Victoria Strait can limit vessels with restricted maneuverability. It is the most popular route for smaller vessels. By the end of 2010, 23 west bound vessels and 27 east bound vessels had transited via this route.

Route D

A variation of Route C – From Lancaster Sound through the Barrow Strait, Peel Sound, Franklin Sound and Larsen Sound, thence through Rae Strait and Simpson Strait into Queen Maud Gulf. A shallow draft variant of Route C with minimum depths of 6·4m in the Simpson Strait. It may be accessible when Victoria Strait is blocked with ice. It affords the opportunity to stop at the Gjøa Haven settlement on King William Island.

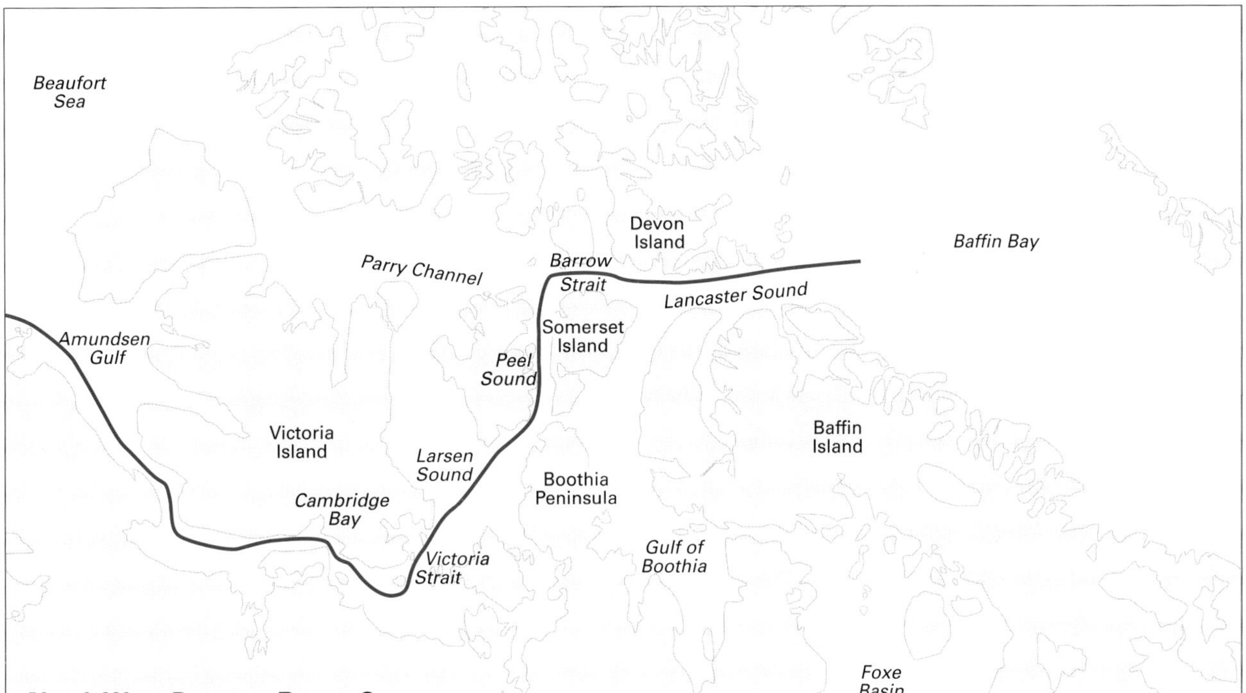

North West Passage Route C

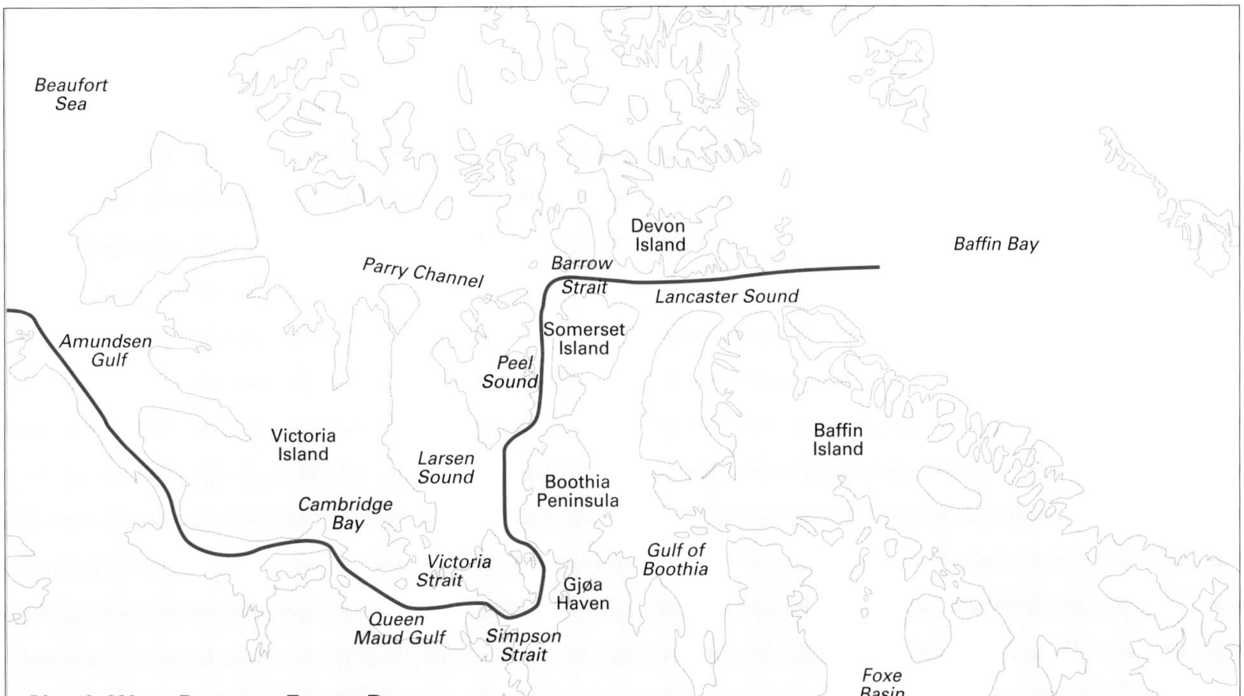

North West Passage Route D

Professor Headland, of the Scott Polar Research Institute, University of Cambridge, documents three additional routes:

Route E

Lancaster Sound, Prince Regent Inlet, Bellot Strait, Franklin Strait, Larsen Sound, Victoria Strait, Coronation Gulf, Amundsen Gulf, Beaufort Sea, Chukchi Sea, Bering Strait. Route E is dependant upon the ice conditions in the Bellot Strait which is also subject to strong currents. As the ice tends to clear later in the navigation season, it is used more frequently by east bound vessels who will be navigating this area slightly later in the season.

Route F

Lancaster Sound, Barrow Strait, Viscount Melville Sound, M'Clure Strait, Beaufort Sea, Chukchi Sea, Bering Strait.

Route F is the deepest and most direct route through the North West Passage. However the M'Clure Strait is very rarely ice-free and only one transit via this route has been documented. This was achieved by the Russian icebreaker, *Kapitan Khlebnikov*, in 2001. The route is used by submarines because of its depth.

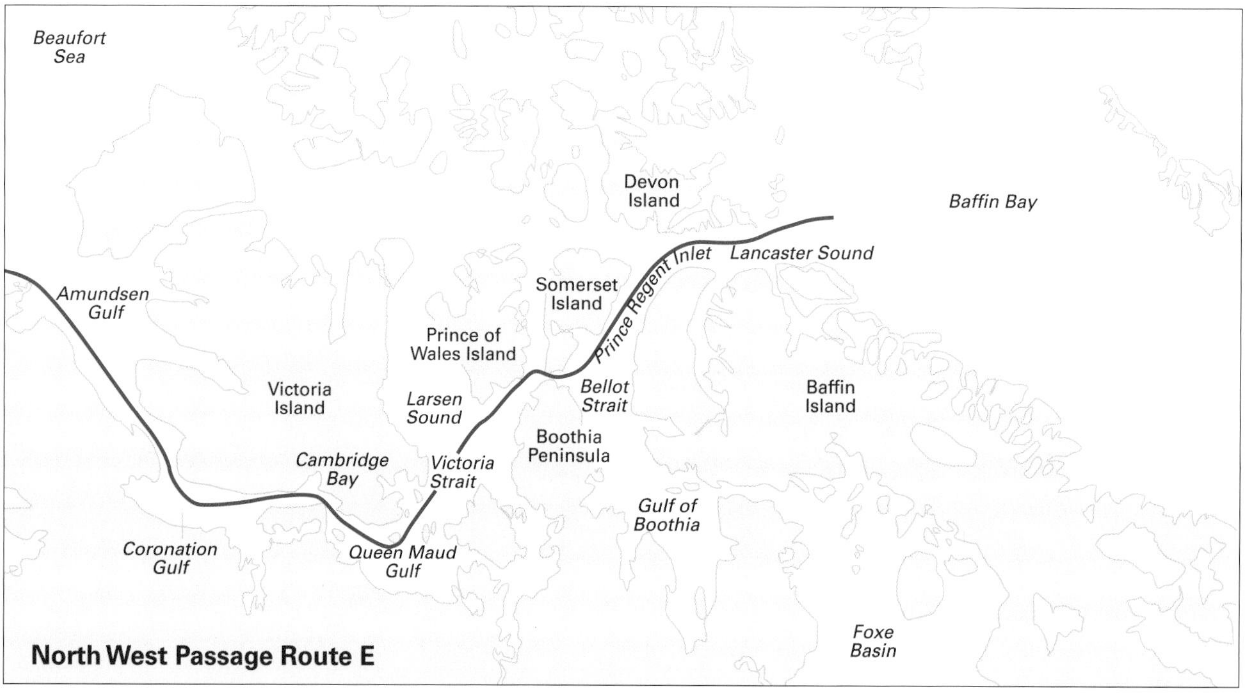

North West Passage Route E

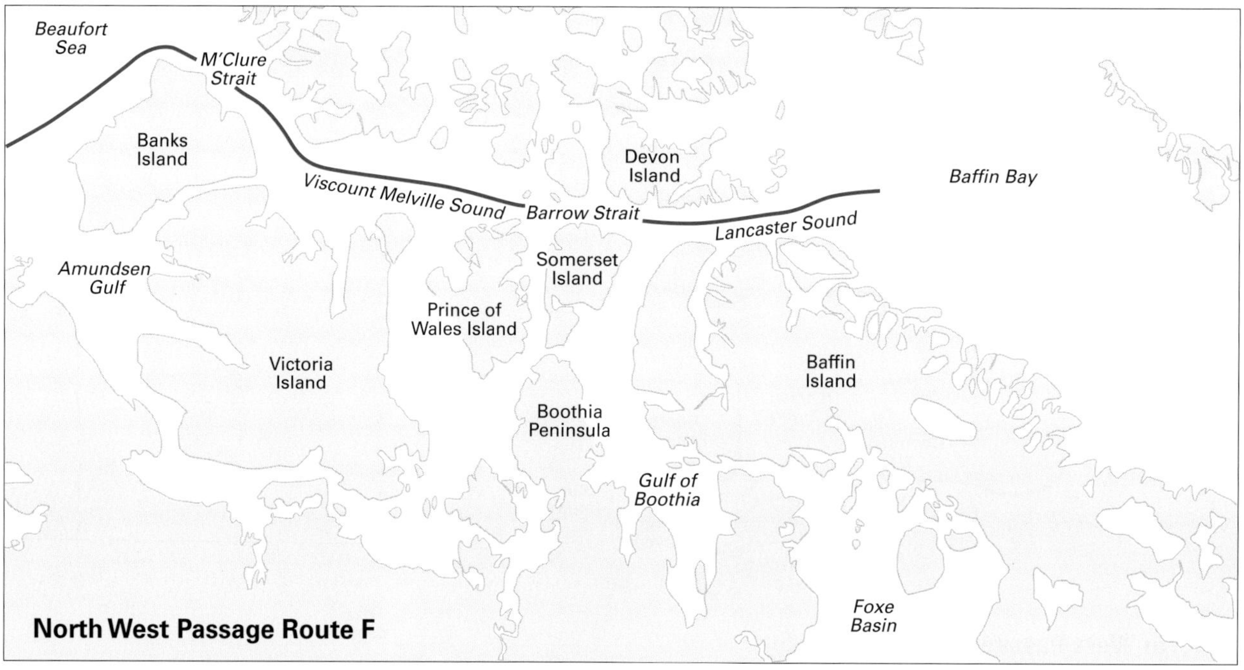

North West Passage Route F

Route G

Hudson Strait, Foxe Basin, Fury and Hecla Strait, Bellot Strait, Franklin Strait, Victoria Strait, Coronation Gulf, Amundsen Gulf, Beaufort Sea, Chukchi Sea, Bering Strait. A difficult route owing to severe ice usually at the west of Fury and Hecla Strait and the currents of Bellot Strait.

Route G is subject to severe sea ice in Fury and Hecla Strait, the Gulf of Boothia and Bellot Strait. Only three transits have been recorded via this route and all of them were east bound.

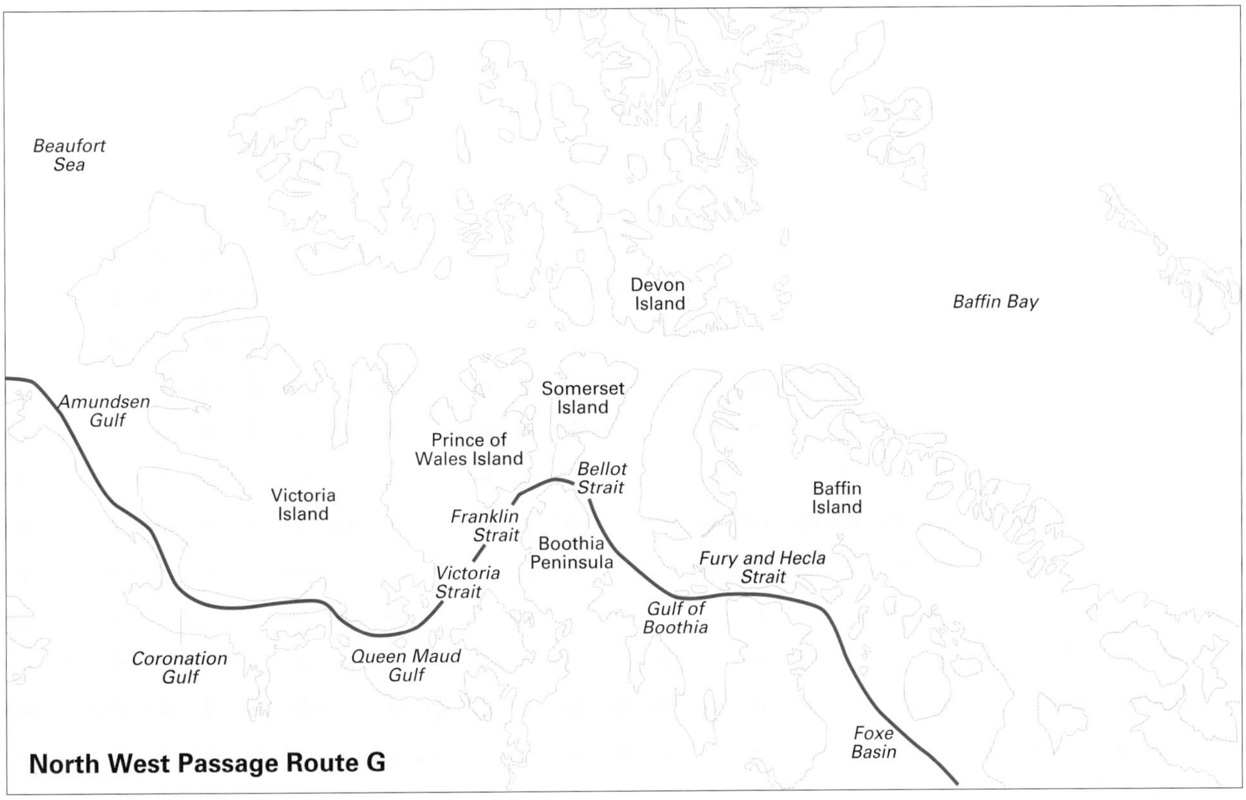

North West Passage Route G

Twilight in Peel Sound *Máire Wilkes*

Pilotage notes

Contents

The notes in this section are designed to be read in conjunction with the relevant coastal pilot or sailing directions and do not replace them.

The major settlements and many anchorages are mentioned in the following pages. However, vessels transiting the North West Passage between Pond Inlet in the east and Nome in the west will log about 3,000 miles and many anchorages have yet to be explored by cruising boats. It is highly likely that, with the aid of NOAA and CHS coastal pilot books and charts, skippers and crews navigating these waters will discover 'new' anchorages. Please refer to the notes concerning 'Selecting an anchorage' on page 36. The author would be very pleased to receive details and photographs of any 'new' harbours, anchorages or routes which can be included in future editions. Contact details can be found on the RCCPF website.

Victor Wejer, a Canadian with considerable Arctic sailing experience, has collected a list of potential anchorages from sailors who have sailed through the North West Passage or in adjacent waters. The list, which includes additional information, can be found on the RCCPF website.

Useful websites – North East and North West Passage pilotage

	Marine Exchange of Alaska Port information, useful links, coastguard and emergency information	www.mxak.org/ports/all_regions.html
	Alaska Association of Harbormasters. The site includes contact details for harbourmasters in Alaska	www.alaskaharbors.org/index.html
	RCC Pilotage Foundation	www.rccpf.org.uk/passage-planning/arctic

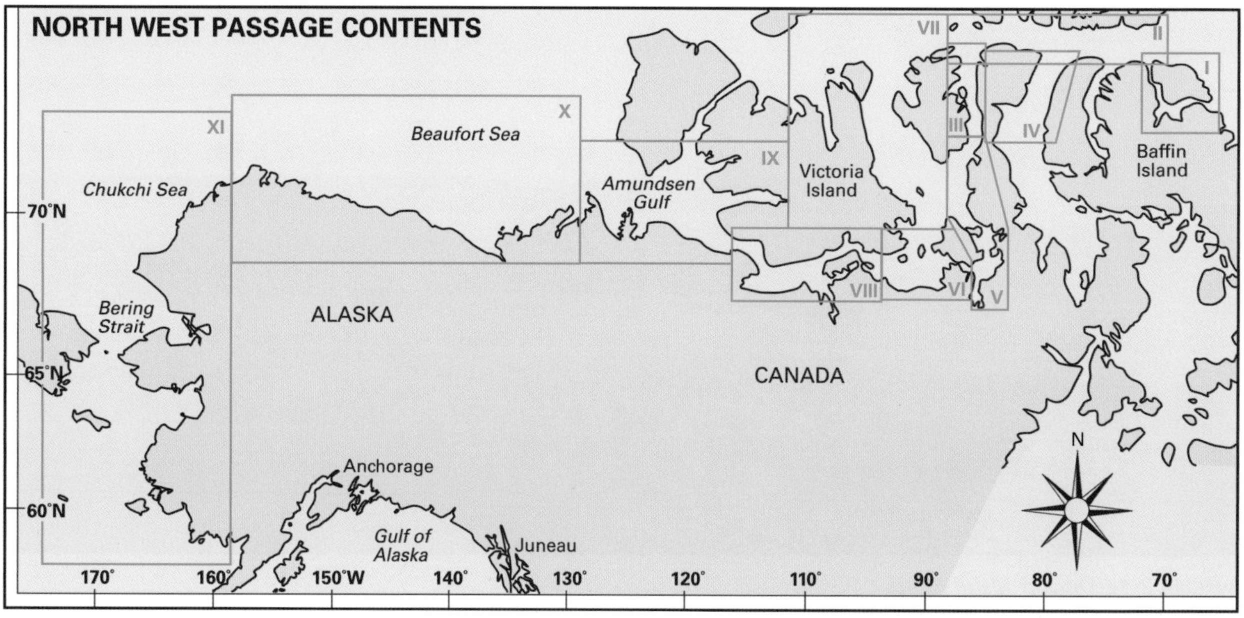

I Pond Inlet, Eclipse Sound and Navy Board Inlet

Pond Inlet was named in 1818 by explorer John Ross after English astronomer John Pond. The Inuktitut name for Pond Inlet is 'Mittimatalik,' which means the place where Mitima is buried.

Ice break-up commences in July when the North Water polynya in Baffin Bay reaches the eastern entrance to Pond Inlet. The ice in Pond Inlet and Eclipse Sound normally breaks up and disperses in mid-July. The W end of Eclipse Sound is normally the last area to become ice-free. Freeze-up occurs in early October. Several glaciers on both the north and south shores calve icebergs. Ice bergs and floes move in the anti-clockwise current which circulates in Pond Inlet and Eclipse Sound.

In addition to the numbered anchorages, cruising boats are reported to have anchored in Emerson Island (72°22′N 79°03′W), White Bay (72°26′N 79°25′W) and Deep Cove off Milne Inlet (72°11′N 80°24′W).

Navy Board Inlet *Sibéal Turraoin*

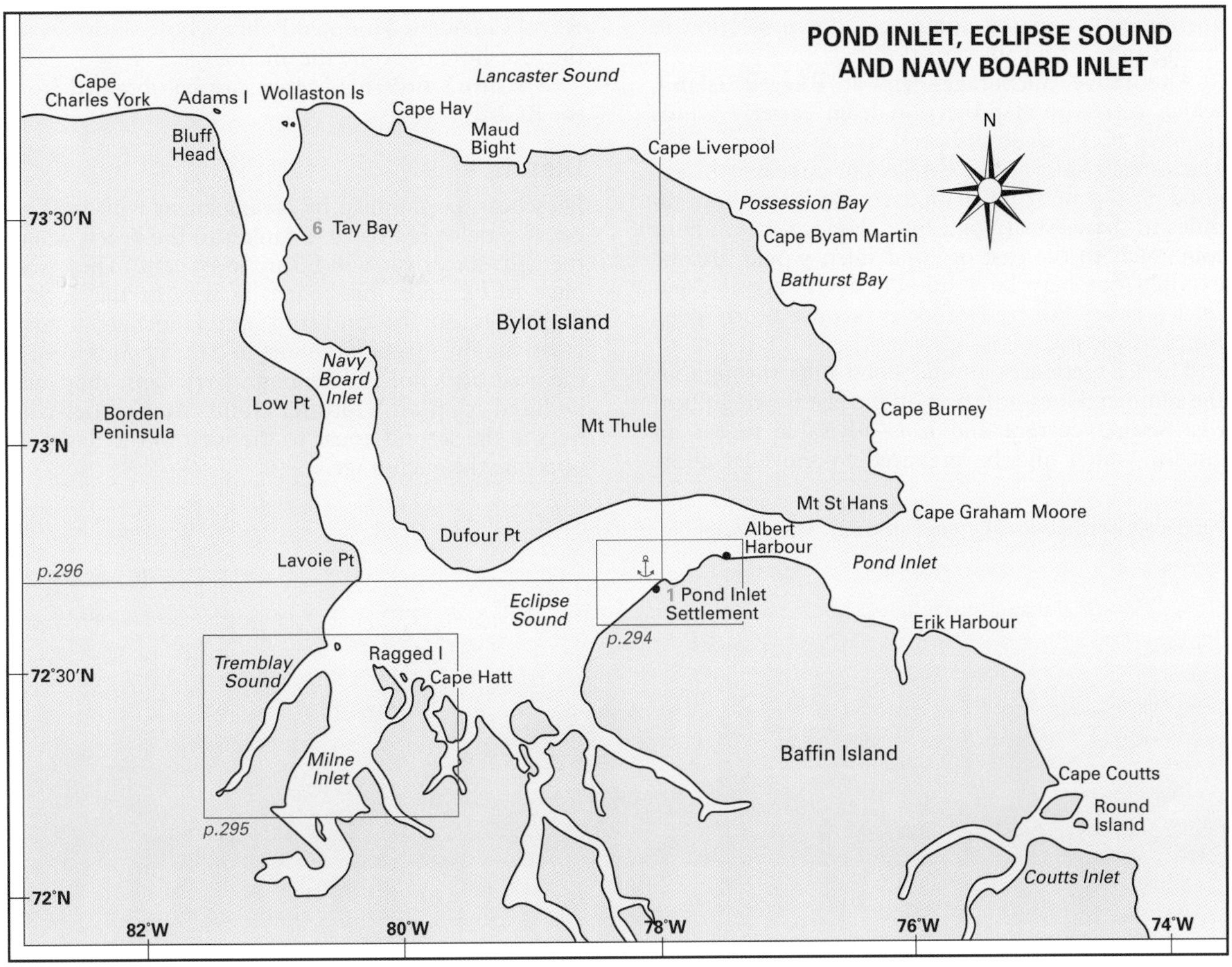

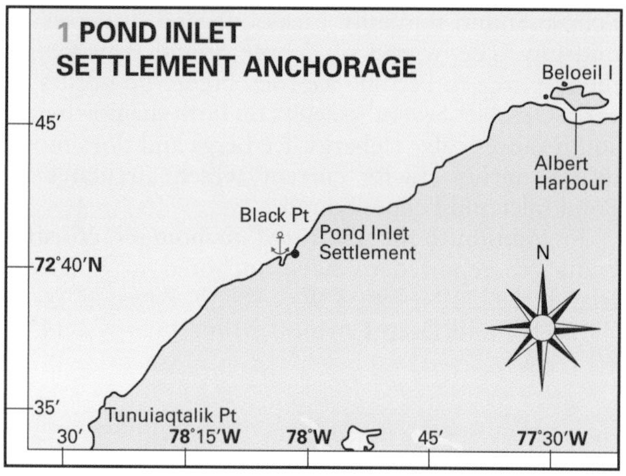

1 Pond Inlet Settlement

72°42′N 77°59′W

Approach

Accessible when the ice melts in July, August and September. Enter from Baffin Bay from the east or Navy Board Inlet from Lancaster Sound in the north. The former is likely to be ice-free earlier in the year and reference to ice-charts is advisable for both.

Anchorages

Anchor in 6–15m off the beach opposite the radio mast and church. Good holding in sand. The anchorage is exposed and gives poor protection in strong winds from any direction.

Alternative anchorages are at Ragged Island, which offers good protection from easterly winds (beware rocks close inshore), or the inlet at Cape Hatt which has varying depths but appears to have good protection from all quarters. Both are about 40 miles to the west of Pond Inlet. James Creek, about four miles to the east of Pond Inlet, would also be exposed but may be a suitable anchorage if Pond Inlet is beset. Albert Harbor is inconveniently deep for most yachts.

The ice circulates around Pond Inlet throughout the summer. Floes drift past on the fast flowing (2kn) east setting current and it is advisable to set an anchor watch and be prepared to move at short notice. It may be sensible to lay less anchor scope than normal so that, if the vessel is hit by a floe, the anchor will drag easily. If the boat is securely anchored, the floe may cause more damage. Less chain is also quicker to recover if time is short.

Pond Inlet roadstead *Sibéal Turraoin*

Formalities

Customs and Immigration are dealt with by the Royal Canadian Mounted Police whose station is on the foreshore opposite the anchorage.

A visitor's firearms licence can be obtained from the RCMP.

Diesel

Diesel can be supplied by arrangement with the Co-op. It is delivered by road tanker to the beach where the delivery driver will fill up jerry cans. These will have to be taken on board by way of the yacht's dinghy. It can be cold and wet launching a fully laden dinghy through the surf in windy conditions. If the boat does not have enough jerry cans, they may be hired from an 'Outfitter' (Inuit tour guide) who lives in the second house to the west of the flag pole opposite the anchorage.

Pond Inlet landfall viewed from Baffin Bay *Máire Wilkes*

Settlement of Pond Inlet *Dermot O'Riordan*

Facilities

Pond Inlet (population 1,550) has relatively good facilities for visitors. One of the hotels may be able to help with showers, laundry and use of their Wi-Fi internet connection. Pond Inlet has elected to be a damp settlement, that is alcohol is not illegal but may not be sold or purchased. There are two supermarkets: the Co-op and the Northern Store. Fresh food, including fruit, vegetables and milk, is flown to Pond Inlet several times a week. There is a museum and a nursing station. Pond Inlet settlement not recommended (locally) for fresh water.

The hotel contact details are:

Sauniq Hotel ✆ (867) 899-6500
Email sauniq-innsnorth@Arcticco-op.com

Black Point Lodge Hotel ✆ (867) 899-8008
Email blackpointlodge@qiniq.com

Transport connections

The airport has connections to other Nunavut settlements with onward connections to Ottawa.

Yacht crews land ashore by dinghy. Local children are likely to play with any dinghy and life-jackets left unattended.

Bylot Island

Bylot Island, the Borden Peninsula to its west and the land between Oliver Sound and Paquet Sound lies within the Sirmilik National Park. Special regulations may apply and one should contact the National Park if planning to go ashore in these areas. The visitor information pack, which can be downloaded from their website is informative. The Pond Inlet office contact details are:

✆ (867) 899-8092
Email sirmilik.info@pc.gc.ca

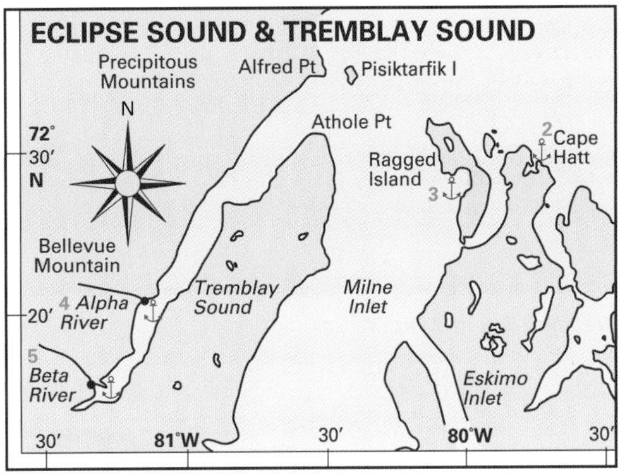

Eclipse Sound, Milne Inlet and Tremblay Sound

The scenery is beautiful. Although much of the water is deep, there are suitable anchorages which can be identified with careful study of chart *7212*. In the summer, one is likely to see Inuit hunting camps throughout the region.

2 Cape Hatt 72°29′N 079°43′W

The small, almost landlocked, bay to the east of Cape Hatt is navigable for small vessels. It is a favourite camp site for Inuit hunters in the summer. Depths vary throughout the bay and caution should be exercised. A yacht drawing 2.8m has anchored comfortably in the bay. Good protection from all directions.

3 Ragged Island 72°28′N 080°00′W

The bay to the west of Ragged Island can provide a sheltered anchorage when the wind is from the north through east to south. There are several rocky outcrops extending from the shore and a good lookout is required before anchoring. Good holding in silt, 10m.

Ragged Island *Máire Wilkes*

Tremblay Sound *Máire Wilkes*

Alpha River, Tremblay Sound, with an Inuit hunting party camping in the delta *Máire Wilkes*

Southern entrance to Navy Board Inlet *Sibéal Turraoin*

Tremblay Sound

4 Alpha River 72°N 26′W 080°N 57′W

The Alpha River delta is a favourite campsite for Inuit hunters in the summer.

Anchor in 15–20m off the river delta.

5 Beta River 72°17′N 081°13′W

The river delta is at the head of Tremblay Sound. Anchor in 15–20m either side of the spit. It is a good place to take on fresh water.

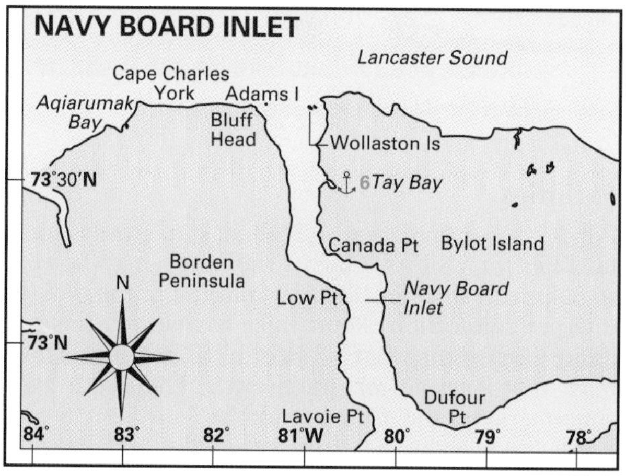

Navy Board Inlet

The ice in Navy Board Inlet is one of the last areas of ice to clear in the Eclipse Bay/Pond Inlet area. This normally happens in early/mid August. If planning to leave Pond Inlet for a passage through the North West Passage, it may not have cleared when one plans to leave and a passage around the east and north of Bylot Island will be necessary to gain Lancaster Sound. See the Canadian Sailing Directions for hazards and potential anchorages. It is a very pretty passage with steeply rising land to east and west.

The high elevations can accelerate winds dramatically.

6 Tay Bay 73°29′N 80°45′W

A convenient anchorage at northern end of Navy Board Inlet. Shallow water comes a fair way out on north side past the entrance; good for anchoring but can shelve rapidly. Good shelter can be found whilst sheltering from an easterly gale, however, the anchorage is exposed to strong winds from the S/SE which enter the anchorage over the saddle at the head of the bay. Alvah Simon over wintered here in 2011 and wrote about the experience in his book *North into the Night*.

II Lancaster Sound and Barrow Strait

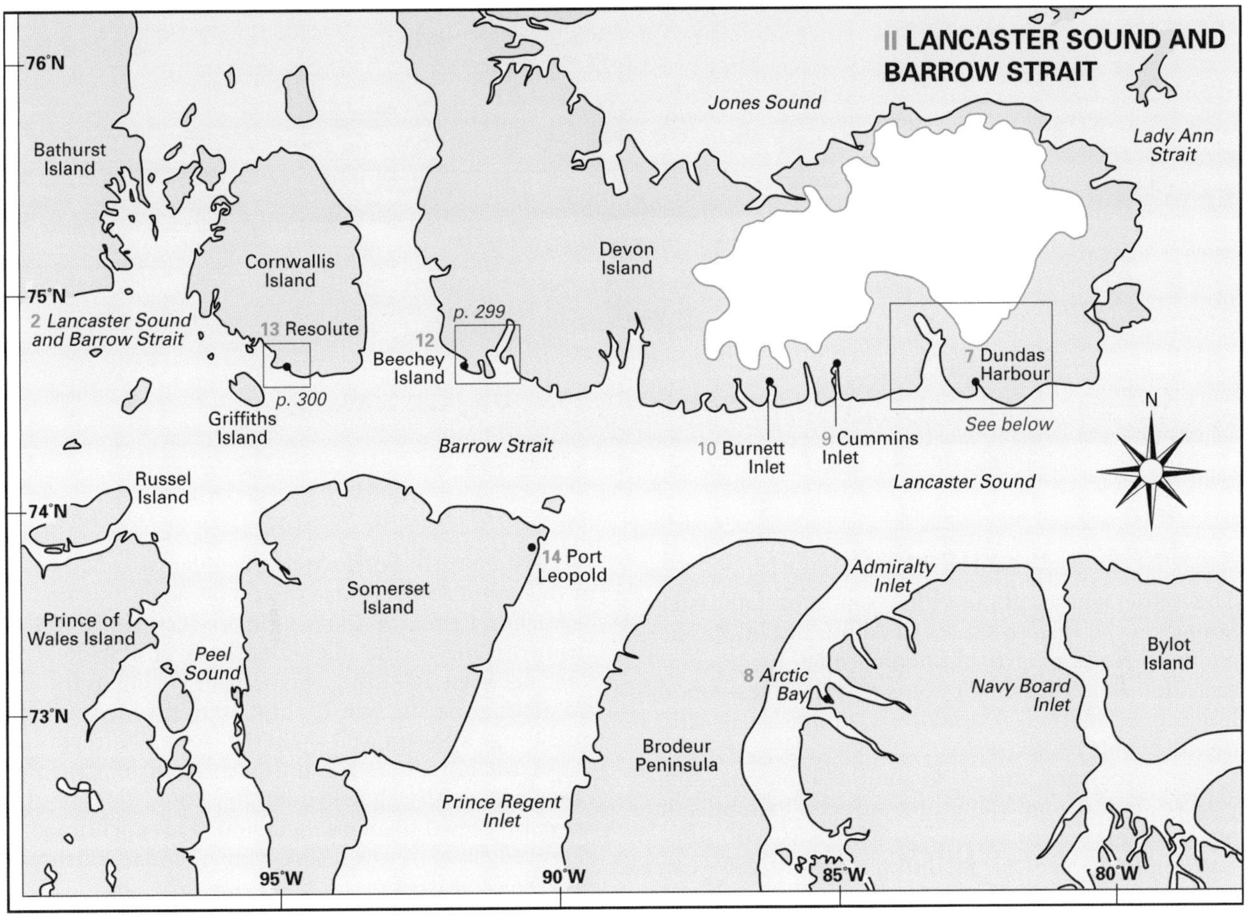

Water can be collected from the glacial river estuary at the entrance. Take a rifle ashore; polar bears have been sighted.

The ice in Lancaster Sound clears between the end of June and mid August. It clears sooner if the wind is from the northwest and later if it is from the southeast. A strong surface current moves eastwards along the southern side of the sound. Warmer water in the northern and eastern parts of Lancaster Sound should mean that they are ice-free before the southern areas. However, this should be verified with ice charts, keeping a sharp look out from on high and looking out for 'ice blink' and 'water skies.' A more northern route should avoid the strong east-going current on the south coast.

There are many potential anchorages on the south coast of Devon Island and the following are known to have been used by cruising boats: Cuming Inlet (74°34'N 85°00'W), Stratton Inlet (74°30'N 86°38'W), Blanley Bay (74°30'N 87°24'·4W), Graham Harbour (74°30'·7N 88°09'·7W), Rigby Bay (74°34'N 90°03'W) and Radstock Bay (74°45'·40N 91°10'·70W and 74°43'·6N 90°45'·2W).

7 Dundas Harbour 74°32'N 82°26'W

On the northern side of Lancaster Sound. Reported to offer good shelter with a choice of two anchorages. Good holding in 12m with some kelp. Katabatic winds from the ENE can be very strong. There is an abandoned RCMP outpost and deserted Inuit settlement but no facilities.

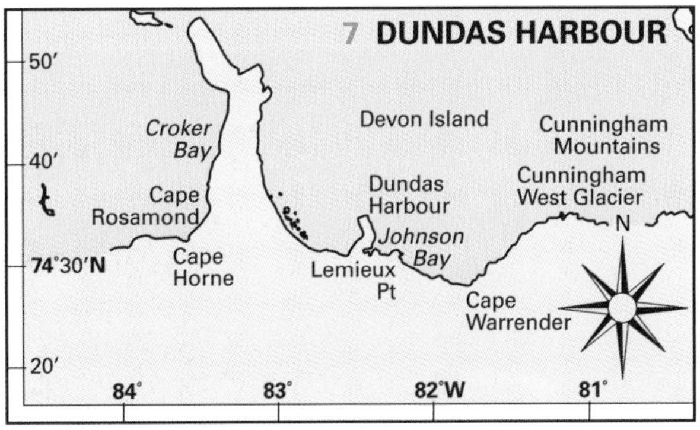

Lancaster Sound *Máire Wilkes*

8 Arctic Bay 73°02'N 85°10'W

The settlement is about 50M south of Lancaster Sound on the eastern shores of Admiralty Inlet. The anchorage is in the bay although a small breakwater provides shelter for small boats and dinghies. Good holding is reported. Alternatively, dinghies can land on the pebble beach.

The settlement, known in Inuit as Ikpiarjuk, 'the pocket', is surrounded on three sides by high hills. It has a population of about 750 with a RCMP office and limited medical facilities. The RCMP can arrange customs clearance if required. Diesel supplies can be arranged at the hotel. A tanker will fill up jerry cans which have to be relayed to the anchored vessel. Water from village. Flights are available from First Air.

9 Cuming Inlet 74°39'N 84°59'W

Proceed up the centre of Cuming Inlet. The Canadian pilot reports a rock ½M off the shore at about the point where a glacier enters on the west side. It does not, however, say which shore the rock is half a mile off. Fortunately, the inlet is 1.6M broad at this point so the centre should be safe.

Arctic Bay - the settlement

Anchor behind a spit on the eastern shore 2·4M from the end of the inlet. Depths over a wide area vary between 10–15m. The bottom is kelp and rock so getting an anchor to bite is not so easy. The anchorage appears well sheltered from all directions.

The anchorage at the northern head of the inlet comprises gently shelving silt and could possibly be more protected from ice incursion. This anchorage is reported to be more secure than Dundas Harbour, 40M to the east.

10 Burnett Inlet 74°36'N 86°10'W

The anchorage is in the pool at the head of the inlet, on the east side of the island. The chart has soundings up to the island but none thereafter. Turn to starboard on entering the pool keeping about midway between the coast and the island. Depths should not be less than 10m. About 200m due east of the island is a large area of water 10–15m in depth. Holding is excellent in mud and fine mud. The water shallows towards the north and the outfall of the two rivers there.

Reported to give good shelter in both southerly and northerly gales with a slight swell making in round the corner. Shelter from the southerly winds however, is only apparent when almost in the pool. The anchorage has been reported as almost ice-free when there was thick ice at the mouth of the inlet.

11 Gascoyne Inlet 74°41'N 91°17'W

Gascoyne Inlet is an alternative anchorage to Beechey Island, and is sometimes used by Canadian Coastguard vessels. It is 5M to the east of Beechey Island. Depths are 10m or less.

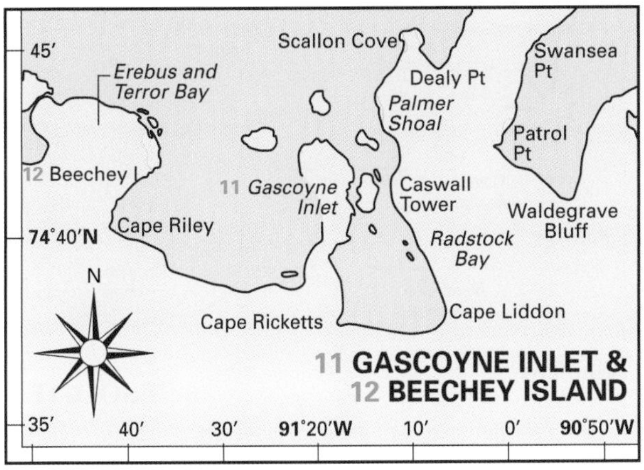

12 Beechey Island – Erebus and Terror Bay 74°43′N 91°42′W

Used by Franklin's expedition when they over wintered here in 1845–46. The bay is named after Franklin's two ships: HMS *Terror* and HMS *Erebus*. It was also the base for one of the Franklin rescue attempts. This is a useful anchorage if a vessel has to wait for ice conditions to improve in Peel Sound. A vessel is less likely to become trapped by ice in Erebus and Terror Bay than in Resolute. There are no facilities ashore although water may be obtained from streams.

Anchorage

Often used by Canadian coastguard vessels, the bay affords reasonable protection. The normal anchorage is in the northwest part of the bay in 10–18m. The eastern side can be used in easterly winds however it is shoal for some distance from the eastern shore. The holding is good in shale.

Ice dangers

Ice enters the bay and circulates around it, dependent upon wind and current. The tidal range appears to be about 2m. Floes ground at low water and re-float at high water. A constant anchor watch should be kept and it may be necessary to re-anchor frequently.

John Torrington's grave at Erebus and Terror Bay, Beechey Island *Sibéal Turraoin*

Ashore

On the north shore there are five graves. One is unmarked, the others are of Thomas Morgan of HMS *Investigator*, William Braine, John Hartnell and John Torrington who were all part of the Franklin expedition. The graves were exhumed in 1981 and the bodies were found to be very well preserved by the perma-frost. Autopsies revealed high levels of lead in the bodies, probably from the tin cans used by the expedition, which may have contributed to their deaths. The story is recounted in

The remains of barrels and tin cans used by the crew of HMS *Investigator* whilst searching for the Franklin expedition. The lead solder used to seal the tin can be seen *Sibéal Turraoin*

Erebus and Terror Bay, Beechey Island *Sibéal Turraoin*

Northumberland House, Erebus and Terror Bay, Beechey Island *Sibéal Turraoin*

Owen Beattie and John Geiger's book, *Frozen in Time*. A navigation cairn, built by the crews of the *Erebus* and *Terror*, can be reached by a short climb on the hill above the graves.

On the southern side of Erebus and Terror Bay are the remains of one of the Franklin rescue mission camps. Northumberland House was constructed by the crew of HMS *Investigator* in 1854. The site is littered with the hoops and staiths which made up the mission's supply barrels. There are also many first generation tin cans: red-lead paint having prolonged their decay. There are several memorials dedicated to the Franklin expedition and those who tried to rescue them.

13 Resolute (Cornwallis Island)

74°41'N 94°53'W

Resolute is named after HMS *Resolute* one of the vessels who searched for the lost Franklin expedition. Resolute is a centre for transport, communications and administration for the high Arctic. In 2013 it had a population of 243. There are plans to build a 100 strong military training base.

The small boat anchorage, in the centre and north of the bay, has depths from 18–27m. The approach has greater depth on the western side. It is reported to have poor holding in mud and shale. Vessels with a draught greater than 8·5m, anchor in the open roadstead 1M south of Sight Point. The harbour ice is normally broken up by ice breaker in early August but may become blocked again after prolonged periods of westerly winds. The ice will depart again when the prevailing northeast and easterly winds return. **More than one yacht has become trapped in the harbour by ice.** It may be necessary to re-anchor several times to avoid ice floes.

There are two landing beaches but no dock.

Diesel is transferred by jerry cans and dinghy or by anchoring the parent vessel close to shore and using a hose. Anchoring close to shore may be difficult in windy conditions.

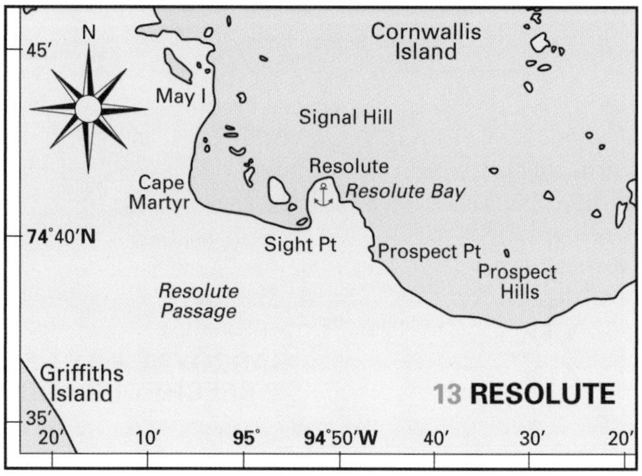

A supermarket, the Tadjaat Co-op, provides basic provisions. An Anglican church welcomes worshippers.

There is a nursing station and a Royal Canadian Mounted Police office.

The airport is served by Kenn Borek Air and First Air and there are plans to expand the airport as part of the proposed military training project.

The hotels number four and are: the Narwhale Inn (✆ 867 252 3968), Qausuittuq Inn North (*Email* coophotel@polarland.com), South Camp Inn (✆ 867 252 3737, *Email* scinn@internorth.com) and the Airport Hotel (✆ 867 252 3968). They may be able to help provide internet access.

Sea ice off Griffiths Island, Barrow Strait *Máire Wilkes*

The settlement of Resolute as seen from the south *Máire Wilkes*

III Peel Sound

Peel Sound connects Barrow Strait in the north to Franklin Strait in the south. Ice break up occurs during August and freeze up begins during the third week of September. Vessels transiting the North West Passage from the east may find that they are waiting in Resolute, Beechy Island or Pond Inlet monitoring ice forecasts and waiting until the waters in Peel Sound are navigable. The coast of Somerset Island is rocky rising to 100m close to the sea and 300m inland. Prince of Wales Island, to the west, is rather lower and undulating. There is a slight (0·3kn) current setting southwards on the west side of the sound and northwards on the east side.

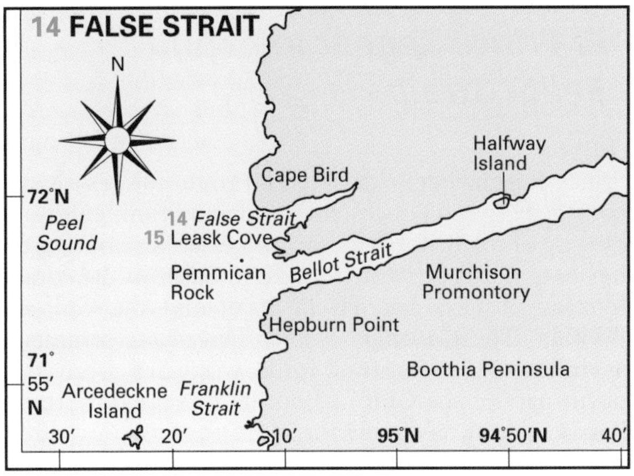

Sea ice in Peel Sound *Máire Wilkes*

Leask Cove *Bob Shepton*

In addition to the numbered anchorages, cruising boats are reported to have anchored in Batty Bay (73°14′N 91°24′W), Fitzgerald Bay (72°09′N 89°45′W), Cresswell Bay (72°40′N 93°00′W) and Port Neill (73°09′N 89°10′W).

14 False Strait 71°59′N 95°11′W

A useful anchorage at the western end of the Bellot Strait, just north of the entrance, for vessels waiting for ice conditions to improve in Peel Sound or the Bellot Strait. Shelter reported to be good from all but westerly winds with good holding.

15 Leask Cove 71°59′N 95°08′W

Leask Cove on the southern side of False Strait has been reported as a well protected and snug anchorage. Anchor in 7–10m. It is a good place to await a favourable tide if transiting the Bellot Strait.

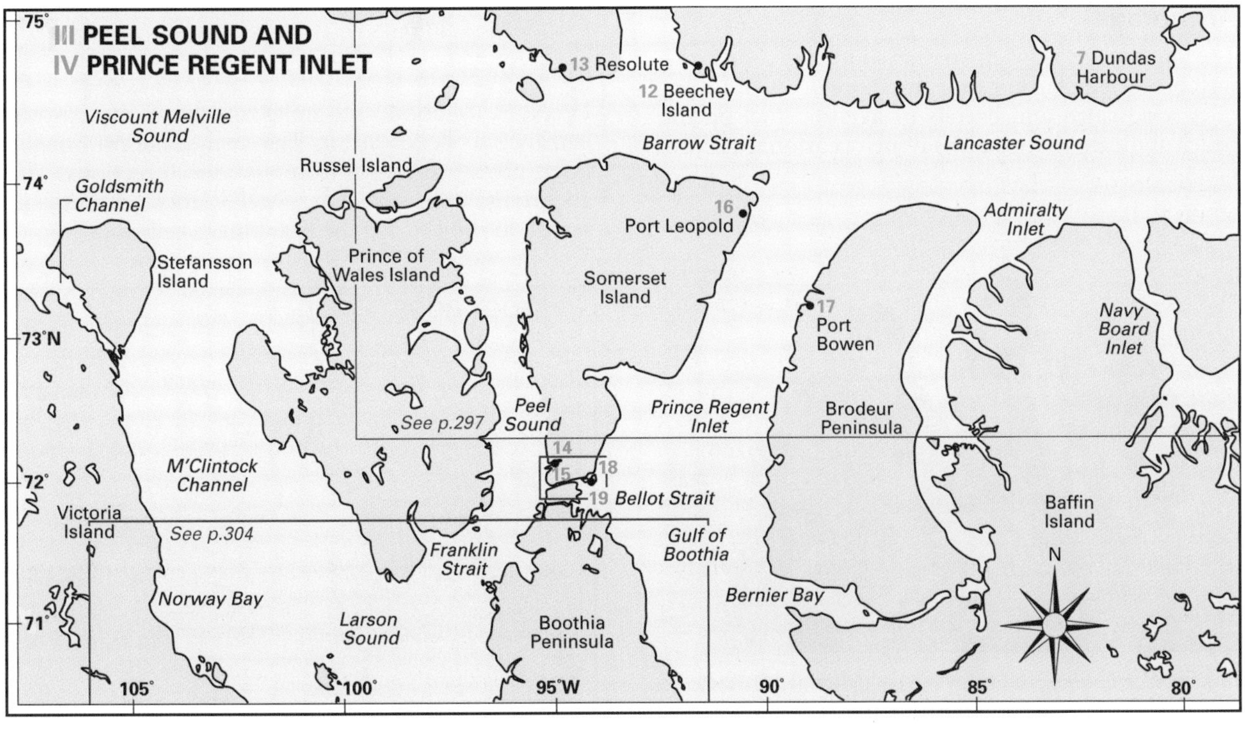

6. THE NORTH WEST PASSAGE

IV Prince Regent Inlet and Bellot Strait

Prince Regent Inlet is a potential route for vessels on passage between Lancaster Sound and Franklin Strait, by way of the Bellot Strait or for vessels attempting to navigate north or west from Foxe Basin in the south by way of Fury and Hecla Strait and the Gulf of Boothia. The *Canadian Sailing Directions* comment as follows: 'Bellot Strait leads westward from the north part of the Gulf of Boothia to Franklin Strait, but is seldom navigable for more than two or three days without icebreaker assistance.'

Despite this foreboding advice, at the end of 2012, 41 of the 88 successful east bound transits of the North West Passage had used the Bellot Strait and 19 of the 95 successful westbound transits had used the Strait. A greater number of eastbound vessels used the Strait because they would be transiting this part of the North West Passage at a later time in the season when the ice is more likely to have broken up.

In addition to the numbered anchorages, cruising boats are reported to have anchored in Nansivik Mine (73°04'N 84°33'W).

16 Port Leopold 73°52'N 90°18'W

Port Leopold is at the northern end of Prince Regent Inlet. The bay is well protected by dramatically sculptured cliffs. Pods of beluga whales are known to visit the bay. There is a small hut on the shore.

HMS *Enterprise* and HMS *Investigator*, both of which were searching for the Franklin expedition, were here and 'EI 1849' is engraved on a rock on the shore.

Anchorage

The anchorage is open to the south but otherwise well protected. Anchor near the shore in 6–7m (20ft).

A food cairn and barrels of aviation fuel on the beach indicate that there may be occasional visitors here.

Crew of *Northabout* resting on the rock inscribed 'EI 1849' at Port Leopold *Jarleth Cunnane*

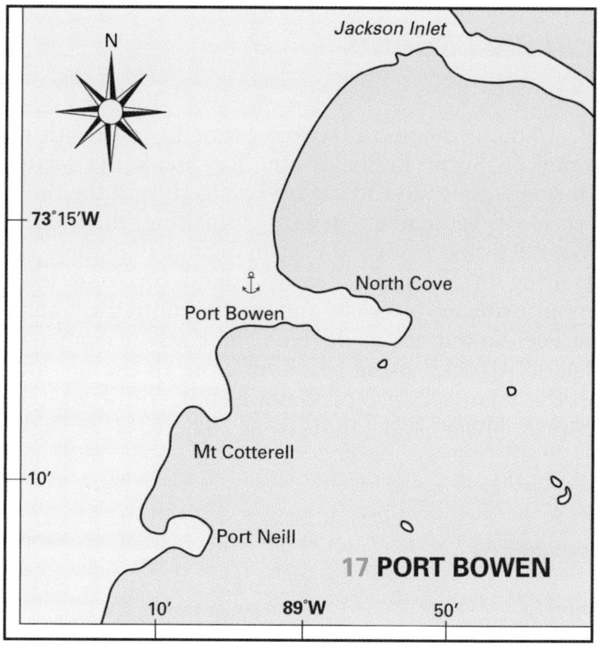

17 Port Bowen 73°14'N 88°58'W

Port Bowen is a safe anchorage on the east side of Prince Regent Sound. Parry overwintered here in 1824.

18 Fort Ross 72°00'N 94°14'W

This marks the eastern end of the Bellot Strait and is a good place to wait for ice conditions to improve. There are many anchorages available in the harbour depending on the wind direction. It is feasible to walk up onto high ground and look westwards into the Bellot Strait to assess the ice. There are two small buildings on the shore, remnants of a Hudson's Bay Company trading post. One has been maintained as an outpost and has a stove, fuel and some stores. Windows are well boarded to keep out bears.

19 Levesque Harbour 71°55'N 94°28'W

Levesque is about six miles south of the eastern entrance to Bellot Strait. The anchorage off Smellie Point gives protection from all wind directions. The anchorage was used by McClintock during his search in the *Fox* for the Franklin expedition.

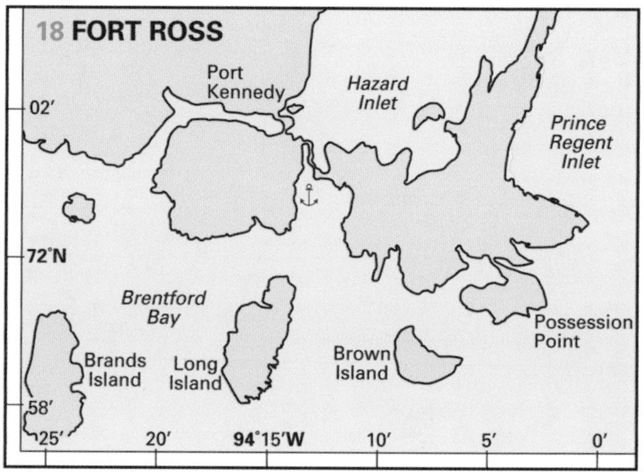

The old Hudson's Bay Company store at Fort Ross
Bob Shepton

Magpie Rock *Richard Hudson*

Bellot Strait

The Bellot Strait is a 17M-long, narrow stretch of water connecting Franklin Strait on the western end with Prince Regent Inlet to the east. It can completely plug up or clear of ice within twenty four hours. It has notoriously strong tidal currents (up to 8–9kns in places) and it is essential to take these into account when transiting the strait (see website addresses for predicted tide times). Barely submerged Magpie Rock is a danger to navigation at the eastern end. It is marked with range marks but these are very difficult to see and would be impossible to locate in poor visibility. Half way through the strait, Zenith Point (72°N) marks the most northerly tip of the North American mainland at the top of the Boothia Peninsula.

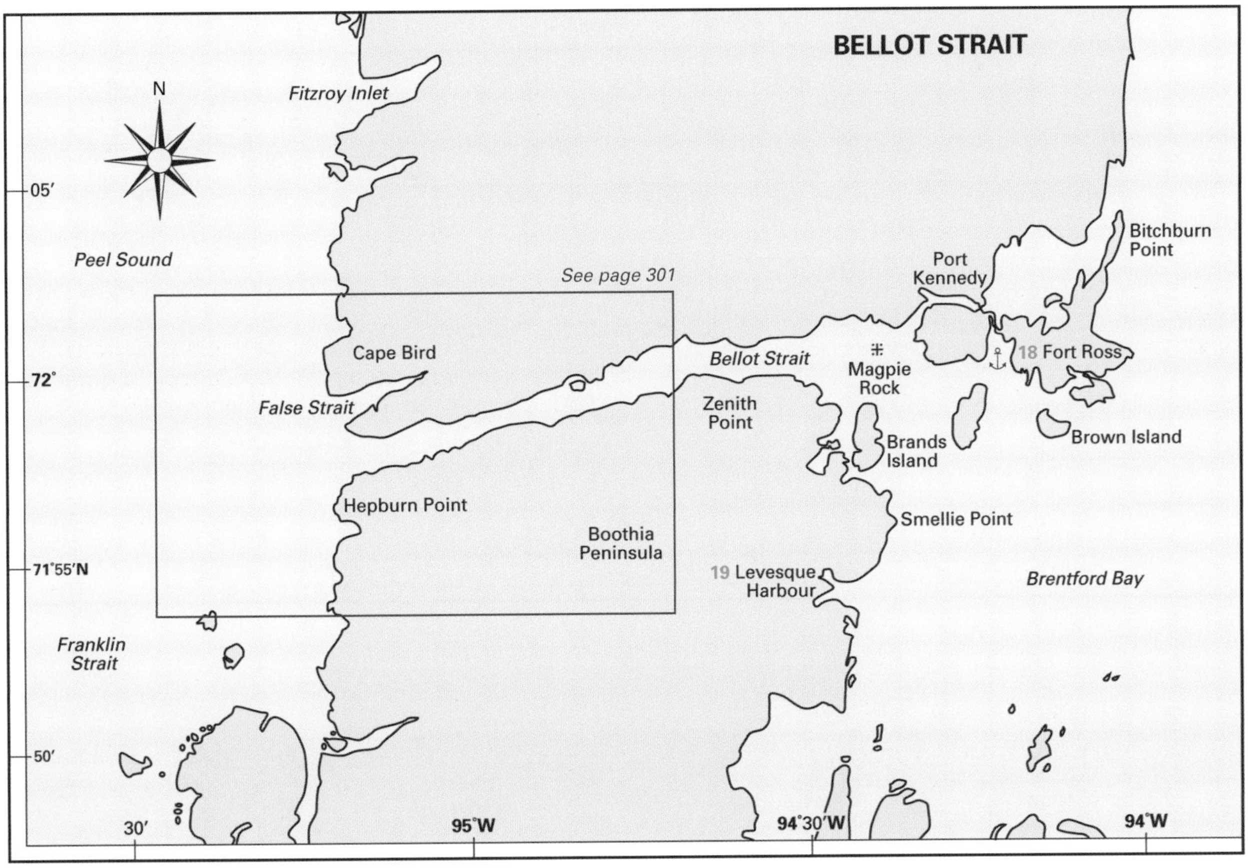

V Franklin Strait, Larsen Sound and King William Island

The charts and *Canadian Sailing Directions* will yield a number of potential anchorages. The surface water colour will indicate whether the bottom is rock or mud/sand. Most of the mud is good holding.

20 Camilla Cove 71°43′N 95°30′W

Camilla Cove anchorage is in the southeast corner of a small bay about 16M south of the western entrance of Bellot Strait. It reportedly a good anchorage with 3·5m (12ft) at the entrance at high tide. There is a fresh water spring. Approach with caution as larger vessels may run aground on a rock reef near the entrance (depth not known).

An uncharted intertidal rock (of which there are many) has been reported in 71°19′·7N 96°41′·0W.

Remnants of sea ice in Larsen Sound *Máire Wilkes*

In addition to the numbered anchorages, cruising boats are reported to have anchored in Cape Victoria* (69°52′N 96°08′W), Oscar Bay* (69°45′N 95°39′W) and Josephine Bay* (69°38′·57N 94°43′·8W).

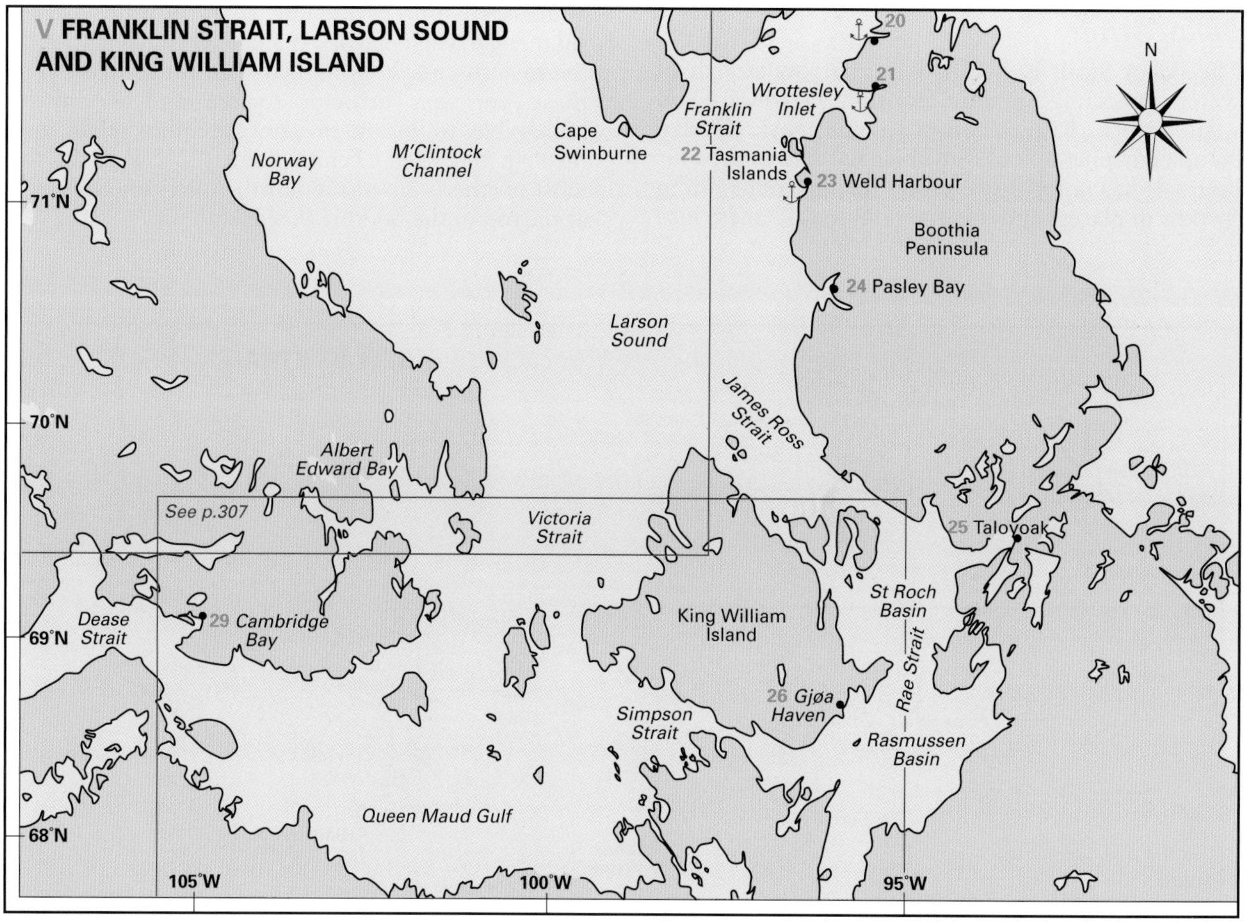

Pasley Bay

21 Pattinson Harbor, Wrottesley Inlet 71°30'N 95°27'W

This anchorage is a short distance up the Point Liardet channel in the northeast corner of Wrottesley Inlet. It is about 40M south of the western entrance of Bellot Strait. It is not a particularly good anchorage, but vessels have sheltered in depths shallow enough to anchor in some extremely bad weather. The inlet is a long, deep fjord, with further anchorage possible towards its eastern end.

22 Tasmania Islands

71°14'N 96°32'W

The Tasmania Islands, on the eastern side of Franklin Strait, are relatively high (170m) and of rock thereby offering a good radar target.

The islands are likely to offer a number of anchorages, one of which is reported in the position quoted above and described as a pleasant anchorage by a beach at the far western end of the cove. However ice floes on the unpredictable tidal currents can be a problem. Note an unmarked shoal is reported in position 71°19'·66N 96°41'·03W.

Shotland Channel, Tasmania Islands *Bob Shepton*

Ice floes in Sophie Louise Bay, Tasmania Islands *Bob Shepton*

It may be no coincidence that Sir John Franklin was the Lieutenant-Governor of Tasmania, south of Australia, from 1836 to 1843. The epitaph on a statue of Sir John Franklin in Tasmania, Australia was written by Tennyson and reads: 'Not here! The white north hath thy bones and thou, Heroic sailor soul, Art passing on thine happier voyage now, Toward no earthly pole'.

23 Weld Harbour 71°07'N 096°22'W

Good holding and shelter. A favourite haunt for Muskox.

24 Pasley Bay 70°36'N 96°09'W

Pasley Bay was used by Larsen in the St Roch to over-winter in 1941/1942. During their stay, the St Roch crew erected four cairns in the vicinity of the bay. An old cabin is reported to be on the south shore of the SE arm of the bay where there are a number of islets and shoals. Fair holding and shelter from all except W winds.

25 Taloyoak (Spence Bay)

69°32'N 93°31'W

Taloyoak is a village (2011 population 899) with an airport, two supermarkets, two hotels, Royal Canadian Mounted Police and limited medical facilities. The settlement, which was originally called Spence Bay, was formed in 1947 when the Fort Ross settlement was closed down and the inhabitants relocated. The word 'Taloyoak', or 'Talurjuaq', originates from the Inuit word meaning 'large screen' or a screen used when hunting caribou.

There are numerous shoal areas in the approaches and *CHS Sailing Directions* should be studied carefully. Good anchorage except in SW winds. Diesel and water available from the village.

Taloyoak *Bob Shepton*

26 Gjøa Haven 68°37'N 95°53'W

Originally a camping site for the Netsilik Inuit. The settlement is known in Inuit as *Uqsuqtuuq* which means 'lots of fat', a reference to the good hunting which can be expected here. It was, and is, also a centre for traditional crafts.

Amundsen sailed into Gjøa Haven in 1903 and spent two winters there. He divided his time between carrying out scientific experiments and learning traditional survival, travel and hunting techniques from the Inuit. Sheltered from all winds, this harbour was described by one of Amundsen's crew as, 'The most perfect little harbour in the world'.

In 2011, the population was 1,279.

Approach

Enter using the unlit leading marks on 358°. Entry at night is possible with caution. Resist any temptation to cut between the main island and the small island which stands a few miles off the eastern head of the bay – yachts have run aground here.

Anchorage

Anchor in 8–12m off the town past the narrows near the head of the bay. Note small craft moorings at the extreme head of the bay. Good holding in mud. Well protected from all winds.

Airport

The airport is served by Canadian North and First Air airlines.

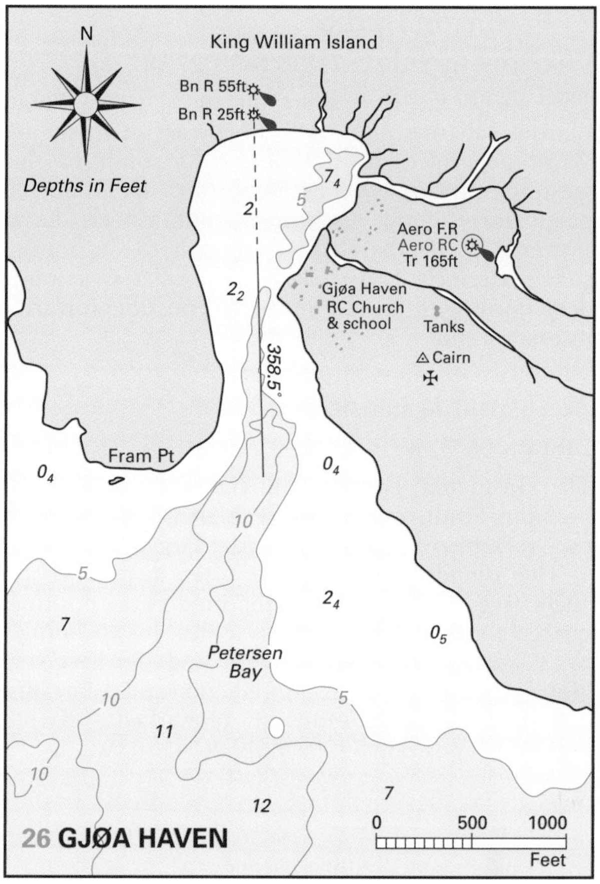

Gjøa Haven *Dermot O'Riordan*

Gjøa Haven craftsman
Sibéal Turraoin

Useful websites

	Gjøa Haven Gjøa Haven community website	www.gjoahaven.net/the-community.html

Two yachts anchored in Gjøa Haven *Máire Wilkes*

Facilities

There are two supermarkets: the Co-op and Northern Store.

The Amundsen Hotel (✆ 867 360 6176) may be able to provide showers, laundry and wireless internet access.

Outfitters can organise trekking, sledding and hunting trips. There are opportunities to buy local Inuit arts and craft. Craftsmen in Gjøa Haven are particularly well known for their fine stone sculptures and ivory carvings. There is even an 18 hole golf course!

There is a medical centre, school and Royal Canadian Mounted Police station.

Diesel can be bought and transferred by jerry can.

VI Simpson Strait and Queen Maud Gulf

Simpson Strait lies between King William Island to the north and the Canadian mainland to the south. It is about 45 miles long. At its narrowest point, about 16 miles from the western end, it is about two miles wide but the shallow water restricts the channel to five cables wide. The Strait has many shoals, strong tides and relatively narrow channels.

During the navigation season, the channels are marked by buoys (IALA system B) however they would be easily displaced by ice. Several ranges (or transits) mark the channels but, in conditions of poor visibility, they can be very difficult to see. Much of the land is low lying which makes distinctive features difficult to recognise. Charts are not surveyed to GPS levels of accuracy. Use every available means to navigate safely. Best to navigate these waters during daylight.

Tidal streams of up to 7kns have been reported near Eta Island with associated rip tides and back eddies around shoals.

The least depth through the eastern part of Queen Maud Gulf and Simpson Strait is 7·3m (24ft) however the Sailing Directions say the maximum draft of vessels using this route has been 5m (16ft).

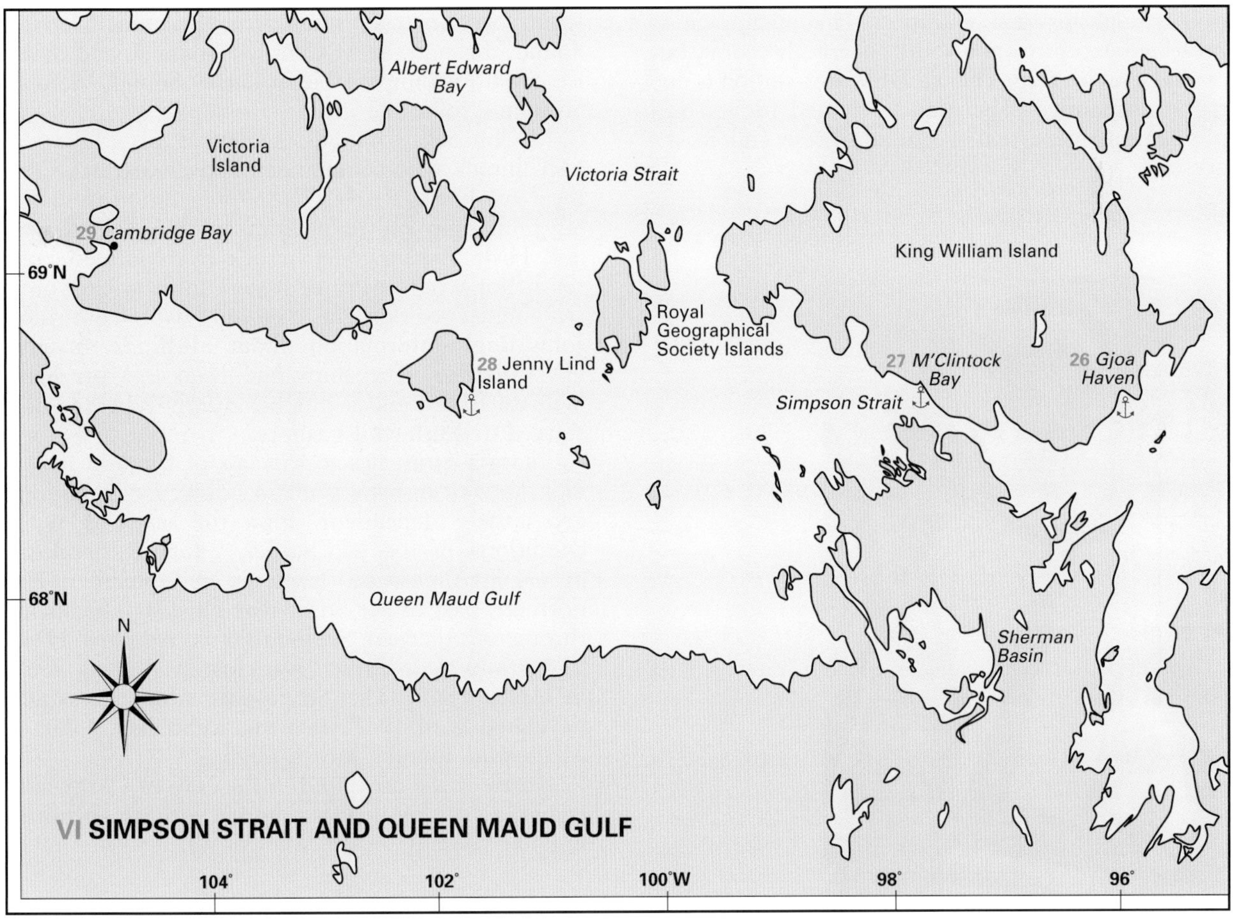

Simpson Strait transit (or range) marks *Máire Wilkes*

Queen Maud Gulf presents fewer hazards however it is more prone to ice drifting south from the M'Clintock Channel.

27 M'Clintock Bay 68°39'N 097°44'W

M'Clintock Bay lies at the western end of the Simpson Strait on the south shore of King William Island. It is reported to be a secure and sheltered anchorage.

The old DEW line station here was demolished in 2004–2005 by digging a big hole, lining it and pushing everything into it. Entrance may be blocked by ice.

28 Jenny Lind Island 68°43'N 101°58'W

The anchorage at Jenny Lind Island, which is named after the Swedish opera singer, is reported to be an easy straightforward entrance. The anchorage is protected except from a southeasterly direction, but could be an ice trap. The old DEW line station is due to be dismantled. The island is noted for its bird population, in particular Canada geese and Ross's geese.

Sibéal Turraoin

VII Viscount Melville Sound, M'Clintock Channel and Victoria Strait

Viscount Melville Sound is that part of the Parry Channel which is to the north of Victoria Island and the M'Clintock Channel. Melville Island, one of the Parry Islands, lies to the north of the Sound. Ice break-up occurs in early/mid August and progresses from east and west towards the middle of the Sound. The north side of the channel normally has less ice. Freeze-up starts in early/mid September. There is a slight east setting current and ice movement is predominately determined by wind.

Commander Robert McClure and his crew in HMS *Investigator* over-wintered off Banks Island in the western part of the Sound for three years whilst attempting to locate the Franklin expedition. They were rescued by a sledge party from HMS *Resolute* in 1853 and in doing so, became the first people to transit the North West Passage; albeit by a combination of ship and sledge.

The M'Clintock Channel leads south from Viscount Melville Sound to Larsen Sound. Break-up progresses from the south in early August. Freeze-up begins in mid to late September. Ice in the M'Clintock Channel is largely determined by wind direction, strength and duration. The prevailing NW winds can drive ice south from Viscount Melville Sound, through the M'Clintock Channel, and make ice conditions impassable in Larsen Sound, Victoria Strait and John Rae Strait.

M'Clintock Channel is named after Francis McClintock who commanded Lady Franklin's ship, the *Fox*, during the 1857/1859 expedition to locate Sir John Franklin's expedition in the HMS *Terror* and HMS *Erebus*. McClintock overwintered near the Bellot Strait in Prince Regent Inlet, where, on a sledging expedition, he met Inuit who confirmed John Rae's information about HMS *Terror* and HMS *Erebus*. The ships had been lost off King William Island and a number of white people had starved to death whilst ashore.

Victoria Strait lies to the east of Victoria Island and the west of King William Island. Ice conditions are largely dependent upon the ice and wind conditions in the M'Clintock Channel. Break-up occurs in August and freeze-up in September. The northern part of the Strait may have significant ice throughout the year. Sir John Franklin's ships' HMS *Terror* and HMS *Erebus* were lost in Victoria Strait in April 1848. The Strait was not successfully navigated until 1967 when the icebreaker, *John A. McDonald*, found a way through.

North of the area, and to the NW of Cornwallis Island, a cruising boat is reported to have anchored in Polaris Mines (75°23'N 96°53'W).

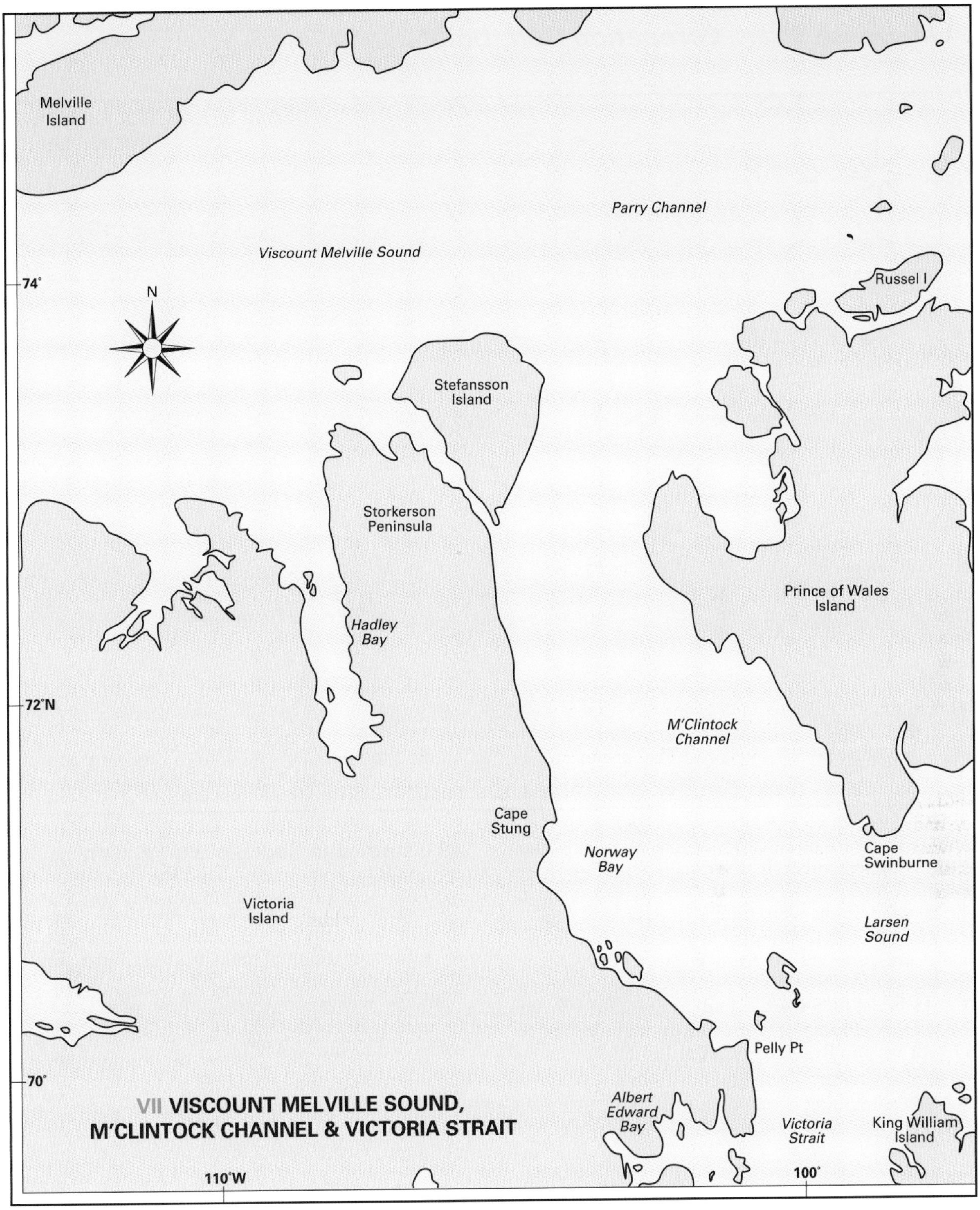

VII VISCOUNT MELVILLE SOUND, M'CLINTOCK CHANNEL & VICTORIA STRAIT

VIII Dease Strait, Coronation Gulf, Dolphin and Union Strait

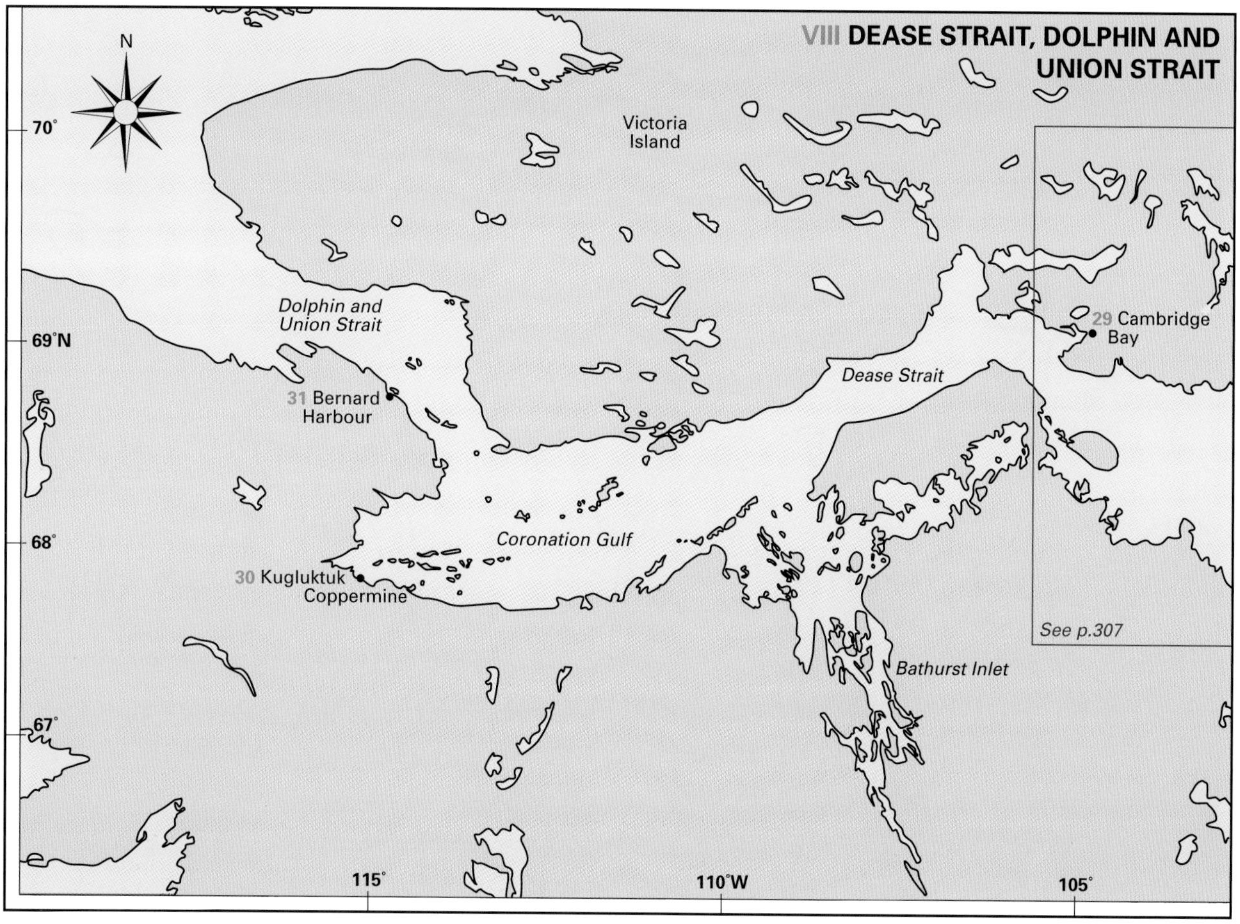

The ice in Dease Strait clears at the end of July and reforms in September. It is normally frozen over by the third week of October. The land is low lying in the east and, in the west, shingle slopes rise to 46m.

In addition to the numbered anchorages, cruising boats are reported to have anchored in Sinclair Creek (68°44'N 108°57'·6W), Port Epworth (67°43'N 111°54'W), Lady Franklin Point (68°29'·1N 113°14'·5W), Muskox Bay (69°13'N 113°40'W) and Read Is. (69°13'N 113°53'W).

29 Cambridge Bay 69°03'N 105°02'W

Charts 7750, 7782

Cambridge Bay is located on the south coast of Victoria Island and is the administration centre for the Kitikmeot region of the Northwest Territories. In 2011, the population was 1,375.

In the navigation season, there is a Canadian Coastguard radio station which is remotely controlled by Inuvik MCTS.

Cambridge Bay *Sibéal Turraoin*

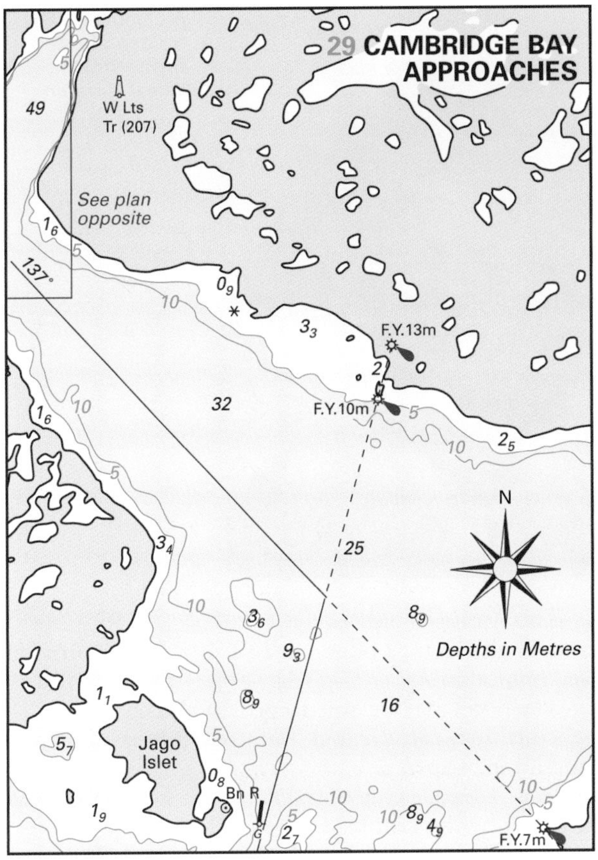

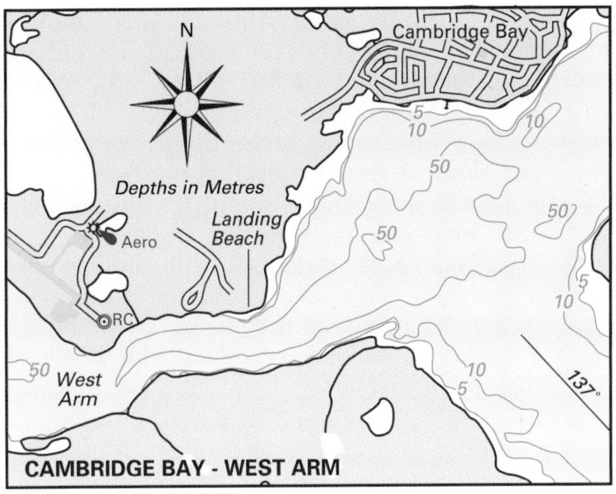

Approach

Approach using the various leading lights which make the entrance straight forward by day or night.

Note that the two unlit port and one unlit starboard buoys are close to the transit off Jago Islet and, in darkness, a good watch should be kept for them.

Mooring alongside

Vessels can moor alongside the public quay when not in use by supply vessels. There is approximately 6m of water alongside the southern edge but it is shoal at the west and east faces. Craft using the quay can expect frequent visitors and on-lookers. Children congregate on the quay at night-time and there have been reports of them throwing pebbles onto visiting boats.

Anchorages

Boats can anchor off the quay in about 7m. Good holding. The wider area of Cambridge Bay has many anchorages, from Carl Bay (where the *Maud* is) to the end of the West Arm. Cambridge Bay has over 30km of mostly navigable shoreline. There is good arctic char fishing in the bay.

Diesel

Diesel can be obtained from the Kitimuth office who will arrange for a road tanker to visit the quay. There is a call-out charge for this service if fuel is required out of normal office hours. In 2012 this was $156 per boat (even if more than one boat is refuelling at the same time).

Facilities

Northern Store and Co-op supermarkets are well stocked by northern standards. Kitimuth Supplies stocks a range of hardware and tools. Opposite is a workshop whose mechanics are very helpful and well equipped. Musk ox, arctic char, caribou, etc. can be obtained from a shop which specialises in local food stuffs. There is a gift shop which sells local craftwork. Wireless internet (free) available at the Kitikmeot Heritage Society Centre which is part of the high school library.

Cambridge Bay quay *Dermot O'Riordan*

Useful websites – Cambridge Bay

	Cambridge Bay	www.cambridgebay.ca
	Maud Returns Home - a plan to salvage the sunken ship wreck of Roald Amundsens polar ship *Maud* and bring her back to Norway	www.maudreturnshome.no

There is a delivery fee of $100 for water supplied at the dock. Propane bottles can normally be refilled.

The Visitor's Centre (✆ 867 983 2224), at the east side of town, is very welcoming and has a shower. They open a file each year in which they print out blogs of vessels transiting the North West Passage. There are displays about Cambridge Bay and other Inuit communities, the Copper Inuit, a large stuffed polar bear (which will confirm any doubts you may have held about the wisdom of carrying a rifle on board), the history of the North West Passage and Amundsen's *Maud*, the wreck of which lies in the harbour.

The *Maud*, named after Queen Maud of Norway, was built in 1916 for Roald Amundsen's expedition to transit the North East Passage.

She was launched in Norway and christened by Amundsen by crushing a chunk of ice against her bow with the following words:

> 'It is not my intention to dishonour the glorious grape, but already now you shall get the taste of your real environment. For the ice you have been built, and in the ice you shall stay most of your life, and in the ice you shall solve your tasks. With the permission of our queen, I christen you: *Maud*.'

After a six year transit of the North East Passage, between 1918 and 1924, she ended up in Nome, Alaska and in August 1925 was sold on behalf of Amundsen's U.S. creditors.

The buyer was the Hudson's Bay Company which renamed her *Baymaud*. She was to be used as a supply vessel for their outposts in the western Arctic. However, in the winter of 1926 she was frozen in the ice at Cambridge Bay, where she sank in 1930.

The ship currently lies just off the shore in the bay, across the inlet from Cambridge Bay's former Hudson's Bay Company store. However, in 2011 a Norwegian company proposed to salvage the *Maud* and return her to Norway. This met with opposition from the inhabitants of Cambridge Bay and the Canadian government refused to issue an export licence. The Norwegian company appealed this decision in 2012 and won their appeal. An archeological survey of the *Maud* is planned to take place in 2014 after which she is expected to be salvaged and taken to Vollen in Norway where a new museum is to be built for her.

Quad bikes outside a house in Cambridge Bay. Note the caribou antlers near the entrance *Máire Wilkes*

A Cambridge Bay resident dressed for warmth *Sibeal Turraoin*

The Arctic Islands Lodge hotel (✆ 867 983 2345) and High Arctic Lodge (✆ 250 497 2000) provide accommodation.

The hotel may be able to provide Wi-Fi.

Outfitters can arrange hunting, fishing, dog sled and hiking trips.

Inuk Charlie is a noted sculptor whose work is inspired by the Cambridge Bay wild life.

The Ovayok (Mount Pelly) National Park lies about 15km to the east of Cambridge Bay.

There is a medical centre, school, library and Royal Canadian Mounted Police station.

The airport is served by Canadian North and First Air airlines.

Coronation Gulf

Clearing of the ice begins in the beginning of July and is normally navigable in the first week of August. Freeze-up occurs from mid October. Elevations rise to 300m on the south coast but are generally low lying. The main route along the northern shores is buoyed as is the route along the west shore between Dolphin and Union Strait and Coppermine.

Coronation Gulf made the news in 2010 when the cruise liner, *Clipper Adventurer* hit a rock. The 128 passengers were evacuated by a canadian Coastguard vessel. Initial reports indicated that the rock was 'uncharted' however the following navigation warning had been issued in 2007:

Navigation Warning: A102/07 – Western Arctic - Coronation Gulf – September 16, 2007: A shoal was discovered between the Lawson Islands and the Home Islands in the Southern Coronation Gulf in position 67°58'·25N 112°40'·39W. Charted depth in area 29m. Least depth found 3.3m. Isolated rock. Refer to NAD83 Datum.

Coronation Gulf, like most of the Arctic, is still in the process of being accurately charted and vessels should navigate with caution at all times. The *Clipper Adventurer* had not heeded the navigation warning and her forward looking sonar was unserviceable. Fortunately, no lives were lost.

30 Kugluktuk (Coppermine)

67°50'N 115°06'W

'Kugluktuk' means 'the place of moving water' which probably refers to the Bloody Falls about nine miles up the Coppermine River. Its population in 2011 was 1,450 and it boasts an airstrip, post office, two supermarkets, two schools, two hotels, RCMP detachment, and a health centre. Diesel and water are available. Internet at school and library.

The approaches are shoal and a rock with less than 2m over it is in mid channel between Cape Kendall and Kigirktaryuk Island. Careful study of *CHS Sailing Directions* is required.

Good holding is reported in the anchorage 0·8M NW of the hamlet.

Dolphin and Union Strait

Ice clears during July and refreezes in October. The 123 mile strait is marked by racons and day beacons. The Canadian sailing directions recommend navigation by daylight because of uncertainty regarding tidal streams and the difficulty of obtaining good radar fixes due to low lying land. There appears to be a southeast setting current.

The remains of the distmantled DEW station at Bernard Harbour *Sibéal Turraoin*

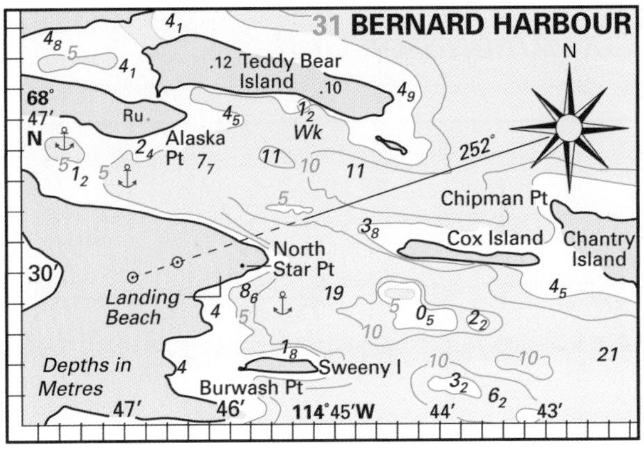

31 Bernard Harbour 68°47'N 114°47'W

Charts 7776, 7710 – which has a detailed chartlet of the harbour

Bernard Harbour is at the eastern end of Dolphin and Union Strait and is a pleasant overnight stop. There is an abandoned trading station and disused DEW station.

Approach

Enter either through the main northern entrance on the leading marks (252°) or via the unmarked southern entrance.

Anchorage

Anchor in 8m between Alaska Pt and North Star Pt. Good holding and reasonable shelter from all winds except NW gales.

Ashore

It is well worth going ashore to see the abandoned DEW station. As always in this area, shore parties should take precautions against polar bear attacks.

Bernard Harbour *Sibéal Turraoin*

IX Amundsen Gulf

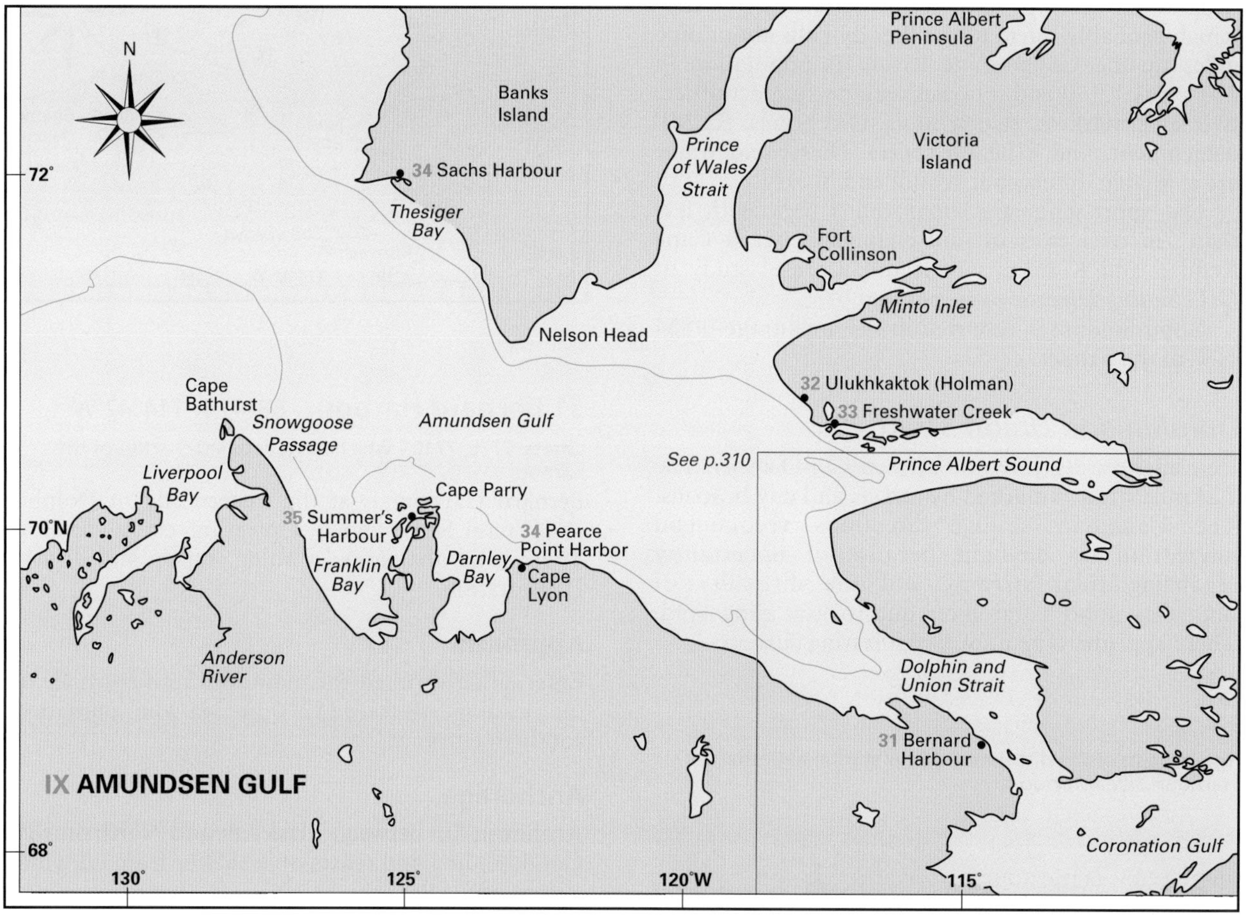

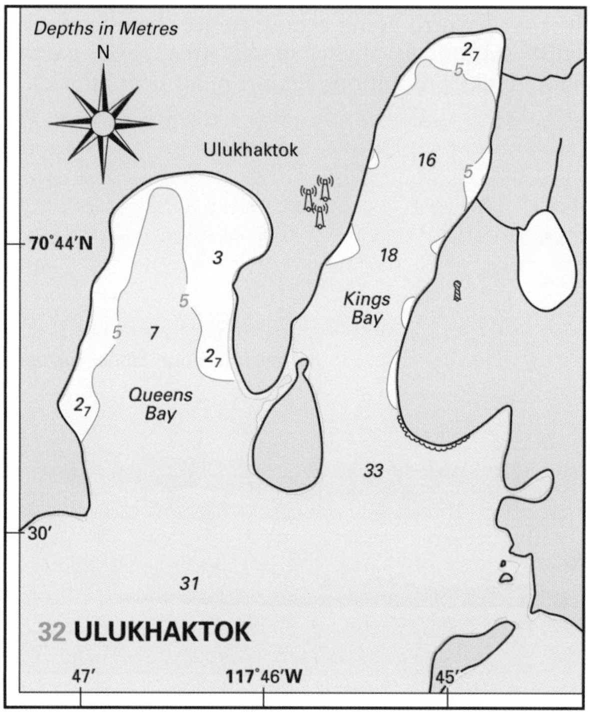

A counter-clockwise current circulates in the Gulf which will set against vessels working westwards along the southern coast. A polynya develops near Cape Bathurst in May and June which is followed by break up in July with the area normally being ice free in August. Freeze up is in October.

In addition to the numbered anchorages, cruising boats are reported to have anchored in Fresh Water Bay (70°36′N 117°28′W), De Salis Bay, Banks Is. (71°26′·9N 121°37′·2W), Pearce Point Harbour (69°49′·4N 122°41′·4W), Darnley Bay (69°45′N 123°40′W), Cape Parry (70°11′·8N 124°32′·3W) and Summer's Harbour(70°07′·7N 125°04′·6W).

32 Ulukhaktok (Holman)

70°44′N 117°46′W

Ulukhaktok is a small Inuit settlement with an airstrip and landing beach on the Diamond Jenness Peninsula of Victoria Island. CHS *Chart 7668* Prince Albert Sound covers the area and has an insert for Holman. The hamlet of Holman officially changed its name back to the traditional name of Ulukhaktok in 2006. Charts and uncorrected *Canadian Sailing Directions* still refer to it as Holman.

Queen's Bay, Ulukhaktok *Richard Hudson*

Vessels may anchor in Queen's Bay to the west or in Kings Bay to the east. Small craft may prefer to anchor in the shallower waters of Queens Bay where there is good holding in 6m.

Ulukhaktok has two RCMP officers, a school (computers with internet access available in the adjoining library), a Northern store and a Co-op store, also an art store. Prices at the stores are generally higher than at Cambridge Bay. There is a hotel, the Arctic Char Inn (✆ 867 396 3501), with a restaurant. While the hotel has Wi-Fi, they may only allow hotel guests to use it (not restaurant patrons). It is believed that diesel is available.

In King's Bay there is a wall where barges berth, however, it is not suitable for a yacht (nothing to tie dock lines to and quite shallow). King's Bay has more shelter than Queen's Bay.

Cruise ships commonly visit Ulukhaktok, yachts are rare.

The settlement is served by First Air and Kenn Borek airlines.

Pearce Point Harbor *Máire Wilkes*

33 Freshwater Creek

70°38'N 117°30'W

Freshwater Creek, in Freshwater Bay on the north side of Prince Albert Sound on Victoria Island, is about 15 miles from Ulukhaktok (Holman). CHS *Chart 7668* does not give much detail, but the middle of the channel is reported as having at least 13m until close to Freshwater Creek. Freshwater Creek is in the north extremity of the west arm of Freshwater Bay.

Anchor in approximately in 5m, loose gravel/poor holding. Good drinking water is reportedly available.

34 Pearce Point Harbor

69°49'N 122°41'W

Pearce Harbor is the only sheltered harbour on the mainland coast between Darnley Bay and Bernard Harbor some 200M to the east. Pearce Harbor is described in the Admiralty Pilot *NP12* as 'one of the finest harbours along the Arctic coast of Canada, with room for at least 10 small vessels.' However, small vessels in recent years have reported poor holding in the gravel bottom and a good anchor watch should be kept.

Landing is on the gravel beach. There is an abandoned airstrip and buildings.

35 Summer's Harbour

70°07'N 125°04'W

Henry Larsen, of *St Roch* fame, described Summer's Harbour as the best harbour in the Canadian arctic. Oil exploration vessels were over-wintered there in the 1980's and the wide bay can provide shelter to vessels big and small. There is 14m of water in the centre of the harbour but smaller craft many wish to anchor in shallower depths close to the shore. The wind can be very strong but boats can anchor so they are not on a lee shore and the holding is reported to be good.

The Smoking Hills, Cape Bathurst *Sibéal Turraoin*

Smoking Hills south of Cape Bathurst

70°11'N 127°04'W

Charts 7664

No anchorage but interesting to see. Underground coal and bitumen deposits here burn continually. They were discovered by Franklin in 1826. In 2010, several jets of smoke were seen in the vicinity of Fritton Pt (70°11'N 127°04'W).

Snowgoose Passage 70°32'N 128°05'W

Snowgoose Passage lies between Cape Bathurst and the Ballie Islands at the western end of Amundsen Gulf. A vessel viewing the Smoking Hills will save approximately eight miles by taking the passage. Least depth in 2010 was 3·4m. However, like many spits, one good storm could change the bathymetry significantly. The passage should only be attempted in good visibility and clement weather.

Note the radar indicates that the chart, based on WGS84, is incorrect in several places.

Cape Bathhurst from seaward *Máire Wilkes*

X The Beaufort Sea

The Canadian/USA border is at Demarcation Point. Pilotage to the east is documented in the *Canadian Sailing Directions* and west of Demarcation Point is covered by *U.S. Pilot Number 9*.

Navigation hazards in this area of the Beaufort Sea include off lying pingos or 'Pingo Like Features' (PLFs). In sea areas where the mean depth is some 50m, the depth can suddenly reduce to 10–15m. The least depth found in these areas is 9·4m.

Of more importance to smaller vessels are existing and abandoned oil drilling operations. These operations were facilitated by building artificial islands from sand and gravel dredged from the sea bed. When the drilling was finished, the islands were left to erode naturally. Details are given in the sailing directions and coastal pilot book.

In addition to the numbered anchorages, cruising boats are reported to have anchored in Shingle Point (68°58'·8N 137°16'W).

36 Sachs Harbour, Banks Is.

71°59'N 125°17'W

Sachs Harbour was named after the *Mary Sachs* an expedition vessel which was part of the Canadian Arctic Expedition of 1913. It is the only permanent settlement on Banks Island and, in 2011, had a population of 112 people. 75% of the world's muskoxen live on Banks Island and Sachs Harbour is a centre for hunting and trapping. In 2006 a wild crossbred grizzly/polar bear was shot nearby. The town is the headquarters for the Aulavik National Park and the visitor centre is well worth visiting.

There is a post office, shop, guest house, RCMP detachment, hunting outfitters, limited medial facilities and an airport (Aklak Air). Diesel and water are available.

Approaches are shallow and liable to change due to weather and ice. An approach in poor weather is not recommended. *CHS Sailing Directions* should be studied carefully. The anchorage is exposed to N winds and an alternative, six miles to the W, may be preferable.

37 MacKinley Bay 69° 56'N 131° 09'W

This is a manmade harbour which is no longer in use. It was used by oil field support vessels and has a dredged entrance channel. There is a breakwater offering protection for the swell and a concrete wharf.

38 Tuktoyaktuk 69°27'N 133°02'W

Tuktoyaktuk is known as 'Tuk' to its 900 residents. It is a major supply base for the western Canadian Arctic. In the navigation season, outlying settlements are supplied by way of shallow draft barges towed by Tuk based tugs. Around the harbour there are

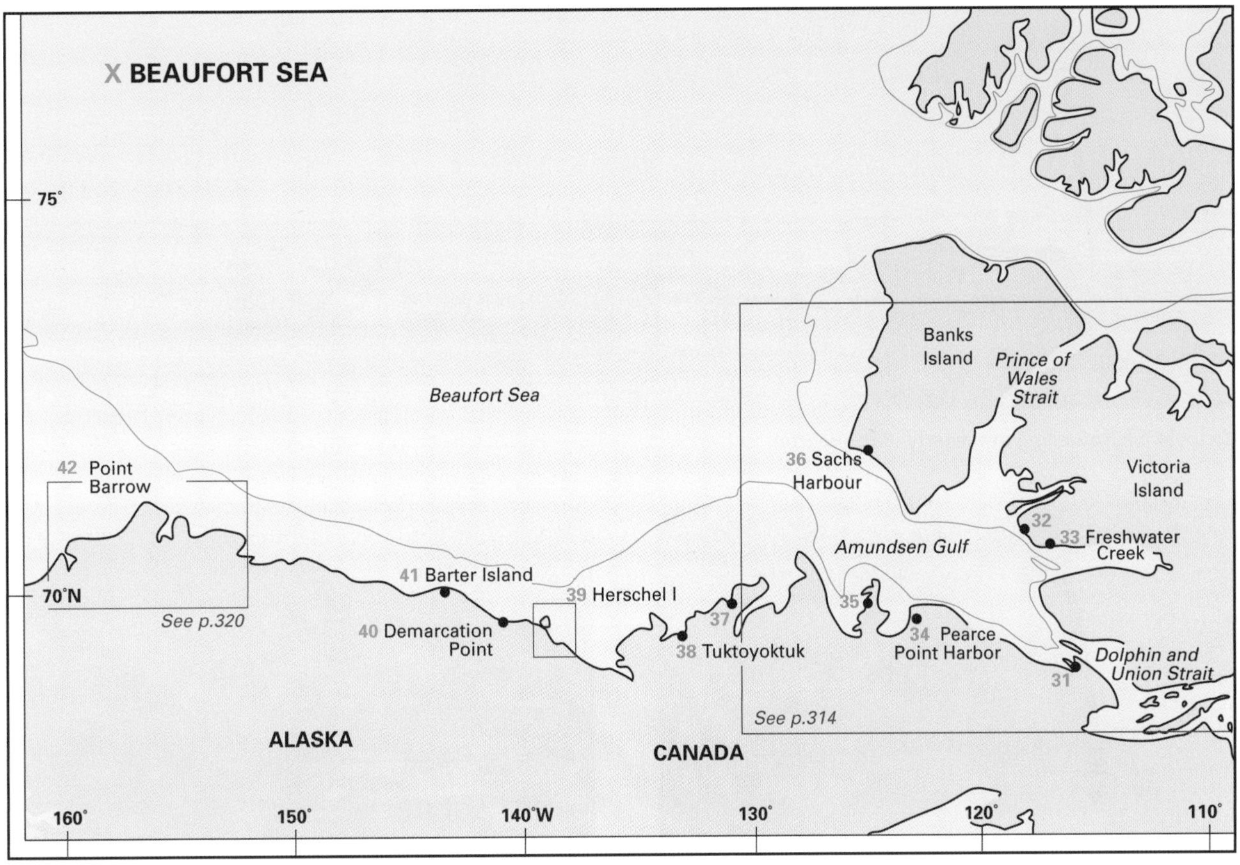

Tuktoyaktuk pingo *Sibéal Turraoin*

many unused wharfs left over from a past boom in oil exploration.

Tuk is a potential overwintering location.

It lies at the northern end of an ice road which is operational in the winter and was the subject of a reality TV series. There are plans to build an all-weather road to Inuvik which is scheduled for completion in 2018.

Approach

The main harbour in the east is a supply hub for much of the Canadian Arctic. Both the eastern and western entrances are shallow. The eastern entrance is the main entrance. Once through the main entrance, use the transits (ranges) to navigate to the small boat anchorage off the settlement in the west of the harbour.

Tuktoyaktuk anchorage *Dermot O'Riordan*

The western entrance is very narrow and the transit close to the spit must the followed very closely. It is easy to run aground here!

Anchorage

Anchor off the settlement or moor alongside a wharf or barge.

Diesel

Fuel (by jerry can) can be obtained from the supermarket opposite the landing pontoon. Smaller vessels can go alongside the jetty.

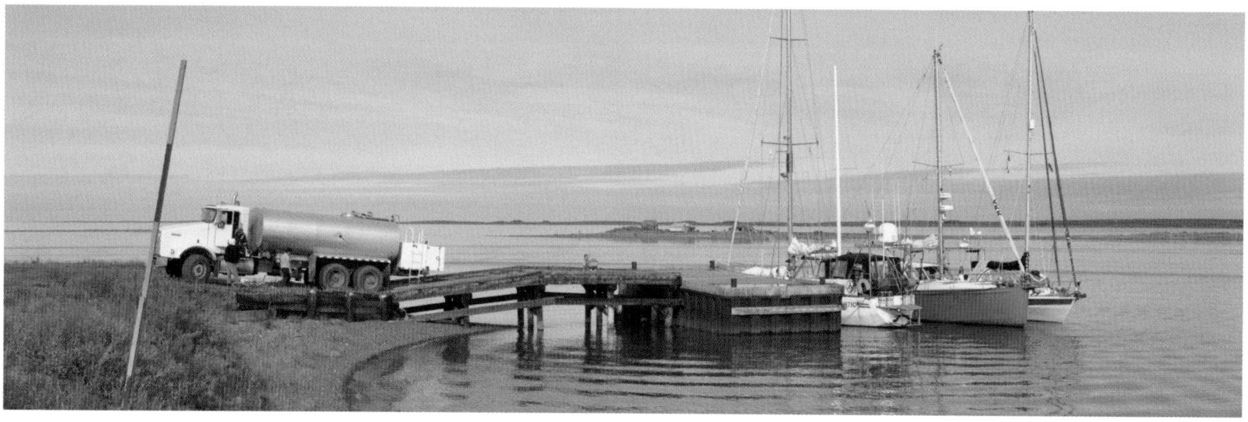

Tuktoyaktuk, refuelling at the jetty *Bob Shepton*

Tuktoyaktuk ice house *Bob Shepton*

Herschel Island *Sibéal Turraoin*

Facilities

Supermarket opposite the landing pontoon.

There are two hotels; the Hotel Tuk (✆ 867 977 2381) and Pingo Park Lodge (✆ 867 977 2155).

The 'ice-house' is well worth seeing. It is a series of underground rooms build in the permafrost. Residents use it to store food.

Tuk is famous for its 'Pingos' and is the centre for the Pingo Canadian Landmark National Park.

The airport is served by Kenn Borek and Aklak Air airlines.

39 Herschel Island

Pauline Cove 69°34'N 138°55'W

Herschel Island is an abandoned whaling station and trading post. In its heyday hundreds of boats congregated here to trade. Today, several wooden buildings remain which are kept in repair by Canadian Rangers. There is an old customs house, a sauna, a couple of houses beside the old whalers graves, ice houses and native driftwood shelters. Although not always occupied, there is a sign outside one of the houses offering visitors use of the shelter. Visitors may also use the sauna. Beluga whales may be sighted in the anchorage. There is an airstrip.

Herschel Island *Dermot O'Riordan*

Anchorage

Anchor in 6m off the whaling station. Excellent shelter.

Useful websites

	Parks Canada Pingo Canadian Landmark	www.pc.gc.ca/eng/docs/v-g/pingo/index.aspx
	Tuktoyaktuk	www.tuk.ca

Herschel Island buildings *Dermot O'Riordan*

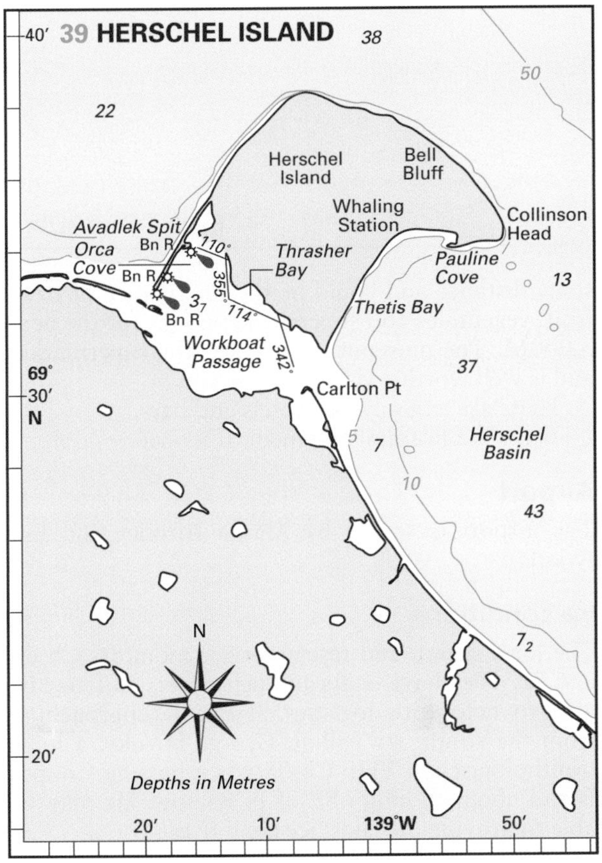

40 Demarcation Point 69°41′N 141°17′W

The border between Canada and the USA lies 6·5 miles to the east of Demarkation Point and is marked by a 1·2m obelisk 30m inland.

Demarcation Bay, 0·5M W of Demarkation Point, is reported to give good shelter and good holding in 5m, sticky mud.

41 Barter Island 70°07′N 143°47′W

In the eighteen and nineteenth centuries, Barter Island was a major trade centre between the Canadian Inuit and Alaskan Inupiat peoples. The island has a land area of only a few square miles, the northeastern quarter of which is occupied by the settlement of Kaktovik. Kaktovik, which means 'seining place' is a fishing centre. In 2010, the population was 239 people, 75% of whom were indigenous eskimos. Hunting of whales and caribou is an important part of their livelihood. There is a post office, store, health clinic and an airstrip.

The harbour to the east of Kaktovik is called Barnard Harbor but is only suitable for the shallowest draft vessels (1·2m or less). Cruising boats have anchored off the west side of Barter Island and reported good shelter in strong winds. The bay is quite shallow and care is required.

42 Barrow 71°18′N 156°50′W

Charts NOAA 16082

The anchorage is an open roadstead off the main town and it is not advisable to plan on re-supplying here as it may not be possible to stop with bad ice, wind or sea conditions. Shoal draft vessels may be able to tuck around behind Point Barrow and the crew can then hike to town. If approaching from the west, Barrow is a good introduction to the hunting society of the north. Animal bones, skins and bowhead whale remains are much in evidence.

Approach

Barrow is an exposed open roadstead. There are no fixed off-shore dangers on approach. Sea-ice is the main hazard and is a particular threat in northerly or westerly winds.

Anchorage

Anchor anywhere in front of the town, weather and ice permitting. There is no accurate depth charting here as ice can change the sea floor every year. The bottom is good holding in mud. The main commercial part of town is easily identified by the large buildings. Approximately one mile further to the east an anchorage can be found which is closer to the fuel station. It can be recognised by a substantial launching ramp/landing area. Vessels can anchor 100m offshore in water 3m deep.

Shoal draft vessels may want to attempt an entry into Elson Lagoon. Note there is a shoal directly N of the entrance. Approach from the NW. The pass is very deep but shoals up within 1km of the lagoon entrance. Most of the lagoon has depths of more than 1·8m.

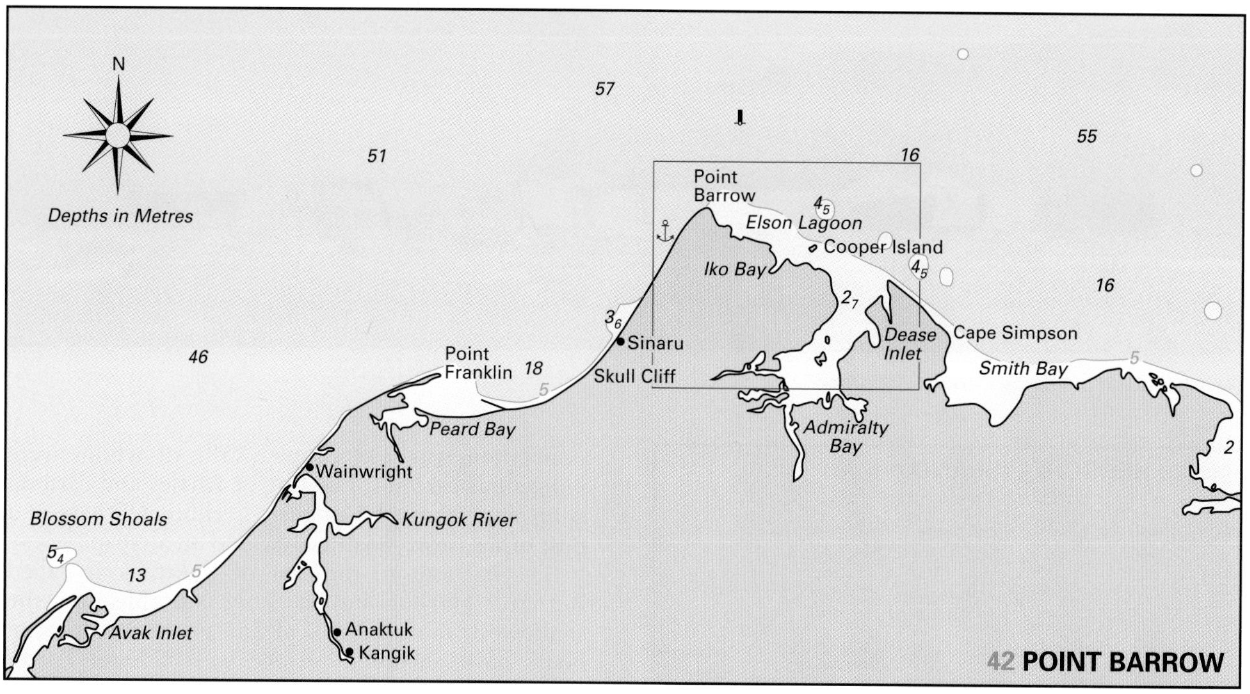

42 POINT BARROW

Diesel

The fuel station is about 50m from the beach next to the NAPA auto parts store. This is at the northern group of the two clusters of buildings within the area called 'Browerville'. It can be accessed from the substantial launching ramp/landing area.

Facilities

The main supermarket is in the same area as the fuel station, two blocks in from the beach. If heading east this is the last place to buy fresh supplies for quite some distance and could be the best choice of fresh fruit, vegetables and supermarket goods for the next 3,000M. The museum is also near the supermarket and is well worth a visit.

There are a number of hotels and bars.

There is a hospital and medical service.

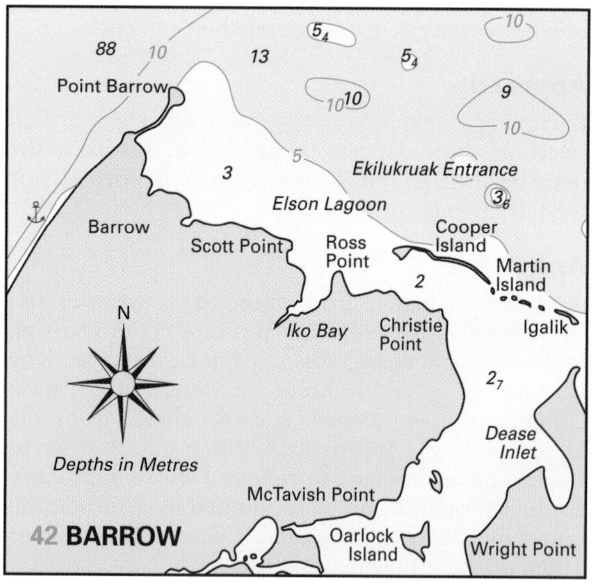

42 BARROW

Airport

The airport is served by Alaska Airlines and Era Aviation.

Ice conditions

The local search and rescue service monitors Ch 68 and 72. They have boats and helicopters and may be able to help with logistics. If one is approaching from the south, try calling George Divoky, a local ornithologist, on VHF Ch 08 when passing Cooper Island about 25 miles SE of Pt Barrow. He may be able to provide the latest ice conditions.

The Barrow webcam is a good source of current weather and ice information.

Ice may not clear around Barrow until late July but the time constraints of an eastbound North West Passage transit make it prudent to sail east as far as possible whilst waiting for it to clear. To the west of Barrow, it may be possible for a shallow draught vessel to anchor off Peard Bay in settled conditions. Careful pilotage will be required. If the weather is good it is also possible to anchor off Pt Lay or Wainwright.

Useful websites

	University of Alaska Barrow ice web cam	http://seaice.alaska.edu/gi/observatories/barrow_webcam

XI Chukchi Sea and Bering Sea

43 Point Hope 68°20′N 116°46′W

Point Hope is the prominent headland about 200M north of the Bering Strait. It juts out into the Chukchi Sea and it's Inupiat name is 'Tikigaq' which means 'forefinger.' The headland attracted whales close to the shore and it became a hunting ground for the Inupiat people. The settlement (2010 population 674), which lies to the SE of the point has a police station, airstrip, school and a famous basket ball team. To the NE of the point is a lagoon.

Small craft can anchor in gravel or hard mud with fair holding either to the north or south of Point Hope as wind and ice dictate.

The northern anchorage (68°27′N 166°19′W) is off the curved beach in about 7m. To the south of Point Hope, the water off the settlement may be too deep for anchoring. A recommended anchorage is in approximate position 60°20′N 166°37′W, about 3M E of the settlement.

44 Port Clarence 65°17′N 166°50′W

Charts NOAA 16204

There are many possible anchorages in Port Clarence which is an excellent natural harbour. The bay is formed by a large sand spit, near the end of which is built a loran station with a 420m high tower. There is a road between Teller, the settlement associated with Port Clarence, and Nome.

Amundsen landed at Teller (70km by road) after his first balloon flight over the pole.

In addition to the numbered anchorages, cruising boats are reported to have anchored in Cross Is. (70°29′N 147°57′W) and Cape Halkett (70°46′·12N 152°15′·2W).

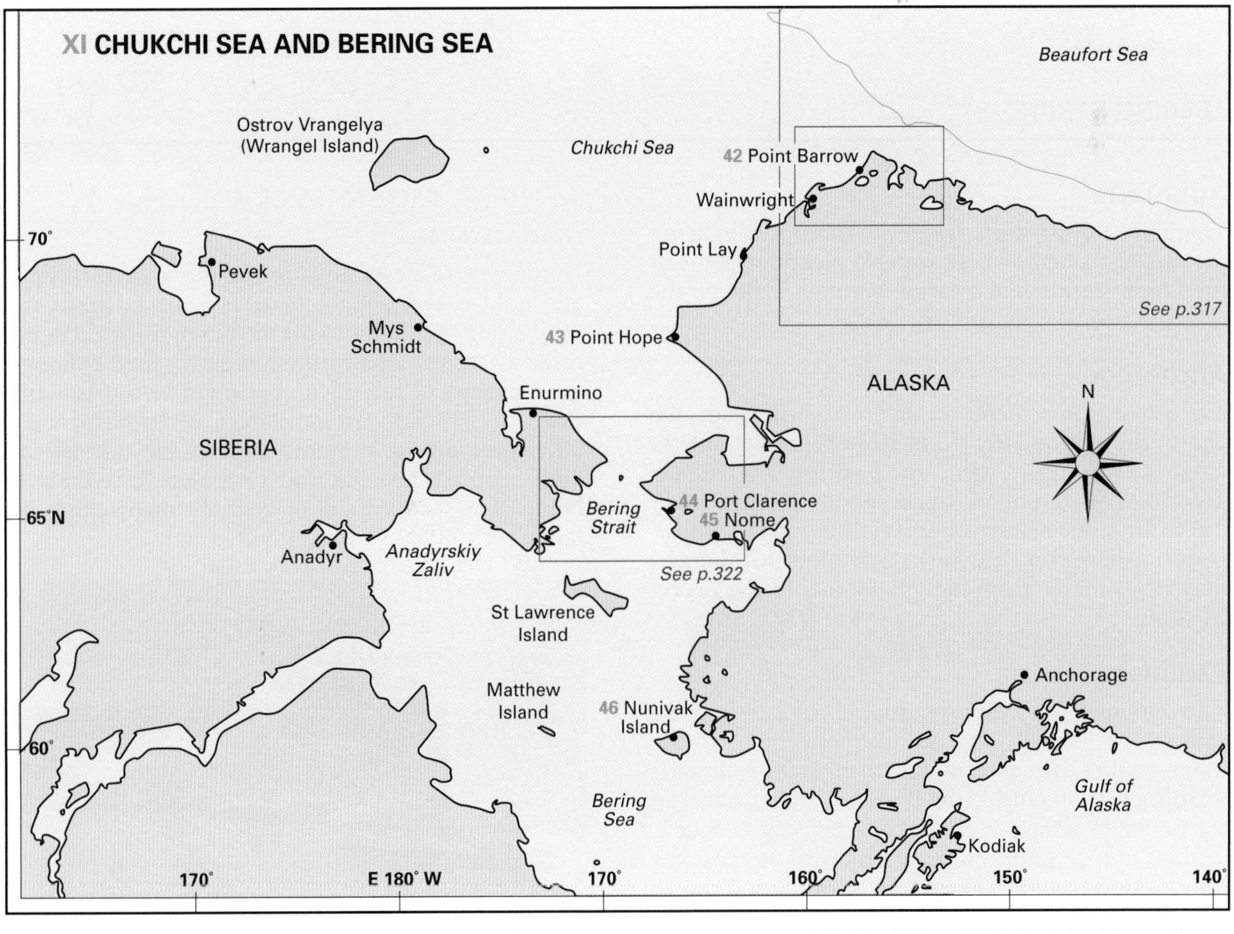

Cape Prince of Wales, Bering Strait *Sibéal Turraoin*

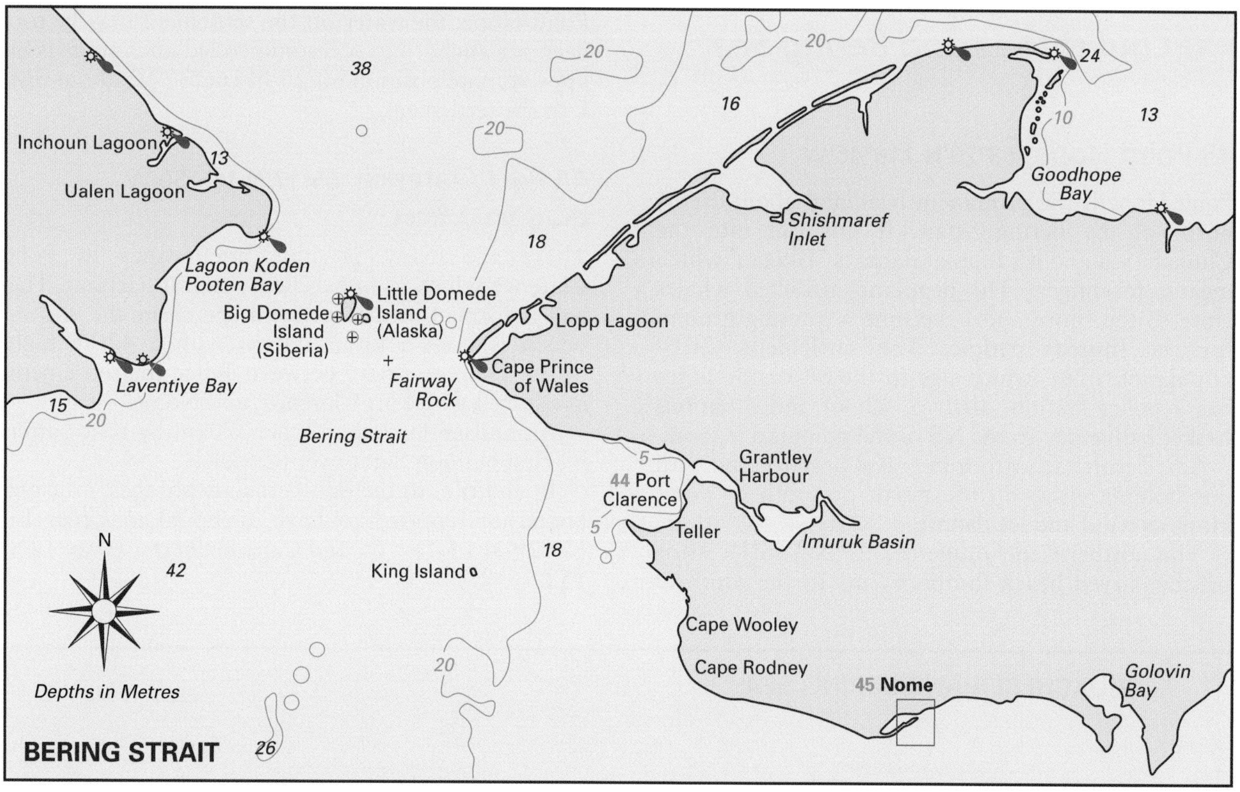

Approach

There are no off-shore dangers. There is a light on the end of the spit. There are also plenty of lights at the Loran station and aviation warning lights on the tower.

Anchorage

The yacht *Fine Tolerance* anchored just inside the end of the spit and tucked in close behind to shelter from a southerly wind in position 65°16'·4N 166°50'·6W in 6m of thick, good holding mud. There are some below water reefs close in to shore.

Scrimshawed walrus tusks and other local crafts may be available from the inhabitants of the Brevig Mission.

Facilities

The settlement of Teller (population of 229 in 2010 census) is located on the southern half of the 'Nooke' spit. It was established in 1900 following the discovery of gold at the Bluestone River mine. In the boom days the population numbered over 5,000. Today, its population depends on subsistence hunting and fishing. There is a post office and shop.

45 Nome 64°30'N 165°26'W

Charts NOAA 16206

Nome was made famous in the old gold rush days and gold is still sought here. It is sieved from the sand along the shallows off the beach using dredging rafts. There is a small fishing industry here although the mainstay of the town appears to be tourism and mining. The wild-west gunslinger, Wyatt Earp, had a hotel here during the gold rush at the turn of the 20th century. The Iditarod Dog Sled Race ends in Nome. For such a small place it has many claims to fame, yet still has a pioneering feel to it.

Nome small boat harbour *Bob Shepton*

Useful websites

	City of Nome website	www.nomealaska.org/
	City of Nome harbourmaster	www.nomealaska.org/department/index.php?structureid=15

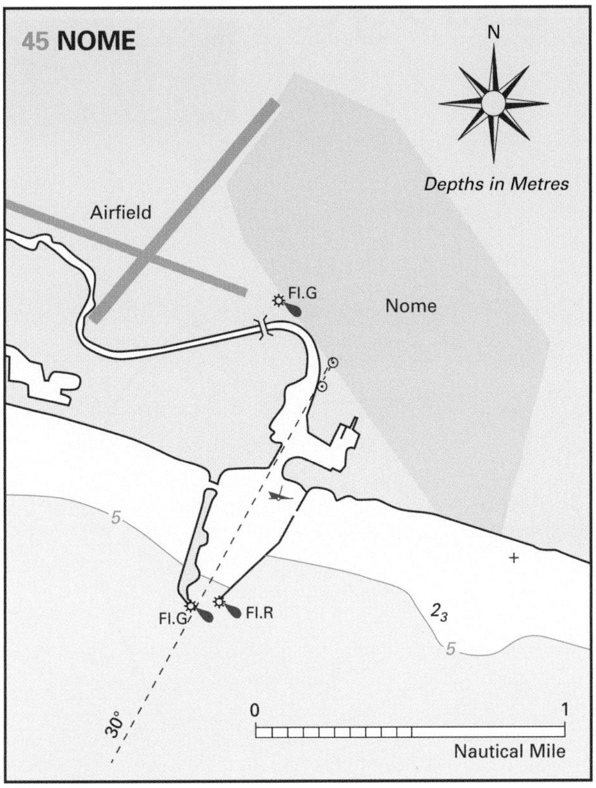

Approach

There are no off-shore dangers here other than the shallow waters. The new outer harbour is dredged and there should be no draft problems for yachts. There is a tidal range of 0·5m, although the normal caution concerning tidal heights during prolonged periods of high winds or high pressure applies. The small boat harbour has a depth of 3m (10ft) .

Formalities

Contact the harbourmaster before arrival (24 hours is requested), particularly if entering at a weekend. The harbourmaster contact details are:

Office ✆ 443-6619, Mobile (907) 304 1906
VHF Ch 12 or 16
Email istotts@nomealaska.org

The harbourmaster will, if asked, contact Customs. If this is the boat's first U.S. port, the skipper should make contact with Customs at the earliest possible opportunity.

Mooring

Smaller vessels may use the pontoons in the small boat harbour. Alternatively yachts can berth alongside the quay wall. Larger vessels use the outer harbour. The harbourmaster reports that he now has a dozen yachts visiting each year and he does his best to accommodate them.

Diesel

Alongside berth for main fuel tanks however the operator will not refill jerry cans for 'environmental reasons'. Jerry cans can be filled at a nearby gas station, but you'll need to get a lift or hire a taxi. Fuel is expensive.

Facilities

There are three supermarkets and numerous small shops and restaurants. There is an internet service available at the library.

The airport is served by Alaska Airlines, Berins Air and Era Aviation.

There is a hospital (✆ 443 3311) and most of the facilities one would expect in a medium sized town. If this is the first port of call after transiting the North West Passage from the east, the tarmac roads and choice of drinking establishments will be impressive!

Vessels can be over wintered in Nome. There is no crane but vessels can be hauled out using a trailer. This service is run by Rolland Trowbridge (✆ 907 434 1516) and vessels are stored over the winter in a locked yard.

Fuel: Bonanza ✆ 907 387 1201, Crowley ✆ 907 443 2219.

Potential vessel crane haulouts: STG ✆ 907 644 4664.

Water: Delivery (by truck) Moonlight Springs ✆ 907 443 2620. Free water is available by hose at the floating docks with limited reach. The Port also has a large water trailer that pulls water directly from the city's treated water main. This is for larger volumes of water, 1,000gal and more.

Welding/Diving: Rolland Trowbridge ✆ 907 434 1516. Alaskan Arctic Marine Divers: (Gene Fenton) ✆ 928 380 4990. Seakers ✆ 907 562 7099.

46 Etolin Anchorage, Nunivak Island

60°26'·N 166°09'W

Charts NOAA 16006

The anchorage is exposed to the northeast but makes for a pleasant stopover roughly half way between False Pass and Nome. Although the low island offers no protection from a strong northwest wind, seas are reported as flat in these conditions and the anchorage comfortable. The currents in Etolin Strait are strong but they do not appear to extend into the bay.

An alternative anchorage can be found close to Nash Harbour at 60°20'N 166°37'W where kelp on the southern shore may hinder secure anchoring.

Approach

There are no offshore dangers directly out from the anchorage however the area north of Cape Etolin has many rocks and shallow areas which should be avoided. There is also a reef a few miles to the south of the anchorage. Etolin Strait is very wide but is subject to strong tidal currents (2–3kns).

Anchorage

Anchor in 5m with a rocky bottom. The flashing light on top of a small tower is clearly visible at night from the anchorage point.

Points of Interest

Mekoryuk Village is about 3km away. The houses are visible from the anchorage. Mekoryuk is one of only two villages on the island.

7. The North East Passage

or Northern Sea Route

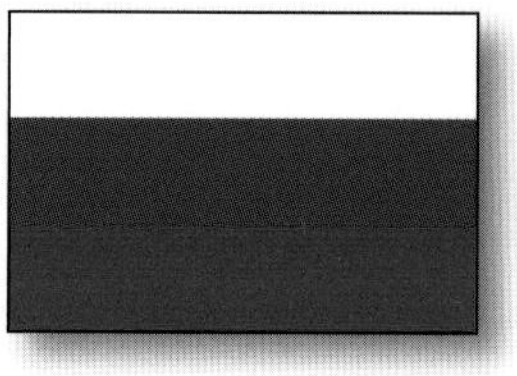

Contents

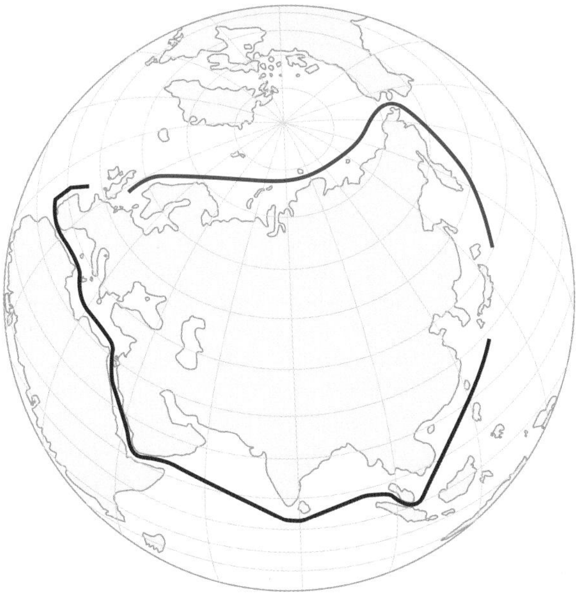

Europe to 'Far East' distance saved by using the North East Passage

Introduction

In the West, the route north of Russia connecting the Atlantic to the Pacific Oceans is known as the North East Passage. In Russia, through whose waters the route passes, the route is known as the 'Severniy morskoy put', the 'Sevmorput' or the 'Northern Sea Route.' The Northern Sea Route is approximately 3,500 miles which is longer than the North West Passage. It can be divided, from west to east, into the following seas: the Barents Sea, the Kara Sea, the Laptev Sea and the East Siberian Sea. It is rarely navigated by small vessels due to the harshness of the environment, almost impenetrable sea ice and formidable Russian bureaucracy. The sea ice north of the Taymyr Peninsula can remain impenetrable year round.

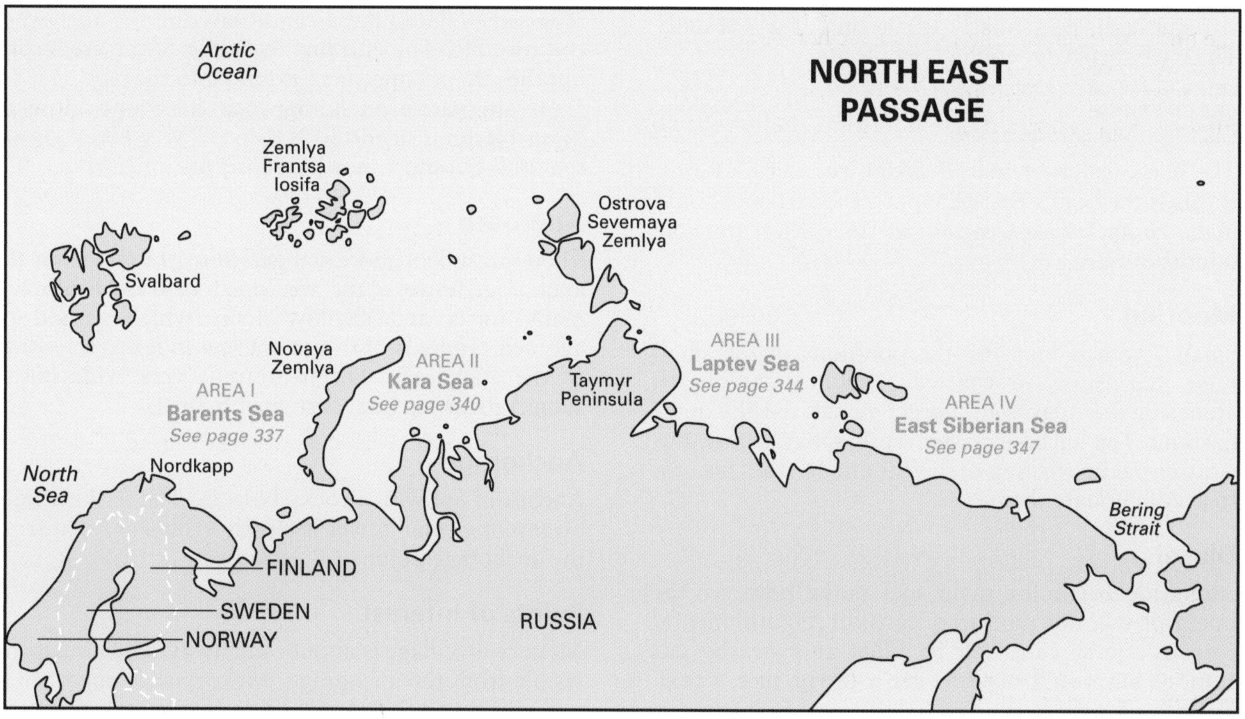

History of the Northern Sea Route

Like the North West Passage, the Northern Sea Route had been speculated about since the 15th century. At that time, an alternative route from the Atlantic to the Pacific Oceans was eagerly sought by European nations wishing to trade with China. It was hoped to find a route avoiding the great southern capes of Cape Horn and the Cape of Good Hope which were dangerous, controlled by the Spanish or Portuguese and not the most direct route. Some of these problems still exist today.

In 1553 the English navigators, Sir Hugh Willoughby and Richard Chancellor doubled the North Cape (Nordkapp) in their vessel the *Edward Bonaventure*, entered the White Sea and sighted the coast of Novaya Zemlya. In 1594, Willem Barents explored the sea which now bears his name. Three year's later he and fellow Dutchman Heemskerck sailed around Novaya Zemlya, overwintered there before sailing onto Lapland, unfortunately Barents lost his life on the final passage.

The problem was approached from the other direction in 1728 when, under the orders of Peter I the Great, the great Danish Navigator, Vitus Bering, sailed northwards through the strait which now bears his name and established that Asia and North America were two separate continents. This was verified in 1778 by Captain James Cook who was the first person to chart both sides of the strait.

Several Russian and Austrian expeditions resulted in the northern coast of Russia being explored in the 18th and mid 19th centuries but it was not until 1879 that the first successful transit was made by the Swedish explorer Baron Adolf Erik Nordenskold.

In 1893, the Norwegian explorer, Dr Nansen left the New Siberian Islands in an attempt to be the first person to reach the North Pole. His vessel, the *Fram*, was specially designed to pop up above the sea ice when beset. He deliberated froze the *Fram* into the ice and waited until the current set her towards the Pole. After eighteen months, he attempted to walk to the Pole and reached 86°13′·6N, the furthest north anyone had ventured at that time, before being forced to retreat to Franz Josef Land. The *Fram* meanwhile drifted westwards and eventually emerged in the North Atlantic Ocean.

A convoy being led by the icebreaker, *Kapitan Babich*, through the Chukchi Sea *Jarlath Cunnane*

The Russian revolution in 1917 resulted in the newly formed USSR looking with renewed interest for a navigable Northern Sea Route. In 1932 the Soviet expedition led by Professor Otto Schmidt transited the Northern Sea Route in one season. This paved the way for hopes of a commercial route and a governing body, the Glavsevmorput, was established with Professor Schmidt as it's first Director. Glavsevmorput supervised navigation through the Northern Sea Route and built the northern sea ports.

In the early part of the Second World War, Russian icebreakers escorted the German cruiser, *Komet*, from the Atlantic Ocean to the Pacific so that it could attack the British Royal Navy in the Pacific. Later in the war, when the USSR was fighting with the Allies, the Northern Sea Route was used by the Soviets to transfer naval ships and supplies from the Pacific to the Atlantic Oceans.

The Northern Sea Route continued to be used by the Soviets and commercial traffic peaked in 1987 when 6·6m tons of cargo was carried on the route. Following the break up of the USSR in the early 1990s commercial traffic using the route declined. In 1993, a Russian, Japanese and Norwegian body, the International Northern Sea Route Programme, (INSROP) was formed. INSROP made available much information about the Northern Sea Route but eventually determined that the route was not commercially viable for international trade at that time. This was because of the high cost associated with deploying icebreakers and producing ice strengthened ships to the size and draught restrictions determined by INSROP (50,000 tons, with a beam of 30m and a draught of 12·5m).

However, climate change and exploration for natural gas in the Arctic has prompted renewed interest in the route. In 1997 the Finnish vessel, *Uikku*, became the first non-Russian tanker to transit the Northern Sea Route. The largest ship to transit the Northern Sea Route was the 117,000 ton *SCF Baltica* in 2011. In 2012, 1·1m tons of cargo was carried through the Northern Sea Route by forty six commercial ships including the 288m LNG carrier, *Ob River*.

Major commercial interests in the region, such as the oil companies, are building their own smaller icebreakers. A new fleet of ice breakers, discussed in more detail later in this chapter, was ordered in the 2000s and 2010s which reflects Russia's commitment to the Northern Sea Route.

Up to date statistics and port information concerning commercial traffic in the Northern Sea Route can be found on the Northern Sea Route Information Office's website.

Small vessel transits of the Northern Sea Route

Year	Vessel	Registry	Master	Route	Notes
1991–1993	*Yakutia*	Russia		West	1991 Tiksi-Chukotka, 1992 Cargoed back to Tiksi, 1993 Tiksi-Murmansk
1998–1999	*Apostol Andrey* (16·2m yacht)	Russia	Nikolay Latau	West	Wintered Tiksi
2000–2002	*Sibir*	Russia	Sergei Cherbakov	East	Two winters
2002	*Vagabond* (15·3m yacht)	France	Eric Brossier	East	Circumnavigated the Arctic First single season transit
2002	*Dagmar Aaen* (27m yacht)	Germany	Arved Fuchs	East	Circumnavigated the Arctic
2004–2005	*Northabout* (14·9m yacht)	Ireland	Jarlath Cunnane	West	Wintered Khatanga Circumnavigated the Arctic
2009	*RX II*	Norwegian	Trond Aasvoll	East	
2010	*Peter 1* (18·5m yacht)	Russia	Daniel Gavrilov	East	Circumnavigated the Arctic in one season
2010	*Northern Passage* (9·6m trimaran)	Norway	Borge Ousland	East	Circumnavigated the Arctic in one season
2010	*Explorer of Sweden*	Sweden	Ola Skinnarmo	East	
2011	*Eshamy*	UK	Jeffrey Allison	West	
2011/2012	*Lena*	Finland	Veli Karkkainen	East	
2012	*Scorpius*	Russia	Sergey Nizovtsev		
2013	*Lady Dana*	Poland	Ryszard Wojnowski	East	
2013	*Tara*	France		East	

Others that were cargoed, thereby not completing the passage 'on their own keel'

Year	Vessel	Registry	Master	Route	Notes
2003–2004	*Campina* (Steel yacht)	Netherlands	Henke de Velde	West	
2007	*Barrabas* (12m yacht)	UK	Adrian Flanagan	West	

Useful websites – Commercial traffic Information

	Northern Sea Route Information NSR	www.arctic-lio.com

Useful websites

	Northabout Blog of the *Northabout* expedition through the North West and North East Passages	www.northabout.com

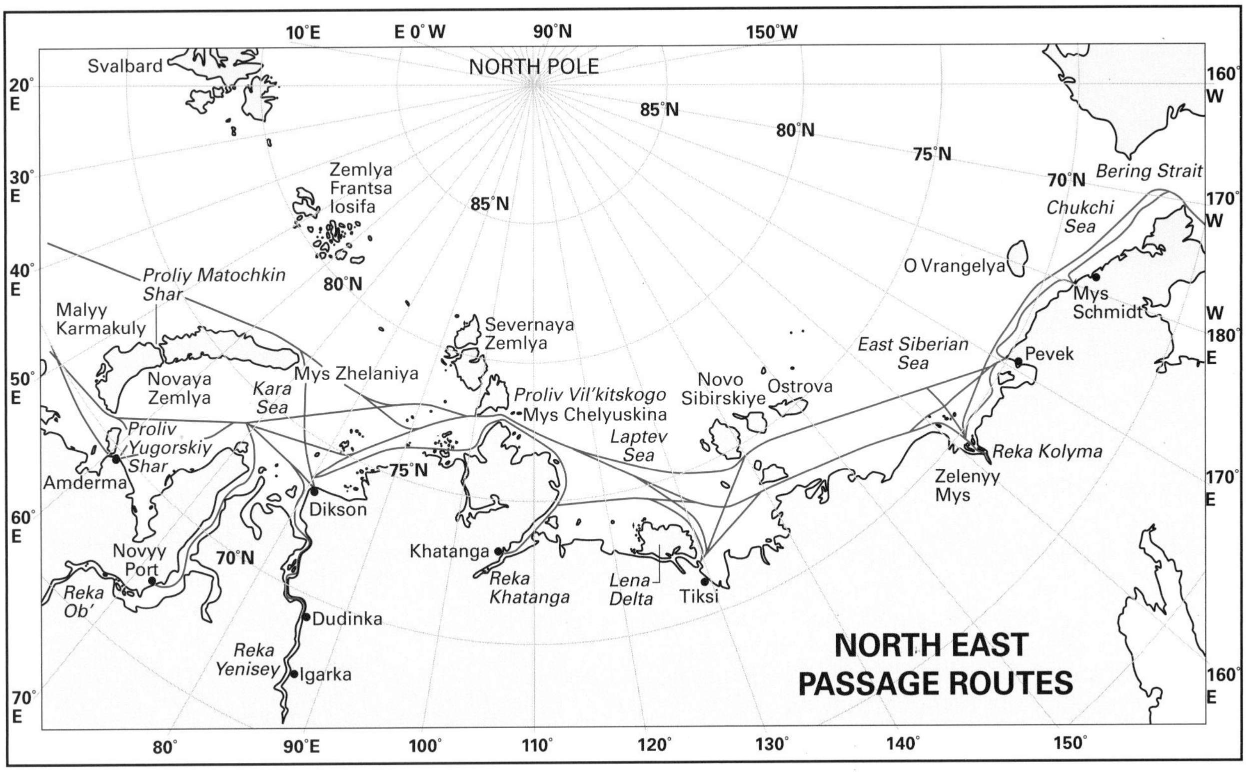

Routes

The British Admiralty Sailing Directions (*NP10*) identifies four potential routes:

- The Coastal Route – which is about 3,500M
- The Central Route – which is about 3,200M
- The High Latitude Route – which is about 2,900M
- North Pole Route – which is about 2,700M

The most navigable route for a small vessel is likely to be the Coastal Route as it is probable there will be less ice and access to shore-side support is more readily available.

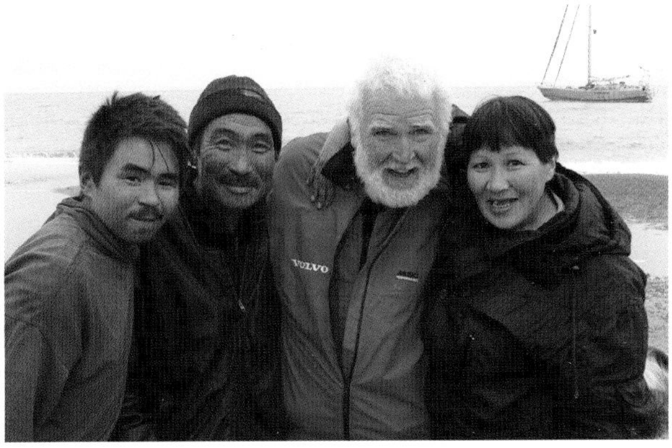

Chukchi people welcome Jarlath Cunnane, the skipper of *Northabout Jarlath Cunnane*

People and culture

Of the 2,000,000 people living in Arctic Russia, less than 70,000 are indigenous. From west to east, these are the Saami peoples in the Murmansk region, the Nenets in Novaya Zemlya and the Kara Sea, the Dolgan on the Taymyr Peninsula, Evenk and Even in the Sakha Republic bordering the Laptev and East Siberian Seas and the Chukchi on the shores of the East Siberian and Chukchi Seas. Seventy-five percent of indigenous people live in rural areas and it was the ancestors of these peoples who moved in the last ice age to populate the Canadian arctic. The Chukchi and Siberian Yupik people living at the eastern side of the Northern Sea Route are members of the Inuit Circumpolar Council (ICC) as are the indigenous people of Canada, Alaska and Greenland.

Reindeer meat is traditionally an important source of food for all the indigenous peoples and the reindeer are often kept in herds. This is supplemented by fishing and hunting for moose, seals and various birds. Today both indigenous and non-indigenous people rely heavily on cereals, dairy products, potatoes, fruit and vegetables imported from more southern regions of Russia.

The majority of the non-indigenous population originate from all over Russia and live in urban areas on the Northern Sea Route coast. In the Murmansk area the main industry is metal processing which has caused much pollution in the vicinity. The Kara Sea has extensive oil and gas production industries and mining and metal processing is important in the Taymyr Peninsula.

Cities along the route, which in reality are broken down and largely abandoned towns, occur every 500 miles or so. Settlements and old polar stations exist sporadically, also mostly abandoned. During Stalin's great northern expansion of the 1950s and subsequently during the Cold War these were places of importance.

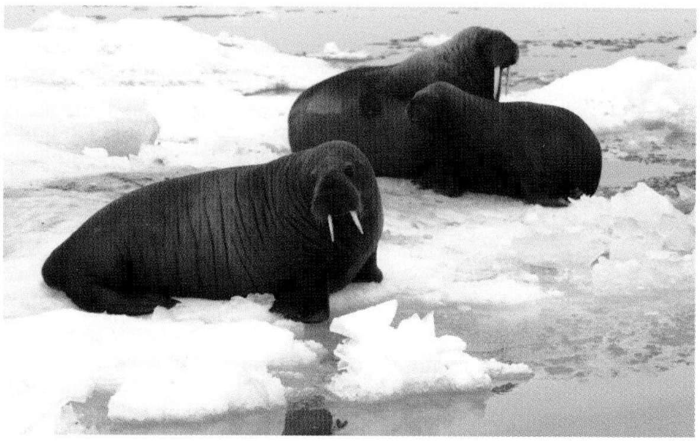

Walrus in the East Siberian Sea *Jarlath Cunnane*

Terrain and flora

In Paddy Barry's words, 'these lands are not celebrated for their scenic character!' The majority of the land is subject to permafrost leaving less than 1% which can sustain plant life. Vegetation comprises mainly tundra plants such as mosses, lichens and fungi. Flowering plants bloom in the short arctic summer. In wetlands, marsh plants grow and in warmer dry areas, there are extensive grasslands. There are no trees.

The Reka Ob', Reka Yenisey, Rena Indirka, Reka Pyasina, Reka Kolyma, Reka Yana and Reka Lena are great rivers which flow into the Northern Sea Route waters and bring with them changes in both the flora and fauna.

Wildlife

Polar bears, wild reindeer, arctic fox, lemmings, arctic wolves and arctic hares are found in most areas. Polar bears are everywhere in the winter but move with the ice in the summer.

Cod, arctic char and capelin are plentiful and are an important link in the food chain. Squid range in size from 15cm to the very large Breachioteuthis which measure 4m from tentacle to tentacle.

Whales, seals and walrus found in the North West Passage are also found in the Northern Sea Route. Details are given elsewhere in this book.

Numerous avian life is supported on the Northern Sea Route shores. These include arctic terns, Ross's ivory, sabines, herring gulls, glaucous gulls, kittiwakes, guillemots, little auks, snipe, geese, eider duck, arctic owls, eagles and tundra partridge.

Cruising information

Ice regime

A detailed explanation of the ice regime in these waters is given in *NP10*.

Ice coverage in the region can be divided into three areas:

- Semi-permanent area of ice in the central Arctic where water depths are greater than 600m. Although

KEY (%)

- >95
- 95
- 75
- 50
- <10

Average sea ice concentration JANUARY (1984 - 2003)

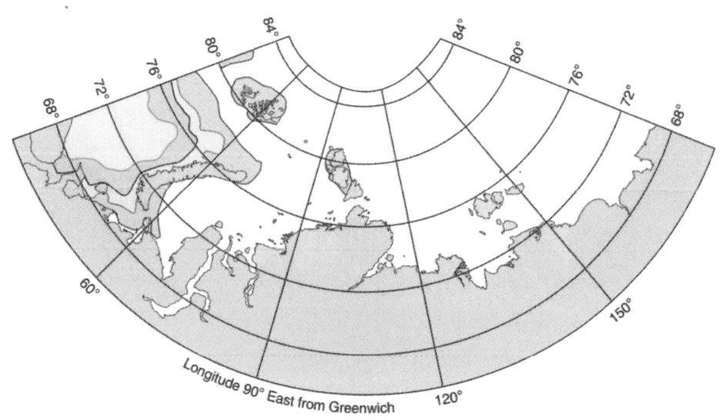

Average sea ice concentration FEBRUARY (1984 - 2003)

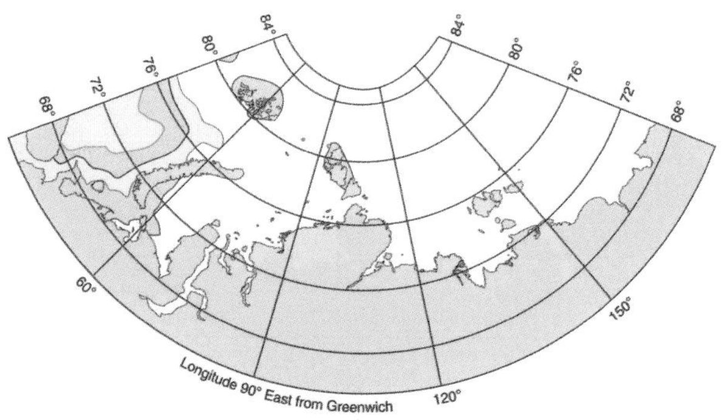

Average sea ice concentration MARCH (1984 - 2003)

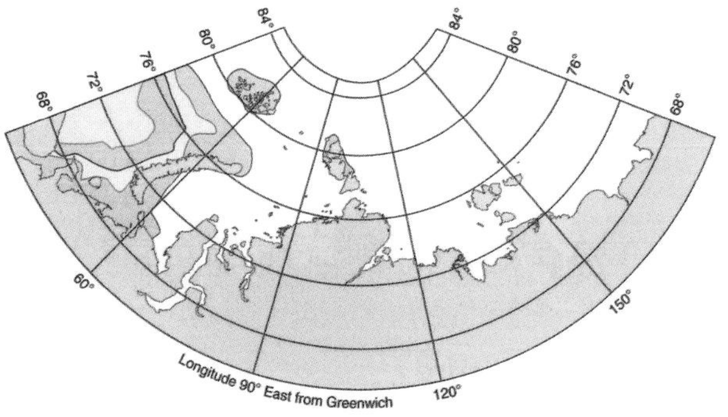

Average sea ice concentration APRIL (1984 - 2003)

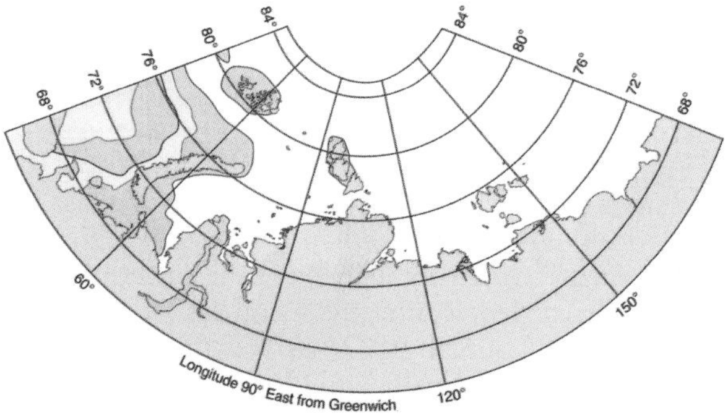

Illustrations from *Admiralty Pilot NP10*

Average sea ice concentration MAY (1984 - 2003)

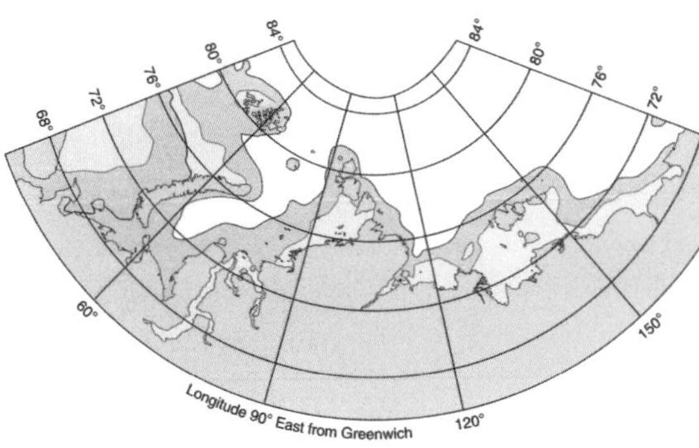

Average sea ice concentration JUNE (1984 - 2003)

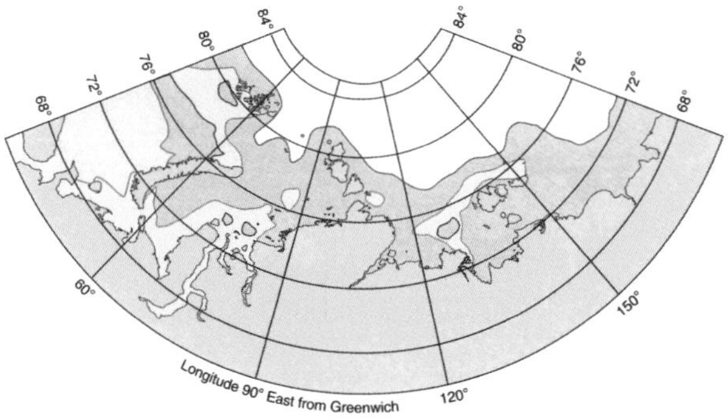

Average sea ice concentration JULY (1984 - 2003)

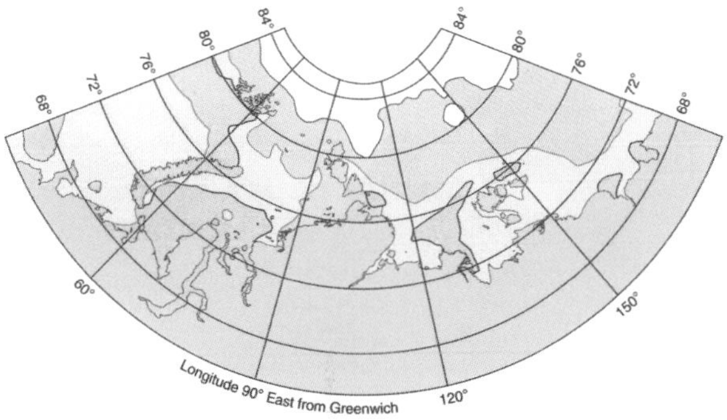

Average sea ice concentration AUGUST (1984 - 2003)

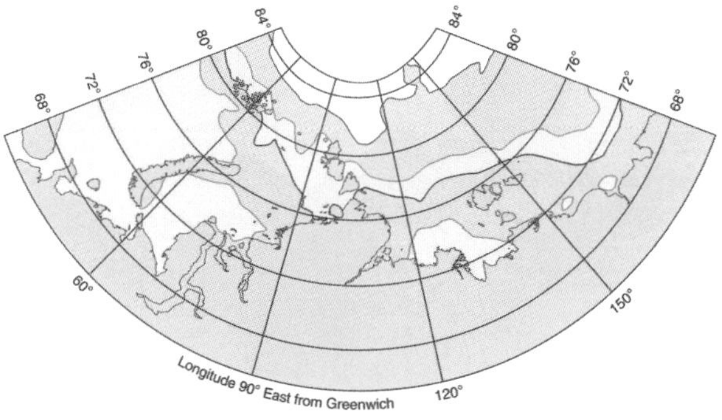

Average sea ice concentration SEPTEMBER (1984 - 2003)

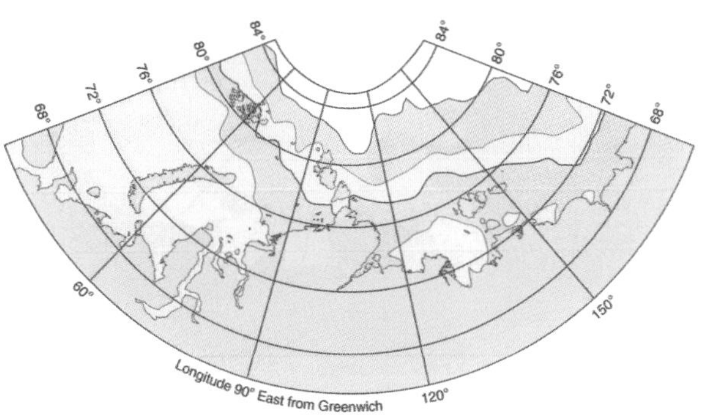

Average sea ice concentration OCTOBER (1984 - 2003)

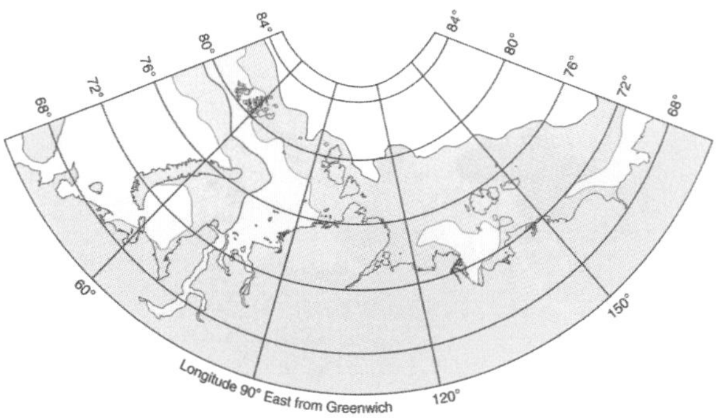

Average sea ice concentration NOVEMBER (1984 - 2003)

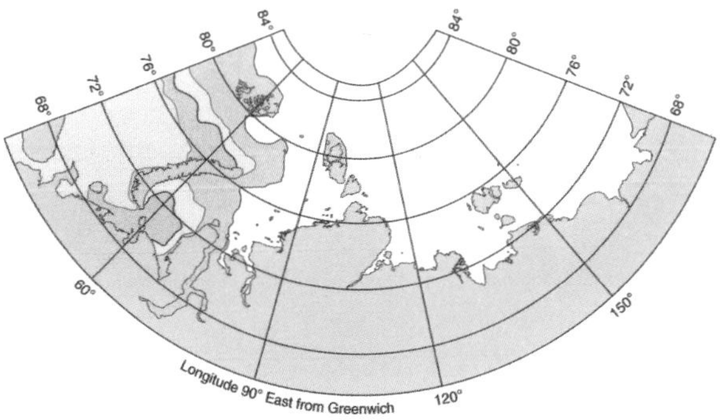

Average sea ice concentration DECEMBER (1984 - 2003)

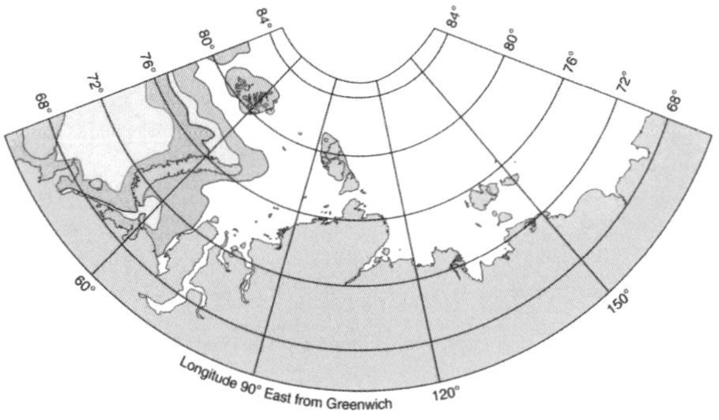

Kara Sea sea ice *Jarlath Cunnane*

global warming is reducing both the thickness of this ice and its area, the ice is always present.

- The waters between the 25m and 600m depth contours comprise mainly first year ice much of which breaks up in the navigation season.
- Shore-fast ice from the shore to the 25m contour. Most, but not all, of this ice will break up in the summer. Break-up is enhanced by outflow from the many rivers which discharge into the Arctic seas.

Ice drifts slowly across the Arctic Ocean from Siberia, across the North Pole to northern Greenland where it travels south on the East Greenland Current. This process takes from three to five years and will, hopefully, not be a significant navigation feature.

In winter the entire Northern Sea Route is covered in ice and no navigation is possible. In most areas, break-up starts in May and the ice is at a minimum in September. Break-up starts with the shore-fast ice between the coast and the 25m contour. The last area to clear, if it does, is normally the Proliv Matisena which separates the Kara and Laptev Seas north of the Taymyr Peninsula.

Currents and tidal streams

The current along the coast of the Northern Sea Route sets in a generally easterly direction.

In general, tidal streams are weak except near headlands, straits and islands where they may be much stronger. Tidal height information is rarely available and best established by experience.

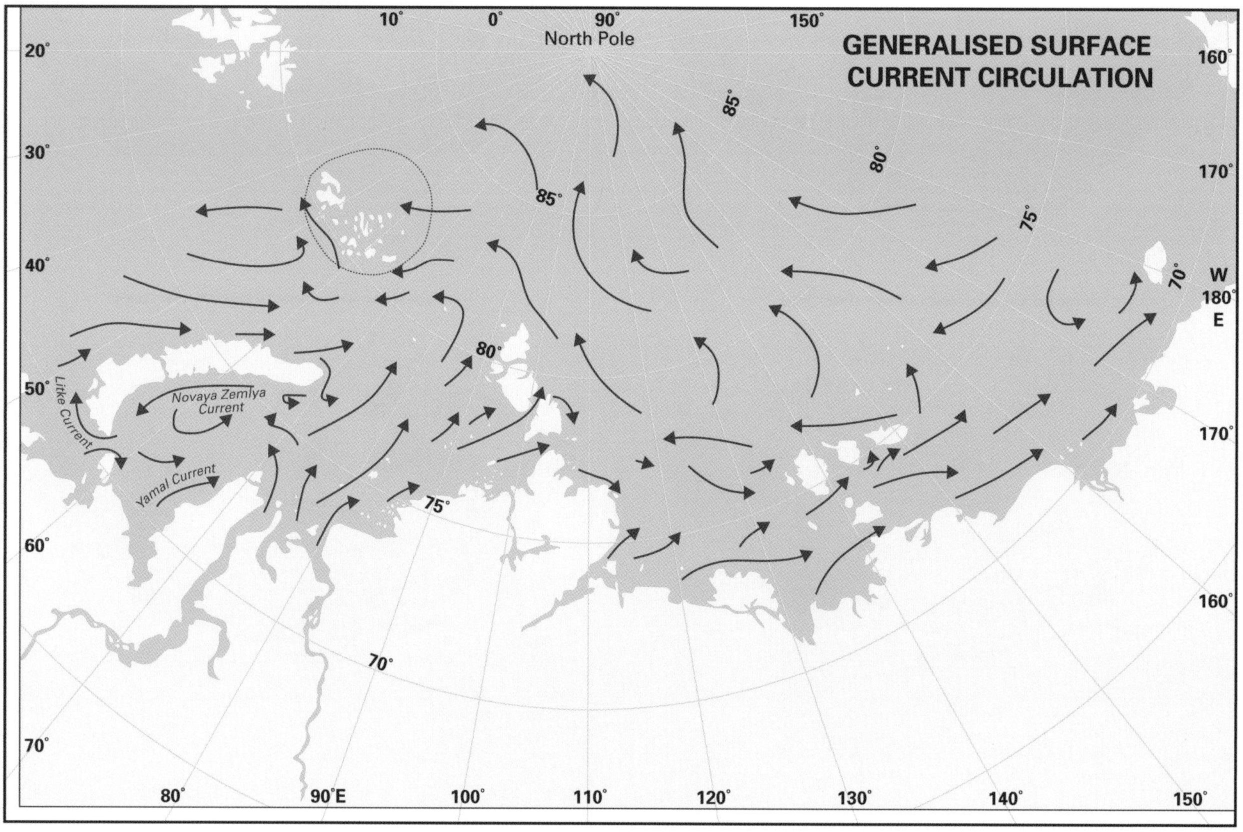

Procedures and regulations

Visas

Visas are required for all foreigners visiting Russia. They should be obtained from the visitor's country of permanent residence and can take up to a month to arrange. They are obtained directly from the Russian embassy or by a visa agency. Embassy fees for processing visa applications vary from country to country. A specialised visa agency is more expensive but should be quicker and less troublesome.

There are three main types of visa: a tourist visa, business (long term) visa and a transit visa. Tourist visas are more easily obtainable but are restricted to a maximum of 30 days and are valid for one or two visits to the country. Business visas are issued for periods of up two years and may be valid for multiple visits. Transit visas are valid for a few hours or days and are designed for people traveling by air or train who are only in the country for a short period of time. Crew attempting the Northern Sea Route are advised to obtain a business (long term) visa.

Visa timescales may be extended but the process is difficult and time consuming. It is therefore best to apply for a visa for a longer period of time than is anticipated.

Part of the paperwork which has to be submitted with a visa application is an 'invitation'. Invitations for tourist visas are obtainable from Russian hotels, travel agencies or specialised visa agencies. Hotels may provide the service free of charge, otherwise they are likely to cost about US$40 or be included as part of the service provided by a visa procurement agency. Invitations to accompany business visas must be obtained from a registered Russian company or from one of the visa agencies.

Moscow - one or more visits may be necessary to obtain paperwork when planning a Northern Sea Route Passage
Jarlath Cunnane

Many yachtsmen and women visiting Russia have been helped by Vladimir Ivankiv who is the Honorary Port Representative for the RCC and the OCC Port Officer for Saint Petersburg. He is currently able to arrange invitations at €30/person. For each crew member visa he needs their full name, passport number, date of birth, and nationality.

Vladimir Ivankiv
Email vladimir@sailrussia.spb.ru

Permit to transit the Northern Sea Route

Vessels attempting to transit the Northern Sea Route require a permit from the Northern Sea Route Administration (NSRA). New rules were published in 2013 appertaining to navigation through the

Useful websites – Russian procedures, regulations and visas

	Russian Embassy in London Russian Visa application	http://ru.vfsglobal.co.uk
	Russian Embassy in the UK Visa help links	www.russialink.org.uk/embassy
	Universal Travel Service Visa support	www.russianvisas.org
	Way to Russia A commercial agency offering useful advice and visa services	www.waytorussia.net/Travel/VisaSupport.html
	Express to Russia Tourist and visa agency	www.expresstorussia.com
	Northern Sea Route Administration The official web site for applications to transit the NSR	www.nsra.ru/en/celi_funktsii/

Northern Sea Route. The rules, and permit application process, are designed for commercial shipping and applications relating to foreign yachts are uncommon. At the time of writing, it is uncertain as to how the new rules will be interpreted for smaller vessels attempting a transit of the Northern Sea Route.

Ships navigating the Northern Sea Route in waters with ice present and without ice-breaker assistance must be ice-strengthened to at least category Arc4 (ICE1). The implementation of the rules for smaller vessels with no ice-strengthening categorisation is open to interpretation by the officials dealing with the application.

In the past, an application had to be made, in Russian, by a 'Russian Partner.' The Russian Partner was likely to be a professional person familiar with the bureaucracy and a good communicator in both Russian and the vessel's crew language. The Partner submitted the application, followed its progress, submitted additional information as required and expedited the application when it was delayed. The process was time consuming and the Partner's fees were likely to be several thousand US dollars. This may well still be the best approach.

Since 2013, the application form, which is in English and initially appears quite straightforward, is available on the NSRA website. It is not easy to quantify what additional information is likely to be required, however, applicants ought to include:

- Proof of the crew's competence. The NSRA is used to dealing with professional mariners and it may be difficult for yachtsmen to convince them of their ability to operate safely in the Northern Sea Route. Evidence of successful North West Passage or antarctic passages may be useful but will not be conclusive proof.
- Vessel details. This should include drawings, photographs, construction details and details of safety equipment.
- Evidence that the Northern Sea Route rules are being complied with as much as possible (see website)

Paperwork *Jarlath Cunnane*

- Port of entry, intended stops *en route*, dates of entry *en route* stops and final destination ETA, proposed route, etc.
- Crew lists with full names, DOBs, place of birth, occupation, place of employment, citizenship, passport details, visas, etc

The application is dealt with by the NSRA who consult with other organisations including the border guard, FSB (the Russia Security Service), Department of Tourism, and Murmansk Shipping Company.

The permit application process is likely to take at least twelve months. The application process is liable to change.

Murmansk Shipping Company

The Murmansk Shipping Company controls and directs all shipping within the Northern Sea Route. A likely condition of a vessel's permit to transit the Northern Sea Route is that a vessel contacts the Murmansk Shipping Company every day by satphone to report on the vessel's position, ice conditions, weather conditions, etc. In return, the vessel will receive ice/weather forecasts and routing guidance. In the past, this role has been fulfilled by Mr Nicolai Babich who is a most experienced Arctic navigator and whose knowledge of the route is profound.

Ice pilot

Another likely condition of a vessel's permit to transit the Northern Sea Route is that a Russian ice pilot, who will be nominated by the Murmansk Shipping Company, is appointed onboard for the duration of the transit.

The ice pilot will probably be the best person to talk to the Murmansk Shipping Company every day and may be invaluable when dealing with customs and border patrols, coastguards, local police, etc.

The ice pilot is likely to have many year's experience of navigation within the Northern Sea Route but he may not be familiar with small vessel operations and culture. This may be a challenge for the boat's crew but is likely to be far outweighed by his knowledge of local customs and bureaucracy.

Local officials and the Russian language

The Russian Federation comprises 83 republics, each to a large degree autonomous, and its officialdom is equally so. Russian immigration, police and customs agencies are quite hierarchical and one may have to deal with people at a number of different levels within the organisation. Whenever possible, one is advised go straight to 'the man at the top'. That way there should only be one set of negotiations. Skippers may be expected to 'ease the path of bureaucracy'.

It is important that a Russian speaker is part of the crew. Great confusion will result without this skill.

RUSSIAN Print	RUSSIAN Script	Transliteration	Cyrillic Morse Code Symbol
А а	А а	a	· —
Б б	Б б	b	— · · ·
В в	В в	v	· — —
Г г	Г г	g	— — ·
Д д	Д д	d	— · ·
Е е	Е е	e (ye)[2]	·
Ж ж	Ж ж	zh	· · · —
З з	З з	z	— — · ·
И и	И и	i	· ·
Й[1] й	й	y	· — — —
К к	К к	k	— · —
Л л	Л л	l	· — · ·
М м	М м	m	— —
Н н	Н н	n	— ·
О о	О о	o	— — —
П п	П п	p	· — — ·
Р р	Р р	r	· — ·
С с	С с	s	· · ·
Т т	Т т	t	—
У у	У у	u	· · —
Ф ф	Ф ф	f	· · — ·
Х х	Х х	kh	· · · ·
Ц ц	Ц ц	ts	— · — ·
Ч ч	Ч ч	ch	— — — ·
Ш ш	Ш ш	sh	— — — —
Щ щ	Щ щ	shch	— — · —
Ъ[3] ъ	ъ	"	· — — · — ·
Ы[1] ы	Ы ы	y	— · — —
Ь ь	ь	'	— · · —
Э э	Э э	e	· · — · ·
Ю ю	Ю ю	yu	· · — —
Я я	Я я	ya	· — · —

Marine safety information

Weather, ice and navigation warnings are primarily available through the Inmarsat-C system (Navareas XX and XXI). Weather reports are transmitted twice a day at 0600 and 1800 hours UTC. Ice reports are transmitted at 1800z on Mondays, Wednesdays and Fridays.

Russian geographic names

The following translations may be useful:

arkhipelag	archipelago
banka	shoal, bank
guba	bay
led	ice
mayak	lighthouse
more	sea
mys	cape or headland
novi	new
oblast'	province
obryv	bluff
ostrov	island
proliv	strait
recka or rechka	river
severnay	north
vodka	vodka
vostok	east
yug	south
zaliv	gulf, bay, inlet
zapad	west

There is a Navtex transmitter at Tiksi Port which transmits on 518KHz with the identifier 'Q'. It has a nominal range of 300M. Other Navtex transmitters are reported to be operational at Arkhangelsk ('L'), and Murmansk ('K'). Transmitters are planned for Amderma, Dikson, Mys Sterlegova, Bol'shoy Begichev and Ostrova Andrea.

Marine Safety Information is transmitted by facsimile from Murmansk Radio (UDK/UDK2) on 6,446KHz, 7,907KHz and 8,444KHz at 0700 UTC, 0800 UTC, 1400 UTC and 1430 UTC. The RPM/IOC is120/576.

Reporting

Vessels are expected to report twice a day through Amderma, Dikson, Tiksi or Pevek radio stations (*ALRS Vol.1*).

Vessels are required to carry a satellite 'phone (Iridium) and report to the Murmansk Shipping Company daily.

Useful websites – marine safety information

	Bremen University Small scale ice charts	www.iup.uni-bremen.de:8084/amsr2/
	Athropolis Current Arctic weather reports	www.athropolis.com/map2.htm
	Northern Sea Route Administration Official and current weather and ice information for the NSR	www.nsra.ru/en/meteoinfo/

7. THE NORTH EAST PASSAGE

Charts and publications

The following publications are informative:

- *British Admiralty Sailing Directions for the White Sea (P72), Arctic Pilot Volumes 1 (NP10) and 2 (NP11), Bering Sea and Strait Pilot (NP23)*
- *Russian Guide to Navigating through the Northern Sea Route No 4151B* (in English)
- *Admiralty List of Radio Signals*
- *International Code of Signals* (for signals between ice breakers and assisted vessels)
- *Northabout - Sailing the North East and North West Passages* by Jarlath Cunnane (ISBN-13 978-1905172238).

In addition, the following Russian publications are recommended if transiting the Northern Sea Route:

- 7107 Catalogue of maps and books on the Arctic Ocean
- 4151B Guide to Navigating through the Northern Sea Route (English)
- 1115 Kara Sea Pilot. Part I. Kara Sea except Ob'-Yeniseyskiy Area
- 1116 Kara Sea Pilot. Part II. Kara Sea Ob'-Yeniseyskiy Area
- 1118 Laptev Sea Pilot
- 1119 East Siberian Sea Pilot
- 1120 Western Part of Chukchi Sea, Bering Strait & North-West Part of Bering Sea Pilot
- 4140 Navigation Regulations of Vessels in Barents, White and Kara Seas (Summary)
- 9956.01 Notice to Mariners No.1 by the MoD GUNiO
- Latest coastal warnings in the navigation area (Murmansk, Arkhangelsk, coastal warning West: 45° Kanin Cape – 86° Dudinka; eastward – coastal warning East)
- 2111 List of Lights. Northern Sea Route
- 2103 List of Lights. Russian coast of Barents Sea
- Radio communications regulations of maritime mobile service and maritime mobile satellite service.
- Communication instructions for the period of Arctic navigation 2010–2011.

British Admiralty charts are suitable for passage planning but the Russian charts are the preferred navigation medium. Both are available from Imray.

Russian digital charts are excellent and are annotated with recommended routes. Following is a list of the recommended Russian charts:

10100, 10103, 10104, 10105, 10106, 11114, 11115, 11116, 11122, 11124, 11126, 11127, 11129, 11130, 11132, 11133, 11136, 11137, 11138, 11140, 11141, 11142, 11143, 11144, 11145, 11146, 11147, 11148, 11149, 11150, 11151, 11155, 11164, 12000, 12001, 12002, 12003, 12011, 12014, 12015, 12016, 12305, 12306, 12307, 12309, 12310, 12311, 12312, 12321, 12322, 12327, 12328, 12329, 12330, 12331, 12332, 12333, 12334, 12340, 12346, 12347, 12406, 12407, 12408, 12414, 12420, 12422, 12423, 12424, 12425, 12426, 12427, 12428, 12429, 12431, 12432, 12433, 12437, 14315, 14316, 15004, 15005, 15006, 61001, 61002, 61003, 61004, 61018, 61030, 61035, 61036, 61037, 61039, 61040, 61041, 61043, 61045, 61047.

Buoyage

IALA region A buoyage applies throughout the Northern Sea Route. This is the opposite to the North West Passage which uses region B buoyage (red right returning). Buoys are removed outside the navigation season and are subject to being moved by ice movements.

Fuel, water and supplies

The crew of *Northabout* reports that they were able to obtain diesel in the ports visited. The trade was usually with ship's captains and sometimes with ship's engineers. The currency was a combination of Irish whiskey, vodka, and US Dollars.

Anadyr - refuelling following negotiations with the tug skipper *Jarlath Cunnane*

The shop in the village of Enuremo *Jarlath Cunnane*

Russian icebreaker in the Chukchi Sea *Jarlath Cunnane*

Fresh water is sometimes available ashore but it's quality is variable being sometimes contaminated with bird excrement. It can also be expensive.

Food is available in the settlements although mariners may prefer to take an adequate quantity of stores on board.

Icebreakers

In 2014, most of Russia's icebreakers had been built in the 1970s. A notable exception being the most powerful icebreaker ever built, the 2007 nuclear powered *Pyat'desyat' Let Pobedy*, or *50 Years of Victory*, which first reached the North Pole in 2008.

A major icebreaker construction programme commenced at the beginning of the century. The flagship being the LK-60 class nuclear icebreaker. This will measure 173m x 34m and will become the most powerful icebreaker ever built. Two nuclear reactors will produce 60MW of power driving three propellor shafts. It will need refuelling with uranium-235 every seven years and it's 33,450 tonne displacement will be capable of crushing ice up to 4m thick. An innovative ballast system will vary the draft between 8·5m and 10·5m which will enable the vessel to operate in both river estuaries and deep sea. Three LK-60 vessels are planned to be built between 2018 and 2020.

50 Years of Victory nuclear icebreaker. *ROSATOM*

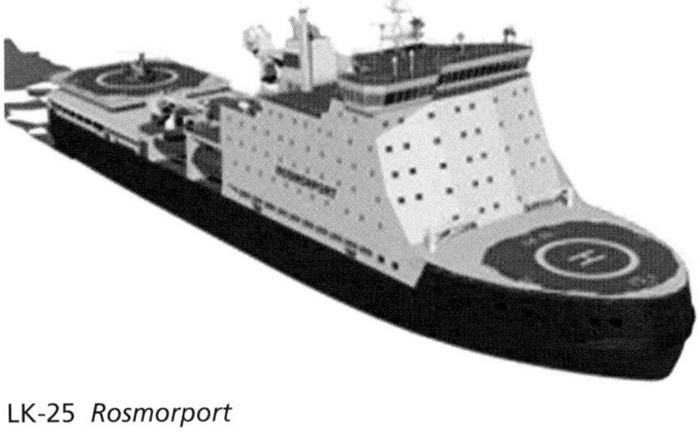

LK-25 *Rosmorport*

Useful websites - Icebreakers

	Rosatom Flot The nuclear ice-breaker company website	www.rosatomflot.ru/index.php?menuid=20&lang=en

Other icebreakers planned are the LK-25, LK-16 and a unique 'skew-going' icebreaker.

The 22,130 tonne displacement LK-25 is powered by a 25MW diesel-electric engine and will come into service in 2015. In addition to its main engine, it will have two 7·5MW Azipod thrusters which will allow the vessel to break ice up to 2m thick whilst moving ahead or astern at a speed of 2 knots.

The LK-16 will have a displacement of 14,000 tonnes and is also powered by a diesel-electric plant. It will have two azimuthing propellors and a bow thruster which will enable it to break ice up to 1.5m thick.

The 'skew-going' icebreaker is a new concept. It will have an asymmetric hull powered by three diesel-electric power plants developing 12,000 HP. It will have a LOA of 76m and a beam of 20·5m. The asymmetric hull will move forwards, backwards and sideways to clear a path 50m wide in ice up to 0·6m thick

The new fleet will also provide search and rescue, oil-spill response, fire-fighting and salvage capabilities.

Icebreaker pilotage is available on request for commercial vessels at a price. If a smaller vessel is in need of assistance, the service may be made available if it is convenient to do so. It is a very hazardous experience following an icebreaker as huge blocks of ice are spewed out behind it which present a danger to small craft. This is mitigated to some extent if one is lucky enough to follow a nuclear icebreaker such as the *Sovetsky Soyuz* as she has air jets which push the broken ice to the edge of the new channel leaving a clear path to follow. The skipper and expedition leader on *Northabout* both emphasise how fraught with danger it is following a conventional icebreaker like the *Captain Babich*.

Principal ports

Port	Position	Remarks
Murmansk	69°00'N 33°06'E	Ice-free all year and the biggest city north of the Arctic Circle
Amderma	69°46'N 61°38'E	Relatively small port
Novyy Port	67°39'N 72°29'E	Mouth of River Ob'
Dikson	73°30'N 80°30'E	Major port and HQ for E Arctic
Ust'Port	69°40'N 84°25'E	Summer HQ for river pilotage. On the shores of Reka Yenisey
Dudinka	69°24'N 86°10'E	Mineral exports from Noril'sk. On the shores of Reka Yenisey
Igarka	67°27'N 86°35'E	Timber exports. On the shores of Reka Yenisey
Tiksi	71°39'N 128°53'E	Mouth of the River Lena
Khatanga	71°59'N 102°28'E	Relatively small port. (*Northabout* over-wintered here)
Zelenomyss kiy Port	68°45'N 161°18'E	River Kolyma
Pevek	69°43'N 170°17'E	Mineral exports

Sea ice forming off the stern of *Northabout*, East Siberian Sea
Jarlath Cunnane

Pilotage and harbour information

The official pilots, charts and sailing directions referred to elsewhere in this chapter are, of course, essential for navigation.

From west to east, the Northern Sea Route can be divided into four areas:

Area I. Barents Sea

Area II. Kara Sea

Area III. Laptev Sea

Area IV. East Siberian Sea

AREA I. BARENTS SEA

Eastbound vessels entering the Barents Sea may enter either from the west by way of Norway and the Nordkapp (North Cape) or from the south by way of the White Sea.

Barents Sea pilotage directions are given in the *Admiralty Sailing Directions for the Southern Barents Sea* and *Beloye More Pilot* (NP72). Vessels approaching the Barents Sea from the west may wish to consult the *Norway Cruising Guide* by Judy Lomax (ISBN: 978 184623 284 8) and the *Admiralty Sailing Directions for Norway Pilot Vol 3B* (NP58B).

Barents Sea climate

Atlantic depressions move over the area from west to east. Associated cold and warm fronts are often occluded and approach from the southwest. The Arctic front lies near Nordkapp in the winter and moves to the south in the summer. Depressions often form on the front and move southeast across the Barents Sea.

Prevailing winds are from the south and southwest in the winter. In the summer they are often variable or from the northeast.

Fog is more frequent in the summer than in the winter. In August, in the western Barents Sea, near Murmansk, it is foggy for about 2% and in the east, off the coast of Novaya Zemlya, it is foggy for about 8% of the time.

Sea ice forms first on the southeast coasts in late October and progresses westwards throughout the winter. At its peak, the pack ice extends northeastwards from Murmanskiy Berreg to northern Novaya Zemlya. The break-up starts in May and the area is usually ice-free by late July. The port of Murmansk is normally ice-free at all times.

Barents Sea points of interest

The Barents Sea is named after Willem Barentsz a Dutch explorer who was born in 1550. He led three voyages, in 1594, 1595 and 1596, which attempted to find the Northern Sea Route to the Pacific. Although he did not sail any further than Novaya Zemlya, the islands between the Barents and Kara

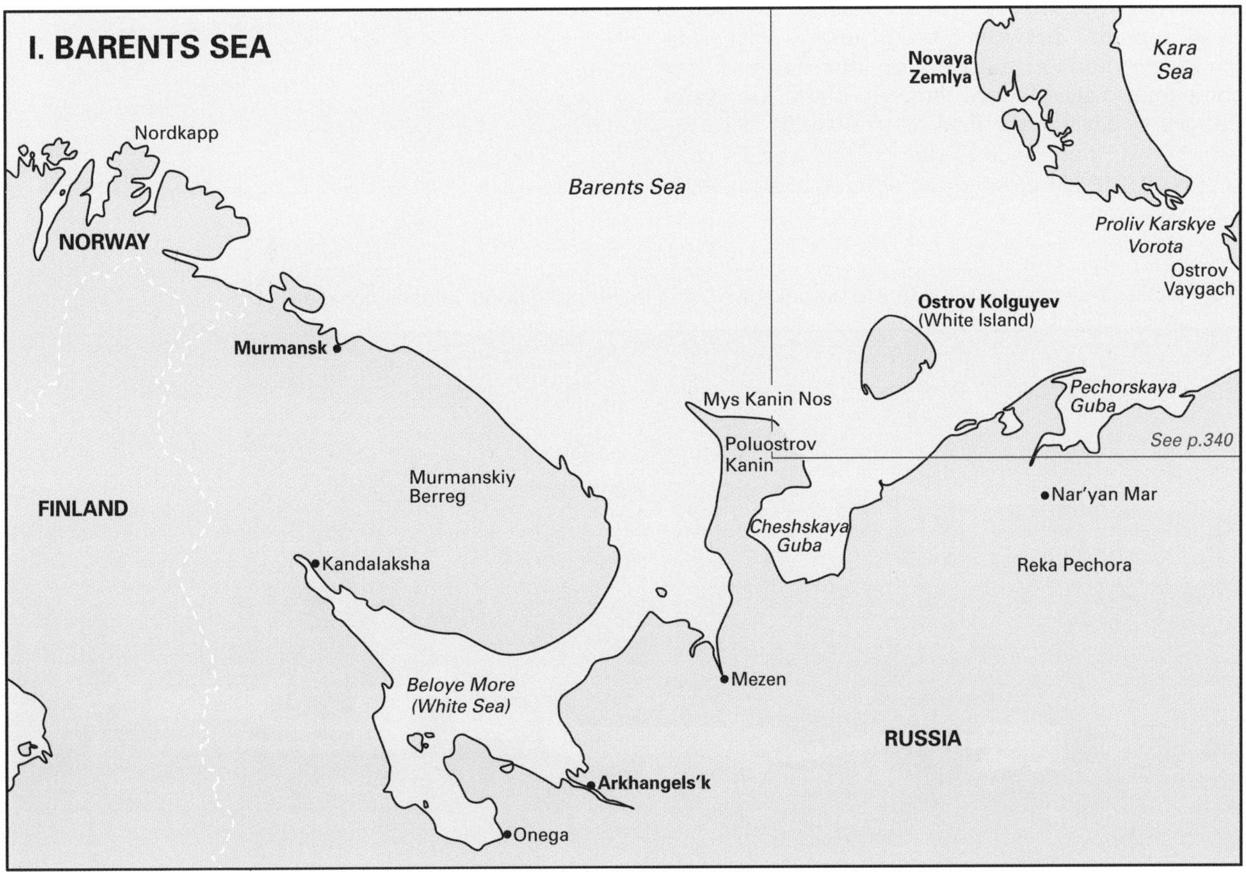

Seas, he charted much of the sea which, in due course, was named after him. On his last voyage, his ship became beset and Barentsz and his crew were forced to over-winter on the ice off the northeast shore of Novaya Zemlya. They survived the winter but Barentsz died the following June whilst attempting to navigate one of the ship's small boats to the Russian mainland.

On new year's eve in 1942, German warships attacked a British convey en-route to Murmansk. The ensuing battle became known as 'The Battle of the Barents Sea'. The British minelayer, HMS *Bramble* and a destroyer HMS *Achates* were sunk as well as the German destroyer *Friedrich Eckoldt*. The German heavy cruiser *Admiral Hipper* was severely damaged. However, the entire convoy of 14 merchant ships made it safely to Murmansk with their cargos comprising 202 tanks, 2,000 military vehicles and 33 bombers. Hitler was so infuriated by the German navy's failure that he changed the German offensive strategy to one relying on U-boats rather than surface ships.

Novaya Zemlya, the islands between the Barents and Kara Seas, were used by the USSR as a nuclear test site during the Cold War. 224 nuclear explosions were detonated with a total explosive energy equivalent to 265 megatons of TNT. That is over 100 times the total explosive power used in the Second World War (including the two Second World War atom bombs).

Oil and natural gas were discovered in the Barents Sea in the 1970s. The Shtokman Field gas reserves are estimated to be 3·2 trillion cubic metres, making it one of the world's largest gas fields. Development between Gazprom, a Russian company, and a number of international oil companies was planned but, in 2006, Gazprom decided to develop the field on its own. In 2012 the project was put on hold due to the world's over supply of natural gas and the development of shale gas extraction.

In September 2013, and shortly after being forced by the Russian coastguard to leave the Kara Sea, three crew members from the Greenpeace icebreaker *Arctic Sunrise* attempted to land on a Gazprom oil rig in the Pechora Sea, the southeastern part of the Barents Sea. The Russian Coastguard responded by seizing the ship and initially charging the Greenpeace activists with 'piracy', which carries a maximum prison term of 15 years. In November of that year the 'pirates' were released on bail.

Search and Rescue

The MRCC for the Barents Sea is based in Murmansk. The contact details are given below:

1	Name of centre(s) MRCC/MRSC/JRCC /JRSC	MRCC Murmansk
2	MMSI-call sign-VHF voice call sign	VHF – 16 CHANNEL MMSI:002734420 VHF voice call sign: Murmansk-MRCC HF/MF – FREQUENCY 2182 KHZ MMSI: 002734420 Voice call sign: Murmansk-Radio
3	Landline communications	✆ +7 8152 428307 ✆ */Fax* +7 8152 423256 *Telex* +64 126178 MAPMU RU *Email* rcc@mapm.ru Inmarsat Mini-M: ✆ +870-762-137-155 *Fax* +870-762-137-157 (*Fax*)

Murmansk approaches with the statue to the unknown solder in the background *Jarlath Cunnane*

Murmansk

68°58′N 33° 05′E

Murmansk is the largest city north of the Arctic Circle. However, like all of the Russian settlements in the Arctic, its population is declining. In 1989 it had 468,000 inhabitants which was reduced to 307,000 in 2010.

Founded by the Russian Empire in 1915, the city has a history of conflict. It was occupied by the British in the First World War and during the Russian Civil War from 1918 to 1920. During the Second World War, the city became an important port for the Russians importing military equipment and exporting raw materials to the Allies. The city was badly damaged by a German offensive in 1941 but was not occupied. A feat which was recognised in 1985 by designating Murmansk a 'Hero City.' In the Cold War, the port became an important submarine base.

Murmansk is dominated by Alyosha, a 35·5m (116ft) tall statue of a First World War soldier which was erected in 1974. In Russia, the Second World War is known as 'The Great Patriotic War'. The statue faces west, towards Reka Lebyazhka and the 'Valley of Glory' where the Russians repelled a German offensive to occupy Murmansk in 1941.

There are several museums in Murmansk. The Naval History Museum of the Red Banner Northern Fleet, PINRO marine culture museum, Murmansk Oceanarium and Murmansk lighthouse may appeal to people with a nautical bent. The lighthouse is home to a book of remembrance which records the names of the submariners lost in the nuclear submarine *Kursk* in August 2000. All 118 crew on the *Kursk* were lost when she sank in shallow water near Murmansk following an explosion. The Russian authorities were criticised at the time for refusing offers of help from the American, Norwegian and British governments.

The port is ice-free all year round.

Alyosha - statue of a First World War soldier *Andrew Syria*

The lighthouse on Ostrov Kolguyev (White Is.) *Jarlath Cunnane*

Lighthouse at Murmansk *Tupungato | Dreamstime.com*

Pilotage is compulsory and there are two TSS in the approaches to Kol'skiy Zaliv, the 33M fjord-like inlet leading to Murmansk. Hydrofoils and seaplanes operate on the Kol'skiy Zaliv. Vessels are required to give the port notice of their ETA 12 days, four days and 12 hours before arrival. Regulations are plentiful.

The port is a major one and has every facility for commercial and fishing craft.

Atomflot, which owns the Russian ice-breaker fleet, is based in the city as is Sevmorput, the administration responsible for the Northern Sea Route.

The airport has flights to Moscow and Tromso, Norway.

Ostrov Kolguyev (White Island)

69°00′N 49°00′E

Ostrov Kolguyev lies in the southeast part of the Barents Sea. It has a population of about 300 people, most of whom live in Bugrino on the southeast of the island. Leading beacons lead to the anchorage off Bugrino which has depths of 5.2m (17ft) in mud. There are plenty of alternative anchorages in the area.

Novaya Zemlya

Novaya Zemlya lies between the Barents and Kara Seas and comprises two main islands: Severny in the north and Yuzhny in the south. The total land area is about 35,000 square miles (90,650 square kilometres), which, as a comparison, is slightly bigger than Ireland.

1,972 of the 2,400 people living on Novaya Zemlya live in Belushya Guba (Belgula Whale Bay) on the southwest corner of Yuzhny (2010 census). The original indigenous population was resettled to the mainland in the 1950s when the islands were used for military and nuclear testing purposes. The last nuclear test was in 1990 but the islands are still a high security military base. The islands remain a restricted area and visitors are not allowed.

The routes around Novaya Zemlya are described briefly in the Kara Sea section of this chapter.

AREA II. KARA SEA

Pilotage directions for the Kara Sea can be found in *Admiralty Sailing Directions Arctic Pilot Volume 1* (NP10).

Kara Sea climate

The climate is influenced by the Siberian high pressure system which lies over the Siberian mainland and the low pressure systems associated with the Atlantic. Low pressure systems move from west to east and tend to bring milder, if windy, weather. The climate is harsher than the Barents Sea but not as severe as the Laptev Sea which is dominated by the Siberian continental air masses.

In Popova, Ostrov Belyy, the average daily temperature in July is 3°C to 8°C. In December it is -18°C to -25°C. There are about 60 days fog per year, the foggiest month being July when it is, on average, foggy for 12 days. Winds are variable with a slight tendency to be southerly in the winter and northeasterly in the summer. Winds are generally light and, on average, there are only about five days a year when a gale blows.

The outflow of fresh water from the Ob, Yenesey, Pyasina and Taimyra rivers is significant. It affects the sea's salinity and currents.

Break-up generally starts in June and the sea starts to freeze again in September. August is the month with the least amount of ice present.

Mother bear and cubs, Kara Sea *Jarlath Cunnane*

Kara Sea points of interest

The first known European explorer to investigate the Kara Sea was the Englishman Stephen Borough who discovered the Kara Strait (Proliv Karskiye Vorota) whilst attempting to reach Reka Ob in 1556 in the *Serchthrift*. The task was completed by the Russian Admiral Stepan Malygin who charted the waters of the Barents and Kara Seas in 1736–1737. Limited exploration expeditions continued throughout the 18th and 19th centuries.

Since the USSR was formed in 1917, scientific research and exploration increased steadily and by

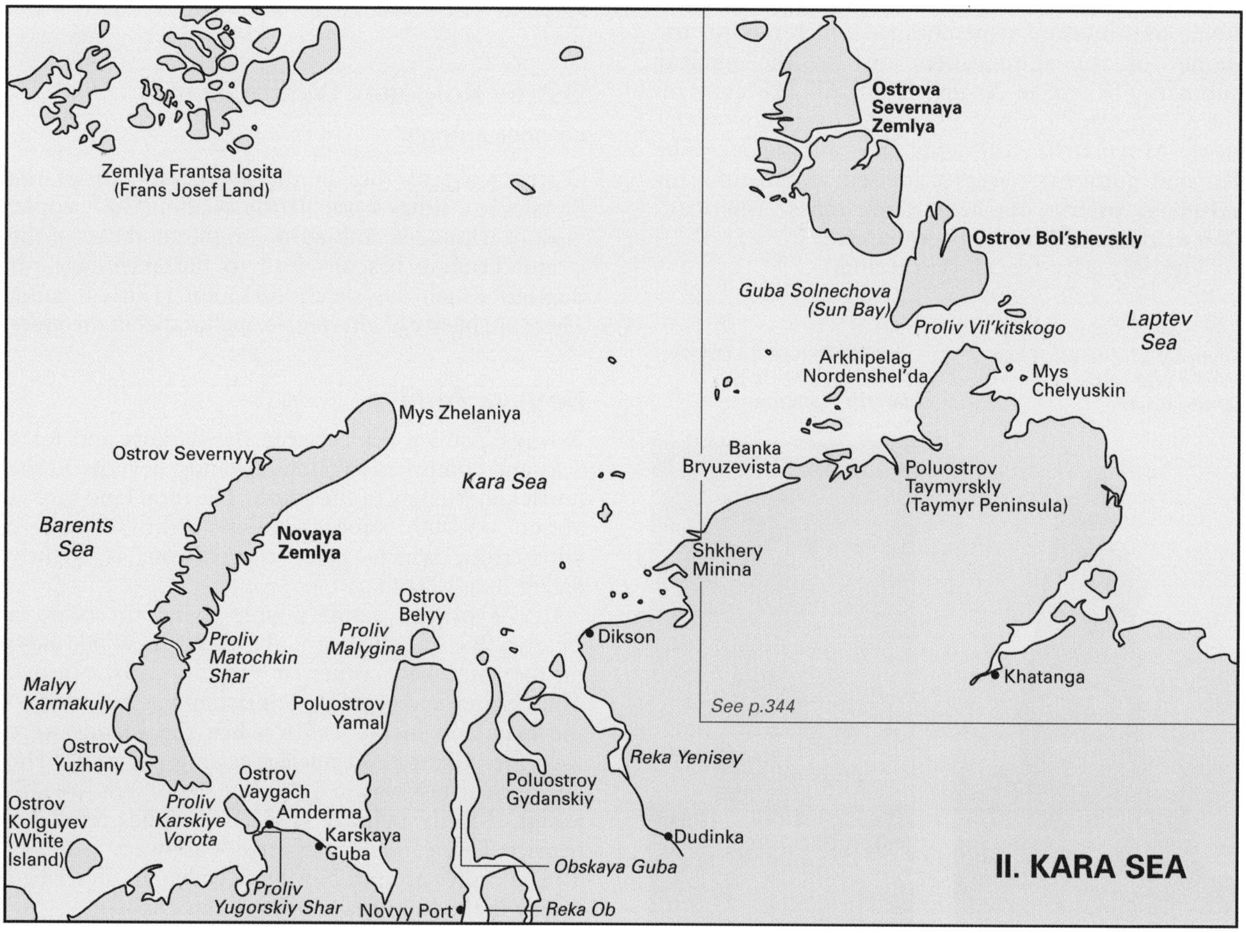

the 1970s there were more than a hundred polar research stations in the Kara Sea. Meteorology, ice reconnaissance and radio services supported both the commercial and military presence in the area.

In 1942 the Germans launched 'Operation Wunderland' where German warships and submarines attempted to destroy Russian ships in the Kara Sea. The operation was only partially successful, the Germans being hampered by ice and bad weather.

Parts of the Kara Sea were used as a nuclear dumping ground and between 1965 and 1988 six nuclear submarine reactors and ten nuclear reactors were dumped in the Novaya Zemlya area. The nuclear submarine K-27 was scuttled on the northeastern coast of Novaya Zemlya on 6th September 1982. Its two nuclear reactors, which contain highly enriched uranium fuel, are of some concern to environmentalists.

Oil has been discovered in the Kara Sea and licences for its extraction were granted in 2010. The developments are being opposed by Greenpeace whose ship, the *Arctic Sunrise*, was escorted out of the Kara Sea in August 2013.

Search and Rescue

The MRCC for the Kara Sea is based in Dikson. The contact details are given below:

1	Name of centre(s) MRCC/MRSC/JRCC /JRSC	MRCC Dikson Lat. 73°30'23N; Long. 080°31'35E
2	MMSI-call sign-VHF voice call sign	VHF – 16 CHANNEL MMSI: 002731107 VHF voice call sign: Dikson-MRCC HF/MF – FREQUENCY 2182 KHZ MMSI: 002733717 Voice call sign: Dikson-Radio
3	Landline communications	✆ +7(39152) 2-41-00 *Mobile* +7 906 903 06 57 ✆ */Fax* +7(39152) 2-42-00 *Telex* 788790 SPAS *Email* mrcc-dikson@mail.ru INMARSAT BGAN ICCID: 870772397954 (Voice, Voice Mail, SMS, GPRS)
4	Types of SAR facilities normally available	Rescue boat, rescue vessel, long range aircraft

Western approaches to the Kara Sea

The Barents Sea and Kara Sea are separated by two islands north of mainland Russia which are collectively known as Novaya Zemlya. Eastbound vessels entering the Kara Sea from the Barents Sea may take one of four routes:

1. North of Novaya Zemlya (*NP10*, chapter 7) where higher concentrations of sea ice are likely to be encountered.
2. Transit the Proliv Matochkin Shar (*NP10*, chapter 6) – a 55M strait between Ostrov Yuzhuny (the southern island of Novaya Zemlya) and Ostrov Severnyy (the northern island of Novaya Zemlya). The strait is designated as an area temporary prohibited to navigation. This appears to be a semi-permanent restriction.
3. Proliv Karskiye Vorota (*NP10*, chapter 4) – the waters south of Novaya Zemlya and north of the island of Ostrov Vaygach. This is the main shipping route for vessels transiting the Northern Sea Route and a traffic separation scheme is in operation. Tidal streams reach a maximum of 1.3kns. The current flows westwards along the Ostrov Yuzhnyy coast (northern side of the strait) and eastwards along the Ostrov Vaygach shores (southern side of the strait). Drifting sea ice is borne by the tide. New ice normally forms each year in November and break-up occurs between mid June and late July. There are a number of anchorages, subject to ice, within the strait.
4. Proliv Yugorskiy Shar (*NP10*, chapter 4) – the 28M strait between Ostrov Vaygach and mainland Russia. Proliv Yugorskiy Shar is normally covered in fast sea-ice from October to late June. The strait is marked with transits (ranges) and navigation buoys which are subject to movement by ice. Pilotage is compulsory for larger vessels, the pilot authority being either Proliv Yugorskiy Shar or Proliv Matochkin Shar. Tidal streams reach 2·8 knots. Sea-ice drifting on the tide may cause an anchored vessel to break her anchor chain and be swept into shallow water. Subject to ice conditions, there are a number of anchorages in the strait, the bottom being sand or pebbles, which are reported to provide good holding.

Mountain Zenith and a glacier, Shumniy, in a bay the Guba Juzhnaja Sulmeneva on Northern island of Novaya Zemlya (New Land) *Sergey33 | Dreamstime.com*

Amderma 69°46′N 61°40′E

The village of Amderma, which means 'a walrus rookery' in the Nenets language, is situated about 20M to the east of Proliv Yugorskiy Shar. The population in 2002 was 650 people. Fluorite mining in the area was abandoned in the 1990s when the settlement's population peaked at about 6,000 people. It has a military and civilian airport with regular flights to Arkhangel'sk. There is a post office and a hospital.

The anchorage is an unprotected roadstead which is subject to strong winds and drift ice.

Karskaya Guba 69°17′N 64°59′E

The small village of Karskaya Guba, or Kara-Guba, has a few log houses, a trading post and is home to the Ust'Kara Polar Station. A submerged meteorite crater lies 15km east of Karskaya Guba which was formed about 70 million years ago. The 65m diameter crater is one of the biggest meteor craters on earth.

The anchorage is reported to provide good holding in mud and sand although it is exposed in strong winds. There is a pier with depths of 1·5m and a pontoon. There is an airport.

Proliv Malygina 72°57′N 69°25′E

Proliv Malygina is the 10M strait north of the Poluostrov Yamal peninsula and south of the island of Ostrov Belyy. It is the shortest route from Proliv Karskiye Vorota or Proliv Yugorskiy Shar to Dikson. Much of the strait is shoal however there is sufficient water for vessels with drafts up to 4m. The west going tidal stream lasts for 8–9 hours with mean rates of 2–3kns. The east going tidal stream is of a shorter duration and is much weaker. The island of Ostrov Belyy may provide some protection from northerly winds and ice. There are a number of anchorages within the strait.

Obskaya Guba and Novyy Port

Obskaya Guba is the 400M inlet to the east of the Poluostrov Yamal peninsula. It is the world's longest estuary. At its head is the Reka Ob which, with a length of 2,625M, is one of the longest rivers in Russia. The river is navigable for nearly all its length.

Parts of the Obskaya Guba entrance are mined. Obskaya Guba freezes in early November and break-up occurs in early June.

Novyy Port (67°41′N 73°05′E) lies on the western shores of the Obskaya Guba some 300M from the Kara Sea. The town, which has a population of about 500, is a supply base for the Obskaya Guba and Kara Sea settlements and a fishing port. Ice break-up is in early July and it usually re-freezes in late October. A bank at the harbour entrance has a least depth of 3·4m.

Dikson and Reka Yenisey

73°30′N 80°25′E

Dikson lies at the mouth of Reka Yenisey, the Yenisey River. Reka Yenisey is about 2,500M long and originates in NW Mongolia. It is an important communication route through Siberia and links with the trans-Siberian railway at Krasnoyarsk. The river freezes during the winter and break-up usually occurs in June. Large ice floes are then expelled into the Yenisey basin near Dikson at speeds of about 4kns.

The (comparatively) major river ports of Ust'Port, Dudinka and Igarka lie on the shores of Reka Yenisey.

Dikson is the most northern port in Russia and is named after the Swedish explorer, Baron Oscar Dickson. It was an important military base which has now been greatly reduced in size. In the 1990s over 5,000 people lived there but this declined to less than 700 people in 2010. Its shipping movements have drastically declined in sympathy with the town's fortunes.

The approaches were mined and anchoring is prohibited.

Although the town is very dilapidated, is does boast a civic sauna, or banya, where crews can wash and steam themselves courtesy of a byproduct of the power station. There is a small airport. Diesel and supplies can be obtained. There are engineering workshops which can carry out marine repairs. The MRCC for the Kara Sea is based in Dikson.

Eastern Kara Sea

From Dikson to Mys Chelyuskin is about 450M. There are no major settlements or ports *en route* although a study of the charts and pilot books will reveal a number of anchorages.

Westerly and northerly winds tend to concentrate sea-ice. It may be possible to seek a more ice-free route in the lee of the various islands.

The Shkhery Minina archipelago lies approximately 90M NE of Dikson. The most prominent landmark in the archipelago is the hill Gora Minina (148m AMSL) in position 74°43′N 86°16′E which can be seen from 30M away. The islands are quite low lying being between 40m to 80m AMSL. There are a number of routes through the archipelago which are described in the pilot books and shown on the Russian charts. There are no major settlements however there are many anchorages. The Ostrov Plavnikovyy (74°26′N 85°00′E), Ostrov Pervomayskiy and Ostrov Gavrilova (75°59′N 92°39′E), and Ostrov Yarzhinskogo and Ostrov Rykachéva (75°51′N 92°50′E) are marine nature reserves and are restricted areas.

There are a number of shoal patches at Banka Bryuzevista and the recommended routes shown on the Russian charts should be followed.

New Siberian Islands *Jarlath Cunnane*

The Arkhipelag Nordenshel'da archipelago is approximately 300M from Dikson and 100M from Proliv Vil'kitskogo, the gateway to the Laptev Sea. There are three recommended routes though the archipelago and a number of anchorages.

Sun Bay, Ostrov Bol'shevik *Jarlath Cunnane*

Dikson - the crew of *Northabout* and a local motorbike
Jarlath Cunnane

AREA III. LAPTEV SEA

Pilotage directions for the Laptev Sea can be found in *Admiralty Sailing Directions Arctic Pilot Volume 1* (NP10).

Laptev Sea climate

The Laptev Sea climate is one of the most severe amongst the Arctic seas. Air temperatures stay below 0°C for 9–11 months of the year and temperatures as low as -50°C (-58°F) have been recorded. The coldest month is January. In the summer, the average temperatures rise to between 0°C in the north and 5°C in the south. Snow can occur at any time of the year and average 70–105 days per annum. Winds can blow from any direction and are normally light for most of the time. Strong northerly winds move the pack ice towards the Russian shore and may make the sea routes impassable.

Sea ice forms in September in the north and October in the south. Break-up is normally in early June. Warm southerly winds help form several polynyas close to the Russian mainland. The Proliv Vil'kitskogo channel, which links the Kara and Laptev Seas, is the most northern part of the North Sea Route and is often impassable. This area and the western Laptev Sea are the most ice-ridden waters of the Northern Sea Route.

Icebergs and growlers are found near Ostrov Severnaya Zemlya and Poluostrov Taymyrskiy.

Laptev Sea points of interest

The coasts of the Laptev Sea were inhabited, in approximate chronological order, by the Yukaghir, Chuvan, Even, Evenk and Yakut tribes from earliest times. Like their counterparts who lived along the route of the North West Passage, these people practiced a variation of the shamanism religion.

Various Russian expeditions explored the area in the 17th and 18th centuries. The Ostrov Lyakhovskiye islands, which lie between the Laptev and East Siberian Seas, were named by Catherine II after the ivory merchant Ivan Lyakhov who established the first settlements in that area. The Great Northern Expedition in 1739–1742, which charted much of the Laptev Sea coastline, was led by Vice Admiral Dmitry Laptev who gave his name to the Dmitry Laptev Strait linking the Laptev and East Siberian Seas. Dmitry Laptev's cousin, Khariton Laptev, led a second part of the Great Northern Expedition and the Sea was eventually named after

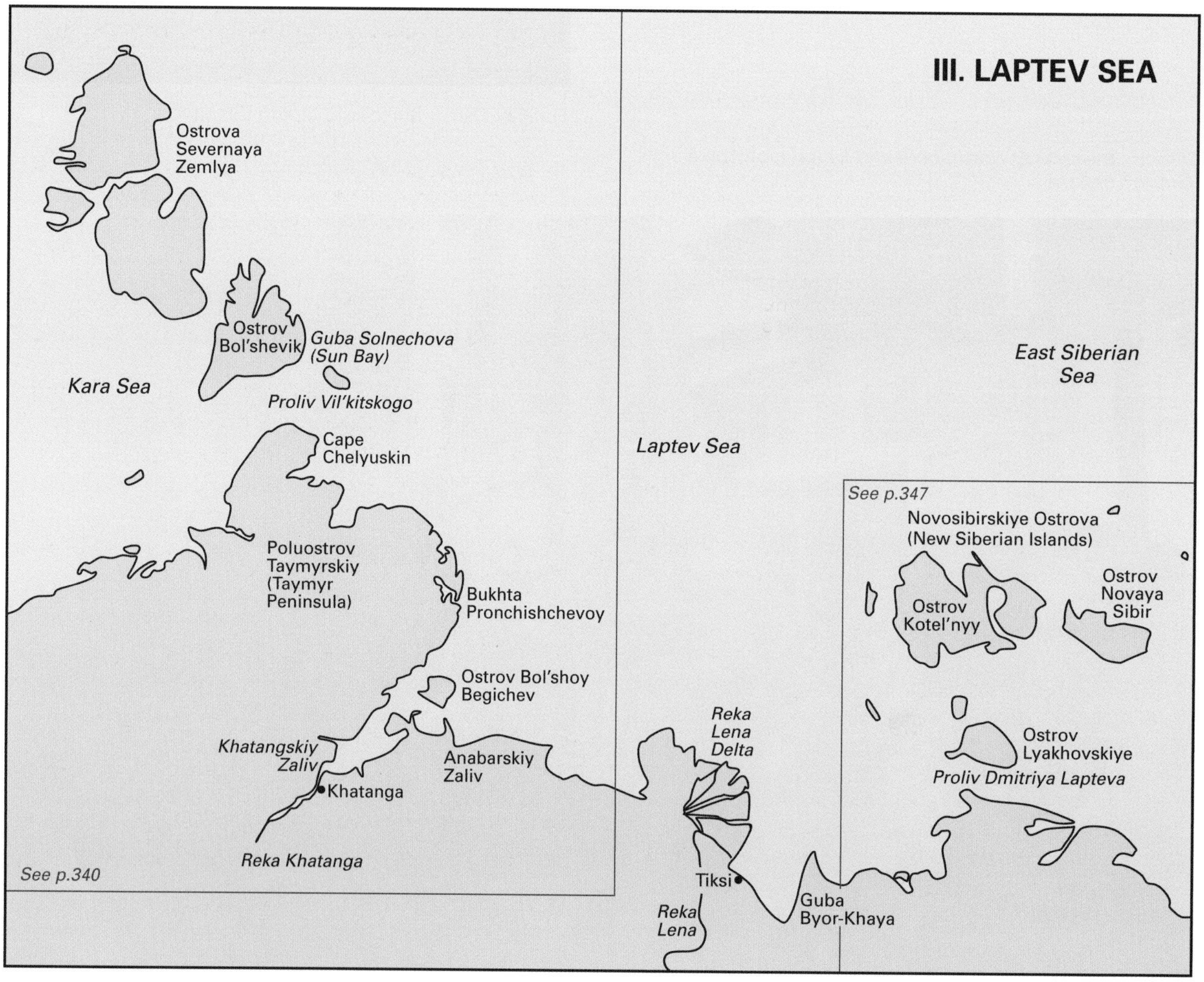

them both in 1935. The first known crossing of the Laptev Sea was accomplished by Adolf Erik Nordenskiold in 1875 in the steamship *Vega*.

Baron Eduard von Toll led two expeditions in 1892–1894 and in 1900–1902. He perished on the last expedition in mysterious circumstances but not before discovering large quantities of fossilised ivory in Novosibirskiye Ostrova (the New Siberian Islands). Some of the ivory is 200,000 years old.

Search and Rescue

The MRCC for the Laptev Sea is based in Tiksi. The contact details are given below:

1	Name of centre(s) MRCC/MRSC/JRCC/JRSC	MRSC Tiksi Lat. 71°41'36N; Long. 128°52'21E (MRCC Dikson)
2	MMSI-call sign-VHF voices call sign	VHF – 16 CHANNEL MMSI: 002731196 Voices call sign: Tiksi-MRSC HF/MF - FREQUENCY 2182 KHZ MMSI: 002733718 Call sign: Tiksi-radio-7
3	Landline communications	✆ +7 924 321 20 90 (Head) +7 41167 530 65 (Duty Officer) *Fax* +7 41167 523 90 *Mobile* +7 924 321 20 90 *Email* tiksi@smpcsa.ru Inmarsat- C:427351446 Inmarsat BGAN ICCID: 870772397397 (Voice,Voice Mail, SMS, GPRS)
4	Types of SAR facilities normally available	Rescue boat, rescue vessel, long range aircraft, medium range helicopter
5	Remarks	MRSC's service time period during summer navigation (approx. July–October)

Proliv Vil'kitskogo 78°00'N 104°00'E

Cape Chelyuskina is the most northern point on mainland Russia and lies between the Kara and Laptev Seas. Proliv Vil'kitskogo is the strait between Cape Chelyuskina and the archipelago of Ostrova Severnaya Zemlya to the north. The recommended navigation tracks for vessels transiting the Northern Sea Route pass through Proliv Vil'kitskogo.

Proliv Vil'kitskogo is rarely ice-free and is probably the most critical section of a Northern Sea Route transit. Commercial ice strengthened vessels routinely require ice-breaker assistance and the strait is quite likely to prove impassable for small vessels. It may be possible to follow an ice-breaker convoy although the dangers of doing so, and previously mentioned in the section about ice-breakers, should be born in mind.

Maximum tidal streams are 1·0kn to 1·5kn.

In 2005, the expedition yacht *Northabout* spent several days sheltering from ice and bad weather at anchor in Guba Solnechova (Sun Bay) on Ostrov Bol'shevik, the southern most of the three main islands which comprise Ostrova Severnaya Zemlya. She eventually transited the Proliv Vil'kitskogo and sailed into the Kara Sea with the aid of a Russian ice-breaker.

Khatangskiy Zaliv and Reka Khatanga

Khatangskiy Zaliv is the wide inlet at the mouth of the Reka Khatanga river. Spring tidal streams attain 2.8kns. Although comparatively shallow, the river and inlet are frequented by both river and sea going craft going to and from Khatanga.

The SE side of the estuary is populated with nomadic Khatangskiy Oblast' indigenous peoples who hunt the wild reindeer, arctic fox, hare and walrus which are found there.

In the 1930s deposits of coal, oil and salt were discovered in Norvik Bay which is on the eastern shores of Khatangskiy Zaliv. A Gulag penal labour camp was established to work the mines. The coal and oil reserves proved to be disappointing but salt was mined there by forced labour until the 1940s when the camp and village of Norvik were dismantled.

The Reka Khatanga has minimum depths of 3·6m and pilotage is compulsory.

Khatanga 71°59'N 102°40'E

Khatanga, which means 'Large Water' in the Evenki language, is 113M from the Laptev Sea and is a possible port of refuge. It is an important regional center with a sea port, fishing port, airport and various administration centers. The port handles coal, metal scrap, crushed stone, iron-ore concentrate, schungite, salt, vehicles, and home trade general cargoes which are delivered to smaller settlements in the Laptev Sea.

Khatanga is the nearest town to the Popigai crater, an asteroid crater which is reputed to be rich in industrial diamonds.

Caribou swimming the river at Khatanga *Jarlath Cunnane*

Khatanga *Jarlath Cunanne*

Khatanga *Jarlath Cunanne*

Diesel, supplies and marine repairs can be found there. There is an airport.

The expedition yacht, *Northabout*, over-wintered In Khatanga in 2004/2005. The problems caused by a 10m surge in water levels as a result of ice melting in the spring, were overcome by overwintering the yacht in an enclosed steel barge.

Tiksi 71°39'N 128°48'E

Tiksi, which means 'a moorage place' in the Sakha language, is the principal port in the Laptev Sea and is about half way through the Northern Sea Route. It is close to the Reka Lena river delta. The Reka Lena being the second largest Russian river, after Reka Yenisey, flowing into the Arctic.

Like many of the settlements along the Northern Sea Route, since the dissolution of the Soviet Union in the early 1990s, the military presence in the area has much diminished and population levels have dropped dramatically. Between 1989 and 2010 the population decreased from nearly 12,000 to about 5,000 people. There are several abandoned apartment blocks in the city. The airport was shut down by the Defense Ministry in October 2012 but, following widespread criticism, it was re-opened in June 2013.

The port is accessible to vessels drawing up to 5·6m. Various cranes are available.

Diesel, supplies and marine repairs are available.

Tiksi is home to one of four meteorological research stations studying clouds, radiation, aerosols, surface energy fluxes and chemistry in the arctic. The other three are in the USA and Canada.

The MRCC for the Laptev Sea is based in Tiksi.

Tiksi *Jarlath Cunnane*

Tiksi – potential future icebreaker captains *Jarlath Cunnane*

AREA IV. EAST SIBERIAN SEA

Pilotage directions for the East Siberian Sea can be found in *Admiralty Sailing Directions Arctic Pilot Volume 1* (NP10). Directions for the Chukchi Sea can be found in *Admiralty Sailing Directions Bering Sea and Strait Pilot* (NP23).

East Siberian Sea climate

Average temperatures are -30°C in January and 0°C–3°C in July. Prevailing winds are S and SW in winter and from the N in summer. The western part of the East Siberian Sea is one of the windiest areas on the Russian arctic coast. Fog occurs 90–100 days per annum, mainly in the summer months.

New sea ice forms in October/November to a thickness of up to 2m. In addition, there is a lot of multiyear ice with thicknesses up to 2·5m. Multiyear ice is particularly hard. Break-up starts in May. By August, the average concentration of ice along the shore line is usually 4-tenths. In bad years, however, the average concentration will be greater than 7- tenths and many areas will be impassable.

East Siberian Sea points of interest

From early times the East Siberian shores were populated with the Yukaghir and Chukchi people. In the second century they were joined by the Even and

Sea ice in East Siberian Sea *Jarlath Cunnane*

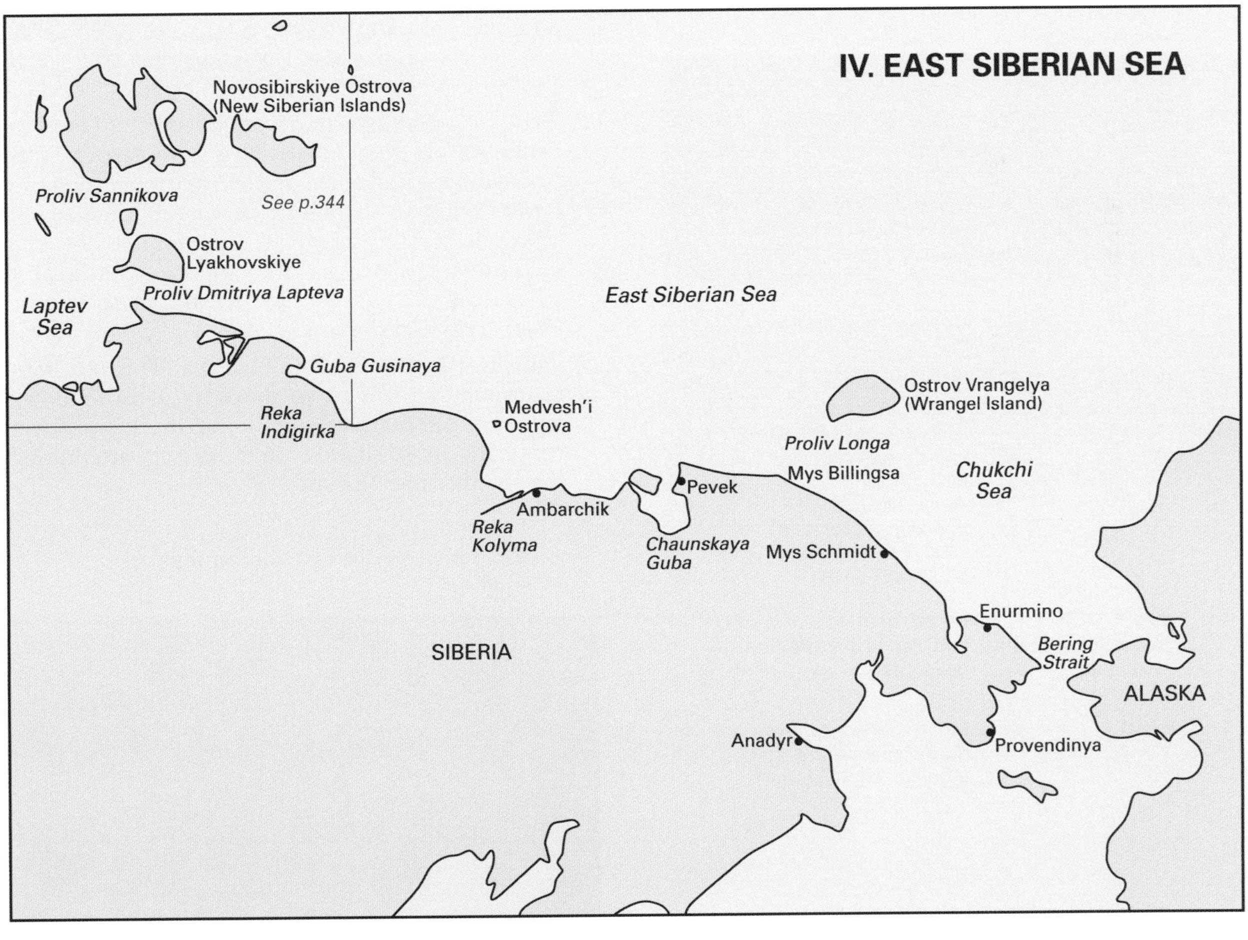

Evenk people and in the 9th and 15th centuries by the Yakut. All of these people were displaced from the Lake Baikal region, some 1,500 miles to the south, by the Mongols. Modern exploration of the area commenced in the 17th century and continued until the 20th century.

Semyon Dezhnyov was a Russian explorer who, in 1648, sailed from the Kolyma River to Anadyr in the Pacific. In doing so he apparently sailed through the Bering Strait almost a hundred years before Vitus Bering did so.

Many of the Gulag forced labour prison camps were in Siberia, particularly along the Kolyma River. About 14 million people were imprisoned in Gulags between 1929 and 1953. Their use peaked in the 1950s. The inmates were normal criminals as well as political prisoners who were forced to work in the mines. The locations were chosen for their remoteness and harsh environment which made prison walls, to some degree, unnecessary. If a prisoner did try to escape, he would be tracked down with dogs and a bounty offered for his capture.

Since the 1990s the use of the Northern Sea Route has declined, the military presence in the area decreased and the populations in the few East Siberian coastal settlements has declined.

Search and Rescue

The MRCC for the East Siberian Sea is based in Pevek. The contact details are given below:

1	Name of centre(s) MRCC/MRSC/JRCC/ JRSC	MRSC Pevek Lat. 69°42'03N; Long. 170°15'26E (MRCC Dikson)
2	MMSI-call sign-VHF voices call sign	VHF – 16 CHANNEL MMSI: 002731117 call sign: Pevek MRSC MF/HF – FREQUENCY 2182 KHZ MMSI: 002733730 Call sign: Pevek-Radio-3
3	Landline communications	✆ +7 42737 42113 *Fax* +7 42737 42114 *Mobile* +7 918 416 41 75 *Email* pevek@morflot.ru pevek87@inbox.ru *Telex* 354471 Inmarsat BGAN ICCID: 870772397870 (Voice,Voice Mail, SMS, GPRS)
4	Types of SAR facilities normally available	Rescue boat, rescue vessel, long range aircraft, light helicopter
5	Remarks	MRSC's service time period during summer navigation (approx. July–October)

East Siberian Sea shipping *Jarlath Cunnane*

Western approaches to the East Siberian Sea

The islands of Novosibirskiye Ostrova (New Siberian Islands) and Ostrova Lyakhovskiye lie between the Laptev and East Siberian Seas. Vessels may navigate through one of three different routes:

1. Proliv Dmitrya Lapteva, between the mainland and Ostrova Lyakhovskiye. Minimum depths are 9m. Ice is nearly always present and, in some years, the passage is impassable without ice-breaker assistance. Currents reach a maximum of 1·3kns and are wind driven. Anchorages may be possible at the Mys Kigilyakh (73°20′N 139°54′E) and Mys Shalaurova (73°11′N 143°14′E) polar stations.
2. Proliv Sannikova, between Ostrova Lyakhovskiye and Novosibirskiye Ostrova. The passage has similar ice and current conditions to Proliv Dmitrya Lapteva. Minimum depths are 11m. If vessels have to deviate from the recommended track due to ice conditions, navigators are warned to beware of the many shoal areas and shallow banks.
3. North of Novosibirskiye Ostrova. This northern route may be subject to more pack ice than the southern alternatives and is not the most direct route for most shallow draft vessels attempting the Northern Sea Route.

Pancake ice forming in the East Siberian Sea
Jarlath Cunnane

Reka Kolyma 69° 54′N 162° 23′E

This major river is about 2,000M long and originates in the Khrebet Tas-Kystabyt mountains. It is navigable for about 70M and has two ports on its shores: Zelenomysskiy Port (68°45′N 161°18′E) and Nizhnekolymsk (68°32′N 160°55′E). Minimum depths are 4·2m. Pilotage for vessels greater than 10m in length is compulsory. In summer the Luoraventlani people graze reindeer along the banks of the Reka Kolyma. In the winter, the Luoraventlani camp and hunt. Their hunting camps, or *yarangi*, are left unoccupied in the summer.

Pevek apartments, Chukchi Sea *Jarlath Cunnane*

Ambarchik 69°38′N 162°18′E

A lighthouse at Ambarchik has been in existence for several hundred years and the area was populated since at least the 18th century. Ambarchik has now been abandoned however and is desolate. In the past, it has been a transit camp for Gulag prisoners, weather station, military base, trading center and polar research station.

In the winter of 1933–34, it is alleged that 12,000 Gulag prisoners were trapped when their transportation ship became beset. All 12,000 prisoners are supposed to have perished due to hyperthermia and starvation.

Coal plant , Pevek

Pevek 69°43′N 170°18′E

The name *Pevek* may have come from the Chukchi word for fat. Alternatively, it may originate from the Chukchi word *Pagytkenay* which means 'smelly mountain.' The smell is supposed to be from the rotting bodies of slaughtered Chukchi and Yukaghir people who fought a battle against each other at Pevek.

Pevek is the principal port in the East Siberian Sea and has a population of about 4,000 people. It imports solid and liquid fuels, industrial equipment and general cargo. Exports include mining products and scrap metal. Many of the tin, mercury, gold, uranium and coal mines are now uneconomic and have closed.

The Gulag labour camp at nearby Chaunlag existed between 1951 and 1953. Its 10,000

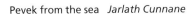

Pevek from the sea *Jarlath Cunnane*

7. THE NORTH EAST PASSAGE

Mys Schmidt from the sea, Chukchi Sea *Jarlath Cunnane*

prisoners were used in the mining and construction industries.

Like most ports along the Northern Sea Route, Pevek's population has declined substantially since the 1990s.

Pevek airport has regular flights to Anadyr and Moscow. Diesel, supplies and marine repairs are available.

The MRCC for the East Siberian Sea is in Pevek.

Proliv Longa 69°53'N 176°06'E

The Proliv Longa is the water connecting the East Siberian Sea to the Chukchi Sea. The principal navigation aid is the Mys Billingsa Lighthouse and racon (69°53'N 176°06'E). The recommended tracks are shown on the Russian charts. There are a number of banks and shoal areas to either side of the recommended track.

Mys Shmidt 68°52'N 179°22'W

Mys Shmidt was a port of call for Captain James Cook in 1778 when he sailed through the Bering Strait into the Chukchi Sea. It grew in prominence during the 20th century as a result of the militarisation of the Northern Sea Route at the time of the Cold War and the USSR's attempts to exploit the tin and gold reserves in the area. Since the Cold War ended the population has declined from 4,600 people in 1989 to less than 500 people in 2010. Much of the town is derelict, apartments are in ruins and there are abandoned rusting military installations everywhere.

Diesel and supplies are available. There is an airport with flights to Anadyr.

Enurmino 66°57'N 171°49'W

Enurmino is a small village, with a population of about 300 people, on the shores of the Chukchi Sea. The people, most of whom are Chukchi, are hunters and they are allowed to harvest three whales, 30 walrus and as many seal as they wish each year.

The anchorage is an open roadstead off a mile long sandy beach.

Roald Amundsen overwintered the *Maud* in Enurmino in 1920–1921.

There is a small shop, a school, post office and limited medical care. There is no airport, however helicopters bring supplies and passengers about once a fortnight.

Mys Schmidt, Chukchi Sea *Jarlath Cunnane*

Enuremo, a village on the Chukchi Sea *Jarlath Cunnane*

Index

Placenames starting with the Icelandic Þ 'thorn' character are at the end after 'z'

INDEX